TEXTBOOK

FOR

EMPLOYEE BENEFIT PLAN

TRUSTEES,

ADMINISTRATORS

AND ADVISORS

This book consists of edited texts of speakers' presentations at the Annual Educational Conference of the International Foundation of Employee Benefit Plans held November 14-19, 1980, in Honolulu, Hawaii.

Elizabeth A. Hieb, Editor

TEXTBOOK FOR EMPLOYEE BENEFIT PLAN TRUSTEES, ADMINISTRATORS AND ADVISORS

volume twenty-two

PROCEEDINGS OF THE 1980
ANNUAL EDUCATIONAL CONFERENCE
HONOLULU, HAWAII

international foundation of employee benefit plans
18700 WEST BLUEMOUND ROAD • P.O. BOX 69 • BROOKFIELD, WISCONSIN 53005 • PHONE 414 786-6700

ANNUAL CONFERENCE PROCEEDINGS SERIES

1956 Workshop . . . . Chicago . . . . Out of Print
1957 Workshop . . . . Denver . . . . Out of Print
1960 Workshop . . . . Miami . . . . Out of Print
1961 Workshop . . . . Philadelphia . . . . Out of Print
1962 Workshop . . . . Denver . . . . Out of Print
1963 Workshop . . . . Miami . . . . Out of Print
1964 Conference . . . . New York . . . . Available
1965 Conference . . . . San Francisco . . . . Available
1966 Conference . . . . Montreal . . . . Out of Print
1967 Conference . . . . Miami Beach . . . . Available
1968 Conference . . . . San Francisco . . . . Available
1969 Conference . . . . New York . . . . Available
1970 Conference . . . . Honolulu . . . . Available
1971 Conference . . . . Miami Beach . . . . Available
1972 Conference . . . . San Diego . . . . Available
1973 Conference . . . . San Francisco . . . . Available
1974 Conference . . . . Toronto . . . . Available
1975 Conference . . . . Honolulu . . . . Available
1976 Conference . . . . Miami Beach . . . . Available
1977 Conference . . . . San Francisco . . . . Available
1978 Conference . . . . Atlanta . . . . Available
1979 Conference . . . . New York . . . . Available

The statements or opinions expressed in any papers or discussions contained herein reflect the views of the authors and do not necessarily represent the views or positions of their firms or organizations or of the International Foundation, its officers, directors or staff.

Reprint of material contained herein permissible if source is acknowledged.

Copies of this textbook may be obtained from the International Foundation of Employee Benefit Plans, 18700 West Bluemound Road, P.O. Box 69, Brookfield, Wisconsin 53005

    $18.00 each for Foundation members

    $30.00 each for Non-members

© 1981 International Foundation of Employee Benefit Plans, Inc. (formerly the National Foundation of Health, Welfare and Pension Plans) International Standard Book Number 0-89154-150-0 Printed in the United States of America

*The Board of Directors
of the International Foundation of Employee Benefit Plans,
on behalf of the entire membership,
wishes to express its gratitude
to the many persons
who contributed so generously
to the 1980 Annual Educational Conference
and to this volume of proceedings*

Officers and Directors—1980

Officers

Helen K. Morton
President and Chairman of the Board

John L. Watts
President Elect

Wesley G. Jeltema
Secretary-Treasurer

Lee R. Polacheck
Executive Vice President

Leonard Zarzynski
Vice President of Finance and Administration

Voting Directors

Irving Baldinger

Arnaldo F. Espinosa

John W. Bernard

Raymond F. Gabel

John E. Boyd

Joseph Hellman

Frank Calegory

C. V. Holder

Thomas F. Courtney

Henry S. Hunt

James M. Dawson

Donald G. Jackman

Advisory Directors

 James Kemp

 Henry A. Scheyer

 H. J. Brownlee

 Robert B. Lashly

 Joseph E. Mastrangelo

 William J. Taylor

 William J. Chadwick

 Albert Morrison, Jr.

 Vernon J. Menard

 Len Teeuws

 D. Richard Dobie

 Robert G. Shortreed

 Theodore P. Picard

 Gerry V. Thibault

 Thomas E. Funk

Donald A. Walters

 Herbert R. Ricklin

Arnold E. Weinstein

James D. Hutchinson

D. H. Rowcliffe, Jr.

Edward D. Zacharko

President's Introduction

A key concept at many levels of business and government is embodied in the phrase "need to know." It is a means of defining responsibility, trustworthiness and accountability. In the employee benefits field, it may take on a very special meaning. As we operate in our world of ever-broadening complexity, bounded by high standards governing both performance and intent, we must, indeed, "know"—we cannot afford to be ignorant. We want, and need, to fulfill the benefit promises made to our plan participants. Such promises become especially vital in today's uncertain environment—and in today's uncertain environment, yesterday's knowledge is not good enough.

International Foundation members have recognized that need. The 1980 Annual Conference brought together nearly 6,000 registrants—the largest number ever. Speakers and panelists explored more than 80 separate topics covering the entire employee benefits spectrum, from techniques of day-to-day plan operation to broad issues—inflation, the international economy, social and demographic changes—having far-reaching effects on plan design. Our theme, "New Horizons," was a hopeful one—while it is a time of uncertainty, we see it as a time of promise, as well.

In this context, we might cite a very special event at this year's Conference—the first CEBS conferment, recognizing the achievement of the first group of CEBS registrants to successfully complete all ten examinations and receive their designation. The ceremony, which will become an annual event, marks a new standard of leadership and professionalism in the employee benefits field. The International Foundation is deeply proud of its role in bringing the CEBS program to fruition. It represents a new and vital expression of our 26 year old belief in, and commitment to, education in the employee benefits field.

In closing, a heartfelt expression of thanks. To those involved in planning, organizing, and finally presenting the 1980 Annual Conference, we wish to express our appreciation for a difficult and important task well done. It is our sincere hope and goal that the skills, information and knowledge contributed so generously here will go out to benefit not only the Conference attendees but also, ultimately, the millions of plan participants and beneficiaries whose interests they represent.

Helen K. Morton
President and
Chairman of the Board
1980

Contents

CHAPTER 1	THE VIEW FROM HERE		
	Freedom, Liberty and Individuals	Pierre A. Rinfret, Ph.D.	3
	The Promises of the '80s— The Perils in Between	Harold B. Ehrlich, Ph.D.	9
	Labor and Business: A Community of Interest	Robert A. Georgine	16
CHAPTER 2	THE LEGISLATIVE ENVIRONMENT		
	The Legislative Process— How to Make Your Voice Heard	Malcolm L. Pritzker	23
	Overview of the Multiemployer Pension Plan Amendments Act of 1980	Robert E. Nagle	27
	Withdrawal Liability	Carlton R. Sickles	36
	The Withdrawal Liability Process	Gerald E. Cole, Jr.	40
	National Health Insurance: Changes in Concerns, Concepts and Content	Steven E. Schanes, Ph.D.	43
	NHI Legislative Update	Joseph Eichenholz	48
	State Health Insurance Mandates: The Hawaii Prepaid Health Care Act— A Model for National Health Insurance	John van Steenwyk, Patricia K. Putman and Orlando K. Watanabe	52
CHAPTER 3	THE LEGAL CONTEXT		
	Recent Decisions Affecting Negotiated Employee Benefit Plans and Joint Trusts	Richard P. Donaldson	61
	Legal Odds and Ends: Issues and Decisions	Hugh J. McCarthy, Jr.	73
	Liabilities of the Contributing Employer	David W. Silverman	77
	ERISA Preemption of State Laws— Crowning Achievement or Empty Promise?	Thomas E. Stanton, Jr.	86
	Participation of Owners in Taft-Hartley Funds— The Legal Considerations	Warren H. Saltzman and Richard C. Johnson	93
	Participation of Owners in Taft-Hartley Trusts— The Administrative Considerations	Phil E. Davidson	99
	When the IRS Knocks: The TCMP Audit Program	Leo Brown	102
CHAPTER 4	RETIREMENT INCOME ISSUES AND PENSION PLAN DESIGN		
	Multiemployer Plans in the '80s— Will They Survive?	Matthew M. Lind, Ph.D.	129
	The Future of Pensions— Federal Government Impact	Ronald L. Haneberg	136
	What's Happening With Social Security	Kenneth P. Shapiro	144

	Retirement Income Adequacy: How Much Pension Is Enough?	David A. Giuntoli	149
	Inflation, COLAs and Retirement Age	John S. Perreca	165
	The Defined Contribution Alternative: Can It Solve All the Problems?	John K. Ware	175
	Reciprocity and Mergers	James M. Dawson	181
	Reciprocity of Pension Benefits— A Combination Approach	Robert J. Duffey	185
	A New Look at Disability Pensions	Siegfried O. Hillmer	190
	Disability Pensions: Competing Benefits and Their Effect on One Another	Mark H. Lipton	194
CHAPTER 5	OPTIONS IN WELFARE BENEFITS DESIGN		
	Flexible Benefit Programs— Has the Time Come?	Ronald D. Wackett	203
	Taxation of Employee Benefits	Daniel H. Mundt	209
	SUB Funds 1980	Harold G. Korbee	214
	Retiree Benefits— Considering the Commitment	William C. Earhart	219
	Prepaid Legal Services Plans	Sidney Gaines	221
	Prepaid Legal Plans— A Growing Benefit	Stanley Howitt	225
CHAPTER 6	HEALTH CARE BENEFITS AND COST CONTAINMENT TECHNIQUES		
	Future Trends in Benefits: Wellness Intervention	Steven E. Schanes, Ph.D.	233
	Prescription Drug Plans— A Cost-Effective Benefit	Ben D. Ward, Sr.	236
	Assisting the Troubled Employee: Alcoholism and Counseling Programs as a Plan Benefit	George A. Frank	240
	Prepaid Dental Care Plans	Kenneth A. Tannenbaum, D.D.S.	243
	COB, Subrogation and Hospital Audits: A Means to Cost Control	Douglas F. Matook	251
	Coping With Hospital Costs— The New York Approach	Richard A. Berman	304
	Second Surgical Opinion Programs— A Cost/Benefit Study	Eugene G. McCarthy, M.D., M.P.H. and Hirsch S. Ruchlin, Ph.D.	308
	A Second Opinion Podiatry Program	Madelon Lubin Finkel, Ph.D., Eugene G. McCarthy, M.D., M.P.H. and Dan Miller	314
	HMOs and Multiemployer Funds— Do They Mix?	Carlton R. Sherman	320
	Health Systems Agencies: Health Planning and Interaction With Welfare Plans	Bernard Handel	327

CHAPTER 7	TOPICS IN PLAN ADMINISTRATION		
	Effects of a Recessionary Economy on Plan Administration	Lee F. Jost	335
	Trustee Responsibilities: Communications to Participants	Robert A. Bohrer	344
	Trustees' Responsibility for Collection of Employer Contributions	Howard S. Susskind	359
	Developing a Welfare Plan Reserve Model and Level	Marc Gertner	367
	Insurance vs. Self-Insurance: A Case Study	Walter J. Butler	383
	Funding Arrangements	Joseph Eichenholz	392
	An Analysis of the Senate Report on Labor Union Insurance	Marc Gertner	401
	Basic Concepts of Accounting for Trustees	Sheldon P. Lewis	425
	The FASB for Non-Accountants	Jonathan F. Haber	429
	Understanding Unfunded Liabilities	Lawrence N. Bader	445
	Reporting and Disclosure of Unfunded Liabilities	Robert A. Semenza	454
	Administrative Costs of Pension Plans	Robert D. Cooper, Ph.D.	459
CHAPTER 8	COMPUTERS AND DATA PROCESSING		
	Solving Administrative Problems Through EDP	Robert A. DeCori	481
	Solving Administrative Problems Through EDP—The Positive Side	Robert J. Beres	486
	Solving EDP Problems Through Administration	Donald H. Rowcliffe, Jr.	490
	EDP: What Goes On in the Little Black Box?	G. A. Mele	494
	Mini and Microcomputers— Data Processing for Small Funds	Spencer V. Bell and Bennie Jones	515
CHAPTER 9	INVESTMENTS		
	Developing the Investment Policy Statement	Peter Ladd Gilsey	531
	Spectrum of Investments 1980	Eugene D. Burroughs	544
	Insurance Company Investment Products	Jon S. Brightman	554
	Real Estate as a Pension Fund Investment	Paul Sack	561
	Investment Targeting: Is There a RAM in Your Future?	Donald A. Smart	566
	Selecting an Investment Manager	Roger C. Bransford	572
	The Investment Manager— Differences in Philosophy and Style	Robert S. Waill	578

CHAPTER 1

The View From Here

Pierre A. Rinfret, Ph.D.

President and Chief Executive Officer
Rinfret Associates, Inc.
New York, New York

Harold B. Ehrlich, Ph.D.

Chairman of the Board and
Chief Executive Officer
Bernstein-Macaulay, Inc.
New York, New York

Robert A. Georgine

President
Building and Construction Trades Department,
AFL-CIO
Washington, D.C.

Freedom, Liberty and Individuals

BY PIERRE A. RINFRET, Ph.D.

I WANT to talk to you about three basic things today. Helen Morton said the economy gives her the impression of watching a yo-yo. I don't think that she could describe it better.

But let me remind you that if you study the history of mankind, it has never been different. What you are living with today is not abnormal, it is normal. Discontinuities, disruptions, war, inflation, defense, enemies, friends, strangleholds, these are the history of the world. I think we've become spoiled. Look at this country and you'll see behind you 35 years of virtually uninterrupted prosperity. No society, no country in the history of the world, has achieved 35 years of uninterrupted prosperity without a major financial crash and without a depression. We Americans really don't appreciate that we have made history. We are rewriting the history books, we are in a totally new era unknown to man, we are crossing new frontiers.

There are three things I want to discuss. First, I want to talk to you about something that very few people talk about. I want to talk about the strength of the United States, in fact, to put it in the plural, the strengths of the United States. In our masochism, in our self-flagellation, all we talk about are our problems. Very seldom do we say how much we've accomplished, so I want to talk about that. Second, of course we face problems, and I want to talk about these problems. Third, and I offer no magic formulas, I want to talk about some ways to resolve the problems we face, using the strengths we have.

I will offer you neither pessimism nor optimism, but realism. I have a fundamental belief, a very simple fundamental faith. My faith is not in the American government, my faith is not in any one sector of our society, my faith is in the American people. I believe very strongly with all my intellect and all my heart that our 225 million Americans are as good as any people that have ever been put on the face of this earth. I'm going to take you

©1981 by Rinfret Associates, Inc. All rights reserved. Reprinted by permission.

Dr. Rinfret, the keynote speaker at the Conference, is president and chief executive officer of Rinfret Associates, Inc., an International economic and financial intelligence firm. Prior to founding his own firm, he was associated for 15 years with Lionel D. Edie & Co., Inc., serving as chairman of the board from 1963-67. Dr. Rinfret served as economic counsel to President Nixon and provided analyses for use by Presidents Johnson and Kennedy. He has lectured at academic institutions too numerous to mention, both in the United States and overseas, and received his doctorate in political economy from the University of Dijon, France. An active International Foundation member during the 1960s, Dr. Rinfret has served on committees and as an advisory member of the Board of Directors.

through some of my reasons for saying why this country is unique and why we have no parallel.

American Strengths as Seen From Abroad

Let me start off by saying something about travel. My wife Ida and I travel outside the United States for about three to four months of the year. There is virtually no major country that we have not visited on numerous occasions. For example, we have made six trips abroad for the U.S. Department of State. We have visited many of the minor countries of the world. One thing we have learned is that if you want to understand foreign countries, you must go there. So I want to talk about our strengths not only from a domestic point of view but also from an international point of view, from my observations of the way the rest of the world looks at us and what it sees about us that we don't see.

I want to read you a movie review that was written in London in March 1979. This review is rather incredible. It appeared in the *Evening Standard,* a British newspaper. The date is March 13, 1979, and this is what they said:

> President Carter's frantic effort to get Egypt and Israel to sign a peace treaty is in response to a growing demand among American voters that the United States must be seen to take a bigger part in world affairs. The mood of neurotic introspection and defeatism induced by the Vietnamese mess and the shame of Watergate has vanished as though it had never been. Americans are once again demonstrating their extraordinary resilience and their refreshing ability to wipe out the past and start afresh. They want the United States to start behaving like a great power again and make its weight felt in the world. Opinion polls show that this is what Americans demand and expect to happen and they are prepared to put their money where their mouth is. Their attitude can be summed up by Theodore Roosevelt's famous admonition: "Speak softly and carry a big stick."

In March 1979, a British writer reviewed an American movie called "The Deer Hunter." This review, dated March 18, 1979, appeared in the *London Sunday Telegraph.* Those of us who fought in World War II or Korea and Viet Nam, those of us who were wounded and lost family, as I did, look at war with horror. But one also realizes that the price of freedom is eternal vigilance. Let's look at what the *Sunday Telegraph* said about the United States:

> At the end of "The Deer Hunter" . . . a group of Americans, mourning a fallen comrade, sing "God Bless America." They do so in a reverential manner. Watching this scene last week, I waited for some ironic undertone to surface . . . but in the event no attempt was made to mock the propriety of patriotic prayer. The scene was played straight, as it might have been in the aftermath of the Second World War. Even more surprising, the London audience—mostly young—did not hiss or giggle. Many of them were clearly deeply moved. Apparently American audiences are reacting in the same way, crying their eyes out over a film which makes no attempt to portray the American intervention in Viet Nam as a crime against humanity. The hero, incredibly enough, is a good American. Perhaps one "The Deer Hunter" does not by itself add up to a new American springtime of confident virility. Fortunately there are other signs, too, of a return to buoyancy. . . . Disarmament, too, has once again become a politically dirty word with Congress threatening to veto SALT II. . . . Up to a point, of course, such a reaction was inevitable, for there never was any likelihood that the American policeman could safely withdraw from the international beat. Sooner or later the resulting dangers were bound to provoke a demand for his return. There never was any cause for Americans to feel guilty. The emperor, so to speak, always had a perfectly respectable set of clothes.

Don't Underestimate Our Free Market System

Let me tell you about a trip to Africa that my wife and I just finished. We went to Guinea, we went to Zaire and we went to South Africa. Guinea and Zaire are underdeveloped countries.

Guinea is Marxist-oriented, Soviet-oriented. The Soviet Union has poured economic aid on the order of $50-100 million a year into that country for years. There are two bauxite mines in Guinea. Both were constructed ten years ago. One mine is 51% owned by an American consortium. The other mine is run by a Soviet group. Five years ago both these operations went into production, each with a rated output of 10 million tons of bauxite a year. In the year 1980, after five years in full operation, the American-managed mine produced 11.5 million tons of bauxite versus its rated capacity of 10 million tons. The Soviet-managed operation, with a rated capacity of 10 million tons, after five years of operation will produce slightly less than 3 million tons.

When we were in Guinea, Mrs. Rinfret and I met one Cabinet Minister after another. I will condense what one Cabinet Minister said to me. For 35 minutes he pounded me. You know the phrases:

"The United States is an imperialistic war-mongering country that rapes the poor for the benefit of the rich." The standard line, for 35 minutes.

At the end of 35 minutes I stood up and said, "Mr. Cabinet Minister, thank you very much. I've taken too much of your time. I'd like to thank you. Good-bye, sir."

"Where are you going?" he said.

I said, "Mr. Cabinet Minister, there is nothing to talk about. You have one view of the United States, I have another. You have one ideology, I have another. With all due respect, you don't know anything about the United States. Your facts are wrong, you don't know who we are or what we are."

"Sit down," he said.

"No, I'm not going to sit down," I said.

"Sit down," he said. Now there were 14 of them and there were my wife and I. Guess what I did? I sat down.

I said, "Mr. Cabinet Minister, do you want a dialogue?"

With tears in his eyes, he said, "Dr. Rinfret, help us. Help us. We desperately need help. We need American assistance. We need your technology. We need your investment. What we need is Americans to teach us how to produce because we are not successful and we are slipping every year. America must help."

That's a country which has been dominated for 20 years by the Soviet Union, and it's now turning to the United States. In Zaire, we found the same situation.

Now let me tell you a story about the People's Republic of China. There are 1.020 billion people in China. Until six months ago the Chinese government had said there were only 800 million. About a month ago they admitted that the figure was over 1 billion: 25% of the total world population.

Incidentally, if you're interested in China, may I suggest a publication for you to read. It's called the *Beijing Review*. It costs $13.50 a year for 52 issues. It's all about what is going on in China, written in English.

The Chinese are looking toward the West. When a Vice Premier of China was in the U.S. recently on an official visit, he told President Carter that he and his delegation wanted to call on the Ingersoll-Rand Company. So arrangements were made for the Vice Premier and 40 other Chinese to visit Ingersoll-Rand. The people at Ingersoll-Rand asked the Vice Premier of China why he wanted to visit their company.

He said, "It's very simple. You've been around since 1890. You have never abandoned an investment, you have persisted. We want to talk to people who invest for the long run."

The Vice Premier took his group to some Ingersoll-Rand factories. He walked through one factory, and he said, "Would you mind telling me the depreciation schedule on this factory?" Well, you have to admit that sounds like a real capitalistic remark.

Then he said, "How is it that you can take an old factory, put new machinery in it and make it work? We buy new factories but we can't get them to work. How come the American system works?"

The Ingersoll-Rand people explained how they do that.

The Vice Premier of China then said to the Chairman and Chief Executive Officer of Ingersoll-Rand, Mr. William Wearly, "I wonder if I might have the honor of addressing your staff?" Mr. Wearly said, "It would be an honor for us."

The Vice Premier gave a talk to the people at Ingersoll-Rand. Would you like to know the title of his talk? The title of the talk given by a Vice Premier of China to members of the Ingersoll-Rand Company staff was: "Communism Does Not Work."

If you read the *Beijing Review*, you'll see that the Chinese, 25% of the world's population, are going to an open market, free market system. Why? Because it produces. Because we Americans produce. The only ideology we have is freedom. Not government control, but individual freedom. And we produce.

If you look at the war in the Persian Gulf, between Iran and Iraq, let me ask you a question: To whom did the Saudi Arabians turn when they were worried about their security? Did they turn to Japan for military assistance? Did they turn to France for military assistance? Did they turn to West Germany for military assistance? Did they turn to the United Kingdom or Canada or Australia? To whom did they turn to stabilize the area? They turned to the United States. President Carter put in 32 U.S. Navy ships. The British contributed six ships. The Australian navy is "coincidentally" on maneuvers. Now we have a base in Saudia Arabia.

When the pinch came in the Middle East, and war broke out between Iran and Iraq, did the Saudis turn to Japan, which some people call Number One in the world? No. They turned to the United States. And *Time* magazine says, "We are going to lose as a result of the war in Iran and Iraq." We have a masochistic streak within us. Instead of recognizing that when other people are in trouble, they turn to us, what do we do? We cry about our weaknesses.

Think of it this way. When Castro let some of his people leave Cuba, where did they go? Did they go to Puerto Rico, Guatemala, Venezuela or Brazil? They came to the United States. We took in thousands of Cubans. When people left Viet Nam in sinking boats, which navy was detached by its government to pick up those "boat people" and find refuge for them? The United States Navy.

So I want to make a very simple point: This country that we love to whip, this country that we love to criticize is, in fact, far stronger than we realize. Of course, we've had our moments of anguish, and we've gone through a few living hells. But the fact of the matter is that there's no power in the world like this country. There is no power like it anywhere, in my judgment. The point I want to make is this: Don't underestimate our strengths.

Yes, We Have Some Serious Economic Problems

At the same time, don't underestimate our problems. We have some very serious problems. I don't need to tell you what they are. You know—you live with them, day in, day out. The current rate of inflation in the United States as measured by the Consumer Price Index is 14%. For the year 1980, the Consumer Price Index will be up about 14% over the previous year. If you get double-digit inflation, you get double-digit interest rates. It's that simple. Single-digit inflation, single-digit interest rates.

We have the problem of what I call Presidential promises. That's a euphemism. Mr. Reagan has promised exactly the same thing that Mr. Carter promised in 1976, what one can politely call irreconcilable goals. Let's look at the record. First, he's going to cut taxes. And who isn't for that? Mr. Reagan has said he will cut taxes. He has proposed to introduce legislation to cut taxes by $35-40 billion. He promises to reduce federal spending. He promises at the same time that he's going to raise defense spending and deregulate industry.

Mr. Reagan's promises in 1980 are identical to Mr. Carter's in 1976. But the problems are insoluble in the short run. I think we have to face that fact. Don't expect miracles from Mr. Reagan. Don't expect the economic problems to be solved overnight. Don't expect inflation to be beaten down in one year or two years.

There's another element. Mr. Reagan gets in with an advantage: He carried 44 states. He has 53 Republican seats in the Senate. The House still has a Democratic majority, but Mr. Reagan gets in with the Senate under his control. He has an advantage. I'm very serious about this, and it's not a partisan remark: Mr. Carter came in as a non-politician. Remember, he used to say, "I never worked in Washington." We found out how true that was. He didn't want to work with Congress, he didn't need Congress, he thought. He appointed inexperienced people to his Cabinet.

What's fascinating is what Mr. Reagan is going to do. Many of the appointees that we hear about today are former members of the Cabinet under either Mr. Ford or Mr. Nixon. Apparently there will be only several really new appointees. Now, I have to admit that bothers me a little bit. But on the other hand I know this: He hits the ground running, he hits the ground with a Cabinet of professionals in the political arena, people who have been there before.

We have another problem. Now I am going to say some nasty things about everybody, I want to be non-partisan. The problem is bureaucracy: This country has become a nation of bureaucrats. You have them in the unions, you have them in the corporations.

We have bureaucracy in government, we have bureaucracy in industry, we have it in unions. We have it in splinter groups and we have it in the special-interest groups. We face a serious problem of special interests. I'll give you one illustration: the Alaska pipeline. The first estimate for the Alaska pipeline was that it would cost $900 million. As you will recall, the Alaska pipeline construction was held up for a very important environmental reason. It's true. The environmentalists refused to allow the pipeline to be built until we knew the migratory habits of the caribou. Why? The environmentalists were worried: If you build the pipeline, where will the caribou go? How will they migrate? Can they jump over the pipeline? Where will they jump over it? Where do you build the ramps for the caribou? Can they get on the ramps? What will the pipeline do to the caribou?

So the United States Congress, in a moment of grand generosity, allocated a million dollars to the study of the migratory habits of the caribou. And for three years we held up the pipeline construction. The $900 million construction cost estimate escalated to $7.8 billion. Do you want to know what happened to the caribou? They love the pipeline. They go underneath it, they don't use any of the ramps. They breed beside the pipeline. Why? Because the pipeline repels insects, for some unknown reason.

Would you like to guess where geologists think the biggest new petroleum reserves in the United

States are located? In Alaska's William O. Douglas Wildlife Preserve. Now the environmentalists say, "Uh-uh, you're not going to drill for oil there." So we may be starting another controversy.

We have problems. Inflation, high interest rates, irreconcilable goals, bureaucracy, a lack of entrepreneurial drive on the part of industry, particularly big industry, a failure to serve the marketplace. How do you reconcile them?

Let me give you a very simple concept. I'm told there's an old Chinese proverb that says problems are opportunities. Problems are opportunities. Joseph Schumpeter, a great economic historian, a great analyst, was once asked the question, "What is profit?" He said, "Profit is the end result of the friction of change." Well, if that's true, we have lots of opportunities in front of us because goodness knows we've got enough friction of change. Are there answers to our problems? Yes.

One Solution: More Self-Reliance

I want to give you a very simple concept as my point number three: I think we Americans have somehow lost our way in one area. Very simply, when industry gets into trouble, the first thing it does is run to the United States Government and say, "Bail me out." Look at Chrysler. Now it may sound antisocial, but I happen to believe in free enterprise. I think Chrysler should have gone under. I think the City of New York should have gone under. When the U.S. steel industry cannot compete because its management is one of the most backward, in my judgment, in this country, and when General Motors pays $3 in extra dividends while it is investing only a million dollars a year in research and development, we have a right to ask, "How come?" But Chrysler runs to the government and says, "Bail us out. If you don't, the social costs will kill you." And the government bails them out.

When productivity drops, the unions say, "Restrict employment." We all do the same thing, we run to the government for solutions. Let me ask you this simple question: What solution has the American government been able to put across in the last five years? Has it solved inflation? Has it solved high interest rates? Has it solved the loss of respect for the American people in the rest of the world?

Have we forgotten something? *We* are the strengths. *We* are the people, and we have to rely on *ourselves*. Jimmy Carter can't walk down a production line and say to a businessman, "Get rid of that machine, it's too old." President Reagan can't walk down a production line and say, "Increase productivity, or you'll miss out on a market." He can't say, "Your R&D is inadequate, you're not on the frontier of technology." We've got to do that ourselves. May I suggest to you one solution that's so simple but so often forgotten: it's called self-reliance. Do it yourself. Let me give you some do-it-yourself formulas.

Formula Number One: I believe that in every investment account there should be both gold and silver. Let me make a point to you that many people do not know. From the year 1540 to 1973, 433 years, the price of gold was fixed, first by merchant bankers and later by governments, by the Bank of England or the United States Treasury. If you look at the price of gold over those years, it was virtually flat. In 1973, in a mind-boggling break with history, for the first time in over 430 years the price of gold was determined by the marketplace. It went from an official price of $72 per ounce to $600, where it is now. As for silver, there's a 200 year-old argument in the United States about silver. Here's a very simple rule: Gold and silver move together.

I believe in gold. I believe in gold not because I'm a gold fanatic or a gold bug, but because everybody in the world believes in gold. They buy it. They hide money in gold holdings. Why? Because they don't trust paper money that governments issue.

Formula Number Two: Land and real estate investment. One can joke about land. You know that wonderful line, "They ain't making any more of it." Let me remind you of a very simple fact of life: There are 2 billion people in this world who cannot feed themselves. Over a billion are in China. The food deficit in Africa in 1980 was 20%: they produce only 80% of their own food. In the year 2000, the world food deficit will be 40%, according to the Food and Agriculture Organization. There are only three countries in the world that have surplus quantities of wheat today, the United States, Canada and Argentina. We are now feeding the world and we are now running into our limits on capability and production. Land is becoming a scarce resource, particularly farmland.

Formula Number Three: Growth areas in common stocks. I think the Dow Jones Industrial Average is the most inaccurate, misleading indicator of equities performance in the United States today. Who is in the Dow Jones? The Dow Jones, as I see it, is the bureaucracy of America. It's the giants, the multibillion-dollar companies. They're not the real entrepreneurs of this country. They're not the real movers and the shakers. They rarely rock the boat. They don't take many risks. They don't do anything that may get them a nasty letter from a stockholder. They play it safe.

Go look at those $400 million companies out there and watch the real entrepreneurs of this country. Do we have entrepreneurs? You better believe it. We have one emerging area after another, one emerging company after another, all finding gaps in the market, finding new technologies. We've been looking at the big companies when we should be looking at the small ones.

Formula Number Four: Go abroad. We have a patriotic myopia that only the United States can be successful. Japan, West Germany, France, Australia, Hong Kong, the United Kingdom have incredibly successful industries. Unfortunately, most Americans think investing in the United States is the only game.

Formula Number Five, and let me put it this way: In an inflationary era, anyone who holds a debt instrument beyond 91 days is an optimist, in my judgment. I limit all my investments in debt instruments to 91 days. I call that a relatively long term! But I think that while we have inflation, we're going to a prime rate of 17-18% again. We're going to see those interest rates stay up.

There is a solution to our problems, and I think it is very simple. It's self-reliance. It's we who have survived. The government didn't give that to us, the politicians didn't give that to us. We have adaptability, we have flexibility, we've certainly got perseverance. We've been able to stay with it. That's what free enterprise is called, that's what a free market system is called.

I want to conclude with another fact of life. What has our society accomplished? Nothing much. It has produced the highest standard of living for the largest population ever known in the history of the world, under the banner of freedom. If you think of it this way, it's an incredible accomplishment: This country has the oldest existing written constitution in the world today. The West German constitution dates from 1949, the French constitution from 1958, the Italian constitution, 1948. The Canadians don't have their own constitution yet.

Some people think we are in a state of turmoil. I think we're in a state of social, economic and financial transition. I leave you with this thought: We have democracy, freedom, change, opportunity and, above all else, guts and courage.

The Promises of the '80s— The Perils in Between

BY HAROLD B. EHRLICH, Ph.D.

Prologue

Many people believe that once the strongly business-oriented Reagan Administration, backed by a conservatively constituted Congress, has taken a firm hold on the reins of government, they will go a long way toward overcoming the economic malaise which has plagued our country. And yet, regardless of the strength of their resolve to set things right, is it realistic to expect any great improvement before several years have passed, and without experiencing a period of further hardships in the meantime? After all, when dealing with forces far more powerful than themselves, even the ablest leaders can do only so much. Besides, the techniques employed for battling the problems at hand may well produce unpleasant side effects at the same time or later on.

By analogy, remember that the election of the Nixon Administration in 1968, which many of its supporters believed would produce better conditions practically right away, led instead during 1969 to "tight money," rapidly rising interest rates, falling securities prices and declining profit margins for business, and was followed in 1970 by a severe recession. Looking ahead, we wonder whether it will be possible to pursue the policies outlined during the presidential campaign without creating a lot of pain and/or disappointment.

For example, tramping down hard on the monetary brakes is not likely to curb this particular round of inflation any time soon.[1] To the contrary, employing such stringent measures in the present environment could well make matters worse by driving up the costs of doing business. As for any early substantial reduction in taxes, in view of a prospective federal deficit of $60 billion or more for fiscal 1981, even before factoring in anything for

Dr. Ehrlich is chairman of the board and chief executive officer of Bernstein-Macaulay, Inc., in New York City. The firm manages security portfolios totaling more than $1.5 billion. Most accounts are related to employee benefit plans or other institutional funds. Dr. Ehrlich, who was trained in and taught economics, has spent 22 years in the investment industry. He has been a security analyst, director of research, an advisor to many institutional investment firms and a portfolio manager. Dr. Ehrlich has addressed meetings of many professional organizations, such as the National Association of Business Economists, the Financial Analysts Federation, the New York Society of Security Analysts, the Institutional Investor Conference, Pensions Conference, and the Investments Institute of the International Foundation of Employee Benefit Plans. Articles by Dr. Ehrlich have been published in the Financial Analysts Journal, the Journal of Business Economics, Pensions & Investments, Finance, Intellect, New York and The New York Times.

either reduced revenues or greater expenditures on defense, is the new Congress certain to support such an experiment in "supply side" economics regardless of how bad inflation may be at that time?

Besides, as we have pointed out previously,[2] by no means are Mr. Reagan's closest advisors, who

---

This article, an expansion upon Dr. Ehrlich's Annual Conference presentation, appeared as the Bernstein-Macaulay Client Letter of December 1, 1980.

1. Client Letter, "Federal Reserve Financial Follies," November 1, 1980.

2. Cf., ibid., as well as "Investor Psychology vs. Economic Reality—Forces at Work in the Stock Market," August 1, 1980, and "Rates of Inflation, Recession and Taxes—Where Do They Go From Here?" September 1, 1980.

are mainly traditional fiscal conservatives, committed to cutting taxes come what may—for example, in the event of accelerating inflation. Again, with the overwhelming proportion of federal expenditures now mandated by law, how can the budget be brought into balance within the foreseeable future? Is it not likely that the federal deficit will grow worse first? So, short of such harsh measures as super-tight money, severe recession, drastic cuts in social services or the imposition of an "incomes policy," what would cause an early and material decline in the rate of inflation?

Moreover, given the fragile state of finances—personal, business, and even within the banking system—surely any sustained and serious effort to cut inflation must carry the risk of getting out of hand, of bringing about *de*flation. Finally, considering the political forces loose in this world—forces over which the so-called western governments seem to have precious little control—the risk of massive and *unexpected* social change is great. So, no matter which way we look, we see the potential for a variety of "disappointments" in the next several years.

Nevertheless, later on in this decade, conditions could be much better than at present—which, let's be honest, are not at all bad right now for most Americans, or for people living in other industrialized nations. Let us now examine those developments, both sociological and technological, that hold great promise for the future. Keep in mind, however, that "getting from here to there" without too much trauma is the real problem.

The Promises of the '80s

People

Rather than just technology providing the engine for societal advance, it seems to us that major changes already underway in the composition of our population, in the "demographics," may give business profitability and living standards the greatest boost later in this decade. Specifically, over the course of the 1980s, the following social developments should make for better productivity, strong consumer spending and, hence, higher profits after a time.

- There will be fewer young people as a percentage of the total population in the U.S. Thus, the heavy cost of educating and training workers will level off, so that some of our resources can be redeployed to applications that are productive more immediately.
- The growth rate of the overall work force will slow down dramatically, because there will be *proportionately* fewer *new* entrants of both women and young people. Again, the heavy costs of training will subside. So, the work force as a whole, being older, better trained and presumably more stable, should be more productive on the job.
- The rate of unemployment should decline as the flow of new workers moderates, and as our population becomes more skilled overall. At the same time, the "two earner" family phenomenon should continue apace. The combination of these two trends should stimulate family incomes.
- Total population should grow at least at the same rate as in the 1970s, despite a declining birth rate, simply because so many more people will reach childbearing age. However, there will be more adults in relation to the number of children. The combination of these two forces should buoy total national consumption.
- The age group between 25 and 45, who normally earn more than others, will increase the most rapidly of all. So, provided there are enough jobs to go around, the growth of personal income could accelerate. In addition, this age group tends to have a higher spending rate, to work harder and to be more stable than the younger people who were such a dominant part of the population in the 1970s.
- The rate of increase in unemployment compensation, family welfare and other so-called transfer payments should taper off under the impact of a combination of these forces. This change should help to hold the tax burden in check, and help to improve the productivity of our population as a whole.

In a word, provided that the problems we face can be overcome without suffering a "financial accident" or some other major damage to our economy, i.e., provided there are enough well-paying jobs for all, then personal incomes and spending could flourish later on. Productivity, profit margins, and living standards could improve markedly. Even the rate of inflation could wind down a lot, as it usually does during periods of balanced "real" growth.

Government

Tax Credits and Incentives. Maybe we are guilty of wishful thinking, or perhaps just plain naivete, but changes in government could also promote productivity, increased profit margins, improved living standards and balanced real growth. For example, once beyond the potential traumas of the next year or two, major tax reform, as well as some reduction of the total tax burden, seem like good bets. Specifically, during the next several years, Congress should pass several pieces of legislation designed to promote capital formation. For example, there could be another reduction in capital gains rates, an increase in tax credits for physical investment, liberalized rules for depreciating hard assets and more incentives for specific sectors such as energy development.

In addition, we may see direct promotion of research and development, both generally and within specific sectors. Certain industries may get relief from excessive foreign competition, either through restrictions on imports, or even through subsidies for exports. Finally, possibly in the *second* half of 1981 and certainly by some time in 1982, we should see an across-the-board and perhaps major cut in income taxes designed to foster real growth.

Please understand that we still do not believe that the odds for this kind of tax cut during the first half of 1981 are all that great. Within the next few months, the rate of inflation is likely to remain uncomfortably high, while the federal deficit may balloon further. Besides, given the mood of the people, which clearly favors balancing the budget as well as other conservative moves, Congressmen may be reluctant to vote for any measure that seems fiscally "irresponsible."

Besides, would it not be wise to hold off until it is patently obvious that a tax cut is needed to get the economy going again? Wouldn't it be only politically sensible for them to wait a while—to wait for inflation to die down, for more people to demand tax cuts—and to derive some political benefit for the 1982 elections? Moreover, Professor Laffer's theories to the contrary notwithstanding, how easy would it be to *justify* cutting income taxes in a major way during the first part of 1981, at a time when the Federal Reserve will be striving to curb inflation? Nevertheless, major reduction as well as reform of taxes is on the way. Business may receive some material benefits, particularly in the form of aids to capital formation, even in 1981.

Reduced Regulation. In addition, considering the sympathies generally associated with the incoming Administration, further deregulation of industry is highly likely. For example, we would not be surprised to see the restrictions on pipeline and utility plant construction relaxed considerably. In all probability, the use of coal and atomic power to generate electricity will be pushed, and perhaps vigorously.

The standards for automobile gasoline mileage and for exhaust emission could be softened or at least stretched out further in time. There will be deregulation of transportation and other industries, while the burden of government-required paperwork could be reduced measurably. Above all, we believe that the Reagan Administration, as he committed, will rely far more heavily upon private initiative for the development of oil and gas reserves. So, we could see the reduction or even the elimination of the windfall profits tax, the "mini" tax on intangible drilling expenses, and even some liberalization of depletion allowances.

All in all, regardless of the specific measures taken, government is likely to act far more favorably toward business interests, at least for the next several years. Therefore, regardless of how it all turns out in the long run, on an "expectational" basis, people should be more willing to exert entrepreneurial efforts. For the promotion of real growth, the longevity of our capitalist system and the ultimate health of our financial markets, the recent political shift could turn out to be quite favorable.

Technology

Scientific advances accomplished in the 1970s, as well as others in the works right now, should also prove beneficial to our society. For example, computers are being reduced both in size and price, and so dramatically that most offices, stores, factory work stations and private homes may employ one or more units within a very few years. The art of telecommunications is advancing so rapidly that a great many first class letters may be transmitted rather than carried. In short, electronic science is rapidly removing a good part of the drudgery from people's lives, while enabling them to be more economically productive.

Advances in the biological sciences also offer great potential. Specifically, improvements in surgical techniques are making operations more reliable and less traumatic. Thus, recovery rates are speeding up. Sophisticated instruments are providing earlier detection of illness, better diagnosis, and improved treatment. With the synthesis of new substances like interferon, we may be able to arrest or even to "cure" a variety of viral-related disorders, ranging from the common cold to cancer. As these things are perfected and become used more widely in the 1980s, people should live longer and more comfortably, and be more productive.

Surely, there will be major advances in the use of energy as well as in the development of new energy sources. For example, we will improve the generation, transmission and especially the employment of electrical power. Already, buildings are being heated partially by "excess" energy from lighting systems. On a relative basis, even the cost of producing electricity from *existing* plants will be held in check by various new techniques. Transportation vehicles of all kinds, from automobiles and trucks to airplanes and railroad engines, which have already become more fuel efficient, will be improved further. Certainly, a great deal of money will be expended in finding and developing new supplies of energy. Specifically, drilling activity is bound to continue increasing, the windfall profits tax notwithstanding, and major efforts will be made to extract hydrocarbons from coal, shale, tar sands, and older oil fields.

In its way, the government's "synfuels" program could become the "inner space" exploration project of the 1980s. Admittedly, there could be immense wastage associated with developing these technologies, if only because such huge sums will be deployed as the result of governmental spending and other incentives. Nevertheless, our society as a whole, and certainly private industry, should benefit enormously. By analogy, the U.S. space program, which took many billions from the stream of GNP in order to put a few men in orbit and then on the moon, provided the computer and other scientifically-oriented industries with exceedingly valuable knowledge—plus mighty good profits.

Investment

Looking ahead, all of this technological activity should help to generate a whole new round of investment in plant and equipment; i.e., a round of capital formation. For one thing, new facilities will be required in order to employ these scientific advances productively. Second, provided we are right about the tax incentives and governmental funding that industry will receive, management will have the incentive to modernize and, in many cases, even to expand. Third, the relaxation of governmental regulations should also encourage capital expenditures.

Fourth, considering the population trends described earlier, and provided that our economic system surmounts the difficulties of the next year or so without being stalled unduly, consumer demand should expand more than enough to generate a new round of capital investment. Fifth, in this decade, the shift from manufacturing to service industries should slow down, and the service sector will need more physical investment per employee anyway.

Finally, aside from the fact that much of the existing plant and equipment in America is so obsolete that considerable upgrading is required just to maintain profit margins, some industries—such as aerospace and energy—are truly short of capacity. Thus, without meaning to be overly optimistic, we think that a new and perhaps powerful cycle of capital formation is quite likely to occur, although it may not begin in earnest for another year or two. Admittedly, it could be difficult to finance, for reasons discussed later and, of course, any sort of serious economic setback could postpone the whole process.

Productivity

In many ways, the combination of all these technological advances and capital spending projects should enhance both productivity and the quality of life. Surely, increasing computerization can aid output per man-hour in offices and factories. The use of high-speed digital telecommunications can cut paper shuffling considerably, and can make people more directly productive in other ways. Further development of conservation techniques as well as new energy sources can cut costs and make production more efficient. In other words, our society should be able to get more *output* from each unit of labor *input*.

In addition, from an overall point of view, advances in medicine should help people to be more productive. For example, just reducing the average duration of the common cold could add many more days of work per year. Along more exotic lines, slowing down the aging process and/or enabling older people to work more should do the same. Finally, while it is hard to assert with great conviction, we still believe that—in general—job attitudes will improve during this decade. Not only will the population be more mature chronologically, but today's young people seem more achievement-oriented than at any other time since the immediate postwar period.

The Perils in Between

Profit Margins

In the meantime, until these technological advances take hold, until a good deal of new plant and equipment has been put in place and especially until the volume of output picks up considerably, productivity is likely to remain low. In addition, at least for the time being, the cost of energy is likely to continue rising, even per unit of production. Finally, we do not expect the costs of financing business activity and investment, which have been going up rapidly, to decline much any time soon. For all of these reasons, then, profit margins could remain under pressure, especially in the event that final sales slacken off again, as we expect.

Double Dip

We believe that the odds for another recession—probably in the first half of 1981—are high, for the following reasons. First and foremost, by running up faster than the average disposable income, inflation continues to siphon off consumer buying power. In fact, a great many people have been keeping up with escalating living costs only through some combination of increased borrowing and reduced savings. Both of these avenues for maintaining consumption have finite limits, although rapidly rising prices in both the real estate and the equity markets have allowed this process to persist longer than at some other times in the past.

Second, in relative terms, business spending on new plant and equipment, one of the main forces of economic advance, has been winding down because final demand has remained sluggish, and because profit margins have remained soft. Looking into the immediate future, most signs point toward a further weakening of such expenditures. Third, the Federal Reserve's tight money program is bound to place additional downward pressure on both consumer and business spending. Fourth, in the absence of new moves by Congress, the burden of taxes will increase automatically in 1980 as inflation pushes people into higher brackets, and as higher rates for Social Security deductions take effect.[3]

Finally, barring a *substantial* and near-term cut in tax rates, which we question, those rebounds in housing and autos, which led the economic recovery in the fall of 1980, should peter out shortly because of high interest rates as well as declining "real" spendable incomes. And, without the impetus of both these forces, surely the U.S. economy will run down again, if only because there is no big stimulus—other than greater defense spending—coming on to keep things going.

However, having taken this position, we hasten to add that we have no further judgment about this projected recession. It might be worse, not so severe, or about the same as the last one. There are too many crosscurrents at work, and too many political possibilities—not only domestically, but overseas—for us to have a clear picture of the future. For example, passage of a substantial tax cut early in the 97th Congress would tend to cushion any downturn, and to foster a fast recovery subsequently. By contrast, additional monetary tightening by the Fed might cause a "financial accident," which could lead to a much worse recession than anything experienced since the 1930s.

Financial Accident

In fact, the greatest peril we face is the chance that something might go seriously wrong with our financial system. For, by every standard measure, such as current ratio, quick ratio, acid test and ratio of total debt to equity, American industry as a whole presently exhibits the worst balance sheet position of the postwar period. In general, our banks are no better off, with extraordinarily high ratios of loans to deposits and a paucity of equity capital, not to mention that raft of LDC paper which may not be worth anywhere near face value.

True enough, since 1973, the monetary system of the western nations has held up well under the pressures of huge outflows to the Middle East, two severe recessions, rounds of hyperinflation, the insolvency of several borrowing countries and even the failures of several large banks. However, just because the "unthinkable" has not happened during these trying times is no reason to assume that things will continue fortuitously in the future.

To the contrary, complacency itself, toward either inflation or the progress of the recovery, could well lead to an unexpected trauma. Even today, without much fanfare, the rate of bankruptcies—personal as well as business—has been rising at a time when economic pressures are making it even more difficult to pay bills.

Disinflation

In this vein, the prevalent assumption that a good strong dose of disinflationary medicine will cure most of our economic ills could prove dangerous. After all, during the past several years, consumer spending has been spurred by increasing amounts of borrowing on asset values driven ever higher by inflation. At the same time, businessmen have also borrowed heavily for new plant and equipment, going on the premise that such goods would only cost more in the future, while their loans would be paid back in currency worth less and less all the time.

---

3. As estimated by the U.S. Congress Joint Committee on Taxation, the combination of higher payroll taxes and inflation will push individual income taxes up $35 billion in 1981. In addition, Social Security taxes could rise about $19 billion and the further deregulation of oil prices will boost windfall profits taxes by $11 billion. All told, the Committee estimates, federal taxes are slated to rise as much as $85 billion in 1981.

Yes, in large part, inflationary *expectations,* as well as the functional aspects of inflation, have prolonged the economic advance that began in 1975. Moreover, we are convinced that once the Fed removed credit controls and began stimulating the money supply in May 1980, the general expectation of renewed inflation helped to power the subsequent recovery. At present, even with real incomes falling and the profits of many companies none too robust, people are spending heavily for *things,* which they feel must go up in value, and reducing cash reserves, which they feel can only decline in buying power.

Assuming this perception of the current scene is correct, what would happen in the event that prices stopped rising so fast? Inflationary expectations and purchasing patterns might remain high for a time. But, should disinflation persist for very long, then would people be quite so eager to consume, to borrow even more, to reduce savings? Suppose that the prices of single family houses leveled off for a while, or even declined markedly (horrors!), would homeowners feel quite so comfortable about spending more and more for goods and services?

In essence, the process of *dis*inflation—especially if it takes place fast enough—can choke off economic growth and can cause a recession just as effectively, if not more so, than rampant inflation. For most people, rapid disinflation can be even more damaging than equally rapid inflation, because at such times jobs are lost, pay can be cut and the value of most "hard assets" tends to decline. Inflation may erode real incomes and living standards, but disinflation can knock them both off—and in *absolute* terms.

So, we see disinflation as a potential peril rather than as the unabashed positive force perceived by so many others. In fact, perhaps because most people believe that material disinflation is only a remote possibility, precious little attention has been paid to its negative aspects. Moreover, again because most people believe that the chances for this scenario are low, we think it could happen. And, if it does, it would do a lot of damage because so many people would be caught by surprise. Precisely how such a process of rapid disinflation might start is hard to pinpoint in advance although, in the present situation, it could be triggered by misguided governmental policies such as excessive contraction of money supply growth.

Hyperinflation?

Suppose, just suppose, that this view of how things may go in the next year or so proves wrong—in fact, exactly backward. Specifically, suppose that Congress soon enacts a broadly based tax cut of $35 billion or more for 1981, and that the Administration pushes hard for further cuts of $100-150 billion over the course of several years. At the same time, suppose that there are major reductions in welfare expenditures, as promised, but that spending on defense rises materially, and probably more than the savings affected elsewhere. Finally, suppose that Mr. Reagan pursues "hard line" policies overseas, which would mean even more spending to support foreign commitments.

Given these developments, with all due respect for the theories of supply side economics, chances are that the federal deficit would burgeon mightily—at least for a while. Given this scenario, is it not reasonable to think that inflation might also run away again? For, at least on an "expectational" basis, people would have every reason to act as though prices were headed ever higher. Playing out this line of thought a bit further, given such an environment, the Federal Reserve would surely bend every effort to curb money supply growth, provided the present leadership remains in power.

So, hyperinflation, accompanied by super-high interest rates, is another peril that we might face during the next year or two. For, in the event that Congress and the new Administration provide consumers and businessmen with all of these financial incentives, as well as a slew of new defense spending, both private and governmental borrowing could go through the roof.

After a while, of course, economic growth might be great enough to cover all of these prospective deficits, public and private. But, in the meantime (and with all due respect to the arguments of supply side economics), the combination of massive tax cuts and greater expenditures for defense could very well worsen inflationary expectations and drive interest rates higher, regardless of countervailing moves by the Fed and/or concurrent reductions in spending for social services.

Social Unrest

Speaking of reductions in governmental services, should the campaign pledge to cut welfare spending deeply be carried out, many people could become truly unhappy—especially during a period of disinflation. For it is bad enough to lose purchasing power during a period of inflation, when unemployment is usually low; but, it is far worse to lose income and/or wealth—in *absolute* terms—during a period of disinflation, when unemployment is often high. So, regardless of how positive people may feel right now, when—let's face it—things are going relatively well for most of us, they may turn nasty during an economic setback, with unemployment and other social benefit programs reduced materially.

Surely, the notion that people should be more self-reliant is a welcome change from the welfarism that prevailed in the 1960s and even in the 1970s. However, that present sentiment presumes the availability of plenty of jobs. In tougher times, those who suffer economic adversity may well feel cheated, and could react angrily at the polls, or even in the streets. Thus, social unrest could prove to be one of the perils of the next several years.

Political Upheavals

Turning to foreign affairs, things are getting no better and, if anything, even worse. For example, nations in the Middle East are at war once again. The "have nots" are forming new alliances, presumably against the "haves." Not only in the U.S. but in many other places, spending on "defense" is bound to increase, with no assurances regarding how or when the weapons and forces accumulated may be used. With a demonstration of strong leadership, and after they are carrying a "bigger stick," perhaps the Reagan Administration can reassert American dominance in world affairs. At that time, clashing interests may be forced to resolve their differences, and peacefully. However, neither Russia nor China, not to mention the more militant Middle Eastern powers, are likely to remain idle while the U.S. builds up its military capabilities.

In any event, for at least the next several years, foreign political upheavals are likely to prove perils to our economic progress, whether from further curtailment of the flow of oil or from other disruptions. Above all, just going on the recent record, these sorts of troubles are likely to take most of us by surprise, to catch us unprepared.

Yes, the "promises" of the '80s are magnificent indeed, for they could improve the quality of our lives, as well as our standards of living, immeasurably. However, getting from here to there *safely*, without a lot of anguish, even if possible is not likely to be at all easy.

Labor and Business: A Community of Interest

BY ROBERT A. GEORGINE

I AM GOING to address myself to a subject that I believe is most appropriate for our first Annual Conference of the 1980s. That subject is the growing community of interest between labor and management with respect to employee benefit plans.

For many years, it has been evident that labor and management have mutual interests with respect to collectively bargained plans, especially jointly trusteed plans. The International Foundation of Employee Benefit Plans is, itself, an outgrowth of that community of interest.

The 1970s, with the enactment of ERISA, saw the continued growth of our shared concerns in this area, and I believe that the coming decade will see an even more dramatic increase in the recognition of this community of interest.

Two Key Developments

Two unrelated developments in the employee benefit plan field are at center stage as we enter the '80s. These two unrelated developments underscore the existence of this community of interest and the need for cooperation between labor and management.

The first development is the enactment of termination insurance legislation for multiemployer plans, legislation that will have a significant impact on labor and management, and on institutions which have never before felt themselves touched by multiemployer plans. The other development is the increasing desire on the part of workers and their representatives for greater control over the investment of their benefit plan assets.

The Employer Liability Issue

The Way It Was

Jointly trusteed plans, as most of you know, were for the most part originally established by unions which, through collective bargaining, secured agreements from a number of otherwise-unrelated employers to contribute a specified amount of money to a multiemployer plan. The contribution formula may have been in terms of

Mr. Georgine is president of the Building and Construction Trades Department, AFL-CIO, which has 15 affiliated unions with 4.1 million members. He graduated from DePaul Academy and attended the University of Illinois and DePaul University. Mr. Georgine began his career as an apprentice in Lathers' Local Union #74 in Chicago and became a journeyman in 1953. After two years in the U.S. Army, he worked his way up through the elected offices in Lathers' Local Union #74. Mr. Georgine was assistant business manager of the Lathing Foundation in Chicago in 1962 and 1963. In 1964, he became international representative of the Wood, Wire and Metal Lathers' International Union. Later, he served as assistant to the general president and was elected general president in 1970. Mr. Georgine was elected secretary-treasurer of the Building and Construction Trades Department in May 1971 and served in that capacity until June 1, 1974, when he was unanimously elected president of the Department. He also serves on the AFL-CIO standing committees on education and housing. Mr. Georgine is a director or member of numerous labor, government and business organizations including the U.S. Department of Labor ERISA Advisory Council, Construction Industry Stabilization Committee and the Collective Bargaining Committee on Construction. He is chairman of the National Coordinating Committee for Multiemployer Plans.

cents per hour, dollars per week, or cents per ton of coal. Whatever the method of determining contributions, the employers' only obligation was to make that fixed contribution. They could walk away from the plan with no further liability.

Under these circumstances, employers had little reason to be concerned about the administration of those plans, nor were they overly concerned with whether the plans were well funded or partly funded, or whether they promised too much. From management's perspective, those were labor's headaches. Once the employer had made his monthly contribution he was free, for the most part, to ignore the pension plan that promised his employees a retirement benefit.

Indeed, the system also permitted unions to be unconcerned about the levels of funding, or promising a greater benefit than could be afforded in the short range, for you could always pay tomorrow for the benefits earned today. Furthermore, if necessary, plans that found themselves in financial distress could always reduce benefits, even retroactively.

Most trustees, both union and management, were responsible and, by and large, the record of our multiemployer trusts prior to the enactment of ERISA was admirable. However, the system was one which permitted a lackadaisical attitude.

Enter ERISA

ERISA, of course, changed all that. Three of its provisions were to have a direct and significant impact on thinking in the multiemployer plan universe.

First, ERISA prohibited retroactive reductions of accrued benefits. Therefore, a plan in short term financial distress, or a plan in a declining industry, could no longer reduce the level of benefits in order to keep the plan alive.

Secondly, ERISA imposed minimum funding requirements, which you all know require regular funding of future and past service benefits. In some industries, this new funding burden, when coupled with the prohibition on the retroactive reduction of accrued benefits, forced increases in employer contributions by as much as 40%. These mandatory increases had a direct impact on labor as well as management, for in most industries, at least part of the increase came out of the next collectively bargained wage package.

The third of ERISA's provisions that had a significant impact concerned plan termination insurance and employer liability.

Faulty Incentives

Specifically, the termination insurance program under ERISA, as enacted in 1974, provided that an employer who remained with a plan until it terminated, or who withdrew from a plan within five years of its termination, was liable to the Pension Benefit Guaranty Corporation for unfunded guaranteed benefits in an amount up to 30% of the employer's net worth. However, an employer who withdrew more than five years before termination escaped liability entirely.

This system generated the infamous "last man out" syndrome. Fear of being one of the unfortunate few who might be stuck paying everyone else's liability was rampant in industries affected by multiemployer plans. I am sure that many employers withdrew, hoping that the plan would not terminate within five years.

Even more important than the actual withdrawals was the climate which existed in industries such as the construction industry. Whether a legitimate issue or not, many groups of employers fanned the flames generated by fear of contingent employer liability until it became an impediment to effective collective bargaining. Indeed, in many instances, the threat of contingent employer liability became the rallying cry for those who wished to go open shop to begin with. And, even where this was not the case, there was great reluctance on management's part to increase benefits—thereby increasing unfunded liability—so long as the possibility of contingent employer liability existed.

The incentive to abandon a plan which was generated by contingent employer liability was compounded by the 30% net worth cap that applied to an employer's liability. For some employers, the cost of *maintaining* the plan exceeded 30% of their net worth. Under those circumstances, it became economically worthwhile to terminate the plan and shift the pension burden onto the PBGC insurance program which, as you all know, is paid for by our plans in the form of premium dollars.

Surprising as it may seem, in some of these plans it might have seemed beneficial even to *labor* to terminate, since benefits were guaranteed 100%.

Adding to these difficulties were the threats from dying industries. The Pension Benefit Guaranty Corporation, in one of its many analyses of potential terminations in dying industries, suggested a possible premium cost of $80.00 per participant per year. If that prognosis were ever realized, 7% of the average multiemployer plan participant's annual pension contribution would have gone to finance benefits for workers in dying industries.

Between the prohibition on benefit reductions, the funding requirements, and the structure of employer termination liability, the multiemployer system was in serious jeopardy. Both management and labor had an economic incentive to terminate: management because it could throw off part of its liability on others, and labor because its benefits were guaranteed 100%.

Shared Concerns—And an Effective Coalition

Labor and management had a shared perception of the basic problems facing multiemployer plans and, for the most part, each recognized the legitimate concerns of the other. As a result, an unprecedented coalition of the major elements of labor and management was formed. It is with pride that I can point to the fact that the National Coordinating Committee for Multiemployer Plans was instrumental in putting together this coalition and keeping it together through exceptionally trying circumstances. As a matter of fact, it is this experience which offers some hope for labor and management cooperation as we enter the '80s. I won't take time to describe for you all the gory details—suffice it to point out that we were able to include in our coalition the Coordinating Committee; the National Construction Employers Council and, ultimately, all of its affiliated construction employer trade associations; both labor and management in the food marketing and retail industries; labor and management in the trucking, mining and food service and lodging industries; the AFL-CIO; and ERIC, the ERISA Regulations Industry Committee, not only in behalf of its member corporations but also in behalf of the National Association of Manufacturers, the Chamber of Commerce, the American Bankers' Association and the life insurance industry.

The Amendments—A Source of Discord. However difficult it was to put together this coalition, it was infinitely more difficult to *keep* it together through the legislative process, as each side, periodically, found itself with an opportunity to secure some related (or unrelated) legislative advantage.

Let me provide an example.

During the last stages of the legislative battle, certain non-germane amendments were tacked onto the bill in the Senate. These included an amendment to sharply curtail the enforcement of the Occupational Safety and Health Act, which I will refer to as the OSHA amendment; an amendment to transfer jurisdiction for safety and health in sand and gravel pits from the Mine Safety Administration to the Occupational Safety and Health Administration (the so-called MSHA transfer amendment); and an amendment to exempt the Hawaii Health Care Act from the preemption provisions of ERISA (the Matsunaga amendment, named after its principal sponsor in the Senate).

The Matsunaga amendment was supported by some people in labor; indeed, I had agreed with Senator Matsunaga even before the termination insurance legislation reached the Senate floor to support his amendment. But it was strongly opposed by the NAM and ERIC, and we had made a commitment to the coalition bill which of course did not include the Matsunaga amendment. We not only had to let the NAM and ERIC fight to get it dropped from the bill; to keep faith with the coalition, we had to actively support their effort—and we did.

To cite another example, the OSHA amendment, frankly, almost succeeded in splintering the coalition. Certain elements of the small business community were so enthralled with the prospect of gutting OSHA that they forgot how imperative it was that we get relief from the contingent employer liability provisions of Title IV of ERISA. The Chamber of Commerce and the AGC strayed from the coalition for several painful weeks while they flirted with the non-germane amendments. As a matter of fact, it was during this period that Title IV went into effect for six weeks. Only then did they realize the importance of keeping the coalition together.

The MSHA amendment offered an example of a deliberate effort to extract from the coalition both labor and management in the construction industry. It was generally known that we in the building trades supported an MSHA transfer. But others in labor were opposed, and the cardinal principle of keeping the coalition together dominated our thinking.

A Law We Can Live With. Eventually, we succeeded. Together, this coalition faced and survived one of the toughest legislative battles in recent memory. Many compromises were necessary on both sides, but the result was a termination insurance law that fosters the growth of multiemployer plans. The incentives existing under the old law for employers to withdraw from plans or to terminate them, as well as the incentives for labor to go along with plan termination, are gone. They are replaced by withdrawal liability and reduced guarantees that act as *dis*incentives to abandonment of plans on the part of both management and labor. Stricter funding requirements for all multiemployer plans, as well as special funding requirements for plans in financial trouble, will aid in providing greater strength and vitality to plans, and a better assurance of benefits for those to whom pension promises were made.

This was all possible despite what many felt to be overwhelming odds—odds against sustaining a cooperative and coordinated front between unions and employers. But, by recognizing our community of interest, we succeeded.

Investment Targeting

The second major development which will, I believe, further increase the community of interest between labor and management concerns the investment of plan assets, both with respect to the return provided to the fund and the secondary effects of these investments. This development is, as I mentioned at the beginning, the increasing desire on the part of workers and their representatives to exercise greater control over the investment of their pension plan assets.

Most discussions of what has become known as social investing focus on the benefits to be provided to workers. However, I believe that the potential benefits that can be derived from an active and positive investment policy will be of equal importance to both labor and management.

At the outset, let me make it clear that I am not referring to the entire range of investments generally referred to as social investments, but rather to the kinds of investment practices that have positive secondary results for participants and employers alike. That is, those investments that preserve and expand jobs, and thus a plan's contribution base, or otherwise promote the well-being of participants, employers and the communities from which they come.

Pension Funds as a Capital Source

Pension funds, as many of you know, are the single most important source of external financing that corporations have today, providing one-half of new, externally generated capital and one-quarter of all new capital generated in our economy. Private and state and local pension funds are worth some $450 billion; they will contribute some 50 billion new dollars to the economy this year. They own 20-25% of the stock of American corporations, and 40% of corporate bonds. Growing at a rate of 10% per year, pension funds will invest $750 billion in the economy over the next ten years. Pension funds presently account for 9% of net personal income, and 25% of net household assets. Today, pension funds literally dominate the trading on our nation's stock and bond exchanges.

Although unions represent only about 20% of the private sector work force, almost two-thirds of all private sector workers who belong to a pension plan are in collectively bargained funds. While unions are the single most important factor in the creation of pension funds as we know them today, in practice, a worker-oriented investment philosophy is almost non-existent for these funds.

The largest single category of pension funds are the single employer funds. At least half of their $250 billion in assets are collectively bargained, but the employer has sole discretion in the investment policies of these funds.

Public employees have, at least potentially, more control over their funds, but the $150 billion in public funds are often tightly restricted by state legislation that usually accepts Wall Street wisdom at face value.

Some unions, especially those in the construction industry, do have a significant role in the control of pension assets, through $50 billion in jointly trusteed funds. However, the investment community still dominates the investment policies of these funds.

Investment Biases

As with all other institutional monies, pension funds generally have been controlled by investment experts who adhere to a philosophy of efficient capital markets. In theory, these monies are invested in the nation's capital markets with a view of bringing about the greatest return, with the most ease and the least risk. However, in fact, institutional investors, on the whole, have been unable to match the return of even a passbook savings account over the last 15 years.

Moreover, their investments are heavily weighted in favor of the nation's largest corporations, especially those that have massive investments in advanced technology and automation, and those that have been effective and mobile allocators of resources on a global scale. Small and medium-sized firms, whose risk-adjusted return has consistently outperformed that of the blue chip corporations, have been largely unable to tap this increasingly important source of capital, and instead have been forced to rely on far more expensive sources of capital.

Union Involvement: A Changing Role

Even where union trustees have a significant voice in pension fund management, they have usually relied on these institutional investors every bit as much as have the state and local governments and the employer-controlled funds. There seem to be two reasons for this. First, union officials are not investment experts. The political as well as legal responsibility of investing millions of dollars in members' deferred wages weighs very heavily. And, since the so-called investment experts are the standard for the measurement of prudence, union trustees have felt that they have no other choice but to turn over complete investment discretion to their investment professionals.

The second major factor is that unions traditionally have avoided involvement in the management end of the economy. With investment policy so closely linked with management decisions, union officials have felt that they should have no significant role beyond expecting a decent return on their money.

Today, however, the situation is fast changing. Many labor trustees are dissatisfied with the performance of their funds, both in terms of the return provided and in the types of investments made. It has become increasingly clear that, left to their own devices, investment professionals generally prefer to put money in non-union companies over unionized ones. Their professional bias appears to favor companies that enjoy a "union-free environment."

Combined with this realization is the growing awareness on the part of the unions that they have no choice if they are to survive, much less grow, but to demand that their members' deferred wages be used to promote their interests and not be used to undermine their present as well as future economic security. While there are numerous legal, political, economic and practical questions related to the effective investment of pension capital, more and more union officials, on the national and local level, are exploring specific steps that can be taken.

Nowhere is this more evident than in the building and construction trades. There are several reasons for this. First, we historically have been involved exclusively with jointly trusteed funds, giving us a great deal of firsthand experience over the past 30 years. Second, there is a more direct and visible relationship between a construction investment and a job for an individual worker than is the case for other sectors of the economy.

A Natural Alliance

Whether union pension fund trustees want to invest pension fund assets as part of a joint venture to keep a plant from relocating, or whether they want to stimulate the union side of construction, they are finding a natural ally in the management with which they have working relationships. After all, both labor and management in those sectors of the economy in which collectively bargained plans proliferate have a direct interest in sound investments which stimulate their sector of the economy. Trustees are finding that they can provide a better return than the so-called investment experts *and* provide secondary benefits for their participants and contributing employers.

In the past decade, the building and construction industry has been harder hit by the economic roller coaster than any other segment of the economy. Once again, as we enter the '80s, we appear to be at the cutting edge of the financial community's tunnel-visioned approach to controlling inflation: high interest rates. Faced with this threat, labor and management in the construction industry are recognizing the imperative of financial cooperation. In this effort, we will need the cooperation of the executive branch of government in granting the necessary exemptions and issuing the appropriate rulings, without which our efforts may not succeed. To achieve those exemptions and rulings will require a united effort on the part of labor and management.

I believe that, as both labor and management become increasingly aware of the vast potential for mutual benefit that can be derived from imaginative investment of pension plan assets, the community of interest concerning these issues will continue to grow. And, in my view, active and positive investment policies that reflect these shared concerns will become a dominant feature of collectively bargained plans in the coming decade. Without such policies, the very existence of collectively bargained plans and the industries with which they are associated may be in doubt. But with those active and positive investment policies, we can share a period of enormous growth.

In closing, I call upon the International Foundation to join with us in realizing the benefits promised by cooperation in the coming decade. I know that with your cooperation, we will all succeed in our common goal of nurturing our collectively bargained plans so that they may offer greater retirement security to millions of American working families.

CHAPTER 2

The Legislative Environment

Malcolm L. Pritzker

Partner
Zimmerman and Obadal
Washington, D.C.

Robert E. Nagle

Executive Director
Pension Benefit Guaranty Corporation
Washington, D.C.

Carlton R. Sickles

President
Carday Associates, Inc.
Landover, Maryland

Gerald E. Cole, Jr.

Assistant Executive Director
Pension Benefit Guaranty Corporation
Washington, D.C.

Steven E. Schanes, Ph.D.

President
Schanes Associates
San Diego, California

Joseph Eichenholz

Director of Health Policy Analysis
Connecticut General Life Insurance Company
Hartford, Connecticut

John van Steenwyk

Vice President
Martin E. Segal Company
New York, New York

Patricia K. Putman

Associate Dean, Legal and Legislative Affairs
University of Hawaii
Honolulu, Hawaii

Orlando K. Watanabe

Administrator, Disability Compensation Division
State of Hawaii
Department of Labor and Human Relations
Honolulu, Hawaii

The Legislative Process—
How to Make Your Voice Heard

BY MALCOLM L. PRITZKER

Introduction

I moved to Washington, D.C. four years ago to be a partner in a Washington, D.C. law firm. As a fairly recent addition to what is referred to by the newspapers as the "Washington scene," I brought my own perceptions and prejudices about the government, and especially the legislative process, with me. The image of so-called inner circle denizens of Capitol Hill in the Congress and on the staffs of the Congress, and the Congressmen imposing their inefficient and overbearing will on those of us in the real world, was strong. The real world was defined, in my mind, as any city outside of Washington, D.C.

For many years, I had been the attorney for a number of local multiemployer pension and welfare plans. In addition, for over ten years, I have been one of the management trustees and have done some legal work for the Graphic Arts International Union Supplemental Retirement and Disability Fund.

The Graphic Arts plan has approximately 50,000 participants in both the United States and Canada. Over 8,000 former employees of participating unionized employers in the graphic arts industry are receiving retirement benefits from the fund. The fund has assets in excess of $170 million. Each month the fund office sends out approximately $750,000 to pensioners. Contributions by the over 1,500 participating employers exceed $2 million per month. The average participating employer employs 33 covered employees.

It is also important to note that the assets of the fund exceed termination liability. If the fund terminated tomorrow, we have enough assets to pay all vested participants all of the benefits due them. This is, as I am sure you know, a unique position for a pension plan to be in.

The Multiemployer Amendments: A Matter of Concern

It will come as no surprise to those of you who are trustees that the trustees of our fund became

Mr. Pritzker is a partner in the Washington, D.C. law firm of Zimmerman and Obadal. He is a trustee of a national pension plan (GAIU Early Retirement) and serves as legal counsel to other funds. He received a B.A. degree in Labor-Management Relations from Pennsylvania State University, did graduate work at the Wharton School of the University of Pennsylvania and received his J.D. degree from Temple University Law School. He has written numerous articles, and a book entitled Collective Bargaining Manual. *He is on the Panel of Labor Arbitrators of the Federal Mediation and Conciliation Service and the American Arbitration Association. Mr. Pritzker has appeared on previous Foundation educational programs.*

concerned about some of the provisions initially proposed in H.R. 3904 and S.1076—the Multiemployer Pension Plan Amendments Act. The trustees of the fund assigned a committee of professionals to study the proposed bill. The committee consisted of the general attorney for the fund, the fund actuary, myself and one other trustee.

A complete report was made by this committee to the full board of trustees, which consists of 14 management and 14 union trustees from all over the United States and Canada. The report analyzed the bill and contrasted it to the portion of ERISA which would go into effect if a bill of some kind was not passed. The committee's report pointed out the practical impact of some provisions in the bill upon the workings of the fund.

The trustees had never previously gotten involved in the legislative process, and therefore had to think through just what their responsibilities—both fiduciary and practical—were in the face of a proposed bill that clearly would have been harmful in its initial form.

ERISA—which contains so much language relating to the responsibilities of trustees—is silent on the issue of trustee involvement in the legislative process.

Our trustees decided that we would be negligent in carrying out our responsibilities to the employee participants and the contributing employers if we did not attempt to shape the legislation to meet the needs of the participants and the employers. For us to merely accept what was decided by others could have meant the expenditure of large sums of money which, in our opinion, would be better spent to improve benefits. We were also fearful that some of the provisions of the initially proposed bill might have eroded some of our current benefits.

We decided that employer contributions and investment returns should, to the maximum extent possible, be used to benefit fund participants rather than to fund compliance with unnecessary regulation. We felt that for us to not even attempt to make our voice heard would be an abdication of our responsibilities. The comparison would be for a private citizen not to vote, and then complain about the competence of the Congressman elected to represent him.

A Plan of Action

Once having decided that we had to do something, the questions became:
1. What changes did we think should be made in the bill?
2. How could we achieve these changes most effectively?

We first analyzed the Congressional Committees which would conduct hearings on the proposed legislation. We found that there was no one committee involved in this legislation: the Pension Task Force, House Committee on Education and Labor, House Ways and Means Committee, Senate Labor Committee and Senate Finance Committee were all involved. Hearings before most of these committees would be held.

Preparing a Position Paper

We had to develop a position paper which would be given to the members of each committee and their staffs. We also had to develop testimony which would communicate our concerns and our objectives. I was assigned the task of writing the initial draft of our position paper. The rest of the committee members critiqued the position paper and recommended changes.

There are several ways you can write a position paper. A position paper can be written—
- For posterity
- For a law review article
- To massage the egos of trustees
- To educate the Congress and committee staff.

Obviously, the most effective way to write a position paper is to identify who you are, what impact some aspects of the legislation would have on your fund and what recommendations you have to change these provisions.

You must remember that you are not writing on a clean slate. You are dealing with proposed legislation, which in this case was the product of an enormous amount of work done by the staff of the various Congressional Committees. Unless you think it is desirable and possible to attempt to defeat the entire legislation, you should select the real problem areas for discussion in the position paper. It is counterproductive to nitpick every minor annoying section of a bill.

Presenting Effective Testimony

The process of presenting testimony before several Congressional Committees who are considering a proposed bill is quite interesting. Once your position paper is in final form, 30 or 40 copies of your paper must be delivered to the staff of the committee before which you will testify. The staff of a committee, such as the House Pension Task Force Committee, is very different from the staff of an individual Congressman. The committee's staff becomes extremely knowledgeable about the legislation before it, because they have often discussed, considered and perhaps even written the bill. Bills are not often written on the back of an envelope by Congressmen scurrying to their next meeting.

When the day of the hearing comes, you arrive at the committee room, which is often a long room with a judicial bench on a raised platform behind which the Representatives and the committee staff sit. A hearing table is before the raised platform from which witnesses testify. It is very much of a courtroom type setting. It is a setting that I am used to, and therefore, as the person who would testify for our fund, I was able to keep from hyperventilating.

I watched a number of presentations made before the several Congressional Committees which considered this bill, and reached several conclusions about the most effective way to give testimony.

Some witnesses read the same statement that they already had had delivered to the committee staff. This is a waste of time. You possibly will be surprised to know that the staff has read and considered each position paper well before the hearing. The staff has carefully briefed and summarized each position paper for the Congressmen. Some Congressmen have read each paper. Obviously, the most effective way to testify is to get the attention of the Congressmen and staff. The way to do that is to establish eye contact, then to give a precise summary of your written testimony and add a number of practical examples not in your paper which will bring your points home.

Some of the witnesses I heard adopted the classic approaches of viewing with alarm or pointing with pride. Either the Republic was doomed by the bill, or the bill was a great creation by historic statesmen.

The attitude of the several Congressmen was interesting. Most were briefed, most listened, most understood and several asked detailed questions. The questions and answers are more helpful in some respects than the formal oral testimony. There were, to be candid, a few Congressmen who would pop in to the committee hearing room from time to time to deliver a politically self-serving declaration of their interest in and love for—fill in the blank—unions, old people, pensioners, employers—and then leave, without hearing the testimony, caring little about the testimony or, indeed, the bill itself.

Before and after each presentation of testimony before a committee, our group met with the staffs of each committee. As I pointed out previously, the staffs impressed us with their knowledge of the proposed bill, and seemed genuinely concerned about those relatively few areas of the bill we viewed as major problems, once we advised them of the practical impact these sections would have on our fund and its participants. The fact that we could speak with one voice, including both management and labor concerns, was quite helpful.

The testimony before the Senate Committee followed the same format, except that only one Senator—the chairman of the committee—was in attendance. He was knowledgeable about the bill and our presentation. We were advised that the other Senators would read the testimony, the formal presentations and the transcript of the hearing.

Follow-Up and Communication

We decided not to personally contact any of the Congressmen or Senators who were on the committees considering this legislation. We felt that, at least initially, the most effective procedure was to make our formal written and oral presentations and to further explain our position to the staffs of the committees.

Once the bill was reported out of the House Committees, we analyzed it carefully and were gratified to find that our real areas of concern were addressed in a substantially modified version of the bill. In other words, all of the presentations and all of the witnesses did succeed in modifying the bill. We made a difference.

However, we discovered that one very harmful change was made in the bill which would have changed our fund from its enviable position of having no liquidation liability and therefore no possible employer liability to a fund which had more liabilities than assets. The change to which I refer was buried in some obscure clause in the bill, and we did not discover the possible impact of the change for several weeks.

At that time, after advising the staffs of both the House and Senate Committees of our great concern, we launched into a program of communicating directly with the Senators on the committee then considering the bill that had already been passed by the House, so that we could attempt to substantially change or entirely delete the harmful provision of the bill. We got together a list of all of the Senators whom we thought could play a role in achieving the desired modification. We really did not care whether the Senators were Republicans or Democrats so long as they were in a position to listen to our pleas—and, if we could be persuasive enough, we hoped, to agree with our position. We then thought through which of the 30 trustees scattered throughout the United States would be best able to communicate with each Senator. We prepared a short position paper. We coached each trustee about the problem and the telephone presentation we wanted him to make.

The trustees called the Senator or House member to whom they were assigned and told the Senator or Congressman or their key administrative assistants of this particular problem in the bill. They told them that a letter would be delivered by the end of that same day explaining in detail the fund's problem with that portion of the legislation. The trustees were surprised that in a number of instances they could get Senators on the telephone and discuss the problem with them. If a Senator was not available, his administrative assistant was available. The administrative assistants were courteous and helpful. The trustees were convinced that the Senators and their administrative assistants sincerely cared about the harmful impact on our fund and its participants.

We were successful and the offending clause was substantially modified.

Conclusion: Continued Involvement

Our trustees came full circle from a cynicism over the Washington scene to a practical realization that—at least sometimes, on some issues—we could make a difference in a proposed piece of legislation and thereby fulfill our obligations as trustees.

We intend to stay involved in the legislative process. I would urge you and your board of trustees to examine each piece of proposed legislation and to get involved in protecting your funds as part of your duty to safeguard the assets of your funds and provide maximum protection to the participants and to the contributing employers.

Overview of the Multiemployer Pension Plan Amendments Act of 1980

BY ROBERT E. NAGLE

MY REMARKS are intended as an overview of the multiemployer legislation, in an effort to hit the highlights and alert you to some of the aspects with which you should be particularly concerned. The outline which appears in the Appendix to this article contrasts provisions of prior law to the new law; this was done by way of underscoring the areas in which the new legislation represents departures from the previous provisions of ERISA.

ERISA Title IV as Background

I might say by way of background that when the original provisions of ERISA were being considered in 1973 and 1974, one of the issues in great contention was whether the guarantee program of Title IV should be made applicable to multiemployer plans. Congress finally made the judgment that it should be, but because the matter had been in dispute and because there was uncertainty as to just what the impact of Title IV would be on multiemployer plans, the coverage of Title IV for such plans was not made fully effective at that time. Rather, there was provided a period of several years during which, if a multiemployer plan terminated, PBGC would have discretionary authority to decide whether to guarantee the benefits of the participants in that plan.

This period of discretionary coverage was initially scheduled to expire on January 1, 1978, but subsequently was extended in several stages until August 1, 1980. During this period of discretionary coverage, it became apparent that there are a significant number of multiemployer plans which are experiencing various degrees of financial difficulty. It also became clear that the existing provisions of Title IV, if they were to be made fully applicable to multiemployer plans, would in all likelihood have an adverse effect on many such plans, particularly on those in financial difficulty, and in many cases would encourage their termination rather than their continuance.

Mr. Nagle is the executive director of the Pension Benefit Guaranty Corporation (PBGC), a self-financing government corporation established to administer pension plan termination insurance under ERISA. Mr. Nagle was appointed to this position in September 1979. Before joining PBGC, Mr. Nagle had been a partner at the Washington, D.C. law firm of Wald, Harkrader and Ross, where he specialized in employee benefit plans and labor law. From 1969-1974 Mr. Nagle was on the staff of the Senate Committee on Labor and Public Welfare, serving as general counsel from 1971-1974. During this period he was responsible for much of the staff work performed during the consideration and adoption of the 1974 pension reform legislation. He was also extensively involved as a staff member in the development and passage of the Occupational Safety and Health Act of 1969, and the Equal Employment Enforcement Amendments of 1972. From 1963-1969, Mr. Nagle was counsel for appellate litigation in the Solicitor's Office of the Department of Labor, and served as associate special counsel to the President's Committee on Equal Employment Opportunity for the two prior years. Mr. Nagle received his J.D. degree from the University of Chicago. He also has an LL.M. from Georgetown University Law School and a B.A. from Wesleyan University.

The primary reason for this conclusion lies with the employer liability provisions of the original legislation. If a multiemployer plan were to terminate, those employers who were contributing to the plan at the time it terminated would be subject to liability to the PBGC. In addition, liability could be assessed against those employers who withdrew during the five years prior to the plan's termination. But the earlier within that five year period that the withdrawal occurred, the less would be the employer's liability. If the withdrawal occurred more than five years before termination, the employer withdrawing would be home free, with no liability.

Under those circumstances, if a plan appeared to be encountering financial problems, the shrewd employer would seek to get out as soon as possible and leave others to bear the potential burden of employer liability. And, if enough employers were seized with this "rush to the door" psychology, the plan's financial difficulties would be compounded, with increasing likelihood that the prospect of termination would become a reality. In addition, when a plan did terminate, ERISA limited any employer's liability to 30% of net worth. This meant that PBGC was not likely to recover all of the costs that it would incur in taking over a terminated plan. Those costs would therefore be thrust on the insurance system, meaning that they ultimately would be borne by the other plans which pay premiums to the PBGC.

Everyone who considered the matter agreed this was a bad situation all around. An effort therefore was made to devise new legislation which would tend to strengthen multiemployer plans, encourage their continuance rather than their termination, and remove from the statute those unfortunate incentives which I have described. That legislation was finally enacted on September 26, 1980, and is called the Multiemployer Pension Plan Amendments Act of 1980. It incorporates basic revisions to ERISA which will be applicable to all multiemployer pension plans, and many of these revisions are of critical significance.

Key Provisions of the MPPAA

Listed in the outline are 11 areas in which the new legislation represents substantial departures from the prior law. It might be said that the first six items are directly essential to the new guarantee program; the remaining five, although of substantial significance, are included in the law for reasons which are not necessarily related to the new guarantee program.

Withdrawal Liability

By far the most significant feature of the new legislation is the provision for withdrawal liability. It is also the most complex creation of the legislation and, in addition, is the area of the law with which you as trustees will have your most immediate and urgent concerns.

What is withdrawal liability? Well, simply put, it is an obligation that the statute imposes upon an employer who withdraws from a multiemployer plan to pay a portion of that plan's unfunded vested benefits. The withdrawal liability is calculated as an annual amount which is to be paid on a quarterly basis by that employer over a period of up to 20 years. This concept of withdrawal liability is really something quite new under Title IV. You will recall that under previous law, employer liability arose only if a plan terminated. Now, withdrawal liability will be imposed when an employer withdraws from a plan *without regard* to whether the plan terminates. The reasons for the new liability rules are simply put. One is to discourage withdrawal from multiemployer plans, and the other is to protect the plan and the other contributing employers from the impact of those withdrawals that do occur.

There are several basic questions that are presented by the withdrawal liability concept. One is what constitutes a withdrawal. The statute defines a full withdrawal as well as a partial withdrawal, both of which may give rise to liability.

The calculation of withdrawal liability is a highly complex matter. How do we determine a withdrawing employer's share of the unfunded vested benefits? There are various alternative methods for doing that. There is also a question of how the payments are to be made and how the payment obligation will be enforced.

There are two points I might stress before leaving the topic. One is that there are special rules for plans in the construction industry, in the entertainment industry, and in the trucking, moving and warehousing industry. If your plan is in one of those industries, it is important for you to become familiar with the special rules which pertain.

I should also stress that administration of withdrawal liability is going to be your responsibility as plan trustees. Under the original ERISA provisions, employer liability would be collected by PBGC. That is not the case now. When an employer withdraws, the *plan trustees* are the ones who will collect the withdrawal liability. And, the trustees are also responsible for making choices among the various options that the act provides with respect to the calculation and collection of withdrawal liability. What is more, the obligation to pay withdrawal liability arises with respect to withdrawals that occur subsequent to April 28, 1980. Since some of your plans may, therefore, already have withdrawal liability to collect, it is important that you become familiar with the applicable rules as soon as possible.

Funding Standards and Plan Reorganization

There was also concern in Congress that multiemployer plans generally should be subject to somewhat more stringent funding requirements. As a consequence, the act was amended to provide that unfunded past service costs attributable to new benefit increases are to be amortized over 30 years rather than 40 years, and experience losses amortized over 15 years rather than 20 years, as had been the case.

The next subject on the outline is that of plan reorganization. This is a matter addressed to those plans which are experiencing some degree of financial difficulty, particularly plans whose unfunded vested benefits in pay status have become particularly high in relation to contributions and plan assets. In such cases, the act attempts to bring about a better balance between plan assets and contributions on the one hand, and benefit levels on the other. It does this in two ways. One is to tighten the funding requirements for plans in reorganization, and the other is to give those plans some flexibility in reducing or eliminating recent benefit increases.

Now, how do you know if your plan is in reorganization? You make a calculation to determine what amount would be required in any year to amortize unfunded vested benefits in pay status over ten years and all other unfunded vested benefits over 25 years. If that amount is higher than the amount produced by the otherwise applicable minimum funding standards, you are by definition a plan in reorganization. That new funding test becomes the controlling funding standard, and is called the minimum contribution requirement or MCR.

Insolvency: An Insurable Event

I will move next to the matter of the insurable event. The legislation changes the nature of that event. Under the prior law, and this is still true for single employer plans, if a plan terminates with insufficient assets to pay guaranteed benefits, the PBGC takes over the plan and makes up any amounts required to pay guaranteed benefits. Plan termination was therefore the insurable event. This has been changed in the future for multiemployer plans; the insurable event will now be plan insolvency.

An insolvent plan is one that is unable to meet its benefit obligations as they become due. It is not necessary for such a plan to terminate, and we hope it will not. The new law provides for an insolvent plan to reduce its benefit payments to levels which it can pay. If those levels are below the amounts guaranteed under the new legislation, PBGC will provide financial assistance to the plan to enable it to pay guaranteed benefits. If the plan's insolvency is only a temporary condition, that financial assistance will probably be in the form of a loan. But if insolvency is a permanent condition, the financial assistance undoubtedly will be an outright grant. In either case, the idea is to make it possible for even an insolvent plan to continue, rather than be forced to terminate.

Guarantees and Premium Levels

Let me turn to the matter of guarantees for multiemployer plan participants. The level of guarantees provided under the new legislation is somewhat less than what was provided under prior law, and is also less than what is still provided for single employer plan participants. The level has been affected in two respects. One is that the maximum amount that is guaranteed has been reduced, and an element of coinsurance has been added. In addition, no benefit increases are guaranteed until they have been in effect for five years.

The act also increases the premium for multiemployer plans. Until now, that premium has been 50¢ annually per participant. That rate is going up in stages over a period of nine years to a level of $2.60. There will be an initial increase to $1.00 for the plan year in which the date of the enactment (September 26, 1980) falls, prorated in accordance with how much of the plan year remains after that date. For the next four plan years, the annual rate will be $1.40.

'Multiemployer' Definition

The definition of multiemployer plans has changed by the elimination of ERISA's 50% of contributions test, so that essentially any plan to which two or more unrelated employers contribute and which has been negotiated with a union will probably be a multiemployer plan. The legislation does provide an election option for those plans which were not multiemployer plans under the prior legislation because they did not meet the 50% of contributions test. Such plans will have a period of time in which they may elect to continue as non-multiemployer plans.

Contributions

With regard to delinquent contributions, there are some very significant provisions in the legislation which enhance the remedies available to a multiemployer plan. Fulfillment of an obligation to make contributions became a requirement under ERISA. A plan will be authorized to enforce that obligation in federal court, and the statute makes provision for the collection of interest and attorneys' fees and also for a penalty.

The matter of mistaken contributions is of recurring interest. The legislation will now make it possible for a multiemployer plan to return contributions found to have been made as a result of a mistake of law *or* fact, and such return may be made within six months after the plan discovers that the contribution was mistaken.

Severance Pay Plans

There are new provisions relating to severance pay arrangements and supplemental retirement income plans. The Department of Labor is authorized to prescribe regulations under which such plans may be treated as welfare rather than pension plans. This, of course, would have a significant impact with respect to the funding and vesting rules applicable to those plans.

Appendix

Multiemployer Pension Legislation

I. Employee Retirement Income Security Act of 1974 (ERISA)
   - Enacted September 2, 1974
   - Discretionary coverage of multiemployer plans until August 1, 1980
   - Mandatory coverage from August 1, 1980 until September 26, 1980

II. Multiemployer Pension Plan Amendments Act of 1980 (MPPAA)
   - Enacted September 26, 1980
   - Basic revisions in rules for all multiemployer plans

III. The Multiemployer Pension Plan Amendments Act of 1980 revised existing law in these areas:
   - Withdrawal liability
   - Plan reorganization
   - Insurable event
   - Guarantees
   - Funding
   - Premiums
   - Definition of multiemployer plan
   - Mergers and transfers
   - Delinquent contributions
   - Mistaken contributions
   - Severance pay plans

WITHDRAWAL LIABILITY

	Old Law	New Law
Definition of withdrawal	Not defined	Permanent cessation of (1) the obligation to contribute or (2) all covered operations; partial withdrawals also covered
Liable employer	Only 10% contributors	All withdrawing employers
Amount of liability	Share of the unfunded guaranteed benefits	Share of the unfunded vested benefits
Form of payment	Bond or escrow for five years	Quarterly installments paid directly to plan
Special industry rules	None	Special rules for construction, entertainment, trucking, moving, and warehousing industries
Administration of withdrawal liability	PBGC	Joint board of trustees

REORGANIZATION

	Old Law	New Law
• What does reorganization do?	No provision	Balances contribution and benefit levels
• When is a plan in reorganization?	No provision	When regular minimum funding will not fund unfunded retirees' benefits over ten years and actives' vested benefits over 25 years
• Minimum contribution requirement (MCR)	No provision	Fund unfunded retirees' benefits over ten years and actives' vested benefits over 25 years
• Overburden credit	No provision	Reduces the MCR when the number of retirees exceeds the number of actives and the employer contribution rate has not decreased
• Benefit reductions	Very limited reductions of accrued benefits permitted	Permits reduction of benefits increased in prior five years if the employer contribution rate is maintained

INSURABLE EVENT

	Old Law	New Law
• Insurable event	Plan termination	Plan insolvency
• Employer liability	Share of unfunded guaranteed benefits, limited to 30% of the employer's net worth, due in a lump sum to PBGC	Continued payment of required contributions to the plan
• Participants' benefits	Reduced to the guaranteed level if the plan is insufficient; no restoration	Same; benefits may be restored if the plan's financial condition improves
• Plan administration	PBGC generally becomes trustee	Plan sponsor continues to administer the plan
• PBGC premium funds	Pay the difference between the unfunded guaranteed benefits and employer liability	Provide financial assistance, if necessary, so plan can pay out guaranteed benefits when due

FUNDING

	Old Law	New Law
• Unfunded past service liability due to new benefit increases	Amortized over 40 years	Amortized over 30 years; grandfather provision for multilevel plans
• Experience losses	Amortized over 20 years	Amortized over 15 years

MULTIEMPLOYER GUARANTEES

	Old Law	New Law
• Benefits guaranteed	All nonforfeitable benefits, up to $1,159	(1) 100% of the monthly accrual rate up to $5, plus 75% of the accrual rate above $5 up to $20 times (2) a participant's years of service
• Guarantee of new benefits and benefit increases	Benefits under five years old at the greater of $20 or 20% per year	Five year cliff

PREMIUMS

	Old Law	New Law
• Premium rate	50¢ per participant	$1 per participant immediately; increases in steps to $2.60 over nine years

DEFINITION OF MULTIEMPLOYER PLAN

	Old Law	New Law
• Number of employers	More than one employer required to contribute	Same
• Bargaining status	Maintained pursuant to one or more collective bargaining agreements	Same
• Percent contributions test	No one employer contributes more than 50% of the total contributions	Provision dropped
• Shared liabilities test	Plan pays participants' benefits, even if employer withdraws, except for benefits resulting from service before the employer joined the plan	Provision dropped
• Transition rule	Not applicable	Plans that were not multiemployer plans under the old definition because of contributions test, have one year to elect to remain in the single employer program

MERGERS AND TRANSFERS

	Old Law	New Law
• Between multiemployer plans	Titles I and II rules to the extent applied by PBGC	Generally, allowed if (1) 120 day advance notice to PBGC; (2) no participant's accrued benefit lower after the merger or transfer; (3) plan insolvency unlikely; and (4) recent actuarial valuation has been made
• Between a multiemployer and a single employer plan	Same	Generally, allowed if no participant's accrued benefit would be lower
		If transfer to single employer plan, multiemployer plan contingently liable if single employer plan terminates within five years; PBGC may waive contingent liability

DELINQUENT CONTRIBUTIONS

	Old Law	New Law
• Legal requirement to make contributions	No ERISA provision	Makes the contractual obligation to contribute an ERISA requirement
• Action to enforce delinquent contributions	No ERISA provision	Plan fiduciary can initiate action in Federal Court to recover delinquent contributions
• Remedies	No ERISA provision	Mandatory award of interest, penalty, and attorney's fees; penalty is the greater of the interest or 20% of the unpaid contributions

MISTAKEN CONTRIBUTIONS

	Old Law	New Law
• Return of mistaken contributions	No provision	Return within six months after mistake found; does not violate Code restrictions on use of plan funds solely for benefit of participants and beneficiaries

SEVERANCE PAY PLANS

	Old Law	New Law
• Tax treatment	Severance pay and supplemental retirement income plans treated as pension plans	Secretary of Labor may issue rules for treating certain severance pay and supplemental retirement income plans as welfare plans

Withdrawal Liability

BY CARLTON R. SICKLES

Introduction

This article is not designed to tell you everything you will ever want to know about employer withdrawal liability, but it is a good first starter. While much of the law is detailed in nature, there is a tremendous amount of latitude on the part of trustees, and a great deal of authority given to the Pension Benefit Guaranty Corporation to add to and modify the provisions of the law. PBGC representatives at this Annual Conference have indicated their determination to produce their rules and regulations as soon as possible because of the impact the rules will have upon the early compliance with the law by trustees.

The first task of the trustees is to identify the withdrawn employer. Two kinds of withdrawal are defined in the law, complete withdrawal and partial withdrawal. There is a general rule with specified exceptions for each class of withdrawal.

Complete Withdrawal

The exceptions with respect to complete withdrawal involve the construction industry and portions of the entertainment industry and the trucking industry. Any employer or fund not affected by a special industry rule is subject to the general rule, namely that liability attaches when an employer contributing to a multiemployer plan after April 28, 1980, either permanently ceases its obligation to contribute to the plan or permanently ceases all its covered operations (after May 3, 1979, for substantial contributors to a plan covering West Coast sea-going employment).

Construction Industry. The construction industry exemption applies to an employer if substantially all of the employees for whom it has an obligation to contribute perform work in the building and construction industry and are party to a plan which primarily covers building and construction employees. A non-construction employer paying into such plan is not covered by such special provision; however, a non-construction fund may authorize a construction employer to be subject to the special provisions. The special treatment is that

Mr. Sickles, an attorney, is president of Carday Associates, Inc., a consulting and administration firm. He holds a B.S.S. cum laude and a J.D. degree from Georgetown University, and is a member of the firm of Goldberg, Thompson & Sickles. Mr. Sickles was a delegate in the Maryland House of Delegates from 1955 to 1962; a member of the United States House of Representatives, 1963-1967; and a delegate to the Maryland Constitutional Convention, 1967-1968. He is chairman of the Administrative Advisory Committee of the National Coordinating Committee for Multiemployer Plans. A member of the International Foundation since its inception, Mr. Sickles has served two terms on the Board of Directors and was president and chairman of the Board in 1974. Former chairman of the Past Chairmen's Council, Administrative Cost Study, Educational Program and Governmental Affairs Committees, he currently serves as a member of the Employer Liability Committee.

such an employer will be liable for withdrawal liability only in the event that it ceases its obligations to contribute and continues the same type of work in the jurisdiction of its collective bargaining agreement within five years thereafter without renewing its obligation.

Entertainment Industry. The special provision for the entertainment industry is similar in character to the construction industry provisions. However, it applies only to a segment of the entertainment industry with employment usually temporary in nature as listed in the law. Its application may be substantially modified by PBGC, and the trustees may limit or terminate all or part of the exemption.

Trucking Industry. The trucking industry exemption applies to a portion of the trucking industry, and is similar in nature. For the provisions to apply, substantially all of a plan's contributions must be made by employers primarily engaged in long and short-haul trucking, household goods moving or public warehouse industries. To benefit from these special provisions, an employer withdrawing from such plan will be required to post a bond in the amount of 50% of the withdrawal liability, and if the PBGC does not determine that the withdrawal has an adverse impact upon the plan within 60 months, the bond may be canceled. Otherwise, the employer will have to pay the normal withdrawal liability.

Other industries, or parts thereof, may be subject to special rules if PBGC determines that similar characteristics exist.

Partial Withdrawal

Partial withdrawal liability results from a substantial decline in the operations of a contributing employer. It is measured in two ways, either a reduction in the base units (hours, days, weeks, tons of coal, etc.) being reported to the plan over an extended period, or a partial termination of the collective bargaining obligation to contribute, or reduction in the number of the employer's facilities covered by the plan.

Just as in complete withdrawal, there are a number of special exceptions to the general application of the partial withdrawal rules.

Construction Industry. A construction employer is considered to have partially withdrawn only when it contributes for an insubstantial portion of the total number of base units (hours, weeks, etc.) currently being worked by it in the area subject to the terms of the collective bargaining agreement.

Entertainment Industry. There are no specific provisions for partial withdrawal in the entertainment industry. PBGC is charged with developing specific rules for this industry.

All other employers and funds will be subject to the general applicability of the partial withdrawal provisions.

Base Units Decline

The base units decline method of determining partial withdrawal liability will not be effective until the first plan year beginning after April 28, 1982. For this purpose, an eight year period is examined. At the end of the eighth year, the number of employment units reported each year of the last three years is compared with an average of the number of units that were reported in the two highest years of the previous five years, called the high base year. If the amount reported in each of the last three years is 70% less than in the high base year, partial withdrawal liability will result.

A special exception is provided in the case of a plan covering retail food industry employees, where the amount of reduction can be changed to 35% if the board of trustees so determines. If this procedure is established by the trustees, special abatement rules will apply.

Reduction of Agreements or Facilities

The other method of determining partial withdrawal liability, namely the reduction in the number of collective bargaining agreements or facilities of an employer, attaches withdrawal liability in the event that there is more than one such agreement or facility and there is a termination of at least one, but not all, of such agreements or facilities, with a continuation of the work which was previously covered.

Naturally, if there is partial withdrawal liability, the amount of liability is a relative share of the employer's full withdrawal liability.

Abatement

The resumption of employment or increased employment after a withdrawal determination may cause an abatement of the amount to be paid into the fund. With respect to abatement of complete withdrawal liability, the PBGC is charged with establishing such rules and regulations. With respect to abatement of partial withdrawal liability, there are four separate systems in the law for determining all or partial abatement of such liability.

Liability Limitations

Once the withdrawing employer has been identified, it is possible that certain limitations set out in the act will preclude the necessity of any withdrawal liability payment by the employer. For instance, a labor dispute will not trigger withdrawal liability, nor will a change in corporate structure or sales of assets whereby the new structure or employer assumes the responsibility that would otherwise attach to the terminating employer. A so-called free look provision, if adopted by trustees in very limited circumstances, could result in no liability.

Determining Liability

If the withdrawing employer is not so excused, the next major task is to determine the amount of its liability. The objective is to determine the withdrawing employer's share of the plan's unfunded vested liability. The act authorizes four different methods of making such a determination. It also authorizes PBGC to establish additional methods, and even authorizes trustees to develop their own method subject to approval by PBGC.

Choosing the Method

At the outset, it is important to note that *the construction fund is limited to using the first, or presumptive, method of determining allocation.* Construction funds may, however, provide a different allocation formula to other than construction employers contributing to the plan under such regulations as are established by PBGC.

The presumptive method is the one which is in effect for all plans until such time as a board of trustees selects some other method. When a fund changes the method, the new method is only applicable to withdrawals which occur on and after that date. Since the principle of withdrawal liability applies to employers that terminated after April 28, 1980, long before the law was enacted, the law provides the exception that if a fund were to adopt other than the presumptive method prior to January 31, 1981, then such adopted method would be applicable to any employer who withdrew after April 28, 1980. After January 31, 1981, for a change to be retroactive, it must be agreed to by the employer involved. A fund may change its method at any time, but after September 1983, any change would be subject to PBGC approval. Any change made by the trustees would require a notice of its adoption to all employers and labor organizations representing the employees covered by the plan.

The purpose of each allocation formula is to establish the withdrawing employer's share of the unfunded vested liabilities of the plan (vested liabilities less assets on hand). Each method described in the law is technical and detailed, but their provisions are generally as follows.

Presumptive Method. The presumptive method divides the unfunded vested liabilities of a plan into two parts, (1) that accumulated through the last plan year ending prior to April 29, 1980, and (2) that accumulated thereafter. All withdrawing employers who are in the plan after April 28, 1980, are subject to paying a proportionate share of the latter, but only those who contributed to the fund in plan years ending prior to April 29, 1980, are subject to the former. The post-April 28, 1980, liability is computed on a year by year basis.

Modified Presumptive Method. The modified presumptive method is similar to the presumptive method except that instead of handling the post-April 28, 1980, liability on a year by year basis, it is calculated in the aggregate.

Five Year Rollover Method. The five year rollover method does not make a distinction between plan years ending before April 29, 1980, and those thereafter in determining a withdrawing employer's liability.

Direct Attribution Method. In each of the methods described above, the employer's liability is generally the ratio of the employer's contributions to the total contributions in the previous five year period. The direct attribution method is substantially different in that liability is based upon the unfunded vested benefits directly attributable to participants' service with the employer.

In addition, in each method pursued, a portion of any previously uncollectible withdrawal liability will have to be assigned to each subsequently withdrawing employer.

It is obvious that the result would be different for a particular employer depending upon the method which has been adopted by the trustees, and the particular work history of the withdrawing employer.

More Liability Limitations

Once the appropriate method has been applied to the employer who has been identified as a withdrawing employer, there are some limitations in the law which can reduce the amount of withdrawal liability of an employer as determined so far. The first such limitation is known as the *de minimis* or *deductible* rule. This is a mandatory deductible provision which cannot be ignored by the trustees. The deductible amount is $50,000 (or 0.75% of a plan's unfunded vested benefits, whichever is less), but if the indebtedness is in excess of $100,000, for every dollar of indebtedness thereafter one dollar of the deductible is removed, and by the time an indebtedness of $150,000 has been established, the original deductible of $50,000 has been canceled.

There is also a discretionary de minimis provision which authorizes a board of trustees to increase the deductible amount from $50,000 to $100,000 (or 0.75% of a plan's unfunded vested benefits, whichever is less). This also has the feature that if the indebtedness is over $150,000, thereafter for every dollar of indebtedness one dollar of the deductible is removed and, if the indebtedness is $250,000, then there is no deductible.

Other reductions in the amount of withdrawal liability are provided in the law and may occur in situations resulting from a sale of assets to an unrelated party, employer insolvency, or if an individual or partnership is involved.

Annual Payments

Once the total amount due from a withdrawing employer has finally been determined, it is necessary to determine the amount to be paid each year (in quarterly installments). This determination is made completely independent of the previous calculations, and is based upon the work history of the employer during the last ten years preceding the date of withdrawal. To determine this annual amount, the number of work units reported in the highest three consecutive years is multiplied by the highest rate of contribution. In the event that it takes more than 20 years to amortize the withdrawal liability at this annual rate, the amount payable on the twenty-first year and thereafter would be forgiven, since there is a 20 year cap on the number of years that an employer is required to make payments.

Collection Procedures

It is the trustees' responsibility to collect the withdrawal payments due. The employer is required to furnish necessary information to the trustees upon request.

The plan sponsors advise the employer of the amount of its liability, the amount of its annual payment and the quarterly payment schedule. The first payment will be due 60 days after notice. The employer has a 90 day period to request a review of any specific matter regarding the liability amount or the payment schedule.

Arbitration

If the employer and the board of trustees do not reach an agreement as to the amount of the employer's liability or the amount of its annual payments, either party may then request that the dispute be put to arbitration. The arbitration proceeding is to be conducted in accordance with procedures prescribed by PBGC.

The plan may purchase fiduciary insurance for the arbitrator if the insurance is available. If the parties haven't agreed as to how the cost of the arbitration will be borne, the arbitrator may assess the cost of the arbitration. The arbitrator may also award reasonable attorneys' fees.

In the proceedings, the employer will have to show by a preponderance of the evidence that the decisions of the trustees were unreasonable or clearly erroneous. If the employer is challenging the plan's determination of the unfunded vested benefits, then the employer will have to show by a preponderance of the evidence that, in the aggregate, the actuarial methods and assumptions which were used were unreasonable, or else that the actuary made a significant error.

Court Action

After the arbitration, there is a 30 day appeal period during which either party can appeal to federal court requesting either enforcement, vacation or modification of the arbitrator's award. In this proceeding, the arbitrator's findings of fact are presumed correct, rebuttable only by a clear preponderance of the evidence.

Default

The law defines a default as a failure to cure a delinquency within 60 days after the trustees have given the employer notice of the late payment. The law also provides that the trustees can define a default as any other event which indicates a substantial likelihood that the employer will be unable to pay. Upon default, interest will accrue on the unpaid monies due to the plan at a market rate for comparable obligations, as provided by PBGC. The trustees may then accelerate all monies due and owing to the plan.

More Court Action

If payment is not made, the trustees have access to the courts. If the court finds that the employer owes the money, the court is required to hold the employer liable for the unpaid contribution, interest, a penalty then of an amount equal to the greater of that interest charge again or liquidated damages of up to 20%, plus attorneys' fees and any other appropriate legal or equitable relief.

Conclusion

In conclusion, please be reminded that this is a very complicated piece of legislation. The attempt here has been to discuss it in broad, general terms. For that reason, many of the minor details have been omitted, but they may be of significance in a particular case. In excess of 60 regulations have to be adopted by PBGC pursuant to the terms of the act and, of course, there is some general authority that PBGC has which may bring about additional regulations.

PBGC has already issued some of these regulations and is seeking outside professional help in concluding this large task.

The Withdrawal Liability Process

BY GERALD E. COLE, JR.

The Act: Development and Purpose

The Multiemployer Pension Plan Amendments Act is the result of three years of intensive discussions and compromise between labor and management. One of the reasons that it is so exceedingly complex is that it represents an attempt to deal with all of the different industries and all of the different situations covered by multiemployer plans.

Both Congress and the PBGC recognized that because of the diversity among multiemployer plans and the potential impact of any legislation, we had to provide a great deal of latitude to plan trustees. We recognized that we didn't know all the answers and certainly didn't know how to deal with all of the problems of multiemployer plans.

We have also recognized that in order for there to be any sort of sound insurance program, one that is not going to result in $50 per year premiums, we had to have a program that stressed the continuation of plans and gave trustees enough flexibility to fit the requirements of the law to the particular circumstances of their plan.

The whole purpose of this legislation is to encourage, in some instances to force, multiemployer plans to continue rather than dump their liabilities on the PBGC.

Now, who is the PBGC? Who is the premium system? It is all of you. You pay the freight for this program. There was a tremendous effort during development of the legislation to isolate the instances in which PBGC paid insurance to cases where plans became unable to meet benefit payments because of extended declines in their contribution base. That principle is the essence of the new law.

It is built on two pillars. The first is some tightening in the funding rules for all plans, with an even tighter funding standard for those plans that are in bad financial condition. The new funding standards are intended to require adequate funding for plans which might otherwise terminate and which, according to some estimates, could drop somewhere between $1-4 billion on the rest of the plans through increased premiums. So better funding is one of the pillars of the new law.

Mr. Cole, assistant executive director for policy and planning for the PBGC, is responsible for coordinating overall corporate policy and for developing PBGC regulations and legislative programs, including matters involving the Multiemployer Pension Plan Amendments Act of 1980. Mr. Cole previously served as special counsel for PBGC, as assistant general counsel at the Cost of Living Council, and as an associate in a private law firm engaged in the practice of labor law. Mr. Cole graduated from the University of Pennsylvania (Wharton) and Harvard Law School. He has spoken at previous Foundation and other educational programs.

The other pillar is withdrawal liability. The purpose of withdrawal liability is to make sure that the employers that stay in the plan are not the ones that end up holding the bag. Withdrawal liability ensures that the burden of funding the plan is shared by all employers. Plans have been given great latitude in deciding how to apportion the liability, and Congress added a whole host of special rules. Thus, withdrawal liability is complex. The law is going to have to evolve here in major respects. Thus the extent to which the new law is successful in achieving its goal of creating stability in multiemployer plans is going to depend on the genius and devotion with which you, the trustees, carry out your responsibilities.

We at PBGC will seek to help by promulgating necessary regulations and, where we have the authority to do so, by creating additional options needed to make the law fair and administrable. We want to hear from you. We already have a *Federal Register* publication asking for comments on where people want regulations. We want to hear from you so that we can ease the way, but it is not our responsibility to administer this law—it is yours.

What Is Withdrawal Liability?

What is withdrawal liability? What are we talking about? Withdrawal liability is an employer's legal obligation to continue to make payments to the plan after it withdraws. The payments must continue for the number of years necessary to finish funding the withdrawn employer's share of the unfunded vested benefits. Thus, the allocation of unfunded vested benefits determines how many years an employer that withdraws has to continue payments to the plan.

In the course of the legislative process, a number of special interest groups came forward. There were claims that withdrawal liability wasn't equitable in this situation, it wasn't equitable in that situation, it wasn't necessary here, there, etc. These concerns were addressed in defining what constitutes a withdrawal and by creating a number of limitations on withdrawal liability.

So in the withdrawal liability process, the first step is to determine whether an employer who has ceased contributions has withdrawn. That is not always going to be an instant or easy process.

The next step is to compute that employer's share of the unfunded vested benefits. The share will depend on the allocation method chosen by the plan. Those of you who are in the building and construction industry can forget about choosing an allocation method. You don't have any choice. Construction employers wanted the presumptive allocation rule to be the only rule for the construction industry, and they got it.

After you've computed an employer's share of unfunded vested benefits, you have to apply any relevant limitations, such as the sale rule or the net worth rule. After applying the limitations, you finally get the bottom line, the liability of the employer.

Then you must collect the liability. That's what withdrawal liability is all about: collecting money for the plan.

A Step by Step Process

Has a Withdrawal Occurred?

Very quickly, let's review each of the steps and see what is involved. First, determine whether the employer has withdrawn. There is a general rule for withdrawal, and then there are special rules.

There is a special rule for construction. There is a special rule for entertainment. There is a special rule where an employer transfers its liabilities to another employer who agrees to continue contributing to the plan. There is a special, optional, free-look rule, which will exempt a newly entering employer from any liability if the employer withdraws within six years.

How, then, do you identify a withdrawal? You have to find out when an employer's contributions cease, and you have to know why those contributions cease.

Computing Liability

Once you've determined that the employer has withdrawn, you have to compute its share of liability. The liability is based on unfunded vested benefits. So you need to have your actuary determine the value of vested benefits (that is already generally required in Schedule B to the Form 5500), and the value of plan assets. The choice of actuarial assumptions is critical. Depending on which assumptions you choose, the amount of unfunded vested benefits in the plan can go up or down dramatically.

Having determined the unfunded vested benefits for the plan as a whole, you next allocate the total among employers. There is a presumptive allocation rule; it is the rule that will apply if you do not choose another option. There are three statutory options that may be adopted by plan amendment. Also, a plan is permitted to develop its own allocation method and submit it to PBGC for approval.

Finally, the PBGC was given authority to develop some additional allocation rules that plans could choose. We probably won't develop our rules for a while, because the plan can develop its own allocation rules and submit them to us for approval. The law says that PBGC may not disapprove plan rules unless it finds they create an unreasonable risk of loss to participants or the PBGC. What that means, generally, is that as long as you're not trying any funny business with your allocation rule, the PBGC is going to have to approve it.

The law provides that if a plan isn't amended to adopt another allocation rule before February 1, 1981, it may only apply an optional allocation rule to withdrawals that occur after the plan is amended, unless the withdrawn employer agrees otherwise. Failing to act before February 1, 1981, does not lock you into the presumptive method. Nonetheless, it may be advisable to avoid computing liability using two different methods, one way for old withdrawals and another way for new withdrawals. So you may wish to act by February 1, 1981, but in some instances that is just not going to be possible.

But, let me repeat, failure to act on an allocation method by February 1, 1981, will not cause a disaster.

Apply Relevant Limitations

Having determined an employer's allocable share of unfunded vested benefits, you must then apply any relevant limitations to determine the actual liability. There is a special rule for the trucking industry that limits the liability. There is a special sale rule that applies in the event all or substantially all of the assets of a business are sold. There is the de minimis rule, which is really a deductible in the amount of $50,000 or three-quarters of 1% of the unfunded vested benefits, whichever is less. So if ¾% of the unfunded vested benefits is greater than $50,000, then the deduction is $50,000. The plan may be amended to increase that deduction up to $100,000, subject to the ¾% limitation. There's a special limitation for bankruptcy: one-half of the liability has general creditor status and the other half is limited to the remaining equity, if any. Thus, you still may be able to get a substantial amount of money from a bankrupt employer.

Finally, there is the 20 year cap, which limits the obligation to continue payments to a maximum of 20 years. That can result in lessening the liability. In the great majority of plans, however, the 20 year cap won't even come into play. If a plan is not funding its unfunded vested benefits over 20 years or less, the plan is in bad shape.

Some important limitations don't apply in mass withdrawal. The de minimis rule doesn't apply, and the 20 year cap doesn't apply. This is to prevent creating an incentive to dump the plan on the insurance system, which would then need to increase every other plan's premiums.

Notification and Collection

The final stage in the withdrawal liability process is to notify the employer and collect the liability. The first step in this stage is to request any additional information you may need from the employer. The second step is to notify the employer of the liability amount and the schedule of annual payments. Unless the employer defaults, its obligation is to make a series of annual payments. The annual payment amount is based on what the employer was contributing before it withdrew. The employer's withdrawal liability does not affect the annual payment. The liability affects the number of years those payments must continue.

If the employer fails to make a payment when due, and then doesn't pay within 60 days after notice from the plan administrator, the plan may sue for the entire amount of the liability.

After the plan administrator demands payment from the employer, the employer has the right to raise matters that it thinks are wrong. The trustees must respond to those matters. Either party may then go to arbitration. Failure to make a payment after arbitration is treated as a delinquent contribution under the new rules in Title IV of ERISA, which means the court must award the plan interest, attorney fees and penalty up to 20% of the delinquency.

National Health Insurance: Changes in Concerns, Concepts and Content

BY STEVEN E. SCHANES, Ph.D.

FROM COMMENTS and questions heard about the country, it appears that there is wide misunderstanding with respect to the type of "national health insurance" toward which we are now heading. These misconceptions have their roots in the fact that we have been considering national health insurance in some form or other for approximately 30 years and, generally speaking, the public has lost interest in the details, having heard the issues discussed so many times in the past. Therefore, most people seem to be unaware of the fact that the entire structure of a national health care package may well be significantly different from the popular understanding of "national health insurance." As will be developed below, changes in the health care picture and in national priorities have led to broad acceptance among the nation's leaders of a program which is significantly different from the proposals which have caused such great controversy over the years.

Pre-1969 Issues

Early Concepts

From the time of the enactment of the British National Health program and the initial experience under it (the late 1940s and early '50s), our early concentration was on the possible adoption of a similar program. National health insurance (NHI) was envisioned, by both opponents and proponents, as a federal takeover of the private health insurance system under which the government would provide comprehensive benefits to the entire population. In keeping with the British model, this would be "womb to tomb" coverage. The issue was whether or not medical care should be "socialized"; and "socialized medicine" became the issue. Much of the argument focused on the potential impact of government control over doctors: i.e., services provided, individual patient load and charges. The

Dr. Schanes is president of Schanes Associates, advisors on employee benefit policy, with offices in San Diego, California. From 1974 to February 1976, Dr. Schanes served as the first Executive Director of the Pension Benefit Guaranty Corporation. Between 1969 and 1974, he held various positions in the U.S. Department of Commerce, including Special Assistant to the Secretary for Policy Development. In this period he represented the Department of Commerce in the development of ERISA and national health insurance. From 1958 to 1969, Dr. Schanes was vice president of the Martin E. Segal Company, consultants to public and private pension and welfare funds. He also held the positions of academic dean, professor of political science and chairman of the Division of Economics and Business Administration of the University of San Diego from 1966 to 1969. From 1952 to 1958, he served as the first director of the New Jersey State Division of Pensions. He holds a Ph.D. in International and Constitutional Law from Cornell University and is on the labor-management panel of the American Arbitration Association. He has held offices in various professional organizations, including president, National Association of State Social Security Administrators, and vice president, National Association of State Retirement Administrators. He currently serves on the International Foundation's Government/Industry Relations Committee. Dr. Schanes has lectured extensively on employee benefits, and was the recipient of Pension World's *1976 Employee Benefits Award of the Year.*

battle against this concept was led, of course, by the American Medical Association. However, there also was a general fear on the part of the public with regard to direct government operation and control of a major profession.

The major issue arose out of the concern for the great number of Americans who are unprotected for the cost of medical care. Of course, with the passage of Medicare, many elderly individuals now had health insurance of a fairly far-reaching nature. Still, there were others who had not been covered by Social Security and many individuals in the under age 65 category who had no systematic way of providing for the cost impact of possible large medical bills. It was generally felt that most of these individuals would forego medical treatment when it was needed, with adverse individual and public consequences. Others would meet these costs out of personal savings and might well end up in the poverty class, requiring public assistance over the long run.

Structure and Funding

The proponents of national health insurance wanted to see a universal, standardized level of benefit protection which would cover both minor and major cost areas. While there was disagreement as to the range of benefits which would be covered, the definition of NHI included "standard" hospital and medical expenses.

An important question was the way in which universal medical care would be paid. In light of the level of current expenses, it is a little hard to appreciate that the medical expenses of 25 years ago were *then* deemed to be very great. Generally, the issue has been whether the cost should be met through general taxation or through the Social Security system, with premiums paid by both employers and employees. Those advocating a universal program generally called for the entire program to be funded out of general taxation, with benefits available to persons in all categories of life on a low individual cost basis. There might be some small personal payment at the outset and some copayment feature—both of these designed to avoid excess utilization. However, the federal government would run the system and would find the resources from general taxes.

As part of the overall structure, there was need to control developing costs and to plan for a rational health delivery system. Legislation was enacted which provided for planning agencies at the local and state level which would operate under general federal guidelines. These structures would attempt to establish controls over the growth of hospitals and the duplication of services and equipment. Thought was also given to the numbers of doctors being produced by the medical schools. It was suggested that there be greater emphasis on the general practitioner, with a subsidy for individuals who studied to become general practitioners and who stayed in that profession. There is now general agreement that this structure of planning and cost controls was ineffective, largely because there was little implementing authority given to the planning agencies.

Medicare as Model

At the same time, Medicare was a new program, viewed in many quarters as a demonstration of the experience that might develop in an overall NHI program. While it was clear that the immediate impact was that of reducing the problems confronted by the elderly in the health care area, it was too early to determine whether this would be a short or long term effect. It should be noted that, as developed, Medicare largely relied on the private insurance sector for payment and control of the system, with payments coming out of the Social Security collections—through the carriers, to the providers. As enacted, Medicare preserved the relationship between the insurance carriers, the Blues and the hospitals and doctors. In fact, in order to qualify to serve as a third-party intermediary in the case of payments to hospitals, the insurance carrier or Blue had to be satisfactory to the specific hospital. Many questioned, and continue to question, whether this relationship can produce effective cost control mechanisms and procedures.

Underlying the entire consideration of NHI was the fact that our health care system had developed in a "free market" environment. This had proven successful in providing a good level of medical care to great numbers of people, but left out those who could not compete for services in the marketplace. Certainly, the forces which had gained economically through this structure used their financial power to dominate political decisions, naturally preserving the favorable position in which they found themselves. The campaign against "socialized medicine" was largely successful.

1969-77 Developments

FHIP and FAP

Under the Nixon Administration, a new approach to NHI was developed. Basically, this program would have mandated a certain level of benefits to be provided by employers, with or without employee cost-sharing. The benefits which were proposed were largely those applicable to federal employees, who already had group health insurance coverage on a large scale. For those employers who were financially unable to provide the mandated benefits, "pools" would be established, which would be subsidized as needed. There was debate as to the source of this subsidy—whether it would come from the larger employers who were providing their own benefits, or from federal sources.

For those persons who were not employed, or who were underemployed, there would be a "Family Health Insurance Plan" (FHIP). This would consist of the same level of benefits which would be mandated for employers, but would be provided from federal funds to persons who were under the Family Assistance Plan (FAP). Persons receiving family assistance would receive graduated assistance with regard to health insurance coverage, depending upon the level of income. The idea was to prevent a large discrimination between those who were marginally underemployed as compared to those who were fully employed. Unfortunately, the complications of "FHIP" and "FAP" bogged down the development of the total NHI program so that the entire scheme never did receive full national attention.

At the same time, while an overall comprehensive NHI plan was being developed, a debate began with regard to the ultimate level of benefits which might be provided and the possible phasing in of benefits over a period of time. Out of this came the issue of whether the federal government should concentrate its attention on catastrophic coverage—assistance in meeting major bills—as opposed to comprehensive coverage. There was a large body of thought to the effect that the basic weakness in the present system was that of meeting the unexpected large medical bill—that the government could provide for this in one way or another without disturbing the basic relationships and structures which had developed over the years. However, while these issues were being debated, a number of other developments caused NHI to lose its priority status in terms of national need.

A Changing Climate

Health Care Developments. Several new and socially important developments did take place. The first of these was the HMO initiative. The Administration became convinced that health maintenance organizations (HMOs) could provide an alternative health delivery system at lower cost. Monies were available from HEW for the establishment of HMOs around the country, and there was a major federal initiative on sponsoring various groups which might be interested in establishing HMOs.

At the same time, a renal dialysis program became effective. This was a "model" demonstration of national health insurance applicable to one medical problem. It was viewed as an experiment of a federally run program out of which experience with respect to a total federal program might be garnered. The renal dialysis program started off at a cost of about $250 million per year and has rapidly risen to $2 billion. The administrators found themselves involved with very heavy social decisions with respect to services to be provided, as well as costs which grew well beyond predictions.

At the same time, Medicaid—the providing of health care financial assistance to persons on welfare—began to have widespread cost impact. Meanwhile, experience demonstrated that the costs for medical services for those on Medicare were rising quite rapidly, so that the personal level of expenditure was close to what it had been before Medicare was enacted. Both of these programs demonstrated that one of the consequences of the availability of large amounts of governmental funds was an increase in the cost of health care.

Other Events. NHI, like most other domestic affairs programs, was affected by two external events: Watergate and Vietnam. Both caused the attention of policymakers and planners to shift from intensive concentration on any program which could have far-reaching budgetary impacts. For NHI, the period between 1972 and 1976 was largely one of stagnation. However, other developments in this period played an important role in the evolution of present-day positions.

Certainly, the entire employee benefits industry learned a great deal about federal law and regulation upon the passage of ERISA. Other facile students were Congress and other government agencies, such as HEW. While ERISA is complicated, it does not have the far-reaching scope of covering every person in the land. NHI would do this, and the prospects of administrative difficulties—and their implications—become very clear through ERISA. Certainly, a number of key persons who had wanted a completely federally run NHI program moved away from this position as a result of observing the ERISA experience.

Cost Containment: Growing Pressures

Inflation and the rising cost of medical care have served to change the focus of NHI considerations from that of providing health care to that of at least equal concern for cost containment. As the cost of health care has skyrocketed over the past five years, and as the cost of all other living expenses has gone up rapidly, there has been a new national focus on the reduction of costs wherever possible. Of course, Proposition 13 is a manifestation of this public feeling. It has become clear that a totally new federal program involving massive additional outlays and taxes is not acceptable to the majority of American voters.

A new system of local and federal planning and control over hospital costs was introduced. The health systems agency (HSA) is a local planning structure which passes upon the addition of new hospital capacity and facilities, including expensive new equipment. The HSA involves participation by all sectors of the community. This device has not been uniformly successful—in fact, it has had some notable failures—but the concept of careful community review and understanding of hospital-bed capacity has undoubtedly caused a rethinking of hospital expansion plans.

At the same time, medical technology has continued to grow more and more sophisticated. With this sophistication have come increased costs of equipment and procedures. While each of these is designed to save lives and to extend years of life, large and difficult social questions have arisen as to our ability to pay for these valuable gains. Further, we have begun addressing the question of whether specific new (and old) techniques are actually useful. This type of questioning has led to a number of changes in practices by health care providers and the insurance industry in terms of reviewing, eliminating or changing formerly acceptable services.

The necessary emphasis on cost containment has brought about innovations on the part of corporate plan sponsors and multiemployer benefit plans. Among these are health education, second surgical opinion programs, emphasis on generic drugs, and alternative delivery systems (such as various types of HMOs, surgical procedures performed on an outpatient basis or in the doctor's office, and home health care as opposed to institutional stays).

With the election of President Carter in 1976, there appeared to be a commitment to "National Health Insurance"—which most observers understood to mean the initial concept of a government-run structure. In 1977, the new Administration tackled the question of meeting the NHI commitment in light of budgetary considerations. With health care costs rising at the rate of 15-20% a year, it was clear that, whatever the original concept might have been, financial reality would dictate the manner in which the Administration would seek to meet a social goal. Certainly, the Administration was not alone in this. A number of major conferences were held on the subject throughout the country, with serious rethinking of the entire subject. Clearly, cost containment had now become a matter of first priority, and any national program would have to address this issue at the outset.

1978-80—Years of Reconsideration and Negotiation

The year 1978 saw a redefining of the need for NHI. Clearly, government financial intervention is to be directed at the uninsured and underinsured, with emphasis on the former. Reliance will be placed upon the private sector to cover the employed with a level of benefits to be mandated by the government. Where industry cannot meet the prescribed goals, based upon certain tests of financial ability, a subsidy would be provided so that the same benefits would be available to all. In essence, the federal government would be substituting a new national program for Medicare and Medicaid and ensuring that the private sector provided at least the same level of benefits for the employed.

It is interesting to note that this path to national health insurance has now been adopted by all the principal advocates of NHI, and that we are actually looking at various versions of a program which was developed in 1970. Of course, one of the factors is that industry has made tremendous strides in the level of benefits provided to employees (as reflected in their costs for health insurance—and the significant move toward self-funding of benefits as a means of cost saving). In any event, a careful reading of the definition of national health insurance as proposed by President Carter, Senator Kennedy and Senator Long did not reveal a significant difference in this regard. There were, of course, certain differences with regard to level of benefits and other aspects.

As indicated above, cost containment and inflationary pressures became major focal points in the NHI considerations. In 1978, President Carter pressed for legislation which would place certain cost controls on hospitals. (It failed to pass.) Clearly, the Administration viewed this as an important part of the national health care picture. At the same time, both the Administration and Congress were considering other steps which might control provider costs. In answer to these developments, the providers themselves formed an organization called "The Voluntary Effort" which set as its goal reducing the rate of increase in health care costs by 2% per year (beginning with a 16% annual rate of increase between 1977 and 1978).

The strong role which inflation came to play in NHI policy was well indicated by President Carter's proposal that benefit levels be phased in in accordance with certain key inflation indicators. That is, both the federally provided benefits and the federally mandated benefits for the employed would initially have been fixed at certain minimum levels and then increased as the nation as a whole could afford to do so. While this approach was opposed by Senator Kennedy, it seems clear that a less than "total" package of benefits will be provided and/or required at the outset of any program.

Public debate centers on two alternative approaches: the providing of certain basic benefits affecting ordinary health care expenses and extending through major medical insurance; or the providing of some form of major medical insurance alone, with perhaps some special areas of basic benefits (such as child health care). Although Presidential politics obviously plays a role in consideration of the level and type of benefits, it appears that budgetary considerations may very well be the determining factor. Fortunately, or unfortunately, for the private sector, the budgetary considerations are those of the federal government almost exclusively, whereas the far larger burden will fall upon the private sector. Still, the cost implications for the business community have been playing some part in the thinking of policymakers.

With the revised emphasis being placed upon the private sector for the providing of mandated benefits, there has developed a much greater knowledge on the part of the governmental policymakers with respect to the roles of the different elements of the present health care system. It has become clear that neither the plan sponsors (corporations or jointly trusteed plans, for the most part) nor third-party intermediaries (insurance companies or contract administrators) can effectively control the cost of health care. These costs rest with the providers (principally hospitals and doctors) and the way in which they perform their services. Therefore, one of the major issues confronting the policymakers is the question of the degree to which government itself will act to regulate, or to support the regulation of, provider charges.

The Prognosis

It now appears that short of some major national or international crisis (and energy or inflation may be perceived as such a crisis) we will see the enactment of a national health insurance program. Recognizing that this is not strictly a national insurance program, the various sponsors have used other names, such as "National Healthcare." However, the press and the public will undoubtedly continue to use the old term to refer to whatever program is enacted. Without some significant degree of education during the enactment process, the fact that government will not be providing *all* will come as a shock to many who feel that the old definition of national health insurance still applies. Certainly, from a purely political standpoint, it is in the interest of the sponsors of such legislation to have this understood before enactment so as to avoid the heavy price of future disillusionment.

NHI Legislative Update

BY JOSEPH EICHENHOLZ

Introduction

In light of the November election, I have decided to use contingency presentation No. 17 on national health insurance. The topic is, "NHI, You Gotta Be Nuts," or, "Where Have All the Proposals Gone?" As a card-carrying member of the economists' union, I'm not allowed to give a presentation without putting up at least one formula:

$$P_R + S'_R + H''_D = C_H A_O S$$

Translated into English, this formula summarizes the general Washington environment we are likely to see in 1981: a President who is a Republican, a Senate that is Republican for the first time in a long time, a House that is Democratic and, doing a double take about what happened to them, an element expressed in our formula as *chaos* (or *C*arter is *H*ome *a*nd *O*ut of *S*ight).

We are going to have a political situation in this country the likes of which we have not seen in a long time with respect to health legislation. It will be exciting; I'm going to spend my entire year commuting on U.S. Air. We have had generation after generation of health insurance proposals, health proposals, technology assessment proposals, regulatory proposals. For the last decade, the definition of a national health insurance proposal has really been, everything you always wanted to do to the American health care system but didn't have the guts to say openly. NHI is an idea. I'm not sure if it ever came, has been here, went, but the title has worked wonders to give people audiences for debate.

Current Health Care Issues

Let me talk very briefly about the issues of 1981 in the health care system and what we have to look forward to. I can't tell you what is going to happen, if anything, but the ground rules of the debate are now being drawn up.

First, there is the insurance aspect of national health insurance. Most people in this country today have health insurance in one form or another. There are only about 11-18 million people, de-

Mr. Eichenholz is director of health policy analysis for the Connecticut General Life Insurance Company. He is responsible for economic, legislative and political analysis of health issues; application of external environment in company activities, and education of external (public and private) policymakers in the aspects of insurance impacting on their decisions. Previously, Mr. Eichenholz was director of economic analysis and policy planning in the office of the assistant secretary for health with the U.S. Department of Health, Education and Welfare. He received his B.S. from the State University of New York and his M.A. in economics from Brown University. Mr. Eichenholz is a member of the health care management committee of the Health Insurance Association of America and the liaison between the commercial insurance industry and the U.S. Department of Health and Human Services on technology assessment.

pending on whose economist you swear by, who do not have any health coverage. Those people tend to be migrants, seasonal workers, part-time workers, underemployed people, workers in high-turnover industries and low wage workers. Those are the folks who don't have any coverage. By and large, most people today do have something. For many the catastrophic coverage, the high-end expense kind of coverage, is somewhat limited, but this is getting better all the time.

NHI: Where Are the Real Needs?

So where are the gaps? If you want to have national health insurance or insurance legislation, who are you trying to help? First, we've got people we call uninsurable. Those are people who, because of medical conditions, risky occupations or experience, cannot find private health coverage. A company might refuse to cover them except at a very high rate compared to the average. They may be sick people. The company knows it may have a lot of expenses; they underwrite accordingly. There are about 900,000 around the country who are uninsurable at any price. Next, we have the unemployed. There are people who lose their coverage when they lose their jobs, as do their dependents; the extent of this problem depends on the recession and depends on economic conditions, as to how many lose benefits, and for how long. Widows, divorcees and their dependents often lack coverage. These are the people we need to help. An NHI proposal that affects the coverage of others by and large is superfluous to the vital needs of our nation.

We have also seen a change in the sense of crisis about the uncovered in these groups. In 1975, we felt that there were tremendous numbers of people losing their coverage due to unemployment. We never saw the data in time to want to do anything. The government simply couldn't respond that quickly. I'll just tell you that from having been there. The joke that some people make—I don't think it's a joke—but the comment, "Thank goodness I don't get all the government I pay for"—believe me, it's true. In 1975, the problem came and went before the federal government could do anything about it. By 1979, we found that 16 states had mandated some form of conversion or continuation coverage for unemployed workers. Most major carriers have some kind of conversion privilege in their contracts. In the past year, many of them have waived their standard policy language to allow broader benefits upon termination, but there is still a gap.

We also still have a gap represented by widows, divorcees and dependents of deceased workers. These are the kinds of people who fall through the cracks in any kind of legislation. They tend to be small groups, but they are important groups to help. And finally, we have the gaps in the public programs. Medicare does not cover outpatient drugs. Medicare does not have as progressive a home health benefit as one ought to think about. Medicaid has very uneven benefits across the states. There are millions of people who lose their coverage because of changes in categorical status—that's what Medicaid is. The income cutoffs differ by state. There are millions of people who need additional help. The cost is tremendous, but there is a recognized gap. This last item is really income redistribution, and is what has made most NHI proposals prohibitively expensive.

Thinking about it for 1981, what are our resources as a country? We don't have a lot of free cash, so most of what we'd like to do as a people to help other people, we can't afford as a country. So the debate will really be, what can you pick off? What gaps can you fill at reasonable cost, relying primarily on the private sector to the greatest possible extent? Where can you make progress without starting whole new federal programs?

The Great Cost Debate

Let me give you the second dimension of the national health debate, and this is the one of costs. Steve pointed out that health inflation has begun to drive the national health insurance debate. (I will continue to use the term national health insurance because I'm sure you all understand by now that it is merely representative terminology.) Actually, I would disagree with Steve in one respect: it was not the later 1970s but the early 1970s where we saw the first health cost inflation horror stories. In 1971, in the context of economy-wide wage and price controls, we had separate controls on the health sector. In 1972, we saw passage of a large number of Medicare amendments. These included the renal disease program on the one hand, which was a new benefit; but also included were a number of control mechanisms. These were the PSROs, the professional standards review organizations, to monitor quality and cost, as well as a tremendous number of economic regulations directed at Medicare and Medicaid patients but with tremendous implications for the entire regulatory system: limits on hospital reimbursement, limits on physician reimbursement, limits on expenditures for capital, limits on payment for teaching physicians in medical centers. All sorts of limits.

The debate slid by because it was economic regulation, not legislation, and the Social Security Administration just kept grinding away, chopping down dollar by dollar, with all the money they saved transferred to the private sector. By now, Medicare and Medicaid are paying far less than their fair share as originally envisioned by Congress, and those of us with private sector coverage are paying a disproportionate share of health costs, particularly in the hospital—a hidden tax, if you will.

Current Priorities

What about now? Well, we know the economic conditions. The first priority in 1981 without a doubt is going to be economic legislation. Senator

Dole, the new Chairman of the Senate Finance Committee, has said that his first priority will be tax cut legislation. His second priority, and this gets us back into the national health insurance debate, his second priority will be catastrophic health insurance legislation, although prospects must be considered dim. Senator Dole wants to do something positive. He will call it national health insurance if it helps. He will call it something else if it helps, but it really is catastrophic coverage and gap fillers, a phrase I'm coining. Gap fillers: doing what you can do at relatively low cost to help somebody and not be paralyzed by economic conditions. Comprehensive proposals, such as the Health Security Act, are dead. Senator Kennedy is now a member of the opposition in the Senate. Congressman Corman was defeated for reelection. There's going to be a whole new generation.

People and Proposals

Who were the young Turks in the national health insurance debate? Who have you got to watch? In the Senate, as I've said, Senator Dole is going to be a key factor. He worked very closely with Senator Long last year in framing the health insurance legislation that almost worked its way through the Senate and was stopped really only because of economic conditions and the pressure to balance the federal budget. In the Senate Finance Committee and on the House side you've got some new people who are going to be leaders in the national health insurance debate. They are called the "pro competition" advocates, and they have a number of different proposals which are designed to, in their own words, foster greater competition in the health care system.

This is the new buzz word—pro competition. We all favor competition; it would be hard to find an insurance or business company representative who doesn't favor competition. But each of us is now beginning to define competition in our own way, just as we've always defined national health insurance in our own way. Pro competition to Congressman Al Ullman, former Congressman who chaired the House Ways and Means Committee, meant tax legislation, for that was the committee he had jurisdiction over. He proposed to limit the deductibility of employer contributions for health insurance benefits. Pro competition to Congressman Jimmy Jones from Oklahoma, also on the Ways and Means Committee, and now Chairman of the House Budget Committee, means voluntary standards for those employers who choose to offer health insurance (which they must meet in order to get a deduction), along with a federal program (owned and operated by the federal government) to provide coverage for those who don't have access to employer plans. Now, that's a funny way of favoring competition, to actually set up a federal government program, a new Medicare, but let's leave that to the 1981 debate.

Senator David Durenburger, a first-term senator from Minnesota, has proposed legislation favoring competition through multiple choice of carriers. Every employer or multiemployer trust would have to offer three different options to employees through three different carriers, and somebody would have to administer it. I have a feeling that that legislation would become the "Third-Party Administrators' Full Employment Act," if it ever got passed. But, that's the concept—multiple choice with, again, limits on the deductibility, and employee rebates. Finally, we have the newest big actors on the scene, former Congressman Dave Stockman, now director of the Office of Management and Budget, and Congressman Gephardt from Missouri. The Stockman-Gephardt bill combines bits and pieces of all the other pro competition bills and fits them in with a framework espoused by Allen Enthoven from Stanford. It would basically set up the entire world into these little health care corporations—a corporation here run by an insurance company, a corporation here run by a third-party administrator, a corporation here run by a medical society, a corporation here run by a hospital, a corporation here run by my brother-in-law. Anybody who wants to can sell a plan, can provide benefits. Any employee can elect to belong to any plan. Congressman Gephardt never quite tells you how he's going to implement and administer it. However, there's going to be a new health care court to adjudicate all this stuff. No more regulatory bureaucracy, he's going to wipe out all forms of regulation, but there will be a health care court set up patterned after the tax court, and I don't have to tell you what happens when you get into tax court.

Competing Issues

There is one little complicating factor in the health area, which is that in addition to health insurance type legislation, there is going to be an awful lot of busywork that Congress has to do in 1981. For example: The Public Health Service Act goes back to 1798. The PHS started as a system of hospitals to care for merchant seamen. Today it's an agency of over 50,000 people, which still runs hospitals, clinics, nursing homes, neighborhood health centers, community mental health centers, health planning, etc. Fifteen major Public Health

Service Act authorities expire in 1981.

Funding for HMOs, funding for health planning and so on, are woven into this tremendous economic policy debate to which health care planning per se will have to take a back seat. Then there is the national health insurance debate—on the Senate side, the focal point being gap fillers and catastrophic coverage, and on the House side the focal point being pro competition. There will also be 15 different pieces of legislation or legislation on 15 different provisions of the Public Health Service Act. That will take up an awful lot of time. So I would guess that we're going to have a busy season. The kind of legislation that will impact on you will clearly be the national health insurance pieces; HMO legislation; and the health planning legislation.

Let me also mention that the Clean Air Act comes up for renewal in 1981, and that's also, as it happens, under the jurisdiction of the House Commerce Committee. The subcommittee that has to look at that law will be the Health and Environment Subcommittee. Henry Waxman of California is the chairman. So that committee, which would have to look at some health insurance legislation, will also have the Public Health Service renewals to worry about and the Clean Air Act—and what gets on the agenda first, behind the economy, is anybody's bet.

Conclusion

I would guess that we're not going to see an awful lot of legislation passed, because of that formula that I began with. All I can tell you is that the environmental interests and the health interests are going to be competing for time in the House of Representatives. In the Senate, it's going to be Senator Dole competing with Senator Hatch, who now will be chairing the Labor and Health Committee, so we're in for a very confusing, I think, but exciting time.

In the history of this long national health insurance debate, remember, it didn't start or it isn't going to start with 1981. The issues have been around for a long time. Their development as issues has gone on for a long time, and it's surely not going to end.

State Health Insurance Mandates: The Hawaii Prepaid Health Care Act— A Model for National Health Insurance

BY JOHN VAN STEENWYK,
PATRICIA K. PUTMAN and
ORLANDO K. WATANABE

JOHN VAN STEENWYK

PATRICIA K. PUTMAN

Mr. van Steenwyk is vice president of Martin E. Segal Company, with responsibility for coordinating direct-service health care programs, including HMOs, and developing and implementing cost containment plans for clients. He received his A.B. degree from Oberlin College and his M.B.A. from the Wharton School of the University of Pennsylvania. Mr. van Steenwyk is a fellow of the Society for Advanced Medical Systems and a clinical assistant professor of community and preventive medicine, New York Medical College.

Ms. Putman, an associate dean of legal and legislative affairs at the University of Hawaii, serves as attorney for the medical school and has been involved in the employee benefits field for over 13 years. Prior to assuming her current position, she served as attorney for the Legislative Reference Bureau, State of Hawaii. Ms. Putman earned her B.A. and J.D. degrees at the University of California, Berkeley, and is active as a member of numerous professional and service organizations including the bar associations of California and Hawaii; the American Bar Association Committee on Medicine and Law and Forum Committee on Health Law; American Judicature Society; American College of Legal Medicine; American Society of Law and Medicine; American Society of Hospital Attorneys; and Council on Prepaid Health Care. She is president of the American Lung Association of Hawaii, and serves as chairperson of the Hawaii Advisory Committee to the U.S. Civil Rights Commission.

Mr. Watanabe, administrator of the disability compensation division, State of Hawaii Department of Labor and Industrial Relations, previously served as administrator of the temporary disability insurance and workers' compensation divisions and, prior to that, as labor law inspector and wage claims examiner, all for the State of Hawaii. He graduated from the University of Hawaii and received specialized training from the U.S. Army Command and General Staff College, the College of Workers' Compensation, the U.S. Army Inspector General course, and numerous civilian and military seminars and workshops. Mr. Watanabe currently is a member of the Hawaii State Comprehensive Health Planning Council, which is charged with statewide health planning, the Hawaii Government Employees' Association, the International and Western Region Association of Industrial Accident Boards and Commissions, the Hawaii State Committee on Health Insurance, the State Advisory Committee on Vocational Rehabilitation, the board of the Rehabilitation Hospital of the Pacific, and other organizations.

State Health Insurance Mandates

In the past decade, state legislatures have been very busy on the subject of health insurance. While the great debate on national health insurance has languished and fizzled in Washington, many quiet and decisive actions have been taken at the state level.

With the sole exception of the Hawaii Prepaid Health Care Act, none of these state laws require that an employer provide group insurance to its employees: they answer, in one way or another, the question of what *kind* of health insurance coverage we should have—supposing that we have health insurance in the first place.

Here is a box score or overview:
- 18 states require coverage for the treatment of alcoholism; an additional 11 require that insurers offer coverage for this purpose.
- 25 states require group insurance policies to provide conversion privileges to those who leave covered employment.
- 40 states require coverage of newborns from birth.
- 29 states require continued coverage (beyond age 18) of children who are mentally or physically handicapped and who rely on their parents for support.
- 20 states require varying degrees of coverage for mental and nervous disorders; an additional ten require that such coverage be made available for purchase.
- 12 states require that specified procedures, such as surgical operations, be paid for whether performed inside or outside of a usual hospital setting.

An additional series of laws provide for the recognition of various health professionals including chiropractors, psychologists, podiatrists, social workers and practitioners of Oriental medicine. Three states—Rhode Island, Maine and Minnesota—have catastrophic health insurance laws. These do not represent any requirement on employers, but rather provide stopgap coverage, paid for from the state treasuries, for the relatively few individuals, not on Medicaid, who incur very high expenses and who may exceed the limits of their private coverage. Three state laws—those in Connecticut, Wisconsin and Minnesota—require insurers to make qualified comprehensive plans available.

One state—Hawaii—has a comprehensive health insurance law that is frequently classified with those of the others. But it is not like these; it is absolutely unique. It is important. It is the first application, in this country, of the requirements that would prevail if the national health insurance legislation, as most recently proposed by Senator Kennedy, and as proposed by the Carter Administration, were to be enacted. These proposals—like the Hawaii Prepaid Health Care Act—require that employers provide a certain set level of health insurance coverage for their employees.

As we have gradually become aware, the concept of national health insurance has gradually been transformed. It used to be conceived of as a government-run program, most likely tied in with Social Security, leaving employee benefit coverage in a supplemental role, if not entirely obsolete. This view of national health insurance is still held by some—but the prevailing consensus, now, is that it would be difficult to find enough tax financing for an extensive new government program. Hence, the backbone of NHI is suggested to be the already-existing coverage provided by employee benefit plans.

This is what has been put into effect for Hawaii.

The compulsory health insurance law has worked well in Hawaii; it has resulted in the intended expansion of coverage, both in terms of numbers of people covered and the extent of their benefits. Health insurance in Hawaii is now just short of being universal, including private coverage, Medicare and Medicaid. These results have been achieved without noticeable price inflation, widespread hardship on employers, onerous administrative requirements or other untoward consequences.

Orlando Watanabe, of the Hawaii Department of Labor and Industrial Relations, will explain the requirements and administration of the Hawaii Prepaid Health Care Act. Mr. Watanabe is directly responsible for the enforcement and administration of the requirements of the act.

The Hawaii Prepaid Health Care Act

Requirements of the Act

The Hawaii Prepaid Health Care Act was enacted in June 1974 and became effective January 1, 1975. It requires that employers provide full-time employees (20 hours or more per week) with health insurance coverage; and that the employer pay at least half of the premium cost of the coverage for the employee. Coverage for employees' dependents is not required, although almost all employers make this available and a majority pay part or all of the cost. The law also provides subsidies to employers who can prove economic hardship as a result of the health insurance requirements.

The insurance coverage is required to meet prevailing standards, equivalent to that held by the majority of the subscribers to the Hawaii Medical Service Association (as to fee-for-service coverage) and the Kaiser Foundation Health Plan (as to prepaid group practice or HMO benefits). Variations in coverage are explicitly allowed, but must be approved by the Prepaid Health Care Advisory Council. The benefits provided must include hospitalization, surgery, anaesthesia, medical services both inpatient and outpatient, maternity benefits, treatment for substance abuse and diagnostic examinations. Employees who already have coverage through another family member, or through Medicare, may waive coverage.

A 1977 amendment to the act puts real teeth in its enforcement provisions: "Any employer who fails to provide coverage as required . . . shall be liable to pay for the health care costs incurred by an eligible employee. . . ."

Administration of the Act

The act is administered by the Hawaii Department of Labor and Industrial Relations, in conjunction with the requirements for two other sets of requirements on employers: workers' compensation and temporary disability insurance. There are some 20,000 employers in Hawaii. All three requirements affecting employers, while different, involve essentially the same administrative procedure: that is, interpreting and explaining the requirements, monitoring compliance, and administering sanctions and penalties on those employers that fail to comply. More specifically, the activities include: informing employers of the requirements of the act; approving or disapproving plans presented by health insurance companies and employers to meet the standards of the act; determining whether there has been compliance with the act; enforcing penalties where there is no compliance; and handling complaints and inquiries. The Department of Labor and Industrial Relations also has the responsibility for administering requests for state subsidies for employers who demonstrate financial hardships arising from compliance with the act.

Many observers have remarked on the fact that the administration of the Hawaii Prepaid Health Care Act requires very little additional effort on the part of the state government. Since the workers' compensation and temporary disability requirements were already in force, no substantial additions to the staff of the Department of Labor and Industrial Relations were required in order to handle the health insurance requirements.

It has often been said that a compulsory health insurance requirement would involve an extensive government bureaucracy. This has not been the case in Hawaii.

Patricia K. Putman, who played a vital role in studying the need for the legislation and in shaping its provisions, will discuss the history of the Hawaii Prepaid Health Care Act.

History of the Prepaid Health Care Act

Consideration of this legislation was based largely on a 1969-71 study conducted under the direction of Professor Stefan Riesenfeld for Hawaii's Legislative Reference Bureau. Professor Riesenfeld, now an Emeritus Professor of Law at the University of California, Berkeley, is a widely respected expert on social legislation. The study pointed out the gaps in the population which had no insurance coverage—including approximately 40,000-50,000 people in the work group.

The study posed a choice: either to expand medical assistance through Medicaid, or to require universal coverage by employers. The second alternative was recommended. Medicaid in Hawaii was already at the limit of the national standard, and further expansion would not have allowed federal participation in the additional cost. A draft of the legislation was proposed and championed by State Senator Nadao Yoshinaga. Discussion of the legislation continued through the 1971-74 sessions of the Hawaii Legislature. In 1974, "with the strength of the long distance runner," the legislation was enacted.

The legislative discussions were active, but marked by an absence of heated debate. No major interest group in Hawaii voiced strong opposition. The main idea expressed in opposition was that national health insurance was "just around the corner" and, accordingly, it would be a waste of time for one state to enact such legislation. In retrospect, the passage of legislation may be viewed as a logical extension of existing public and private health insurance. It was also an extension of the strong tradition established early in Hawaii's statehood, for social welfare legislation providing for universal protection.

ERISA and Current Status

The legal and legislative history of the Hawaii Prepaid Health Care Act is not altogether smooth and lacking in controversy. During the period in which the Hawaii law was under consideration, the U.S. Congress was studying the Employee Retirement Income Security Act of 1974 (ERISA). The U.S. Congress was not aware of Hawaii's consideration of compulsory health insurance. The

Hawaii Legislature, for its part, thought of the ERISA legislation as concerning retirement plans only, and not relevant to group insurance.

In enacting ERISA, Congress reserved for itself jurisdiction on the content of all employee benefit plans, including group insurance: ERISA expressly prohibits the states from making contrary requirements in this regard. A legal challenge to the enforcement of the Hawaii Prepaid Health Care Act was made by the Standard Oil Company of California, based on Section 514(a) of the ERISA legislation. In confirming this, Judge Charles A. Renfrew of the Federal District Court, Northern District of California, quoted Justice Brandeis, who said in a 1932 Supreme Court dissent *(New State Ice Company v. Liebman,* 285 U.S. 261, 311): "It is one of the happy incidents of the federal system that a single courageous state may, if its citizens choose, serve as a laboratory; and try novel social and economic experiments without risk to the rest of the country." Judge Renfrew affirmed the applicability of the ERISA requirement, but noted that ERISA had been enacted without considering the Hawaii law. Hawaii's remedy, he suggested, "is not in this court but in Congress."

With the cooperation of the Hawaii Congressional delegation, Senators Inouye and Matsunaga, and Representatives Akaka and Heftel, remedial legislation is under consideration. In the meantime, the State of Hawaii has made appeal to the legal decision rendered by Judge Renfrew and will make further legal appeals as necessary, while continuing to enforce the law.

The provisions of the act, and how it applies, and its possible usefulness as a model for national health insurance have to be understood in light of the particular conditions which prevail in Hawaii. These will be discussed next by John van Steenwyk.

Health Care in Hawaii

Hawaii's geography, economy, population and climate are, of course, unique. But Hawaii is not "foreign." It is one of the 50 states. Patterns of disease and of medical practice are substantially the same as those of the U.S. mainland, but with some important differences in emphasis. The organization and economics of health care also are essentially similar to those prevailing in the rest of the U.S.—here, with crucial differences in emphasis.

Characteristics of the Population

There is no denying the fact, however, that Hawaii is different. It is an island state, in the middle of the ocean. It has about 900,000 residents; the U.S. mainland has over 220 million. Hawaii's economy is unique, and much less diverse than that of the U.S. mainland. Tourism, military activities and agriculture are the major industries. Hawaii's principal products are unique, a direct result of location and climate. There is no domestic competition with its main products. Living costs are higher than on the U.S. mainland, as are family incomes. Wages, however, tend to be lower and there is a high proportion of multiple-worker families.

The population includes several distinct ethnic groups. Caucasians account for about one-fourth of the population; Japanese for another fourth. The remaining half is composed mainly of distinct ethnic groups, including people of Hawaiian descent, Filipinos and Chinese. In terms of age, the statistics show Hawaii residents to be somewhat younger than those of the U.S. generally.

A remarkable fact is the lower death rate in Hawaii. Data from the National Center for Health Statistics indicate that Hawaii's death rate, adjusted for age and sex, is about 65% of the national standard. This has some apparent relation to race and ethnicity: the death rates for Caucasians in Hawaii were 81% of the expected rate; the rate was 60% for non-Caucasians. Hawaii deaths from cancer were about 85% of the U.S. average rate; from heart disease, about 74%; from motor vehicle accidents, 69%. Infant mortality rates for Hawaii were about 80% of the overall U.S. rate.

While mortality is low, morbidity is very close to the U.S. average. Surveys conducted by the U.S. Department of Health and Human Services and by the Hawaii Department of Health list illnesses at about the same rate in Hawaii as in the overall U.S.—just under 200 acute conditions per 1,000 persons per year. Disability rates, from health surveys, are also essentially the same.

Health Care Delivery System

Outpatient Emphasis. While the gross rates of morbidity and disability are approximately the same as in the U.S. generally, there are key differences in health care delivery. Hawaii has more physicians, in relation to the overall population, than does the overall U.S. Moreover, a greater portion of Hawaii's physicians practice in groups. Most striking is the fact that Hawaii has a very low supply of hospital beds—just about 70% of the overall U.S. average. The low supply of hospital beds in Hawaii can be traced, in part, to the long existence of multispecialty group clinics, in which referral practice, for acute illness, tends to be concentrated. Medical centers such as the Straub

Clinic and Honolulu Medical Group are staffed in just about all specialties, and have facilities for doing a great deal of work on an outpatient basis. Historically, Hawaii's physicians, having good outpatient facilities to use, have not overemphasized the use of the hospital.

All of this, and other factors which we will cite, have resulted in remarkably low hospital utilization in Hawaii. Hawaii Medical Service Association, the Blue Shield affiliate which is Hawaii's major prepayment carrier, reports utilization at the rate of approximately 360 bed-days per 1,000 enrollees per year. This is in contrast to the experience of U.S. Blue Cross plans, which varies by region but which averaged 736 days per 1,000 last year. It also is lower than the average of U.S. health maintenance organizations, which was about 400 bed-days per 1,000 according to a recent tally.

Provider Competition. Hawaii's health care system is marked by effective competition, and has been cited as a significant example of how competition can work. Part of this is between the physicians in multispecialty group practice and those practicing solo or as members of smaller groups.

There is also competition between the Kaiser Foundation Health Plan, a large group practice health maintenance organization serving over 100,000 people, and the Hawaii Medical Service Association, or HMSA, which serves over 500,000 people under private contracts and, in addition, serves about 60,000 Medicare beneficiaries, over 90,000 Medicaid recipients and some 65,000 military dependents. The dynamic tension between the two locally based health plans—Kaiser and HMSA—is real. Kaiser provides somewhat broader benefits than HMSA and is under considerable pressure to exert strict budget discipline. In turn, HMSA must keep a rein on utilization and fees so that its rates won't get too far above Kaiser's.

Competition between two dominant carriers and two different delivery systems has forced fee-for-service medicine to maintain a great deal of economic discipline. Added to that is the fact of carrier dominance. The Hawaii Medical Service Association, since it handles health care financing for so many people, is able to exert a significant degree of economic influence on providers.

All in all, the situation is markedly different from, say, that of California, in which no carrier has a significant part of the market.

Benefits and Coverage Patterns. Differences in medical practice and prepayment have an undoubted influence. So does the pattern of benefits in Hawaii. Employee benefits "grew up" somewhat differently in Hawaii than on the mainland: coverage for doctors' office care and other outpatient services was an early development ... not something added later. The pattern of first dollar coverage for outpatient care was established many years ago in Hawaii. This was influenced primarily by the group practice physicians, who opposed the establishment of a prepayment plan which discriminated in favor of inpatient care. In other words, when prepayment was established in Hawaii, doctors had more to say about the matter than did hospitals. Also, the pattern was influenced by labor unions, which favored inclusive coverage.

In order to make the available health insurance dollars stretch to include outpatient services, most health insurance in Hawaii (except that provided through Kaiser) has involved patient copayments. The currently prevailing HMSA contract calls for patient copayments of 50% for x-rays and lab tests, and 10% for a semiprivate hospital room. The latter is especially unusual. As we all know, the major pattern in the U.S. generally has been toward full payment for the cost of hospital care.

All of these influences have led, in one way or another, in the direction of significant economies in hospital bed-day use, and in overall lower costs for comprehensive insurance coverage.

Impacts of the Act

Now it is time to turn to a discussion of the various effects of the Hawaii Prepaid Health Care Act.

We have determined, after extensive study, that the percentage of the civilian population covered by health care insurance rose from 95.3% in 1974—before the act was effective—to 98.2% in 1977. These results are documented more fully in a report we prepared in 1978 for the U.S. Department of Health, Education and Welfare, and in a paper prepared with Dr. Raymond Fink and presented last year at the American Public Health Association's annual meeting. Group coverage, the subject of the act's requirement, can be related further to jobs. Here we see a somewhat more dramatic example of the impact of the act: an increase from 70.2% of jobs covered in 1974 to 77.8% in 1977—almost an 11% increase.

But what's going on here? If health insurance is required to be universal, why does group coverage total less than 100% of jobs? The main explanation is that about 50% of workers in Hawaii are part of multiple-worker families; and, in another feature which contrasts with the U.S. mainland, not everyone accepts duplicate coverage. In fact, our studies indicate that over 75,000 workers had waived duplicate coverage, as of the end of 1977.

This, in turn, can be understood from the fact that the dominant carriers—HMSA and Kaiser—each make an effort to review their membership lists to identify duplicate coverage. Unlike most carriers elsewhere, they actively call attention to the fact that being covered twice, for service benefits, presents no advantage. In addition to this, "family coverage" such as would involve a working spouse often costs the worker something: employee contributions toward the cost of dependent coverage are the prevailing pattern in Hawaii.

Summary of Results

In summary, it can be said that Hawaii has a controlled health care system with extensive existing coverage. Hence, the requirement of health insurance, through the Hawaii Prepaid Health Care Act, has had marginal cost and no adverse impact on the economy. The intent of the law—that of expanding coverage—has been accomplished without fuss or dislocation. The mandated coverages were precisely those which were most prevalent. (However, the Prepaid Health Care Advisory Council, charged under the act with reviewing coverage, has required detailed changes in the benefits afforded to employees of many employers, most of these based on the mainland.)

There have been no noticeable effects on the economy, or on employment. Health care costs have increased in Hawaii, as they have in the rest of the U.S. But they have not increased at a special rate, which would be the expected result from increased coverage resulting from the requirement of such a law.

While some significant gaps in coverage remain and Hawaii's arrangements cannot be said to match every aspiration, it is clear that Hawaii has accomplished in large measure what is being sought for the rest of the country:

1. Relative economy—to the extent achieved by a health care delivery system which is organized and rationalized in such a way that hospital bed-day use for the entire population is kept to a level generally achieved only by health maintenance organizations;
2. Comprehensive prepayment—in the sense that most of the health insurance in Hawaii includes coverage for outpatient treatment and does not involve pernicious economic incentives to excessive hospital use;
3. Coverage which comes very close to being universal, with the major gap being coverage for persons who are unemployed, but not yet eligible for Medicaid;
4. The health insurance requirements of the act have found acceptance, and there is no substantial problem with compliance.

The Hawaiian situation is unique mainly in that it was receptive to a mandated health insurance plan. The delivery system absorbed whatever additional burden may have been involved. The employers affected were relatively few, and they apparently absorbed the extra costs. The state readily absorbed the administrative tasks involved. The whole plan went into effect without substantial hitch or complaint.

This smooth transition can be contrasted with the "big deal" that national legislation on this subject is thought to be—fraught with great danger of uncontrollable costs. It is, of course, a far different thing to mandate a substantial increase in coverage than to mandate a marginal one. For some areas of the U.S., and for some industry segments, comprehensive coverage, if mandated, would represent substantial change, with implications both for the economy and for the delivery system. Hawaii, by contrast, had extensive existing coverage and effective health care cost controls.

In summary, the question of transferability involves consideration of the *comparative extent and scope of existing coverage.* It also involves consideration of what cost controls are available; these are relatively well developed in Hawaii. The existing situation in terms of benefit coverage and in terms of the health care delivery and financing system determines the results which can be expected for mandated coverage.

In conclusion, one of the 50 states, unique as it may be, does have the economics reasonably under control. As suggested long ago by Justice Brandeis, one state can "serve as a laboratory" for the rest of the nation. There is a great deal to be learned here, which can help us develop our understanding of the interrelationship between health care prepayment financing and the provision of health care services.

CHAPTER 3

The Legal Context

Richard P. Donaldson

Partner
Donaldson & Kiel, P.S.
Seattle, Washington

Hugh J. McCarthy, Jr.

Director
Hugh J. McCarthy & Associates
Chicago, Illinois

David W. Silverman

Partner
Granik, Silverman, Sandberg, Kirschner,
Campbell & Nowicki
New City, New York

Thomas E. Stanton, Jr.

Partner
Johnson & Stanton
San Francisco, California

Warren H. Saltzman

President
Saltzman & Johnson Law Corporation
San Francisco, California

Richard C. Johnson

Vice President
Saltzman & Johnson Law Corporation
San Francisco, California

Phil E. Davidson

Account Executive
Martin E. Segal Company
San Francisco, California

Leo Brown

Employee Benefits Consultant
Vedder, Price, Kaufman,
Kammholz & Day
New York, New York

Recent Decisions Affecting Negotiated Employee Benefit Plans and Joint Trusts

BY RICHARD P. DONALDSON

Introduction

In the 13 months since the last International Foundation Annual Conference (October 1979), there have been approximately 300 court, arbitration and administrative agency decisions which involve or affect negotiated employee benefit plans and joint trusts.

The 20 decisions selected for this presentation are deemed to be among the most significant.

Time considerations permit only a brief mention of each decision, and we would caution those of you who are not attorneys to review these decisions carefully with your attorneys before applying them to any situation or problem in which you may be involved. Many of the decisions are still on appeal and the ultimate result will not be known for some time. Other decisions are such that attorneys may have differing views as to the meaning of the rules being announced or applied.

Statutory Regulations— Other Than ERISA

The National Labor Relations Act

1. *Amax Coal Company v. National Labor Relations Board,* ___ F.2d ___, 280 BNA BPR D-4 (3rd Cir. 1980).

It is an unfair labor practice under Sections 8(b)(1)(B) and 8(b)(3) of the National Labor Relations Act for a union to coerce an employer in the selection of his representatives for the purposes of collective bargaining. In prior years, the National Labor Relations Board held that these sections were violated in instances where a union insisted, to point of impasse, that an employer participate in a jointly trusteed multiemployer fringe benefit fund where the employer trustees were selected by other parties. Then, in the 1978 *Sheetmetal Workers Local 493* case, the board backed away

Mr. Donaldson is a partner in the law firm of Donaldson & Kiel, P.S., with offices in Seattle, San Diego and Washington, D.C. The firm limits its practice to employee benefit plan law. Mr. Donaldson is an honor graduate of the University of Wisconsin Law School and has taught labor relations subjects at Seattle University and the University of Washington. He has also lectured at the University of Texas and New York University. Mr. Donaldson was founding editor of the International Foundation's Legal-Legislative Reporter *news bulletin. He is a former member of the Foundation's Advisory Board of Directors, Attorneys Committee, Trustees Committee, and Research and Information Committee, and is a frequent speaker at Foundation meetings. A member of the American Bar Association Labor Law Section, he formerly served as co-chairman of its Welfare and Pension Plan Subcommittee.*

from that position, indicating that trustees of a fringe benefit trust fund are, while serving as such, independent fiduciaries and are not collective bargaining representatives.

In the instant case, the United Mine Workers Union was accused of violating Sections 8(b)(1)(B) and 8(b)(3) by insisting to impasse and striking an independent coal company for the purpose of forcing the coal company to participate in a certain pension and welfare fund, the management trustee of which was appointed by companies other than the independent company. Based on its view that trustees are fiduciaries and not collective bargaining representatives, the NLRB found no such violation.

However, on appeal to the Third Circuit Court of Appeals, the court reversed the board. The court said that, while trustees normally function as fiduciaries, they also serve as representatives of the parties who appoint them and can be expected to advance the interests of those parties. The court concluded:

> Because we hold that the management trustee of this Union's pension and welfare fund is a collective bargaining representative within the meaning of Section 8(b)(1)(B), we conclude that the Union violated the Act by striking to obtain Amax's participation in the fund whose management trustee is not selected by Amax.

Update: Under ERISA, and under Section 302 of Taft-Hartley, it is abundantly clear that trustees, while serving as such, are to function as independent fiduciaries and not as collective bargaining representatives. The *Amax* decision is an undermining of that concept and has been severely criticized. In the recent debate on the Multiemployer Pension Plan Amendments Act of 1980, Congressman Frank Thompson commented that *Amax* was wrongly decided and does not reflect Congressional intent (House floor debate 8/25/80).

Veterans Reemployment Rights Act

2. *Bunnell v. New England Teamsters and Trucking Industry Pension Fund,* ___ F.Supp. ___, 286 BNA BPR D-1 (D.C. Mass. 1980).

We reported two years ago on *Alabama Power Co. v. Davis,* 431 U.S. 581 (U.S. Sup. Ct. 1977), wherein the Supreme Court ruled that the federal selective service laws require that a reemployed veteran is entitled to benefit credit, under a defined benefit pension plan, for time spent in the military service. The *Alabama Power* case involved a single employer pension plan, but we predicted that the same requirements might be made applicable to jointly administered multiemployer plans.

Bunnell is a fulfillment of the earlier prediction. Here, the plaintiff started working for Brock Hall Dairy (later purchased by Knudsen Dairy) in May 1944. In October 1944, during the course of World War II, he was inducted into the army, where he served until he was honorably discharged on December 18, 1945. On the very next day, for the convenience of the government, he reenlisted voluntarily and served until October 28, 1948. He then returned to his job at the dairy company.

Knudsen Dairy participated in the New England Teamsters and Trucking Industry Pension Fund. In 1974, the plaintiff applied to the pension fund for pension benefits, under a special 30 year service pension formula. He was advised that under a plan rule he would get credit for the time which he spent on active military duty, in World War II, but not for the time during which he served as a voluntary enlistee following the end of the war. Thus, he was short the required 30 years and could not retire. He continued working, however, until 1978, when he had the necessary service and he then retired.

The plaintiff brought suit against Knudsen Dairy and the pension fund contending that under the Veterans Reemployment Rights Act, 38 U.S.C. Section 2021, *et seq.,* he should have been credited with the full time of his enlistment. The court readily agreed with this contention, pointing out that under the statute benefits are equally available to voluntary enlistees as well as to those inducted in the draft.

The difficult issue, however, was whether the pension fund had the burden of restoring the missing credited service. The pension fund argued that, under the statute, it is the responsibility of an ex-veteran's "employer" to restore all rights to which he is entitled. The court agreed that the technical statutory burden falls on the employer but, looking at the total relationship between Knudsen Dairy and the pension fund, the court found that the pension fund was the operative agency insofar as the design and administration of the pension plan was concerned. The court noted that Knudsen, being only one of many contributing employers, was not in a position to control the activities or decisions of the pension fund. The court said:

> If the Fund were not required to comply with the statute, an employer would either have to drop out of the Plan and provide retirement benefits directly in order to control the terms of eligibility, or reimburse veterans in Bunnell's position in a piecemeal fashion for the difference between amounts provided by a union's pension plan and amounts due under the statute. Either course of action would undermine the integrity of collective bargaining agreements and so frustrate federal labor policies.

Pointing out that veterans' reemployment statutes are to be liberally construed, the court concluded that the "appropriate remedy" is to require the pension fund to recompute the plaintiff's credited service and award him retroactive pension benefit payments.

Criminal Statutes

3. *United States v. Andreen,* and *United States v. Ford, et al.,* ___ F.2d ___, 80 Daily Journal D.A.R. 2723 and 2739 (9th Cir. 1980).

Previous mention has been made of indictments issued, in 1976, against 16 of the union and management trustees who were serving or had served on one or more of the San Diego Laborers Trust Funds (Pension, Welfare, Vacation and Training), and the attorney for the funds. The primary charge against the defendants was that they had conspired to embezzle, and did embezzle, monies from the trust funds in violation of Section 664 of the United States Criminal Code, by the following conduct:

a. Voting themselves special pension credits, for service as trustees, not authorized by the pension plan and not made available to the plan participants;
b. Approving expensive medical examinations for themselves at a medical clinic, not authorized in the welfare plan, and not made available to the plan participants;
c. Approving excessive expense allowances for attendance at International Foundation meetings and keeping the difference between the allowances and the actual expenses (allowances ranged up to $2,500 per trustee per meeting).

The criminal trial was held in the spring of 1977. Just prior to the trial, seven of the defendant trustees pleaded guilty. The nine remaining defendant trustees, and the attorney, went to trial, but were found guilty. Jail sentences ranging from one to ten years were imposed and certain defendants were also assessed $10,000 fines.

Most of those who were convicted at the trial took appeals to the Ninth Circuit Court of Appeals. In decisions dated September 26, 1980, the appeals court affirmed all of the convictions, although certain defendants did win reversals as to certain counts of the indictments.

The trust attorney argued that he should be relieved of criminal responsibility with respect to the unauthorized pension credits, as he did not personally gain from this transaction. In rejecting this contention, the court noted that the attorney was deeply involved in creating and implementing the special pension program, even though he was not a participant therein. Said the court:

> It is not necessary, however, that one have an active stake in the outcome of the crime [citing authority]. It is sufficient if [the attorney] acted with criminal intent to further the crime or that his purpose was to take part in its commission.

. . .

> The trial judge was justified in inferring that [the attorney] acted to aid and abet the violation, by counseling the trustees and concealing the activities from outside inquiries. His conviction on count 2 is therefore affirmed.

In determining that the excessive expense allowances violated the statute, the court observed that:

> ... as reimbursement for attendance at educational conferences, the board of trustees would grant themselves large sums of money and would keep any money not spent at the conference. Evidence in the record suggests that more than half of such expense allowances was excessive.

Collections

4. *Washington Area Carpenters Welfare Fund v. Overhead Door Company of Metropolitan Washington,* ___ F.Supp. ___, 289 BNA BPR D-12 (D.C. D.C. 1980).

5. *Western Washington Cement Masons Welfare Trust v. Hillis Homes,* 26 Wn. App. 224; ___ BNA BPR ___ (Wn. Ct. App. Div. 1 1980), petition for review denied (Wash. Sup. Ct. 1980; Dkt. No. 47200-9).

Perhaps the most important issue being litigated in construction industry collection cases is the defense, based on Section 8(f) of the Labor-Management Relations Act, that a prehire collective bargaining agreement may be voidable, at the option of the employer, where the union does not represent a majority of the employees. This defense is based upon the analysis of Section 8(f) made in *N.L.R.B. v. Iron Workers Local 103 (Higdon Contracting)* 434 U.S. 335 (1978). Last year, we cited a Florida collection case *(Florida Viking Sauna)* in which this defense was rejected but, since then, there have been additional cases. The following are examples.

In the *Overhead Door Company* case, a construction employer signed a collective bargaining agreement with the Carpenters union, in 1969, at a point in time when he was starting a construction project. The employer signed successor agreements in 1972 and 1976. When the agreement was originally signed, the union represented only three of the company's 13 employees.

Subsequently, the trust funds audited the employer's payroll records and determined that the employer owed approximately $14,000 in delinquent contributions. Suit was then brought to collect. The employer raised the *Higdon* defense, arguing that the Carpenters union had never obtained majority support among its employees and, hence, the collective bargaining agreements were unenforceable. The court sustained this defense and dismissed the action.

The trust funds emphasized that the union was not a party to the collection suit and defenses which might otherwise be available against the union should not be recognized in a suit by the funds, citing a number of previously decided cases. The court distinguished the earlier cases, suggesting they did not involve the concept of a "voidable" agreement as was present here. The court concluded:

> The *Iron Workers (Higdon)* case teaches that majority support is a crucial element of an enforceable prehire agreement. Such support must be established affirmatively by the party suing to enforce the agreement ... As majority support has not been shown, the agreement is unenforceable against Overhead. Consequently, [the] Funds have no claim for insufficient contributions with respect to the three employees on whose behalf some contributions were made nor any right to examine Overhead's payroll records for other employees.

Other decisions to the same effect are *Health and Welfare Plan v. Associated Wrecking Company,* ____ F.Supp. ____, 291 BNA BPR A-23 (D.C. Nebr. 1980) and *Western Washington Laborers Employers Trust Funds v. McDowell,* ____ F.Supp. ____, 103 LRRM 2219 (D.C. W.D. Wash. 1979).

On the other hand, the Washington Court of Appeals in *Hillis Homes* squarely rejected the employer's Section 8(f) defense to a collection suit. *Higdon,* said the court, "... is authority only for the proposition that pre-hire arrangements are not enforceable by picketing ..." and does not bar the enforcement of a prehire agreement by third-party beneficiaries such as the trust funds. The court went on to state that the rights of third-party beneficiaries in labor contracts are strongly supported by labor policy, and that by enacting ERISA, Congress had declared "... a national public interest in the protection of employee benefit rights...." Accordingly, the court concluded that the funds were entitled to recover the contributions under the agreement, including contributions for non-union employees.

The *Higdon* defense was also rejected in *Western Washington Laborers Employers Trust Funds v. Newman,* ____ F.Supp. ____ (D.C. W.D. Wash. 1980 DKT. No. C79-858V). The court expressly declined to follow the *McDowell* case decided previously in the same district.

Update: In the recently enacted Multiemployer Pension Plan Amendments Act of 1980, Congress added, in Section 515, a provision obligating all employers who are parties to multiemployer plans to make the contributions to such plans as required by the terms of their collective bargaining agreements. Collection actions can now be litigated under Section 502 of ERISA. In any judgment entered in such an action, certain statutory surcharges can be included. Congressman Frank Thompson, in explaining this new addition to ERISA, emphasized the need for allowing trustees of plans to recover delinquent contributions without regard to issues which might arise under labor-management relations law and he specifically commented that Congress considered the *Overhead Door* case and the *McDowell* case to have been "incorrectly decided." The new legislation, he said, is intended to clarify the law in this respect. (House floor debate 8/25/80.)

Employee Retirement Income Security Act

Refund of Erroneous Employer Contributions

6. *Martin v. Hamil,* ____ F.2d ____, 273 BNA BPR D-4 (7th Cir. 1979).

A major headache, in living with ERISA, has been the handling of employer contributions paid by mistake. Normally, one would expect that erroneously paid contributions could be "backed out" of the plan's records and refunded to the employer. However, ERISA Section 403(c)(2)(A) put an end to this practice, for it provided that no contributions could be refunded to an employer, with the exception that if contributions were paid by mistake of fact such contributions could be returned, but only within one year after the date of payment.

Inasmuch as errors of this kind are frequently not discovered until many months or years after they are made, the ERISA refund restriction had the effect of forfeiting large amounts of erroneously made contributions. Some relief was recognized in the *Reuther* and *Bacon* cases, both decided in 1978, wherein it was held that the restriction on employer refunds was not retroactive prior to January 1, 1975.

Nonetheless, the §403(c)(2)(A) restriction has continued to trouble employers, plan trustees, administrators and attorneys and, when it has been literally enforced, it has led to some harsh results. A case in point is *Martin v. Hamil.* Here a partnership made contributions to a pension fund for two owner-partners, as well as for its employees. In the course of a payroll audit, the payments for the partners were discovered. The trustees then brought a declaratory judgment action, which resulted in a decree that the partners were not entitled to participation and, further, that they could not obtain a refund of their post-ERISA contributions. The Seventh Circuit Court of Appeals affirmed.

Update: Congress, in the recently enacted Multiemployer Pension Plan Amendments Act of 1980, undertook to correct the inequity of the refund rule, insofar as multiemployer plans are concerned. Congress has rewritten Section 403(c)(2)(A) to eliminate the distinction between mistakes of law and mistakes of fact and to remove the one year time limitation. Contributions made after September 26, 1980, under either a mistake of law or of fact, may be refunded within six months of the date when the trustees determine that such contributions were made by mistake. Further, trustees are allowed to refund contributions mistakenly paid before September 26, 1980, under either a mistake of law or fact, if the refund is made on or before March 26, 1981. *See* new act, Section 410.

Splitting of Pension Plan Benefits

7. *Stone v. Stone and S.I.U.-P.M.A. Pension Plan,* ___ F.2d ___, 80 Daily Journal D.A.R. 2802 (9th Cir. 1980).

State courts have consistently affirmed their authority to order pension plans to divide present or future pension benefit payments pursuant to decrees entered in marital dissolution or child support cases. Although a division of pension benefits conflicts with anti-alienation provisions in trust and plan documents, and with ERISA Section 206(d)(1), which mandates such antialienation provisions, the courts have ruled that ERISA does not preempt the state's divorce or community property laws or that there is an implied exception, in Section 206(d)(1), with respect to claims of spouses and children.

The situation has been particularly acute in California. It was hoped that the United States Supreme Court would agree to review the California state court decisions, but it has declined to do so. See *Retirement Fund of Plumbing Industry of Southern California v. Johns; Carpenters Pension Fund for Northern California v. Campa;* and *Southern California IBEW-NECA Pension Plan v. Johnston,* appeals or petitions denied 1/14/80, 274 BNA BPR A-20; *Operating Engineers Pension Trust v. Lionberger,* appeal denied 5/19/80, 292 BNA BPR A-22.

Contemporaneously, some of the state court divorce litigation was removed to federal court, in the hope of getting a contrary declaration. There was inconsistency in the district court decisions but in the most publicized decision, *Stone v. Stone,* federal judge Charles Renfrew took the position that ERISA did not preempt the California community property law. On September 29, 1980, the Ninth Circuit Court of Appeals affirmed *Stone v. Stone* as well as a similar decision in *Carpenters Pension Trust for Southern California v. Kronschnabel.* The court said:

> The district court's ruling on the merits was clearly correct ... the Supreme Court's summary dismissal of the appeal in (the *Campa* case) binds district and circuit courts to the view that ERISA does not preempt state-court orders requiring a pension plan to pay a community property share of a plan participant's monthly benefit payments directly to his or her ex-spouse.

Other decisions make it clear that the exemption engrafted upon Section 206(d)(1), for the benefit of spouses and children, does not extend to garnishments or attachments initiated by other creditors. Pension benefits will not be forfeited or divided to satisfy creditors' claims. The leading case is *General Motors Corp. v. Buha,* 623 F.2d 455 (6th Cir. 1980).

An extreme but illustrative case is *Helmsley-Spear, Inc. v. Winter,* 290 BNA BPR D-6 (N.Y.

App. Div. 1980). Here, an employee had committed fraud against an employer, including the theft of certain checks totalling $8,500. The employer obtained a judgment of restitution but, under the principle of ERISA Section 206(d), the court would not allow the judgment to be enforced against the employee's interest in the company profit-sharing trust.

Return to Work Following Retirement

8. *Thomson v. I.A.M. National Pension Fund*, ___F.2d___, 282 BNA BPR D-3 (7th Cir. 1980).

Section 203(a)(3)(B)(ii) of ERISA permits a multiemployer plan to suspend a retiree's benefits, if he returns to work,

> ... in the same industry, in the same trade or craft, in the same geographic area covered by the plan, as when such benefits commenced.

It has been held that this nonforfeiture rule applies only "upon the attainment of normal retirement age." More restrictive rules can be written with respect to early retirees. *See* the *Riley* and *Hurn* cases cited in last year's presentation. The Department of Labor has issued proposed regulations dealing with the subject of suspension of benefits. *See* 29 CFR 2530.203-3 (12/13/78). No final regulations have yet been issued.

In the *Thomson* case, the plaintiff was a participant in a nationwide multiemployer plan. On his retirement, the plaintiff was required to sign a "retirement declaration" which, among other things, required that he would accept no employment "without prior written approval of the trustees." It also required that he would have to refrain from taking employment with any employer who contributes to the pension fund or with any noncontributing employer, in the same or related business as those employers who do contribute.

The Seventh Circuit Court of Appeals found these provisions to offend Section 203. The court indicated that the statute does not allow a pension plan to require a retired person to obtain the consent of the pension trustees before reemployment. The court went on to say that inasmuch as the geographical area covered by the plan is the entire United States, it would be permissible to restrict a retiree from returning to work anywhere in the United States. However, the plan restrictions violated the statute as they did not limit the prohibited employment to "the same industry, and in the same trade or craft." The court opinion does not make clear in what "industry" or "trade or craft" the plaintiff was engaged prior to his retirement, but inasmuch as the plan did not mention such concepts, the plan was found to violate ERISA. The case was remanded to a lower district court for further proceedings.

In the course of the opinion, the court added this helpful comment:

> It is permissible for the trustees to require an applicant retiree to furnish, by way of a retirement declaration, information and proof necessary for the administration of any lawful employment restrictions the plan may impose. It is appropriate to include in the declarations a warning informing the retiree of these restrictions. Like the plan itself, however, the declaration must conform with [Section 203(a)(3)(B)].

Duty to Furnish Information

9. *King v. Wagner Electric Corporation Contributory Retirement Plan*, ___F.Supp.___, 274 BNA BPR D-2 (D.C. E.D. Mo. 1979).

Section 502(c) of ERISA provides that if a plan administrator (the definition of which includes a board of trustees) fails, within 30 days of a written request, to furnish statutory information to a plan participant, such administrator may be personally liable to the participant for damages of up to $100 per day.

In the *King* case, an employee retired under a company pension plan in February 1977. Subsequently, he wrote to the plan administrator requesting a copy of the plan document which was in effect at the time he retired. The administrator sent the retiree a copy of the current plan document containing certain ERISA amendments which had been made retroactive to January 1, 1976.

The plaintiff, however, continued to press for a copy of the plan document which was actually in effect in February 1977 when he retired. When he did not receive a copy, litigation was started. While the litigation was pending, the plaintiff was finally furnished with a copy of the text which he wanted. However, it was pointed out that insofar as the retiree's rights were concerned, his rights could have been determined by the document which had been furnished to him earlier.

The court agreed with the plaintiff that he was entitled to receive, upon his written request, a copy of the plan document as it existed at the time of his retirement, regardless of whether the plan was thereafter amended on a retroactive basis.

As to the assessment of a $100 per day penalty,

the court rejected this relief. The court noted that the imposition of the penalty was subject to the discretion of the court and that, in this case, plaintiff had neither "alleged, argued, proved, nor adverted to" any actual pecuniary damage or prejudice resulting from the failure of the administrator to provide the required document. It was also noted that the plaintiff had formerly worked as Industrial Relations Director with the company and was generally conversant with the provisions of the pension plan.

Consider also *Allen v. The Atlantic Richfield Retirement Plan*, ___ F.Supp. ___, 272 BNA BPR D-17 (D.C. E.D. Pa. 1979), *affirmed* 313 BNA BPR A-23 (3d Cir. 1980), where the court considered and rejected an argument that plan fiduciaries have a duty, under ERISA, to counsel individually with plan participants to explain their rights and options under plan documents. The court said:

> ... part of the fiduciary's duty under Section 404 is to provide employees with a comprehensive explanation of the contents of the plan. It is equally clear, however, that Congress did not intend to impose a duty to provide the kind of individualized attention urged by plaintiff here, but rather envisioned that a fiduciary could discharge its obligations through the use of an explanatory booklet, provided that the booklet adequately explained the plan and the bases for disqualification.

Trust and Plan Administration

Plan Design Determinations

10. *Turner v. Teamsters Local 302*, 604 F.2d 1219, 102 LRRM 2548 (9th Cir. 1979).

Health and welfare funds which provide retiree medical benefits have frequently found themselves in a financial squeeze brought about by the increasing numbers of retirees, as compared to actives, and by the high utilization of medical care benefits by the retirees, particularly in certain areas such as prescription drugs. Several boards of trustees have been required to reduce or even eliminate retiree medical benefits amidst a storm of protests and threatened and actual litigation.

This case concerned the operation of a dairy industry retiree welfare fund maintained by Teamsters unions and various dairy industry employers in the San Francisco Bay Area. In the period 1973-1974, as a result of decreasing numbers of contributing employers, the fund was in a precarious financial condition. The parties to the collective bargaining agreement then amended the bargaining agreement to increase the contribution rate and, at the same time, delete a previous requirement which obligated the trustees to maintain a certain level of benefits for retirees. The trustees were given the authority, henceforth, to provide the benefits only within the limit of the funds available.

The trustees of the fund then modified the benefits to which the retirees were entitled, including an elimination of eye care coverage and life insurance benefits. Additionally, a retiree contribution of $20.50 per month was imposed upon retirees who were not covered by Medicare.

A number of retirees brought a class action in federal district court against the unions, the employers and the trustees objecting to the benefit changes. The court dismissed the action insofar as the unions and employers were concerned. This decision was sustained by the Ninth Circuit Court of Appeals.

The appeals court held that, unlike a retirement plan, the participants in a health and welfare plan are not "vested." Such benefits, said the court, are negotiated periodically and are enforceable only for the life of the particular collective bargaining agreement. The court specifically noted that there was "no evidence that appellant was advised by the collective bargaining agreement, the trust agreement, or any plan brochure that health and welfare benefits would be paid for the rest of his life." The court decided:

> We conclude that the amendment to the 1974 collective bargaining agreement by the appellee unions and employers did not constitute a breach of the contract. The health and welfare benefits were not vested property rights but were instead contractual rights subject to amendment by the parties to the agreement.

The retirees' claims against the trustees are still awaiting decision by the federal district court.

11. *Ponce v. Construction Laborers Pension Trust for Southern California*, ___ F.2d ___, 314 BNA BPR D-1 (9th Cir. 1980).

Prior to ERISA, it was the practice of the Laborers Union pension trust funds in the state of California to require 15 years of credited service as a condition for retirement. When ERISA was enacted, the 15 year requirement was reduced to ten years.

The pre-ERISA 15 year rule was challenged in northern California in the case of *Morgan v. Laborers Pension Trust Fund for Northern California,* ___ F.Supp. ___, 279 BNA BPR D-6 (D.C. N.D. Calif. 1979); in the Los Angeles area in the case of *Ponce v. Construction Laborers Pension Trust for Southern California,* ___ F.Supp. ___, ___ BNA BPR ___ (D.C. C.D. 1979; Docket No. CV78-2895 MML); and in the San Diego area in the case of *Miranda v. San Diego County Laborers Pension Trust Fund,* ___ F.Supp. ___, ___ BNA BPR ___ (D.C. S.D. Calif. 1980; Docket No. 75-0517-GT).

In these cases, it was alleged, by laborers who had retired before ERISA became effective, and who were deemed ineligible for benefits because they had less than 15 years of credited service, that it was "arbitrary and capricious" for the boards of trustees to maintain the earlier 15 year rule. These cases were supported by public interest law clinics and groups including the National Senior Citizens Law Center. In all cases, however, the district courts sustained the 15 year eligibility rules.

The *Ponce* case was appealed to the Ninth Circuit Court of Appeals and, recently, the court reversed and remanded. The court noted that because of the 15 year rule, only about 4% of the Southern California plan participants qualified for and began receiving pension benefits and that, while maintaining the 15 year requirement, the trustees also voted to substantially increase the benefit factor. The appeals court concluded that the district court did not fully consider these matters in its earlier decision, and remanded for the taking of further evidence as to the rationale of the trustees. The court said that it could well be "arbitrary and capricious" for trustees to maintain a vesting requirement with a high exclusion rate and at the same time to pay an unusually high level of benefits.

Individual Benefit Determinations

12. *Feher v. Local 381 Pension Fund,* ___ F.2d ___, 292 BNA BPR A-20 (2d Cir. 1980).

This case illustrates the importance of consistency in the evaluation of pension disability applications. Here, the applicant submitted as proof of his disability, a disability pension award from the Social Security Administration. The trustees denied the application, however, on the ground that they could not "find any affirmative proof that [the applicant was] disabled." No clarification of what additional "affirmative proof" was needed was provided.

In a subsequent lawsuit, the federal district court held that the trustees had acted arbitrarily and capriciously because, in other cases, the trustees had accepted a Social Security disability award as evidence of disability under the plan. The court said that the trustees were not bound by Social Security awards but, if there was to be a different test, "basic fairness requires that the higher burden be consistently applied to all similarly situated persons, and that the individual be apprised of this fact, neither of which was done here." The district court awarded the applicant a disability pension and reasonable attorneys' fees, and the Second Circuit Court of Appeals affirmed.

13. *Toland v. McCarthy,* ___ F.Supp. ___, 293 BNA BPR D-3 (D.C. Mass. 1980).

In this pension eligibility determination case, the court found occasion to admonish the trustees for failing to develop all the facts before coming to a conclusion. The plaintiff initiated the court suit after his application for retirement benefits was denied.

The basis for denial was that the applicant was not entitled to certain credited service under the plan as, during the period in question, he had been working as a salaried supervisor rather than as a production employee. Various documentary evidence was presented to the trustees as to the applicant's status, much of which was ambiguous or contradictory. The trustees made no further attempt to resolve the ambiguities which existed, either by calling the applicant to testify or by seeking testimony from other witnesses. The court set aside the trustees' decision denying benefits, but asked for briefs from counsel as to whether the case should be remanded to the trustees for further proceedings or, alternately, whether the court should proceed to decide the merits.

See also *Chastain v. Delta Airlines, Inc.,* ___ F.Supp. ___, 314 BNA BPR A-11 (D.C. N.D. Ga. 1980) in which the court reversed the decision of a health and welfare plan committee, in a contested survivor's benefit case, and remanded for further proceedings, as the committee had failed to fully develop the necessary evidence.

Update: Last year, we reported that in *Wardle v. Teamsters Central States Pension Fund,* ___ F.Supp. ___, 239 BPR D-1 (D.C. S.D. Ind. 1979) a request for a jury trial, in an ERISA benefit claim case, had been denied. This decision has now been affirmed by the Seventh Circuit Court of

Appeals, ___ F.2d ___, 306 BNA BPR A-11 (7th Cir. 1980). Another recent case denying a request for a jury trial is *Rice v. Hutton,* ___ F.Supp. ___, 290 BNA BPR A-20 (D.C. W.D. Mo. 1980).

Exhaustion of all Remedies—Arbitration

14. *Amato v. Bernard,* ___ F.2d ___, 104 LRRM 2719 (9th Cir. 1980).

15. *Challenger v. Local Union No. 1 of the International Bridge, Structural, and Ornamental Iron Workers, A.F.L.-C.I.O., et al.,* ___ F.2d ___, 288 BNA BPR D-1 (7th Cir. 1980).

As reported in previous sessions, it is clear that the courts will disallow ERISA benefit claim litigation unless the plaintiff can establish that he has "exhausted all remedies" provided for in the plan documents. The most extensive endorsement of this principle is in the recent *Amato* decision of the Ninth Circuit Court of Appeals, wherein the court approved the dismissal of an ERISA suit seeking pension benefits because the applicant had failed to follow internal review procedures. The court said that "federal courts have the authority to enforce the exhaustion requirement in suits under ERISA and as a matter of policy, they should usually do so."

The use of mandatory arbitration in resolving disputed benefit claims, a concept still being resisted by the Department of Labor, received major support from the Seventh Circuit Court of Appeals in the *Challenger* case. Here, a participant in a jointly administered pension fund requested information on his pension credits and was advised that his credits were less than he expected, because of a break in service. The participant then sued the trustees and the plan administrator for a declaration that he was entitled to additional credit.

The pension plan document contained a mandatory arbitration provision which recited, in part:

> The applicant may appeal the final decision of the Trustees to final and binding arbitration by notifying the Pension Plan office within thirty (30) days of the date of the decision of his desire to arbitrate.
>
> . . .
>
> The decision of the arbitrator shall be final and binding on the applicant and the Board of Trustees.

Because the participant did not invoke this procedure, a lower district court dismissed his complaint and, on appeal, the court of appeals affirmed. It was argued that the case involved allegations of breaches of fiduciary responsibility, as to which the plaintiff should be entitled to a court trial, but the court found that the essential theme of the complaint was that the trustees had wrongfully interpreted the plan. Inasmuch as the controversy is essentially a contract matter, it is appropriate that it be submitted to arbitration as provided for in the plan document. The court concluded by saying:

> To make every claim dispute into a federal case would undermine the claim procedure contemplated by the Act. It would also burden employee benefit funds with substantial expense.... We believe that Congress, in adopting ERISA, did not require or contemplate such a result.

Two additional ERISA benefit claim cases which were dismissed because the plaintiff failed to follow arbitration procedures provided for in the plan documents are *Sample v. Monsanto Company,* ___ F.Supp. ___, 286 BNA BPR D-7 (D.C. E.D. Mo. 1980) and *Scheider v. United States Steel Corporation,* ___ F.Supp. ___, 285 BNA BPR D-1 (D.C. W.D. Pa. 1980).

The Punitive Damages Issue

16. *Calhoun v. Falstaff Brewing Company,* ___ F.Supp. ___, 262 BNA BPR D-18 (D.C. E.D. Mo. 1979).

In 1977 we reported on two cases, one in Oregon *(Bell)* and one in California *(Hurn),* where the courts ruled that punitive damages are not recoverable under ERISA. The imposition of punitive damages, which often total many times the amount of the actual damages, is allowable in some jurisdictions, and under some statutes, as a means of correcting the defendant's conduct. To impose punitive damages upon plan fiduciaries, under ERISA, would have ominous consequences. Most fiduciary liability insurance policies will not provide coverage for such awards, hence, the fiduciary's personal assets would be at risk.

In *Calhoun,* the court ruled that "punitive damages are not recoverable under ERISA" and granted a motion striking a request for such damages.

Note, however, that in another recent case, *Eaton v. D'Amato,* ___ F.Supp. ___, 291 BNA BPR D-11 (D.C. D.C. 1980) the court indicated, in a preliminary ruling, that "an award of punitive damages (under ERISA) in an appropriate case is not foreclosed." This ruling was requested by the boards of trustees of jointly administered benefit funds, in a suit against the corporation administering such funds, in which it was alleged that the corporation was functioning as a fiduciary and had violated fiduciary responsibilities.

Fiduciary Responsibilities

17. *Gilliam v. Edwards,* ___ F.Supp. ___, 296 BNA BPR D-2 (D.C. N.J. 1980).

We have reported in prior sessions that personal liability has been imposed in judgments entered in ERISA fiduciary responsibility lawsuits, or in settlements entered into to dispose of such lawsuits, including several actions against trustees of labor-management benefit funds.

In *Gilliam,* the court ordered a union trustee, who also served as fund administrator under an administrative services contract, to repay the trust fund for the salary he had thus far drawn under the contract, a sum in excess of $12,000. The contract was for a five year term, with the trustee-administrator having the right to renew for another five years.

The court found that the administrative services contract violated ERISA because:

a. The union trustee who obtained the contract failed to disqualify himself while the other trustees considered the matter. Quite to the contrary, he took an active role in the discussions, encouraging the other trustees to award him the contract. He voted in favor of a motion to instruct the fund attorney to prepare the contract. These actions, said the court, constitute improper "self-dealing" in violation of ERISA Section 406(b)(1).

b. Even if self-dealing had not been involved, the transaction would still be prohibited under Section 406(a)(1)(C), unless exempt by Section 408(b)(2). The latter section allows a plan to contract with a party-in-interest for necessary "services" provided that "no more than reasonable compensation is paid therefor." Citing DOL regulation 29 CFR 2550.408b-2(c), the court said that a contract is not reasonable if it does not permit termination by the plan on reasonably short notice. The five year contract, with a five year option, violates this principle.

c. Additionally, during at least part of the time when the union trustee was serving as fund administrator, he was also being paid a salary by his local union. While it was argued that this was a "part-time" salary, the court found that the payment was substantial enough to qualify as full-time pay for purposes of Section 408(c)(2), which prohibits a fiduciary from receiving any compensation from a plan if he is already receiving full-time pay from an employee organization whose members are plan participants.

The court concluded by saying:

> According to (ERISA) a fiduciary who violates any fiduciary obligations shall be personally liable for resultant losses to the plan and for restoration of profits contingent upon the illegal use of plan assets ... ERISA grants the court wide discretion in fashioning legal and equitable relief to make the plan whole and respect the rights of the beneficiaries, including recision of unlawful transactions and recovery of monetary loss to the plan.

Comment: Those of us who serve trust funds in what we normally consider ministerial or advisory positions should learn, from recent developments, that we are not at all insulated from fiduciary responsibility lawsuits if our activities are found to make us "fiduciaries" or if we are otherwise involved in aiding or abetting the wrongful conduct. Consider *Brink v. DaLesio,* ___ F.Supp. ___, 105 LRRM 2233 (D.C. Md. 1980) — judgment entered against trustee and trust fund administrator for various breaches, including practice of administrator in charging excessive administrative fees; *Trustees of the Retirement Benefit Plan v. Equibank, N.A.,* ___ F.Supp. ___, 286 BNA BPR D-5 (D.C. W.D. Pa. 1980) — court upholds jurisdiction of suit by trustees accusing bank of various breaches including the making of improvident investments and the failure to render proper accounts; *Marshall v. Tolley International Corporation,* ___ F.Supp. ___, 271 BNA BPR A-14 (D.C. S.D. Ind. 1979) — Department of Labor files action against employee benefits consulting firm alleging breaches of fiduciary responsibility in advice given to trust fund concerning termination of certain insurance policies; *Marshall v. Gordon, Marshall v. Florida Administrators, Inc.,* and *Marshall v. Esposito,* ___ F.Supp. ___, 268 BNA BPR A-23 (D.C. S.D. Fla. 1979) — Department of Labor files three actions against two consulting firms, and others, alleging breaches of fiduciary responsibilities in connection with the purchase by certain trust funds of life insurance at an excessive cost; *Southeastern Lumber Manufacturers' Association Voluntary Employee Benefit Plan v. The Walthour Agency,* ___ F.Supp. ___, 289 BNA BPR A-15 (D.C. N.D. Ga. 1980) — court retains jurisdiction of suit including allegations that an accounting firm had been negligent in auditing a trust fund's books and records, thus failing to discover certain mismanagement and missing premiums; *Lentino v. Fringe Employee Plans, Inc.,* ___ F.2d ___, 272 BNA BPR D-6 (1979) — court reviews case which includes allegations that legal counsel to a certain severance pay plan was negligent in handling IRS qualification of plan — court upheld dismissal of the claim against the attorney as plaintiffs failed to present expert testimony necessary to prove malpractice.

18. *American Communications Association, Local 10, I.B.T. v. Retirement Plan for Employees of R.C.A. Corporation,* ___ F.Supp. ___, 290 BNA BPR D-3 (D.C. S.D. N.Y. 1980).

This case will be of comfort to many boards of trustees who have, in recent years, watched their investment portfolios decline in market value and have been concerned over the possibility that the decline in value, by itself, might constitute a breach of fiduciary responsibility. Here, a lawsuit against plan trustees included a charge of imprudent investment. The complaint alleged that the plan assets had been "imprudently invested so as to provide a lower return or yield than could have been obtained by the exercise of prudence." The court found this allegation to be insufficient to constitute a claim under ERISA, and the allegation was dismissed. The court said:

> ... the fourth and fifth causes of action are deficient in that they are utterly without factual content to support the conclusionary allegation of lack of prudent management. A claim of lower return "than could have been obtained by the exercise of prudence" does not set forth in what respect the fiduciaries failed in their duty. The mere fact that there may have been a decline in the value of the Plan's portfolio or a diminution of income in a given year does not by itself establish imprudent management. Indeed, market fluctuations have expressly been rejected as untrustworthy indicia of value—especially in times of economic decline. The standard to be applied is that of conduct, tested at the time of the investment decision, rather than performance, judged from the vantage point of hindsight. The complaint contains no factual specification of any act the trustees took or failed to take that resulted in the lower rate of return alleged by plaintiffs.

Deadlocked Issues

19. *Union Trustees and Employer Trustees of the Operating Engineers Pension Trust,* 80-1 CCH Arb. 8275 (Arbitrator Joseph F. Gentile 1980).

The complications of ERISA caused an arbitrator, in this deadlocked issue case, to approve the retention of additional legal counsel for the board of trustees of a pension fund. The case arose when the union trustees asked for the right to have co-counsel appointed, at the trust fund expense. It was argued that additional legal services were required in view of the highly technical legal issues confronting the trust fund.

The arbitrator approved the retention of additional counsel, for a period of one year, but he denied the proposal that additional counsel should be selected unilaterally by the union trustees. Additional counsel would have to be selected by joint action of both trustees. The justification for approving the hiring of additional legal services was stated as follows:

> It is not uncommon in technical areas of the law, such as trust administration (particularly since the advent of ERISA) that "second opinions" are reasonably necessary and needed. The trustees, by law, have a difficult role to play with respect to the field of labor/management relations... When a person is on the "front line" in trust administration, such as trustees, that person is entitled to be fully satisfied and confident in the legal positions taken...

Miscellaneous

20. *Talarico v. United Furniture Workers Pension Fund A,* ___ F.Supp. ___, 272 BNA BPR D-11 (D.C. Nebr. 1979).

Here, a trust fund was sued by a contributing employer for refusing to accept contributions on behalf of the employer's employees, as provided for in the employer's collective bargaining agreement. The particular bargaining agreement provided that the employer would not begin making contributions, for newly hired personnel, until such persons had been on the payroll for one year and were at least 25 years of age. The trustees refused to accept contributions from this employer, under these circumstances, as other employers were paying for new employees regardless of age or tenure of employment.

Noting that the plan document gave the trustees the power to authorize an employer "to participate in the plan upon appropriate action by the employer acceptable to the board of trustees," the court upheld the action of the trustees. The court also said:

> A multiemployer pension plan such as the Fund cannot be forced to jeopardize (its) actuarial soundness by violating a policy essential to that soundness to accommodate the desires of a single employer. While the contribution program which (the employer) seeks to impose upon the Fund is contained in a collective bargaining agreement, the Fund's trustees have the right under the Plan and the duty under ERISA to exercise their independent judgment on the acceptability of that program. The record shows that their judgment was exercised in a reasonable and well-considered manner.

The employer argued that because the fund had accepted some contributions which it had made, the fund was now estopped to deny the acceptance of further contributions. However, the court found that the fund was not aware of the exact basis on which the contributions were made and that "actions taken due to ignorance or innocent mistakes" are not sufficient to constitute an estoppel.

Conclusion

Just a few years ago, even after ERISA was enacted, there were some 100-150 decisions issued annually which directly involved or affected negotiated employee benefit plans and joint trusts. This past year, there were more than 300 such decisions.

Much of the increased litigation is needed to obtain interpretations or clarification of ERISA, a process that could be partly avoided if the Department of Labor and the Internal Revenue Service would issue regulations that are overdue, and make greater use of interpretive bulletins and other announcements of their positions.

Additionally, there is an increasing number of suits alleging breaches of fiduciary responsibilities, including fiduciary responsibilities in the area of plan design. These suits require careful attention to trust activities and decision making by trustees and by administrators and all other advisors. One principle that is quite clear is that when the fiduciary "hat" is in place, it may fit more like a deep-sea diver's helmet.

There are also a large number of cases dealing with decisions denying benefit claims, but with the emergence of the "exhaustion of remedies" rule and the possibility of using mandatory arbitration, the financial and time-consuming aspects of this type of litigation can be minimized.

As to the most recent case which is likely to have the greatest impact on day-to-day trust and plan administration, we would select *Stone v. Stone and S.I.U.-P.M.A. Pension Plan,* as it provides what may be the last significant court ruling upholding the splitting of pension plan benefits in divorce and child support cases. Pension plans will now have to accept new burdens in the area of keeping records and issuing dual checks.

Legal Odds and Ends: Issues and Decisions

BY HUGH J. McCARTHY, JR.

Introduction

It is widely recognized that under our common law system of jurisprudence, judges do not merely decide individual cases; they do more than that. Judges make law.

Felix Frankfurter addressed this issue in a letter to Hugo Black shortly after he had become an Associate Justice of the Supreme Court. He wrote, "Judges cannot escape the responsibility of filling in the gaps which the finitude of even the most imaginative legislation renders inevitable. So the problem is not whether the Judges make the law, but when and how much ... (law they will make)."

I predict that there will be a great deal of judge-made law as a result of the interpretation not only of ERISA but also in connection with the Multiemployer Pension Plan Amendments Act of 1980. There will soon be cases testing whether or not the 1980 act is unconstitutional under the "contracts" clause of the U.S. Constitution.

One area that continues to be the subject of a great deal of litigation concerns the standard against which trustees' actions are judged. This paper will deal primarily with this standard as it applies to employee welfare benefit plans.

Recent Litigation

Fiduciary Conduct

There are two basic areas of litigation involving employee welfare benefit plans. The first category involves actions brought by the government against trustees and their advisors.

For example, in the fall of 1980, the Department of Labor filed suit in the Southern District of Florida against several former trustees, a current trustee and the fund's consultant. The suit alleges that they all breached their fiduciary duties by allowing or causing the trust fund to pay excessive premiums for life insurance purchased from Farmers National Life Insurance Company. The Depart-

Mr. McCarthy is a director in the law firm of Hugh J. McCarthy & Associates, located in Chicago. He has participated in panel discussions relative to employee benefit plans for programs sponsored by the American Bar Association, Midwest Pension Conference and the Practising Law Institute. He is a graduate of Dartmouth College and received his J.D. degree magna cum laude, Order of the Coif, from the University of Michigan. His firm represents a number of Taft-Hartley trusts, primarily in the construction industry. Mr. McCarthy is a member of the Foundation's Attorneys Committee and has spoken at previous Foundation educational conferences.

ment is asking the court to order the defendants to pay the fund in excess of $240,000. If each defendant were held liable, that would require the trustees and the consultant each to pay over $30,000 to the trust fund. The case is *Marshall v. Breed* (Civ. No. 80-6487, Oct. 3, 1980).

This was the sixth suit filed in 1980 by the DOL in Florida involving health and welfare funds. The other five suits involve over $1 million which the DOL alleges was spent in excess of what should have been spent for various types of insurance benefits.

Eligibility Rulings

The second broad category of litigation is of more significance to trustees in general because it arises much more frequently. This area involves decisions made by trustees as to the adoption and application of eligibility rules.

Prior to ERISA the basic issue was, did the trustees act in an "arbitrary or capricious" manner or in some way not act for the "sole and exclusive benefit" of the participants and their beneficiaries. It seems that the same basic standard still applies today. During 1980, the Court of Appeals for the Ninth Circuit held that the arbitrary and capricious standard still applies to employee welfare benefit plans under ERISA. The plan which was involved in that litigation provided for death benefits to be paid to the spouse of a deceased participant. The participant died, the widow was sent an application form, but before completing the necessary application for the death benefits, the widow also died. Her executor asked that the benefits be paid to her estate. The trust fund's administrative rules were applied and no benefits were paid. The widow's executor filed suit against the trustees.

The district court ruled in favor of the estate. In so ruling, the district court applied the familiar arbitrary and capricious standard, but the court also made analogies to the California law regarding both probate and commercial insurance under which insurance proceeds vest in the beneficiary immediately upon the death of the insured.

The Ninth Circuit reversed and held in favor of the trustees. It too applied the familiar arbitrary and capricious standard. However, the Ninth Circuit also noted that the rule was "reasonable" in light of the policy of the plan to benefit living dependents and not to benefit the estate of a deceased widow. *Gordon v. I.L.W.U.-P.M.A. Benefit Funds* (77-2614, Apr. 3, 1980 9th Cir.) BNA BPR 304 A-17, CCH 22,589.

In another case decided in 1980, the Ninth Circuit again applied the arbitrary and capricious standard to a welfare benefit plan. This time, there was again an overlay of "reasonableness" applied.

A longshoreman died without having designated a beneficiary to receive his welfare benefits. He had been separated from his wife since 1969. He had not been divorced. At the time of his death, he left surviving him his wife, with whom he had not lived for six years, a legitimate minor son, the woman with whom he had been living for the three years prior to his death and an illegitimate daughter who was dependent on him and living in his household at the time of his death.

The plan rule that was challenged provided that death benefits were to be paid first to the participant's legal spouse, if the spouse shared a common domicile with him and they had been married for at least one year. If no benefits became payable under that clause, then the death benefits were to go to the person, if any, who both shared a common domicile with him for the three years prior to his death and was claimed as a dependent on the decedent's tax returns. If no person met the second test, the plan provided that benefits would be paid to unmarried minor persons claimed as dependents on the participant's tax return.

The district court ruled that basing eligibility on information on the tax returns was arbitrary and capricious. The court then awarded the benefits to the woman with whom he had been living at the time of his death. The Ninth Circuit reversed, finding that the use of tax returns as a means of determining dependency was reasonable and that the rule was not arbitrary and capricious. The circuit court then awarded benefits to the legitimate minor son. *Gelfgren v. Republic National Life Insurance Co.,* 78-2418, July 21, 1980 (9th Cir.).

Multiemployer Multiunion Plans

In the last three years another interesting issue has begun to be litigated. It concerns an employee welfare benefit plan that is both a multiemployer plan and a multiunion plan. There are two basic types of these plans. One is a multicraft plan found in one geographic area. The other is a single craft plan covering the geographic jurisdiction of several distinct local unions or councils.

The Problem. The issue that has been raised does not result from the expansion or growth of the plans. It arises when one of the constituent groups decides to terminate participation in the multiunion trust fund to join another plan, or to establish a new welfare plan at the local level.

In the event one of the participating local union areas decides to withdraw from participation and begin a new trust fund for the employees in that local union's area, several things will happen. Effective with the date of withdrawal, no more employer contributions will be coming due to the old multiunion plan from employers in the withdrawing jurisdiction. The supporting cash flow of the trust fund will be reduced. Under the rules of many plans, there is no provision for this occurrence. As a result, benefits may still have to be paid to participants from the withdrawing area in accordance with the regular eligibility rules. At the same time, the new local trust fund is receiving all employer contributions due for the period beginning with the date of withdrawal.

Unless the multiemployer, multiunion trust fund is fully funded, the withdrawing participants would be benefiting disproportionately when compared to those remaining in the multiunion trust. The old fund would be paying claims during a period of time when the other fund, the new fund, is building up reserves. Inasmuch as many, if not most, plans have some form of extension of eligibility rules designed as a protection against participants losing coverage while temporarily unemployed, this skewed financial arrangement could continue for six months, a year, or even longer. During this period of time the old fund could suffer severe financial hardship.

Limiting Liability. It would be good practice for trust funds of this type to do one of two things. One approach would be to fully fund the plan to cover all benefit extensions. Depending on the state of a fund's reserves, this may require an increase in the hourly contribution rate with no increase in current benefits. The other approach would be to amend the trust agreement and/or the plan itself to provide for the elimination of part if not all of this liability if there is a withdrawal from participation by one or more of the local unions involved.

A recent Sixth Circuit Court of Appeals case involved a trust fund that chose to limit their liability to pay welfare benefits in the event of a voluntary withdrawal of a participating local union. (*Pierce v. N.E.C.A.-I.B.E.W. Welfare Trust Fund,* __F.2d. __ 9th Cir., 1980). The trustees in that case terminated eligibility effective on the 31st day after the date of the withdrawal. Applying the same basic test under both Taft-Hartley and ERISA, the court of appeals found that the trustees had not acted in an arbitrary or capricious manner, and upheld the rule. The court also found that the trustees had been prudent and had acted in accordance with the documents governing the plan.

The former participants filed a petition with the Supreme Court asking the Court to issue a writ of certiorari and review the case. This petition was denied on December 1, 1980.

It seems, then, that the arbitrary and capricious standard is still in effect, but, as can be seen by a review of some of the case law, other standards such as "reasonable purpose" or "reasonable justification" may be grafted on to it as the federal common law develops in this area.

Workers' Compensation Offset

In 1980 the United States Supreme Court agreed to hear and decide two cases concerning the following issue: If a participant in a pension plan becomes disabled in an accident and workers' compensation benefits are paid to him, may his pension benefits be reduced by the amount of the workers' compensation benefits received? *Buczynski v. General Motors Corp.,* 80-193; *Alessi v. Raybestos-Manhattan, Inc.,* 79-1943. Where the plan itself, and not the state workers' compensation statute, provides for a reduction in pension benefits, some courts have permitted the offset, while other courts have been holding that such a plan provision is a forfeiture and therefore prohibited under Section 203(a) of ERISA.

In both of the cases that the Supreme Court will decide, the Third Circuit has taken the position that Section 203(a) does not prohibit the offset. Because of the practical workings of the process by which these cases get to the Court, there is speculation that it may well overrule the Third Circuit. Those who feel this way reason as follows: It requires the vote of four of the nine Justices to agree to hear a case in which a petition for writ of certiorari is filed. Of all of the thousands of petitions filed in a year, the Supreme Court grants the writ in only 6% of the cases.

It should be noted that the Court in *Nachman Corp. v. P.B.G.C.,* also decided in 1980, placed a great deal of emphasis on the nonforfeitability of pension benefits.

Guidelines for Trustees

The courts' decisions in these cases could give us all an idea of the standards that may be developed in the future for all employee benefit plans. Since the passage of ERISA, more than 3,000 suits have been filed citing Title I of ERISA as the jurisdictional basis for the action. Different courts will phrase the test differently. However, as can be seen from the cases discussed in this paper, there is one common standard which is at least referred to in almost every case. That is: Were the trustees acting in an arbitrary or capricious manner in taking or failing to take a particular action or making a particular decision? A court will apply the relevant facts concerning the action or decision to this standard.

To protect themselves, it is good practice for a board of trustees to do a number of things.

First, eligibility rules, as well as all other rules of the plan, should be in writing.

Second, when adopting or amending eligibility rules, document the cost considerations and policy considerations underlying the rules adopted. This documentation should be made as a part of the minutes or as an attachment to the minutes of the meeting at which the rule was adopted or amended.

Third, as a general proposition, changes in eligibility rules should be prospective and not retroactive in application. There are, of course, exceptions. For example, a particular claim under a health and welfare fund may have to be denied under the current rules. The trustees, when they see a rule in operation which as applied seems unfair or inequitable, may decide to change the rule to liberalize the plan. At times, they will want to do so retroactively to give the advantage of the changed rule to the person whose particular circumstances pointed up the desirability of a change. The amendment would be made retroactively to a date certain. If so, they must be careful to treat all participants evenhandedly. All other participants whose claims may have been denied under the prior law must be treated the same. Claims which may have been denied which now would be covered, should be paid.

After a rule has been amended, notify all of the participants of the change. If a rule is adopted that is more restrictive than the prior rule, consideration may be given to putting an effective date on it several months into the future so that the receipt of the notice will predate the actual date the rule becomes effective. Again, the reasons for rule changes should be documented so that the trustees can show that their actions were not arbitrary or capricious, but rather that their actions were in accordance with the documents governing the plan and that they were acting with the degree of care and skill that a prudent man would have exercised under like circumstances.

If trustees follow these guidelines, and if they are fair, then their actions should be upheld regardless of the label the courts may place on the standards against which trustees' conduct will be judged.

Liabilities of the Contributing Employer

BY DAVID W. SILVERMAN

A LOSS OF CONTRIBUTIONS to a trust fund must be considered a loss of last resort. It is only after all avenues of collection against any other entity, whether individual or corporate, have been exhausted that the trustees can close the books and accept the loss. Therefore, the prudent trustee, in the performance of his duties of collecting the contributions due the trust fund, should not be willing to accept the loss based upon the single fact that the delinquent contributor is without sufficient funds to make past due contributions. The prudent trustee should look elsewhere before accepting any loss.

We start this analysis with the trustees being informed that not only is a corporate signatory to the labor-management agreement in arrears, but that the business has been terminated, and there are no assets available to pay the fund the amounts due. In this part of the presentation, we examine the personal liability of the officers, directors and stockholders of the corporate contributor who was, or is, a signatory to the labor-management agreement containing an obligation to make contributions to the trust fund.

Incorporation as a Public Policy

The basic purpose of forming a corporation as a vehicle for conducting business revolves around our constitutional and legal history, which provides that a corporation is a separate entity; corporate assets and liabilities are independent and distinct from the assets and liabilities of its individual officers, directors and stockholders. The corporate form of doing business has its great advantage in that there is a line drawn between the corporate assets and liabilities and personal assets and liabilities. As a general rule, those who deal with the corporation must look to the corporation for the payment of just debts. Those who deal with the individual can look only to the individual. Neither can hold the opposite entity responsible for the satisfaction of a debt. The ease of formation of corporations and their constitutional and statutory protection are grounded in the public policy that

Mr. Silverman is a partner in the law firm of Granik, Silverman, Sandberg, Kirschner, Campbell & Nowicki, located in New City, New York. He is responsible for handling litigation for the firm's clients which include public utilities, state insurance departments, insurance companies and banks. Mr. Silverman has served as a management trustee on Local 363 International Brotherhood of Electrical Workers, Local 964 United Brotherhood of Carpenters and Local 29 Bricklayers, Masons, etc., trust funds. He also serves as counsel to various multiemployer funds and management associations. He received his B.S., LL.B. and LL.M. (taxation) degrees from New York University. Mr. Silverman has spoken at previous Foundation educational programs.

business is fostered through the separation of personal assets from corporate assets, and personal liabilities from corporate liabilities.

There is, however, a corresponding public policy throughout this nation that the workman who toils and produces for his corporate employer should be paid his wages, and that the mere interposition of a corporation should not stand in the way of his being paid. The conflict arises between the two public policies when the corporation is without assets and the workman has not been paid. It is then that the separation of personal assets and corporate liabilities becomes an issue.

We include within the term "wages" contributions to all plans which have been negotiated by labor and management in accordance with the relevant terms of the Taft-Hartley Act (pension, welfare, vacation, etc.). Therefore, when the corporation has failed to pay wages and make contributions to these jointly negotiated plans, we are seeking to have the courts determine that, in a conflict between the public policy which fosters the corporate enterprise and the public policy which mandates that employees be paid their wages and fringes, the payment to the employee for his wages and fringes is the paramount public policy. Certain states have clearly indicated the supremacy of the public policy of payment of wages and fringes over insulation from corporate debts; other states may be silent, but the legal theories which would result in a personal liability on the part of an officer, director or stockholder of a corporation permeate the law.

We, therefore, start with a statement by counsel for the trust that the XYZ Company, which has been delinquent, is still delinquent and has now gone out of business. Counsel further states that the corporation is without assets, its secured creditors have taken all of its machinery and equipment, the bank has foreclosed on its building, and all of the work force have now made application for unemployment benefits. Counsel suggests that, under the circumstances, no further action be taken, for to obtain a judgment against the corporation would be a useless act. There is then addressed to counsel the following series of questions for an examination of the law to determine whether or not liability can be imposed upon the officers, directors and stockholders of that now-defunct corporation, to the extent of the delinquency in contributions to the various Taft-Hartley funds.

Criminal Liability for Failure to Pay Benefits

Does your state have a law which provides that failure to pay employee benefits renders corporate officers who deal with the corporate funds liable to criminal prosecution? In such states as New York, the legislature has provided in its labor law (198c):

> ... any employer who is a party to an agreement to pay or provide benefits or wage supplements to employees or to a third party or fund for the benefit of employees and who fails, neglects, or refuses to pay the amount or amounts necessary to provide such benefits ... within thirty days after such payments are required to be made, shall be guilty of a misdemeanor.... Where such employer is a corporation, the president, secretary treasurer, or officers exercising corresponding functions shall each be guilty of a misdemeanor.

The mere fact that the corporate officers set forth in the statute are guilty of a misdemeanor and violate a penal statute does not in itself help the trust fund. Even assuming that the corporate officer goes to jail—a highly unlikely event—that does not help the trust fund collect monies which are due. However, the legal theory which flows from the violation of a penal statute is of assistance to the trustees and counsel for the trust.

The legal theory applied is that if a criminal or penal statute imposes a duty upon a corporate officer, but does not set forth a precise civil remedy for the protection of those benefited by the penal statute, the law will assume such a civil remedy. In other words, the workmen for whose benefit the statute was passed have a *civil* cause of action for the money damages they have sustained. What we are dealing with is the concept that a *civil liability* on the part of these corporate officers is established by virtue of their failure to meet the requirements of the *penal statute.* The officers of the corporation are, therefore, financially responsible to the same extent that they have violated the penal statute.

If any portion of the penal law in your state is directed toward the individual corporate officer, director or stockholder for failure to pay wages, a basis exists for the imposition of personal responsibility and civil liability upon those officers mentioned in the penal statute for the monies due covering the period that they have violated the penal statute. Therefore, trust counsel is asked to determine whether any similar penal statute is in force and effect within the jurisdiction of the trust fund. Prudence will dictate that a proceeding be brought against the same people against whom the state's attorney or the district attorney could commence a criminal action (*see* citation of cases with respect to this theory at footnote 1).

---

1. *Johnson, et al. (Carpenters Fringe Benefit Funds) v. Clay Partition Co., Inc. & Rubin Zimmerman,* 93 Mis.2d 414, 65 A.D.2d 737; and *Excavators Union Local 7311 Welfare Fund v. Zurmuhlen,* 68 A.D.2d 816.

In Pennsylvania, *see* 43 P.S. Section 260.9a, and 43 P.S. Section 260.2a, discussed in detail in *Steamfitters Local Union No. 420 of Philadelphia v. Murdoch International, Inc.,* U.S.D.C., E.D. Pa., No. 77-1716.

See 2A: 1b-90.2 Civil & Criminal Justice, New Jersey 2CV: 1-4 Not a Crime.

Other cases are: *Bel v. Hood,* 327 U.S. 678; *Coal Comy v. Borak,* 377 U.S. 426; *Fischman v. Raytheon Mfg. Co.,* 188 F.2d 783 (2d Cir. 1951); *Brennan v. Emerald Renovators, Inc.,* D.C.N.Y. 410 F.Supp. 1057.

Shareholders' Liability

In the event of a conflict between the insulation of the corporate stockholder from corporate debts and the corresponding public policy that workmen should be paid for their wages and fringes, the conflict in some states has been resolved by statute. As part of the business corporation law which generally governs corporations in the State of New York, there is a provision (Section 630) which provides: "The ten largest shareholders . . . shall jointly and severally be personally liable for all debts, wages or salaries due and owing to any of its laborers, servants or employees . . . (providing that the ten largest shareholders) . . . shall (be given) . . . notice in writing . . . such notice shall be given within ninety days after termination of such services . . ."

The statute further provides that if the ten largest shareholders are not known, the records of the corporation be examined and, thereafter, notices be given. This statute is not applicable to publicly held corporations or to corporations which are traded over any exchange; however, in a state such as New York, of the vast numbers of corporations, only a small number meet the exclusion of being publicly held. As an aside, the notification to the shareholders in such states as New York should be part of the collection procedures. When any corporate contributor is delinquent, and the trust is sending out notices to that effect, it would be wise to have notices sent to the ten largest stockholders as well.

It is obvious that the State of New York and other states have taken the position that the conflict between payment of wages and insulation of shareholders from corporate liabilities is resolved in favor of payment of wages. Therefore, counsel for the trust should investigate the state's statutes and decisional law for any provision which would impose liability upon shareholders of the corporation, even if limited only to wages. If such statutes or decisions have been handed down in the state in which the trust fund operates, then personal liability of the shareholders, however limited, should be explored more fully. (For citation of authority and other cases on this issue, see footnote 2.)

Conversion

The legal name tag given to another theory for proceeding against responsible corporate officers, directors or stockholders is "conversion." Here, we are dealing with a collective bargaining agreement which sets aside a definite weekly or monthly sum for vacation, paid holidays, union checkoff, etc. We are dealing here with sums of money which have actually been credited to the working person and then deducted from the gross wage to provide a net figure. With respect to vacation fund and union checkoff, sums of money, charged to the account of the employee and upon which the employee has paid income and other taxes, are not by agreement paid directly to the employee, but are assigned to others. The same legal argument can be made for contributions to a pension or welfare plan, in that the employee has bargained for a cash hourly rate of so many dollars per hour, but the bargaining process has directed payment to the appropriate fund. The theory of conversion is that immediately upon the payment of the worker at the end of the work week when payroll is computed, the corporation must segregate the sums of money attributable to the worker; some of the sums due the worker are paid in cash, and some are paid in fringe benefits.

There is no doubt or dispute concerning the segregation of funds for fringe benefits such as union checkoff or vacation pay. The law is not as clear, however, with respect to pension and welfare amounts. If the corporate officer does not segregate these amounts and pay them over to the proper trustees, but rather uses these monies for any other purpose, most states will hold that the corporate officer guilty of that diversion or conversion is personally liable (see relevant cases in footnote 3).

Breach of Trust

Though there are those who might disagree, the courts will not countenance unconscionable conduct. As the legislatures pass various laws which reflect the social conscience of the community, the courts write decisions setting forth the legal conscience of the community. It is to this area that lawyers have assigned the name tag, "breach of trust." The concept of trust provides another avenue for the imposition of personal liability upon officers, directors and stockholders who have used the corporate funds to fulfill obligations other than those of wages and fringe benefits.

The argument addressed to the court, in the exercise of its legal conscience, is that in negotiating

---

2. *Arthur Grossman (Graphic Arts International) v. Senor*, 64 A.D.2 561 (1978).
Carpenters Health & Welfare Fund of Phila. v. Ambrose #79-1224 7/11/80 310 BNA A-10.

---

3. *Goldstein (International Production Service Sales Employees) v. Frank Mangano*, 99 Misc.2d 513. *AMF, Inc. v. Algo Distrs.*, 48 A.D.2d 352.

a collective bargaining agreement providing for a total wage package (a portion which is paid to the employee in cash and a portion contributed to a Taft-Hartley trust), the employee has, in effect, assigned part of his hourly or weekly wage irrevocably to the trust, this constituting an equitable assignment. The hallmark of an equitable assignment is that payments to the trust represent a discharge of the obligation to the employee. Operating under the same type of legal theory as previously discussed under conversion, the corporation could not lawfully appropriate the monies equitably assigned to the trust for any other purpose. In the event that the corporation diverted the assigned portions of the employee's wages to any purpose other than the various trust funds, any corporate officer, director or stockholders participating in the diversion of that equitable assignment is personally responsible to the extent of the amounts of money diverted.

In some states the theory of breach of trust has become statutory. Laws setting forth this concept are found in the lien laws, dealing, therefore, primarily in the area of the construction trades. In New York, Section 70 of the lien law provides that any funds received by the owner or contractor, resulting from the improvement of real property, shall constitute a trust fund. The law provides that the trust fund is to be administered by the owner or the contractor, and the only payments which can be made out of that fund are to various subcontractors, contractors, architects, engineers, laborers and material men. Other legitimate amounts which may be taken from that trust fund are taxes, wages, and payment of premiums upon various bonds or insurance policies. Therefore, by statute, if a contractor or owner takes the proceeds of any payment on account, mortgage or construction loan, and uses those proceeds for a purpose other than that specifically set forth in the lien law, such action automatically constitutes a diversion from the trust and renders personal responsibility upon those parties having control of the money. Its corresponding advantage is that if the money has been transferred to anybody else who knew, or should have known, that these funds came as a result of a diversion from the trust, that person who receives the money must return it, providing another deep pocketbook for the satisfaction of any claims of diversion of trust fund monies under the lien law (see citations in footnote 4).

Negligence

In the continuing search for third parties who might be responsible, in a legal sense, for the failure to pay contributions to a trust fund, an action in negligence might be considered. An act which a reasonably prudent person would not have committed under the same facts and circumstances constitutes negligence. Correspondingly, the failure to act, when a reasonably prudent person would have acted—once again keeping in mind the facts and circumstances of the case—constitutes negligence. In other words, negligence is a case tried today which examines in detail an act, or omission to act, in the past.

The theory of negligence is important, for it provides a financially responsible party if the corporate officers maintain a policy of liability insurance covering their negligent acts. Policies covering negligence of the corporation or corporate officers are issued by the insurance carriers. If a lawsuit is structured in negligence, it has its basis in that a reasonably prudent corporate officer, having full knowledge of the circumstances, would have paid the fringe benefit fund rather than other creditors. The paying of others as an act of commission, and the failure to pay the trust funds as an act of omission—which a reasonably prudent person would neither have committed nor omitted—can be considered a negligent act. Assuming the corporation to have a policy of liability insurance covering negligent acts or occurrences and assuming, further, that recovery is made, then the recovery is paid by the insurance company to the extent of the insurance policy.

To date, I know of no action which has been begun strictly on a negligence theory against the corporation or corporate officers. In the event, however, that such an action is required, and assuming dollars and cents justify the expense, an additional avenue for collection is presented. If successful, any judgment will be paid by a solvent insurance carrier to the extent of the loss sustained by the fund (or to the insurance limits). Certain cases which have indicated that this cause of action or this type of lawsuit might be viable are set forth in the citations in footnote 5.

Piercing the Corporate Veil

All lawyers are familiar with the theory of "piercing the corporate veil." Public policy fosters

---

4. *Hinkle Iron Co. v. Kohn*, 229 N.Y. 179; *AMF, Inc. v. Algo Distrs.*, 48 A.D.2d 352. *Bldg. Trades United Pension Trust Fund-Milwaukee v. Schultz*, 315 BNA BPR A-8 Bkrptcy E.D. Wisc. #79-01939.

---

5. *Culinary Workers Local 596 v. Gateway Cafe, Inc.*, 100 L.R.R.M. 2773 (Wa. Sup. Ct. 1979).

corporations and allows them, as business entities, to conduct business and engage in trade with the further advantage of being able to insulate the corporate assets and liabilities from the individual assets and liabilities of the various shareholders, officers and directors. The critical issue is, does the corporation have a legitimate business purpose? In "piercing the corporate veil," it is shown that the corporation was used for an improper purpose, such as violating or evading a duty owed, making fraudulent transfers or, if it is a successor corporation, perhaps reincarnating the disbanded corporation. In other words, the corporation does not fit the public policy argument which allows it to insulate its assets and liabilities. If one can pierce the corporate veil, then the court disregards the corporation and imposes liability on its stockholders and those engaged in the business in their individual capacity. The most recent cases on this issue, involving contributions to various benefit funds, appear in footnote 6.

Parent Subsidiary Liability

To the same extent that public policy fosters corporations, it also fosters a parent subsidiary relationship. This deals with the area where one corporation is the owner of stock in another corporation, or perhaps one corporation forms another corporation to carry on some specific aspects of its business. The same public policy applies to a parent subsidiary corporation as to a corporation owned by several stockholders or by a single individual stockholder. The trust fund is often placed in a situation where the subsidiary has been formed for the specific job in question and is without funds, but the parent corporation is financially responsible.

Here, the courts are asked to disregard the corporate status of the subsidiary and allow the trust fund's attorney to proceed against the parent presumed to be more financially solvent. Before the court will disregard the separation of parent and subsidiary, it will look at the relationship between the two entities. If the subsidiary company's whole business is determined by its parent corporation, or the parent exercises control in everyday operation, or if the subsidiary is only a "dummy" for the parent, then the courts have no difficulty in holding that the subsidiary's contracts are those of the parent. In such a situation, the failure to pay will be transferred from the subsidiary to the parent. Once again, counsel is given an opportunity to proceed against someone outside the labor-management agreement for payment of the amounts due the trust fund.

The same type of argument would be made by counsel for the trust fund against a controlled group of corporations, as PBGC and other government agencies do when they are seeking to impose the statutory liability upon other corporations in the controlled group, when one corporation is forced to discontinue the pension plan. The theory is the same. There is by statute a difference in definition of employer in Title I and Title IV of ERISA. PBGC can proceed against the controlled group by statute. Counsel for the fund must resort to existing case law to see if action can be brought against another corporate entity (see *PBGC v. Ouimet*, 307 BNA BPR D-1 8/29/80 1st Cir.; *Steamfitters v. Murdoch*, #77-1716 (U.S.D.C. E.D. Pa. 4/25/79).

There is no question that the statutory authorities cited herein and the cases cited in the footnotes are from only a few of this nation's 50 states. It may very well be that the statutory manner of proceeding against officers and directors of a corporation, or stockholders of a corporation, applies to only a few states. However, the legal theories are the same, whether they are incorporated in statutes or not. Since one can always argue that the failure to pay a worker the wages which are inclusive of fringe benefits is a theft of services, the legal theory for liability may be present in all states. Under ERISA, the Congressional mandate to the federal courts—namely, that the federal courts are to fashion a uniform law of trust as it affects these jointly negotiated labor-management trust funds—may result in the application of the legal theory by courts in other jurisdictions, in the absence of statute, in order to form a uniform body of trust law applicable to these Taft-Hartley type trusts. It may be that the initial decisions are based upon state statutes; but the *theory* of the statute remains in all other jurisdictions, even though not expressed by that state's legislature. Under the circumstances, the mere fact of absence of statutory requirements, as set forth herein, should not deter counsel from proceeding upon the theory involved, in order to secure personal liability of corporate officers, directors, and shareholders or any other third party who may be able to make up the loss involved.

---

6. *Bekey v. Third Ave. KY Co.*, 244 N.Y. 84; *Van Valkenburgh Nooger, Nivelle v. Hayden Publishing Co.*, 30 N.Y.2d 34; *Rapid Transit Subway Constr. Co. v. City of N.Y.*, 259 N.Y. 472; *Port Chester Elec. v. Allan*, 40 N.Y.2d 652; *Astrocom Electronics v. Lafayette Radio*, 63 A.D.2d 765. *Steamfitters Local Union No. 420 of Philadelphia v. Murdoch International, Inc.* #77-1716 U.S.D.C. E.D. Penn. 4/25/79.

Problems With the Closely Held Corporation

'Opposing' Decisions

The contributing employer of a small closely held corporation has presented problems to the courts and to trust funds with respect to the corporate contributions which are made on behalf of a stockholder or officer of a small corporation. A corporation which is owned by one or two people, who work just as hard as any other union participant, who work with the tools of the trade and who have made contributions on their behalf, is faced with additional problems under ERISA. When the time comes for the stockholders to retire or make an application for welfare benefits, the problem arises as to whether the stockholders are covered persons. The situation is best illustrated by two cases. The first is *Brauer v. Sheet Metal Workers Pension Plan of Southern California, Arizona and Nevada* (82 Cal. App.3rd 159) (certiorari to the United States Supreme Court denied). Brauer, as a 50% stockholder of the corporation, paid his contributions to the trust fund but was denied his pension. The denial of benefits resulted from an interpretation of the Taft-Hartley Act (the act under which all jointly administered funds draw their legal authority) to the effect that notwithstanding his work, and notwithstanding his contribution, he was to be treated as an employer. Since the Taft-Hartley Act legitimatizes trust funds only on behalf of employees, he could not recover the benefits he claimed due.

Diametrically opposed is the case from the Seventh Circuit of *Reiherzer v. Shannon and Central States Southeast and Southwest Areas Pension Funds* (581 F.2d 126). Here, Reiherzer was a 90% shareholder in his small corporation, had made the required contributions, and was likewise seeking retirement benefits. In this case, the court held that Mr. Reiherzer was entitled to those benefits. Judging his eligibility under the Internal Revenue Code rulings (Revenue Rulings 69-421j), Reiherzer was a participant and entitled to his benefits.

The difficulty is reconciliation of the two views, and each case, whether it be *Brauer* or *Reiherzer*, stresses the same point. Brauer, who was denied benefits, was the subject of the following language by the court:

> Finally, as set out in the agreement and declaration of trust establishing Sheet Metal Workers Pension Plan of Southern California, Arizona and Nevada dated August 11, 1972, the powers of the pension plan's trustees include the power "to construe the provisions of this trust agreement and the pension plan and any such construction adopted by the Board in good faith shall be binding upon any and all parties or persons affected thereby."

Here the trustees determined appellant (Brauer) was not eligible for benefits based upon their acceptance of the definition of the term employee as outlined above (speaking of the definition under the Labor Law). Under such circumstances, where there is no showing nor any sufficient allegations . . . that the trustees acted arbitrarily, capriciously or in bad faith, their actions are final and not subject to judicial review.

So Brauer, in accordance with the trust instrument, was not entitled to the benefits he sought, notwithstanding the contributions, and the court could find nothing wrong with the decision rendered by the trustees in denial of benefits. The Taft-Hartley Act said the trustees were legally correct.

Reiherzer, who received the benefits he sought, was subject to the following language of the court:

> This Court, in deciding this case, under Federal common law principles, of course, cannot replace its judgment for the considered judgment of the plan's trustees. Rather we are required to uphold the trustees' decisions unless it was arbitrary and capricious in light of the language of the plan.

As far as Reiherzer was concerned, the court then looked at the plan to see whether there was a definition of "self-employed" and found there to be an absence of such definition. The court also found that the initial decision of the trustees was inconsistent, and concluded that the "ability of the trustees to blow hot or cold on the definition of 'self-employed' under the plan demonstrates the arbitrariness of their denial of Reiherzer's pension on the ground that he was self-employed."

In each instance, the court examined the plan for arbitrary, capricious or improper conduct of the trustees in rendering their decision.

Consistent Policy Needed

What the contributing employer must do and what the various pension funds and welfare funds must do is to establish a clearly defined policy as to how they will treat the worker who also owns stock or controls the small corporation. The courts have repeated time after time that as long as the plan is clear, as long as the trustees act in a similar manner under similar circumstances, their determination will be upheld. This is the advice to trustees and to the management contributor of a corporation.

No such ameliorating circumstances are available for the partnership or for the individual who has not incorporated. Perhaps it is best stated by the United States Court of Appeals for the Ninth Circuit in *Aitken v. I.P. & G.C.U.-Employer Retirement Fund* (87 L.C. 22401) where the court held: "to uphold the decision of the fund and its interpretation of the agreement we need not decide that to pay benefits to Aitken would be illegal. It is sufficient that Appellee's (the Fund) interpretation of the eligibility provisions is reasonable ... the language of the plan agreement is not ambiguous ... the committee's interpretation of the agreement was reasonable...." But the handwriting is on the wall for the corporate contributor of a small closely held corporation and the trustees in the performance of their fiduciary duties. For the Ninth Circuit concluded its determination with the following statement:

> The Eighth Circuit has held that administrators of a Section 302 (Taft-Hartley) Trust have an obligation to make periodic determinations of eligibility ... we decline at this time to detail the precise boundaries of the duty imposed ... a duty enforceable in this Circuit as well as the Eighth. Encompassed within this duty, however, is the obligation to inform an applicant, and his contributing employer, of the applicant's ineligibility within a reasonable time after the committee acquires knowledge of that ineligibility.

It seems obvious that contributing employers from small closely held corporations should make positive inquiry as to the rules and regulations of the trust fund, and find out how these small corporate contributors are treated pursuant to rules and regulations. There will correspondingly be imposed upon the trustees or the administrators of the trust a duty to notify participants and contributing employers if they feel that the contributions are not in accordance with the trust instruments, or that the party on whose behalf contributions are made will not be recognized as a participant. If the small corporate contributor would do his part, and if the trustees or administrators would do their part, there should be a cessation of such cases as *Brauer* and *Reiherzer*. Then the only question will be whether the rules and regulations are clear and explicit; whether similar circumstances dictate similar decisions; and whether there is any reason to hold that a particular determination by the trustees is arbitrary and capricious when examined by a court.

The Audit of the Employer's Books

The trustees of a trust fund, to act prudently, should already have developed a reasonable and systematic plan for the auditing of contributions made by corporate employers. Each audit plan, in order to be reasonable and prudent, should be worked out by the trustees in conjunction with their accountants, with their administrators and other experts, so as to be reasonable in cost and scope as dictated by the size of the plan. The costs of any audit program and the anticipated benefits to be accomplished by such a program determine the scope, extent and regularity of the audit.

Written Authorization

When an employer receives notice from a trust fund or from its administrator that his books are going to be subject to audit, one cannot do away with the initial reaction of any contributing employer that his books are a private affair and not subject to scrutiny by any third party. If the employer, in signing the labor-management agreement, has agreed that not only would contributions be made, but that there is a complete right of audit by the fund's accountants and that books and records will be made available on demand, legally there is nothing which can prohibit the inspection of the books. The problems arise when the clear language authorizing such an audit is missing from either the labor-management agreement or from the trust agreement which would be incorporated in the labor-management agreement. Here, the corporate contributor looks to the body of established law for reasons which would prohibit the the trust fund's audit of its books.

Such a defense on the part of any employer would start with the case of *Moglia v. Geoghegan*, 207 F.Supp. 641, *aff'd* 403 F.2nd 110, where the court has held that any payment made by an employer to a trust is forbidden unless there is a written agreement between the employer and the union. If the employer claims that there is no written agreement, and should this be acknowledged as correct, there is no right of collection and there would be no subsidiary right of audit. If an agreement is in writing, and it covers the construction industry, and there has never been shown certification or majority representation by the construction industry union involved, the employer will take the position that such a contract was governed under Section 8F of the Taft-Hartley Act, and therefore is terminable at will and no audit could be had of his books. Therefore, since the agreement is in writing, but the necessary prerequisite of certification or majority representation is missing, the agreement is not sufficient to support an audit of the books or payment of benefits (see *Washington Area Carpenters Welfare Fund v. Overhead Door Company,* D.C., April 22, 1980, 289 BNA BPR D-12).

If the employer is not a signatory to the labor-management agreement, this does not spell the end of the opportunity to audit his books. Certainly, many corporate contributors bargain as a member of an association. The question of authorization to the association to bargain on his behalf, or perhaps authorization once given and withdrawn, becomes a critical issue in determining whether or not the agreement that the association signed is binding upon the employer (see *Garment Workers v. Miami Casuals, Inc.,* 456 F.2d 799; *Paul v. Lindgren,* 375 F.Supp. 843; *Rizzuto (Operating Engineers) v. Vacar Construction,* 69 A.D. 2nd (N.Y.); *Cement Masons v. Venezia Cement,* 302 BNA, BPR A-15).

Scope of Audit

Assuming all of the hurdles have been overcome with respect to either a signed labor-management agreement or an agreement binding upon the employer signed by the association, the next area of defense deals with the scope of the examination and which of the employer's books may be examined by the auditors. Certainly, under the federal rules of discovery, items which deal not only with evidence which is material and necessary may be examined; those books which may lead to the discovery of evidence are also germane and may be examined by the fund's accountant (*Central States, etc. v. Fairway Transit,* D.C.E.D. Wisconsin, 78 C.641; 22, 333 P.H.). Whether or not the refusal to have one's books examined would be construed an unfair labor practice (though initially held to be so in *Detroit Cabinet and Door v. Millmans Local,* 1452 247 N.L.R.B. 186) is still debatable. That the Detroit Cabinet Company did not even bother to interpose any defense to the proceedings before the National Labor Relations Board detracts from the force and validity of the uncontested decision.

It should be brought out, as a note of caution, that in those states where by statute it is a crime not to pay contributions to the various funds, and where the contributor does business in his own name, or perhaps as a partnership, and there is an absence of a written agreement allowing audits of the books, one defense available to the individual entrepreneur (or perhaps to the partner) is that any examination of the books would violate the individual's rights under the 4th and 5th Amendments to the Constitution—namely, those amendments dealing with self-incrimination and improper search and seizure. If the trust fund deals with contributors who do business either individually or as a partnership, the trust fund and/or the labor-management agreement should clearly and precisely stipulate that the individual contributor consents to an examination of its books of account so as to verify the accuracy of the contributions.

The Employer's Knowledge of His Total Liability to the Trust Fund

This section of the presentation is not a detailed analysis of withdrawal liability or the liability of an employer when the trust fund becomes insolvent, nor is it a dissertation upon the rights of PBGC and the various statutory liabilities imposed upon the employer for his pro-rata share of liabilities which have been accrued because of vested benefits promised by the trust instrument. The fact that there is potential liability on the part of the management contributor is well known to all. The recent amendments to ERISA dealing with employer liability affect the salability of a contributing employer's business. There are certain exemptions available to those in the construction industry, certain aspects of the trucking industry, or the entertainment industry. Congress with respect to a limited group of employers has provided for an exemption from withdrawal liability. The exemption of these businesses, however, is limited to situations where the contributing employer does not continue, after withdrawal, to work in the area. However, to the vast number of contributing employers who have not been favored with an exemption, this withdrawal liability directly impacts upon the value of their businesses.

Trustees still collect the contributions, pay benefits and incur liabilities when the amounts of benefits are determined by them. More important now is the fact that the trustees' actions directly impinge upon the contributing employer. Every time the trustees vote a general increase in benefits, it creates a liability which directly impinges on the value of the contributing employer's business.

The issue is crystal clear as to what the trustees are to do with increases in contributions: use the funds to reduce unfunded vested benefits, or increase benefits. The answer depends on which side of the bargaining table you sit at, or who designated the trustees. The question that the contributing employer must ask is: What do I do with the profits of my business? Do I allow them to remain within the corporation, increase its net worth, and thereby stand as further security for a liability determined by another? Or do I withdraw the profits from the business and distribute its annual profits, so that if liability is ever imposed, it can be imposed only upon the assets existing at the time? At least the profits made now or in the future, having been withdrawn, have been used by the contributing employer for purposes he considers more important. In essence, the employer with a 100% withdrawal liability is faced with some serious questions as to reinvestment of accumulated profits.

ERISA Preemption of State Laws—Crowning Achievement or Empty Promise?

BY THOMAS E. STANTON, JR.

Introduction

Title I of ERISA provides for the detailed and specific regulation of covered employee benefit plans under the headings of reporting and disclosure, participation and vesting, funding, fiduciary responsibility and administration and enforcement. These regulatory provisions were a deliberate departure from the Welfare and Pension Plans Disclosure Act of 1958, "which clearly anticipated a broad regulatory role for the States" over employee benefit plans, including plans established in interstate industries regulated by the National Labor Relations Act and the Taft-Hartley Act.[1]

Congress intended that Title I should preempt the state regulation of covered employee benefit plans, with narrowly limited exceptions. It said this in so many words in Section 514 of ERISA, which provides that, subject to those limited exceptions, "the provisions of [Title I] shall supersede any and all State laws insofar as they may now or hereafter relate to any [covered] employee benefit plan." Section 514 emphasized the breadth of its purpose by defining "State law" as including "all laws, decisions, rules, regulations, or other State action having the effect of law."

Congressman Dent, one of the principal authors of ERISA, hailed this preemption provision as "the *crowning achievement* of this legislation, the reservation to Federal authority [of] the sole power to regulate the field of employee benefit plans." He added: "With the preemption of the field, we round out the protection afforded participants by eliminating the threat of conflicting and inconsistent State and local regulation."[2]

Mr. Stanton is a partner in the law firm of Johnson & Stanton, in San Francisco. He is involved in general legal practice with an emphasis on the construction industry. He has served as co-counsel for a number of jointly trusteed benefit plans in California for nearly 27 years. Mr. Stanton received his A.B. and LL.B. degrees from the University of California at Berkeley and his LL.M. degree from Harvard University.

The views of Congressman Dent were echoed by Senator Javits, another of the authors of ERISA. Expressing fear that a less comprehensive preemption provision would lead to "endless litigation over the validity of State action that might impinge on Federal regulation," the Senator said that "the emergence of a comprehensive and pervasive Federal interest and the interests of uniformity with respect to interstate plans required—but for certain exceptions—the displacement of State action in the field of private employee benefit programs."[3]

Impact on State Domestic Relations Laws

State domestic relations laws are not within the narrow exceptions from preemption provided in

---

1. *Malone v. White Motor Corp.* (1978) 435 U.S. 497, 512, 98 S.Ct. 1185, 1194.
2. *Hewlett-Packard Co. v. Barnes* (N.D. Cal. 1977) 425 F.Supp. 1294, 1299, aff'd, (9th C.A. 1978) 571 F.2d 502, *cert. den.* 99 S.Ct. 108.

3. *Ibid*

Section 514. The conclusion should follow logically, therefore, that ERISA has preempted those laws as they relate to employee benefit plans. This has not been the holding of the majority of courts to date, however, and the result has been the "endless litigation" feared by Senator Javits and the threatened destruction of the national uniformity in the regulation of employee benefit plans which ERISA was intended to achieve.

The courts initially interpreted and enforced the preemption provisions of ERISA in accordance with long-established judicial principles. They started with the language of the statute—which the United States Supreme Court has repeatedly admonished them to do[4]—reviewed the legislative history of Section 514, and held that ERISA preempted such state laws as the California Knox-Keene Act regulating health care service plans and the Hawaii Prepaid Health Care Act.[5]

When the courts faced the question as to whether ERISA preempted state domestic relations laws, however, many of them faltered. In common-law as well as community property states, domestic relations courts have routinely entered and enforced orders against pensioners as well as employed persons for the support of separated or divorced spouses. In community property states, and in the increasing number of other states which have adopted marital property laws patterned after the community property laws, domestic relations courts have also entered and enforced orders dividing between divorcing spouses the entitlement to, and the ownership of, pension benefits (or prospective pension benefits). The laws which provide for the entry and enforcement of these orders probably have more all-pervasive and direct impact upon employee pension benefit plans than any other state laws.

Issues and Decisions

An accepted judicial procedure for a court troubled by the impact of ERISA upon state domestic relations laws would have been to hold that ERISA had clearly preempted those laws and to call upon Congress to correct whatever judicially perceived inequity had resulted from such preemption. While this procedure would have delayed and perhaps even have prevented correction of the inequity in the particular case before the court, the procedure would have preserved the integrity of the judicial process and might have spurred Congress to enact legislation correcting the inequity on a uniform national basis consistent with the fundamental concept of ERISA.[6]

Instead of following this accepted procedure, the courts that dispute the wisdom of Congress' decision to preempt state domestic relations laws as they relate to ERISA plans have ignored the plain words of Section 514 and have engaged in strained reasoning to reach a result more to their liking. Courts in common-law states have perceived an implied exception to the antiassignment provision of Section 206(d)(1) of ERISA which allows enforcement of support orders against pensions that are in pay status; and, having perceived this exception to one section, they have held that the exception, although written by Congress in invisible ink, overrides conflicting language in other Sections of ERISA, such as Sections 403(c), 404(a), 502 and 514.[7] In community property states, the courts have given the domestic relations laws a far greater impact upon ERISA plans by holding that the divorcing or divorced spouse of a plan participant is the owner of a community property share not only in the participant's pension when in pay status but also in the participant's unmatured rights under the pension plan.[8] This holding not only circumvents the antiassignment provision of ERISA but it also, according to the courts, quali-

---

4. The United States Supreme Court has recently reaffirmed that

> Logic and precedent dictate that "[t] the starting point in every case involving construction of a statute is the language itself" [*Santa Fe Industries, Inc. v. Green*, 430 U.S. 462, 472 (1977), and *Ernst & Ernst v. Hochfelder*, 425 U.S. 185, 197 (1976), each quoting *Blue Chip Stamps v. Manor Drug Stores*, 421 U.S. 723, 756 (1975) (Powell, J., concurring); *The Greyhound Corporation v. Mt. Hood Stages, Inc.* (1978) 437 U.S. 322, 330, 98 S.Ct. 2370, 2375] and where the words of a statute "are clear and unequivocal on their face" *(United States v. Oregon* (1961) 366 U.S. 643, 648, 81 S.Ct. 1278, 1281), those words are controlling [*Ernst & Ernst v. Hochfelder* (1975) 425 U.S. 185, 200-201, 98 S.Ct. 1375, 1384-1385].

5. *Hewlett-Packard Co. v. Barnes*, supra; *Standard Oil Co. of California v. Agsalud* (D.N.D. Cal. 1977) 442 F.Supp. 695, aff'd, (9th C.A. 1980) 633 F.2d 760.

6. Congress anticipated that the broad scope of the preemption provision of ERISA might present problems, and set up a Joint Pension Task Force to study and review, among other things, "the effects and desirability of the Federal preemption of State and local law with respect to matters relating to pension and similar plans [ERISA, Section 3033(a)(4), 29 U.S.C. §1222(a)(4)].

7. *American Tel. & Tel. Co. v. Merry* (2d C.A. 1979) 592 F.2d 118, 121; *Cody v. Rieker* (2d C.A. 1979) 594 F.2d 314, 316.

8. *In re Marriage of Pilatti* (1979) 96 C.A. 3d 63, 67; *In re Marriage of Lionberger* (1979) 97 C.A. 3d 56, 68.

fies the ex-spouse as a plan participant notwithstanding the fact that she does not come within the plain words of ERISA.[9]

In *Stone v. Stone,* a federal district court held that the transfer of pension benefits under state community property laws to a divorced spouse is not an "assignment" of such benefits prohibited by Section 206(d)(1); that since such a transfer is not expressly prohibited, the transfer is permitted by ERISA; that since Congress intended to permit the transfer of the pension benefit, it must also have intended to permit the transfer to the divorced spouse of the participant's right to sue under Section 502(a)(1)(B) of ERISA to recover the benefits; and that therefore the divorced spouse was herself a participant as defined in ERISA and entitled to bring an action in a federal district court against the pension plan pursuant to Section 502(a)(1)(B) to recover her community property share of the benefit.[10]

On appeal, the United States Court of Appeals for the Ninth Circuit affirmed the holding of the district court. The court of appeals first held in a companion case, *Carpenters Pension Trust for Southern California v. Kronschnabel,*[11] that the summary dismissal by the United States Supreme Court of an appeal from the decision of the California court of appeal in *In re Marriage of Campa*[12] for "lack of a substantial federal question" was a holding by the Supreme Court that a state court had jurisdiction to order the board of trustees of an ERISA pension plan to make benefit payments in violation of the provisions of the documents and instruments governing the plan, and that this holding was binding upon all lower courts. The court then ruled that, because of the holding of the United States Supreme Court in the *Campa* case, the divorced spouse of a plan participant came within the term "participant" as defined in ERISA, namely, "any employee or former employee of an employer, or any member or former member of an employee organization, who is or may become eligible to receive a benefit" from an ERISA plan,[13] notwithstanding that this interpretation of "participant" made that term "mean something other than what the plain words of the statute generally convey."[14]

Problems for Fiduciaries

This judicial tinkering with and twisting of the plain words of ERISA presents serious problems from the standpoint of the fiduciaries of ERISA plans. Section 404(a)(1) of ERISA requires that a plan fiduciary "discharge his duties with respect to a plan solely in the interest of the participants and beneficiaries" of the plan, "for the exclusive purpose of providing benefits to such participants and beneficiaries" and defraying administrative expenses, and "in accordance with the documents and instruments governing the plan insofar as the documents and instruments are consistent with the provisions" of ERISA. Any breach of this fiduciary obligation subjects the fiduciary to personal liability to make good to the plan any losses to the plan resulting from the breach, and to such other equitable or remedial relief as a court may deem appropriate.[15] Thus, if the words of ERISA do not mean what they clearly say, and even then are subject to "implied exceptions," plan fiduciaries are exposed to unacceptable risks of personal liability, and the plans themselves are exposed to the "endless litigation" feared by Senator Javits.

California Laws. The problems created by the zeal of the courts to protect the interests of divorcing or divorced spouses against the broad sweep of ERISA preemption are particularly acute in community property states such as California. California has a unique statute which provides that no domestic relations order or judgment shall be enforceable against an employee pension benefit plan unless the plan has been joined as a party to the proceeding in which the order is entered.[16] In addition, the California courts have held that an attorney who fails to take appropriate steps in a marriage dissolution proceeding to protect the interest of a non-employee spouse in the employee spouse's pension is liable for malpractice.[17] The result has been that a large pension plan, such as the Carpenters Pension Trust Fund for Northern California, has been joined as a party to more than 100 marriage dissolution proceedings since the effective date of ERISA, and summonses in one or more new proceedings are being received on a weekly basis.

The California joinder statute[18] provides that an employee pension benefit plan is not required to appear at any hearing in the marriage dissolution proceeding, although it may do so. If the plan does

---

9. *In re Marriage of Pilatti, supra,* p. 67.
10. (N.D. Cal. 1978) 450 F.Supp. 919.
11. (9th C.A. 1980) 632 F.2d 745, 747.
12. (1979) 89 C.A. 3d 113, *app. dism.,* 444 U.S. 1028, 100 S.Ct. 696.
13. ERISA Section 3(7), 29 U.S.C. §1002(7).
14. (9th C.A. 1980) 632 F.2d 740, at p. 743.

15. ERISA Section 409(a), 29 U.S.C. §1109(a).
16. California Civil Code, Section 4351.
17. *Smith v. Lewis* (1975) 13 C.3d 349, 360.
18. California Civil Code, Section 4363.2.

not appear at a hearing, an order entered as a result of the hearing must be served upon it, and the plan is allowed 30 days within which to move to set aside or modify the provisions of the order affecting it. If within this 30 day period the plan moves to set aside or modify the provisions of the order affecting it, such provisions cannot become effective until the court has resolved the motion. An ERISA plan served with an order requiring it to make payments other than for the exclusive benefit of a plan participant or beneficiary or otherwise in violation of the documents and instruments governing the plan is faced with the alternatives of either (a) moving to set aside or modify the order and risking an adverse ruling by the domestic relations court and the assessment of attorneys' fees against the plan under Section 502(g) of ERISA, or (b) complying with the order and exposing the plan administrator to liability for breach of fiduciary duty if the United States Supreme Court should ultimately hold that the plain words of ERISA must be obeyed.

This effort by the courts to legislate by "implied exception" and by departing from the "plain words" of the statute is not only unfair to ERISA plan administrators, participants and beneficiaries; the effort has also defeated rather than advanced the national uniformity in the regulation of employee benefit plans which Congress so clearly intended to achieve.

Subchapter II. In 1968, Congress enacted Subchapter II of the Consumer Credit Protection Act for the purpose of protecting wage earners and pensioners against oppression and eventual bankruptcy as a result of the demands of their creditors.[19] As originally enacted, Subchapter II excluded support orders from its protective provisions.[20] In 1977, however, the subchapter was amended to protect 35-50% of the disposable portion of a pensioner's benefit from garnishment for a support order, depending upon whether or not the pensioner was supporting another spouse or dependent child and depending upon the currency of the pensioner's arrearages.[21] In a common-law state, the pensioner receives the full benefit of the protection provided by Subchapter II, since any payments pursuant to a support order are deducted from the pension benefits subject to garnishment by other creditors.[22] In community property states, however, the portion of the pension benefit transferred to a divorced spouse pursuant to the community property laws is deducted *before* determination of the percentage of the benefit protected from garnishment by Subchapter II.[23]

The Evans Case. Both the inequity to plan participants and the defeat of national uniformity resulting from this judicial legislation are illustrated by the case of Herman Eugene Evans, a participant in the pension plan of the Carpenters Pension Trust Fund for Northern California.

Herman was entitled under the terms of the Carpenters plan to a single life benefit of $650 per month based upon 25 years of covered work as a carpenter. He elected a husband and wife benefit for the protection of his wife, Opal Arletha Evans, thereby reducing his benefit by 21% to $513.50 per month and giving Opal the right after his death to a benefit for life of 50% of this amount, or $250.75 per month, provided that Opal remained married to him at his death. Opal knew of this election and signed the form by which the election was made.

Shortly after Herman's retirement, Opal sued him for the dissolution of their marriage. The Carpenters Fund was joined as a party to the marital dissolution proceeding, and the domestic relations court, having determined that Opal had a one-half community property interest in Herman's benefit, ordered the fund to pay 50% of the benefit directly to Opal forthwith and without awaiting Herman's death. Opal thereafter levied execution upon Herman's remaining benefit of $265.75 per month for the enforcement of arrearages under a support order totaling $1,816.40. The domestic relations court held that, under the Consumer Credit Protection Act, the execution was enforceable against 55% of the remaining benefit, or $141.21 per month, leaving Herman $115.54 per month or approximately 18% of the pension he had earned through work as a carpenter for 25 years, until the arrearages under the support order have been paid.[24]

If Herman and Opal had been residents of a common-law state, the protection of the Consumer

---

19. 15 U.S.C. §1671 *et seq.*
20. P.L. 90-321, Title III, §303, May 29, 1968, 82 Stat. 163, 15 U.S.C. §1673(b).
21. P.L. 95-30, Title V, §501(e)(1)-(3), May 23, 1977, 91 Stat. 161, 162; 15 U.S.C. §1673(b)(2).

22. *Marshall v. Dist. Ct. for Forty-First-6 Jud. Dist.* (E.D. Mich. 1978) 444 F.Supp., 1110, 1115-1116; *General Motors Acceptance Corp. v. Metropolitan Opera* (1978) 413 N.Y.S.2d 818, 820.
23. *See* Order on Motion for New Trial or Alternative Relief and Order of Modification filed on May 20, 1980, in *In re Marriage of Evans,* Sacramento Superior Court No. 732405.
24. *Ibid.*

Credit Protection Act would have extended to the full amount of Herman's monthly benefit. Under uniform rulings of the Wage and Hour Administrator and court rulings secured by the Secretary of Labor, the amount garnished by a family support decree in a common-law state would not be deducted from the retirement benefit of a pensioner before computation of the maximum percentage of the benefit subject to garnishment to enforce a support order.[25] Thus, in such a state, only 55% of the full benefit of $513.50 per month, or $282.42, could have been subjected to garnishment. Of this amount, $256.75 would have been absorbed by the marital dissolution award to Opal and only $25.67 per month would have remained subject to garnishment to enforce the support order.

Far-Reaching Effects

This judicial legislation in behalf of divorcing or divorced spouses of plan participants has had other adverse consequences for ERISA plans and the objectives Congress sought to achieve by enacting ERISA. The judicial legislation has eroded and will continue to erode the protection provided by ERISA to surviving spouses. The California courts have held that, in order to protect the community property interest of a divorcing spouse, a domestic relations court may enjoin a plan participant from exercising the joint and survivor option mandated by ERISA for the benefit of his surviving spouse.[26] Also, in an increasing number of cases like the case of Herman Evans, a spouse who has consented to the election by her husband of the joint and survivor option, with a concomitant reduction in the husband's monthly benefit, has subsequently sued for the dissolution of the marriage and a community property share of her husband's reduced pension. ERISA requires that a participant be given a reasonable opportunity to reject the joint and survivor annuity after he has received a written explanation of the terms and conditions of the annuity,[27] and if such explanation must include advice that his spouse may nullify his acceptance of the annuity by suing for a dissolution of their marriage and obtaining a community property share of the reduced pension, he will be encouraged to reject the annuity.

Further, the holding that the divorced spouse of a participant is a participant in the plan in her own right has substantially and onerously expanded the reporting and disclosure requirements of ERISA Sections 101, 102, 104(b) and (c), and 105. Those requirements apply to such a spouse whether or not she is receiving benefits under the plan, and plan administrators will be faced with the necessity of keeping track of and otherwise dealing with persons whose only connection with the plan is that they once were married to participants. In addition, under such holding, every divorcing or divorced spouse who joins an employee pension benefit plan as a party to a marriage dissolution proceeding, or otherwise sues the plan in a state court for all or a portion of a participant's pension benefit, can claim an award of an attorney's fee against the plan pursuant to Section 502(g) of ERISA.[28]

Explicit vs. Implied Exception

In November 1979, the Senate Committee on Labor and Human Resources submitted a report on Section 209, entitled, "The ERISA Improvements Act of 1979: Summary and Analysis of Considerations," in which it proposed to replace the "implied exception" legislated by certain courts with what was described in the report as "an explicit and carefully delineated statutory exception."[29] This exception would exclude from the preemption provisions of Section 514 a judgment, decree or order (including an approval of a property settlement agreement) relating to child support, alimony payments or marital property rights, pursuant to a state domestic relations law (whether of the common-law or community property type), which—

> (A) creates or recognizes the existence of an individual's right to receive all or a portion of the benefits to which a participant or a participant's designated beneficiary would otherwise be entitled under a pension plan,
> (B) clearly identifies such participant, the amount or percentage of such benefits to be paid to such individual,

---

25. Opinion Letters Nos. 1151, 1158, 1159, 1229, CCH Labor Law Rep., Wages-Hours Administrative Rulings, #30,721, #30,726, #30,727 and #30,813; authorities, *supra,* Note 22.
26. *In re Marriage of Lionberger* (1979) 97 C.A.3d 56, 68, *supra.*
27. Internal Revenue Service Regulations 1.401(a)-(11)(c)(3).

---

28. In *In re Marriage of Reyes* (1979) 96 C.A. 876, 880, the court rejected a contention that a divorced spouse was entitled to an award of attorneys' fees under ERISA, commenting that the spouse had failed to establish that she was a participant, beneficiary or fiduciary within the meaning of ERISA. When the case was remanded to the superior court, however, the court found that the spouse was a "beneficiary" within the meaning of ERISA and awarded her an attorney's fee notwithstanding the appellate ruling. The case is again on appeal.
29. Report, p. 30.

the number of payments to which such judgment, decree or order applies, and the name and mailing address of such individual, and

(C) does not require such plan to alter the effective date, timing, form, duration, or amount of any benefit payments under the plan or to honor any election which is not provided for under the plan or which is made by a person other than a participant or beneficiary.[30]

In its report, the Senate Committee affirms that the "national interest in uniform federal regulation of ERISA-covered employee benefit plans is still generally paramount."[31] The effect of the amendment to Section 514 proposed in the report, however, would be to give the divorced spouses of participants in employee pension benefit plans greater and more immediate rights than those given by ERISA to the surviving spouses of participants. In effect, Congress will have turned over to the individual states the definition and enforcement of the rights to plan benefits of the divorcing and divorced spouses under the worst possible conditions from the standpoint of employee pension benefit plans, the participants and beneficiaries of such plans, and the employers who contribute to and sustain the plans. In such a situation, the following concerns become very real:

1. In a marital dissolution proceeding, the principal if not the only concern of the domestic relations court is with the rights of the parties before it at the time and, where an interest under an employee pension benefit plan is involved, with the rights of the non-employee spouse with respect to the plan. The court gives little if any attention to the interests of the employers who contribute to the plan, the employees covered by the plan (other than the employee who is a party to the proceedings), the person or persons who may subsequently marry the party employee, and the administrators of the plan.

2. The employers who contribute to an employee pension benefit plan are interested in reducing employee turnover and training costs and in maintaining a stable work force.[32] Where, as under California law, the spouse of a plan participant acquires an enforceable property interest in the participant's prospective pension as soon as the participant earns a single pension credit,[33] an employee who has had his prospective pension benefits cut in half by a divorce decree during the early years of his employment is discouraged from continuing in that employment. By obtaining employment with another employer or in another industry, he can start accruing benefits under another plan free of the decree, and thus obtain greater assurance of an adequate pension when he reaches retirement age. If he is vindictive in nature, he may also be motivated by the opportunity to leave his divorced spouse with an empty bag.

3. Conversely, if the divorce occurs later in the employee's working career, the halving of his prospective pension discourages the employee, even though his efficiency may be on the decline, from retiring and making way for younger workers,[34] to the detriment not only of the employer but also of the other employees participating in the plan. Many pension benefit plans provide for a service pension, which permits an employee to retire at any age with a full pension after 25 or 30 years of credit. The purpose of this provision is to encourage longtime employees to retire and open job opportunities for younger workers—a purpose which is defeated in the case of an employee who has had his pension benefit divided by a divorce decree.

4. When a divorced plan participant remarries, his new spouse acquires an enforceable property interest under California law in his prospective pension as soon as he earns a single pension credit after the remarriage, and this process can continue through successive divorces and remarriages until his retirement or death. Also under California law, the first years of service under a pension plan are given the same weight in the division of pension rights between spouses as later years of service, even where the participant's earnings in the later years are significantly greater than his earnings during the first years.[35]

---

30. Report, p. 118.
31. Report, p. 47.
32. See *Alabama Power Co. v. Davis* (1977) 431 U.S. 581, 594, 97 S.Ct. 2002, 2009.
33. *In re Marriage of Brown* (1976) 15 C.3d 838, 842.
34. See *Alabama Power Co. v. Davis, supra,* note 32.
35. *In re Marriage of Anderson* (1976) 64 C.A.3d 36, 39; *In re Marriage of Judd* (1977) 68 C.A.3d 515, 523.

It has not been unusual for the rate of employer contributions to an employee pension benefit plan to increase over a period of 20 years from 10¢ per hour to $2.00 per hour. If such contributions are to be considered compensation for services rendered by the employee, it seems obvious that a spouse who was married to the employee while his work generated contributions at the rate of $2.00 per hour would be entitled to a greater proportionate share in the employee's pension than a prior spouse who was married to the employee when his work generated contributions at the rate of 10¢ per hour. If the second spouse's marriage to the employee is in turn dissolved, she may well obtain a judgment, decree or order which conflicts with the judgment, decree or order in favor of the first spouse. If the marriage is not dissolved and the second spouse becomes the surviving spouse and the beneficiary of a joint and survivor option, she will doubtless claim her survivor's benefit freed of any interest of the first spouse. In either event, the proposal that the definition and enforcement of the rights of divorcing or divorced spouses in plan benefits be turned over to the individual states will lead to endless litigation and lifelong recrimination between the employee (so long as he survives) and his successive spouses.

Conclusion

What has been said above demonstrates that the matter of defining and enforcing the rights of divorcing and divorced spouses in pension plan benefits presents major policy considerations, the resolution of which should not be left to state legislatures and to state domestic relations courts. The problems involved are not confined to California and the other community property states, but also extend to common-law states, which increasingly are enacting marital property laws patterned after community property laws.[36] In view of the objective of ERISA to secure national uniformity in the regulation of employee benefit plans, Congress alone has the incentive and the ability to evaluate and adjust all of the conflicting interests involved, including the interests of the immediate parties to a marital dissolution proceeding and those of contributing employers, plan participants generally, subsequently acquired spouses of the participant party, the plans and the plan fiduciaries.

Based upon experience in California, such Congressional legislation might well:

a. Limit the interest of a spouse to a community property interest in a vested benefit. This was the California law for more than 17 years and was only changed in 1976.
b. Require that the divorcing spouse's community property interest be satisfied out of other property before resorting to a pension benefit
c. Provide that in the absence of other assets of a participant which would justify a support order, the spouse's interest in the pension shall be in lieu of a support order
d. Provide that the ex-spouse's interest in the pension terminates upon remarriage
e. Impose a statute of limitations upon the assertion by an ex-spouse of a community property interest in a pension
f. Provide that an ex-spouse's interest shall be proportional to the contribution rate in effect when the community was in existence
g. Prohibit joinder of a pension plan as a party to a marriage dissolution proceeding.

Petitions for certiorari have been filed in both the *Stone* and *Kronschnabel* cases seeking plenary review by the United States Supreme Court of the decisions of the court of appeals in those cases. It is vitally important to plan fiduciaries that these petitions be granted, since only the Supreme Court can resolve the uncertainties resulting from those decisions and give the fiduciaries the needed guidance which Congress intended that they should have. Granting of the petitions is of equal importance to the plans and their participants and beneficiaries, since an opinion of the Supreme Court on the merits in these cases will focus the attention of Congress, and all other concerned persons, upon the issues to be resolved in defining the interests, if any, of divorcing or divorced spouses of plan participants in the benefits provided by ERISA plans.

---

36. *See* Prager, "Future Sharing Principles and the Future of Marital Property Law," (1977) 25 U.C.L.A. Rev. 1, 3.

Participation of Owners in Taft-Hartley Funds— The Legal Considerations

BY WARREN H. SALTZMAN and
RICHARD C. JOHNSON

Introduction

The participation of persons with ownership interests in businesses contributing to Taft-Hartley trusts presents problems under three different statutes:
1. Section 501 of the Internal Revenue Code. Section 501 governs the tax exempt status of pension, welfare and group legal trusts.
2. Section 401 of the Internal Revenue Code. Section 401 sets forth the requirements for obtaining favorable tax treatment for pension plans.
3. Section 302 of the Taft-Hartley Act, 29 U.S.C. §186. Section 302 sets forth additional requirements which must be met by a collectively bargained plan if the union is at all involved in its administration. (Plans which are subject to this law are referred to as "Taft-Hartley trusts.")

Each of these three problem areas is discussed in detail below, followed by a discussion of some miscellaneous problems applicable to owner participation.

IRC Section 501

This is the section of the Internal Revenue Code which governs the taxability of income earned by trust funds.

IRC Section 501(a) applies to pension plans. It makes them tax exempt so long as they meet the requirements of Section 401 of the Internal Revenue Code (discussed below). Loss of tax exempt status for a pension plan involves a substantial additional expense which would significantly reduce the benefits the plan could otherwise provide.

Mr. Saltzman is president of Saltzman & Johnson Law Corporation, a San Francisco firm which specializes in Taft-Hartley trust funds in various industries. He received his B.A. degree from the University of California-Berkeley and his LL.B. from the Yale Law School. He was a teaching fellow at Stanford Law School and taught trust law at Golden Gate University School of Law for several years. Mr. Saltzman has spoken at numerous International Foundation educational meetings.

IRC Section 501(c)(9) applies to welfare plans. Under newly issued regulations, participation of owners will not affect the trust's tax exempt status so long as they do not exceed 10% of the total plan participants.[1] These regulations also prohibit eligibility rules which would limit membership or benefits to officers, shareholders or highly compensated employees:

> Eligibility for membership may be restricted by ... objective conditions or limitations reasonably related to employment. ... Any objective criteria used to restrict eligibility for membership or benefits may not, how-

---

Richard C. Johnson is vice president of the Saltzman & Johnson Law Corporation. As one of the principal attorneys for the firm, he shares overall responsibility for providing services to clients in the employee benefits area.

---

1. Regs. §1.501(c)(9)(2)(a) 46 *Federal Register* 1719, January 7, 1981.

ever, be selected or administered in a manner that limits membership or benefits [to a contributing employer's] officers, shareholders or highly compensated employees.... Restrictions or conditions on eligibility for membership or benefits [will generally be considered consistent with these rules if they are determined] through collective bargaining, by trustees designated pursuant to a collective bargaining agreement, or by the collective bargaining agents of the members . . .

Thus, although these proposed regulations apply a "discrimination" rule similar to the one discussed below in connection with IRC §401, discrimination will generally not be found to result from rules adopted by a Taft-Hartley trust. Nevertheless, it may be advisable to minimize any possible discrimination argument by adopting eligibility rules along the same lines recommended below at the end of the discussion of the Section 401 discrimination problem.

If the requirements of §501(c)(9) are not met, the tax would only be levied on net income from trust reserves, i.e., gross earnings reduced by plan expenses and perhaps even by benefits paid. Therefore, the amount of the tax would not be likely to affect the trust's ability to pay plan benefits.

IRC Section 501(c)(20) applies to group legal plans. It states that they are tax exempt so long as they meet the requirements of IRC Section 120. Section 120 permits owners to participate so long as no more than 25% of all participants are owners who (with their families) own more than 5% of the business. Section 120 also requires that a group legal plan not discriminate in favor of owners, officers and highly compensated personnel—a provision which, like the one discussed above, parallels Section 401's prohibition of discrimination in pension plans.

IRC Section 401

This provision of the law applies only to pension plans (including both defined benefit and defined contribution plans) but, as noted above, the philosophy of its non-discrimination requirements have been read into the requirements which must be met by welfare and group legal plans if they are to receive tax exempt status. Pension plans which meet Section 401's requirements receive the following tax advantages, without the first three of which the typical Taft-Hartley pension plan could not exist:

- Current deductibility of employer contributions (IRC §404)
- No current taxation to employees of sums contributed for them (IRC §402)
- Tax free accumulation of income [IRC §501(a)]
- Exemption from federal estate tax of distributions to beneficiaries (other than lump sum distributions) [IRC §2039(c)].

IRC §401(a) requires that a qualified plan be for the "exclusive benefit of the employees and their beneficiaries." As explained in more detail below, the practical result of this requirement on owner participation in a Taft-Hartley pension trust is clear: (1) Persons owning more than 10% of an *un*incorporated business *can't* participate; (2) shareholder-owners of regular corporations (and shareholders of Subchapter S corporations who own 5% or less of the stock) *can* participate even if they own 100% of the business; and (3) persons owning 10% or less of an unincorporated business and shareholders of a Subchapter S corporation who own more than 5% of the stock *may be* permitted to participate if the trust adopts special rules (which are particularly complex for defined benefit plans). However, for the reasons set forth below, owners who cannot participate (whether because it would violate the law or because the plan does not permit such participation) may nevertheless be able to continue to vest in benefits accrued while in the bargaining unit.

Unincorporated Owners and Shareholders of Subchapter S Corporations

A fundamental problem for both defined benefit and defined contribution plans is being able to meet the requirements of IRC §401(d), which applies to plans covering "owner-employees." "Owner-employees" are sole proprietors or partners owning more than a 10% interest in the business. The rules of Code Section 401(d) are practically impossible for Taft-Hartley retirement plans of any type to meet, so they should not permit unincorporated owners owning more than a 10% interest of the business to participate.[2]

---

2. It should be noted that a defined contribution plan that does not cover any partner owning more than 10% of the business need not comply with either §401(d) or §401(j). Therefore, under the Internal Revenue Code, such a plan could cover partners owning 10% or less of a business if it meets the requirements of Code Section 401(a)(9) (distributions to such partners must begin by age 70½ whether or not they are still working) and Code Section 401(c)(17) (limiting their annual compensation taken into account under the plan to $100,000).

Furthermore, IRC §401(a)(18), combined with the other Code sections referred to therein, provides that unincorporated owners (no matter how small their ownership interest) and shareholders of Subchapter S corporations who own more than 5% of the stock of the corporation cannot participate in a *defined benefit* pension trust unless various special requirements of the law set forth in IRC §401(j) and Regs. §1.401-11 are complied with. Compliance with these requirements is administratively difficult for Taft-Hartley defined benefit pension plans. The full extent of such difficulty will not be known until regulations are issued under Internal Revenue Code §401(j).

Incorporated Owners (Other Than Subchapter S)

General Rule. For purposes of the Internal Revenue Code, individuals who are employed by a regular corporation are all considered "employees," no matter how much stock they may own. Therefore, shareholder participation is not prohibited by §401's requirement that a pension plan be for the "exclusive benefit of [the employer's] employees or their beneficiaries."

Discrimination Problem. The only potential problem arising under Section 401 with respect to the coverage of corporate shareholders (except for the "Subchapter S" problem mentioned above) is the possibility that their participation may violate the statutory prohibition in Section 401 against discrimination in favor of shareholders, officers and highly compensated personnel. For example, if the owner participates without including his other non-bargaining unit employees, there may be discrimination in favor of the owner in relation to those other employees. This danger can probably be avoided by not permitting owners to participate as such, but instead permitting participation only on behalf of *all* those employees of contributing employers outside the bargaining unit who fall within a non-discriminatory classification—e.g., permitting their participation only if they perform bargaining unit work or were participants in the plan prior to leaving the bargaining unit. Allowing participation by corporate owners who have never done bargaining unit work would be inadvisable from this standpoint.

(Since discrimination also presents problems for group legal plans and welfare plans, as discussed above, it is similarly advisable that such plans permit owners to participate only insofar as they are part of a non-discriminatory classification of eligible participants.)

Vesting Problem. The question here is whether the plan can permit participants to count time worked as unincorporated owners toward any minimum eligibility requirements for participation or—more importantly—toward the vesting of whatever benefits they may have accrued while working under the bargaining unit. The plan is certainly not required to credit such time (unless the contiguous non-covered service rules discussed below require it to do so), but it may wish to do so. The law on this point is not yet settled. The Internal Revenue Service used to hold that vesting was a form of benefit and therefore could not be given for time worked as an unincorporated owner, but it appears that the IRS's position may have changed in light of Code Section 414(a), which provides that certain service with predecessor employers must be counted as service by a current employer. There is no problem in giving such credit for periods during which an owner was incorporated, so long as no "discrimination" is involved.

Section 203(b)(1) of ERISA, as interpreted by Regs. §2530.210(c), requires Taft-Hartley trusts to give vesting credit for "contiguous non-covered service"; the same rule appears in IRC §411(a)(4) and Regs. §1.411(a)-5(b)(3)(iv)(C). These rules arguably *require* that eligibility and vesting credit be given for certain periods of ownership—e.g., where the period of time as an owner directly precedes or follows time spent in the bargaining unit with the same employer.

Taft-Hartley Section 302, 29 U.S.C. §186

General Rule

This is the provision of the law whose applicability to owner participation has been the most confusing. Section 302 of Taft-Hartley is a statute originally designed to prevent payment of bribes by employers to union representatives. The history of this statute and its purposes are summarized in *Blassie v. Kroger* (footnote 5).

Section 302 makes unlawful any type of payment from an employer to a union representative unless certain specified requirements are met. It should be noted that Section 302 applies to all kinds of trusts referred to therein—pension plans, vacation plans, health care plans, group legal plans,

---

Such a plan could also cover shareholders of a Subchapter S corporation who own more than 5% of the corporation's stock if it complies with Code Section 401(c)(17); if it is a profit sharing plan, it must also comply with Code Section 1379(a) (restricting allocations of forfeitures to shareholder-employees).

etc. It also should be noted that Section 302 will not apply at all if union representatives have no role in the administration of the plan—as might be the case, for example, where the collective bargaining contract simply requires employers to send their money to insurance companies or service organizations which in turn provide the benefits specified in the bargaining agreement.

Sole and Exclusive Benefit of Employees Rule

Although payments to a trust fund in whose administration union representatives have any role is prohibited by Section 302, there is an exception in §302(c)(5) [29 U.S.C. §186(c)(5)] for payments to funds which are jointly administered and meet certain other specified requirements. One of these other requirements is that the trust must be for the "sole and exclusive benefit of the employees of such employers and their families and dependents." Again, then, the question is whether or not owners are "employees."

Section 302 does not contain its own definition of the word "employee," but when the Taft-Hartley Act was amended in 1947 (which is when Section 302 first appeared) a new Section 501(3)[3] stated that "employee" would have the same meaning under the amended act as it had in the National Labor Relations Act prior to its amendment by Taft-Hartley. This picked up the definition of employee in Section 2(3) of the original law—29 U.S.C. §152(3)—which states that

> the term "employee" shall include any employee . . . but shall not include any individual . . . employed by his parent or spouse, or any individual having the status of independent contractor or any individual employed as a supervisor. . . .

There is no question but that this definition is significant in deciding who is entitled to vote in a representation election, and most of the cases interpreting this definition arise in the context of such elections. However, other cases indicate that the definition cannot be applied strictly to all areas of Taft-Hartley. For example, there are cases which hold that, despite the clear statutory language in the definition, an owner's spouse and children who work for the owner can vote in representation elections under certain circumstances.[4] Supervisors have also had their participation in Taft-Hartley trusts approved despite the fact that they too are not considered "employees" under the above-quoted definition, as have other non-bargaining unit employees such as trust fund employees and retired employees.[5]

Another case indicating that the statutory definition of "employee" may have no relevance to Taft-Hartley trusts is *Allied Chemical and Alkali Workers v. Pittsburgh Plate Glass Co.*, 404 U.S. 157 (1971). Here the United States Supreme Court held that although retired personnel could not be considered "employees" under 29 U.S.C. §152(3), and therefore their interests were not the subject of mandatory collective bargaining, they could nevertheless still be "employees" for purposes of Section 302 and participate in a collectively bargained pension plan. Notice, however, that this case involved individuals who were former bargaining unit members and were never owners, as is the case with several of the other decisions which suggest that the statutory definition should not be read literally into Section 302.

The argument that stockholders are not "employees" and therefore cannot participate in a Section 302 trust stems primarily from NLRB cases involving representation elections.[6] In the

---

3. This Section 501(3) was never codified in 29 U.S. Code, presumably because those responsible for codification thought it unnecessary. This has led to confusion in the cases, since the definition it picks up, which appears at 29 U.S.C. 152(3), states that it applies only for purposes of Subchapter II, whereas Section 302 appears in Subchapter IV. The *Brauer* case (*see* footnote 8) concluded that this definition applied without attempting to explain why the limitation to Subchapter II should be ignored. Although the court in the *Waggoner* case (*see* footnote 9) correctly noted that *Brauer* was wrong in ignoring this limiting language, the *Waggoner* court in turn was apparently unaware of the uncodified language of Section 502(3) of the original Taft-Hartley Act which does, indeed, make the definition in 29 U.S.C. §152(3) applicable.

4. *See*, for example, *NLRB v. Caravelle Wood Products, Inc.*, 466 F.2d 675 (7th Cir. 1972) and *Cerni Motor Sales*, 201 N.L.R.B. 133 (1973).

5. *Blassie v. Kroger Co.*, 345 F.2d 58 (8th Cir. 1965); *Moglia v. Geoghegan*, 403 F.2d 110 (2d Cir. 1968), *cert. denied* 394 U.S. 919; *Reiherzer v. Shannon, infra,* footnote 11.

6. Key cases in chronological order are *Cherrin Corp. v. NLRB*, 349 F.2d 1001 (6th Cir. 1965); *Foam Rubber City No. 2,* 167 N.L.R.B. 81 (1967); *Lake City Foundry Co. v. NLRB*, 432 F.2d 1162 (7th Cir. 1970); *NLRB v. Caravelle Wood Products, Inc.*, 466 F.2d 675 (7th Cir. 1972); *Cerni Motor Sales,* 201 N.L.R.B. 133 (1973); *NLRB v. Wood Products, Inc.*, 504 F.2d 1181 (7th Cir. 1974); *Weyerhauser Company*, 211 N.L.R.B. 140 (1974); *Toyota Midtown, Inc.*, 233 N.L.R.B. 106 (1977); *Webco Bodies, Inc.,* 237 N.L.R.B. 192 (1978); *Tops Club, Inc.,* 238 N.L.R.B. 130 (1978); *Hoalthouse Furniture Corp.,* 249 N.L.R.B. 58 (1979).

earlier cases, the Board took the position that any stockholder/employee who had a "substantial" stock interest was not an "employee" under 29 U.S.C. §152(3), and for that reason could not vote in a representation election. The Seventh Circuit, however, consistently rejected this view, holding that stockholder-employees might be excluded from representation elections on other theories, but that there was no basis for holding that they were not as much "employees" as any other employees of the corporation.[7] The Board's most recent statement on this point appears in the *Webco* case (*see* footnote 6), which indicates that the Board is unlikely to exclude stockholders as such, but will instead rely on other available theories to keep them from participating in representation elections. Even in the *Webco* case the Board clearly indicated that it would not, in any event, automatically conclude that a stockholder owning less than 50% of the stock is not an "employee."

The only court case specifically stating that a 50% stockholder is not an "employee" under Section 302 and is therefore not eligible to participate in a Taft-Hartley trust is the recent California case of *Brauer v. Sheet Metal Workers*.[8] The court in that case relied primarily on the earlier NLRB *Foam City Rubber* case (*see* footnote 6), whose theory had been rejected by federal circuit courts and is only barely alive even with the NLRB. In *Waggoner v. Skytt*,[9] another California court specifically disapproved *Brauer*, relying in part on the erroneous conclusion that the statutory definition of employee in U.S.C. §152(3) does not apply to Section 302.[10]

The best-reasoned cases, and the ones which are most likely to eventually prevail, are *Sanchez v. Trustees of the Pension Plan, et al.* and *Reiherzer v. Shannon*.[11] These cases specifically held that Section 302 does not prohibit participation by a stockholder-employee. However, when it comes to unincorporated owners, all reported cases hold that Section 302 prohibits their participation.[12] *Aitken v. IP&GCU-Employees Retirement Fund*[13] sets forth as dicta compelling reasons why Section 302 need not have been interpreted to prohibit participation by unincorporated owners; however, this issue is not particularly significant for pension plans because of the Internal Revenue Code problems which participation of unincorporated owners would present.

Trustees' Discretion and Written Agreement Requirement

Whether or not it is legally permissible for owners to participate in Taft-Hartley trusts, the law is certainly clear that the trustees have discretion as to whether or not to allow persons who are excluded from the bargaining unit to participate, and the trustees' decision on this point will be upheld by the courts.[14] Some of the cases make it clear that even when there are allegations that union business representatives, or even trustees or their agents, told the individuals that their participation was permissible (when in fact it was not), it would be a violation of Section 302 to pay the benefits;[15] the rationale is that Section 302 requires that the contributions be subject to a "written agreement," so if the only applicable written agreement (e.g., the plan or trust agreement) prohibits participation by owners, the trustees have no authority to pay them benefits.

Miscellaneous

Return of Contributions

Until the advent of ERISA, it was at least possible to return contributions improperly paid by owners, but Section 403(c)(2) of ERISA as originally enacted prohibited the return of contributions

---

7. *Lake City Foundry Co. v. NLRB*, 432 F.2d 1162 (7th Cir., 1970); *NLRB v. Caravelle Wood Products, Inc.*, 466 F.2d 675 (7th Cir., 1972).

8. 146 Cal. Reporter 844 (1978), *cert. denied*, 99 S.Ct. 1033 (1979).

9. *Waggoner v. Skytt* (Partial Summary Judgment, U.S.D.C., Central District of California; Case No. CV 77-1550-AMT, August 30, 1979); published in BNA *Pension Reporter* of December 17, 1979, at page D-2.

10. *See* footnote 3.

11. *Sanchez v. Trustees of the Pension Plan*, 353 So.2d 327 (La. Sup. Ct., 1978); *Reiherzer v. Shannon*, (581 F.2d 1266 7th Cir., 1978). See also *Rockey v. Western Conference of Teamsters*, 595 P.2d 557 (Wash. Ct. of App., 1979).

12. *Melang v. I.B.E.W. Pacific Coast Pension Fund*, 93 L.R.R.M. 2389 (Western District Wash. 1976); *Dohrer v. Wakeman*, 14 Wash. App. 157, 539 P.2d 91 (1975); *Martin v. Hamil*, 608 F.2d 225 (7th Cir. 1979); and *Reiherzer v. Shannon, supra*.

13. 604 F.2d 1261 (9th Cir. 1979).

14. See *Martin v. Hamil*, footnote 12; *Bacon v. Wong*, 445 F.Supp. 1189 (U.S.D.C. N.D. Cal. 1978); and *Wong v. Bacon*, 445 F.Supp. 1177 (U.S.D.C. N.D. Cal. 1977); *Central States Southeast and Southwest Areas Pension Fund, et al. v. Wholesale Produce Supply*, 478 F.Supp. 884 (U.S.D.C. Minn. 1979), *aff'd*. 611 F.2d 694 (8th Cir. 1979); *Thurber v. Western Conference of Teamsters Pension Plan*, 542 F.2d 1100 (9th Cir. 1976) and the *Aitken* case referred to above at footnote 13.

15. *See* the following cases: *Thurber* (footnote 14); *Aitken* (footnote 13); *Moglia* (footnote 5). See also *Phillip v. Kennedy*, 542 F.2d 52, 55 n.8, (8th Cir., 1976). *See also* the *Blassie* case at footnote 5.

to employers. An exception was made for contributions made as a result of a "mistake of fact"; these could be returned within one year after the mistaken contributions were made.

In interpreting this provision of ERISA, the courts consistently held that contributions made by owners under the mistaken belief that they were permitted to participate were made under a "mistake of law," so that any such contributions made after ERISA became effective could not be returned at all.[16] This harsh rule was amended as part of the Multiemployer Pension Plan Amendments Act of 1980,[17] so that any kind of mistaken contribution to a multiemployer plan can now be returned within six months after the mistake is discovered; a special provision in the amending law gave all plans until March 26, 1981, to return mistaken contributions whose return was prohibited before the amendment. (Welfare plans may not want to return contributions improperly made by owners if they have provided insurance coverage for the period for which the contributions were received, whether or not the coverage actually resulted in the payment of dollar benefits; in such cases, the welfare plan should also consider seeking the return of any benefits paid in excess of the contributions received.)

Dangers If Participation Unlawful

It appears highly unlikely that the case law relating to Section 302 of Taft-Hartley will develop so as to prohibit the participation of stockholder-employees in Taft-Hartley trusts. Even if such a development occurs, the trustees probably need fear nothing more than a cease and desist order prohibiting such participation.

Permitting participation by even 10% owners of unincorporated businesses presents a different problem. Their participation should never be permitted by pension plans, for the reasons set forth above relating to Internal Revenue Code problems. So far as welfare plans are concerned, even if the Internal Revenue Code presents no problem, most cases still indicate that participation by unincorporated owners in any Taft-Hartley trust would violate Taft-Hartley Section 302. Again, however, there is little danger to the trustees other than a cease and desist order. It would be very difficult to establish any monetary damage to the welfare plan, since premiums would have been received for the coverage provided, and criminal sanctions would certainly be inappropriate in the absence of highly unusual circumstances.[18]

There is, however, a potential danger for unincorporated owners who contribute to a welfare plan. If their participation is ever successfully challenged, the plan may be unable either to reimburse them for incurred claims or to refund their contributions, and/or they may have become uninsurable; thus they would have been better off had they previously obtained other health insurance coverage. (The same danger exists when owner-participants lose coverage for *any* reason, except to the extent that the plan allows them extended self-coverage.)

Summary and Conclusions

1. Because of both the tax laws and the labor laws, it generally will not be advisable or practical for a Taft-Hartley pension trust to permit participation by unincorporated owners. Welfare trusts and group legal trusts can permit unincorporated owners to participate, provided the non-discrimination requirements of IRCS 501 are met, subject to the dangers just mentioned in the event that the Taft-Hartley Act should ever be interpreted to prohibit their participation under Section 302.

2. Participation of stockholder-employees should present no problem (except for the Subchapter S shareholder as mentioned above), but care must be taken to avoid any possible discrimination of the type prohibited by the Internal Revenue Code.

3. Whenever owner participation is to be allowed, it is essential that the language of the plan clearly permit such participation, since benefits cannot be paid to individuals whose participation is not permitted by the terms of the plan itself. In addition, the eligibility requirements for owner participation should be reviewed to be sure they meet the legal requirements described above.

4. Since the participation of owners in Taft-Hartley trusts presents practical as well as legal problems (*see* Mr. Davidson's article, which follows), it is the authors' recommendation that plans which do not presently give owners the right to participate continue to not do so, and that plans which presently permit owner participation should not extend this right beyond what their plans have historically provided.

---

16. *See*, e.g., *Martin v. Hamil* at footnote 12.
17. Act Section 410, amending ERISA §403(c) and IRC §401(a)(2).
18. Plans which want to be absolutely safe often experience-rate the non-bargaining group separately and set its premiums in accordance with its own experience; but this approach may not be practical if the group is small (or becomes small through attrition), since the premiums on a separately experienced basis may become too high for anyone to afford.

Participation of Owners in Taft-Hartley Trusts— The Administrative Considerations

BY PHIL E. DAVIDSON

THE DECISION as to whether or not a multi-employer pension or health and welfare trust is going to allow participation by owners or other non-bargaining employees should not be taken lightly. In addition to the legal aspects discussed in Mr. Saltzman's article, there are administrative implications and possible cost considerations involved in this decision.

Documentation Needed

If trustees decide to allow this kind of participation, first the trust and the plan document both have to specifically allow for it. Second, and very important, is that a subscription or participation agreement is necessary if the trustees are going to allow participation by employees not covered by a bargaining agreement. In a typical trust, all employers that contribute on behalf of their bargaining unit employees are signatory to a bargaining agreement covering those employees. In lieu of the bargaining agreement that would normally exist, the trust fund would have them sign a subscription agreement. Such a written agreement is necessary to comply with Section 302 of the Taft-Hartley Act. Further, it is an effective way for the trustees to establish the ground rules for the participation by employers for employees other than those covered by a bargaining agreement.

Some of the ground rules that need to be specified in the subscription agreement would be, first of all, that the employer would agree to be bound by the terms of the plan and the trust agreement for those particular employees. Second, the trustees would want to describe the basis on which contributions are going to be made by that employer to the trust; for example, on an hourly or a monthly flat rate basis. Third, the subscription agreement should indicate who must participate in the plan. For example, the trustees may wish to require for employees of a corporation that all non-bargaining employees of that corporation must participate.

Mr. Davidson is an account executive for Martin E. Segal Company, with responsibility for designing and maintaining health and welfare, pension, annuity and SUB plans. Previously, he served as a group sales representative for Pacific Mutual Life Insurance Co. Mr. Davidson received his B.A. degree in political science from Arizona State University and has done graduate work in business administration at Arizona State University.

For pension plans, it is important to require participation for at least as long as that employer is signatory to a collective bargaining agreement which requires him to contribute for his bargaining unit employees.

Who Should Be Allowed to Participate?

Health and Welfare Plans

One of the first questions to be addressed in making the decision to allow participation by other than bargaining unit employees concerns who should be allowed to participate in the plan. For health and welfare plans, from a legal standpoint there are no particular problems in allowing either owner-operators or other non-bargaining employees of a corporation (including the stockholders of that corporation) to participate. This coverage is quite commonly allowed in Taft-Hartley trusts. From an administrative and benefit standpoint, however, there can be some additional costs involved. Administratively, the trustees have to set up policing procedures so they know who these participants are. From a benefit cost standpoint, there is always the possibility that there could be some selection against the plan. This is one of the major areas of concern in allowing the participation of non-bargaining unit employees, in that the trustees have to be aware that there is the possibility of abuse or selection against the plan unless the proper controls are established.

Pension Plans

The question of who should be allowed to participate in pension plans is more complex. First, participation should definitely not be allowed for *sole proprietors or owner-operators*. It can be allowed for *partners* if it is limited to those partners that own 10% or less of the business. If partners are allowed to participate in a pension plan, it is probably a good idea to require, as part of the subscription agreement, a certified list from that partnership specifying by name who the partners are and what percent of the business they own. Although it is difficult to police, many funds go one step further and, in addition to applying the required 10% rule, they only allow partners to participate if the partners are working under the bargaining agreement.

For *employees of corporations* (including stockholders) there are no particular problems in allowing coverage in a pension plan other than avoiding discrimination under the Internal Revenue Code. If discrimination is present, it can not only affect the employer but also can cause problems for the fund. Ideally, in order to avoid this discrimination problem, the trustees should require that all non-bargaining unit employees of a corporation participate in the plan. This is not always practical, however, and it is probably not fair to either the lower-paid employees or the employer. First, it is expensive for the employer to contribute at the same hourly rate for his lower-paid, perhaps clerical, employees as he does for his bargaining unit employees. In addition, many of those employees will not stay around long enough to vest, since many multiemployer pension plans use the ten year cliff vesting rule. To require participation on behalf of those employees by an employer is probably not fair to the employees, since they would be much better off if their employer established an IRA for them.

Some funds that do allow participation by corporate employees limit such participation to those employees in the corporation that do bargaining unit work. Another way to do it is to establish a different schedule of benefits and contribution rates for those lower-paid employees which is more related to their wages or salaries. This can become a little complicated, and therefore an administrative burden; but, as an example, if the contribution rate for the bargaining unit employees is $1.00 per hour, the trustees could establish a sliding contribution and benefit schedule for all other employees that relates their annual income to that of a steadily employed bargaining unit employee. Under this approach, the contribution rate for a clerical employee could be at the 20-30¢/hour level, with benefits appropriately reduced from the bargaining unit employee level.

How to Charge for Coverage

The next question to be addressed by trustees is how to charge for coverage. In a health and welfare plan, the most common way to charge non-bargaining employees of a corporation is a flat monthly rate. This "flat rate" is simply the cost of the benefits, whether insured or self-insured, plus a charge to cover the cost of administration. Coverage usually is provided only on a month-to-month basis, with no provision for an hour bank reserve. Since these employees usually work on a different basis than most bargaining unit employees, it is not necessary to have the same eligibility rules as you would for bargaining unit employees. For owner-operators or others that work under the bargaining agreement, it is more common to charge for coverage on an hourly basis, the same as with regular bargaining unit employees. If this is the method used, the subscription agreement should specify that the actual number of hours worked are to be reported. Whether or not a fund allows an hour bank under this kind of arrangement is generally a policy matter for the trustees.

The actual benefit and administrative costs for owner-operators or other non-bargaining employees can either be pooled with the regular group of bargaining unit employees, or an attempt can be made to determine these costs separately. Overall, however, pooling is usually more common, since it is certainly easier. In some situations, a particular board of trustees may feel that there could be specific identifiable additional costs for allowing participation by non-bargaining employees, and therefore may want to set up a separate rating arrangement. This certainly can be done where warranted, and where it is relatively easy to determine the additional costs.

In many multiemployer pension plans, benefit

and vesting credit are granted on the basis of some unit of work. For example, in the construction industry, credit is generally based on hours of work. Therefore, for ease of including non-bargaining unit personnel, trusts are generally better off to grant their credit and base their contributions on the same unit of work. To do otherwise can create administrative complications for the plan. If coverage is allowed only for those that do bargaining unit work, the fund can use the actual hours of work. If coverage is extended to all non-bargaining employees in a corporation, then the fund might want to use a specific number of hours, which should be specified in the subscription agreement.

Special Rules

Participation and Enrollment

Next, the trustees should consider some special rules to help prevent selection against the plan (health and welfare or pension). One of the most important rules is to require a specified time for allowing participation: i.e., sort of an open enrollment period. What can be done here is to send out a notice to all contributing employers advising them that coverage will be allowed for non-bargaining unit employees and requiring participation by a certain date. Accompanying the notice should be a sample subscription agreement, a copy of the trust agreement and a copy of the plan. What the trustees do *not* want to do is allow owner-operators or other non-bargaining employees to come into the plan, withdraw from the plan and come back in, which is where abuses can occur. If the trustees do want to allow people to come back into a health and welfare plan after they have withdrawn, the fund should require some sort of evidence of insurability.

Another thing the trust should have is a strongly enforced delinquency rule, tied to an active payroll audit program. The payroll audit program provides the necessary policing to help prevent abuse, first by ensuring that coverage is only provided to those people that the plan allows for, and second, by ensuring that all people in a particular group who are required to be covered are, in fact, being covered.

Withdrawal of Employer

As indicated earlier, one of the main problems in allowing non-bargaining unit participation concerns withdrawal by an employer of these employees. In a pension plan, this can present particular problems in the area of past service credit that the trustees may have granted. To help solve this problem, some plans provide that if employers withdraw their non-bargaining employees, the plan will cancel all past service credit previously granted to those employees. Another method, which is a bit more complicated, is to provide for lower benefits for those non-bargaining employees that have been withdrawn from the plan. This could be tied to an age or service requirement; for example, if they are above a certain age they are given a lower benefit, or if they have not met a certain participation or service requirement they are given a lower benefit. In any event, it is important to have some restrictions for those employees that might be withdrawn from the plan.

Written Notice

One final point, which could be helpful in avoiding communication problems in the future, is to advise all contributing employers, either annually or on some other regular basis, exactly what the rules are for participation in the plan. This can be done whether or not the fund allows participation for any non-bargaining employees. The administrative or fund office knows who the contributing employers are, and these notices can be included with the monthly reporting forms. A regular notice specifically advising all employers that contribute to the plan as to exactly what is and what is not allowed should help protect the fund if disputes arise later.

When the IRS Knocks: The TCMP Audit Program

BY LEO BROWN

Introduction

The Internal Revenue Service has begun an intensive 22 month audit of 22,500 employee benefit plans under its Taxpayer Compliance Measurement Program (TCMP). This is the first time that the IRS is auditing employee benefit plans on such a comprehensive scale. For example, while the usual IRS audit is limited to time and issues which the agent is permitted to examine, the TCMP audit has no time constraints and is all-inclusive.

The TCMP, which has traditionally been used in connection with income tax audits, is being applied for the first time to employee benefit plans. It is used both as an enforcement and long range research program tool for the measurement and evaluation of compliance by employee benefit plans and gaps in their administration. These data will be used to identify areas of non-compliance and to provide an objective basis for planning the Employee Plans Examination Program.

Examinations will concentrate heavily on the effects of the plan in operation along with a review of plan document provisions—notwithstanding that the plan in question may have obtained a favorable IRS determination letter. The audit will be thorough and involve the collection of comprehensive plan data on Form 6080, the TCMP Employee Plans Examination Document—an eight page, 313 question form that must be completed by the IRS examiner. For example, the form requires an examination of return data on Form 5500; a review of service crediting procedures, vesting, accruals, discrimination, integration and funding methods and how they have been working in operation; prohibited transaction findings and related/delinquent returns. A detailed overview of Form 6080 is included in the Appendix to this article.

Reprinted from *Pension World* July and August 1980. Copyright 1980. All rights reserved. Printed in U.S.A. Communication Channels, Inc., 6285 Barfield Road, Atlanta, Georgia 30328.

Mr. Brown is an employee benefits consultant (legal assistant) with the law firm of Vedder, Price, Kaufman, Kammholz & Day in New York and Washington, D.C., and Vedder, Price, Kaufman & Kammholz in Chicago. He was formerly with the management consulting firm of Towers, Perrin, Forster & Crosby, Inc., and chief of the Pension Trust Group of the Manhattan district office of the Internal Revenue Service in New York. He began his IRS service as an Internal Revenue agent in 1946 and became an IRS pension trust specialist in 1953. Mr. Brown was a member of the faculty of the Graduate School of Business of Pace University in New York where he taught courses in executive compensation, pensions and employee benefits. He has lectured at the New York University Annual Institute on Federal Taxation, Practising Law Institute, Pension & Welfare News Conference, Tax Executive Institute and many other professional income tax and pension trust forums. He has co-authored two folios for the American Law Institute-American Bar Association Pension and Profit-Sharing Plans and is the senior editor of the ERISA Source Manual, *a publication of the Law Journal Seminars-Press. In addition, he has edited* Employee Benefits Law—ERISA and Beyond *by J. D. Mamorsky, Esq., and several other books and publications.*

In most instances, the IRS will be examining employers who have received advance favorable determination letters stating that their plans of deferred compensation are qualified under IRC

§401(a). The TCMP audit program is designed to help the Employee Plans Specialist uncover developments that have taken place in operation which adversely affect the qualified status of the employer's plan and/or trust. The situations which will most likely confront the Specialist during the course of the examination are reviewed below.*

Coverage

Every plan approved under IRC §401(a) must contain adequate provisions to ensure that nondiscriminatory eligibility requirements are met. The employment records of the adopting employer will be test-checked to see if the coverage approved in the plan instrument is being followed in operation and continues to meet the statutory requirements. For example, the Specialist will analyze the payroll records to ascertain whether the employees excluded by the employer as having less than the definitions set forth in the statute and regulations and whether those excluded by reason of length of service did not, in fact, meet the service time requirement stipulated in the plan.

Plans which were initially qualified on the basis that coverage thereunder met the classification requirements imposed by IRC §401(b)(1)(B) will be given particular attention. In many instances, minor operational changes such as number of employees covered, compensation levels, unionization, and other pertinent factors can easily upset the qualified status of such plans. For example, a salaried-only plan may have been approved on the basis that the compensation of the salaried participants was substantially the same as that of the excluded employees and that the plan coverage included employees in all compensation ranges. However, personnel changes may have occurred in operation which considerably alter the coverage picture, such as promotions, disproportionate increases in compensation, employee cutbacks, sale of a division, transfer between parent and subsidiary, and interdepartmental transfers.

Finally, the coverage trend in all contributory deferred compensation plans will be particularly analyzed to determine if the lower-paid employees are being kept out of the plan because of the mandatory contribution requirement. If such exclusions are occurring in operation, and it is determined that the situation is being caused by the required contribution being burdensome to the rank and file employees, the plan may lose its qualified status.

---

* These examples are taken from the *IRS Employee Plans Audit Guidelines Handbook.*

Omission of Eligible Employees

1. Varied corporate enterprises. Corporations are frequently engaged in a variety of activities. The employees who operate such activities are all employees of the corporation and must be considered for coverage purposes. In many instances, the payroll records of these employees are located at different sites, and the employer could easily omit eligible employees from participation. The Specialist will be particularly alert for such omissions.

2. Are they really self-employed? Many employers, in an effort to avoid the expense and responsibility of paying FICA and withholding tax on wages paid to their employees, will require them to sign an employment agreement of some kind which states that they are self-employed individuals. Furthermore, since these workers are labeled by the employer as self-employed, they are excluded from consideration for plan qualification purposes, a fact unknown by the IRS at the time the determination letter was issued. A contractual arrangement is not determinative of the employer-employee relationship where the realities of the situation conflict with the terms of the contract. If the Specialist determines that a taxpayer has gained a coverage advantage using such deceptive devices, disqualification of the plan and trust may be in order.

3. Who is the employer? Employer A may physically transfer his employees to Employer B pursuant to a contract but continue to exercise control and supervision over the employees transferred. Under these circumstances, Employer A is still the employer, and the transferred employees must be considered when determining whether his plan meets the coverage requirements of qualification.

4. Is the plan being followed? These are situations where the plan instrument provides for coverage of all employees and the favorable determination letter was issued on that basis. In operation, however, only salaried employees or some other limited group were actually being included.

Inclusion of Ineligible Employees

The IRS examiner is attentive to situations where ineligible employees are included as plan participants for reasons which are to the advantage of the employer. For example, frequently an attorney, accountant, or other professional persons will perform services for the employer on an annual fee basis, but the employer does not direct and control their activities with respect to such services. These persons are not common-law employees and are not eligible to participate in the employer's plan. The employer, however, may have made a deal to include a professional in the plan for obvious tax advantages in exchange for a reduction in fee or other consideration. The names of such professionals may be obtained from statements, letterheads, legal documents, job descriptions, interviews with the plan sponsor, etc., for comparison with payroll records or the plan participants list.

Persons who serve the employer only as outside non-employee members of the board of directors are not common-law employees and, therefore, are not eligible for plan participation. However, these persons are usually very powerful and influential individuals and, for this reason, it is not uncommon to find them included in the plan on the basis of the director's fees received.

A retired executive may have terminated employment and enjoyed the advantages of a lump sum distribution only to return to render part-time consulting services for the same employer. The fees paid for such services do not constitute wages and, therefore, such individuals may not again participate in the plan.

The IRS examiner will also be alert in identifying relatives of the officers and shareholders who appear on the list of plan participants. There have been instances where parents, sons, daughters and wives of the key personnel, though they perform no services whatsoever for the employer, are paid a salary and are covered under the plan.

Slow Vesting—High Turnover

Careful attention will be given to determine if the facts indicate that only the prohibited group will ever receive a benefit because of turnover of the rank and file participants. Indications of rapid employee turnover can be readily determined from analysis of the employee participation list, and evidence that the rank and file employees have or have not received benefits from the plan upon severance of employment can be ascertained from an audit of the trust's distribution records and/or the employer's records of plan operation.

Imputed Compensation

In reconciling non-deferred compensation paid or accrued for all employees under the plan with the records of the employer, the Specialist will be alert for imputed compensation included in the total. Inasmuch as imputed compensation is not consistently and uniformly applicable to all employees under the plan, discrimination may arise.

Money Purchase Pension Plans

1. Weighted formulas. Money purchase pension plans which contain a benefit formula weighted on the basis of years of service as well as compensation can become discriminatory in operation if the service factor operates to favor the prohibited employees. Therefore, the Employee Plans Specialist will test the current year under examination for evidence of such discrimination by comparing the ratio of benefits to compensation for each employee group. (*See* Rev. Ruls. 68-652, 653 and 654.)

2. Manipulation of compensation. The dollar amount of compensation upon which the annual contribution rate is applied is sometimes manipulated in order to provide the principal employees with a greater benefit. One of the more common methods used involves the application of the contribution rate to annual compensation in effect on the last day of the year or some other specified time. In this manner, an executive who earns $50,000 per year can be paid at the rate of $10,000 for the month of December, which is annualized to $120,000 for contribution purposes. The Specialist can detect these maneuvers by comparing the payroll records with those used in computing the amount of annual contribution to the pension plan.

3. Allocation of forfeitures. Despite the fact that it is prohibited by the plan, some employers allocate the forfeitures generated in their money purchase pension plans to the accounts of the participants. In most instances, this occurs where the employer has both a pension and a profit-sharing plan, since allocation of forfeitures is permitted in a profit-sharing plan.

Profit-Sharing Plans

1. Are contributions allocated according to plan formula? (a) If the formula is based on allocating contributions in proportion to compensation, the Specialist will test-check the allocations made to ensure that the plan instrument complies in operation and remains non-discriminatory. (b) Where the formula is weighted on the basis of compensation and years of service, experience points or other similar criteria, the Specialist will determine that the result of the application of the formula does not produce discrimination. (*See* Rev. Ruls. 68-652, 653 and 654.)

2. Forfeitures based on account or weighted balances. Many plans have been approved allocating forfeitures on account balances. Presumably, the plan instrument did not provide for allocation to the remaining participants in such a manner as to effect discrimination in favor of officers, shareholders, or highly compensated employees. The Specialist will examine the allocations of forfeitures to make sure that the approved method has not resulted in discrimination. A test check of several different classes of participants will show whether discrimination has occurred in operation. This determination is made on a year-to-year basis. If the employer has a high turnover rate and there is slow vesting in the plan, this method of allocating forfeitures tends to result in allocations to the prohibited group in a manner that produces discrimination. (See Rev. Ruls. 68-302 and 71-4.)

3. Multicorporation forfeiture problems. A profit-sharing plan and trust is adopted by a parent corporation. The instrument permits subsidiary or other corporations to adopt the plan. The plan has all the safeguard provisions as to eligibility, coverage, contributions, forfeitures, etc. If the parent and subsidiary or other corporations adopting the plan are in an industry where the rank and file employees turn over rapidly, then substantial forfeitures are likely to occur. If these corporations are related by stock ownership, common officers, common directors, etc., and employees are transferred between participating corporations, then the identity of individual forfeitures may become lost in the shuffle.

In similar situations, the Specialist will determine that forfeitures are not being allocated in contravention of the terms of the plan. In this, the Specialist will determine that no part of the corpus or income is being used for, or diverted to, purposes other than for the exclusive benefit of the participating employees of the employer where the forfeiture occurs. In certain situations where the source of forfeitures cannot be identified because of constant movement of employees between corporations, it is satisfactory if the forfeitures are allocated in accordance with the plan formula for allocating contributions. (See Rev. Rul. 71-148.)

4. Rapid turnover plus slow vesting. In situations where turnover is high, the Specialist will test the vesting provisions to see whether there is resulting discrimination in favor of the prohibited group. Inasmuch as the presence or absence of discrimination in any case depends on the facts of the individual case, no specific guideline is applicable to all situations. The general rule, i.e., funds arising under a profit-sharing plan from forfeitures of participants' interest must not be allocated to the remaining participants in such a way as to result in discrimination in favor of officers, shareholders, or highly paid employees, prevails in this area. Depending on the facts, the Specialist may recommend revocation or cause the plan to be amended to increase the vesting rate that will prevent buildup of forfeitures in subsequent years.

Definition of Compensation

Discrimination in contributions or benefits can be caused by the definition of compensation used in computing the retirement benefits. The facts may show that, at the time the favorable letter was issued, the restrictive definition of compensation used in the plan (such as basic pay only, etc.) was not discriminatory. Subsequently, the situation changed and now the payroll records reveal that the ratio of restricted compensation to total remuneration is higher proportionately for the prohibited employees than for the rank and file.

Initially, the rank and file employees may have been receiving all of their pay in the form of a basic salary, while currently, commissions and overtime account for a large share of their total compensation. The same rationale would apply if the pension benefits are based on salary only when, for example, most of the total compensation is from tips and such tips are paid over by the employee to the employer; paid by the patron to the employer as a service charge; or accounted for by the employee to the employer (as opposed to merely being reported).

Not Following the Plan

Many times, the employers do not really understand the meaning of the amendments which they were required to make in order to qualify. They merely incorporated the words contained in the IRS letter into the amendments requested. Consequently, many do not follow the plan as perfected. The Specialist, therefore, will pay particular attention to the early misconceptions which the employers had about the plan's operation.

1. Credit with a proprietorship or partnership. Despite IRS correction of this common error at qualification time, there are still instances where the benefits of prior owners of non-corporate entities are being based on service time with such predecessor companies.

2. Integrated variable benefit plans. In pension plans of the variable benefit type, the employer will probably understand that greater benefits will be derived from the application of the excess earnings to provide additional benefits for his participants, but may not understand the complex mechanics of limiting the amount of excess earnings that may be credited to a participant's account in an integrated plan. Consequently, the plan operates in a discriminatory manner.

3. Duplication of benefits. In flat benefit pension plans, a rehired participant would automatically receive a duplicate benefit if the employer did not understand what the Specialist meant when requiring the no duplication amendment at initial qualification time. Also, in multiple corporate groups, the Specialist will ascertain what controls are maintained by the employer to ensure that duplication of benefits does not result from the transfer of employees from one member corporation to another, where service with each predecessor employer is recognized without an offset of benefits earned under the predecessor employer's plan.

4. Subchapter S corporations. There have been instances where an employer erroneously included the shareholders' share of distributable taxable income due from a Subchapter S corporation in the total compensation figure used in the computation of their pension benefits. Of course, since these are not wages, the plan may lose its qualification. The Specialist can detect this error by perusing the corporate payroll records, the Form 1120-S, or the shareholder's Form 1140s.

The Tax Reform Act of 1969 limited the amount which could be contributed tax free for all shareholder employees of a Subchapter S corporation owning more than 5% of the corporate stock to the lesser of 10% of compensation or $2,500. Since many employers may not be aware of this change, when examining a Subchapter S corporation the Specialist should ascertain that all amounts contributed for the benefit of these restricted employees in excess of such limitations were included in their income.

Terminations

General

Where coverage is reduced because of discharge by an employer, by amendment to the plan, or other circumstances such as a plant closing, relocation, decrease in business, financial difficulties, etc., a partial termination may occur which requires the rights of each participant in the part of the plan terminated to become nonforfeitable. Accordingly, the Specialist will inspect the coverage schedules for the year(s) examined and, if a substantial decrease of participants has occurred, will determine if a partial termination has resulted and, if so, that nonforfeitability has been granted to the terminated participants involved.

Permanency

Do the facts reveal that the plan was abandoned within a few years after it was established? If so, was there a valid business reason? These facts will be determined by examining records such as the corporate minutes, pertinent correspondence between the employer and third parties on subjects relating to the termination, and the employer's financial statements (if finances are a factor in the termination). If the facts reveal that taxpayer's plan was not a permanent and continuing program, the Specialist will initiate disqualification proceedings.

Discrimination

Discrimination in favor of the prohibited group may result when a pension plan is prematurely terminated. This is especially true in plans which are funded at a faster rate for the prohibited employees than for the rank and file. The Specialist will gather and analyze all of the data specified in Section 4.04 of Rev. Proc. 72-6 to test for such discrimination. [*See* Regs. 1.401-4(c)(1) and Rev. Rul. 55-60.] In addition, when examining such terminations, the Specialist will keep in mind the restrictions in benefits contained in Regs. 1.401-4(c)(2).

If it is discovered that the taxpayer has already made distributions to the participants (other than through the purchase of insurance contracts), the Specialist should also verify that the benefits were not computed using assumptions which were less conservative in any respect than were used in determining costs during the previous life of the trust, and no discount for severance other than death was assumed. (*See* Rev. Rul. 71-152.)

Contribution Deduction

General

The Employee Plans Specialist will ascertain whether the plan contribution was properly established, the contribution was made timely in cash or other acceptable property to the proper recipient, and the amount paid and deducted did not exceed the limitations imposed by IRC §404(a)(1), (2) or (3).

Establishment of a Liability

Whether an employer is on the cash or accrual basis, he must establish a valid liability before a deduction claimed for a contribution to the plan can be allowed.

The first element to establish the liability is that

there must be a plan in effect before the end of the taxable year in which a deduction is claimed. In the case of a trusteed plan, a valid trust must be in existence and evidenced by a written instrument executed before the close of the taxable year. In the case of a non-trusteed annuity plan evidenced only by contracts with an insurance company, the plan is not in effect until such contracts are executed and issued. (Where the plan is separate and apart from a group annuity or annuity contracts, see Rev. Rul. 59-402.) In most instances, all pertinent documents will have been inspected by the Specialist if a determination letter was issued. In other situations, the Specialist should carefully check the dates and signatures on all essential documents if one of the open years under examination includes the year the plan was established.

In a pension plan, the plan instrument itself establishes the liability for a deductible contribution. But when a plan is amended, the date of its formal adoption has a significant bearing on what constitutes the liability. For instance, it is not uncommon for an employer to amend a plan to increase the benefits for all participants on a retroactive basis (exclusive of freeze period). The resulting increase in contributions would not be deductible until the year the amendment was formally adopted, even if its effective date is prior to that time—this means on or before the last day of the taxpayer's taxable year. Therefore, the dates and signatures on such amendments will be verified.

Timely Payments

The Specialist will also verify that the contributions made to the plan in the form of cash or other property were made timely and, for both the cash and accrual basis taxpayer, this means within the taxable year or within the grace period provided by IRC §404(a)(6)—i.e., not later than the time prescribed by law for filing the tax return, including extensions.

Furthermore, a contribution will not be considered timely made unless it is paid to the proper recipient as opposed to some intermediary—in a trusteed plan, this means to the trustee; in a wholly insured plan, this means to the insurance company.

Contributions in the Form of Property Other Than Cash

General

When a taxpayer makes a contribution in the form of property other than cash, all elements of the transaction will be carefully scrutinized by the Specialist. There are numerous violations in the area, not only with regard to the fair market value (FMV) of the property claimed as the deduction, but also the acceptability of the transferred asset as an exempt employees' trust investment.

Employer's Notes

The delivery of an employer's own promissory note to an employees' trust does not constitute a payment for purposes of IRC §404(a). Payments against such notes are deductible as cash contributions in the year or years actually paid. (See Rev. Ruls. 55-608 and 71-95.) In addition, it will be determined whether this transaction is prohibited by IRC §4975.

Real or Personal Property

In order to avoid the payment of brokers' commissions and other fees incident to the sale of property, employers will often transfer stock, bonds, mortgages and other personal or real property directly to the trust rather than sell them and contribute the cash proceeds. If stocks or bonds are transferred (other than securities issued by the employer corporation), the employer realizes a taxable gain if the FMV at the time of the transfer exceeded the cost. However, if the opposite were true, the resulting loss sustained would not be deductible, since this is a transaction between related taxpayers as defined in IRC §267. (See Rev. Rul. 61-163.)

Mortgages require special scrutiny. IRC §267 appears to be more often overlooked when mortgages are transferred to an exempt employees' trust than other types of property. Not only is it difficult to determine the FMV of a mortgage on the date of transfer, but the Specialist will also determine whether such an investment in the hands of the trust qualifies under the exclusive benefit rule. For instance, a $100,000 second mortgage was included in the employer's income at face value. Ten years later, after payments have reduced it to $90,000, the mortgage is contributed to the trust. As a result of this transaction, the employer claims a contribution deduction of $80,000, on the basis that this is the FMV on the date of the transfer, and claims a loss on the exchange. IRC §267 prohibits the deduction of the loss. With regard to the other problems mentioned, the Specialist should include the following criteria in his determination.

— Is the interest rate adequate?
— Is the security sufficient to cover the outstanding balances of the second mortgage?
  Was the transfer recorded?
— Was the debtor notified of the transfer so

that all future mortgage payments would be made to the trust? (*See* Rev. Rul. 69-494.)

In addition to verifying the FMV of real property claimed by an employer as an IRC §404(a) contribution, the following effects will also be considered:

- The value of the property conveyed may exceed the deduction limitations imposed by IRC §404(a).
- If the real property has appreciated in value, the employer realizes a taxable gain upon transfer. No loss is allowable.
- If there is a mortgage on the real property conveyed and the trust rents or leases such property, unrelated business taxable income may be generated. If there is a leaseback or other arrangement of the property to the employer, the Specialist will determine whether the transaction is arm's-length.

Revocation for Failure to Qualify in Operation

The end result of a TCMP audit could be the retroactive disqualification of a plan that has received a determination letter but is being operated in a discriminatory manner. The IRS has recently been successful in disqualifying plans even where (1) inadvertent errors caused discrimination in operation, (2) there was an innocent misstatement or omission of material facts and (3) a defective plan provision never became operative.

Inadvertent Error

Ludden v. Commr. (9th Cir., No. 77-3895, Feb. 4, 1980).

The taxpayers were the officers of a corporation and each owned half of the outstanding stock. The corporation established IRS-approved pension and profit-sharing plans for the benefit of employees. Due to an inadvertent administrative error by an accountant, the corporation only made contributions to the plans on behalf of the Luddens for the 1972 tax year and not on behalf of the only other eligible employee, a secretary. IRS determined that the plans did not qualify for that year and asserted a deficiency against the Luddens for income tax on the contributions made on their behalf. The U.S. Tax Court upheld the IRS [68 T.C. 826 (1977)].

The Ninth Circuit affirmed the tax court, stating that to gain the tax benefits of qualification, plans must satisfy IRC Section 401(a) in operation as well as in their plan provisions. The court said that a deviation may not be "sufficiently substantial" to disqualify the plan where it results in no harm to anyone and is voluntarily corrected by the parties themselves. Here, the Luddens only offered to reallocate contributions to the secretary's account upon an agreement by IRS to hold the plans qualified if a retroactive reallocation were made. The court also dismissed the taxpayer's argument that IRS' refusal to rule the plans qualified upon retroactive reallocation is arbitrary and unreasonable, stating that: "There is no provision in the Internal Revenue Code governing the retroactive correction of errors in the administration of employee plans." [*See*, however, IRC Sec. 401(b), which allows retroactive effect of amendments to the *terms* of employee plans.]

Misstatement or Omission of Material Facts

Oakton Distributors, Inc. v. Commr. (U.S. Tax Court, 73 T.C. No. 18, Jan. 30, 1980).

In 1970, Oakton Distributors, Inc., established a money purchase pension plan which was integrated with Social Security to the maximum extent possible. In September of that year, the IRS determined the plan was qualified and tax exempt. In 1972, Oakton adopted a profit-sharing plan which was also fully integrated with Social Security. In seeking qualification of the profit-sharing plan, Oakton misstated that its contribution to the pension plan was on a non-integrated basis. The Commissioner, on the basis of Oakton's answers, qualified the profit-sharing plan, although, in fact, the two plans when aggregated resulted in excessive integration.

Upon submission of the ERISA-fied plans in 1976, IRS discovered the excessive integration and so advised Oakton. In response, Oakton abandoned the integration of the profit-sharing plan for years prior to 1978 and reallocated contributions without integration and adopted a non-integrated contribution formula for the money purchase pension plan effective May 1, 1977. Notwithstanding these amendments, the IRS disqualified the profit-sharing plan for 1977.

The tax court rejected Oakton's contention that its retroactive amendment of the plan removed any improprieties prior to the revocation of qualification by the IRS, thereby rendering such revocation unlawful. Although IRC Sec. 401(b) allows retroactive amendments to qualify an otherwise nonqualifying plan, such amendments must be made within a "remedial amendment period" or within an extended period for amendment as determined by the discretionary authority of the Commissioner. Oakton had, in fact, never requested an extension of the remedial period as required by regulations. Furthermore, Oakton's proposed amendments to the plans occurred some three years after the initial determination of qualified status—well beyond the period established for requesting an extension of time to amend a plan.

The court also rejected petitioner's argument that the failure of the Commissioner to further extend the remedial amendment period at his discretion pursuant to Reg. Sec. 1.401(b)-1(e) would create "substantial hardship to the employer" and would not be in the "best interest of plan participants." The court concluded that Oakton failed to demonstrate any hardships except those normally attendant to the loss of qualified status.

Also rejected was Oakton's attempt to circumvent Sec. 401(b) by relying on cases which permitted retroactive correction of plan defects. The court noted that, in such cases, courts have sustained retroactive amendments when the objectionable provisions had never become operative, when the employer acted with reasonable diligence in seeking a determination letter with respect to the plan [see, e.g., *Aero Rental v. Commr.*, 64 T.C. 331 (1975)] and when a voluntary correction was made prior to a final adverse determination and without bargaining for a favorable determination [see dictum in *Ludden v. Commr.*, 68 T.C. 826 (1977)]. Oakton satisfied none of these tests. Contributions to the plan had been made on the basis of impermissible provisions of the plan; Oakton waited three and a half years after the favorable determination in 1972 before proposing any remedial action; and the adoption of remedial amendments was made as part of the bargaining process with the Internal Revenue Service.

Oakton's objection to the retroactive disqualification of the profit-sharing plan was also rejected. The court found no abuse of discretion on the part of the IRS in retroactively disqualifying the plan, since the initial determination of qualification was made on the basis of a material misrepresentation by Oakton. Moreover, the IRS was entitled to rely on the information supplied by Oakton and was not required to verify the information against the documents submitted to IRS.

Defective Plan Provision

Tionesta Sand and Gravel, Inc., v. Commr. (U.S. Tax Court, 73 T.C. No. 60, Jan. 31, 1980).

Tionesta had a profit-sharing plan that called for complete vesting upon (1) notice of termination to the trustee from the employer, (2) adjudication of the employee as a bankrupt or (3) dissolution of the employer. There was no provision for full vesting when contributions were completely discontinued. Although the plan came into existence in 1968, no determination letter was requested until 1978. The plan was approved for plan years beginning in 1976, but IRS challenged the employer's prior deductions.

The court held that Tionesta's profit-sharing plan was not qualified because the trust agreement did not provide for full vesting of participants' interests on complete discontinuation of contributions as required by Sec. 411(d)(3) of the Internal Revenue Code. This was so even though the plan was not terminated, contributions were not discontinued, and the plan was since amended to comply with the statutory requirements. The court explained that Congress had not intended a plan which contained a defective provision to be considered qualified even if the defective provision never became operative.

Conclusion

Plan sponsors should be concerned that their plans are being operated in a discriminatory manner. As discussed above, the courts have upheld IRS' contention that the plan can be retroactively disqualified as the result of inadvertent and honest mistakes notwithstanding the plan sponsor's willingness to correct the mistake.

The preferable approach is to use care in operating a plan and to correct mistakes before an IRS audit. Correction of any identified errors indicates to an examining agent a willingness to operate the plan in a non-discriminatory manner and in strict accord with the plan document. In sum, a "pre-audit" review would uncover deficiencies and save considerable time arguing the case before IRS and, most importantly, would safeguard the qualified status of the plan.

Appendix A

Overview of Form 6080
(The TCMP Employee Plans Examination Document)

Part I—Entity Data

The examination is conducted by an Employee Plans Specialist who is instructed to review the information reported on Forms 5500/5500-C and to indicate whether the information is correct as reported and, if not, the corrected response.

Questions in this part relate to lines 4, 6, 18 and 20 of Forms 5500/5500-C with reference to the type of sponsor and plan, plan form, plan model and whether sponsored by one or more employers. In addition, the examiner is required to indicate who the plan administrator is, if a professional association, if the plan is collectively bargained, whether a pre-ERISA plan, and whether a determination letter was issued.

Part II—Control Data

This part is for internal use with regard to personnel, time spent and results of the TCMP audit.

Part III—Return Data

The examiner is required to verify the accuracy of the information reported on line 7 of Forms 5500/5500-C with regard to the number of plan participants, their vesting, terminated and retired status, and line 17 with regard to the eligibility of employees for participation. He is also required to verify the funding, integration and other data represented on lines 8, 9, 10, 11, 12, 16, 20 and 23 of Forms 5500/5500-C.

In this part the examiner is called upon to audit the plan income and expenses and to record the beginning and ending balance sheets reported on lines 13 and 14 of the Form. Apparently, he is not precluded from conducting a balance sheet audit.

Part IV—Results of Examinations (TCMP)

Section A—Eligibility/Participation Standards and Coverage—This section is a review of the plan provisions dealing with the crediting of years of service, breaks in service and coverage requirements of Code Section 410(a). The examiner is also required to verify that all eligible employees are covered in the plan and those persons ineligible are excluded. Also, he must determine whether members of controlled groups are included and whether the plan meets the percentage or classification test of Code Section 410(b)(1).

Section B—Vesting Standards—The examiner is required to review the plan vesting provisions, determine whether they have been followed in operation, and whether employees have been discharged to avoid vesting.

Section C—Vesting Discrimination—This section is limited to plans covering fewer than 100 participants, to determine whether the vesting provisions under the plan deprive rank and file employees of benefits.

Section D—Accrued Benefit Requirements—The examiner is required to determine whether employee contributions are separately accounted for or otherwise identifiable, how benefits are provided and which of the three accrual methods is used.

Section E—Discrimination-Benefits or Contributions—A review of the following is required:
a) Whether compensation used is discriminatory; b) If two plans are required to meet the coverage requirements, whether the benefits are comparable; c) Whether the benefit formula is non-discriminatory; d) Whether an allocation of contributions was made in the case of unreasonable compensation; e) Whether the allocation of contributions and forfeitures was non-discriminatory; f) Other problem areas.

Section F—Integrated Plans—Integrated plan benefit provisions are reviewed as to type of integration with Social Security, integration levels and integration percentage rates. If the plan is an excess benefit plan, the number of employees who are otherwise eligible but do not earn any plan benefits must be shown.

Section G—Modes of Distribution/Benefit and Contribution Limits—The plan provisions and compliance therewith dealing with the statutorily required joint and survivor benefits, and limitations on benefits and contributions are reviewed.

Section H—Minimum Funding Standards—The auditor is required to determine whether the charges and credits to the minimum funding standard have been satisfied, if any deficiency has been approved by an IRS waiver and whether the alternative minimum funding standard has been used.

Section I—Funding and Actuarial Methods—The examiner is required to review and report on the funding methods used, the actuarial experience of the plan and the actuarial methods, factors and assumptions. In addition, he is required to determine whether the funding of projected benefits is subject to the Code Section 415 limitations and to record the assets, liabilities, normal cost, gains and losses shown on the actuarial balance sheet, if applicable.

Section J—Deduction Limitation—Questions required to be furnished concern the timeliness of the payment of contributions, accuracy of fair market value of non-cash contributions, whether contribution or credit carry-overs were proper and if ESOP contributions were improperly claimed as a tax deduction.

If the examiner determines that an adjustment to the deduction claimed is required, the amount of the adjustment and the appropriate subsection of Code Section 404 which limits the deduction is recommended.

Section K—Miscellaneous—Other operational and plan provisions which are to be reviewed and reported are: the non-diversion requirement; the prohibited alienation and assignment requirement; the reversion of contributions permitted by ERISA Section 403(c)(2); the annual valuation of defined contribution plan assets; the merger, consolidation or transfer of liability provisions of Code Sections 401(a)(12) and 414(1) and compliance with the filing requirements, PBGC coverage, and payment of premiums, taxability of trust income as unrelated business taxable income and filing of Form 990-T; the limitation of contributions to profits in the case of a profit-sharing plan; compliance of a TRASOP with the provisions of section 301(d) of the Tax Reduction Act of 1975; the fiduciary requirements of ERISA Sections 402(a), 402(b)(4), 404, 406, 407, 412, and 503, whether information required to be filed under ERISA Section 101(b) has been complied with and whether penalties are recommended for failure to file various reports, statements, notices and information returns to the IRS.

Part V—Results of Examination-Prohibited Transaction Findings

The examiner is required to report the results of the audit of the trust under the plan relating to self dealing transactions prohibited by Code Section 4975(c)(1), whether any administrative exemptions granted under Code Section 4975(c)(2) were complied with and any other prohibited transaction problems.

Part VI—Related and Delinquent Returns

Finally, the examiner is required to report on related returns required to be filed, the results of an examination of these returns, the additional tax and/or penalties recommended for deficiencies and failure to file, and adjustments and referrals to other examiners to determine additional tax and/or penalties.

Appendix B

TCMP EMPLOYEE PLANS EXAMINATION DOCUMENT PART I—ENTITY DATA								2. Data Center Use Only		
1. Sponsor				3. Annual Report Form (1) ☐ 5500 (2) ☐ 5500C						
				4. Name of Plan:						
				5. Correct Business Code: *(See Exhibit)*		6. Effective Date of Plan: Y Y M M			7. Date Incorp. Y Y M M	

Enter "x" in 9-12	PLAN ENTITY					PLAN FORM			8. Type of Employer/Plan Sponsor		
	(1) Single Employer	(2) Controlled Grp.	(3) Multi-Employer	(4) Multiple Collect. Barg.	(5) Multiple (Other)	(6) Defined Benefit (DB)	(7) Defined Contr. (DC)	(8) Other (Explain)	(1) ☐ Sole Proprietor (2) ☐ Partnership (3) ☐ Subchapter S (4) ☐ Tax Exempt Organ. (5) ☐ Corp. *(not (3) or (4))* (6) ☐ Administrator/Joint Board		
9. Reported											
10. After Audit											
PLAN FORM											
11. Reported											
12. After Audit									Tab No. 13.		

PLAN TYPE Enter "x" in 14-15	(1) N.A.	(2) Fixed Benefit	(3) Unit Benefit	(4) Flat Benefit	(5) Profit-Sharing	(6) Stock Bonus	(7) Target Benefit	(8) Other Money Purch.	(9) Thrift-Savings	(10) ESOP 401(a)	(11) Other
14. Reported											
15. After Audit											

PLAN INDICATOR Enter "x" in 16-17	(1) N.A.	(2) M&P	(3) Field Proto	(4) Pattern	(5) Model Plan	(6) Bond Purchase		Tab No. 18.
16. Reported								
17. After Audit								

MISCELLANEOUS DATA *Place an "x" mark in appropriate column.*		(1) Yes	(2) No	(3) N.A.
19. Is there a plan administrator other than the plan sponsor indicated in item 1?	19.			
20. If there is an "x" in item 8(1) through (5), is the employer part of a controlled group of corp. or common control employers? *(Not per Line 4 of Return)*	20.			
21. If there is an "x" in item 8 (2), (3) or (5), is the employer a professional association?	21.			
22. If single employer plan *(Item 10(1))*, is the plan collectively bargained?	22.			
23. Does this return cover an "Old Law" plan?	23.			
24. Has a determination letter been issued?	24.			
25. If item 24 is "yes", enter date of issue:	25.	Y Y M M		
26. If item 24 is "yes", what were caveats? ("x" mark one or more) (1) ☐ "C" (2) ☐ "D" (3) ☐ "E" (4) ☐ "F" (5) ☐ "G" (6) ☐ "H" (7) ☐ "I" (8) ☐ "J" (9) ☐ "K" (10) ☐ Other ("M") (11) ☐ None				

PART II—CONTROL DATA						
27. Examining Officer's Name	28. Grade G.S.	29. Time Hrs.	30. Closing Code	31. Penalties $	32(1). Issue Code	32(2). R/P
33. Group Manager's Initials	34. Date	35. Form 6080 Reviewed (1) ☐ Yes (2) ☐ No				
36. Reviewer's Initials	37. Date	38. Time /10	39. Disposal Code	40. Closing Assoc. District	41. Closing Key District	

Form 6080 (7-79)   —1—   Department of the Treasury – Internal Revenue Service

PART III—RETURN DATA

Items marked with "*" should not be completed in Col. (1) for 5500-C

	Section A—Participants *(End of Year)* [Line 7 of Return]		(1) Reported	(2) After Audit
42.	Active participants *(employed or carried as active)* Number fully vested	42.		
43.	Number partially vested	43.		
44.	Number nonvested	44.		
45.	Total *(Items 42, 43 and 44)*	45.		
46.	Retired or separated participants receiving benefits	*46.		
47.	Retired or separated participants entitled to future benefits	*47.		
48.	Subtotal *(Items 45, 46 and 47)*	48.		
49.	Deceased participants whose beneficiaries are receiving or are entitled to receive benefits	*49.		
50.	Total, *(Items 48 and 49)*	50.		

	Section B—Employee Information [Line 17 of Return]		(1) Reported	(2) After Audit
51.	Total number of employees	51.		
	Number of employees excluded under the plan—			
52.	Minimum age or years of service	52.		
53.	Employees on whose behalf retirement benefits were the subject of collective bargaining	53.		
54.	Nonresident aliens who receive no earned income from United States sources	54.		
55.	Total excluded *(Items 52, 53 and 54)*	55.		
56.	Total number of employees not excluded, *(Item 51 less 55)*	56.		
57.	Employees ineligible	57.		
58.	Employees eligible to participate, *(Item 56 less 57)*	58.		
59.	Employees eligible but not participating	59.		
60.	Employees participating, *(Item 58 less 59)*	60.		

Enter "x" mark in Appropriate Column in Sections C, D and E

	Section C—Funding Arrangement [Line 11 of Return]		(1) Reported	(2) After Audit
61.	Trust *(benefits provided in whole from trust funds)*	61.		
62.	Trust/arrangement providing benefits partially through ins. and/or annuity contracts/combination	62.		
63.	Trust/arrangement providing benefits exclusively through ins. and/or annuity contracts	63.		
64.	Custodial account described in section 401(f) of the Code and not included in item 63	*64.		
65.	Other	65.		

	Section D—Integrated Plan [Line 20 of Return] 66. ☐ Not Applicable		(1) Reported	(2) After Audit
67.	Social Security	67.		
68.	Railroad Retirement	68.		
69.	Other	69.		

	Section E—Other Return Data		Reported		After Audit		
			(1) Yes	(2) No	(3) Yes	(4) No	(5) N.A.
70.	Was any plan amendment adopted in this plan year? [Line 8 of Return]	70.					
71.	Does any such amendment result in the reduction of the accrued benefit of any participant under the plan? [Line 8 of Return]	71.					
72.	Will amendment result in a reduction of current or future benefits? [Line 8 of Return]	72.					
73.	In this plan year, was this plan merged or consolidated into another plan or were assets or liabilities transferred to another plan? [Line 10 of Return]	73.					
74.	Did any person who rendered services to the plan receive, directly or indirectly, compensation from the plan in the plan year? [Line 12, 5500; Line 19, 5500-C]	74.					
75.	Does the plan, or a known party-in-interest with respect to the plan, have any control or significant financial interest, direct or indirect, in the surety company or its agents or brokers? [Line 16 of Return]	75.					
76.	Was the plan terminated during this plan year or any prior plan year? [Line 9a of return]	76.					
77.	If "yes" were all trust assets distributed to participants or beneficiaries or transferred to another plan? [Line 9b of return]	77.					
78.	Was a resolution to terminate this plan adopted during this plan year or any prior plan year? [Line 9c of return]	78.					
79.	If defined benefit, did one or more reportable events or other events requiring notice to PBGC occur during this plan year? [Line 23, 5500; Line 22, 5500-C]	79.					
80.	If item 79(3) is "Yes", what was reportable event(s)? 1) ☐ "a" 2) ☐ "b" 3) ☐ "c" 4) ☐ "d" 5) ☐ "e" 6) ☐ "f" 7) ☐ "g" 8) ☐ "h" 9) ☐ "i"		Tab No. 81.				

Form 6080 (7-79)   —2—

Part III (continued)		Items marked with "*" should not be completed for 5500-C				
Section F—Balance Sheet (Per Return) Assets		(1) Beginning	(2) Ending	Section H—Plan Income	(1) Reported	(2) After Audit
Total Cash	82.	$	$	Contributions from:		
Receivables				Employers 106.	$	$
Employer cont.	*83.			Employees 107.		
Employee cont.	*84.			Others 108.		
Other	*85.			Non-Cash contr. 109.		
Net Receivables	86.			Total cont. (Sum of 106-109) 110.		
General Investments				Earnings from Invest.		
Real Estate	*87.			Rents *111.		
Mortgages	*88.			Royalties *112.		
Loans	*89.			Total Earn.—Invest. 113.		
Value-pooled Funds	*90.			Net Realized Gain (Loss) on sale/exchg. assets 114.		
Other Invest.	91.					
Total Gen. Invest.	92.			Other Income 115.		
Total Party-in-int. invest.	*93.			Total Income (Sum of 110 113, 114 and 115) 116.		
Bldgs. & other deprec. Drop	94.					
Total value unalloc. ins. contracts	95.			Section I—Expenses	(1) Reported	(2) After Audit
Other Assets	96.			Distribution of Benefits and Payments		
Total Assets (Sum of 82, 86, 92, 93, 94, 95 and 96)	97.			Directly to Part. or Benefit 117.		
Memo Entry: Total Party-in-int. on 5500-C	98.			Total Dist. of Ben. & Pay. 118.		
Section G—Balance Sheet Per Return Liabilities		(1) Beginning	(2) Ending	Interest Expense 119.		
Payables				Admin. Expenses		
Plan Claims	*99.			Salaries & Allow. *120.		
Other Payables	*100.			Fees & Commissions *121.		
Total Payables	101.			Other Admin. Exp. *122.		
Acquisition in Debt.	102.			Total Admin. Exp. *123.		
Other Liabilities	103.			Other Expenses 124.		
Total Liab. (Sum of 101, 102 and 103)	104.			Total Expenses (Sum of 118, 119, 123 & 124) 125.		
Net Assets (Item 97 less 104)	105.			Net Income (Expense) (Item 116 less 125) 126.		

PART IV—RESULTS OF EXAMINATIONS (TCMP) *See exhibit for action codes*

Section A—Eligibility/Participation Standards and Coverage	Tab. No. 127.

128. How does Plan Determine Credit for Year of Service?
   (1) ☐ Not Applicable   (3) ☐ Elapsed Time   (5) ☐ Combination
   (2) ☐ 1000 or less Actual Hours/Year   (4) ☐ Other Equivalency   (6) ☐ Other

129. If item 128 is any of (2) through (6), enter appropriate action code other than "N.A."   129.

For items 130-138 enter an "x" in Column (1) or (2), as appropriate, and enter the appropriate action code in Column (3).

		(1) Yes	(2) No	(3) Action Code
130.	Are breaks in service rules utilized by plan? 130.			
131.	Is service with predecessor employer credited? 131.			
132.	Were other problems relative to IRC 410(a) encountered? 132.			
133.	Are all employees who met plan eligibility requirements in fact covered? 133.			
134.	Were independent contractor/employee issues encountered? 134.			
135.	Were shared employees considered by the employer to be "employees"? 135.			
136.	Were all employees of controlled group considered by the employer in applying the coverage tests? 136.			
137.	Did plan purport to meet the percentage test of IRC 410(b)(1)(A)? 137.			
138.	Did plan purport to meet classification test of IRC 410(b)(1)(B)? 138.			

139. If item 138 is "Yes" what were the exclusions:
   (1) ☐ Hourly   (3) ☐ Department or Division   (6) ☐ Other
   (2) ☐ Salaried   (4) ☐ Job Classification
                    (5) ☐ Union (Other than by Statute Per 410(b)(2)(A))

Form 6080 (7-79)

Part IV (continued) — Section B—Vesting Standards
Tab. No. 140.

141. Vesting schedule applicable to all plan participants:
 (1) ☐ Full and Immediate (3) ☐ Rule of 45 (5) ☐ 10-year cliff vesting (7) ☐ 4-40 vesting (9) ☐ Other
 (2) ☐ 5 to 15 years (4) ☐ Graduated (6) ☐ Class year vesting (8) ☐ Multiple

142. For item 141 enter appropriate action code other than "N.A." 142.

143. How is credit for year of service determined? (1) ☐ Not Applicable (3) ☐ Elapsed Time (5) ☐ Combination
 (2) ☐ 1000 or less actual hours/years (4) ☐ Other Equivalency (6) ☐ Other

144. If item 143 is any of "(2)" through "(6)"; enter appropriate action code other than "N.A." 144.

For item 145-151, enter an "x" in Column (1) or (2), as appropriate, and enter the appropriate action code in Column (3).

	(1) Yes	(2) No	(3) Action Code
145. Does plan exclude service as allowed under §411(a)(4)?			
146. Are forfeitures limited to those allowable under IRC 411(a)(2) and (3)?			
147. Is service with predecessor employer credited?			
148. Does plan attempt to use cash out/buy back to exclude service for vesting?			
149. Does plan provide full vesting at NRA per 411(a)(8)?			
150. Were any other problems relative to IRC 411(a) encountered?			
151. Did discrimination result per IRC 411(d)(1)?			

Section C—Vesting Discrimination (5500-C only)   152. ☐ N/A
Tab No. 153.

Number of Active Participants (Before Adjustments)	Top 3rd (1)	Middle 3rd (2)	Bottom 3rd (3)	Total (4)
154. 100% Vested				
155. 51-99% Vested				
156. 1-50% Vested				
157. 0% Vested				
158. Total				
No. Separated W/Forfeitures 159. ☐ Not Applicable				
160. Year Audited				
161. Preceding Plan Year				
162. 2nd Preceding Plan Year				
163. Total				
Amt. Forfeitures (Defined Contribution Plans) 164. ☐ Not Applicable				
165. Year Audited				
166. Preceding Plan Year				
167. 2nd Preceding Plan Year				
168. Total				

Section D—Accrued Benefit Requirements
Tab No. 169.

For items 170-172 and 174, enter an "x" in Column (1) or (2), as appropriate, and enter applicable code in Column (3).

	(1) Yes	(2) No	(3) Action Code
170. Where the plan provides for voluntary and/or mandatory employee contributions are separate accounts for each participant maintained for employee and for employer contributions?			
171. If item 170 is "no", was rule of 411(c)(2) applied?			
172. Were other problems encountered relative to accrued benefits?			

Defined Benefit Plans: 173. ☐ Not Applicable

174. Is plan fully insured per 412(i)?   174.

175. If item 174 is "No", what is accrual method?
 (1) ☐ 133-1/3% method (2) ☐ 3% method (3) ☐ Fractional Rule (4) ☐ Multiple methods

176. For item 175 enter appropriate action code other than "N.A":   176.

Section E—Discrimination-Benefits or Contributions
Tab No. 177.

For item 178-184, enter an "x" in Column (1) or (2), as appropriate, and enter applicable code in Column (3).

	(1) Yes	(2) No	(3) Action Code
178. Is the definition of compensation nondiscriminatory?			
179. Where two plans are treated as one plan to satisfy coverage, are the plans comparable?			
180. If defined benefit plan, is plan benefit formula nondiscriminatory?			
181. If there was unreasonable compensation, was there a reallocation?			

Defined Contribution Plans:

	(1) Yes	(2) No	(3) Action Code
182. Is the allocation of employer contributions nondiscriminatory?			
183. Is the allocation of forfeitures in a P/S plan nondiscriminatory?			
184. Were any other problems encountered relative to discrimination in benefits or contributions?			

Form 6080 (7-79)   — 4 —

Part IV (continued)   Section F—Integrated Plans (Social Security)   185. ☐ Not Applicable

186. Type of Integration
(1) ☐ Pure Excess   (2) ☐ Step-Rate   (3) ☐ Offset   (4) ☐ Other

187. Plan Integration Level—Dollar Amounts
(1) ☐ RR 71-446 Table   (3) ☐ RR 78-92 Table   (5) ☐ Dollar Amounts   (7) ☐ Not Applicable
(2) ☐ RR 69-4 Table   (4) ☐ Current FICA Taxable Wage   (6) ☐ Other

If "x" in item 187 (5), enter the following		(1) Dollars	(2) Action Code
188. One Integration Level	188.	$	
Multiple Integration Levels:			
189. High Level	189.	$	
190. Low Level	190.	$	

Plan Integration Percentage Rates		(1) Rate	(2) Action Code
191. Pure Excess	191.	%	
Step-Rate:			
192. Lower	192.	%	
193. Higher	193.	%	
Offset			
194. Percentage of Compensation	194.	%	
195. Percentage of Offset	195.	%	
196. Other	196.	%	
197. If the plan is a pure excess plan, number of employees included in Item 60 which received no contributions or benefits under the plan because their compensation is less than the integration level.	197.		

Section G—Modes of Distribution/Benefit and Contribution Limits   Tab No. 198.

For items 199-202, enter an "x" in Column (1) or (2), as appropriate, and enter the appropriate action code in Column (3).		(1) Yes	(2) No	Action Code
199. If plan provides benefits in form of a life annuity, does the plan contain language intended to satisfy the "qualified J. & S. annuity" requirements (§401(a)(11))	199.			
200. Were there any excessive annual additions or excessive annual benefits?	200.			
201. If defined contribution plan does the plan in form provide a method for dealing with amounts found to be in excess of the prescribed limitations?	201.			
202. Is application of "limitation year" rules correct?	202.			

Section H—Minimum Funding Standards   203. ☐ Not applicable (See Instructions)   Tab No. 204.

For items 205-214, enter an "x" in Columns (1) or (2), as appropriate, and enter the appropriate action code in Column (3).		(1) Yes	(2) No	(3) Action Code
205. Did the contribution satisfy the minimum funding requirement for the year?	205.			
206. Does the plan have an approved waiver of a funding deficiency for the current year?	206.			
Defined Benefit Plans: (Items 208-214) 207. ☐ Not Applicable				
208. Has the alternative minimum funding standard account been used?	208.			
209. If the funding method was changed during the year, was the change approved?	209.			
210. Were there any changes in the actuarial assumptions during the year?	210.			
211. Was the method of valuing plan assets changed during the year?	211.			
212. Are there any "other" credits to the Funding Standard Account on Schedule B of Form 5500?	212.			
213. Have there been recurring actuarial losses?	213.			
214. Have plan amendments been properly taken into account for purposes of the FSA?	214.			

Minimum Funding Standards Account		(1) Reported	(2) After Audit	(3) Action Code
215. Charges required under IRC 412	215.			
216. Credits made (not including credit from waiver)	216.			
217. Funding Deficiency (Excess, if any, of Item 215 over 216)	217.			
218. Amount of waiver (IRS approval LTR.)	218.			
219. Net Funding Deficiency (Excess, if any, of Item 217 over 218)	219.			

220. What years are covered by the most recent actuarial valuation?
(1) ☐ Current year   (2) ☐ 1st prior year   (3) ☐ 2nd prior year   (4) ☐ None of these.

For item 220, enter action code   221.

222. If item 208 is "yes", when was the alternative minimum funding standard used?
(1) ☐ Current year   (2) ☐ 1st prior year   (3) ☐ 2nd prior year   (4) ☐ None of these

From 6080 (7-79)

| Part IV (continued) | Section I—Funding and Actuarial Methods (Defined Benefit Plans Only) | 223. ☐ N.A. | Tab No. 224. |

225. What was the funding method used:
   (1) ☐ ILP   (3) ☐ EAN   (5) ☐ Frozen Initial Liability   (7) ☐ Other
   (2) ☐ Unit credit (4) ☐ Attained age normal (6) ☐ Aggregate

		226.	
For item 225 enter appropriate action code other than "N.A."			

For items 227-237, enter an "x" in Column (1) or (2), as appropriate and enter appropriate action code in Column (3).

		(1) Yes	(2) No	(3) Action Code
227.	If item 225 is "4", "5", or "6" was there a decrease in accrual rates? 227.			
228.	If 227 is "yes", was the decrease greater than .05 percent? 228.			
229.	If 228 is "yes", were there recurring decreases? 229.			
230.	If item 225 is "1", "2" or "3" was there actuarial gain in excess of 2% of accrued liability? 230.			
231.	If 230 is "yes", have there been recurring actuarial gains? 231.			
232.	If item 225 is "1" "2", or "3" was full funding limit exceeded? 232.			
233.	If the actuarial method used does not allow computation of the full funding limit, was a test made to determine the full funding limit during the current or prior year? 233.			
234.	Are participants' projected benefits included in actuarial calculations limited to amounts not in excess of section 415 limitations? 234.			
235.	Do the funding assumptions use a: (Items 235-237)			
235.	Salary Scale 235.			
236.	Preretirement Mortality Table 236.			
237.	Turnover Table 237.			
238.	Enter the preretirement interest rate used: 238.			%
239.	Enter action code other than "N.A." for item 238: 239.			

Enter the following amounts used in the actuarial valuations:

		(1) Dollars	(2) Action Code
240.	Value of assets 240.		
241.	Accrued liability (if calculated) 241.		
242.	Normal cost 242.		
243.	Actuarial Gain (if calculated) 243.		
244.	Actuarial Loss (if calculated) 244.		

| Section J—Deduction Limitation | 245 ☐ N.A. | Tab No. 246. |

For items 247-252, enter an "x" in Columns (1) or (2) and enter the appropriate action code in Column (3).

		(1) Yes	(2) No	(3) Action Code
247.	Was the contribution timely paid? 247.			
248.	For noncash contribution was FMV correct as claimed? 248.			
249.	If deduction was to a profit-sharing or stock bonus plan were contribution carryovers proper? 249.			
250.	If deduction was to a profit-sharing or stock bonus plan were credit carryovers proper? 250.			
251.	In the case of an ESOP, was a deduction improperly claimed for an amount that was the basis for additional TRASOP invest. credit? 251.			
252.	Was deduction adjustment recommended to audit? 252.			

253. Indicate the appropriate section(s) which limit deduction claimed:
   (1) ☐ 404(a)(1)(A)(i)   (4) ☐ 404(a)(1)(B or C)   (7) ☐ 404(a)(3)(A)   (10) ☐ 404(a)(7)
   (2) ☐ 404(a)(1)(A)(ii)   (5) ☐ 404(a)(1)(D)   (8) ☐ 404(a)(3)(B)
   (3) ☐ 404(a)(1)(A)(iii) (6) ☐ 404(a)(2)   (9) ☐ 404(a)(5)

| For item 250 enter appropriate Action Code other than "N.A." | 254. | |

255. If item 252 is "yes" indicate amount of adjustment for appropriate Code Section.

	Code Section	Adjustment
(1)	404(a)(1 or 2)	$
(2)	404(a)(3)	$
(3)	404(a)(5)	$
(4)	404(a)(7)	$
(5)	Total	$

Form 6080 (7-79)

Part IV (continued)	Section K—Miscellaneous		Tab No. 256.		
For items 257-282, enter an "x" in Column (1) or (2) and enter the applicable Action Code in Column (3).			(1) Yes	(2) No	(3) Action Code
257. Was there a violation of the exclusive benefit rule of IRC 401(a)(2)?		257.			
258. Is the assignment or alienation of an employee's interest in excess of statutory limits prohibited?		258.			
Does the plan permit or has there been a return of contributions because of:					
259. Nonqualification		259.			
260. Nondeductibility		260.			
Mistake of fact		261.			
262. If a defined contribution plan, was the annual valuation of assets and allocation of appreciation/depreciation proper?		262.			
263. If there was a plan merger or spin-off or transfer of assets or liability was Form 5310 filed?		263.			
264. Was Form 5310 filed as a result of termination?		264.			
265. Is the plan covered under PBGC Termination Insurance Program?		265.			
266. If item 265 is "yes" or undetermined, was PBGC-1 Premium Form filed?		266.			
267. Was any of the trust income subject to taxation as unrelated business taxable income under Code section 511-514?		267.			
268. If item 267 is "yes", was Form 990-T filed?		268.			
269. Are employer contributions to a profit-sharing plan made from current or accumulated profits?		269.			
270. If a TRASOP qualified under 401(a) are all provisions of 301(d) satisfied?		270.			
271. Was the plan established under a written instrument which named fiduciaries and specified a basis on which payments are made to and from the plan?		271.			
272. Are there indications that the administrative expenses of the plan, particularly compensation of plan fiduciaries, employees, professional or service providers may be unreasonable? (Act Sec. 404)		272.			
273. Does the plan appear to have diversified its investments? (Act Sec. 404)		273.			
274. Does the plan seem to have suitable procedures to investigate prospective investments and to monitor the performance of its investment portfolio? (Act Sec. 404)		274.			
275. Are there indications that the plan lacks procedures for collection of contributions and other amounts due the plan or that such procedures have not been enforced? (Act Section 404)		275.			
276. Are all plan personnel who are handling plan funds covered by a fidelity bond? (Act Section 412)		276.			
277. Has the plan/Trust invested in employer securities (including debt obligations) or employer real property?		277.			
278. Is there any indication that a Plan Fiduciary has dealt with plan assets in his own interest, represented a party with adverse interests in a transaction involving the plan, or received personal consideration from a party dealing with the plan in a transaction involving plan assets?		278.			
279. Are there indications that the plan does not have reasonable procedures for handling claims, denial of claims, and review of claims after denial?		279.			
Have the following reports been filed in a timely manner?	SPD	280.			
	SAR	281.			
	SMM	282.			
Were any other problems encountered which have not been specifically identified elsewhere on Form 6080 (Explain in Remarks)		283.			
Penalties for failure to timely file the following:			(1) Amount Recommended		(2) N.A.
284. Annual registration statement, §6652(e)(1)		284.	$		
285. Individual registration statement for each participant, §6690		285.	$		
286. Actuarial report for defined benefit plan, §6692		286.	$		
287. Notification of change in status §6652(e)(2)		287.	$		
288. Actuarial statement in case of mergers, §6652(f)		288.	$		
289. Information relating to certain trustee and annuity and bond purchase plans, §6652(f)		289.	$		
290. Total		290.	$		

Form 6080 (7-79)

PART V—RESULTS OF EXAMINATION—PROHIBITED TRANSACTIONS FINDINGS		Tab No. 291.		
For items 292-300 enter an "x" in Column (1) or (2) and enter appropriate action code in Column (3)		(1) Yes	(2) No	(3) Action Code
292. Were there any transactions between plan and employer, subsidiary, affiliate or parent of employer, or officer, director, ten percent or more shareholder or highly compensated employee of employer?	292.			
293. If item 292 is "yes", were the transactions prohibited by 4975 (c)(1)?	293.			
294. Were there any transactions between plan and plan fiduciaries?	294.			
295. If item 294 is "yes", were the transactions prohibited by 4975(c)(1)?	295.			
296. Were any fiduciaries full-time employees of the employer or of a union whose members are covered by the plan?	296.			
297. If item 296 is "yes", was their compensation as fiduciaries limited to reimbursement of expenses properly and actually incurred?	297.			
298. If the plan is an ESOP, did it engage in a loan transaction with a disqualified person to purchase employer securities?	298.			
299. If plan was ever granted an administrative exemption under 4975(c)(2), were all the conditions contained in the exemption met?	299.			
300. Were any other problems encountered relative to prohibited transactions?	300.			

PART VI—RELATED AND DELINQUENT RETURNS

Related Returns 301. ☐ N.A. Delinquent Returns 309. ☐ N.A.

	Form	302. Filing Req.	303. No.	304. Hrs.	305. No. Chg.	306. No No Chg.	307. Additional Pen. or Tax	308. Adjustment on Referral(s)	310. No.	311. Hrs.	312. Additional Pen. or Tax	313. Adjustment on Referral(s)
(1)	5500						$				$	
(2)	5500C						$				$	
(3)	5330						$				$	
(4)	990T						$				$	
(5)	1041							$				$
(6)	1040							$				$
(7)	1120							$				$
(8)	1120S							$				$
(9)	Total						$	$			$	$

Remarks:

Form 6080 (7-79)

Appendix C

Form **5500** Department of the Treasury Internal Revenue Service Department of Labor Pension and Welfare Benefit Programs Pension Benefit Guaranty Corporation	**Annual Return/Report of Employee Benefit Plan** **(With 100 or more participants)** This form is required to be filed under sections 104 and 4065 of the Employee Retirement Income Security Act of 1974 and sections 6057(b) and 6058(a) of the Internal Revenue Code, referred to as the Code.	**1978** This Form is Open to Public Inspection

For the calendar plan year 1978 or fiscal plan year beginning , 1978 and ending , 19

File original of this form, including schedules and attachments, completed in ink or type.

▶ Keogh (H.R. 10) plans with fewer than 100 participants and with at least one owner-employee participant **do not file this form.** File Form 5500–K instead.
▶ Other pension benefit plans and certain welfare benefit plans with fewer than 100 participants **do not file this form.** File Form 5500–C instead.
▶ Governmental plans and church plans (not electing coverage under section 410(d) of the Code). **Do not file this form.** File Form 5500–G instead.
▶ Welfare benefit plans with 100 or more participants complete only items 1 through 16 and item 22.
▶ Pension benefit plans, unless otherwise excepted, complete all items. Annuity arrangements of certain exempt organizations and individual retirement account trusts of employers complete only items 1 through 6, 9 and 10.
▶ Plan number—Your 3 digit plan number must be entered in item 5(c); see instruction 5(c) for explanation of "plan number."
▶ If any item does not apply, enter "N/A."

1 (a) Name of plan sponsor (employer if for a single employer plan)	**1 (b)** Employer identification number
Address (number and street)	**1 (c)** Telephone number of sponsor ( )
City or town, State and ZIP code	**1 (d)** Employer taxable year ends Month Day Year 19
2 (a) Name of plan administrator (if other than plan sponsor)	**1 (e)** Business code number
Address (number and street)	**2 (b)** Administrator's employer identification no.
City or town, State and ZIP code	**2 (c)** Telephone number of administrator ( )

3 Name, address and identification number of ☐ plan sponsor and/or ☐ plan administrator as they appeared on the last return/report filed for this plan if not the same as in 1 or 2 above ▶

4 Check appropriate box to indicate the type of plan entity (check only one box):
 (a) ☐ Single-employer plan   **(c)** ☐ Multiemployer plan   **(e)** ☐ Multiple-employer plan (other)
 (b) ☐ Plan of controlled group of corporations or common control employers   **(d)** ☐ Multiple-employer-collectively-bargained plan   **(f)** ☐ Group insurance arrangement (of welfare plans)

5 (a) *(i)* Name of plan ▶ ....   **5 (b)** Effective date of plan
 (ii) ☐ Check if name of plan changed since last return/report
 (iii) ☐ Check if plan year changed since last return/report   **5 (c)** Enter three digit plan number ▶

6 Check at least one item in (a) or (b) and applicable items in (c). Item (d) on page 2 must be completed:
 (a) Welfare benefit plan: *(i)* ☐ Health insurance   *(ii)* ☐ Life insurance   *(iii)* ☐ Supplemental unemployment
   (iv) ☐ Other (specify) ▶
 (b) Pension benefit plan:
   (i) Defined benefit plan—(Indicate type of defined benefit plan below):
    (A) ☐ Fixed benefit   (B) ☐ Unit benefit   (C) ☐ Flat benefit   (D) ☐ Other (specify) ▶
   (ii) Defined contribution plan—(indicate type of defined contribution plan below):
    (A) ☐ Profit-sharing   (B) ☐ Stock bonus   (C) ☐ Target benefit   (D) ☐ Other money purchase
    (E) ☐ Other (specify) ▶
   (iii) ☐ Defined benefit plan with benefits based partly on balance of separate account of participant (section 414(k) of the Code)
   (iv) ☐ Annuity arrangement of a certain exempt organization (section 403(b)(1) of the Code)
   (v) ☐ Custodial account for regulated investment company stock (section 403(b)(7) of the Code)
   (vi) ☐ Trust treated as an individual retirement account (section 408(c) of the Code)
   (vii) ☐ Employee stock ownership plan not part of a qualified plan (section 301(d) of the Tax Reduction Act of 1975)
   (viii) ☐ Other (specify) ▶

Under penalties of perjury and other penalties set forth in the instructions, I declare that I have examined this report, including accompanying schedules and statements, and to the best of my knowledge and belief, it is true, correct, and complete.

Date ▶ ....   Signature of employer/plan sponsor ▶ ....

Date ▶ ....   Signature of plan administrator ▶ ....

Form 5500 (1978) Item 6(d) Must be completed   Page 2

6 (Continued)
- (c) Other plan features: (i) ☐ Thrift-savings (ii) ☐ Keogh (H.R. 10) plan
  - (iii) ☐ Employee stock ownership as part of a qualified plan (check only if you checked a box in (b)(ii) above)
- (d) Is this plan covered under the Pension Benefit Guaranty Corporation termination insurance program? . . . . ☐ Yes ☐ No ☐ Not determined

  If "Yes," list employer identification number and/or plan number used in any filing with PBGC if the number was different than the numbers listed in item 1(b) or 5(c) ▶

7 Number of participants as of the end of the plan year (welfare plans complete only (a)(iv), (b), (c) and (d)):
- (a) Active participants (employed or carried as active) (i) Number fully vested . .
  - (ii) Number partially vested .
  - (iii) Number nonvested. . .
  - (iv) Total . . . .
- (b) Retired or separated participants receiving benefits . . . .
- (c) Retired or separated participants entitled to future benefits . . . .
- (d) Subtotal, sum of (a), (b) and (c) . . . .
- (e) Deceased participants whose beneficiaries are receiving or are entitled to receive benefits . . . .
- (f) Total, (d) plus (e) . . . .

		Yes	No
(g)	During the plan year, was any participant(s) separated from service with a deferred vested benefit (if "Yes," see instructions)? . .		

8 Plan amendment information (welfare plans complete only (a), (b)(i) and (c)):
- (a) Was any amendment to this plan adopted in this plan year? . . . .
- (b) If "Yes," (i) And if a material modification, has a summary description of this modification
  - (A) Been sent to plan participants? . . . .
  - (B) Been filed with DOL? . . . .
  - (ii) Does any such amendment result in the reduction of the accrued benefit of any participant under the plan? . .
  - (iii) Will amendment result in a reduction of current or future benefits? . . . .
  - (iv) Has a determination letter been requested from IRS with respect to such amendment? . . . .
- (c) Enter the date the most recent amendment was adopted . . ▶ Month _____ Day _____ Year _____

9 Plan termination information (welfare plans complete only (a), (b), (c) and (f)):
- (a) Was this plan terminated during ☐ this plan year or ☐ any prior plan year? . . . .
- (b) If "Yes," were all trust assets distributed to participants or beneficiaries or transferred to another plan? . .
- (c) Was a resolution to terminate this plan adopted during this plan year or any prior plan year? . . . .
- (d) If (a) or (c) is "Yes," have you received a favorable determination letter from IRS with respect to such termination? . . . . .
- (e) If (d) is "No," has a determination letter been requested from IRS? . . . .
- (f) If (a) or (c) is "Yes," have participants and beneficiaries been notified of the termination or the proposed termination? . . .
- (g) If line 6(d) is "Yes," and either item 9(a) or (c) is "Yes," has a notice of intent to terminate been filed with PBGC? . . . .

10 (a) In this plan year, was this plan merged or consolidated into another plan or were assets or liabilities transferred to another plan? .

If "Yes," identify other plan(s): | (c) Employer identification number(s) | (d) Plan number(s)
(b) Name of plan(s) ▶ ....

- (e) Has Form 5310 been filed with IRS? . . . . ☐ Yes ☐ No

11 Indicate funding arrangement: (a) ☐ Trust (benefits provided in whole from trust funds)
- (b) ☐ Trust or arrangement providing benefits partially through insurance and/or annuity contracts
- (c) ☐ Trust or arrangement providing benefits exclusively through insurance and/or annuity contracts
- (d) ☐ Custodial account described in section 401(f) of the Code and not included in (c) above
- (e) ☐ Other (specify) ▶ ....
- (f) If (b) or (c) is checked, enter the number of Schedule A's (Form 5500) which are attached . . . . . . ▶

12 Did any person who rendered services to the plan receive, directly or indirectly, compensation from the plan in the plan year? . . ☐ Yes ☐ No
If "Yes," furnish the following information:

a. Name	b. Official plan position	c. Relationship to employer, employee organization or person known to be a party-in-interest	d. Gross salary or allowances paid by plan	e. Fees and commissions paid by plan	f. Nature of service code (see instructions)

Form 5500 (1978) Page **3**

13 Plan assets and liabilities at the beginning and the end of the plan year (list all assets and liabilities at current value). A plan with no trust and which is funded entirely by allocated insurance contracts which fully guarantee the amount of benefit payments should check box and not complete this item . . . . ☐

Note: *Include all plan assets and liabilities of a trust or separately maintained fund. (If more than one trust/fund, report on a combined basis.) Include all insurance values except for the value of that portion of an allocated insurance contract which fully guarantees the amount of benefit payments. Round off amounts to nearest dollar. Trusts with no assets at the beginning and the end of the plan year enter zero on line 13(h).*

Assets	a. Beginning of year	b. End of year
(a) Cash: *(i)* On hand		
(ii) In bank: (A) Certificates of deposit		
(B) Other interest bearing		
(C) Noninterest bearing		
(iii) Total cash, sum of (i) and (ii)		
(b) Receivables: *(i)* Employer contributions		
(ii) Employee contributions		
(iii) Other		
(iv) Reserve for doubtful accounts		
(v) Net receivables, sum of (i), (ii) and (iii) minus (iv)		
(c) General investments other than party-in-interest investments:		
(i) U.S. Government securities: (A) Long term		
(B) Short term		
(ii) State and municipal securities		
(iii) Corporate debt instruments: (A) Long term		
(B) Short term		
(iv) Corporate stocks: (A) Preferred		
(B) Common		
(v) Shares of a registered investment company		
(vi) Real estate		
(vii) Mortgages		
(viii) Loans other than mortgages		
(ix) Value of interest in pooled fund(s)		
(x) Other investments		
(xi) Total general investments, sum of (i) through (x)		
(d) Party-in-interest investments:		
(i) Corporate debt instruments		
(ii) Corporate stocks: (A) Preferred		
(B) Common		
(iii) Real estate		
(iv) Mortgages		
(v) Loans other than mortgages		
(vi) Other investments		
(vii) Total party-in-interest investments, sum of (i) through (vi)		
(e) Buildings and other depreciable property		
(f) Value of unallocated insurance contracts (other than pooled separate accounts):		
(i) Separate accounts		
(ii) Other		
(iii) Total, (i) plus (ii)		
(g) Other assets		
(h) Total assets, sum of (a)(iii), (b)(v), (c)(xi), (d)(vii), (e), (f)(iii) and (g)		
Liabilities		
(i) Payables: *(i)* Plan claims		
(ii) Other payables		
(iii) Total payables, (i) plus (ii)		
(j) Acquisition indebtedness		
(k) Other liabilities		
(l) Total liabilities, sum of (i)(iii), (j) and (k)		
(m) Net assets, (h) less (l)		
(n) During the plan year what were the:		
(i) Total cost of acquisitions for common stock?		
(ii) Total proceeds from dispositions of common stock?		

Form 5500 (1978) Page 4

14 Plan income, expenses and changes in net assets for the plan year:
Note: *Include all income and expenses of a trust(s) or separately maintained fund(s) including any payments made for allocated insurance contracts. Round off amounts to nearest dollar.*

Income	a. Amount	b. Total
(a) Contributions received or receivable in cash from—		
(i) Employer(s) (including contributions on behalf of self-employed individuals)		
(ii) Employees		
(iii) Others		
(b) Noncash contributions (specify nature and by whom made) ▶		
(c) Total contributions, sum of (a) and (b)		
(d) Earnings from investments—		
(i) Interest		
(ii) Dividends		
(iii) Rents		
(iv) Royalties		
(e) Net realized gain (loss) on sale or exchange of assets—		
(i) Aggregate proceeds		
(ii) Aggregate costs		
(f) Other income (specify) ▶		
(g) Total income, sum of (c) through (f)		

Expenses	a. Amount	b. Total
(h) Distribution of benefits and payments to provide benefits—		
(i) Directly to participants or their beneficiaries		
(ii) To insurance carrier or similar organization for provision of benefits		
(iii) To other organizations or individuals providing welfare benefits		
(i) Interest expense		
(j) Administrative expenses—		
(i) Salaries and allowances		
(ii) Fees and commissions		
(iii) Insurance premiums for Pension Benefit Guaranty Corporation		
(iv) Insurance premiums for fiduciary insurance other than bonding		
(v) Other administrative expenses		
(k) Other expenses (specify) ▶		
(l) Total expenses, sum of (h) through (k)		
(m) Net income (expenses), (g) minus (l)		

(n) Change in net assets—	a. Amount	b. Total
(i) Unrealized appreciation (depreciation) of assets		
(ii) Other changes (specify) ▶		
(o) Net increase (decrease) in net assets for the year, (m) plus (n)		
(p) Net assets at beginning of year, line 13(m), column a		
(q) Net assets at end of year, (o) plus (p) (equals line 13(m), column b)		

15 Has there been any change since the last report in the appointment of any trustee, accountant, insurance carrier, enrolled actuary, administrator, investment manager or custodian?   Yes | No

If "Yes," explain and include the name, position, address and telephone number of the individual who left or was removed by the plan ▶

Form 5500 (1978) Page **5**

16 Bonding: Yes | No
  (a) Was the plan insured by a fidelity bond against losses through fraud or dishonesty? . . . .
      If "Yes," indicate number of plans covered by this bond ▶ --
  (b) If (a) is "Yes," enter the maximum amount of loss recoverable ▶ -----------------------------
  (c) Enter the name of the surety company ▶ ---
  (d) Does the plan, or a known party-in-interest with respect to the plan, have any control or significant financial interest, direct or indirect, in the surety company or its agents or brokers? . . . .
  (e) If the plan is not insured by a fidelity bond, explain why not ▶ -----------------------------
  (f) In the current plan year was any loss to the plan caused by the fraud or dishonesty of any plan official or employee of the plan or of other person handling funds of the plan? . . . .
      If "Yes," see specific instructions.

17 Information about employees of employer at end of the plan year. (Plans not purporting to satisfy the percentage tests of section 410(b)(1)(A) of the Code complete only (a) below and see specific instructions):
  (a) Total number of employees . . . .
  (b) Number of employees excluded under the plan because of:
      (i) Minimum age or years of service . . . .
      (ii) Employees on whose behalf retirement benefits were the subject of collective bargaining . . .
      (iii) Nonresident aliens who receive no earned income from United States sources . . . .
      (iv) Total excluded, sum of (i), (ii) and (iii) . . . .
  (c) Total number of employees not excluded, (a) less (b)(iv) . . . .
  (d) Employees ineligible (specify reason) ▶ ---
  (e) Employees eligible to participate, (c) less (d) . . . .
  (f) Employees eligible but not participating . . . .
  (g) Employees participating, (e) less (f) . . . .

18 Is this plan an adoption of a: Yes | No
  (a) ☐ Master/prototype, (b) ☐ Field prototype, (c) ☐ Pattern, (d) ☐ Model plan or (e) ☐ Bond purchase plan? .
      If "Yes," enter the four or eight digit IRS serial number (see instructions) ▶

19 (a) Is it intended that this plan qualify under section 401(a) or 405 of the Code? . . . .
  (b) Have you requested or received a determination letter from the IRS for this plan? . . . .

20 If plan is integrated, check appropriate box:
  (a) ☐ Social security   (b) ☐ Railroad retirement   (c) ☐ Other

21 (a) Is this a defined benefit plan subject to the minimum funding standards for this plan year? . . . .
      If "Yes," attach Schedule B (Form 5500).
  (b) Is this a defined contribution plan, i.e., money purchase or target benefit, subject to the minimum funding standards? (If a waiver was granted, see instructions.) . . . .
      If "Yes," complete (i), (ii) and (iii) below:
      (i) Amount of employer contribution required for the plan year under section 412 of the Code . .
      (ii) Amount of contribution paid by the employer for the plan year . . . .
          Enter date of last payment by employer . . . . ▶ Month .... Day .... Year ....
      (iii) Funding deficiency, excess, if any, of (i) over (ii) (file Form 5330 to pay tax on deficiency) . . .

22 The following questions relate to the plan year. If (a)(i), (ii), (iii), (iv) or (v) is checked "Yes," schedules of such   Yes | No
items in the format set forth in the instructions are required to be attached to this form.
  (a) (i) Did the plan have assets held for investment? . . . .
      (ii) Did any non-exempt transaction involving plan assets involve a party known to be a party-in-interest? . .
      (iii) Were any loans by the plan or fixed income obligations due the plan in default as of the close of the plan year or classified during the year as uncollectable? . . . .
      (iv) Were any leases to which the plan was a party in default or classified during the year as uncollectable? . .
      (v) Were any plan transactions or series of transactions in excess of 3% of the current value of plan assets? .
  (b) The accountant's opinion is ☐ not required or ☐ required, attached to this form, and is—
      (i) ☐ Unqualified
      (ii) ☐ Qualified
      (iii) ☐ Adverse
      (iv) ☐ Other (explain)

Form 5500 (1978) Page **6**

23 Complete this item only if you answered "Yes," to Item 6(d) | Yes | No

Did one or more of the following reportable events or other events requiring notice to the Pension Benefit Guaranty Corporation occur during this plan year? . . . .

If "Yes," complete (a) through (h) below.

(a) Notification by the Internal Revenue Service that the plan has ceased to be a plan as described in Section 4021(a)(2) of ERISA or a determination by the Secretary of Labor of non-compliance with Title I of ERISA .

(b) A decrease in active participants to the extent specified in the instructions . . . .

(c) A determination by the Internal Revenue Service that there has been a termination or partial termination of the plan within the meaning of Section 411(d)(3) of the Code . . . .

(d) An inability to pay benefits when due . . . .

(e) A distribution to a Substantial Owner to the extent specified in the instructions . . . .

(f) An alternative method of compliance has been prescribed for this plan by the Secretary of Labor under Section 110 of ERISA . . . .

(g) A cessation of operations at a facility to the extent specified in the instructions . . . .

(h) A withdrawal of a substantial employer . . . .

If additional space is required for any item, attach additional sheets the same size as this form.

☆ U.S. GOVERNMENT PRINTING OFFICE : 1978—O-263-183

23-188 5979

CHAPTER 4

Retirement Income Issues and Pension Plan Design

Matthew M. Lind, Ph.D.

Vice President of Corporate Planning
and Research
The Travelers Insurance Company
Hartford, Connecticut

Ronald L. Haneberg

Consulting Actuary
George B. Buck Consulting Actuaries, Inc.
Dallas, Texas

Kenneth P. Shapiro

Vice President
Huggins & Company
Partner
Hay Associates
Philadelphia, Pennsylvania

David A. Giuntoli

Consultant
Hewitt Associates
Milwaukee, Wisconsin

John S. Perreca

Senior Vice President
Edward H. Friend & Company
Washington, D.C.

John K. Ware

Senior Consultant
A. S. Hansen, Inc.
San Francisco, California

James M. Dawson

President
James M. Dawson Associates, Inc.
Manchester, New Hampshire

Robert J. Duffey

Business Manager/Financial Secretary
Journeymen Plumbers and Steam Fitters
Local Union No. 393
San Jose, California

Siegfried O. Hillmer

Assistant City Attorney
Fire and Police Pension System
and City Employees' Retirement System
Los Angeles, California

Mark H. Lipton

President
Lipton and Lipton, A.P.C.
San Jose, California

Multiemployer Plans in the '80s—Will They Survive?

BY MATTHEW M. LIND, Ph.D.

Introduction

For more than 30 years now, multiemployer pension plans have provided a significant measure of retirement income security for millions of American workers. From fewer than 1 million participants in 1950 and assets of less than $1 billion, multiemployer plans have grown to an estimated 2,000 plans covering 8 million participants for pension benefits backed by more than $22 billion in assets. This growth has increased multiemployer plans' share of all individuals covered by private plans from about one in ten back in 1950 to about one in four today.

Without multiemployer plans, many—perhaps even the vast majority—of the millions of workers who have participated in these plans would not have been able to receive a pension benefit. In those industries where a worker's attachment is primarily to the industry and not to an individual employer or where there is a rapid turnover of employers—and these are the types of industries in which multiemployer plans are concentrated—the portability provisions of multiemployer plans are essential to being able to earn a vested right.

Moreover, the risk-sharing inherent in multiemployer plans has, over the years, protected workers' benefits from the business failure or shutdown of an employer. In the typical single employer plan, termination of the plan due to bankruptcy or some other business hardship often brought with it the anguish of lost benefits. This was often a shattering event for retirees and those workers near retirement, who had built plans around the expectation of receiving their promised benefits. PBGC's insurance program has gone a long way toward giving workers peace of mind in this respect. But PBGC's insurance does not cover all benefits. Moreover, the best protection a worker has is an ongoing pension plan, not only because they may receive their full benefits, but also because where a plan continues there is always the prospect of post-retirement benefit improvements. In these inflationary times, this possibility is no small consideration.

Mr. Lind, as vice president of corporate planning and research for The Travelers Insurance Company, Hartford, Connecticut, is responsible for the strategic and operational planning for The Travelers Insurance Companies and subsidiaries. Prior to joining Travelers, he was the executive director of the Pension Benefit Guaranty Corporation, appointed in November 1977, after having served for a year as acting executive director. Mr. Lind was with PBGC since its inception in September 1974 when he assumed the position as director of the Office of Program Development, with responsibility for the design, development and ongoing evaluation of the Corporation's insurance programs. He also has served as a management associate at the Office of Management and Budget, where he was actively involved in the development of national health insurance legislation, and the policy analysis and implementation of pension reform legislation. He received his S.B. and S.M. degrees in electrical engineering from Massachusetts Institute of Technology and his M.A. and Ph.D. degrees from Harvard in applied mathematics. A frequent lecturer, Mr. Lind has spoken at previous International Foundation and other educational meetings, and is currently a member of the Foundation's Governmental Affairs/Industry Relations Committee.

Multiemployer plans have typically afforded workers greater security as regards plan continuation. Unlike those covered by a single employer plan, workers in a multiemployer plan have looked to their plan—not their current employer—for payment of their pensions. If their employer goes out of business, while they may temporarily lose their job, they typically will not have lost their pension and their ability to carry their credited service elsewhere.

So, when I consider one of the questions posed by this session—"Should multiemployer pension plans survive?"—my answer is a conditional "yes." So long as multiemployer plans answer the needs of workers for pension portability and benefit security, they should survive. However, as I shall discuss a bit later, some of the ideas and proposals now being discussed within the context of the President's Commission on Pension Policy could radically affect the "needs" which multiemployer plans have met so well for so long, and thereby alter the attractiveness of such plans relative to other alternatives.

The Basic Problem

Turning now to the second question posed by this session—"*Will* multiemployer plans survive?"—I'd like to begin by recapping the basic problem facing multiemployer plans.

In its proposals to Congress transmitted roughly two years ago, PBGC said that the basic problem facing multiemployer plans is the problem of a declining contribution base. In practice, multiemployer plans operate on the basis of a relatively stable or growing contribution base. When a protracted decline in that base occurs, several things happen which tend to feed on themselves and make matters worse. Where significant past service liabilities exist, contribution rates go up; eventually, this tends to discourage new employers and their workers from joining the plan. More importantly, perhaps, high contribution rates relative to benefits may encourage withdrawals or, even worse, be a factor in precipitating bankruptcies if overall labor costs get out of line. This adds to the rate of decline in the contribution base, and the cycle repeats itself.

While relatively few multiemployer plans have failed, a number of plans today, for a variety of circumstances, find themselves on the brink of collapse. The recently enacted Multiemployer Amendments to ERISA attempt to address this situation. First, in recognition that ERISA has made matters worse, the bill contains measures aimed at fostering plan continuation and keeping employers within the plans. Second, recognizing that some plans will need help to fulfill their obligations, the bill provides firm statutory guarantees, thereby removing the disruptive uncertainties attendant to the discretionary coverage provisions.

All of this represents a delicate balancing act because, arguably, in its attempts to provide protection and encourage plan continuation, PBGC has provided added obstacles in some industries to building the contribution base through additions of new employers.

But, I'm not here to spend a lot of time debating PBGC's bill. I'm sure you've heard a lot of that. What I am here to do is focus on the basic problem—the declining contribution base. What I hope to do is to begin to address the outlook in the '80s for the contribution base of multiemployer plans in various industries. I use the term "begin" because, first of all, there is a real paucity of relevant data and, second, there are a number of considerations affecting the growth of multiemployer plans about which I can only offer conjecture and speculation. Nevertheless, I believe that the factors and contin-

Table I

Distribution of U.S. Multiemployer Plans
and Participants by Industry, 1976

Industry	Percentage of All U.S. Multiemployer Plans	Percentage of All U.S. Multiemployer Participants
Manufacturing	14.1%	22.7%
Construction	50.3	27.5
Transportation	7.5	20.8
Communication & Utilities	1.5	.3
Services	12.2	10.4
Trade	8.4	8.8
Other and Unknown	6.0	9.5
Total, All Industries	100.0%	100.0%

gencies about which I will be speaking should also enter into the thinking and planning of trustees, plan advisors and the parties to collective bargaining, as they consider the benefits and contributions under their plans in the years to come.

Factors Affecting the Contribution Base

Overall Trends

The future growth or decline in the contribution base of a multiemployer plan is the result of a number of often interrelated factors. First, and perhaps most basic, is the *employment outlook* for the industry; i.e., will there be more or less jobs? The answer to this question will largely rest on such factors as technological change, foreign competition, and both demographic and consumer preference trends as they affect the quantitative and qualitative nature of demand for goods and services. For example, the employment decline in the dry cleaning industry has, in large measure, resulted from permanent press fabrics—a technological development—and also the trend toward leisure fashion, which reflects the growing informality of our society. In the maritime industry, we see both the effects of technology—containerization, for example—and the decline of our merchant fleet as a result of foreign competition.

But the employment outlook for an industry, although important, is not the final determinant of the outlook for the contribution base. Of at least equal importance—perhaps even of greater importance, these days—is the *outlook for unionization* of the industry. Geographic shifts of an industry— for example, the movement of the textile industry away from the Northeast to the South—may signal a decline in the number of unionized workers even where the industry itself may be growing in the aggregate. Government policies can also quite obviously affect the growth of unionization.

And, even where new employment *is* unionized it is possible—in some cases, even likely—that these added workers may not elect to participate in an existing multiemployer plan. In particular where the existing plan is experiencing difficulties, both workers and employers may see it to their advantage to set up their own plan, defined benefit or otherwise.

What, then, is the outlook—or at least, my perspective—for multiemployer plans in the '80s? Let's begin by first examining the dimensions of the multiemployer plan universe.

Table I illustrates the distribution of multiemployer plans and their participants by major industry classifications. As we can see, the plans themselves are concentrated in manufacturing, construction and the service industries, with construction having by far the largest number. However, when we look at how participants are distributed by industry, we find that almost 70% of the participants are found—and in roughly equal proportions—among manufacturing, construction and transportation. These results reflect the relatively local nature of construction plans in contrast to the frequently regional nature and hence larger size of the much smaller number of transportation plans.

Table II illustrates the relative importance of multiemployer plans in the same key industries. It's

Table II

Multiemployer Plans and Participants
as a Percent of All Defined Benefit Plans
and Participants by Industry, 1976

Industry	Multiemployer Plans as a % of All Plans in the Industry	Multiemployer Plans Participants as a % of all Participants in the Industry
Manufacturing	1.3%	12.1%
Construction	24.8	98.6
Transportation	8.4	74.7
Communication & Utilities	1.8	1.4
Services	2.6	46.1
Trades	1.3	28.8
Other and Unknown	.6	10.9
Total, All Industries	2.8%	24.6%

clear that except for construction, where multiemployer plans account for almost one-fourth of all plans, multiemployer plans are generally a small proportion of all defined benefit plans found in an industry. On the other hand, when we look at participant coverage, we find that multiemployer plans are a significant factor in most industries, and a dominant factor in both construction and transportation.

What is the employment outlook through the '80s for key multiemployer industries? Well, to give us some perspective, let's start out by looking at the past record and future prospects for growth in the civilian labor force taken as a whole. As we can see from Table III, the overall rate of increase in the labor force for the 1980s is projected to be much less than has occurred in the past. The rapid employment increase in recent years, which reflects the economic recovery from the significant recession in 1974-75, is expected to drop sharply over the next five years and drop to the extremely low rate of 1.2% during the last half of the decade. Overall, labor force growth during the decade should occur at an annual rate of about 1.5%, which is sharply down from the 2.0% annual rate experienced, for example, over the period 1959-1973. The basic factor underlying this expected decline is that most of the post-World War II baby boom has already been absorbed into the labor force and that future entrants from the post-1957 group will reflect the much lower birth rates experienced since that time.

Table III

Growth in the
Civilian Labor Force

Year Groupings	Average Annual Rate of Growth
1959-1973	2.0%
1973-1974	1.4
1977-1980	2.8
1980-1985	1.9 } 1.8
1985-1990	1.2

Overall, growth in the civilian labor force from 1977 to 1990 is projected at an annual rate of 1.8%. Keep this figure in mind, because the employment projections I have pulled together for key multiemployer industries have been made for the same period. Viewing this 1.8% as an average growth rate will therefore help us to see which multiemployer industries are growing faster or slower than average.

Table IV presents the employment outlook for key multiemployer industries. The base year for all

Table IV

Employment Outlook by Key Multiemployer Industry

	Participants in Multiemployer Plans 1976	Industry Employment 1976	Multi-employer Participants as % of Industry	Industry Employment Projected 1990	Average Annual Rate of Growth 1977-1990
Bituminous Mining	268,847	219,800	100%	354,000	3.7%
Maintenance and Repair Trades	656,426	1,249,000	53	1,482,000	1.3
Heavy Construction	318,306	774,300	42	1,240,000	3.5
Other Construction	1,371,314	1,854,000	74	3,026,000	3.2
Baking & Confectionery	124,502	349,900	35	334,000	−0.2
Apparel & Textiles	617,624	2,236,900	28	2,536,000	1.0
Leather	34,975	23,200	100	16,000	−2.6
Furniture	120,760	305,600	40	502,000	3.7
Printing	229,033	1,099,200	21	1,315,000	1.1
Metal Working	216,526	1,154,900	19	1,358,000	1.1
Trucking	1,439,424	1,149,100	100	1,587,000	2.1
Water Transportation	198,304	195,400	100	192,000	−0.1
Food Retailing	392,966	2,036,600	19	N/A	—
Hotels	319,250	929,400	34	1,747,000	4.8
Hospitals	92,528	2,363,200	4	4,307,000	4.4

employment projections—that's column 1—is year-end 1976. The next two columns are intended to give us some indication of the importance of multiemployer plans in each of the key industries selected. Column 2 shows the total employment for the industry in 1976. Thus, by dividing the number of multiemployer participants—that's column 1—by the total industry employment—that's column 2—we get multiemployer participants as a percent of total key industry employment—and that's displayed in column 3.

This calculation tends to overstate the proportion of workers in multiemployer plans because the participant count in column 1 includes retirees, whereas the industry employment count in column 2 is limited to active workers. That's why, for example, the ratios for bituminous mining and leather actually compute out at greater than 100%. But we needn't let this inaccuracy bother us because the basic objective here is to get some indication of how large a factor multiemployer plans are in an industry. In general, where the proportion in column 3 is high, it is perhaps more likely than not that multiemployer plans will experience growth similar to the industry; where the percentage is low, it is less likely. But this generalization cannot substitute for a careful consideration of those "beneath the surface" forces and trends affecting the contribution base.

Column 4 shows the industry employment projected in 1990 and column 5 shows the average annual growth rate for 1977-1990 which corresponds to this projection. Overall, you can see that half the industries having multiemployer plans are expected to grow faster over the 1977-1990 period than the 1.8% growth rate for the civilian labor force as a whole. The other half are expected to grow less fast than the average with two industries, leather and the baking and confectionery industries, actually showing a decline.

Key Industries Examined

I'd now like to comment on some of the critical factors in several of these industries that—quite apart from the employment growth in the industry as a whole—will determine the growth or decline in the multiemployer plans operating in those industries. After doing this, I want to conclude my remarks with a few observations regarding developments that could impact multiemployer plans as a whole.

Starting with *bituminous mining*—we all know that our energy needs and our evolving national energy policy will place heavy reliance on coal; thus, bituminous employment will probably have rapid growth. This expansion will occur in western states, if environmental obstacles do not stand in the way (and this growth seems increasingly likely, given national needs and political trends). Western miners, however, are not organized to the same degree as those of West Virginia, Pennsylvania and Illinois. Moreover, even if unionization occurs on a wide scale, there may be strong pressures to set up separate plans. In balance—and without respect to the 1950 Mineworkers Plan—I do not think that multiemployer growth will keep pace with the industry, although I do not see any major problems for the existing plans. The industry is basically sound.

In *construction*, where overall growth is projected at well over 3%, the key question is whether this growth will be organized. I expect recent trends toward non-union operations to accelerate. In residential construction, rapid price increases will intensify pressures to control labor costs, leading to non-union or double-breasted operations. In heavy construction, the issue will turn on the extent to which construction in the South and the West is organized. These areas, where so much of our national economic growth is expected to occur, are far less organized than construction elsewhere. In balance, while I don't foresee a problem of national scope, I wouldn't be surprised to see serious financial problems in plans operating in areas where well-below average growth or population decline is expected. These problems may be exacerbated by the increasingly sharp economic cycles we seem to be experiencing, with construction bearing by far the greatest brunt during downturns.

The decline in *baking and confectionery* employment reflects both the use of more capital-intensive equipment and changing dietary habits of the public, especially the trend toward reduced consumption of products high in sugar. This decline may even accelerate, as the number of children declines to record lows as a result of sustained low fertility rates. Children and young adults traditionally have been a large market for baking and confectionery products. I would expect these declines to be more rapid in some areas than others, in keeping with geographic differentials in economic and population growth.

Despite foreign competition, which may have peaked, projections are for a slow but steady increase in the *overall* level of employment in the *apparel and textile industries*. But this growth masks a crucial problem: only about 10-15% of some 600,000 workers in the Southern textile industry are unionized, and that is where the growth is. The key here is likely to be the impact of the

J. P. Stevens breakthrough. Not only will apparel be widely affected in the South by this breakthrough, but other industries probably will experience at least a peripheral effect as well. But even if the South becomes organized, there remains the question of whether these workers will join existing multiemployer plans. Given the problems facing existing plans, there are strong incentives for both workers and employers in the South to establish new and separate plans. I'm not close to this one, but I would not be surprised to see such a development.

A similar situation exists for the *furniture industry,* which is heavily concentrated in Michigan and North Carolina. While Michigan is a highly organized state, North Carolina has traditionally—and, at times, vehemently—been non-union.

Printing, metal working and *water transportation* are expected to show below average growth. All are facing the sort of technological advances and foreign competition which will pose ongoing and persistent problems for many categories of workers covered under multiemployer plans. Although I don't look for any dramatic difficulties—with the possible exception of certain water transportation plans—these problems will pose an ongoing challenge to the prudence and fiscal responsibility of trustees and the parties to collective bargaining.

Food retailing, hotel and *hospital* employment can be expected to exhibit above average growth. Unfortunately, I have been unable to obtain specific data on food retailing because it is placed within the much larger retail trade classification in the projections I have used. Food retailing would seem to be an area where further unionization might appear feasible. There is an incentive in fairly low wage occupations for unionization, although this may be offset somewhat by the large proportion of women workers involved. Women traditionally have been more difficult to organize than men. But then again, traditional attitudes have not been holding up well these days.

Rapid growth is forecast for the hotel industry, reflecting both smaller family size and higher family incomes. What is problematic here is the extent to which energy prices or shortages may blunt this expected growth. In balance, I think the outlook is positive for the industry, and for multiemployer plans in the industry as well.

The growth in hospital employment largely reflects the rapid increase in the number of older Americans, especially the "old old"—those above age 75—whose utilization of hospital care is the highest among any population segment. While much of the employment in this industry is of a professional nature, there would appear to be substantial opportunities for organizing support workers beyond current levels.

Well, that sums up the industry-specific picture. In general, I'm not particularly pessimistic about the outlook in the '80s, at least as regards those factors I have covered. I think that if there *are* going to be problems, they are going to be in smaller local plans operating in those industries and regions experiencing average or below average growth.

National Policies Pose Challenge

What really concerns me are developments in Washington that are just beginning to enter the picture. I'm not thinking here about PBGC's Multiemployer Act. Rather, I'm thinking of the proposals that appear likely to come from the President's Commission. In their interim report, the President's Commission came out tentatively supporting or leaning toward the following key proposals, among others:

- A minimum mandatory private pension plan
- Deductibility of employee contributions to pension plans, and presumably higher contribution limits (i.e., H.R. 10 limits)
- The principle of faster vesting.

Taken together, these proposals and others could make multiemployer plans far less attractive or *necessary* as a primary means for providing retirement income security for workers in a variety of industries. For example, the minimum mandatory private pension plan might provide for full and immediate vesting and a 3% or 4% minimum contribution rate. Furthermore, such a program may provide employers with the option of making contributions to a quasi-government corporation, which would maintain individual accounts for employees and invest funds by means of private sector money managers. Such an arrangement may be especially attractive to small employers, because of potentially low administrative costs.

What does such an arrangement amount to? Well, in a way this minimum plan could operate as a sort of national money purchase type multiple employer plan and, if operating at a 3-4% contribution rate, could provide workers with 15-20% of final pay. Not a rich plan, but then again not a poor one, compared to the benefit levels found in many multiemployer plans.

The point here is that these developments could give employees and workers alike an attractive alternative to a multiemployer plan, and this could serve to undercut efforts in many industries to expand the contribution base. I don't mean to criticize these proposals. In fact, I personally think the Commission is on the right track. But these developments, if they come to pass—and I think they will during this decade—will pose perhaps the most serious challenge to multiemployer plans.

But this brings us back to a basic question posed by this session: Should multiemployer plans survive? I started out by saying "yes." However, if national policy developments create programs which bring to workers many of the same benefits now provided by multiemployer plans, maybe this question will need to be reexamined.

The Future of Pensions—Federal Government Impact

BY RONALD L. HANEBERG

Introduction

Anyone who attempts to look into the future of an economic system must be guided by the well-known principle that he who relies on the crystal ball will eventually eat ground glass. This danger is magnified when the primary thrust of the analysis is designed to estimate the effect of governmental involvement, for it is difficult to avoid personal prejudices in that arena. Perhaps the best way to avoid (or at least lessen) these twin problems is to make certain that the predictions are built upon a firm basis in fact—in this case, the past level of governmental involvement. We will, therefore, proceed by examining present government involvement, and attempt to extrapolate from these facts.

Before embarking upon this historical analysis, political realities must be recognized. The November 1980 election produced major changes at the federal government level. Ronald Reagan campaigned largely on the basis of "getting the government off the people's back," promising a reduction in federal government involvement in the economy. While some of his promises must be dismissed as mere campaign rhetoric, it is clear that there is at least a temporary conservative movement in the country. Substantial additional government involvement in pension plans thus seems highly unlikely, at least over the short and intermediate term future.

There is an even more substantial reason for expecting less activity in the pension area than the election of Mr. Reagan and the Republican control of the Senate. The four major Congressional spokesmen at the time of the enactment of ERISA were Senators Williams (D-New Jersey) and Javits (R-New York) and Representatives Dent (D-Pennsylvania) and Erlenborn (R-Illinois). Representative Dent retired in 1977, and was replaced by Representative Thompson (D-New Jersey) as the major House Democrat spokesman on pensions. The 1980 election resulted in the defeat of Senator Javits and Representative Thompson, while Senator Williams has found himself entangled in Abscam. Of the five major Congressional spokesmen on pensions during the 1970s, only Representative Erlenborn remains as a major leader and Erlenborn has always been an advocate of only limited intervention, rather than substantially increased federal government involvement.

In short, the Congressional experts on pensions have generally disappeared. While new ones may well arise, it must be recognized that pensions are a complex issue and, fortunately or unfortunately, lack political sex appeal. These factors alone would suggest that increased government involvement in pension programs is unlikely. At the same time, the general lack of pension expertise also makes it un-

Mr. Haneberg is a consulting actuary in the Dallas office of George B. Buck Consulting Actuaries, Inc., an actuarial and employee benefits consulting firm. He is a graduate of the University of Cincinnati and the St. Louis University School of Law. A fellow of the Society of Actuaries and the Conference of Actuaries in Public Practice, Mr. Haneberg is also a member of the American Academy of Actuaries, a member of the American Bar Association, and a member of the Kentucky and Missouri Bars. Mr. Haneberg serves on the Foundation's Accountants/Actuaries Committee and is a former member of the Educational Program Committee and the Actuaries Committee, which he chaired in 1979.

likely that there will be major reductions in government involvement, at least from a political standpoint.

Social Security

Impact on Retirement Planning

By any measure, the greatest federal government impact on pensions has been the result of Social Security. Originally signed into law on August 14, 1935, the act is recognized as a direct result of the Depression. At the time Social Security became law, only 6 million people had *any* type of retirement program, with a substantial portion of these being government workers. By 1977, 93% of the people age 65 or older were eligible for Social Security benefits. It is quite clearly the bedrock upon which pension plans in America are based.

The pervasiveness of Social Security goes far beyond the mere number of individuals who are covered by it. An individual retiring in 1980 at age 65 who has always earned the maximum earnings covered by Social Security (which as recently as 1978 was $17,700) could retire on a primary benefit of $653.80 a month. In 1981, if there has been a non-working spouse, the total benefit could exceed $1,000 a month for such a family. Almost as impressive is the fact that the worker who retired in 1965 with a maximum primary benefit of $123.00 will have seen the primary benefit increase to $409.10 by 1980 because of either ad hoc or automatic cost-of-living adjustments. The table indicates the magnitude of these increases. Before leaving the statistical realm, it should also be noted that Social Security estimates that the average worker retiring now has 51.2% of his pre-retirement income replaced by primary Social Security. (It must be added that recent changes in the Social Security law will cause this replacement ratio to decrease to about 42% for the average worker retiring at age 65 in 1986 or later.)

Social Security programs have also tended to influence the timing of benefit payments. The best example is the almost universal recognition that normal retirement age in the United States is age 65. There is no intrinsic medical reason for this age, and some industrialized countries have a different assumed retirement age. Age 65 was established, through political compromise, as the age that benefits would commence under Social Security in 1935, and has become part of the national economic fabric despite substantial increases in longevity during the intervening 45 years. To a lesser extent, Social Security changes permitting early commencement of benefits and providing disability protection in the late 1950s also affected the design of private retirement plans.

Given the economic importance of Social Security, it is somewhat surprising that the first 35 years of the law found only one major change in the method of calculating retirement benefits. In the 1970s, however, two major overhauls occurred. The first, in the early 1970s, was designed to provide automatic cost-of-living increases to retirees, thus protecting them from inflation. The second, in 1977, corrected technical errors in that adjustment procedure, but was also intended to ensure long term sound funding. It attempted to accomplish the latter goal by both substantially increasing future contributions and decreasing the benefits of future retirees. This decrease, already mentioned, is designed to stabilize the income replacement ratio (from *primary* Social Security alone) at about 42% of final pay for the average wage earner who retires at age 65.

Changes Foreseen

The pace of statutory change in Social Security will probably increase in the 1980s. At present, Social Security is confronted with four major concerns:

- Due to recession and inflation, the old age portion of Social Security is confronted with imminent bankruptcy. At present, the total fund assets are less than three months of benefit payments, with the expectation that even this cushion will be eroded. It can be predicted with an almost 100% degree of confidence that Congress will act in 1981 (or early 1982) to prevent this bankruptcy. Among the possible solutions are a temporary loan program (since this phase of the underfunding problem should disappear by 1985), interfund borrowing (since the disability fund is relatively sound), or general revenue financing of a part of the cost of Social Security. The most frequently suggested alternative in the latter area is removal of payroll tax funding of hospital insurance for the aged (Part A of Medicare).
- While the short term financial problems of Social Security are crucial, they also are readily solvable. More perplexing is the projected long term funding difficulty. It will arise after the turn of the century, and will occur through inexorable demographic factors. Quite simply, as the post-World War II "baby boom" reaches retirement age, there will be relatively far fewer active workers to support them. Because this problem is far

Table

Maximum Primary Social Security Amounts for Men Attaining Age 65 in the Years 1949 to 1980

Increase as the Result of Legislation Effective in the Year

Year of Retirement	Maximum Monthly Benefit in Year of Retirement	1950	1952	1954	1958	1965	1968	1970	1971	1972	1974	1975	1976	1977	1978	1979	1980
1949	45.20	68.50	77.10	88.50	95.00	101.70	115.00	132.30	145.60	174.80	194.10	209.70	223.20	236.40	251.80	276.80	316.40
1950	45.60	68.50	77.10	88.50	95.00	101.70	115.00	132.30	145.60	174.80	194.10	209.70	223.20	236.40	251.80	276.80	316.40
1951	68.50		77.10	88.50	95.00	101.70	115.00	132.30	145.60	174.80	194.10	209.70	223.20	236.40	251.80	276.80	316.40
1952	80.00			98.50	105.00	112.40	127.10	146.20	160.90	193.10	214.40	231.60	246.50	261.10	278.10	305.70	349.50
1953	85.00			98.50	105.00	112.40	127.10	146.20	160.90	193.10	214.40	231.60	246.50	261.10	278.10	305.70	349.50
1954	85.00				105.00	112.40	127.10	146.20	160.90	193.10	214.40	231.60	246.50	261.10	278.10	305.70	349.50
1955	98.50				105.00	112.40	127.10	146.20	160.90	193.10	214.40	231.60	246.50	261.10	278.10	305.70	349.50
1956	103.50				111.00	118.80	134.30	154.50	170.00	204.00	226.50	244.70	260.40	275.80	293.80	322.90	369.10
1957	108.50				116.00	124.20	140.40	161.50	177.70	213.30	236.80	255.80	272.20	288.30	307.10	337.50	385.80
1958	116.00					124.20	140.40	161.50	177.70	213.30	236.80	255.80	272.20	288.30	307.10	337.50	385.80
1959	116.00					127.40	144.00	165.60	182.20	218.70	242.80	262.30	279.10	295.60	314.90	346.10	395.60
1960	119.00					128.40	145.10	166.90	183.60	220.40	244.70	264.30	281.30	297.90	317.30	348.80	398.70
1961	120.00					129.50	146.40	168.40	185.30	222.40	246.90	266.70	283.80	300.60	320.20	351.90	402.30
1962	121.00					130.60	147.60	169.80	186.80	224.20	248.90	268.90	286.20	303.10	322.90	354.90	405.70
1963	122.00					131.70	148.90	171.30	188.50	226.20	251.10	271.20	288.60	305.70	325.60	357.90	409.10
1964	123.00					131.70	148.90	171.30	188.50	226.20	251.10	271.20	288.60	305.70	325.60	357.90	409.10
1965	123.00						150.00	172.50	189.80	227.80	252.90	273.20	290.70	307.90	328.00	360.50	412.10
1966	132.70						153.60	176.70	194.40	233.30	259.00	279.80	297.80	315.40	336.00	369.30	422.20
1967	135.90							179.40	197.40	236.90	263.00	284.10	302.30	320.20	341.10	374.90	428.60
1968	138.00							184.60	203.10	243.80	270.70	292.40	311.20	329.60	351.10	385.90	441.10
1969	160.50								208.80	250.60	278.20	300.50	319.80	338.70	360.80	396.60	453.40
1970	189.80									255.80	284.00	306.80	326.50	345.80	368.30	404.80	462.70
1971	213.10									259.40	288.00	311.10	331.10	350.70	373.50	410.50	469.20
1972	216.10									266.10	295.40	319.10	339.60	359.70	383.10	421.10	481.40
1973	266.10										304.90	329.30	350.40	371.10	395.30	434.50	496.70
1974	304.90											341.70	363.60	385.10	410.20	450.90	515.40
1975	341.70												387.30	410.20	436.90	480.20	548.90
1976	387.30													437.10	465.60	511.70	584.90
1977	437.10														489.70	538.20	615.20
1978	489.70															553.30	632.50
1979	553.30																653.80
1980	653.80																

in the future (particularly in political terms), it is unlikely that Congress will feel much pressure to solve it within the next few years. The most likely ultimate solution is the gradual increase in normal retirement age to 68 beginning about the year 2000. Opponents of the proposal have pointed out that this is a benefit reduction in disguise.

- When Social Security was established, a married woman was deemed dependent upon her husband. This concept has become largely antiquated, suggesting that much of the theoretical basis for Social Security benefits is no longer appropriate. There appears to be slowly building support for an earnings sharing concept, whereby the married couple is considered an economic unit. Even if the idea is ultimately accepted by a majority of Congressmen, the practical difficulties in implementing it in Social Security are legion. Thus, serious consideration of this fundamental change is also likely to be deferred for some years by Congress.
- Universal Social Security coverage has not been achieved, primarily because most civilian federal government employees and many state and local government employees do not participate in Social Security at their primary job. (It is interesting to note that neither the Congressmen who vote on Social Security nor the bureaucracy which administers it are covered by it.) Studies have demonstrated that a substantial majority of these workers do ultimately acquire Social Security protection, generally from a second job. Because these individuals often qualify for far greater benefits than their contribution justifies (due to the low-paid tilt of the Social Security formula), their benefits are frequently referred to as either "windfall" benefits or "double-dipping." It is clear that eventually either the Social Security law will be amended to prohibit these abuses or universal Social Security will be mandated. While the second alternative may appear preferable, the leaders of non-covered employees are extremely outspoken in their denunciation of required universal coverage. The issue will not be resolved easily, but Congressional action should be expected within five years. The most likely course is eventual universal coverage, with present employees (and their present programs) being allowed to continue outside the system.

Income Tax Laws

Plan Regulation

While Social Security is clearly the most fundamental source of federal government impact on pensions, the income tax laws have probably influenced the development of private employer plans almost as substantially. If it were not for the three major tax implications of pension programs—immediate deductibility of employer contributions, postponed recognition by the employee for income purposes until actual receipt of benefit, and tax-free accumulations of earnings on contributions—it is unlikely that employer-provided pension plans would be widespread. When the fact that *employee* retirement savings are not deductible (except for the relatively recent adoption of limited IRAs, discussed below) is added, it becomes clear that there has been a powerful impetus given to employer-provided pension plans.

The income tax laws for many years also served as the federal government's primary tool for regulating private pension plans. In order to qualify for those tax advantages cited above (and a number of others primarily of interest to high-paid employees), a myriad of legislated or regulatory standards had to be met. Foremost among these is that "qualified" plans may not discriminate in favor of highly compensated employees, or officers or shareholders. This standard served to guarantee that companies would not establish plans primarily to benefit a select few.

The rather cumbersome tool of income tax laws as *the* primary method of regulating pension programs was largely superseded by the adoption of the Employee Retirement Income Security Act in 1974. On its face, ERISA did not so much supplant tax law regulation as supplement it. In reality, however, attempts by the IRS to expand regulatory provisions beyond statutory language have been confronted with strong arguments that Congress has spoken. ERISA, and its effects and progeny, are discussed further below.

Deductibility of Employee Contributions

Income tax provisions still have one major impact on pension programs which was not effectively preempted by ERISA. Unlike virtually all other industrialized countries, the U.S. does not permit employees covered by retirement plans to make tax deductible contributions to these plans (or other tax-favored programs).

The original absolute prohibition against tax deductible employee savings for retirement has been gradually eroding. Employees of many non-profit organizations have long been allowed to make tax deductible employee contributions to tax-sheltered annuities through salary reduction agreements. More importantly, in 1962, Congress permitted self-employed individuals and partnerships to establish "qualified" retirement plans with, in effect, deductible individual contributions. Although the original permissible level of contribution was small, ERISA increased the amount to as much as $7,500 a year for defined contribution plans, and potentially even more for defined benefit plans. Because of requirements that all other employees of the entity also be covered after a minimal waiting period, these so-called Keogh plans were not pure deductible employee contribution programs. But the longstanding policy prohibiting such deductibility had clearly been weakened.

ERISA also permitted employees who were not active participants in formal retirement systems to make tax deductible contributions to individual retirement accounts. Again, the deductible amount was limited—initially, $1,500 at most, although this subsequently has been slightly increased where the worker's spouse also is not covered by a retirement system.

During the past two years, there has been increasing pressure to permit employees who are covered under pension programs to make similar deductible contributions. With the conservative tilt in the next Congress, it is highly likely that even greater interest in this concept will surface. Although there are arguments against such deductibility (primarily the loss of tax revenue), it should be expected that some form of limited employee contribution deduction will be enacted during the next four years. Other major changes in the income tax laws as they affect pension plans should not be anticipated during that period.

Employee Retirement Income Security Act

Background

The Employee Retirement Income Security Act became law in 1974, after a gestation period of almost ten years. Much of the impetus for legislation came from President Kennedy's Committee on Public Policy and Private Pension Programs, which did not issue its final report until 1965. Although supportive of the importance of private plans, the Committee also suggested that major legislation was needed in order to better protect the interests of the participants. It is perhaps informative to note that the nine years of debate resulted in only one major recommendation being completely dropped. The potential difficulties with portability encouraged Congress in 1974 to require only further study, an assignment which has not been carried out with a good deal of vigor.

The major areas of ERISA—fiduciary standards, participation and vesting requirements, reporting and disclosure, funding standards and plan termination insurance—need not be reviewed further here. However, a few observations about post-ERISA activity should be noted. Perhaps most importantly, ERISA did not sound the death knell of private plans. While relatively few new major defined benefit plans have been established, it is also true that only relatively few major ones have been terminated. An effective argument can be made that the trying economic circumstances of the past decade have had a greater effect on both the birth and death of plans than has ERISA. While problems do exist with ERISA, most observers have come to accept the major premises of the law.

More encouraging for those who oppose further government involvement in private pension plans is that Congress has shown virtually no interest in tinkering with ERISA's provisions. The only major change has been the revamping of multiemployer plan termination insurance and the addition of employer withdrawal liability, a change that was virtually forced upon an unwilling Congress by the unworkability of the original law. Even minor changes have been extremely sparse—primarily, limited changes in individual retirement accounts and in the taxation (or deferral of taxation) of lump sum distributions.

Predictions

With this historical background and the practical political observation above, the following predictions can be made about the revisiting of ERISA over the next five years.

- Post-retirement cost-of-living adjustments for private plans will not be seriously considered by Congress, and will not be adopted.
- Liberalized vesting standards will be debated, but again not adopted.
- Improved spouse's benefits will prove of no interest to Congress.
- Dual administration (by the IRS and the Labor Department) will remain unless the conservative trend broadens in 1982. Even then, the absence of any clearly preferable alternative suggests continuation of the status quo.
- Changes in single employer plan termination insurance, to parallel the recently adopted multiemployer changes, should be

anticipated within the next two years. The possible bankruptcy of Chrysler could hasten the reexamination of plan termination protection; the unfamiliarity of new Congressional leaders with the details of the problem could delay it.

A companion area of interest to ERISA is the possibility of adoption of a similar law dealing with public employee retirement plans. Many observers had expected a consensus to build over the past two or three years toward the adoption of a PERISA. No such activity has taken place. With no major supporters of such legislation, and with state and local systems almost unanimously opposing it, PERISA seems to be an idea whose time has come ... and gone.

Age Discrimination in Employment Act

During the decade of the 1960s, Congress became increasingly concerned with discrimination based on sex, religion, color or age, which resulted in the passage of a number of laws prohibiting discrimination in employment. From a pension standpoint, one would have anticipated that the Age Discrimination in Employment Act of 1967 would have been extremely important. Surprisingly, its passage had relatively little effect on benefit plans in general, partially because of less-than-vigorous enforcement by the Department of Labor in the benefits area and partially because of specific statutory language. Mandatory retirement at age 65 was permissible, and retirement before that age could also be forced, provided it was pursuant to a bona fide retirement plan which was not intended as a subterfuge to evade the purposes of the act.

In 1978, Congress acted to extend the protection of the law by (1) prohibiting mandatory retirement prior to age 70 and (2) specifically outlawing the use of retirement plans to accomplish early forced retirement. Employers were not overly concerned with the effect of these amendments on their pension plans because, prior to passage of the amendments, both the Department of Labor and the House Report indicated that these "amendments do not require that any additional benefit, benefit accruals or actuarial adjustment be provided other than those required under ERISA." A revised Interpretive Bulletin of the Department of Labor followed these guidelines, and many employers (but only a few Taft-Hartley jointly trusteed plans) continued to disregard service rendered and compensation after age 65 in calculating plan benefits.

On July 1, 1979, the Equal Employment Opportunity Commission became the administrative agency responsible for enforcing ADEA. Since the EEOC has frequently suffered from the delusion that it is a legislative body, it was not surprising that shortly thereafter the EEOC announced that it was considering changes in the DOL guidelines. By early 1980, the EEOC was hinting of major changes in the guidelines. By the fall of 1980, the vice chairman of the EEOC was publicly indicating that within a couple of weeks, proposed regulations would be issued making three changes. The most important was that, under defined benefit plans, employees must *either* be credited with additional pension increments (reflecting service, and compensation increases and benefit improvements, if appropriate) or have benefits increased actuarially if they continue working. The vice chairman was also quoted as indicating that under some circumstances the EEOC has reserved the right to require *both* additional accruals and actuarial increases. These proposals had not been issued by mid-November 1980. Although the reasons are unclear, there were potentially three factors. First, the EEOC was inundated with complaints from employers that this continual and costly tinkering with clear Congressional intent was unfounded. Second, the Secretary of Labor, Ray Marshall, sent a long and quite unfavorable letter to EEOC Chairperson Eleanor Holmes Norton opposing the changes. Finally, the EEOC also can read election results.

It seems that the formal proposal will not be introduced and that, even if proposed, it will not be adopted. Longer term, however, it is quite possible that the age 70 mandatory retirement age will be removed in its entirety and that Congress will require pension accruals beyond age 65 (subject to any plan-prescribed maximum). As noted above, the graying of America will present economic difficulties that may be solved largely by encouraging longer working careers. For the first time in 23 years, the number of *retired* men age 55-64 has leveled off instead of increasing, with government statistics indicating that about 45% of salaried employees who reach age 65 are now continuing to work. Better health, inflation, greater longevity and, ultimately, the needs of the economy may all combine to encourage continued employment beyond age 65. Legislative action may have little effect on these trends.

Miscellaneous Governmental Involvement

An outline of government impact to date would not be complete without briefly mentioning two other areas. The 1947 Taft-Hartley Act was important in establishing the legal framework under which collectively bargained industry or area-wide pension plans operated. Quite simply, employer contributions to a fund managed jointly by a board of trustees with an equal number of labor and management personnel was specifically approved.

The second cornerstone to collectively bargained pension programs was the court of appeals decree in 1948 in *Inland Steel Co. v. N.L.R.B.* This case determined that pension plans are a proper bargaining subject, since a pension plan is within the scope of the term "wages" and also within the scope of "other conditions of employment." Both of these are mandatory subjects for bargaining under the National Labor Relations Act. The Supreme Court refused to review the findings, although more than two decades later it did find that bargaining with regard to retiree benefits was *not* mandatory.

These principles have become such an integral part of the pension fabric that they are primarily of historical interest. It seems unlikely that either legislative or judicial action will change the principles in any meaningful manner.

The President's Commission on Pension Policy

One final source of potential future government impact on private pensions must be examined. President Carter in 1979 approved a ten person Commission to examine pension policy, under the chairmanship of C. Peter McColough of the Xerox Corporation. The origins of the Commission are somewhat murky, since President Carter had shown relatively little interest in, or knowledge of, the pension issue. In fact, it has been suggested that the Commission resulted from an offhand response of the President to a question on pensions where, rather than admit his ignorance, the President suggested this need for a high-level committee to examine all issues. Whatever its origin, the Commission has gathered substantial publicity. Its final report is due in February of 1981, but two interim reports were issued in May and November of 1980.

Reports and Comments

The first Interim Report indicated, among other things, that the Commission was quite taken with the idea of mandatory second tier pension plans. This minimum universal pension system (labeled MUPS) would be in addition to Social Security, and would be fully vested. Employers with already-existing pension programs could modify these plans (or a part of them) to satisfy the requirements. Employers without plans would be required to adopt the equivalent of a defined contribution plan with 2-3% of pay as the employer contribution.

While the MUPS issue dominated the first report, the Commission also developed a retirement income goal of 100% replacement of pre-retirement disposable income. Somewhat surprisingly, it is not enamored with post-retirement pension increases, believing that broader coverage is a far more important issue. The first Interim Report also avoided a number of issues, after some initial dabbling. For example, to quote the Commission on "social investments":

> The Commission believes that issues related to the ownership and control of pension fund assets are extremely important. Therefore, the Commission recommends that issues related to the ownership, control and investment of pension fund assets, including the question of non-traditional investment criteria, be investigated to identify and clarify areas for further study.

The second Interim Report indicated that the Commission remained intrigued with the MUPS idea, even though it recognized some of the problems with the proposal. Most importantly, it threatened to back away from the "universal" component by suggesting coverage only for employees who meet certain age, service and hours-of-employment criteria. More interestingly, the second Report was largely concerned with the impact of Social Security. The Commission reversed itself by indicating that it was now leaning in the direction of discouraging early retirement by increasing the normal retirement age under Social Security from 65 to 68 beginning with the period from 2000 to 2012. It further recommended changes in both the early retirement age under Social Security and the retirement criteria under Civil Service to "push back" retirement ages.

A Lasting Effect?

It is difficult to predict the contents of the Commission's final report. Some commentators have suggested that it will ask for its life to be extended, since it has not adequately analyzed a number of crucial issues. Others believe that the Commission will recommend a new committee to consider further the issues raised, perhaps with an orientation that more nearly parallels that of the new President. Most commentators believe that the MUPS recommendation will be the keystone of the Report. A minority of commentators disagrees (including the author). The Commission is also capable of understanding the tides of the country. As noted, the

MUPS proposal is already being reexamined to determine the appropriateness of coverage of a 17-year-old, fast-food counterperson and millions of others of that ilk. Probably the Commission will "suggest" the desirability of a detailed feasibility analysis of the limited MUPS alternative.

It is somewhat easier to estimate the effect of the Report. President Reagan will accept it with thanks, and be little influenced by its findings. Congress will consider some of the conclusions of the Commission, but will show little interest in the major findings. The Commission suffers from a dual problem even more pressing than those encountered by an author predicting the probable course of government involvement. First, it was appointed by a President who has been dismissed from office partially because of his inability to deal with major economic issues. Second, the thoroughness of the analysis of the Commission is subject to severe challenge. The Report will provide one set of viewpoints; it will serve only as a basis for sporadic talk.

The Pension Plan in the Year 2000

Extrapolating that there will be very little additional government involvement in pension plans over the next few years does not, however, indicate the probable status of pension plans at the turn of the century. A few random predictions (in the absolute certainty that no one will verify their ultimate accuracy) are not easily avoided.

- Social Security will have adopted an earnings sharing approach, will provide universal coverage with an upcoming normal retirement age of 68, and will adjust benefits through a retiree cost-of-living index.
- Private pension plans will provide full and immediate vesting, and generally will be integrated with other benefit programs so that an employee can choose his fringe benefit package annually.
- Employee contributions for retirement purposes will be tax deductible.
- Individual retirement ages will vary widely from as young as age 50 to as late as age 80.
- Public employee retirement plans will still be experiencing funding difficulties.
- Pension plan assets will be invested in a much broader range of alternatives, but "social investing" will be utilized in only limited circumstances.

Evolution, not revolution, will have been the means of getting to that future, with employer and union initiatives largely replacing government mandates.

What's Happening With Social Security

BY KENNETH P. SHAPIRO

Introduction

Social Security is a necessary and important system. It is also a very large one. There are currently 35 million recipients receiving approximately $140 billion in benefits. At present, 110 million Americans contribute taxes to support the system. On this basis, Social Security accounts for approximately 22% of the federal budget.

Social Security is also a very expensive system. For its first 13 years of operation, 1937-1949, the total maximum annual tax was $60 per year. Next year, each executive earning more than $30,000 will pay approximately $2,000 in Social Security taxes—and this individual contribution must be made in aftertax dollars. In addition, the company will be required to match the $2,000 with corporate funds. It is projected that in the next five years, an executive earning more than $40,000 will be required to pay $3,000 in Social Security taxes, and his company will pay a matching sum.

In addition, many company benefit programs (particularly the most expensive portions of benefit programs) are tied directly to Social Security. For example, approximately 90% of the long term disability and pension programs and about one-quarter of the survivor income programs of larger companies are integrated with the Social Security system. That is, in order to hedge against the vast growth of Social Security benefits, these corporate retirement, disability and life insurance plans are calculated with a portion of the employee's Social Security benefits as an offset. Thus, the level of benefits and the cost of these programs are directly tied to the Social Security benefits already available. In this way, the Social Security system makes a major impact on corporate benefit costs, which are roughly 40¢ on each salary dollar.

The benefits provided by Social Security are also significant. At the lower salary levels, Social Security replaces approximately 40-45% of the pre-retirement income. This grades down to about one-quarter of income replacement at the $25,000 salary level. In addition, these retirement benefits are free of federal income tax and are also increased

Mr. Shapiro, vice president of Huggins & Company, Inc., and a partner in Hay Associates (both members of the Hay Group), is a Philadelphia-based consulting actuary working mainly with qualified defined benefit pension plans. In addition, he manages the actuarial and employee benefit consulting business for the firm's Eastern Region. Mr. Shapiro has over ten years' experience in the actuarial and employee benefit fields. He has lectured and written extensively on subjects including actuarial science, Social Security, age discrimination, wage/price controls, demography, ERISA and the integration of pension plans with Social Security. Mr. Shapiro is a fellow of the Society of Actuaries, a member of the American Academy of Actuaries and an enrolled actuary. He earned his B.S. degree in mathematics at Brooklyn College, New York City, and his M.S. degree in mathematics at the University of Michigan, Ann Arbor.

annually by the full amount of the increase in the Consumer Price Index. And, these benefits can be increased by as much as 50% if there is an eligible spouse. Social Security benefits provide a substantial portion of the employee's total retirement income. For example, at the $10,000 salary level, Social Security replaces 39%, while the average private pension plan replaces 31% of the employee's pre-retirement income. At $50,000, Social Security replaces 12% of the employee's pre-retirement income, while the average private pension plan replaces 43%.

Utilizing the example of an employee age 40 survived by a spouse and two dependent children to demonstrate death benefits available, Social Security replaces 76% of the employee's pre-retirement income at the $10,000 salary level. This grades down to a 19% replacement ratio at $50,000.

Financial Background

To understand what's happening with Social Security, we need to address the financing of the system. Social Security is funded on a pay-as-you-go basis. This funding method is a cash flow technique whereby taxes collected each year are approximately equal to benefit payments made during that year. In essence, each tax dollar that comes in during a fiscal year will also go out as a benefit payment. The benefits are financed by a payroll tax to which employees and employers contribute equally. In addition, it has always been the intent that the system be self-supporting and not need general revenue financing.

By funding on a pay-as-you-go basis, Social Security is relying on an intergenerational transfer of wealth to meet its funding commitments. In essence, the working generation pays for the benefits of their parents through their Social Security taxes. As long as the population growth exceeds the interest rate, society can forever postpone the payment of the increased Social Security consumption of prior generations, and all generations will be better off. However, the population growth rate no longer exceeds the interest rate.

This is not the way private pension plans are funded. Private pension plans maintain assets to cover the liabilities for retired benefits already promised. If the Social Security system were funded like a private pension plan, it would need assets of approximately $3¾ trillion to pay for all the benefits earned to date by everyone covered by the system (both retired and currently employed). That's an amount equal to 60% of the net worth of the tangible and financial assets of all U.S. households; or almost five times the national debt; or almost seven times the federal budget.

The Sources of Crisis

Economic and Demographic Factors

As noted above, the system was originally rather small. However, it experienced massive growth through the 1960s, culminating with the 1972 Social Security Amendments. This legislation both changed the method of calculating benefits and provided for automatic indexing of benefits for inflation. And so the problems began.

In 1975, for the first time, the system experienced a negative cash flow. Actuarial projections made at that time anticipated this situation would continue for each of the 75 years in the period study, leaving a $4.3 trillion deficit. The reasons for the financial crisis included:
- Unexpectedly high rates of inflation
- Unexpectedly high rates of unemployment
- Unexpectedly high rates of disability
- Lower projected fertility rates.

One of the impacts of inflation results from the benefit payments being increased annually by the full amount of the Consumer Price Index. Thus, for example, the June 1980, 14.3% cost-of-living increase for benefit recipients added $17 billion to the cost of the system. Since Social Security is funded on a pay-as-you-go basis, this additional $17 billion must be funded through an immediate increase in Social Security taxes of a similar amount.

Unemployment creates a loss of revenue to the system. High rates of disability create both a decrease in revenues and an increase in benefit payments.

Lower fertility rates can result in a future with fewer workers and more retirees. A decade ago, there were four workers for every person receiving Social Security benefits: four persons paying the taxes to support one retired man or woman. Today, there are 3.2 workers for every retired person. By the year 2030 the ratio will be two to one; two people will have to pay for what 3.2 people can hardly afford to pay for now.

The tightening ratio of workers to retired people is based on the drastically changing demographic makeup of the American population. The children born during the baby boom of the post-World War II period are now creating a huge bulge of people in the work force. In reaction to that growing bulge, industry has built financial incentives into their benefit programs to encourage people to retire early to make room for the baby boom adults. However, the generation following the baby boom reflects the return to zero population growth and below, thus generating a much smaller group to replace the baby boom adults who will start retiring soon after the year 2000. In other words, beginning next century, there will be a "retirement boom," with not enough population either to fill up the work force or to pay the cost of the nation's promise of Social Security benefits.

Legislation and Benefit Design

The most important reason for the financial crisis, however, was a technical flaw in the 1972 Social Security Amendments. This bill provided for automatic adjustments in the benefit formula for increases in average wages and in consumer prices. Since each of these factors is affected by inflation, inflation has a compounding effect on the level of benefits. While the mathematics of this "coupling" provide acceptable results in a lower inflation environment, the high inflation levels experienced in the mid-1970s dramatized the problem with the formula. In essence, the benefit levels—and therefore their costs—were becoming uncontrollable. In addition, the formula was providing inconsistent results between different generations of beneficiaries.

In December 1977, President Carter signed the 1977 Social Security Amendments. This bill was enacted to avert the system's bankruptcy. Without this legislation, under the most *optimistic* set of assumptions, the first fund would have gone into bankruptcy in 1979.

The 1977 Amendments addressed the financial problem of the system through a twofold increase in taxes collected, as well as a redesigning of the benefit formula to remove the compounding effect of wages and prices. The new "decoupled" benefit formula also provides consistent results between different generations of beneficiaries. It does, however, result in lower benefits for all future recipients.

It is now roughly three years since the dramatic solutions of 1977, and the Social Security system is again facing financial trouble. Negative cash flows were experienced again in 1979. In addition, the most recent trustee's report anticipates continuing cash flow problems despite the large tax increases that will become effective in 1981 and later. In addition, unless Congress acts, the funds to pay retirement benefits may run out by 1982.

Two Major Issues

The 1977 Amendments also mandated studies of universal coverage and sex discrimination under Social Security. Before addressing the financing options, I will discuss these two subjects.

Universal Coverage

Social Security does not cover the entire work force. At present, 6.5 million workers—representing 90% of the federal work force, 30% of state and local government employees and 10% of those who work for non-profit organizations—are outside of the Social Security system. The lack of universal coverage has created issues that fall broadly into five categories:

1. Windfall benefits
2. Shortfalls in wage tax
3. Redistributive inequities
4. Forfeited contributions
5. Gaps and inadequate benefits.

The first issue, windfall benefits, arises when a worker spends the main part of his working life in non-covered employment, but has a part-time job or secondary career covered under Social Security. That worker benefits from the redistributive nature of the Social Security benefit formula, which is designed to favor lower paid workers. The Social Security system fails to distinguish between the low paid worker it is designed to help, and the worker whose earnings appear to be low because his main career was spent outside of the Social Security system.

Even more expensive than windfall benefits is the problem of shortfalls in the wage tax. The shortfalls arise when a worker spends time in non-covered employment, and then goes on to become fully insured under Social Security. The system pays this worker full benefits, even though the years in non-covered employment were exempt from payroll taxes.

While the Social Security benefit formula is redistributive, most public employee pensions are directly proportional to contributions and to pay. This creates the issue of redistributive inequities, since higher paid government workers are now better off—and lower paid workers worse off—than they would be under a combined system of pensions and Social Security. Another inequity arises when people spend a career in non-covered employment but work for a short time in covered employment, and receive no return on their contribution to Social Security. Finally, because Social Security and non-covered retirement systems are not coordinated, people who move between covered and non-covered employment frequently incur periods when they have no protection. In addition, the benefits of non-coordinated state and local government systems are sometimes inferior to those of combined systems.

If the entire work force were brought under the Social Security system, all these issues could be resolved. Coordination of benefits between the public and private sector would reduce insurance gaps; the benefits of all plans could meet certain minimum standards; benefit and contribution inequities could be eliminated; and the burden of retirement income redistribution would fall evenly on all workers. Before leaving the subject, however, it is important to realize that although universal Social Security coverage could solve the problems outlined above, mandating it would create new problems. These new problems would include substantial additional costs in bringing state and local governments within the system, the setting up of transitional programs, and even the ability of Congress to require coverage for state and local governments, or for tax exempt organizations.

Sex Discrimination

Changing Roles. As mandated by the 1977 Amendments, the Department of Health, Education and Welfare studied the issue of sex discrimination under Social Security last year. Its report concluded that the Social Security program does, in fact, discriminate against women. The report does make clear, however, that none of the inequities of the Social Security program is the result of deliberate policy decisions. Rather, they reflect issues that have arisen as a result of changes in American society reflecting the shift in women's roles over the past 40 years from lifelong homemakers to increased participation in the work force. Currently, almost 90% of all women work for pay at some period during their life. This is compounded by the more recent increases in divorce and remarriage rates.

Because of the changing role of women in our society, there is a growing belief that married women should not be treated as dependent under Social Security, and that the system of dependent benefits designed in the past does not work well today. If dependency is not an appropriate device for providing benefits for many women, then other methods are needed. Two options, earnings sharing and double decker benefits, are presented in this report.

Two Approaches. Under earnings sharing, the total annual earnings of a married couple would be divided equally between the spouses each year. Thus, 50% of the couple's total annual earnings will be credited each year to each spouse. The Social Security benefit of an individual worker then would be based on earnings of the individual worker and his or her spouse while married. Each spouse would therefore get a Social Security benefit in his or her own right. This process reflects the concept of equal financial partnership in a marriage.

The second option, double decker benefits, would establish a two-tier benefit system. Tier I would pay a flat dollar benefit to every United States resident, regardless of earnings, who retires or becomes disabled. An additional, earnings-related benefit, Tier II, would be paid based upon a person's average earnings while in covered employment. The total retirement or disability benefit would be the sum of both tiers.

Both options were designed with the idea that a new benefit system should result in costs that would approximate the long range costs under present law.

Financial Options

Returning to the financial crisis of the system, financial options currently being considered by Congress fall into three major categories.

First, *other sources of revenue* can be found. Although the Social Security system has always been self-supporting, proposals for the use of general revenues as a source of financing for the system are as old as the system itself. The concept of a value added tax (VAT)—a national sales tax, as proposed by Congressmen Long and Ullman—could be partially utilized for Social Security financing. Also, mandatory universal coverage would bring additional tax revenue into the system.

The second financing option is to *reduce the benefits* themselves. This can either be done by altering the benefit formula, altering the age of eligibility, or limiting the automatic benefit increases. The current Social Security formula ties initial benefit levels to average wages. Since, over the long run, wages rise faster than prices, a price-indexing formula would result in lower benefits for future retirees than a wage-indexed system. This alteration of the benefit formula would provide significant long range cost savings.

The long term financial problems of the Social Security system could be handled by *raising the Social Security retirement age*. This would also recognize increased longevity and the recent elimination of mandatory retirement at age 65.

Another method of benefit reduction would be to *limit the automatic benefit increases*. The annual automatic benefit increases provided to Social Security beneficiaries are now the largest factor increasing Social Security costs. As stated above, the June 1980, 14.3% cost-of-living increase added $17 billion to the cost of the system. One financial option, therefore, would be to place limits on these automatic benefit increases and/or to provide for benefit increases of less than 100% of the increases in the Consumer Price Index.

Finally, the overall tax structure could be left in place but *offsetting reductions in income taxes* would be made. Proposals of this nature represent a middle ground between those opposing an explicit payroll tax reduction and those seeking a payroll tax reduction achieved through infusions of general revenues into the system.

The President's Commission's Recommendations

In the May 1980 interim report of the President's Commission on Pension Policy, a number of recommendations concerning the Social Security system were made.

Regarding *universal coverage,* the Commission expressed a strong sentiment in favor of extending Social Security coverage to all new workers who otherwise would not be covered.

The Commission stated that a *change in tax policy* regarding employee contributions should be made so that the tax treatment of both employee and employer contributions to a pension plan, and earnings of these contributions, will be taxed the same. Regarding Social Security, the Commission felt that the tax treatment of all contributions to, and benefits from, the system should receive the same tax treatment as do those of other retirement programs. (If that tax treatment of Social Security benefits were adopted, the Commission then recommends the elimination of the earnings test under Social Security.)

The Commission stated that the earnings-sharing approach for the calculation of benefits under the Social Security system should be adopted.

Finally, the Commission recommended that the *normal retirement age* for Social Security not be raised at this time. This was in recognition of the "social contract" with working people today who are approaching retirement. The Commission felt, however, that serious consideration should be given as to whether this social contract with future generations of retirees should be changed, and concluded that it would be preferable to set the normal retirement age in terms of the proportion of adult life to be spent in retirement, rather than in terms of an arbitrary age.

Summary and Conclusion

After 45 years of experience with Social Security, there has been no serious public debate because not many of us have understood the program and its implications. However, the indestructible pillars of Social Security are beginning to chip. To avoid their crumbling, it is time to return to basic principles and rethink the objectives of the program in a public dialogue.

No longer a "sacred cow," as Milton Friedman once remarked of it, the program has increasingly come under attack. Martha Derthick of The Brookings Institute, in her book entitled *Policymaking for Social Security,* concludes that such criticism is healthy, and that reexamination of long-established doctrines and policies is very much to be desired. In the past, she writes, "the nature of policymaking did little to correct, but instead reinforced, a complacent, poorly informed acceptance of the program—participation was so narrowly confined; expert, proprietary dominance was so complete; debate was so limited; the technicality was so intimidating; the propaganda was so appealing; and the forward steps each seemed so small."

After 4½ decades of experience with a Social Security system in which a small group of lawmakers, actuaries and staff people have been making the decisions with almost no public debate, it is time to step back and ask: What should the Social Security system be? How expensive can we afford it to be? And, is it the best way to provide for the rewards of retirement?

Retirement Income Adequacy: How Much Pension Is Enough?

BY DAVID A. GIUNTOLI

Introduction

Those of us who deal with retirement plans have been much concerned with the issue of pension adequacy. The immediate cause for concern has been inflation. As we're all aware, inflation is working havoc with the employee benefit system. In the health and welfare plan area, inflation has a direct and immediate effect. It boosts plan costs and demands ever-increasing contributions even in the absence of any improvement in benefit levels. Inflation causes more dollars to be paid out of health and welfare plans even though benefit formulas remain unchanged.

The effect of inflation on pension plans is more gradual and indirect. Given the type of pension formulas typically found in the multiemployer sector, inflation tends not to affect required employer contributions. In multiemployer plans, the amount of benefit paid out on retirement is controlled by the plan's formula, and other factors unrelated to inflation. Multiemployer pension plan formulas generally do not adjust automatically for inflation. Inflation affects the recipients of pensions—not the pension itself. The plan is affected when adjustments are made to recognize the impact of inflation on the purchasing power of plan participants.

The intent of this discussion is to focus on the issue of pension adequacy. I will be approaching the issue from two standpoints:
1. Determining how much retirement income is enough, and
2. Examining ways to maintain pension adequacy once retirement benefits begin.

A considerable portion of this discussion will center on the role of Social Security. As most of you are well aware, Social Security is the foundation upon which our private benefit system is built. That foundation has undergone considerable change in recent years. It has moved from a basic system of protection to one providing higher levels of income replacement for the average worker. The

Mr. Giuntoli is a consultant in the Milwaukee office of Hewitt Associates. He assists both multiemployer and single employer benefit plans in the areas of design, funding, communication and administration. Mr. Giuntoli is a member of the Wisconsin Retirement Plan Professionals, Ltd. He received his B.S. degree in finance and his M.B.A. degree from Marquette University.

system also provides a level of post-retirement income protection that is unheard of in the private sector: full cost-of-living adjustment.

Let's talk about pension adequacy or, as I posed the question earlier: How much retirement income is enough? Individually, we might answer, "the more the better." There is nothing wrong with this answer as long as there are unlimited resources with which to work. Of course, this is never the case. Every pension plan operates under economic constraints. Given this fact of life, how can we effectively allocate our scarce resources to provide adequate pensions—and how do we define adequate?

Background

Let's take a brief look at some history. Private pension plans have been in existence in the United States for a long time. The first formal pension program was established by the American Express Company in 1875. The pension formula used by

American Express 106 years ago has a very contemporary look today. The plan provided for 50% of final ten year average pay, to employees over 60 years old with 20 years of service. Though not all early pension plans were designed in the same way, it is interesting to note that one of the first plans of significance recognized the relationship between an employee's final pay and the pension amount.

It is common today to see pension plan formulas directly tied to pay. This is especially true in the corporate sector, where the pension formula for salaried employees is often expressed in terms of a percentage of final pay. In collectively bargained pension plans, the pension formula is most often expressed as a dollar rate multiplied by years of service. In the large "pattern-setting" negotiated pension plans, pension multipliers tend to vary according to pay levels. Ford Motor Company's UAW plan calls for pension multipliers that vary depending on pay. The same is true for plans at G.E. and American Can Company.

My point here is that pension planners generally have accepted the premise that retirement income ought to be measured against the standard of pre-retirement pay. Retirement income needs of individuals vary widely, depending upon personal circumstances and lifestyle. Pay levels while working determine living standard. So, pre-retirement income seems to be an appropriate measure of how much will be needed in retirement.

If we accept the premise that pre-retirement income is a good measure in determining adequate pension levels, two more questions need examination:
1. What are the sources of retirement income that should be recognized in achieving the desired level of pay replacement?
2. How much pre-retirement income should be replaced in retirement?

Determining Retirement Income Targets

Regarding the first question, the sources of income to recognize in achieving the desired level of pay replacement, plan designers consider three principal sources:
1. Social Security
2. Private pensions
3. Personal savings.

As a practical matter, personal savings are becoming less of a source of retirement income for most people. This is a combined result of our tax structure and the emphasis in our society on current consumption. Accordingly, most designers of pension plans today consider only income from Social Security and private pension plans in attempting to achieve a targeted level of pay replacement in retirement.

What Is the Real Retirement Income Gap?

Consider now the second question, how much pre-retirement income should be replaced when combining Social Security and benefits from a private pension plan. Should 40%, 60%, 80%, or 100% of pre-retirement income be replaced?

The first point to make here is that we are most concerned about replacing an employee's pre-retirement "spendable" income. We can work toward identifying spendable income by stripping away the items that come off the top of actual earnings. Social Security and federal income taxes are the most obvious. There are other items that could be considered, but let's stop here to illustrate a point.

The retirement income charts—Exhibits 1-6 in the Appendix—display the relationship between Social Security benefits and aftertax income at pay levels ranging from $500 per month to $3,000 per month.

Exhibit 1. As can be seen from Exhibit 1, net income after federal income and Social Security taxes decreases from 92% of gross pay at a pay level of $500 per month to 77% of pay at $3,000 for a married employee. It also can be seen that Social Security replaces a fairly high 76% of gross pay and 87% of aftertax pay at the $500 per month pay level. The Social Security pay replacement percentage declines thereafter. In effect, Social Security does considerably more for lower-paid people at retirement than for the higher-paid, as a percentage of pay. That's because the monthly Social Security benefit, though pay-related, peaks out at the maximum amount for people with an average monthly wage of around $1,600. In other words, a person with a $1,600 average monthly wage would receive a higher Social Security benefit than someone earning $500, but would receive about the same as someone earning $3,000 or more.

The task of the private pension planner is to close the gap between the shaded areas—that is, between what Social Security provides and aftertax income. The *degree* to which the gap is closed will, of course, depend on the board of trustees' objectives and the financial resources available.

Superimposed on the chart are two sloping lines. Each represents the pay replacement that a $10 per year-of-service pension would provide at different pay levels. The broken line represents the monthly pension for someone with 30 years of service—$300 per month. The solid line represents the pension at 20 years of service—$200 per month. We have assumed retirement at age 65. Obviously, the flat $200 or $300 benefit will replace more pre-retirement pay for the $500 per month person than for the $3,000 employee.

Exhibit 2 presents a similar retirement situation. The only difference is that the two sloping lines represent pay replacement from a $20 per year-of-service pension. That is, $400 per month at 20 years and $600 at 30 years. We can make some general observations by looking at the pension lines. Focus on the 30 year service $600 line for a moment. A $600 pension, when combined with primary Social Security, will provide retirement income *greater* than gross pay for workers earning up to around $1,300 per month. The $600 benefit provides more than the aftertax spendable income of workers earning just over $1,500 per month.

A retiree does not pay income taxes on Social Security benefits. Benefits from a private pension plan are taxed as ordinary income. A retired couple, both over age 65, generally would not pay federal income taxes unless they had taxable income of more than $7,400. So the retiree in our example would not be required to pay any federal income taxes on his $600 per month pension. Of course, each retiree's tax situation is different, but within the context of the problem of how much pension is enough, this type of analysis offers a reasonably accurate way of measuring pension adequacy for a covered group.

Exhibits 3 and 4 introduce a new element to the analysis: the spouse's benefit that Social Security provides. In short, Social Security pays an allowance of 50% of the worker's benefit for a spouse age 65 or older, as long as the spouse is not eligible for a larger benefit based on the spouse's own work history. As can be seen, when the spouse's benefit is included, the retiree's pay-replacement situation greatly improves. Exhibit 4, in particular, illustrates just how much the situation improves at higher pension levels. It shows that the combination of family Social Security (primary and spouse's benefit) plus $600 of pension income replaces 100% of spendable income for someone earning up to about $1,100 per month, and actually offers *more* than the pre-retirement gross income for people at the lower earnings levels.

It should be noted that most designers of pension plans consider only the primary, or worker's, Social Security benefit when establishing a pension formula to achieve a desired pay replacement goal. This is because the spouse's benefit will not apply to every retiree.

The point of this discussion is to offer pension trustees and managers a means of measuring the adequacy of pension plan benefits. You may find, when take-home pay is used as a standard, and Social Security is combined with pension benefits, that the retirement income for your plan participants might be better than had been expected.

Exhibits 5 and 6 illustrate pension amounts for a person who retires early—at age 62—using the same $10 and $20 pension plan benefits. We have assumed benefits are reduced 6% for each year of retirement before age 65—a typical early retirement reduction. In Exhibit 6, the $600 benefit is reduced 18%, to $492, and the $400 benefit is reduced to $328. The retiree at 62 receives only 80% of the Social Security benefit he would have received had he retired at age 65. In this typical retirement at age 62 situation, the retiree suffers a 19% overall reduction in retirement income.

Exhibit 7. Consider carrying the analysis a step further to identify other components of spendable income. Exhibit 7 contains estimates of work-related expenses and personal savings at three pay levels. (Depending on geographic location, state and local income taxes also might be taken into account.) In this analysis, we have arrived at the estimated amount of money available for living expenses, and have subtracted estimated Social Security benefits. The difference is the amount to be made up from a pension plan and personal sources. (*Note:* Exhibit 7 displays *annual* instead of monthly amounts.)

Exhibit 8. Moving along, the government also publishes statistics which can be used as a guide in estimating retirement income needs. Exhibit 8 summarizes the annual consumption budgets for a retired urban couple as compiled by the Bureau of Labor Statistics. Three annual budgets are prepared, representing national averages. Regional budget amounts are also available, but for our purposes, consider only the national budget figures:

Lower Budget	$ 6,023
Intermediate Budget	$ 8,562
Higher Budget	$12,669

These budgets recognize that retired people have different expenses and lifestyles than working people. These differences are reflected in retiree expenditures. This information offers another tool for use in assessing the adequacy of pension benefits.

Social Security Formulas

As illustrated earlier, Social Security plays a large role in retirement income by delivering 25-50% of final average earnings for the majority of workers. Its substantial role deserves further consideration.

At the present time, Social Security benefits

have both minimum and maximum amounts. In between, the benefits depend on the employee's covered earnings. In essence, Social Security benefits are pay-related up to a maximum. The maximum benefit in 1980 is reached at final five year average pay levels of around $17,000.

During the decade of the '70s, the average percentage of pay replacement under Social Security increased from about 32% of pay to about 46%. In 1977, the Social Security Act was amended, changing the formula. The pay replacement ratios for the future—under the new formulas—will remain stable. For someone earning $10,000 a year under the old and new formulas, over a long term period reaching in to the 21st century, the new formula will lower pay replacement levels, although the actual dollar amounts provided will be higher. To some extent, the "old" Social Security formula took pressure off private pension plans to increase benefits during the 1970s. In the future, under the new formula, private pension planners may no longer be able to look to Social Security for higher pay replacement.

We often hear comments about the effects of inflation on retirees—those on fixed incomes. It is exceedingly difficult *not* to be sympathetic to retirees whose purchasing power is being eroded by inflation. But, there is something of a myth about those retirees on "fixed incomes."

- No one retiring from business or industry who is covered by Social Security is on a fixed income.
- Social Security—which represents anywhere from one-quarter to over one-half of most people's retirement income—is fully indexed to changes in the Consumer Price Index.

Exhibit 9 illustrates the point about Social Security indexation. Here we have an example of a person retiring at age 65 in 1965. We have assumed that his pension benefit was $200 per month and his Social Security benefit was $132 per month. Both are reasonable benefit levels for 1965. We have assumed no increases in his pension in order to focus on what happened to his Social Security benefit. The left columns track actual dollars paid over the years. The right columns deflate the actual dollars into 1965 constant dollars.

This retiree received 12 Social Security benefit increases over the years 1965-1980. The $132 benefit in 1965 became $409 in 1980—a 210% increase. His combined benefit increased from $332 to $609 —or over 80%. How do the actual dollars compare on a constant dollar basis? Obviously, not as well. The sample retiree suffered a substantial loss of purchasing power on his $200 pension because he received no increases. But, look at the Social Security benefit. He actually had real gains here. Because of periodic increases, the real value of the Social Security benefit increased from $132 to $156. Social Security increases over this period actually outpaced the rate of inflation as measured by the Consumer Price Index. Because of Social Security increases—which are now fully indexed—this retiree's combined loss of purchasing power was limited to 30%. This compares with an overall 62% decrease during the 1965-1980 time period.

The retirement income charts illustrated how much *more* Social Security does for lower-paid workers in terms of pay replacement. Obviously, the more Social Security represents in terms of one's pay replacement at retirement, the better one is insulated from the effects of inflation.

Plan Design: Adjusting for Inflation

So far, this discussion has focused on pension adequacy and the role of Social Security. The next major topic deals with the avenues private pension plans have available to maintain a level of adequacy when inflation is eroding pension value.

Keeping pensions in step with inflation presents problems at two levels:

1. Retired employees whose benefits are fixed at retirement, and
2. Active employees—or future retirees—whose pensions will be determined by benefit rates in effect at some future date.

In the private sector, the truly "inflation-proof" pension which covers both levels (active and retired employees) is a rarity. Only the government, it seems, can afford such a luxury.

Consider the kinds of pension plans found in the private sector. Each has a different capacity to adjust to inflation. Broadly speaking, there are two kinds of pension plans—defined benefit and defined contribution. Defined benefit plans promise a future benefit. Defined contribution plans promise a current contribution.

Defined Benefit Plans

Some defined benefit plans have a pension formula that is pay-related. A typical formula for someone with 30 years of service might be 50% of final average pay less 50% of Social Security. This type of plan is "inflation-proof" at least up to retirement because the formula tracks with increases in pay.

In the multiemployer field, the most prevalent pension formulas are service-related. That is, the

formulas are expressed as either:
- Dollars times service, or
- Percentage times contributions.

These kinds of plans generally have no built-in inflation protection. Inflation protection comes only through specific board of trustee action as increases in the contribution rate are negotiated. But, what specific actions can be taken?

Focusing on retirees, rapidly rising living costs and improvements in longevity can make benefit levels inadequate over a long retirement period. One approach available is a *periodic revision of benefits.* Benefits can be kept under review and periodically increased when the board of trustees believes that inflation has eroded the value of pensions and additional contribution income is available. The advantages and disadvantages of this approach include:
- The liability for each increase is known at the time of the change and the amount of the increase in benefits can be tailored to the amount of money available.
- The long term liability for a series of unknown changes cannot be funded for in advance, and there is no guarantee to employees that future increases will be given—or that they will be sufficient to keep up with changes in the cost of living.
- This kind of adjustment is totally discretionary and may be based on factors other than the change in the cost of living.

Periodic updating of retiree benefits is by far the most prevalent approach to protecting retirees against inflation. Periodic updating creates an unfunded actuarial liability each time an increase is made. However, the liability can be paid over a period of years.

A second approach is to adopt some method for *increasing benefits based on either a predetermined formula or an index.* There are various versions of this approach. Some examples include:
- An annuity payable at retirement that will be increased by $x\%$ each year. The increase takes place regardless of what happens to the Consumer Price Index. The concept is one of an increasing annuity, rather than indexing. The cost is known, and the implications of an unknown liability are avoided. This could also be offered as an individual retirement option.
- Adjusting pensions in accordance with changes in the Consumer Price Index, but not to exceed $x\%$ per year. This is indexation with a cap. A dollar cap could be used in place of the percentage cap.
- Adjusting retirement benefits in any year in which the Consumer Price Index exceeds say, 5% a year, and to the extent of the excess. This is a catastrophic form of protection.
- Tying the retirement income adjustment directly to changes in the Consumer Price Index. Unquestionably, this alternative would be the most popular with employees, since it would eliminate concerns over the risks of inflation. Purchasing power is fully guaranteed from the date of retirement. From the trustee's point of view, this kind of provision will have costs that are both high and unpredictable. This is essentially the approach used by the government for Social Security and federal employee pensions.

None of the forms of automatic pension increases mentioned are prevalent in the private sector today. The main reason is probably cost. For example, our actuaries tell us that, as a rule of thumb, if retirement benefits were increased at a compounded rate of 3%, the long run cost of the plan will increase by about 30%.

As mentioned earlier, current retirees are not the only group affected by inflation. Future retirees are also affected. If the board of trustees has established a pay replacement objective, then periodic adjustments will be needed in the pension formula to maintain that objective. For example, take an employee who is paid $1,000 in 1979. Assume that the pay replacement objective is 80%. That means we're going to have a pension, after 30 years, of $360, or $12 per year of service. If his pay rises about 7½% per year until 1985, to meet the same pay replacement objective requires $1,264. In order to do this, that pension multiplier has to go from $12 to $21. It is with the active employee where the problem of maintaining pension adequacy, though less obvious, may be the greater.

Defined Contribution Plans

Defined contribution pension plans have become a topic of discussion with boards of trustees lately. Defined contribution plans are individual account plans which do not provide specified benefits. These kinds of plans have become "hot topics" because they are not subject to PBGC jurisdiction. Employers like them because there is no unfunded liability. In fact, they are fully funded at all times. Employees like them because they can see their individual accounts grow.

There is nothing wrong with the concept of

defined contribution plans—they have many good features. The principal concern about defined contribution plans is that they can fall short in periods of high inflation. The basic flaw in a defined contribution arrangement is that the benefits payable at retirement depend on the balance in the account of the retiring employee. Relatively greater weight is given to pay during early years of service, when wages were low, than to the higher earnings of later years. Smaller contributions of the early years are invested at compounded interest for a longer period of time than the larger contributions of later years. In a period of extended inflation, the higher contributions in later years may not offset the low contributions of the early years—unless superior investment results are achieved. The risk rests with the employee, not the plan.

In a defined benefit plan, past service can be given immediate recognition—to adjust for inflation—by increasing the benefit multiplier for *all* service. This is difficult in a defined contribution plan. For these reasons, from a plan design point of view, defined contribution plans usually serve best as a pension supplement rather than as the primary source of retirement income.

Conclusion

Our discussion has focused on two primary issues:
1. Pension adequacy. We discussed the concept of spendable income as a measure that makes some sense. And, we looked at some tools that can be used in evaluating the adequacy of pension amounts.
2. Methods of maintaining the purchasing power of pensions. This is a very difficult subject because the avenues available are generally all expensive.

In the final analysis, what does all this add up to for pension trustees concerned with the issue of adequacy?

I would like to be able to say that pressure for pension adequacy will diminish in the future, but I don't think this will be the case. We've all heard the predictions about inflation over the coming decade. Very few forecasters are optimistic that we can eliminate the upward creep in the cost of living.

We also know that we're moving toward the "graying of America." We won't see a dramatic surge in the proportion of the population over age 65 until after the year 2000, but we're headed in the direction of more people moving into age brackets where the level of future retirement income is a very real concern.

There are no easy answers. The pension adequacy issue is here to stay. But my sense is that careful planning can help us solve the pension adequacy dilemma. Here are some suggested strategies for addressing the issue within different employment environments:

1. *Establish pay replacement targets.* Obviously, establishing objectives is easier for a single employer. However, the principles seem to apply equally in the multiemployer sector. The cents-per-hour figures negotiated at the bargaining table could translate into a target pension level for covered employee groups. In allocating a wage package, it may be appropriate to focus on the target rather than only on a cents-per-hour figure.

2. *Recognize the role of Social Security.* While Social Security integration may be inappropriate for a multiemployer plan, some recognition needs to be given to the level of coverage provided through the public system. Employees covered under multiemployer plans typically have widely varying pay schedules. Some plans may be providing "too much" income at the low end of the pay scale, and others "too little" at the upper end. Monitor the pay system and relate average pay scales to the sloping level of protection provided through Social Security.

3. *Coordinate retirement income planning.* Review retirement policies from a collective perspective. If your concern is pension adequacy, are you also providing generous early retirement "sweeteners" to encourage employees to leave the labor force? Conversely, are you providing inducements for late retirement? These policies may not be appropriate if your overriding concern is adequate basic pension protection for all employees.

4. *Look for compromise in the battle over post-retirement pension protection.* Recognize that pressure for indexing will not go away and that some compromise will be in order. You, as pension trustees, cannot be allocating all of your scarce resources to your retired population at the expense of the actives. Neither can you ignore the legitimate needs of pensioners. Wherever possible, keep increases on an ad hoc basis. Again, nearly full inflation protection is provided through Social Security, especially for retirees who derive most of their retire-

ment income from the public system. As I said earlier, there are no easy answers. But, effective planning is the best way I know out of the pension adequacy dilemma.

156

Appendix

Retirement Income Charts

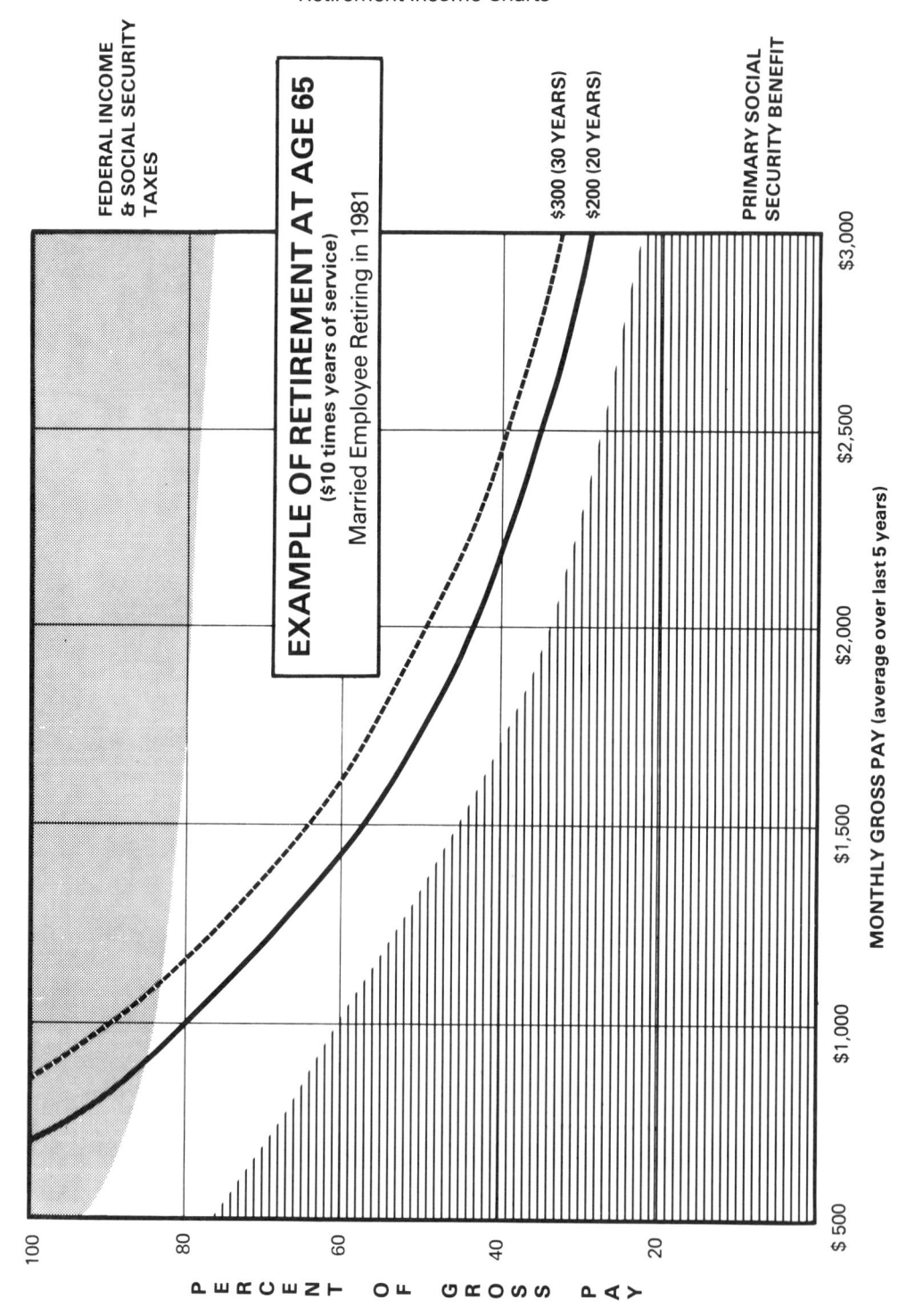

Exhibit 1

EXAMPLE OF RETIREMENT AT AGE 65
($10 times years of service)
Married Employee Retiring in 1981

FEDERAL INCOME & SOCIAL SECURITY TAXES

$300 (30 YEARS)
$200 (20 YEARS)

PRIMARY SOCIAL SECURITY BENEFIT

PERCENT OF GROSS PAY

MONTHLY GROSS PAY (average over last 5 years)

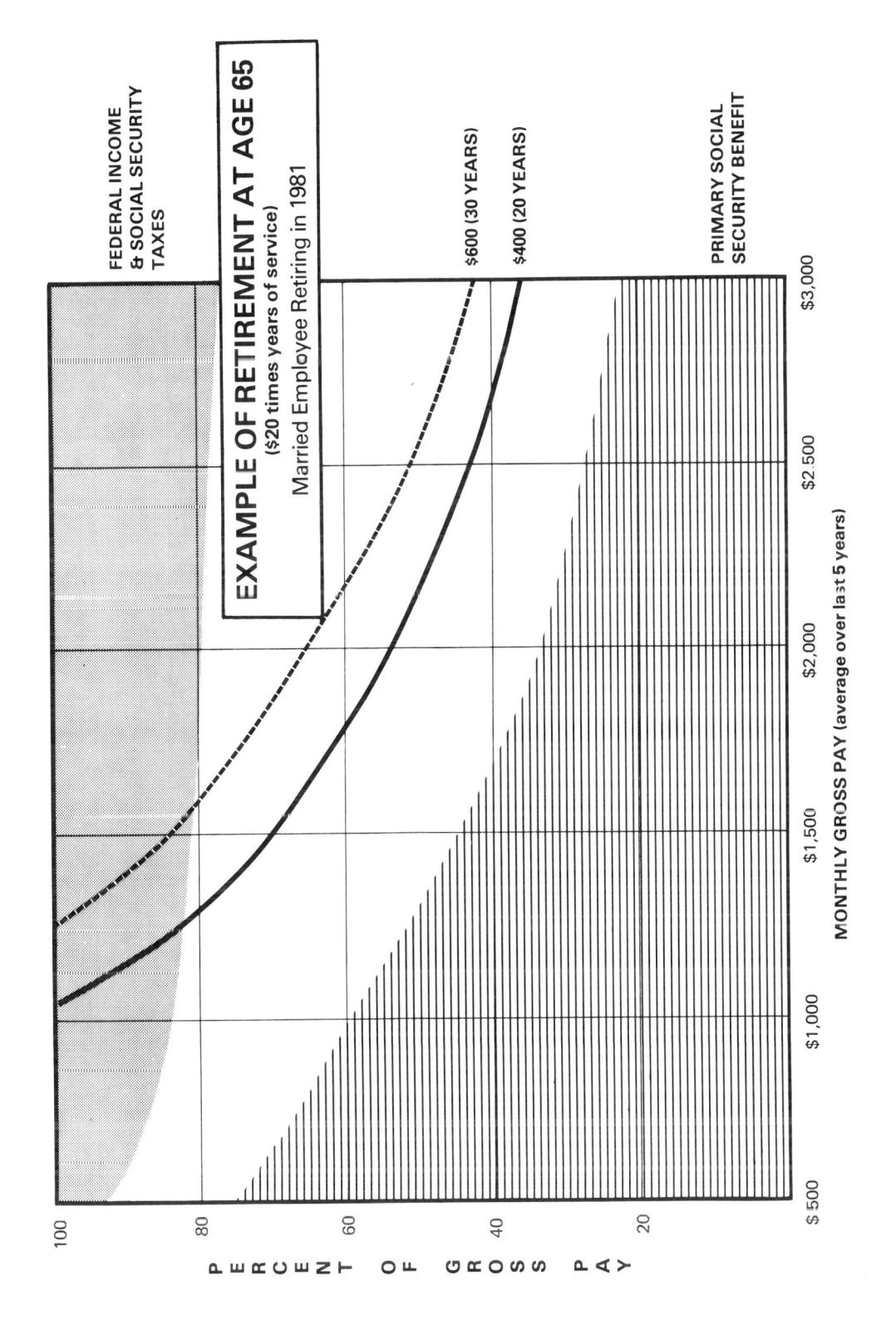

Exhibit 2

EXAMPLE OF RETIREMENT AT AGE 65
($20 times years of service)
Married Employee Retiring in 1981

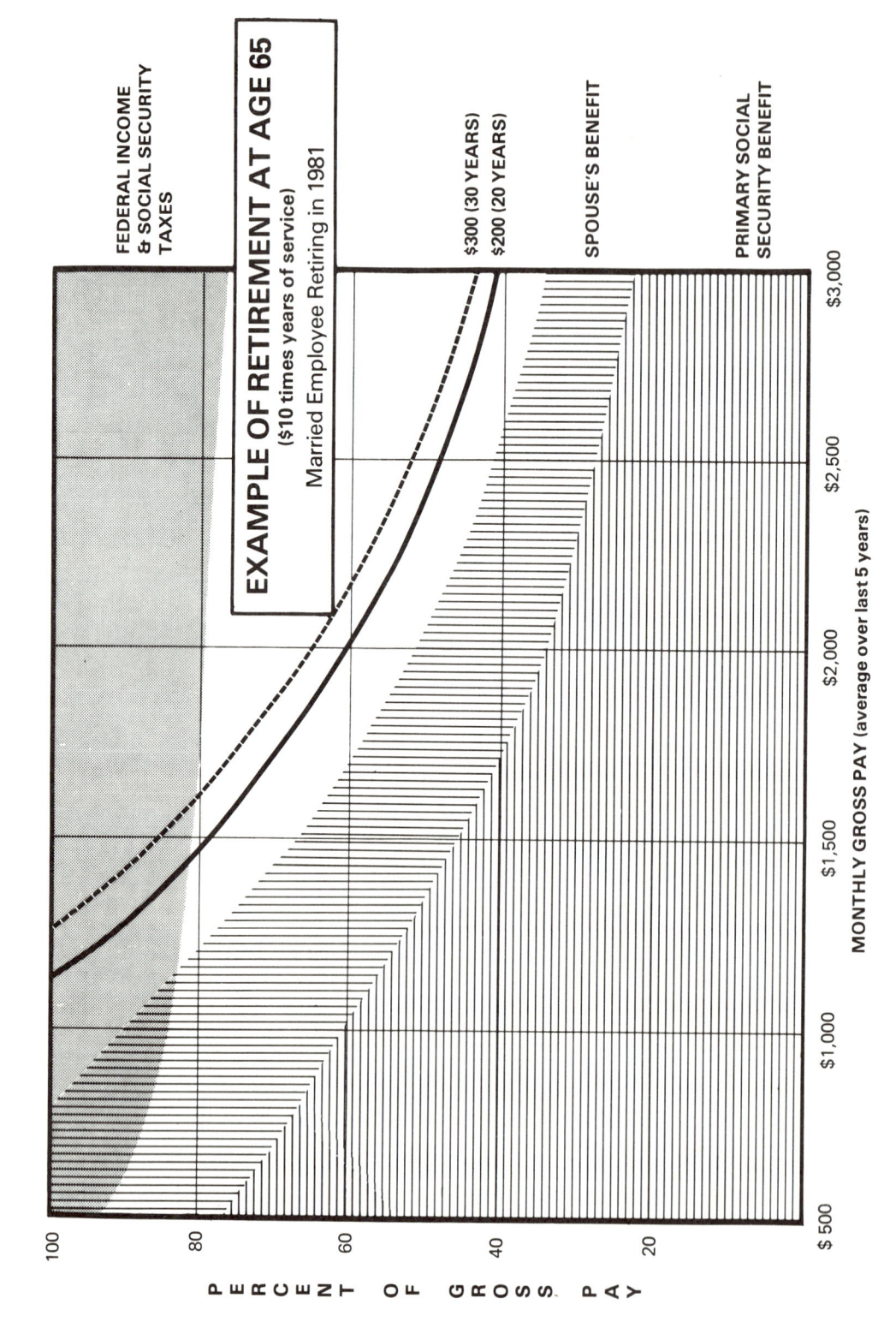

Exhibit 3

EXAMPLE OF RETIREMENT AT AGE 65
($10 times years of service)
Married Employee Retiring in 1981

- FEDERAL INCOME & SOCIAL SECURITY TAXES
- $300 (30 YEARS)
- $200 (20 YEARS)
- SPOUSE'S BENEFIT
- PRIMARY SOCIAL SECURITY BENEFIT

PERCENT OF GROSS PAY: 100, 80, 60, 40, 20

MONTHLY GROSS PAY (average over last 5 years): $500, $1,000, $1,500, $2,000, $2,500, $3,000

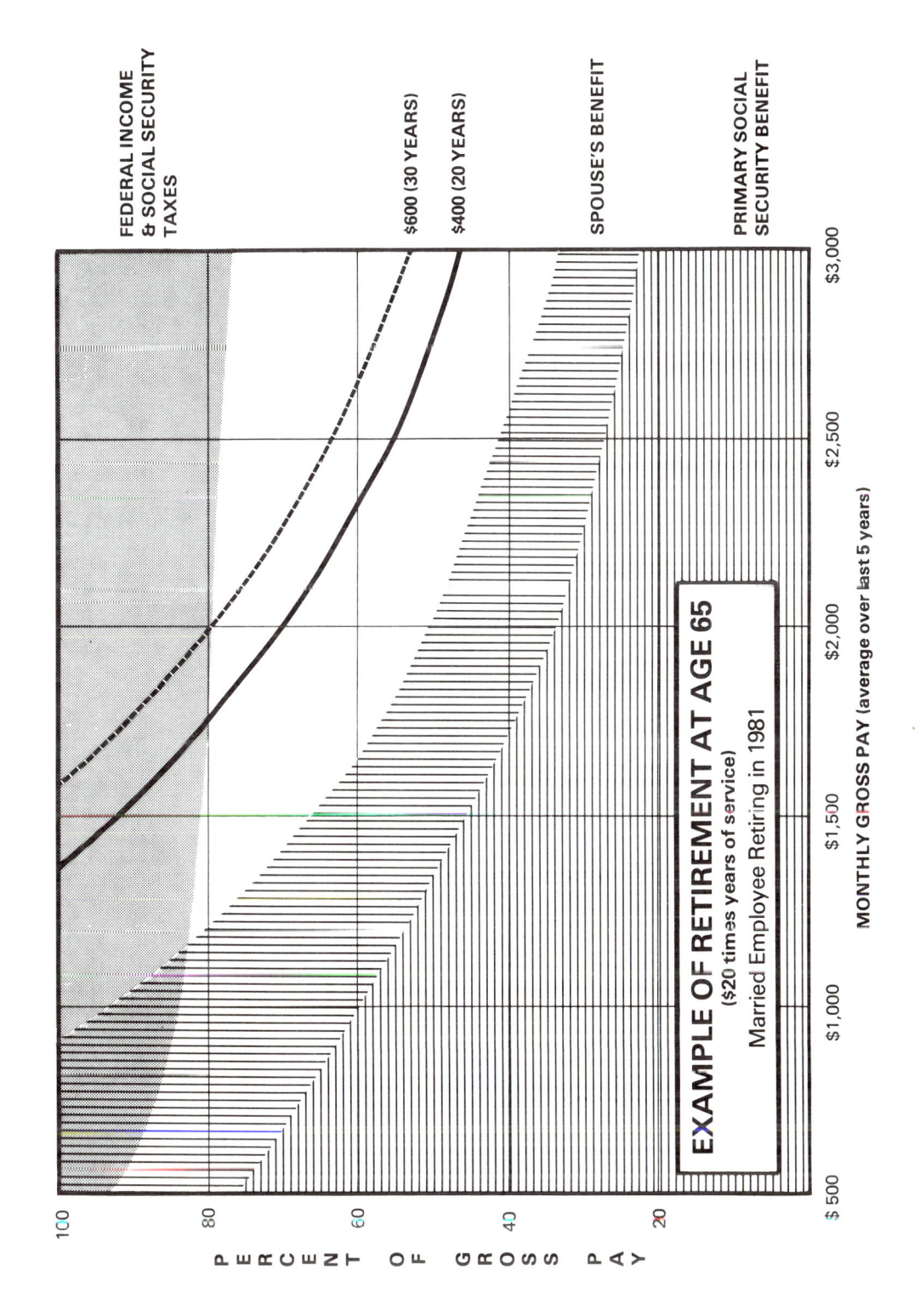

Exhibit 4

EXAMPLE OF RETIREMENT AT AGE 65
($20 times years of service)
Married Employee Retiring in 1981

- FEDERAL INCOME & SOCIAL SECURITY TAXES
- $600 (30 YEARS)
- $400 (20 YEARS)
- SPOUSE'S BENEFIT
- PRIMARY SOCIAL SECURITY BENEFIT

PERCENT OF GROSS PAY

MONTHLY GROSS PAY (average over last 5 years)

1980 Annual Conference 159

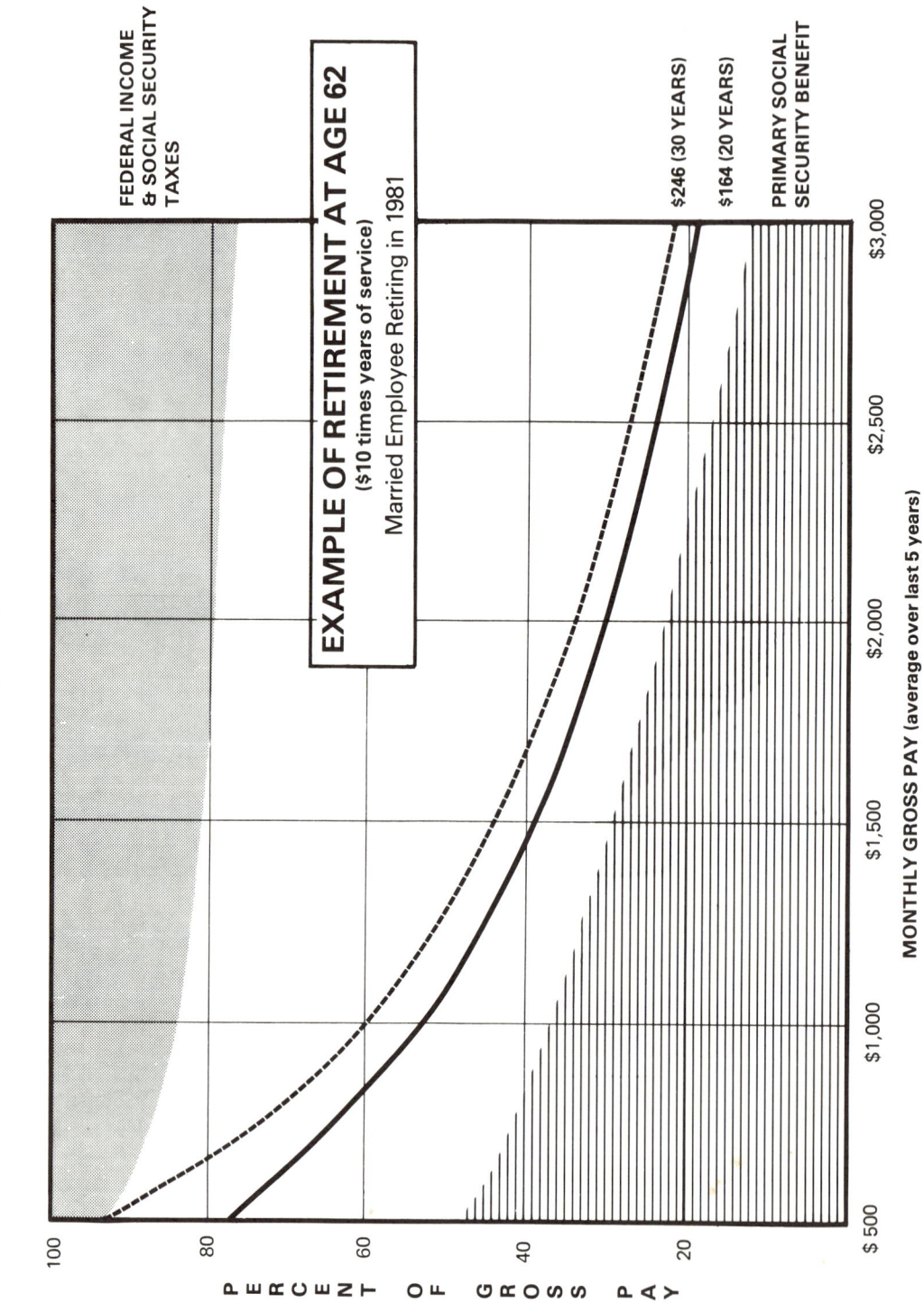

Exhibit 5

EXAMPLE OF RETIREMENT AT AGE 62
($10 times years of service)
Married Employee Retiring in 1981

FEDERAL INCOME & SOCIAL SECURITY TAXES

$246 (30 YEARS)
$164 (20 YEARS)

PRIMARY SOCIAL SECURITY BENEFIT

PERCENT OF GROSS PAY

MONTHLY GROSS PAY (average over last 5 years)

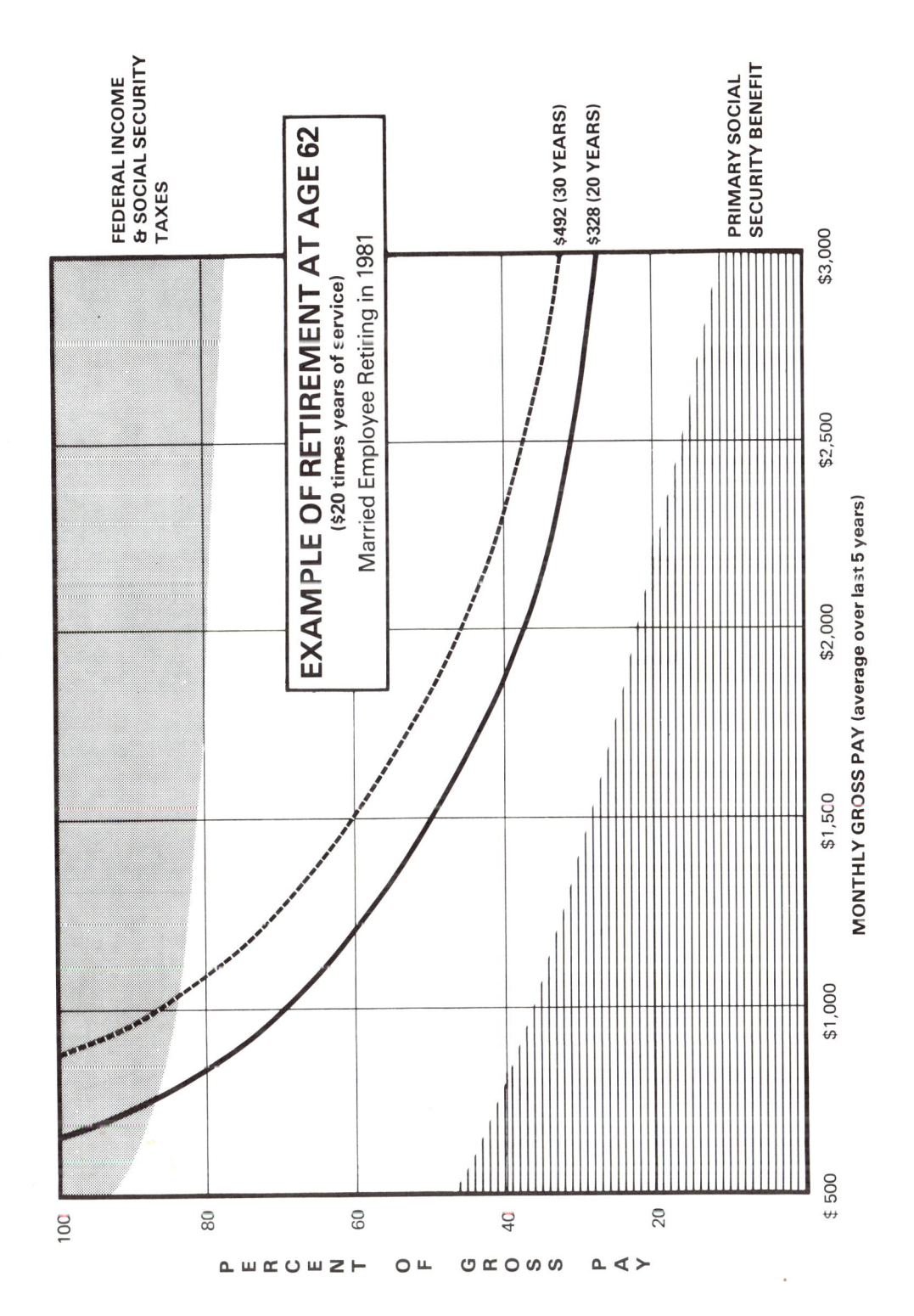

Exhibit 6

EXAMPLE OF RETIREMENT AT AGE 62
($20 times years of service)
Married Employee Retiring in 1981

FEDERAL INCOME & SOCIAL SECURITY TAXES

$492 (30 YEARS)
$328 (20 YEARS)

PRIMARY SOCIAL SECURITY BENEFIT

PERCENT OF GROSS PAY

MONTHLY GROSS PAY (average over last 5 years)

Exhibit 7

Estimated "Spendable Income" While Working
and
Retirement Income Needs
(Married Couple Retiring January 1, 1981)

(1)	Gross earnings—1980	$15,000	$20,000	$30,000
	Less: Federal income tax (a)	1,630	2,740	5,590
	Social Security tax (b)	920	1,230	1,590
	Work-related expenses (c)	1,000	1,200	1,500
	Personal savings (d)	700	1,200	2,400
(2)	Estimated spendable income while working	$10,750	$13,630	$18,920
(3)	Estimated Social Security (e)			
	Primary	$7,510	$7,950	$8,110
	Spouse	3,760	3,980	4,060
	Total	$11,270	$11,930	$12,170
(4)	Needed from pension plan and personal sources (f)	—	$1,700	$6,750
(5)	Percentage (4) to (1)	—	8.5%	22.5%

NOTES:
(a) Joint return, two exemptions, standard deduction.
(b) 6.13% of the first $25,900.
(c) Work-related transportation, meals, clothing, etc.
(d) Highly variable from one couple to another.
(e) Includes both covered worker and spouse, both age 65, 5% pay progression, retirement January 1, 1981.
(f) Up to $7,400 per year—no tax if both age 65.

Exhibit 8

Annual Consumption Budgets for a Retired Couple
Urban United States, Autumn 1979

	Levels of Living		
Component	Lower Budget	Intermediate Budget	Higher Budget
Total Budget[1]	$6,023	$8,562	$12,669
Total family consumption	5,763	8,047	11,719
Food	1,882	2,507	3,149
Housing	1,996	2,862	4,481
Transportation	420	820	1,528
Clothing	225	378	581
Personal care	169	247	362
Medical care[2]	837	842	848
Other family consumption	234	390	770
Other items	259	515	950

[1]Beginning with the Autumn 1973 updating of the budgets for a retired couple, the total budget is defined as the sum of "total family consumption" and "other items." Income taxes are not included in the total budgets.

[2]The Autumn 1979 cost estimates for medical care contain a preliminary estimate for "out-of-pocket" costs for Medicare.

NOTE: Because of rounding, sums for individual items may not equal totals.

Source: Bureau of Labor Statistics.

Exhibit 9

Example
Effects of Inflation on Combined Pension and Social Security Benefit
1965 Through 1980

Retirement on January 1, 1965 at age 65 with pension benefit of $200/month and Social Security benefit of $132/month.

	Actual Monthly Amount			Purchasing Power of Actual Amount[1]			
Year	Pension	Social[2] Security	Total	Pension	Social Security	Total	1965 = 100
1965	$200	$132	$332	$200	$132	$332	100
1966	200	132	332	195	128	323	97
1967	200	132	332	189	125	314	95
1968	200	149	349	181	135	316	95
1969	200	149	349	172	128	300	90
1970	200	171	371	163	139	302	91
1971	200	188	388	156	146	302	91
1972	200	226	426	151	170	321	97
1973	200	226	426	142	160	302	91
1974	200	251	451	128	161	289	87
1975	200	271	471	117	159	276	83
1976	200	289	489	111	160	271	82
1977	200	306	506	104	159	263	79
1978	200	326	526	97	158	255	77
1979	200	358	558	87	156	243	73
1980	200	409	609	76	156	232	70

[1] Purchasing power of the dollar as measured by consumer prices.

[2] Cost-of-living adjustments to monthly Social Security benefits: 2/68, 13%; 1/70, 15%; 1/71, 10%; 2/72, 20%; 3/74, 7%; 6/74, 4%; 6/75, 8%; 6/76, 6.4%; 6/77, 5.9%; 6/78, 6.5%; 6/79, 9.9%; 6/80, 14.3%.

Inflation, COLAs and Retirement Age

BY JOHN S. PERRECA

CORPORATE AND UNION America, together with pension plan sponsors in the public sector, are facing a problem, the implications of which portend a major change in our perception of work, leisure and retirement. Like the big American car, the continuation of traditional retirement ages, and related practices, will make the great American retirement dream a reality for relatively few. Because of the debilitating effect of inflation, most Americans will be unable to retire and maintain their standard of living until their death—this despite Social Security, employer-financed supplemental pension plans (including those with a cost of living adjustment), and individual savings and investments.

What Are the Problems?

What are the specific problems, their causes, and their solutions? First, the problems—I see eight, each of which is intricately caught up with the others.
- A. *Costs:* Corporate and collectively bargained pension costs, and most especially those in the public sector, continue to increase, both in dollars and as a percentage of total covered payroll. (You are, no doubt, acquainted with exceptions to this general statement.)
- B. *Retirement ages:* American workers in the private and public sectors still want to retire sooner, although the trend may be about to shift as the problems about which this presentation is concerned become better known and understood and our perception of the dignity of work increases, most especially during what appears to be unfolding as the conservative '80s.
- C. *Purchasing power:* The purchasing power of fixed pension benefits is being significantly and relentlessly eroded by inflation.
- D. *Cost-of-living adjustments:* Partially or even fully "indexed" pensions (COLAs) can be inadequate and can contribute to the sustained and recently growing rate of inflation.

Mr. Perreca is senior vice president of Edward H. Friend & Company, Washington-based independent actuaries and employee benefit plan consultants. His responsibilities include advising corporate employers, state, county and municipal government officials, hospital, foundation and association executives, as well as Taft-Hartley trustees on the design, financing, implementation and administration of employee benefit programs. Mr. Perreca is a graduate of Allegheny College and has done graduate work at Ohio University and the University of Maryland. He is a frequent lecturer before professional and business groups, and has authored articles for numerous employee benefit and public sector publications, including the International Foundation Digest *and* Employee Benefits Journal. *Mr. Perreca has spoken at many International Foundation educational meetings. He is a member and immediate past chairman of the Public Employees Committee and has taught Certified Employee Benefit Specialist (CEBS) courses on pension plans and Social Security at American University, as adjunct professor.*

- E. *Social Security:* Reliance on Social Security to increasingly offset supplemental private (and some public) pensions is employee savings and security which are more apparent than real.
- F. *Inflation:* The growing impact of inflation places "retirement"—as we know it today—in jeopardy.
- G. *Investment capital:* Private sector investment capital is drying up in our United States, exacerbating the other problems

and contributing to our reduced American worker productivity.

H. *Political expediency:* Our elected officials are contributing to these pension-related financial problems, often at our behest.

What Are Causes of These Problems— and Their Solutions?

While not intended to be all-encompassing, and necessarily sweeping because of the limitations here of time and space, please consider the following causes of these eight problems and a proposed solution to each.

Costs

Corporate and Taft-Hartley negotiated pension plan costs (actuarially calculated costs and actual expenditures, to be more precise) continue to increase, in dollars and often as a percentage of total covered payroll. Yes, you can find exceptions, but the trend is evident, and for some, potentially alarming. Relating these expenditures to corporate income as another measure of the problem, for example, pension expenses for Fortune 500 companies surveyed by Johnson & Higgins averaged 12% of pretax income in 1979 (a significant 45% of pretax income at Firestone and an eye-opening 79% at Bethlehem Steel), this as reported by Mary Greenebaum in her article "Personal Investing" appearing in the December 1, 1980, issue of *Fortune* magazine. Please note that apparent costs do not always reflect actual costs—calculated costs are sometimes deliberately understated or overstated when related to pretax corporate income for corporate dividend and related tax purposes—so many of the exceptions we can each note may be based on a shaky premise.

Actuarial Assumptions. Inadequate actuarial assumptions used in the past are now having their impact felt, with corporate stockholders and, more prevalently, taxpayers in the public sector, being asked to absorb the cost impact of past mistakes. For example, how can you justify an assumption that investment return will, for the long range future, outpace individual growth in salaries by 2% per annum?

How are defined benefit (as distinct from defined contribution) pension plan costs determined? Two ways:

1. *Actual costs* can be determined after the fact and are equal to the benefits actually paid out, plus expenses actually incurred, less the total net (after investment-related expenses) investment performance actually realized on the accumulated funds before disbursement. (Cost = Benefits + Expenses – Investment Return.)

2. *Calculated costs* are those for which your enrolled actuary is responsible, his (or her) calculations made using assumptions as to his best estimate of future experience, but the selection of which should include the active participation of the plan sponsor and/or board of trustees who will be ultimately impacted.

Chart 1

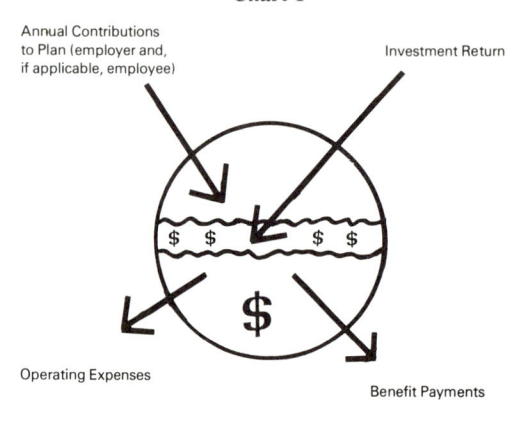

What are these actuarial assumptions? There are nine about which you should be concerned, ranked below in generally decreasing order of significance:

1. Investment performance, based on the total investment concept of interest, dividends, capital gains and/or losses
2. Salary and wage (including hours worked, when applicable) and salary increase projections
3. Social Security benefits and the impact of offsets against employer-provided pension benefits (depending upon the design of your plan)
4. Cost-of-living adjustments after retirement
5. Average age of employee retirement
6. Employee turnover among the non-vested participants
7. Life expectancy both before and after retirement
8. Rate and duration of participant disability
9. Administrative expenses including accounting, actuarial, consulting, and legal fees.

It is important you distinguish between "implicit" and "explicit" actuarial assumptions. "Implicit" actuarial assumptions are those expected to be realistic *in the aggregate,* but individual assumptions may not necessarily be realistic. Using a 6%

Chart 2

Salary Scale

- Salary During 64th Year: $60,510
- Average Last 5 Years: 54,037
- Age 60: 47,930
- 20 Year Average: 36,785
- $20,000 at Age 45
- 6% Per Year Increase

$54,037 Final 5 Year Average Is 47% Higher than $36,785 20 Year Average

Average Final 5 Years (Age 60 to Age 65)

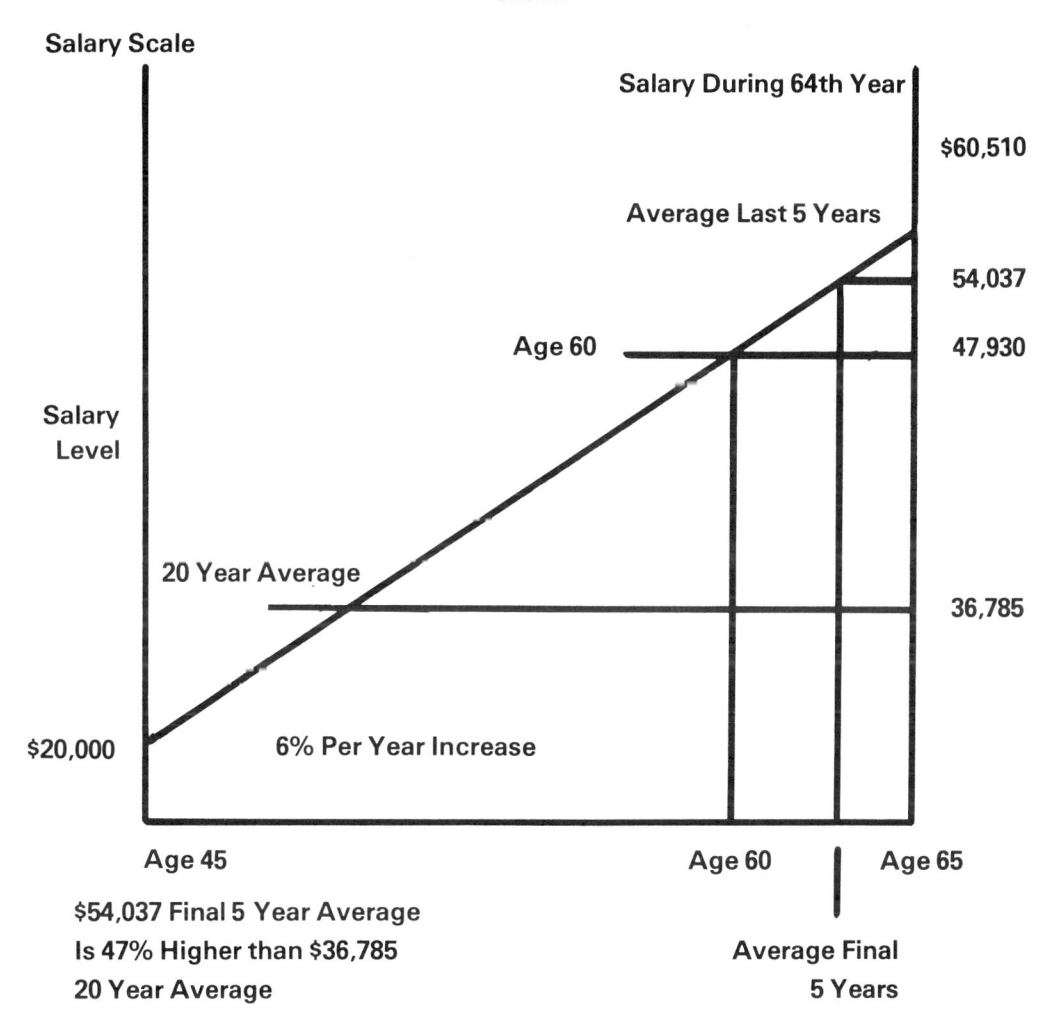

investment performance and 4% salary increase is an example of implicit actuarial assumptions, the presumption being that both are understated, at least in today's economic climate, such that the understated error of one will offset the understated error of the other; in other words, two wrongs might make one right! "Explicit" actuarial assumptions require that *each actuarial assumption* be set realistically. Particularly important among these assumptions are investment performance and salary and wage increase projections.

Why is there a need for a realistic/explicit salary/ wage projection actuarial assumption? Chart 2 illustrates how a pension benefit calculated on the average salary of the last five years, $54,037, is 47% higher than the average salary over 20 years of $36,785 (on which the pension benefit accrual might have been based were a 6% per year salary increase not included).

The need for using a realistic (i.e., explicit) investment performance assumption is similarly significant, noting what small differences an investment performance (assumed or actual) can have, due to compounding, on long range plan costs or benefits:

Consistent Difference in Investment Performance	Probable Effect on Long Range Plan Costs and/or Benefits
.25%	2-6%
.50	4-12
1.00	8-24

Question your actuarial advisor if he proposes the use of implicit, rather than explicit, actuarial assumptions. The alleged "washout" between two implicit assumptions which are understated does not always occur, most especially where your pension fund has grown to a fairly large size in relation to benefits being disbursed; the difference between assumptions (i.e., the delta) does not remain the same as you move these assumptions along a continuum, as is illustrated below for one particular fund:

Salary and Wage Projection	Difference (Delta)	Total Net Investment Performance
3.0%	1.50	4.50%
4.5	1.25	5.75
6.0	1.00	7.00
7.0	.75	7.75
8.0	.50	8.50

Funding Method. The use of an inappropriate funding method is not a frequent problem, but it is one which should be noted if only for the purpose of recognizing the difference in jargon used by your actuary and your other advisors. Remember the funding *method* is the actuarial (i.e., mathematical) basis on which pension and related future benefit costs are calculated. Corporate, Taft-Hartley negotiated, and state and local public employee plans typically use the following three methods, listed in decreasing order of popularity:
   a. Frozen initial liability (most frequently used)
   b. Unit credit (sometimes used)
   c. Aggregate (only occasionally used).

And, while distinguishing terminology, note that the funding *medium* describes the investment vehicle used to accept employer and employee (if required or allowed) contributions and invest them and disburse payments when appropriate under the instruction of the employer or board of trustees. Funding media include the products of life insurance companies, bank trust departments, boards of trustees using an independent investment advisor, or an entirely self-administered plan committed to in-house investment management.

Investment Performance. Deficient investment performance sometimes slips by unnoticed or uncorrected if one or more of the following five common misconceptions are permitted to exist. Don't allow yourself to be lulled into complacency.
   a. "The investment return is sufficient because it meets the actuarial assumed investment performance target." Using implicit actuarial assumptions, this statement is obviously incorrect. Even using explicit actuarial assumptions, your actuary will generally include a margin of conservatism in his selection of the investment return assumption, and your investment manager should not be allowed to use this conservatism as a basis for giving less than his best effort to maximize the investment return.
   b. "Careful consideration has been given to selecting the investment mix appropriate for your plan." According to the Greenwich Research Associates' 1979 Report to Participants for Large Corporate Pension Funds, the following conclusions were drawn from a survey of 1,000 of the largest American companies. The survey found that, for these plans, pension fund asset mix does not vary significantly with the (1) percent of active participants vested; (2) percent of total participants presently retired; (3) benefit formula used; (4) average age of participant; (5) average length of service; or (6) actuarial interest rate assumption. Clearly, you should discuss the selection of investment mix carefully with your investment advisors to ensure it is selected with due deliberation and not merely on the basis of current fashion.
   c. "Anticipated cash flow is an important consideration in setting investment policy." Not necessarily true! The vast majority of pension plans have cash flows which are currently positive and will remain so for the indefinite future. Your actuary can tell you if this is the case and, if so, can set your investment manager's mind at ease with respect to the misperceived need for liquidity and thereby free his energies for achieving the maximum possible investment return within the other investment parameters established by your investment policy.
   d. "Figures don't lie"—but liars can figure. There is often an unreasonable and unconscionable number of methods developed and used to report investment results obtained by various investment advisors and managers. With respect to the actuarial process, however, two should suffice: the internal rate of return and the time-weighted rate of return.
      With respect to a single year, there is seldom a significant difference between the two, and therefore the internal rate can be used as an appropriate estimate of both.

This method is one which determines an investment rate such that when the rate is applied to the market value at the beginning of the period being examined and to all of the cash flow components (taking due recognition of the time at which each cash flow occurred), it will produce an amount of investment return which when added to (1) the market value at the beginning of the period and (2) the net cash flows during the period, will equal the end-of-period market value.

If a period of more than one year is being examined, there is greater likelihood of a significant difference between the two measures. The difference between the two measures is that one (the internal rate of return) recognizes the effect of the timing of cash flows and the other (the time-weighted rate of return) does not. Since the cash flow of the fund is not within the control of the fund manager, the time-weighted rate (which for a period in excess of one year can be acceptably estimated by the geometric average of *annual* internal rates of return) is generally accepted as the best measure of his performance over a period of time. It also has the advantage of being directly comparable between funds, since it is independent of cash flows.

With respect to the actuarial process, the internal rate will provide what is essentially a comparison between actual fund growth over a period of time relative to the rate of growth assumed in the actuarial assumptions. The time-weighted rate, on the other hand, will represent a measure of the average underlying rate available during the period.

It is also important to realize that both of these measures are retrospective in nature and, while they need to be considered in selecting future actuarial assumptions as to expected rates of return, neither should be considered a sole criterion in making that election. This, among other things, implies that the rate of return produced by either measure for a period of less than five years is seldom used in assessing the need to re-evaluate the current actuarial investment return assumption.

e. "Do you understand?" does not communications make. It is important that you take an active interest in both the investment process and the actuarial process. A healthy approach toward such active interest is to start with the assumption that if the material being presented or explained does not make sense, the fault lies with the person doing the explaining. A good practical test of whether you are receiving the full cooperation of your consultant is to observe whether they follow an explanation by asking you, "Do you understand?" or whether they ask, "Have I made myself clear?" The former approach assumes it is your responsibility to figure out what is being said, while the latter recognizes that it is the consultant's responsibility. Don't allow yourself to be intimidated! Ask questions until you know the significance of, and the relationship between, the technical factors about which you are concerned and for which you are responsible. When you are confident you understand, you will come one step closer to your objective of maintaining a financially sound and cost-effective retirement program.

Retirement Ages

American workers, in both the public and private sectors, continue to want to retire sooner, although the trend is changing. Here are the problems:

- Early normal retirement ages are not financially practical. Any private sector shift from age 65 to 60, or to "30 and out," will be financially possible for few—but for those who can afford to and opt to do so, it's their right. In the public sector, the pattern of uniformed personnel seeking to retire at age 50, or even after only 20 years of service, is being found to require substantially increased municipal expenditures (in some extreme cases, in excess of 100% of current payroll). Even non-uniformed public employees seeking to retire at age 60, or at age 55, are facing substantial financial hurdles.
- Life expectancy is growing; more Americans are surviving to older ages, impacting directly on the cost of both Social Security and private and public sector supplemental plans. According to the President's Commission on Pension Policy, demographic projections indicate that the ratio of working population (17-65 year olds) to elderly (over 65) will diminish from today's 4:1 to 2.5:1 by the early part of the 21st century, little more than 20 years from now. What is your perception of the economic and social implications of this trend? Do you expect

to be a payee or payor?

- Our nation's reduced birth rate is apt to contribute to a growing labor shortage between 1980 and the year 2010; this shortage not to be camouflaged by the current high rate of unemployment. Immigration from other nations will mollify the impact of this trend. Exacerbating these demographic and economic problems is the slowing down of American industrial productivity in comparison with other countries.

What solutions does the future portend? Consider the following developments:

a. The federal Age Discrimination in Employment Act (ADEA) Amendments of 1978 (P.L. 95-256) raised the minimum mandatory retirement age for covered employees to 70.

b. The Social Security system provides actuarially increased pension benefits for postponed retirements from age 65 to 68 (but under current law, which is apt to be changed, a better value is realized if benefits commence at age 62 because of actuarial considerations).

c. A necessary and desirable change in our perception of the importance and dignity of work is required. Peculiar to our culture, being able to retire, especially early, is a badge of affluence—it presupposes one has been successful, prepared well, and can now join the leisure class! We should anticipate that retirement ages will be gradually extended; indeed, we should encourage it.

To you who may charge me with threatening an arrangement you have worked hard to achieve, I say, if you can afford it and want to do it, do it! But be mindful of the calculated risk that the eroding effect of inflation may make yours a Pyrrhic victory.

Purchasing Power

The purchasing power of pension benefits commencing at retirement is experiencing significant and increasing erosion. Chart 3 shows the plummeting purchasing power of a fixed pension under various inflation scenarios.

Solutions:

a. Encourage postponed retirements and include, if desirable, additional pension benefit credit to reflect the extended service and, if applicable, the higher average level of compensation on which the pension benefit is calculated. (A further increase in the retiree's monthly pension could be made by reflecting his/her then shorter life expectancy [i.e., an "actuarial increase"], however this would eliminate cost savings.)

b. Introduce, by action of your board of trustees, ad hoc increases in retired employees' pension benefits by increasing only your then unfunded accrued liability—thereby limiting future plan obligations.

c. Add an adequately prefunded and capped cost-of-living adjustment (COLA)—if your contributing employer(s) can afford it and/or is willing to commit himself to future increases in pension costs over which you will be unable to exert direct control.

Chart 3
PORTION OF ONE DOLLAR'S PURCHASING POWER WHICH REMAINS AFTER RETIREMENT UNDER VARIOUS INFLATION SCENARIOS

Number of Years After Retirement	If Annual Rate of Inflation Is:			
	6%	12%	16%	20%
5	75¢	57¢	48¢	40¢
10	56	32	23	16
15	42	18	11	6
20	31	10	5	3
25	23	6	2	1

Cost-of-Living Adjustments

Partially or fully "indexed" pensions (COLAs) can be inadequate and contribute to the sustained and growing rate of inflation.

COLAs are prevalent in public sector employee pension plans, notably the Civil Service Retirement System, Military Retirement System, and many state, county and municipal plans. The aforementioned federal systems remain open-ended (as is the Social Security system), with few state, county or municipal plans so committed, the State of Maryland most recently capping future increases lest the retirement system eventually consume the entire state budget! Annual increases, triggered by increases in the Consumer Price Index (CPI) are usually limited, or capped, to 3%, and certainly no more than 6%, per year. These cost-of-living adjustments are predominantly underfunded and, in the case of the Military Retirement System, entirely unfunded (as is the entire Military Retirement System, its disbursements made from monies provided for through an annual appropriation by the Congress).

Chart 4

PORTION OF ONE DOLLAR'S PURCHASING POWER WHICH REMAINS AFTER RETIREMENT UNDER VARIOUS INFLATION SCENARIOS AND BENEFIT ESCALATION ARRANGEMENTS

Benefit Escalation Arrangement	Number of Years After Retirement	If Annual Rate of Inflation Is 6%	12%	16%	20%
None (Level of Benefits)	5	75^c	57^c	48^c	40^c
	10	56	32	23	16
	15	42	18	11	6
	20	31	10	5	3
	25	23	6	2	1
4% Per Annum	5	91^c	68^c	57^c	48^c
	10	82	46	32	23
	15	74	32	18	11
	20	67	21	10	5
	25	61	15	6	2
6% Per Annum	5	full	75^c	62^c	52^c
	10	full	56	39	27
	15	full	42	24	14
	20	full	31	15	7
	25	full	23	9	4

Automatic COLAs are uncommon in private sector plans principally because of their considerable cost. And, while the manner in which costs are projected may vary, one rule of thumb is that an increase in investment performance of 2-2.5% on a pension fund would be required to finance a COLA provision for retired employees.

Even with COLAs, the immediate future looks grim. Chart 4 shows the portion of one dollar's purchasing power which remains after retirement under various inflation scenarios and benefit escalation arrangements.

The Consumer Price Index does not accurately measure changes in the cost of living, but may overstate it upwards by 2% annually, this overadjustment fueling inflation rather than merely compensating for it. The CPI measures the wrong thing, and is based on the prices of a stated, outdated set of items that are not directly related to the actual cost of living. So the CPI fuels, rather than "adjusts for," inflation. An illustration will make the point, this one reported by futurist Geoffrey N. Calvert in his article "Indexed Induced Inflation" appearing in *The Actuary*, January 1980: In 1935, a four-ply cotton motor tire cost $13, delivered 7,000 miles of useful life and cost .186^c per mile. In 1978, a steel-belted radial motor tire cost $68, had a 40,000 mile useful life, and cost .170^c per mile. The CPI tire price index *rose* 140%, but the cost per mile *fell* by 9%!

Solutions? Two seem to be in order.

a. Approach automatic benefit increase arrangements cautiously and plan to fund them adequately. Introducing ad hoc increases as you can afford them would provide you even greater fiscal control.

b. Recognize that the Consumer Price Index does not accurately measure changes in the cost of living, and urge your elected representatives to demand that establishment technicians develop a more valid and reliable alternative, several of which have already been proposed, including the Product Performance Index (PPI) and the Quality of Life Index (QLI).

Social Security

Reliance on Social Security to increasingly offset supplemental private and public pensions may be security and savings which are more apparent than real.

We have demanded more of Social Security than we are willing to finance. Further, there is confusion between the concept of "individual equity" and "social adequacy," the former a characteristic of private sector plans and the latter a characteristic of social welfare systems. Under individual equity, the contributor receives benefit protection directly related to the amount of his contributions (i.e., actuarially equivalent thereto—characteristic of what is in store when one buys an individual life insurance policy). But under the concept of social adequacy, the benefits paid will provide for all contributors a certain standard of living irrespective of the relationship between what they contributed and what they receive.

The Social Security system is an intergenerational transfer system, marginally financed by employer and employee taxes. According to former Social Security Chief Actuary A. Haeworth Robertson, in his address "Social Security Prospect for Change" to the 66th Annual Meeting of the Chamber of Commerce of the United States, May 1, 1978, "Our Social Security system is an agreement among the people of the nation that one segment of the population will receive certain benefits and that another segment of the population will pay for these benefits, with a certain amount of overlapping."

Coordination, or integration, of Social Security with supplemental employer-sponsored pension plans makes good sense. The offset formula (e.g., 70% of final average compensation inclusive of one-half of primary Social Security) favors higher-paid employees. The step-rate formula is simpler to comprehend (e.g., 1% of final average compensation up to the Social Security wage, plus 2% of the excess, for each year of service at retirement).

Social Security taxes continue to increase dramatically, with $15 billion projected as the combined employer and employee increase for calendar 1980:

Maximum Annual Tax

Year	Employer/Employee	Combined
1937	$ 30	$ 60
1950	45	90
1970	375	750
1979	1,404	2,808
1981	1,975	3,950
1985	2,792	5,584
2000	7,160	14,320

Solutions? While some form of national social insurance may be desirable, if not necessary,

a. The age at which retirement payments commence should be gradually extended to approximately age 70. For example, we could increase the Social Security retirement age upward from 65 by two months for each passing year. If such a procedure were to start in 1981, then by the year 2000, 20 years later, the Social Security retirement age of 65 would have increased to 68 and four months, 40 months of increase over 20 years. This procedure would continue for ten more years, until in the year 2010 the age 70 "normal" retirement age will have been achieved.

b. The size of CPI-triggered retirement payments should not be allowed to increase at current and projected rates.

c. Disability retirement should more intensely emphasize rehabilitation and retraining.

d. Plan provisions and administrative procedures should be simplified so they will be more comprehensible.

e. Employers should endeavor to become more resourceful in the management of their human resources by modifying jobs to accommodate employee skills, physical and mental capacities, schedules and personal preferences where reasonable.

f. Dissuade our elected officials from committing subsequent generations to costs which they may not be able or willing to support. Understandably, general revenue financing has appeal, but it does not solve the problem; extracting money from taxpayers via federal income taxes is no less costly than extracting Social Security taxes from participants and contributing employers. Further, the pressure on public sector employees for universal coverage will not solve the financial difficulties of either the Civil Service Retirement System or the Social Security system, although coordinating Civil Service Retirement System benefits with Social Security, as is typical of private sector plans, will tend to reduce the long term cost (and benefits) of the Civil Service Retirement System.

Inflation

The growing impact of inflation places "retirement"—as we know it today—in jeopardy. Why?

Inflation, according to A. Merriam Webster, is "an increase in the volume of money and credit relative to available goods resulting in a substantial and continuing rise in the general price level." In other words, inflation is too many dollars chasing too few goods. A typical American worker earns more than *twice* as many dollars as he or she did a decade ago, but real income—after taxes and inflation—is 5% *less* than it was in 1970, this according to The Tax Foundation, Inc., and appearing in *The Washington Post,* October 18, 1980.

Social Security's growing disbursements, particularly those reflecting cost-of-living adjustments which represent so-called uncontrollable federal budget items, are exacerbating the inflation problem:
   a. Social Security benefits are indexed upward because of inflation,
   b. Causing higher FICA taxes,
   c. Adding to employer costs (and likely resulting in higher wage demands from workers),
   d. Causing increased prices for goods and services,
   e. Triggering another indexed increase in benefits so recipients will not feel the pinch of inflation,
   f. Causing still higher FICA taxes, ad infinitum!

Automatic retirement at popular retirement ages, irrespective of the new age 70 maximum, compounds the inflation problem by removing from the active work force able-bodied persons who must then be supported by the fewer remaining active workers. Do you believe your attainment of age 65, or even age 70, will preclude your being able to continue to earn an income through gainful employment and make a financial contribution to your family and/or your community?

Inflation-adjusting pay increases force middle class active workers into higher tax brackets where the federal government is the principal beneficiary:
   • In 1971 federal, state, local and Social Security taxes took 16.1% out of the average person's income; in 1979, it increased to 18.5%.
   • A family of four earning $25,000 will need a raise of $3,325 (i.e., 13.3%) in 1980 to keep up with current inflation, but they'll fall behind because the raise will require them to pay $1,271 more in federal taxes!

So, more Americans save even less than they've saved before—5.5% of disposable income in January 1979, vs. 3.3% in January 1980; but the West Germans save 15%, and the Japanese save 25%! In contrast, American consumers' debt payments were 23.5% of disposable income in 1979, and were expected to be higher in 1980.

Solutions? I wish they were simple, but two are well-reasoned and irrefutable:
   a. Support, and promote if you are so inclined, the concept of limiting government disbursements to no more than its receipts, after making allowance for reducing the relative size of our national debt.
   b. Recognize that increased employee productivity can help to reduce inflation and contribute significantly to our becoming more competitive in world markets. It is incontrovertible: there is nothing more unless you produce more; in order to have more, we have to produce more!

Investment Capital

Private sector investment capital is drying up in our United States. Dramatic evidence is our inefficient, and sometimes antiquated, manufacturing machinery and equipment, putting us at a marked disadvantage with our competitors, notably the Japanese and the Germans, whose factories were rebuilt immediately after World War II with the then available state-of-the-art technology, and financed by American taxpayers under the aegis of the Marshall Plan. More evidence?

• Federal government borrowings continue at unprecedented rates, drawing funds away from the private sector where they are needed to generate jobs from which taxes can be exacted, and forcing private sector corporations to pay interest rates at levels higher than what many can earn on their invested assets.

• Foreign competition aggravates our private sector economic problems with their higher levels of productivity, their higher productivity partly reflective of the more modern machinery, equipment and structures following from post-World War II U.S. private-sector-financed Marshall Plan reindustrialization.

• The reduction in citizen savings, reflecting the futility of Benjamin Franklin's frugality because of the confiscatory income tax upon these less-than-inflation-rate savings returns, thereby further denies private sector corporations a source of money they can borrow, money they need to operate, modernize, grow and prosper (along with their employees).

• The possible shift away from equity (e.g., common stock) investments in part because private sector pension fund trustees' perception of their fiduciary responsibility/liability under recent government regulations, notably ERISA, is another exigency with which free enterprise corporate executives are forced to cope, although the overreaction to ERISA appears to be abating, and the investors' perception of stocks, versus bonds, is again rejuvenating.

Solutions? Lend your support to legislation which will promote, rather than undermine, capital formation and efficiency—because a nation that does not save and invest does not grow, and without growth, living standards cannot rise. For example, legislation which will make required and/or voluntary employee contributions to qualified retirement programs tax deductible, if not tax free, will encourage thrift and savings and make investment capital available for borrowing by private sector employers, and thus available to fuel our economic engine. The disinclination of private and public sector pension funds to invest in equities will decline of its own accord as plan sponsors assess their likely return on investment.

Political Expediency

Our elected officials are contributing to these pension-related financial problems, often at our behest—each of us scrambling to get something for nothing! And the problems grow more severe.

- Income transfer payments were $39.0 billion in 1964, increasing to $281.5 billion in 1979, a more than seven-fold increase in 15 years! Today, income transfer payments represent 49% of all federal expenditures, and represent 12% of our total Gross National Product from all levels of government (source: *Business Week,* September 29, 1980).
- The CPI indexing of transfer payments, most notably Social Security, the Civil Service Retirement System and the entirely unfunded Military Retirement System, has resulted in a virtual loss of control over discretionary federal spending. Currently, 75% of all government outlays are tied to the inflation rate, formally or informally. The 28.4% increase in federal spending in the past two years reflects this increase, since few new programs were created (source: *Business Week,* September 22, 1980). Its impact, camouflaged by the post-Vietnam decline of real defense spending, will vanish with the resurgence of defense spending expected in 1981, further accelerating inflation.
- Twenty-five percent of our national budget represents payments due on contracts signed in prior years and interest on the public debt. Fifty percent represents transfer payments to individuals, almost all of which are indexed to inflation (source: *Business Week,* September 22, 1980). Is it any wonder, then, that transfer payments have discouraged people from working, have become an important factor in lowering the long term growth of our economy, have prompted increased Social Security benefits to reduce the incentive to save and invest and, in general, have dampened capital investment?
- No major social programs have been reduced, and several have been increased. The revenue-sharing program to state and municipal governments remains intact at $6.9 billion. And, like the drug addict, state and local governments have grown dependent on these federal funds, enslaved by the bureaucracy they helped to expand by supporting the "something for nothing" philosophy. Lo the pressure on our politicians to produce short term results to ensure their reelection.

Solutions? As a Swiss financier remarked, "It is up to us to pursue our goals by our own efforts and with our own resources"—he from a nation with probably the lowest inflation rate of any worldwide. So-called uncontrollable budget items such as Social Security, Medicare, revenue-sharing and other social programs, in addition to the interest on the national debt, *can* be controlled where we are willing to acknowledge that, like no individual, family or business, no local, state or federal government can long survive if its disbursements regularly exceed its income and assets.

Transfer payments can be reduced by Congressional action. There is no alternative to bringing taxes and inflation under control. According to The Tax Foundation, Inc., (reported in *The Washington Post,* October 18, 1980), federal income taxes for the typical family went up 110% during the ten year period 1970-1980. Social Security taxes increased by 227%. Together, this represents a 147% increase, based on an estimated $19,950 income for one wage earner (compared with $9,750 in 1970).

In conclusion, our elected officials must be held accountable for their financial decisions. We must support those who practice financial restraint.

ns have been around for
The Defined Contribution Alternative: Can It Solve All the Problems?

BY JOHN K. WARE

Introduction

Defined contribution plans have been around for almost as long as defined benefit plans have, but they have never really "caught on" in the Taft-Hartley area. There are many reasons for this, which should become clearer as we discuss the advantages and disadvantages of defined contribution plans later on. Nevertheless, today there is a great deal of renewed interest in defined contribution plans in the following situations:

a. As the type of plan to use when a retirement benefit plan is first being installed
b. As a complementary addition in a situation where a defined benefit plan already exists
c. As a replacement for an existing defined benefit plan.

The main source of this renewed interest in defined contribution plans has come from those associated with Taft-Hartley pension trusts in reaction to the plan termination insurance provisions of the Employee Retirement Income Security Act of 1974. Considerable controversy has been generated regarding how the government should respond to the Pension Benefit Guaranty Corporation's determination that ERISA-mandated termination insurance for Taft-Hartley plans:

a. Represented an attempt to insure an uninsurable risk, and
b. Could actually cause plans to terminate.

The U.S. government's final response was the Multiemployer Pension Plan Amendments Act of 1980. Whether you believe that this latest addition to the area of complex pension legislation was beneficial or detrimental, you surely need to learn more about the alternative many are now looking to: i.e., defined contribution plans.

Definitions

What is a defined contribution plan? ERISA provides a definition in Section 3(34) as follows:

The term ... "defined contribution plan" means a pension plan which provides for an individual account for each participant and for benefits based solely upon the amount contributed to the participant's account, and any income, expenses, gains and losses, and any forfeitures of accounts of other participants which may be allocated to such participant's account.

ERISA describes a defined benefit plan in Section 3(35) this way:

The term "defined benefit plan" means a pension plan other than an individual account plan....

Defined contribution plans are referred to by a variety of different names. Basically, most are divided into the following general categories:

a. Profit-sharing (including stock bonus)
b. Thrift/savings
c. Target benefit
d. Money purchase.

A plan which bases its contributions on company profits is not well suited to the Taft-Hartley situation. Therefore, we will ignore the profit-sharing type in our discussion. Similarly, the thrift/savings type is a retirement plan requiring employee contributions, which is not common under collective bar-

Mr. Ware is senior consultant with A. S. Hansen, Inc., and manager of the actuarial practice in the San Francisco office. An enrolled actuary, he is a fellow of the Society of Actuaries and a member of the American Academy of Actuaries. Mr. Ware received his A.B. degree from San Diego State University.

gaining. The target benefit plan is a special arrangement which attempts to produce benefits similar to a defined benefit plan, but using the defined contribution approach. Later, we will look at target benefit plans.

This leaves us with the money purchase arrangement. Under this plan, a fixed contribution is made to each participant's account annually. It may be a flat dollar amount per month (or hour, shift, ton, etc.) or it may be a percentage of pay. What the participant finally receives upon death, disability, retirement or termination depends on the investment performance and plan expenses which are added to (or subtracted from) the money in his account.

Comparisons

Let us now review the basic plan and benefit features of money purchase defined contribution plans versus defined benefit plans in a Taft-Hartley situation. This will highlight the differences and allow an easier review of the advantages and disadvantages of each.

Participation

Generally, participation would be immediate in both situations.

Vesting

Defined benefit plans usually favor full vesting after ten years of service, with full forfeiture prior to the tenth year. On the other hand, money purchase plans almost always have graded vesting schedules. For example, a simple schedule might be 30% after three years plus 10% more each year thereafter until full vesting is reached after ten years.

The IRS is required to accept any one of the three vesting minimums described in ERISA unless there has been a pattern of abuse or there is reason to believe such schedules would result in prohibited discrimination in favor of shareholders, officers or highly compensated personnel. This general rule applies to both defined contribution and defined benefit plans.

As a practical matter, the highly visible account balances in any defined contribution plan are looked upon as deferred compensation by most participants, and the idea of forfeiture of any part is not well received. Thus, there is a strong trend toward more rapid vesting in defined contribution plans.

Normal Retirement Benefit

A money purchase pension plan really offers only one definitely determinable benefit at retirement—the balance in the account—but most plans permit it to be converted into monthly retirement income. A defined benefit plan offers a definitely determinable monthly retirement income, and conversions to lump sums usually are not allowed.

Early Retirement Benefits

Money purchase pension plans can only offer the account balance in a lump sum, with an "actuarial equivalent" conversion to monthly income. The defined benefit plan usually offers monthly retirement income based on benefits accrued to the date of retirement. If benefits are paid prior to the normal retirement age, they may be reduced to provide an "actuarial equivalent" of the benefits which would normally start later on. Alternatively, there may be smaller "arbitrary" early retirement reductions to subsidize early retirements to some degree. In some cases, additional temporary income is granted at early retirement to provide a "bridge" to Social Security benefits at age 62 or 65.

Termination Prior to Early Retirement

Money purchase pension plans offer a lump sum distribution of the vested portion of the account balance. Defined benefit plans offer the vested portion of accrued benefits payable at normal retirement age, with lump sums available for small or insignificant benefit amounts only.

The impact of more liberal vesting schedules is essentially found here.

Death Benefits

Money purchase pension plans pay out the account balance on death. Defined benefit plans may or may not pay death benefits. Thanks to ERISA, defined benefit plans must offer a special spouse benefit, generally when eligibility for early retirement is reached. Many plans also offer the payment of some portion of contributions made to the plan on behalf of the deceased participant who was not eligible for early retirement. This is done in recognition of the attitudes that many younger participants have about contributions to defined benefit plans: that is, younger participants perceive that retirement is so far off they may never receive any benefit from it, and they are also aware that much of the contribution is being used to pay off the past service benefits of older participants.

Disability Benefits

Again, money purchase pension plans can only pay out the current account balance to participants who become disabled. Defined benefit plans have a very wide latitude with regard to disability. Depending on the financial burden the trustees wish to take on, a defined benefit plan can provide no benefit, or provide as much as a full service monthly benefit payable immediately.

Employer Contributions and Forfeitures

Many may not be aware of a general IRS requirement that pension plans (including both defined benefit and all defined contribution plans except profit-sharing and stock bonus plans) must provide "definitely determinable benefits," and therefore funds arising due to forfeitures must be used to reduce future employer contributions. This was never a problem in defined benefit plans, because the benefit and funding provisions were designed to anticipate forfeitures and could be changed to adjust to the contributions coming in.

In a money purchase pension plan, there is the possibility that the IRS would require the trustees to notify contributing employers that future contributions should be reduced by the level of forfeitures actually being experienced. There are some ways to minimize this result, however. For example, Revenue Ruling 60-73 provides examples of defined contribution plans which anticipate forfeitures in the benefit formula. In addition, forfeitures may be used to help pay plan expenses. Presumably, in operation a money purchase plan would experience forfeitures in excess of plan benefits and expenses in some years and, alternatively, would experience shortages in other years. *The primary question is whether the plan could be worded and operated in such a way as to keep contributions from reverting back to employers. If not, the only alternative is to provide 100% vesting immediately.*

Investment Performance

For defined benefit plans, trustees have the responsibility to watch over investment performance with an eye on emerging liabilities. If significant losses are experienced, there are two courses of action available: (a) attempt to have contributions increased, and (b) reduce benefits (usually only prospectively).

For money purchase pension plans, investment performance, both good and bad, goes directly into the participants' accounts. Unquestionably, trustees would have to be much more careful and conservative with individual account plans.

Inflation

Defined benefit plans can provide very effective protection against inflation, limited by the trustees' assessment of what can be prudently afforded. For example, benefits for service to date can be upgraded. Benefits currently being paid to retirees can be increased, either on a one-shot basis or by providing an automatic escalator. In each case, additional liabilities are created which will claim a share of future contributions.

Money purchase plans allow little flexibility. Past service is not recognized, and retirees do not receive a share of future employer contributions. Generally, all that can be done is to increase contributions to current active participants.

Benefit Communication With Participants

Money purchase plans are relatively easier to communicate to plan participants than defined benefit plans, because each participant has an individual account balance. It is usually much easier for participants to understand and appreciate the value of an account balance than it is for them to understand the value of a monthly pension starting at a future date. Either perceived or actual poor investment performance is therefore highly visible, and may cause problems for trustees (in the form of participant unrest and possible litigation). However, annual benefit statements are a must in money purchase plans, whereas such statements are rarely found in defined benefit plans.

Vesting provisions would be slightly more complex if you are shifting to a graded schedule from the ten year "cliff" schedule.

Administration

The daily administration of a money purchase plan is complicated further by the need to periodically perform careful allocations of investment gains and losses, expenses and (possibly) forfeitures. Whether this should be done annually, semiannually, quarterly or monthly is a matter of balancing individual equity against the added cost of additional allocations.

Conversion: Some Problems

If you are in a situation where you are installing a pension plan for the first time, your decision on the type of plan rests on a careful comparison of the advantages and disadvantages of defined benefit types versus defined contribution types. If you already have a plan in effect, you might review these same advantages and disadvantages and conclude that a plan of each type, operating side by side, gives you the best of both. In either case, a decision to proceed with the installation of a new defined contribution plan is relatively easy.

If you are thinking of *converting* from a defined benefit plan to a defined contribution type, you have the same comparison of advantages and disadvantages to make regarding the plan, but you also face a great wall of government rules and regulations. You need to be aware of these added hindrances, because they may be enough by themselves to discourage all further consideration of conversion.

First, we have the requirement under ERISA that if a plan is converted, benefits under the new plan may not be less after conversion than if the plan had terminated before the conversion. That does not necessarily present a problem, since you would be converting accrued benefits into lump sum values. However, the instant a defined benefit plan becomes a defined contribution plan, the Pension Benefit Guaranty Corporation deems the former plan to have terminated [ERISA Section 4041(f) and Section 4041A(3) added by the Multiemployer Pension Plan Amendments Act of 1980].

The new Multiemployer Pension Plan Amendments would obligate each employer contributor to pay a share of any unfunded vested liability determined as of the conversion date. Additionally, once the PBGC regards the plan to be terminated, the IRS deems it to be terminated as well [IRS Regulation Section 1.411(d)-(2)(c)]. Thus, all benefits accrued to the date of conversion must become fully vested *to the extent funded*, pursuant to IRS termination rules.

Therefore, a conversion creates the following problems:
   a. Extensive reports must be filed with the IRS and the PBGC.
   b. The trustees must assess each contributing employer its share of unfunded vested liabilities, and such amounts will be due and payable regardless of whether employees continue with the plan or with the employer.
   c. As a corollary to (b), employees who have accrued benefits at conversion but who are not vested, will lose all benefits.
   d. If the plan has funds in excess of vested liabilities, any excess must become fully vested with the employees.

The alternative to direct conversion is to phase into the conversion by adding a new money purchase plan alongside the defined benefit plan. Then the objective would be to fully fund the present participants in the old former plan while funneling all new participants into the new money purchase plan. This, of course, assumes that future benefit accruals are suspended and that the money thus diverted will eventually pay off accrued benefits as they continue to vest. An orderly method would have to be devised to transfer current contributions for the original plan participants into the new plan as full funding *and full vesting* of the old plan are achieved. Finally, a merger might take place.

As a final drawback to conversion, the PBGC will likely require on termination that participants be given the option of:
   a. Receiving a lump sum distribution,
   b. Having a guaranteed annuity purchased for them, or
   c. Transferring their interest in the defined benefit plan to an individual account in the new plan.

If such options are required to be given participants upon termination, other problems may arise, such as forced liquidation of assets at possible loss; inadequate benefits at retirement for those who might take the money and spend it; and the administrative burden of communicating the options and obtaining decisions.

Epilogue

The evidence is that, given the present set of rules and regulations governing conversions, one has to be prepared to spend a great deal of time and effort to plan and execute a shift from a defined benefit plan to a defined contribution plan. It probably should not be attempted unless the vested liabilities of the defined benefit plan are fully funded—but, of course, one of the key reasons for considering conversion is eliminated when that enviable position is reached.

The Future

It is now time to ask some questions about our present set of circumstances.
   a. Is the IRS requirement that forfeitures be returned to employers in the form of reduced future contributions really necessary for defined contribution plans in the Taft-Hartley situation?
   b. On conversion, if a commitment is made (and kept) to continue funding all benefits accrued to the conversion date, is it really necessary that the PBGC and IRS consider the defined benefit plan to be terminated?

It would seem that a fairly good case could be made to eliminate these requirements—by introducing legislation, if necessary. Without these government-imposed restrictions as they currently exist, many more would seriously consider converting their defined benefit plans in order to avoid some of the tremendously complicated problems created by the Multiemployer Pension Plan Amendments Act of 1980. These problems are only now beginning to surface, and it will take a few years to fully appreciate them. In the meantime, we must continue to pursue alternatives.

Target Benefit Plans as an Alternative

A target benefit plan is a defined contribution type, but the benefits are described in such a way that they are very similar to "defined" benefits. For example, a very simple benefit formula under such a plan might be $10 per month for each year of service. Each year the actuarial value of the additional benefit earned is the amount that is credited to the participant's account. The expectation is that when the participant finally retires at the normal retirement age, he will have accumulated enough of an investment return on that year's contribution to purchase an income of $10 per month.

Much more complex formulas are also possible. For example, the benefit might be the same as in the first example, but the total benefit at retirement is estimated (including credit for prior service), and a level annual amount necessary to fund this benefit is credited each year to the participant's account. In addition, this projected benefit might be updated periodically—e.g., the benefit level might be increased from $10 to $12 per month for each year of service. Each time benefits are adjusted, an additional level annual increment is added to the participant's account to fund it from the date of the increase.

In this manner, a target benefit plan comes very close to operating the same way a defined benefit plan did before ERISA. However, it does require more recordkeeping effort, and special actuarial determinations would also be needed periodically.

Why would it not be possible to restructure the laws and regulations to allow Taft-Hartley defined benefit pension plans to be transformed into target benefit plans? Participants would be promised only benefits that are paid for, and the need for protective government intervention would be eliminated except for the essential fiduciary obligations already set out in ERISA.

It seems like such a good idea after trying to read through the Multiemployer Pension Plan Amendments Act of 1980!

Summary

REVIEW OF ADVANTAGES AND DISADVANTAGES OF MONEY PURCHASE PENSION PLANS

A. Advantages:
1. Such plans are not subject to the Pension Benefit Guaranty Corporation, either for premiums or for termination liabilities.
2. There are no unfunded past service obligations. By definition, the plan is always fully paid up upon receipt of each year's required contribution.
3. There is no trustee or employer responsibility (other than for ERISA's fiduciary responsibility rules) to restore assets lost through poor market performance; i.e., the participant assumes the investment risk, not the fund.
4. Good investment performance is credited directly to participants.
5. There is no need for annual actuarial reports or periodic valuations.
6. Vesting provisions are more liberal.
7. Participant equity: each participant is credited with the same amount or percentage as every other participant.
8. Individual account balances should be easier to communicate to participants.

B. Disadvantages:
1. More rapid vesting may foster more rapid turnover. The availability of lump sum distributions would increase this tendency.
2. Greater benefits are provided to short-service people than they would otherwise have under a defined benefit plan.
3. Participant attitudes are strongly influenced by poor investment performance. Poor investment performance is especially devastating if it occurs when a person retires or terminates.
4. Smaller benefits at retirement may create pressure for increased contributions.
5. Past service is almost impossible to recognize.
6. It is very difficult to adjust benefits for inflation.
7. There is basically no way to provide cost-of-living increases to retirees.
8. The exact monthly income available at retirement is unknown until the participant actually retires (and actuarial conversion factors are then applied to his account balance).
9. Early retirement benefits cannot be subsidized.
10. Death and disability benefits tend to be inadequate when compared to defined contribution plans.
11. Trustees may be faced with greater fiduciary liability.

Reciprocity and Mergers

BY JAMES M. DAWSON

Reciprocity

Current Status

What is reciprocity? Who will it benefit? And who will it not benefit? What is the attitude of Congress, labor, management and the regulatory agencies?

Reciprocity, by dictionary definition, is *to give and receive. mutually by agreement.* For our purposes, it means a written agreement to mutually return employer contributions or provide equivalent benefits between two or more funds. A recent Congressional committee has stated that such agreements benefit the employer, the employee and the union. The only ones that do not benefit are those funds who refuse to sign a reciprocity agreement. The attitude of Congress can readily be judged by Senate Bill S.209, which would amend ERISA "to encourage collectively bargained plans, particularly multi-employer plans, to establish and maintain reciprocity arrangements which protect an employee's vesting and benefit accrual despite shifts from employment covered by one plan to an employment covered by another plan."

Most international unions are now actively encouraging local unions to sign agreements with all locals within the United States. While management has done little to encourage or discourage reciprocity, it is certainly to their advantage to be able to send workers into the areas covered by funds other than the home fund, as well as to be able to hire outside help and promise that there will be no loss of benefits.

The regulatory agencies at present have no definite rules or regulations to "hang their hats on" except the general rule in LMRA Section 302 that "there must be an agreement in writing." It is hoped that if and when ERISA is amended by S.209 or its equivalent we will be given some helpful regulations regarding reciprocity.

Two Basic Types

First, let's examine the various types of reciprocity agreements in general use at the present time. The two basic types of agreements are "money-

Mr. Dawson is president of James M. Dawson Associates, Inc., in Manchester, New Hampshire. He has been trustee and administrator of welfare, pension, apprentice and industry promotion funds for construction workers in New Hampshire, Maine and Vermont since 1953, and has been a member of the Plumbers Local No. 564 since 1946. He has served as vice president and chairman of its executive board and chairman of the examining board. Mr. Dawson is also a member of the New Hampshire Technical Institute Advisory Council, incorporator of the Manchester Mental Health Program and a member of the board of directors of the Manchester Bank, Southern New Hampshire Planning Council. A member of the International Foundation since 1957, Mr. Dawson has spoken at various Foundation meetings. He is presently a member of the Foundation's Board of Directors, Educational Program Committee and chairman of the Budget and Financial Planning Committee, and a former member of its Administrators, Administrative Cost Study and Financial Review Committees. He is also a member of the board of directors for the Society of Professional Benefit Administrators.

follows-the-man" and "pro-rata." All other agreements appear to be a variation of one or the other, or a combination of both.

Pro-Rata. Basically, the pension pro rata agreements provide for each worker to be credited with credits earned in each fund. No credits or money is ever transferred, and at retirement the worker receives a pro-rata, or proportional, pension from each fund where he has worked during his working life. The advantage is that each fund keeps all contributions and no money is ever transferred between funds. In cases where there are different rates of contribution in each fund, there are few problems because each fund will make payments based on the rate in effect in that fund.

Among the disadvantages are added administration costs due to maintaining the records of employees for a lifetime, even 20, 30 or 40 years after the employee has left the area and is working elsewhere. Few workers will ever remember every place they have worked during a lifetime, and few will enjoy having to file five, ten or 15 different applications for a pension when they retire. It is also a real problem for a worker who moves around a lot to familiarize himself with the rules of each plan where credits have been earned during a lifetime of work.

While all the previous statements refer to a pension plan, we should mention the health and welfare pro-rata agreements, because there are many health and welfare funds using such agreements. The advantages are that no money is ever transferred and no action is ever taken unless there is a claim. The most common practice appears to be that the fund where the worker has the greatest amount of hours will pay the claim. This would appear to make the health and welfare fund pro-rata agreement much less expensive to administer than the money-follows-the-man agreements. This, however, is not always true. Many times, a worker whose home fund has a very meager schedule of benefits finds work in an area where they have an excellent schedule of benefits. He or his family may have been needing surgery but have been postponing it because the home plan paid only a small portion; the new fund with its excellent coverage is just what they have been waiting for. We have seen health and welfare funds with a big construction job and a large influx of workers almost go broke with a flood of claims from itinerant workers.

Money-Follows-the-Man. The money-follows-the-man pension agreement costs less to administer, because hours and money are transferred back to the home fund and as soon as the worker has left the area the records are purged and no further administration charges are incurred. The biggest advantage for the worker is the fact that all his credits are in his home local, where he and his family know the plan, and at retirement he has only one application to make to one fund.

The disadvantage is that many different plans have many different rates of contribution. The question is, if the rate transferred is less than the rate in effect at home, will he receive full credit? Some funds give full credit regardless of the rate reciprocated and find that over the years there will be as many hours at a higher rate as there are at a lower rate, so it all averages out. Even if a reduced credit is given, it is probably equal to the credit the worker would have received from the pro-rata agreement.

In the health and welfare fund, the "cash transfer" or money-follows-the-man arrangement allows the worker and his or her family to file their claims in their home fund, where they are familiar with the coverage and the claim procedures. The administration can become expensive if there is a large influx of workers from outside and no administration fee is charged to cover the cost of the reciprocity payments. Fees as little as 1% and as high as 10% are common. It's a decision for the trustees of each fund to make after careful examination of each situation in each plan.

There is one variation that some funds find acceptable. This is the "case of need" plan, which is still a form of cash-transfer or money-follows-the-man. In practice, no money is transferred unless and until an employee files a claim. At that time, if the home fund does not have enough hours credited to the employee to allow the claim to be paid, the "away" fund will reciprocate just enough money and hours to meet the minimal requirements to cover that claim. Each claim and each employee is treated separately, with the premise that dollars and hours will only be used to prevent a worker from losing his or her coverage if and when a claim actually has been incurred and filed. This type of arrangement never creates a feeling of security on the part of the worker, who always wonders if, "when the chips are down" and he really has a big claim, he will be covered.

Merger as Alternative

We would like to discuss the alternative to any type of reciprocity. We refer to mergers. For many years, small locals in small geographical areas have found that by merging their funds they can reduce administration costs, and therefore increase benefits. Like reciprocity agreements, mergers allow the worker to move around to wherever the work is without fear of losing their benefits. Many locals hesitate to merge funds for fear they will lose their local autonomy, and their international will merge the locals themselves. Actually the reverse is true. We have seen many cases where there was no reciprocity and the international would warn that, unless there were either a merger of the plans or a reciprocity agreement, the international would merge the locals and accomplish the same thing.

While statewide mergers have shown considerable growth, the multistate plans have not proliferated as much. Where they have appeared, there have also been some very healthy side effects. In both the state plans and the multistate plans, there usually develop state councils and multistate councils, and this usually leads to statewide as well as multistate collective bargaining agreements.

Who does this benefit? We submit that the first beneficiary is the employers. They now negotiate one agreement for the whole state or, hopefully, for the whole two or three state area. They now can bid work within the whole area and not worry about a dozen different rates and a dozen different contract expiration dates. There is now a rate of contribution for the whole area and the workers are more relaxed, with fewer worries about coverage for themselves and their families. Arguments about workers moving between locals within the area are minimal and are usually completely eliminated. The workers and locals are certainly happy and everyone seems to benefit.

Legal Requirements

It is important to remember that all mergers are subject to approval of the Pension Benefit Guaranty Corporation. Under Title I—Amendments to Title IV of the Employee Retirement Income Security Act of 1974, "Part A—Mergers or Transfer of Plan Assets or Liabilities," the regulations are as follows:

> Mergers and Transfers Between
> Multi-Employer Plans
>
> Sec. 4231(a)—Unless otherwise provided in regulations prescribed by the Corporation, a plan sponsor may not cause a multi-employer plan to merge with one or more multi-employer plans, or engage in a transfer of assets and liabilities to or from another multi-employer plan, unless such merger or transfer satisfies the requirements of Subsection (b).
>
> (b) A merger or transfer satisfies the requirements of this section if—
>
> (1) In accordance with regulations of the Corporation, the plan sponsor of a multi-employer plan notifies the Corporation of a merger with or transfer of plan assets or liabilities to another multi-employer plan at least 120 days before the effective date of the merger or transfer;
>
> (2) No participant's or beneficiary's accrued benefit will be lower immediately after the effective date of the merger or transfer than the benefit immediately before that date;
>
> (3) The benefits of participants and beneficiaries are not reasonably expected to be subject to suspension under 4245; and
>
> (4) An actuarial valuation of the assets and liabilities of each of the affected plans has been performed during the plan year preceding the effective date of the merger or transfer, based upon the most recent data available as of the day before the start of that plan year, or other valuation of such assets and liabilities performed under such standards and procedures as the Corporation may prescribe by regulation.
>
> (c) The merger of multi-employer plans or the transfer of assets or liabilities between multi-employer plans, shall be deemed not to constitute a violation of the provisions of Section 406(a) or Section 406(b)(2) if the Corporation determines that the merger or transfer otherwise satisfies the requirements of this Section.

Putting It Together

Funding Status. Item 4 above indicates that the actuarial valuation is required, but we suggest it is desirable as well. Some healthy older plans have a small unfunded liability, while many newer funds have large unfunded liabilities. Some use the minimum 30 year funding, while others use the 40 year method. We recently were asked to merge two pension funds. One fund had a contribution rate of 20^c per hour, the other had a rate of 60^c per hour. One had recently had a large construction job with a lot of permit men employed for one to three years, and when these non-vested workers left the fund found itself with almost no unfunded liability. One fund gave credits for all hours worked while the other gave one-tenth credits for each 120 hours, with a maximum of 1,200 hours per year. For many plans—as it developed with these plans—it proves impractical to merge because the differences cannot be worked out to the satisfaction of both parties. Most actuaries will establish a general formula stating the benefit for each 10^c per hour of contribution to account for differences in the rates of contribution, but these rates are based on a definite unfunded liability and a definite set of eligibility rules. If funds desire a merger, there must be a willingness to negotiate with give and take on both sides. Needless to say, a competent attorney, accountant and actuary are absolutely indispensable requirements to any successful merger.

Representation. A major consideration in any merger is the matter of representation on the board of trustees. When local unions merge with national unions, there is usually no local representation, but in area-wide and statewide mergers there is almost always local representation. The weakness is usually too many trustees, rather than not enough, and it usually develops that the unions or employees have more than enough trustees who are willing and eager to serve while the employers will not or cannot find anyone who wants to serve.

One solution is to form a council with one employee representative from each local. Each year a new trustee is elected from the council to serve on the board for three years. Thus, the board of trustees would consist of six trustees: three would represent management, and three would represent labor. At the first meeting, labor would select one trustee to serve for one year, one for two years and one for three years. Annually thereafter, one new trustee would be elected for a three year period.

Size Considerations. The last type of merger is the national plans. Small plans are continuing to join the national plans because of increased government interference and regulations or paperwork and red tape. The most expensive part of the administration today is government paperwork. We personally believe that the government, by design, is forcing small plans out of business or into mergers with big national plans. The real weakness in this trend is that the small plans lose all control with absolutely no local autonomy over their plans. Every area of the country has problems that they feel are peculiar to them, and they are solved best by the people affected. A board of trustees in Washington, D.C., has no real concern for the problems that are peculiar to Bangor, Maine, or Miami Beach, Florida.

The happy medium seems to be a statewide or a two or three state plan which would address the problems of the area, with a local board of trustees representing each local or each state. This type of plan, with the economies of a large fund, yet without the loss of local autonomy, can exemplify the very best kind of reciprocity available.

Documentation. Last but not least, let's examine the actual document. Lawyers never write or say anything in ten words if they can say it in 100, so the introduction is replete with whereases and therefores, but basically we have the official names of the funds which will participate in the agreement. The reason for the agreement and the desired achievements are set forth in legal terms. A list of definitions is given, with a detailed explanation of each term. The definitions are actually very important, and should be prepared carefully. The next section sets forth the duties and responsibilities of each participating fund. How often are payments to be made? How soon after the money is received will it be returned to the home fund? What information will be provided with the money that is reciprocated? How will the money be credited by the home fund? Whose responsibility is it to see that proper credits are given? All these questions should be answered fully.

Will there be a charge for handling or administration? If so, how much? A common practice is to charge 1% of gross wages or 10% of contributions received and reciprocated. Whatever the rate is to be should be plainly spelled out. Section 144 of S.209 specifically states that a reasonable charge for administration may be deducted from the money transferred. The agreement usually requires that each fund provide the other fund with copies of their respective determination letters to prove that they are exempt from taxes [usually under a §501(c)(9) code].

All agreements should provide for amendments and terminations, usually on 60-90 days notice.

Some agreements require the signatures of all trustees, while many require only the respective chairmen's and secretaries' signatures. The choice is up to the participants, and the advice of their attorneys. The important thing is to design and sign these agreements before we find new legislation requiring them in a much less desirable form.

Reciprocity of Pension Benefits— A Combination Approach

BY ROBERT J. DUFFEY

The Problem

Ever since pension programs were developed for multiemployer units, there has been a problem in providing a continuity of pension benefits or credits for those individuals who, through choice or necessity, traveled from one pension trust area to another. In the plumbing and steam fitting industry, most of the pension trusts were formed by individual local unions or a combination of local unions covering an area no greater than one state. This arrangement made it very difficult for an individual who worked in several different areas under several different trust agreements.

Quite early in the history of these pension programs, a system of reciprocity known as "money-follows-the-man" was developed in order to help alleviate this situation. Under this arrangement, when an individual left his home trust area to work temporarily in another trust area, a reciprocity agreement provided for one trust to return to the individual's home trust any contributions made on his behalf. This was, and is, an excellent method of providing continuity of credits or benefits for those individuals who maintained a single home trust throughout their lifetime of employment. However, this program had one serious shortcoming: it did not provide for the needs of an individual who moved permanently from the area of his original home trust and took up residence and membership in another pension trust area.

Quite often, hiring hall agreements require that preferential treatment be given to individuals who reside in the local union area. These types of arrangements made it very beneficial for an individual to take up permanent residence and thereby qualify for the better job opportunities. Under the money-follows-the-man reciprocity program, it is necessary for the individual to maintain his home trust coverage until such time as he earns a vested interest. After having vested in his home local pension program, he could then join another trust and

Mr. Duffey is business manager/financial secretary of the Journeymen Plumbers and Steam Fitters Local Union No. 393 in San Jose, California, a position he has held since December 1972. He is president of the Northern California Pipe Trades Council and chairman of the U.A. Local 393 pension and health and welfare trust funds.

again begin working toward vesting. This type of program generally requires the individual to reside and work in one trust area for at least ten years before moving on. Anyone required to move prior to having vested his pension benefits would, after a period of time, lose them under the break-in-service rules of the individual pension plans.

In attempting to solve this situation, everyone considered various methods of providing portability of benefits. This, of course, had many obvious disadvantages:

1. Contribution rates vary considerably from one area to the other.
2. The trust fund would not be able to determine what assets would be available to it over a long term, and therefore would be unable to project a viable benefit structure.
3. The trust fund had to be able to project its benefit liability and not have this liability subject to rules developed by another fund with an entirely different set of circumstances.

Even transferring the individual's total contribution from one trust fund to the other would not provide equity in that often, benefits had been raised retroactively, thus this contribution would not provide a commensurate benefit in another area.

A Combination Approach

Portability of benefits presents a number of obstacles that are extremely difficult, if not impossible, to overcome. Another avenue is to provide a method of establishing a continuing right to a benefit already earned. The concept of considering an individual's total service within a single industry as if it had been accumulated in one trust rather than a series of trusts is the area we are addressing here.

Background

In order to explain how this concept was developed, I would like to digress for a moment and recap the efforts of two trust funds in the San Francisco Bay area. In 1956, Plumbers and Steam Fitters Local 393 and Local 467 formed a pension trust for the purpose of providing pension benefits for the members of these two local unions. During that time, an individual could transfer from one local union to the other without endangering his pension credits, as both local unions were covered by a single pension trust fund.

A few years ago, there was a disagreement among the trustees of the two local unions as to what constituted the best investment policy for the trust fund assets. After a long discussion, it was determined that the best solution to the problem was to dissolve the joint trust, distribute the assets to the individual organizations, and let each set up an individual pension trust with regulations and investment policies to suit themselves. In order that no member of either organization would suffer a loss of any benefit he had enjoyed in the joint association, it was determined that we would continue to honor credits earned in either of the organizations. This, then, began the original pro-rata vesting reciprocity agreement.

This agreement provided that if any member of Local 467 who was vested in the Local 467 Pension Plan transferred to the Local 393 Pension Plan, he would be immediately vested in the 393 Plan. It also provided that anyone who had *less* than a vested interest in the 467 Pension Plan and transferred to the Local 393 Pension Plan would continue to get a vesting credit equal to the sum of his vesting credits in the two individual trusts. For example, an individual with six years' vesting credit in Local 467 could transfer to Local 393 and, having gained four years' vesting credit in Local 393 Pension Plan, would then be vested in both pension plans. Should he retire at that time, he would be eligible to draw six years of pension benefit from Local 467 pension trust fund at whatever amounts and under whatever terms then prevailed at Local 467 pension trust and four years of pension benefit from Local 393 at whatever amounts and under whatever terms prevailed under Local 393 pension trust at that time.

If the member continued to work and earn credits in either local union, the numbers would change commensurately with the contribution made on his behalf. Basically, the agreement provides that vesting in one plan also vested you in the other plan, and that the total sum of the years in the two plans could be used to achieve the ten year vesting and would vest you in both plans.

An Effective Method

After this system had been in effect for about three years without any complications or problems, the thought arose that anything that can work between two local unions and two pension trust funds should work equally well among any number of trust funds.

The Northern California Pipe Trades Council is an organization of plumbers, steam fitters and fire sprinkler fitters local unions in northern California. This pro-rata vesting reciprocity program was presented to the members of that organization for their approval. Many of the delegates to the Northern California Pipe Trades Council are also trustees in their individual pension trust funds. They took copies of this reciprocity agreement back to their individual trusts for adoption. We are now attempting to reach an agreement with all other United Association pension trust funds in order for this benefit to be available to all the members. We feel it is only fair that this protection be given to those who are required to establish residence in various parts of the United States and who have in the past been unable to secure a sufficient number of pension vesting credits in order to receive pension benefits upon retirement.

Our actuary has determined that the financial impact of this program on our fund will be negligible.

I will give you an illustration of how this plan operates. For purposes of identification, we will call the trust fund the worker is leaving his "home trust fund" and the one he is transferring to the "new trust fund." When an individual transfers from a trust fund participating in this pro-rata vesting program, he brings with him a statement from his home trust fund indicating the number of vesting credits he already has. A copy of this vesting credit statement is deposited with the new trust fund. When the individual receives his annual report from the new trust fund in which he is a member, he sends this report back to his home trust fund so that they will be informed that he is continuing his service within the industry and complying with the requirements of his conditional vesting. When the combination of vesting credits between the two trust funds reaches the required number for vesting, he will be considered vested in each of the trusts.

It may be necessary that some trust funds make amendments to their other benefit programs that are now based on their current vesting rules. These hours can be based on actual credits in the local area, instead of referring to vesting credits. These items are generally financed by other funds and are not a product of pension contributions. The only intent and purpose of the pro-rata reciprocity vesting is to protect the loss of pension benefits. It is obviously not designed to provide windfall benefits in other areas.

All such financial considerations aside, the most important aspect of this program is to establish a method of providing equity in an area where equity has not existed in the past. An individual is entitled to the pension benefit that has been contributed on his behalf. A combination of the money-follows-the-man and the pro-rata vesting approaches to reciprocity will provide this equity.

A copy of the reciprocity agreement drawn up for United Association local unions appears in the Appendix.

Appendix

U. A. Local 393 Pension Trust Fund
Reciprocity Agreement for Pro Rata Pension

Section 1. <u>Purpose</u>

Pro Rata Pensions are provided under this plan for employees who because of transfer of membership from one U. A. Local to another, are not entitled to the reciprocity available to "travelers," and would otherwise be ineligible for a pension because their years of employment have been divided between two or more U. A. Pension Plans.

Section 2. <u>Signatory Plans</u>

A. The provisions contained herein for reciprocity will be available to any other pension trust fund which is established in conformity with Section 302 of the Labor-Management Relations Act, as amended, and Employee Retirement Income Security Act of 1974 and which is a qualified plan under Section 401(a) of the Internal Revenue Code of 1954, created pursuant to a collective bargaining agreement between employers in the Plumbing and Pipefitting Industry and any Local Unions of the United Association. Plans which adopt this agreement for reciprocity shall be hereinafter referred to as "Signatory Plans."

B. Under this reciprocity arrangement, there shall be no transfer of funds between Signatory Plans.

C. Each Signatory Plan will retain its own Plan Year and Fiscal Year.

D. Credited service, whether for purposes of vesting or benefit accrual, will be determined on the basis of the rules of each Signatory Plan.

Section 3. <u>Eligibility for Benefits</u>

If an employee fails to earn at least one full year of vesting credit with a Signatory Plan prior to a break in service, as determined by the rules of the Signatory Plan, no benefits, past or future service credit, will be paid under this reciprocity agreement for the employee's service under said Signatory Plan.

Section 4. <u>Break in Service</u>

Each Signatory Plan will retain its own rules for determining a break in service, except that if,
  (1) a break in service has occurred, and
  (2) the employee subsequently becomes covered under another Signatory Plan, and
  (3) there was no twenty-four month period from last date of employment excluding periods of an excused break during which the employee's total vesting hours from the participating Plans were less than 100 hours,

then such break shall be an "excused break" for purposes of this agreement. Otherwise, the break shall be an "unexcused break."

Section 5. <u>Benefits and Vesting</u>

A. An employee shall be eligible for retirement benefits under this Reciprocity Agreement and his interests in any Signatory Plan under which he has worked shall vest if:

1. He has a total of 10 years of vesting credited service under two or more Signatory Plans in any period of continuous service prior to his retirement, and

2. He has at least one year of vesting credited future service during such period in each of two Signatory Plans.

B. This Reciprocity Agreement shall apply to any employee making application for normal, early, or disability retirement, whose interests have vested as provided in subparagraph A above, regardless of whether or not he is an active participant in the last reciprocating plan at the time of making application. The employee's retirement must occur on or after January 1, 1979. This Reciprocity Agreement shall be applicable for determining vesting as well as eligibility for benefits.

C. If an employee is eligible for a retirement or vested benefit as set forth in subparagraphs A and B above, he shall (except as provided in Section 3 above), be entitled to retirement or vested benefits from each Signatory Plan under which he had any credited service during his period of continuous employment. Each such Signatory Plan shall pay benefits based on its own such credited service, its own benefit formula, and in its own normal form at the time of normal, early or disability retirement. Such benefits shall be inclusive of, and not in addition to, any benefits to which the employee would be entitled from such Plan in the absence of this Agreement.

Section 6. Application for Benefits

Each employee shall make a written application for benefits under this reciprocity agreement, supplying all necessary requested information. Such application shall be made to the last Signatory Plan under which the employee earned at least one full year of future service credit.

Section 7. Optional Benefits

An employee may elect an optional form of pension benefits, such as a joint and survivor option, widow's benefit, etc., from any Signatory Plan if otherwise eligible under the rules and regulations of said Signatory Plan.

Section 8. Payment of Benefits

The payment of benefits shall commence in accordance with the rules of the last Signatory Plan under which the employee earned at least one full year of future service credit. Thereafter, benefits will be paid and benefits may be suspended upon resumption of employment in accordance with the rules and regulations of each Plan.

Section 9. Applicable Law

Any difference, disputes or disagreements that may arise with respect to this reciprocity agreement between any Signatory Plans shall be resolved by arbitration under the auspices of the American Arbitration Association.

IN WITNESS WHEREOF, the duly authorized signatories of the undersigned trusts have executed this agreement on the dates indicated below, to be retroactively effective as of the _____ day of _____, 19____.

U. A. LOCAL NO. 393
PENSION FUND

_____ Date: _____
Chairman

_____
Co-Chairman-Secretary

U. A. LOCAL NO.
PENSION FUND

_____ Date: _____
Chairman

_____
Co-Chairman-Secretary

A New Look at Disability Pensions

BY SIEGFRIED O. HILLMER

Introduction

Disability retirements are on the rise. In some public systems, disability retirements far exceed retirements on account of years of service. This is especially true in fire and police or so-called safety members' pension systems. However, a steady increase of such retirements is noted in private systems too.

A variety of factors are responsible for this phenomenon. Looking at the claimant: he is better educated, more often represented by legal counsel; he is tired of his present job and wants to get out to start a new career, preferably one subsidized by a disability pension (which may provide a means for this as well as for early retirement).

Looking at the other end of the spectrum, we find: vague and ambiguous disability standards in plan provisions or in the applicable statutes, which are liberally interpreted by the courts, as well as overlapping authority to determine disability and to determine fitness to return to work when disability may have ceased. More and more, the plan provisions are not the exclusive basis upon which entitlement to a disability pension can be grounded. The same is true with regard to return-to-work provisions in the plan. Any one or more complicating factors can and often will have a bearing upon the outcome of claims, and will frequently virtually nullify the intent of the underlying plan provisions.

Let me allude to these factors without thereby claiming completeness for my enumeration. I will limit myself mainly to a discussion of those factors that appear to affect pension provisions and conditions of entitlement for disability retirement most significantly.

Workers' Compensation Issues

Conflicting Disability Standards

For some time now, our courts have taken into account decisions made by adjudicatory bodies operating under workers' compensation laws, when called upon to review decisions by pension boards and plan administrators which have resulted in the denial of a disability retirement claim. It is

As Assistant City Attorney, Siegfried O. Hillmer heads the legal department of the Fire and Police Pension System and the City Employees' Retirement System of the City of Los Angeles. He has served in this capacity for more than ten years and is responsible for drafting provisions governing the city's pension plans and defending the pension systems in major litigation. Mr. Hillmer has also served as a Deputy Labor Commissioner for the State of California. Previously, Mr. Hillmer was engaged in labor union work, being affiliated with the DGB, the German equivalent of the AFL-CIO. Educated in Germany, Denmark, England, Canada and the United States, Mr. Hillmer is admitted to practice before the California Bar and the Supreme Court of the United States.

remarkable to observe the frequency with which courts discount the different standards that apply to disability as a basis for a workers' compensation claim vs. disability sufficient to entitle a claimant to early retirement under a pension plan.

The fact of the matter is that the majority of awards under workers' compensation laws are not made to employees who have become disabled—and indeed, this is not the intent of such laws. Workers' compensation laws compensate for industrially-related injuries, regardless of the fault of any person. In other words, it is injury—the impairment of earning capacity—for which monetary compensation is made, not incapacity to work at all, or incapacity to perform the work for which an employee was hired. In contrast, a typical disability retirement pension plan provision will require as a standard that a plan member be "permanently incapacitated for the performance of duty" (Calif. Govt. Code Sec. 31720).

Workers' compensation deals with temporary and permanent disability, as well as partial disability. Workers' compensation usually does not deal with total and permanent disability, which is required to establish eligibility under many disability pension plans.

Although pension plans and workers' compensation laws on principle present different disability standards, different elements of compensation and frequently different issues, there is no question that the courts are heading in the direction of making workers' compensation decisions binding on pension plan administrators.

In *French v. Rishell* (40 Cal. 2d 477), a California supreme court case which is not a disability case but a widow's pension case, the determination by the Industrial Accident Commission that the death of a former captain of the Oakland Fire Department proximately resulted from an injury occurring in the course of and arising out of his employment was found to be res judicata and binding on the trustees of the Oakland Firemen's Relief and Pension Fund. The precedent of *French v. Rishell* has been consistently followed by the California courts, and has been applied with increasing frequency to disability pension claims. One of the latest cases in a long line of such decisions is *Greatorex v. Board of Administration* (91 Cal. App. 3d 54).

It is important to point out that both *French* and *Greatorex*, as well as other cases decided during the 26 years that elapsed between the two decisions, primarily affect pension plans that provide pensions for work-related disability. However, the argument is easily made that once agencies administering workers' compensation benefits decide upon the issue of a compensable injury and the courts apply principles of res judicata or collateral estoppel, disability in a large number of disability pension claims will, for all practical purposes, have been decided by such workers' compensation agencies before a case can ever be considered by the trustees of a pension plan.

Offset Provisions—The 'Windfall' Question

Another aspect of the interaction of workers' compensation and disability pension plans appears to be worthy of mention in this context. When both disability pension benefits and workers' compensation benefits are paid to a person on account of the same disability, it often results in a financial windfall to the disabled employee. Unlike the Social Security Act, few (if any) workers' compensation laws impose limitations on the right to receive both workers' compensation and a disability pension by employing an earnings test; and vice versa, not too many pension plans limit pension amounts because of the receipt of workers' compensation benefits. In California, as in most states, the law specifically provides that the receipt of a disability pension and workers' compensation does not constitute double recovery under the workers' compensation laws (*see:* California Labor Code Section 3752; *City of Palo Alto v. I.A.C. (Gaudin)* (1965), 232 Cal. App. 2d 305).

However, a number of pension plans, in an effort to avoid windfall situations, have been adopting plan provisions requiring an offset, at least for those workers' compensation awards which pertain to the same injury upon which the disability pension is based. At least in the case of public pension plans, the courts have looked with favor upon these offset provisions. To name a few instances: Two 1965 cases established the California trend upholding the validity of offsets by a pension plan for workers' compensation awards to the same person—*City of Los Angeles v. I.A.C. (Fraide)*, 63 Cal. 2d 242 and *City of Los Angeles v. I.A.C. (Morse)*, 63 Cal. 2d 263. (Other cases: *Symington v. City of Albany*, 5 Cal. 3d 23; *City, Etc. of San Francisco v. Workmen's Comp. App. Bd.*, 2 Cal. 3d 1001; *City of Costa Mesa v. McKenzie*, 30 Cal. App. 3d 763.)

The fire and police pension systems of the City of Los Angeles have gone further than most pension plans, with an offset provision which requires not only deductions from pension payments for workers' compensation benefits on account of the same injury but mandates an offset for *any* workers' compensation award, irrespective of the fact that different injuries may be responsible for the award and the disability pension. There are several other California systems with like provisions. California courts not only have upheld such provisions but have approved offsets against disability pensions regardless of *when* the workers' compensation award was granted—even if it was made before the time that the disability pension became effective (see: *Lyons v. Workmen's Comp. Appeals Bd.*, 44 Cal. App. 3d 1007).

Before we leave the subject of deducting workers' compensation awards from pensions, let me direct your attention to two ERISA cases concerning workers' compensation offsets which demonstrate a direction away from my California examples, although the principles involved are also different.

One of these cases arose in Michigan and the other in New Jersey. I am referring to *Utility Workers Union of America, et al. v. Consumers Power Co., et al.*, 453 F.Supp. 447 (1978) and

Henry Buczynski, et al. v. General Motors Corporation, 456 F.Supp. 867 (1978). In the *Utility Workers Union* case, the federal district court differentiated between Social Security and workers' compensation in concluding that an employee was entitled to double pay. Even though the decision is lacking in clarity of expression, it appears that the court experienced no difficulty in ignoring pension plan language which provided for an offset of all workers' compensation payments received by a retiree. The plaintiffs in that case had contended that the offset provisions of the plan violated the antiforfeiture provisions of ERISA §203.

The *Henry Buczynski* case approved and relied upon the holding in the *Utility Workers Union* case, and decided that the offset provisions of the pension plan which allowed the employer to deduct his costs for workers' compensation payments awarded pensioners from their pension retirement benefits was unlawful under ERISA's minimum vesting standards provisions.

Notwithstanding those two cases, I believe that an offset for workers' compensation benefits against a pension plan's disability payments is permissible if the disability benefit exists independent of rights to accrual toward retirement on account of years of service.

The Social Security Disability Standard

In contrast to the disability standards of the workers' compensation laws, which are really standards measuring degrees of impairment, the Social Security Act provides a definition of actual disability which has found favor with many pension plans as a standard of disability. The Social Security Act (Title 42 U.S.C.A.) provides in Section 1382c(3)(A) and (B) as pertinent:

> (3)(A) An individual shall be considered to be disabled for purposes of this subchapter if he is unable to engage in any substantial gainful activity by reason of any medically determinable physical or mental impairment which can be expected to result in death or which has lasted or can be expected to last for a continuous period of not less than twelve months....
>
> (B) For purposes of subparagraph (A), an individual shall be determined to be under a disability only if his physical or mental impairment or impairments are of such severity that he is not only unable to do his previous work but cannot, considering his age, education, and work experience, engage in any kind of substantial gainful work which exists in the national economy, regardless of whether such work exists in the immediate area in which he lives, or whether a specific job vacancy exists for him, or whether he would be hired if he applied for work....

Unfortunately, this seemingly precise formulation of a disability standard is punctured by interpretations, qualifications and regulations prescribed by the Secretary of Health and Human Services. It must therefore be viewed as a standard, to be used with caution: if adopted by a pension plan, there is the danger that, along with the language of the act, one may also have borrowed some unwelcome interpretations of it.

Clarifying Plan Provisions

It may be a good time now to express a few thoughts about drafting pension plan language intended to provide disability pension benefits, whether they be benefits for work-related disability or disability not predicated upon an industrial injury or illness. I cannot do more than touch upon some aspects of disability pension provisions which create problems of challenge and litigation.

Length of Disability

The Social Security Act does not require "permanent" disability to create entitlement to benefits. However, disability must last at least 12 months. This is a condition which, under ordinary circumstances, is fairly easy to prove.

The Internal Revenue Code, although not providing disability benefits but rather an exclusion from gross income on account of disability, provides a definition of disability which may well appeal to those who are inclined to restrict entitlement to a disability pension. It provides in Section 105(d)(5) that a person is:

> ...permanently and totally disabled if he is unable to engage in any substantial gainful activity by reason of any medically determinable physical or mental impairment which can be expected to result in death or which has lasted or can be expected to last for a continuous period of not less than 12 months.

Unless a pension plan is intended to provide liberal disability pension benefits, tailoring plan language after the provisions of the Social Security Act or the Internal Revenue Code should tend to limit disability claims.

Clauses to the effect that a member "who has become disabled" is entitled to a disability pension are often intended to provide a pension for permanent disability only. In actuality, courts usually disagree and find entitlement under such provisions even if the disability is only temporary. One older California case is still relevant: *Tyra v. Board of Police, Etc., Commrs.* (71 Cal. App. 2d 50).

Extent of Disability

Another example of often used and much contested phraseology is the provision that an employee, in order to become entitled to a disability pension, must be "physically or mentally incapacitated and thereby incapable of performing his duties." The difficulty with this type of language is that it is non-specific. Does "duties" mean some particular assignment as part of a particular job, or does it mean *all* possible duties within a specified employment, be it that of electrician, painter or police officer?

It appears that a number of appellate courts have taken a common sense approach to the interpretation of such or similar provisions. In *Craver v. City of Los Angeles* (42 Cal. App. 3d 76), a motorcycle officer injured his back and, having made a reasonable recovery, was assigned to a communications desk. He filed for a disability pension, contending that he was physically no longer able to perform his duties as a motorcycle officer and that he should, therefore, be retired. The pension board denied his application, determining that he was not entitled to disability retirement because he was capable of performing his duties at a communications desk. When the case reached the court of appeal the city prevailed, the court holding that even though a police officer is not able to perform any and all duties usually performed by police officers, he is not entitled to a disability retirement pension if he can perform duties in a given permanent assignment within the police department.

In another case, *Mansperger v. Public Employees' Retirement System* (6 Cal. App. 3d 873), the Public Employees' Retirement System found that a fish and game warden was not physically incapacitated from performing his duties and thus was not eligible for disability retirement. The trial court denied the warden's petition in mandamus to set aside the decision. The evidence showed that in spite of the injury sustained by the employee, he could perform most of the tasks required by his job (although with difficulty in some cases), except for heavy lifting. The court of appeal affirmed the judgment of the trial court, holding that "incapacitated for the performance of duty" within the meaning of the applicable statute meant the substantial inability of the applicant for retirement to perform his usual duties.

Is the Disability Work-Related?

In cases where a pension plan provides two types of disability retirement, i.e., one type for work-related disability and retirement with lesser benefits for non-work-related disability, precise language in the description of disability standards is extremely important. Otherwise, you may soon find that a majority of claims will result in the granting of a work-related disability pension, at least after the case has gone to court following denial by the plan administrators. Typical language to be avoided—if such an outcome is not desired—is a provision whereby entitlement to a work-related disability pension requires that the performance of a person's duties is "*a* cause" of disability. A number of appellate courts have held that *any* cause, even though it only contributed to the disability instead of being exclusively responsible for it, is sufficient under such language to entitle an employee to a work-related disability pension (see: *Heaton v. Marin County Employees Retirement Board,* 63 Cal. App. 3d 421; *Gelman v. Board of Retirement, Etc.,* 85 Cal. App. 3d 92). This also usually results in a finding of entitlement to a work-related pension in cases where the employment aggravated a pre-existing condition of the employee (see: *Kuntz v. Kern County Employees' Retirement Ass'n.,* 64 Cal. App. 3d 414).

On the other hand, it appears that the courts have not as yet gone so far as to hold that minimal industrial contribution to a disability is sufficient to support a claim for a work related disability pension (see: *Colonial Insurance Company v. Industrial Accident Commission,* 29 Cal. 2d 79; *De Puy v. Board of Retirement, Etc.,* 87 Cal. App. 3d 392).

Disability Pensions: Competing Benefits and Their Effect on One Another

BY MARK H. LIPTON

Introduction

Disability benefits are possibly the type of benefits singularly most important to the plan participant. This is so whether the benefits are payable on a short term basis, through a self-funded health and welfare trust or commercial group insurance policy, or on a long term basis through disability pension plan provisions or commercial group long term insurance policies. This is true because disability is unexpected, and the benefits—if available—are there when the participant needs them most. Significantly, the discretion of trustees to structure the provisions of disability benefits is almost unlimited. That is, while ERISA places certain strictures on normal retirement benefit provisions as well as early retirement benefit provisions, including the requirement that a joint and survivor option be made available, disability benefits are governed only minimally by ERISA.

The amount of benefits, short term or long term, the duration and prerequisite requirements, including an immediate connection with the trade, should be considered carefully by all trustees, based on the type of industry the plan covers as well as the assets available to fund disability benefits. In choosing specific plan provisions, trustees should be aware of other disability benefits that may be available to their participants and how they would impact the level of benefits available to the participant. After all, disability benefits are provided as wage replacement, at least prior to age 65, and coordination with other benefits should be considered.

A Multiplicity of Programs

The significance other disability programs will have in providing benefits to a participant should not be underestimated. Testimony before the President's Commission on Pension Policy in October 1979 by the Health Insurance Association of America indicated the following:

> Federal disability programs paid out over $24.8 billion in 1978 to 10.4 million disabled persons and their dependents. These benefits came from Social Security, Civil Service, Military, Veterans, Black Lung and numerous other cash benefit programs operated by the federal government. Not included in this figure are other federal benefit programs such as Medicare and Food Stamps, which many disabled beneficiaries may also receive.
>
> In 1977, an estimated 80 million persons were covered for some form of disability income protection through their employers. This included sick leave and other non-insured plans as well as group short and long term disability programs. Insurance companies alone paid out over $2.2 billion in

Mr. Lipton is president of the law firm of Lipton & Lipton, A.P.C., San Jose, California. He is a graduate of the University of California at Berkeley, and earned his law degree at Boalt Hall. His practice emphasizes employee labor law, including representation of several Taft-Hartley trusts, and Social Security administrative law. Mr. Lipton was the consulting attorney for both the ERISA and Social Security chapters of The Graying of America *published by Dial Press.*

benefits under such programs in 1977.

Workers' Compensation disability benefits and State Cash Sickness programs accounted for an additional $4.2 billion in benefits to disabled workers in 1977.

Individual disability insurance of various kinds covered 36.4 million persons in 1977, while automobile insurance provided disability coverage to an estimated 40 to 50 million persons. Also, there are an indeterminate number of persons who have Waiver of Premium or some other form of disability insurance with their individual and group life insurance programs and large numbers with some type of disability coverage under pension and profit sharing plans.

In recent years, there has been a significant increase in the number of persons utilizing legal action to collect for damages of all types. There has also been an expansion in various welfare programs available to individuals on the basis of need, further expanding total benefits available.

This multiplicity of programs providing income to disabled persons makes the overall disability income system complex and difficult to comprehend. It is further complicated by the varying scope of coverage and benefit levels. The combination of programs for which a single individual may be eligible makes it possible for that individual to intentionally or unintentionally have more disability income protection than is needed. At the same time, an individual who relies on a single program may have inadequate protection. Still others may be overinsured in certain circumstances but underinsured in others. There is a critical need to develop a better understanding of the possibilities of overinsurance, while also being aware of underinsurance, before the multitude of disability insurance programs can be rationalized.

Short Term Disability Programs

Short term disability benefits most often available to plan participants which should be considered by trustees include state disability benefits provided by individual state governments; temporary workers' compensation, which is paid through private insurance carriers in most states; and commercial group short term disability insurance. The benefit levels paid under these various programs differ from state to state. California State Disability Insurance (SDI) pays a maximum of $154.00 per week, while temporary workers' compensation is paid at $154.00 per week to an employee who had prior gross earnings of at least $231.00 per week. Commercial group insurance benefits for short term disability are usually a percentage of the employee's average monthly income, ranging from one-half to two-thirds. Consequently, a Taft-Hartley plan providing for short term disability benefits would usually provide a percentage of average monthly income with a minimum base amount, and should integrate or deduct benefits payable from other sources.

Integration is commonly used by the programs described. California State Disability Insurance is not payable when workers' compensation benefits are available. Commercial group insurance usually excludes any work-related injury and deducts state disability insurance actually received or due, as well as disability benefits payable pursuant to Taft-Hartley plans. Consequently, Taft-Hartley plans should provide benefits *after others have been exhausted* to minimize the liability of the plan. It behooves every trustee to know what benefits his state makes available for short term disabilities incurred by its plan participants.

Short term benefits should not exceed 24 months, and would appropriately be funded by a health and welfare trust fund as an accident or sickness benefit. As liabilities increase dramatically with the length of the disability program, benefits exceeding two years should be covered under a disability pension provision.

Long Term Disability Programs

Long term disability benefits are of equal or greater significance than short term disability benefits. The types of benefits that are available include Social Security disability, permanent/temporary workers' compensation, commercial long term disability insurance and private sector plan disability pensions. The benefit levels vary significantly for these types of programs. Social Security pays a minimum of $122.00 per month primary insurance after 1978, and will pay a maximum primary insurance amount of $1,040.00 per month for those wage earners who have contributed a maximum amount to the Social Security system. The wage earner with a wife who is not working and three or more children will receive a maximum of $1,820.20 per month upon becoming eligible for Social Security disability benefits.

"Temporary" workers' compensation can continue almost indefinitely. As long as the employee's condition is not stationary, temporary benefits will continue. When the employee's condition reaches the point where it is diagnosed as permanent and stationary—that is, it is not expected to get any better or any worse—a rating is given. At that point, permanent benefits are payable based on the percentage rate of disability; e.g., 70% or more qualifies a worker to a lifetime pension in California. The amount of the pension varies depending upon the rating: as the rating goes up, the monthly benefits increase.

Commercial group long term disability insurance benefits are usually a percentage of prior earnings, with a maximum ceiling. Calculation of prior earnings is usually based on the 12 months immediately preceding the date of disability. This may significantly decrease most participants' benefits from commercial group long term disability insurance in that the 12 month period prior to actually ceasing employment usually is peppered with absences because of the disability. Consequently, while two-thirds of the most recent average 12 month salary may be paid, it usually does not equal two-thirds of the highest earnings of the employee.

Most Taft-Hartley plan disability retirement programs provide the same benefits that normal retirement would provide, while allowing the disabled participant to retire due to a disability regardless of his age.

Offsets and Integration

These various benefits interact with one another, in that Social Security will not pay benefits if, when combined with workers' compensation benefits, the amount would exceed 80% of the average monthly earnings of the participant for the five years previous to the disability onset. Commercial group long term disability insurance integrates or deducts Social Security benefits, as well as family benefits, temporary workers' compensation benefits, Taft-Hartley disability pension benefits and all other disability pension benefits. While the commercial group long term disability policies deduct Social Security disability benefits and old age benefits payable under the Social Security Act, cost-of-living annual increases are not deducted.

Taft-Hartley plans usually provide no offsets; when offsets do exist, they usually relate to Social Security or temporary workers' compensation. Again, Taft-Hartley plans should look to the replacement value of earnings they wish to provide and coordinate with other benefits that may be available to the participant.

Disability Standards

Social Security

Undoubtedly, the most significant aspect of plan provisions adopted by a Taft-Hartley trust to regulate the payment of disability benefits is the standard used in determining disability. The Social Security Act defines disability pursuant to 42 U.S.C. Section 416(1) at 42 U.S.C. Section 423(2)(A) as follows:

> (Total disability is the) inability to engage in any substantial, gainful activity by reason of any medically determinable physical or mental impairment which can be expected to result in death or has lasted or can be expected to last for a continuous period of not less than 12 months (and which precludes the claimant from performing not only his previous work, but considering his age, education and work experience any other kind of substantial gainful work which exists in the national economy regardless of whether such work exists in the immediate area in which he lives, or whether a specific job vacancy exists for him or whether he would be hired if he applied for the work).

The "Usual Occupation" Standard

Commercial group long term disability policies usually define disability as the insured's inability to perform his usual occupation for the first 24 months of disability. Thereafter the standard becomes more stringent, although while requiring the insured to be totally disabled it has been held by courts not to be as stringent as the Social Security disability standard. While there is a split among jurisdictions, the majority have concluded that long term disability benefits are payable through commercial group insurance policies if the insured cannot perform "ordinary employment of the particular person insured or such other employment, if any, approximating the same livelihood that the insured might be fairly expected to follow in view of his station, and his physical and mental capabilities." See *Austero v. National Casualty*, 84 C.A.3d 1 (1978), *Erreca v. West States Life Insurance*, 19 C.2d 388 (1942).

What this simply means is that a construction

worker earning $15-20 an hour, limited to light work due to a back injury, cannot be expected to accept a less strenuous job earning only $4 an hour since it does not approximate the same livelihood. A business executive could not be expected to work on an assembly line packaging pharmaceuticals as it is not something that he "might be fairly expected to follow in view of his station...." This court-modified standard of disability is most fairly characterized as being somewhere between the standard requiring inability to perform one's usual occupation and the Social Security disability standard requiring disability from *any* substantial gainful activity based on one's age, education and previous work experience.

Selecting the Plan Standard

The Taft-Hartley plan should adopt either the Social Security disability standard or the standard requiring merely that the participant be unable to perform his usual occupation. If the Social Security standard is adopted, serious consideration should be made to integrating other benefits that are available, particularly benefits available through commercial group long term disability insurance policies. If the latter standard is utilized, it is anticipated that the participant may go back to some other kind of work, and consideration should be given to deducting from the plan benefits such earnings if the participant goes back to work. The plan may want to allow a trial work period for anywhere from six to 18 months during which the participant may keep part of his net earnings in addition to benefits paid by the plan. This is to provide an incentive to go back to work. However, on a long term basis, if an employee has returned to work, the plan trustees should seriously consider offsetting plan benefits by net earnings on a dollar-for-dollar basis.

There are varying considerations facing the plan trustees in selecting the disability standard. If the Social Security standard is selected, the plan will require the obtaining of a Social Security disability award certificate as a prerequisite for obtaining plan benefits. The plan administrators should also consider whether the minimum number of years required to qualify for a disability pension should be equal to, greater than, or less than the number of years required for vesting for normal or early retirement benefits. The trustees should also consider whether a recent connection with the industry will be a prerequisite. For example, do the trustees want to provide disability benefits for an individual who had ten years of covered service under the plan but had been performing non-covered employment for the 15 years immediately prior to disability? Stated simply, do the trustees want to insure for disability purposes individuals who do not have a recent connection with the industry covered by the plan?

If the trustees use the standard merely requiring that the individual be unable to perform his usual occupation to qualify for benefits, the burden of establishing disability will be assumed by the trustees. The trustees cannot then rely on any other body or agency's determination regarding disability. Original medical validation must be obtained either from the participant's treating physician or, if the trustees are not satisfied with the information provided from that source, by medical consultants hired and paid for by the trustees. Continuing medical validation may also be necessary. The Social Security Administration, depending on the type of disability, conducts periodic reviews. If the "usual occupation" standard is utilized by the trustees, it will be their responsibility to monitor the disability and ensure that the medical condition continues.

In using the "usual occupation" standard, a minimum age should more seriously be considered than when the Social Security standard is utilized. As this disability standard is more liberal, the presumption may be made that younger individuals may easily adapt to other employment and therefore should not be eligible on a long term basis for benefits. On the other hand, individuals over 50 having worked in the industry for some time may find it extremely difficult to adjust to other employment and hence be eligible for the disability benefits of the plan. Integration with other benefits, deductions for net earnings, a ceiling on maximum benefits and a requirement of a recent connection with the industry are considerations that should be more seriously evaluated under the "usual occupation" standard than under the Social Security standard.

Rehabilitation and Return to Work Issues

Regardless of which standard is used, the trustees should provide for what will happen to benefits in the event the participant does return to some type of employment. The Social Security Act provides for a nine month trial work period with benefits paid. Workers' compensation provides benefits on the basis of a partial disability while the employee works. Commercial group long term disability continues benefits following a return to work under an approved rehabilitation training program with a deduction of 50-75% of income received under such a program. Private plans can take any of these approaches or others. For instance, in the event an employee returns to work, benefits may be reduced to a minimum amount regardless of the employee's earnings. The plan could provide that earnings and plan benefits combined could not exceed predisability income. To the extent that the total of the two would exceed that amount, plan benefits would be reduced. Combinations and formulas are limitless, and should be structured to meet the unique requirements of the industry covered by the plan.

A parallel consideration to the return to work issue is rehabilitation and the extent to which the plan administrators should be involved in it. In that the Social Security Act contains regulations regarding rehabilitation and both workers' compensation insurance carriers and group long term disability insurance carriers encourage rehabilitation, providing vocational rehabilitation counselors for retraining, the plan should make use of these existing programs.

The Social Security Act relies on the Vocational Rehabilitation Act, 42 U.S.C. Section 422 (a)(b). That provides that any individual receiving Social Security disability benefits who is not precluded because of his disability from entering into a rehabilitation program must enter into such a program approved under the act. The vocational rehabilitation counselors utilized by both the workers' compensation insurance carriers and the group long term disability insurance carriers are familiar with forms of alternative employment which may be feasible for an individual disabled from his previous employment. By utilizing these other rehabilitation programs, Taft-Hartley plans will not expend monies duplicating the efforts undertaken by others, nor will they be faced with having to decide between the claims of the plan participant denying rehabilitation and those of a plan-hired vocational counselor with a different opinion and a competing interest.

Legal Issues and Decisions

Communication to Participants. Regardless of what provisions are selected by the trustees, the participants should receive notice of those provisions. Mere printing of the pension plan booklet without its dissemination is insufficient notice of the plan provisions. One court found that a participant who had no notice of a break-in-service provision could not be subject to the terms of that provision until notice was received. In *Burroughs v. Board of Trustees of the Pension Trust Fund of the Operating Engineers,* 542 F.2d 1128 (1976), the trustees adopted a two year break-in-service rule in 1960 and notice thereof was not communicated to the plan participants. Several years later, a plan participant sought to retire and found that he had lost his credited service because of a two year break. The court held that the two years did not begin to run until he was notified of the break provisions.

Preemption. Probably the most significant case affecting disability pensions in recent years is that of *Buczynski v. General Motors Corporation,* decided by the U.S. Circuit Court for the Third Circuit, 281 BNA BPR D-1, which found invalid a New Jersey statute which would have prohibited deducting workers' compensation benefits received by participants from disability pension benefits. These statutes were found to be preempted by ERISA and thus to be null and void as against plan provisions allowing for deductions of workers' compensation benefits of an ERISA-covered pension plan. This is significant in that traditionally state laws involving regulation of insurance have not been found to be preempted by federal law. *Buczynski* is a significant deviation from that federal hands-off policy in the insurance area. The United States Supreme Court has agreed to hear arguments in the *Buczynski* case by granting certiorari on November 3, 1980. The decision by the United States Supreme Court will significantly impact the states' rights to regulate the specifics of disability plan provisions.

Partial Pensions. Presently a plan may provide for a pro-rata or partial pension for normal or early retirement while not providing a similar disability benefit. In the case of *Streeter v. Board of Trustees of the Construction Laborers Pension Trust for Southern California,* 435 F.Supp. 1148 (1977), that situation arose. A participant argued that he was unable to continue work because of a disability; if he had reached the required age, he would have been eligible for a pro-rata early or normal retirement benefit. Since he could not work to that age because of a disability, he argued that a pro-rata disability provision should be in the plan and allowable to him. The district court disagreed, and upheld the trustees' denial of the pension benefits.

Breaks-in-Service. In that disability pension provisions are optional, the courts have allowed seemingly harsh decisions by trustees to stand in order to encourage inclusion of disability pension plan provisions. The requirement that notice to freeze credits be given trustees in the event of disability, with failure to do so allowing a break, has been upheld. In the case of *Sailer v. Retirement Fund Trust of the Plumbing, Heating and Piping Industry of Southern California,* 599 F.2d 913 (1979), a disabled individual who had not given the trustees the required notice lost all credited service after incurring a break. Had notice of the disability been given to the trustees, credits would have been frozen and the break would not have occurred. In upholding the denial of benefits, the court concluded that the trustees were entitled to insert any stipulations or prerequisites relating to disability benefits they desired in the plan, since a disability pension was in itself not required by either ERISA, Taft-Hartley, or IRS regulations. The courts have held that disability itself does not automatically constitute a suspension of the break-in-service rules, as stated in *Wilson v. Board of Trustees of the Pension Trust for Operating Engineers,* 564 F.2d 1299 (1977).

Connection With the Industry. Another example of unique treatment which may be given disability pension plans is the requirement of a recent connection with the trade in order to be eligible for the benefit. Once a participant has vested his benefits, he may leave the trade or employment covered by the plan and be eligible for the plan benefits upon reaching normal retirement age. This is true even if the participant has not been performing covered employment for many years. However, a vested participant may be required to have been employed in the trade immediately prior to the commencement of his disability in order to be eligible for disability benefits under the plan. In *Vaughan v. Metal Lathers Local No. 46 Pension Fund,* 474 F.Supp. 613 (1979), the district court not only allowed this requirement to be inserted into the plan but allowed it to be retroactive as to those who had left the industry because of unavailability of work and subsequently became disabled. The purpose of the amendment to the plan was specifically to reduce the number of participants able to qualify for disability pension benefits, and had been suggested by the plan actuary because of financial problems the plan was encountering.

Conclusion

It is clear that there are many factors to consider in designing plan benefits for disabilities. It is also clear that disability benefits may have the most significant impact on a plan participant, coming at a time when financial aid is most sorely needed. All plans should strive to have disability provisions. Trustees should become conversant with the different benefits available, monies available for funding and the liberality with which the law treats trustees' decisions in fashioning disability provisions, and then adopt language to provide disability benefits best suited for their plan participants.

CHAPTER 5

Options in Welfare Benefits Design

Ronald D. Wackett

Director, Office of Personnel
and Employee Benefits
United Food and Commercial Workers
International Union
Washington, D.C.

Daniel H. Mundt

Partner
Mundt and Hall
Duluth, Minnesota

Harold G. Korbee

Partner
Korbee & Korbee
Cincinnati, Ohio

William C. Earhart

President
The William C. Earhart Company, Inc.
Portland, Oregon

Sidney Gaines

Senior Partner
Friedlander, Gaines, Cohen,
Rosenthal & Rosenberg
New York, New York

Stanley Howitt

Supervising Attorney and General Counsel
Alaska Electrical Trust Funds
Anchorage, Alaska

Flexible Benefit Programs— Has the Time Come?

BY RONALD D. WACKETT

LOOKING BACKWARD is perhaps the one method we have of viewing the future with any degree of accuracy. And what does retrospective review disclose? It highlights one overriding principle: change is the only constant regardless of the breadth of our observation. The difficulty one encounters when attempting to look into the future lies in attempting to determine the value of past experience while gauging the effect of, and potential for, change in that future.

The central character in our saga is the worker. Whether clothed in jeans or business attire, while benefactor of the past and able to affect the future, this worker is nearly powerless to resist the dynamics of current change or the effect of change from the past. Daniel Yankelovich in his study, "Work, Values and the New Breed," concludes that:

> A new breed of Americans, born out of the social movement of the sixties and grown to majority proportions in the seventies, holds a set of values and beliefs so markedly different from the traditional outlook that they promise to transform the character of work in America.

It is this group, now fast approaching middle age, the majority of whom have never known "want," benefactors of several decades of growth and development in the area of fringe benefits, that is now surveying its environment and beginning to question the status quo of benefit programs that have developed since the mid-1940s.

But why is this challenge appearing? Why, when even now federal regulations are being amended or modified to increase the scope and limits of fringe benefits, does there appear a challenge to the wisdom of the past in the area of employee benefits?

The Challenge of Change

One of the characteristics embodied in the "change" affecting this area is a modification in the

Mr. Wackett is director of benefits for the United Food and Commercial Workers International Union. In addition to staff personnel duties, his responsibilities include administering the international's fringe benefit plans and overseeing 57 pension and 82 health and welfare plans in the United States and Canada. He previously served as contract administrator for the Retail Clerks Unions and Employers Insurance and Pension Fund in Atlanta, Georgia. Mr. Wackett received his B.S. degree from Valparaiso University and his M.A. degree from Antioch University. He is a member of the Industrial Relations Research Association; American Society of Training and Development; National Council on Alternative Work Patterns; and the Gerontological Society. He has spoken at previous Foundation educational meetings.

expectations and values of our beneficiaries. Today's worker accepts and expects certain minimum fringe benefits. As Daniel Bell suggests, "a revolution in rising entitlement" is causing more and more people to become aware of the fateful role work plays in their lives.

Secondly, the general availability of work throughout this group's working lifetime makes the unavailability of work an unthinkable situation. Accordingly, job shopping and change are an accepted and expected characteristic of today's worker.

Thirdly, a change in the focus of contemporary life philosophy from concern for the welfare of society to that of the "self" has resulted in greater opportunity for the individual to live an experiential life with emphasis on personal satisfaction, rather than one dedicated to fostering the traditional values of home, family and community.

And finally, the heavy influx of second wage earners into the economy has changed the need factor of many of today's workers, permitting a potential flexibility in the benefit area heretofore unknown: for example, a husband and wife, both employed on a full-time basis, each entitled to full and often redundant programs of employee fringe benefits.

As we look into the future, we view that future fully expecting that the projections we make today based on past experience may be greatly modified. However, that does not relieve us of the responsibility of making such conjectures. Indeed, planning for future needs and trends is a responsibility none of us can escape if we are truly interested in—and claim to be responsive to—the changing needs of our employees or members.

Historical Perspective

In the past, fringe benefit programs have been attractive to both the employer and employee because:
1. Benefits and their cost generally received favorable tax treatment;
2. The group approach permitted benefits to be purchased at a reduced cost, or permitted the purchase of greater benefits for the same amount;
3. Uniformity of plan design encouraged and permitted actuarial and administrative economies;
4. Attractive benefit programs often provided a recruiting and retention edge in a tight labor market.

To benefit from these efficiencies, benefit programs have tended to adhere to a very traditional design, with employees offered few if any options. As a result, we are today generally providing sound benefit programs at the lowest possible cost—while, at the same time, we are being criticized by some for providing maternity benefits for 60 year old workers and unappreciated retirement benefits to 19 year old students. And, to a degree, this criticism is valid: certainly, older workers espouse improved retirement benefits; the middle-aged, more life insurance and orthodontic benefits; the younger seek expanded medical benefits; and the youngest simply conclude, "Put it in the pocket, baby!"

This can create a tension that may isolate and segment special interest groups within a plant, company or union membership. And yet, while appearing contradictory, one must ask, "Has the end result really been all that bad?" Maybe, maybe not.

As with nearly every idea, a concept once developed immediately becomes subject to modification and refinement. Our approach to employee benefits is no exception. A majority of the working population today enjoys the benefits afforded by health insurance; most have some sort of supplemental retirement scheme in addition to Social Security; and many others, benefits such as long term disability, life insurance, dental and vision benefits.

This refinement then proceeds with new, innovative or unique benefits being added in response to an expressed or perceived need on the part of an employer, employee group or union. Now that the second generation of benefits is making its appearance, so too is the new and varied appetite of today's benefits consumer.

Our responsibility in this session is to survey fringe benefits as we look to the '80s. I am convinced that three specifics will characterize fringe benefits during this decade: (1) There will be pressure to meet more specific or specialized needs of our beneficiaries; (2) A major part of the fringe benefit dollar will be dedicated to benefit communication and member education; (3) That portion of cost dedicated to employee benefits will increase.

The 'Cafeteria' Approach

We will be discussing a number of benefits, some of which are already in operation, some in the development stage, others still in theory. There is one concept that has been around for sometime; one that has received added emphasis because of the changing character of today's worker; an umbrella concept that may be applied to all benefit programs. It is a concept under which the customers serve themselves—elect and select, within certain limits, the benefits that they judge most nearly meet their perceived needs. Cafeteria compensation plans may offer the worker of today what he or she seeks for tomorrow.

In Texas and, I believe, the State of Louisiana, there is a chain of very fine cafeterias. Many years ago, on my first trip to Dallas, being alone in a strange city and not choosing to eat in the hotel dining room, I decided to try one of these cafeterias. You cannot imagine the variety of vegetables, meats and desserts temptingly displayed to whet the appetite of the unwary. And everything seemed so inexpensive—at least, until I received my check from the cashier. Similarly, there are some spokesmen today who believe that, like a cafeteria, we should be offering a greater choice of benefits and more flexibility in plan design if we really intend to satisfy the appetite of our employees and members.

In fact, there are already three fringe benefit cafeterias operating in today's employee benefit dining hall. One has been in operation for the past 20-30 years; a second, a more refined and specialized institution that may now be reaching its zenith; and a third that provides a truly unique menu for the gourmet appetite.

The first cafeteria, developed in the '40s and '50s, has been in operation for years, but selection has been limited to meat or potatoes or vegetables; one, perhaps two, but seldom all three. And, more often than not, the selection was made by someone other than the employee or member. Life insurance, a health insurance plan, a pension plan, disability or a combination of several perhaps; but seldom all of the above.

The second cafeteria, that which served most of us so well during the '60s and '70s, was of course an outgrowth and refinement of these earlier plans. We are now in the '80s. A third dining spot offers a unique menu, truly a gourmet's delight, where the special appetite is appeased: the specialized program for the specialized need. The presentations to follow will explore the third approach, the specialized programs.

You will recall my chagrin when I reached the end of that cafeteria line in Dallas. When the cashier presented my bill, what appeared so desirable at the beginning of that serving line suddenly took on another hue. Therein lies both the strength and the weakness of the cafeteria concept of compensation—it is an opportunity for choice that must be conditioned by the need for satisfaction with one's choice when the time comes to pay the bill; to utilize the benefit selected.

Tax Status

The basic premise upon which the cafeteria form of compensation rests is not new. Interest in and development of this concept has been going on for over ten years. However, the tax status of this approach remains a consideration when evaluating the desirability of this type of employee compensation.

As you are aware, not all employee benefit programs qualify for favorable tax treatment. Prior to the Revenue Act of 1978, an employee or member who had the option to select benefits, some of which were taxable as current income, could be taxed on the value of that benefit even though it was not one chosen as a benefit by the individual. Internal Revenue Service rulings on cafeteria compensation plans have never been clear or uniform. The position of such plans was further clouded by Section 2006 of ERISA, which effectively "froze" cafeteria plans for a time. The problem challenging the existence and growth of cafeteria plans was somewhat clarified with the passage of the Revenue Act of 1978 and, in particular, Section 125 of that act. This provision clarified the tax status of the benefits selected by an individual to whom the cafeteria approach is available. No longer is the employee taxed solely because the participant may choose among the benefits offered by the plan. However, the law does not grant favorable tax treatment to all benefits, only those provided such status under the various Code provisions—life, health, disability, legal, etc.

As indicated earlier, while the tax question relating to optional benefit programs has not been eliminated, one may reasonably expect that if this type of compensation program is one that catches on—is really the program for tomorrow—favorable legislation will not be long in coming. So, let us continue assuming that demand for this form of compensation proves to be as popular as some believe it will be, and that the Code will again be amended to at least ease the way to Internal Revenue Service approval of this type of program.

Implementing the Concept

The flexible benefit program, popularized in professional publications based on experimental programs at American Can Company, TRW and Educational Testing Service, allows an employee to custom design a benefit program that will meet the perceived needs of that employee. This is accomplished by first determining through employee input those benefits the members and employees feel reflect the interest and needs of that working population. Each member is then provided a benefit account, a total dollar amount available to "purchase" benefits, as well as a list of benefits and/or benefit levels available and their associated cost. Employees pick those benefits that appear to be individually desirable. The cost of each benefit selected is then subtracted from his or her benefit account. Taxable benefits are reported as income; benefits provided favorable tax treatment would be treated accordingly.

Though it is perhaps still too early to make an objective evaluation of this approach, it does not seem unreasonable to expect that the component cost of at least some parts of the program will increase. It would appear that there will be a degree of selection against those plans or programs that traditionally benefited from and utilized the concept of spreading, sharing or amortizing the risk. In addition to selection, the broad range of benefits available will almost certainly result in increased cost for administration, insurance company charges, increased data processing expense and legal and audit expense. At a time when *Business Insurance* magazine headlines, "Benefits Getting Too Costly," and estimates that fringe benefit costs may approach 50% of payroll by 1985, the additional cost of a cafeteria-type program, estimated by some to be 10-20% higher to implement than a conventional benefits package, has got to be considered. Whether its cost will be paid by the employer, employee or benefit fund, you may rest assured, it will be paid.

Perceived Benefits...

From the point of view of the employer, union or board of trustees, what is to be gained by implementation of the cafeteria approach to compensation and fringe benefits? What benefits may be realized through this type of plan? What problems may you expect? If adopted, will it really serve to meet a need, or are we merely looking for a need to meet? There may be some positive aspects growing out of its implementation:

1. The employer or trustees, and covered employees for that matter, may for the first time consciously identify the cost of various programs, an important first step in recognizing the need for cost control. If cost increases in a benefit area, the participant may have to make a decision concerning the desirability of the benefit—is it worth the money? If the answer is "yes," he or she may decide to increase their share of the cost of that benefit—probably through a deductible—choose to redirect a portion of subsequent wage increases toward that cost, or even decide to accept a direct share of the cost of the benefit through payroll withholding.
2. Because they now are involved in the decision making process, members may finally begin to question and challenge the expense they are incurring. Is it usual? Is it necessary? Is it reasonable? When about two-thirds of all illness improves on its own without any treatment, these questions should be asked again, and again, and again.
3. Benefits not elected may be terminated and their cost eliminated.
4. Workers selecting benefits based on a per capita cost allowance should have a greater appreciation of not only the benefit but also the cost of these benefits: they are now part of his pay in a very real way.
5. Employee longevity and seniority may be encouraged and recognized through increases in the benefit account—the money available to purchase benefits—based on these factors.
6. Finally, from an employer or trade union point of view, those firms, organizations or trades in the forefront of the flexible compensation parade may temporarily benefit through a competitive edge in recruitment and retention of these employees and members.

...And Potential Problems

There are, however, obstacles to implementation of a flexible compensation program, as well as potential for very real problems. The problem of Internal Revenue Service approval mentioned earlier, although now somewhat clarified, has not been totally resolved and may continue to cause concern for some time. Secondly, difficulty associated with changing a large and already complex benefit program may be a serious obstacle for a large employer or fund, particularly if there are a number of insurance companies or providers involved, varying eligibility rules, deductibles, coverages, policy years, etc.

Third, uncovering the true fringe benefit interests and needs of the employee or member is absolutely essential if the program presupposes to offer options and selection. Developing such a list will require a large investment in time and member input. Once identified, maintaining the currency of desired and needed benefit programs will require ongoing oversight. Fourth, while many laude the accomplishments and potential—too often it is mostly potential and little accomplishment—of data processing systems, the administrator who proposes to administer a sophisticated program of flexible compensation involving both taxable and non-taxable benefits being "purchased" at varying levels from a multitude of benefits, had better have an equally sophisticated data processing system available long before this program becomes effective.

Finally, a large investment will have to be made in providing counseling to each member and/or spouse. I can imagine nothing that would affect the future of such a program more adversely than the specter of the spouse of a plan member who, upon the death of that spouse, finds that he or she failed to "purchase" or select the "right" benefits to provide in such a situation. Or a member testifying before some Congressional committee that he or she was not properly counseled and informed of the implications of a choice by his or her employer or union.

Summary Comments

Where does that leave us? We find ourselves with a question, the answer to which can be determined only in the narrowest extreme. Is flexible compensation a concept appropriate for your employees and members? If the answer is "yes," you may find that the principles upon which employee benefits as we know them today, and which contributed to their acceptance by both employers and their employees—favorable tax treatment of both contributions and benefits, administrative and actuarial economics, cost reduction through risk-sharing—may be thrown out. In their place, we may find increased administrative expense, lower premium volume and adverse selection reflected in higher cost and greatly increased recordkeeping and member counseling responsibilities that may discourage even the most ardent champion of individual choice and selection.

However, if one accepts the premise that fringe benefits are in fact a part of the wage package and subject to discretionary allocation by the receiver, and that the member or employee is in a better position to determine his or her financial needs or goals than some third party, then perhaps flexible compensation may be the answer. After all, who here can authoritatively declare that the traditional format and procedures that have been followed in the past are the correct or even the best methods of establishing employee benefit plans, determining cost and selecting benefits? Perhaps we have been operating in an intellectual vacuum, the limits of which have been determined by tradition, history and legislation.

It is for these reasons that one must conclude that the question of the appropriateness of the flexible compensation concept in your particular situation is one that can only be answered by those whose interests you represent—your members or employees.

The Stay Well Plan — Another Option

With our sensitivity to the popular emphasis on individual freedom and election, there is one additional form of election that, while presently restricted to a much narrower base, may turn out to be one of the more exciting concepts to grow out of our attempts to provide, as one fast food vendor proclaims, "freedom of choice," and which has, as a most important side benefit, a positive emphasis on health education.

In the wake of the panic that beset many governmental bodies following passage of Proposition 13 in the State of California, one of these bodies came up with an idea that could conceivably change our entire approach to health benefit plans in the future. Following a not too uncommon directive to make budget-cutting a top priority, after carefully reviewing all possibilities, the Mendocino County Schools developed a plan that maintains the current level of benefits, rewards those who stay well, takes positive action to encourage good health and just may reduce the cost of medical insurance to that school district.

An Incentive to Stay Well

This plan, since adopted and now marketed by Blue Shield of California, provides for a unique split funding of the cost of medical expense: a portion, currently $500 per employee, is placed in an interest-bearing account in the name of each insured by the employer; the remainder of the usual premium is paid to the provider organization. This effectively provides a comprehensive medical plan with a $500 deductible.

If, during the year, the member incurs covered medical expense totaling less than $500, he has the option of either paying the charge himself or submitting it to the plan office. If he requests reimbursement, the amount of the reimbursement is deducted from his $500 credit. If he elects to pay it himself, his $500 account remains intact. Any expense exceeding the $500 deductible amount is paid under the regular policy. At the end of each year, if the employee has incurred no expense (or less than $500 in covered expense), any balance remaining in his account is carried forward. This amount is invested each year and, upon termination, may be paid as a form of severance pay. The following year another $500 credit will be deposited and available for expense incurred in that year, and so on each year thereafter.

Cost-Effective Utilization Decisions

Experts have concluded that there are three major components in the cost of health care: inflation, facility utilization and technology. The emphasis in this program is on controlling cost generated by excessive utilization. It is estimated that as much as 50-70% of physician/patient contacts are unnecessary—colds, flu, upset stomach, etc. Further, an average family of four may be expected to see a physician or use a hospital emergency room approximately 12 times a year. It is obvious that if only half of these contacts were eliminated, there would be a substantial reduction in medical care costs. If the decision to seek care is based on the individual's view of his condition and the availability of care and its cost, and the facility for care and payment are, in fact, available, it is obvious that something significant must be done if we are to deter utilization. The Stay Well Plan does just that: it rewards those who stay well or treat the routine or inconsequential condition themselves; it pays when a real medical emergency exists; and it encourages good health through an educational program that includes both a published guide to the identification and treatment of common medical problems that is distributed to each employee, and a monthly newsletter that is subject specific.

Further, it allows a type of flexibility in benefit selection: one may request reimbursement or elect to pay the expense himself; when two or more individuals in the same family unit are covered by different group insurance programs, because of the high first dollar deductible, the employee is encouraged to submit charges to the second carrier, thereby maintaining his or her yearly credit. (Since the $500 deposit is not insurance, coordination would not take place until the deductible had been met.) Also, since the insured's expense is being paid as well as a refund of the unused annual deposit, the member has had an opportunity to elect the level of reimbursement desired, while retaining the right to receive a refund of the unused portion of the employer contribution remaining in his benefit account.

While admittedly limited in scope, if widely implemented, this concept appears to hold a promise of comprehensive coverage when needed, an incentive to treat the routine condition at home and the assistance needed to make that decision, i.e., reduced cost through reduced utilization. In addition he may receive a return of the unused deposit or wages in the future.

Conclusion

We have seen in these two approaches a very broad and a rather narrow attempt to meet the challenge or employee need as decided by election and selection. It is my firm belief that as fringe benefits grow in number and scope, there will appear increasing participant pressure for the right to elect and select benefit programs that appeal to individual needs or desires. Whether democracy in the fringe benefits marketplace is desirable is a question that can only be answered by those affected by these benefit programs. Certainly, the future will give us the answer.

Taxation of Employee Benefits

BY DANIEL H. MUNDT

Introduction

The Internal Revenue Service Code of 1954 provides the basic framework for taxation of employee benefits. Over a period of time, the Code sections have been amended by Congress. During the same time period, the Internal Revenue Service has become more and more concerned about what's happening with taxation of employee benefits. The sections of the Code have a good deal of variety in them. Section 401 is probably the primary section, and has a number of subsections dealing with taxation of employee benefits.

The basic concept with respect to qualified plans, and that is our primary focus of concern, was to allow the employer to have a present deduction and defer taxation to the employee for employer contributions to employee benefit plans until the money was actually received in some form by the employee. In some instances, these fringe benefits took the form of a profit-sharing plan, in others, a pension plan, and in some there were vacation benefit plans. Fringe benefit plans now are a regular flower garden of different types and styles of benefits. The idea, of course, was that the amounts contributed by the employer for the employee, and earnings on the same, were taxed at a time when it was most advantageous to the employee. There are also other estate and gift tax advantages that can be realized.

"Fringes"—A Major Compensation Component

A Panorama of Benefits

Why should you and I be concerned about the taxation of employee benefits? Consider the extent of fringe benefits today. Fringe benefits probably no longer can really be considered "fringe benefits." They now occupy something in the area of 40% of salary in many companies. The Table, "Prevalence of Benefits," points up the reason that the Internal Revenue Service and Congress today are becoming more and more concerned about what is being done with respect to the taxation of

Mr. Mundt is a partner in the law firm of Mundt and Hall. He has lectured on business law and industrial relations at the University of Minnesota at Duluth. Mr. Mundt received his B.B.A. degree, J.D. degree and M.A. in psychology from the University of Minnesota. He has been a frequent speaker on labor-management matters, including analysis and application of the Taft-Hartley Act, and has spoken at previous Foundation educational programs.

employee benefits. The issue is not just the taxation of health and welfare or pension or vacation funds, but this whole panorama of what has now become the fringe benefit package. You will notice that these fringe benefits run the gamut from company cafeterias to social activities, to sports activities and physical fitness programs, funeral leave, jury duty, military duty, leaves of absence, professional trade association dues and memberships, employer products or services—and on and on and on. The result of this proliferation has been the Internal Revenue Service's increasing concern about benefits that are being received but are not subject to taxation.

A Benefit for Employers

Employers over a period of time have been interested in contributing to qualified plans because contributions made to pension and health and welfare and profit-sharing plans did not carry with

Table

Prevalence of Benefits

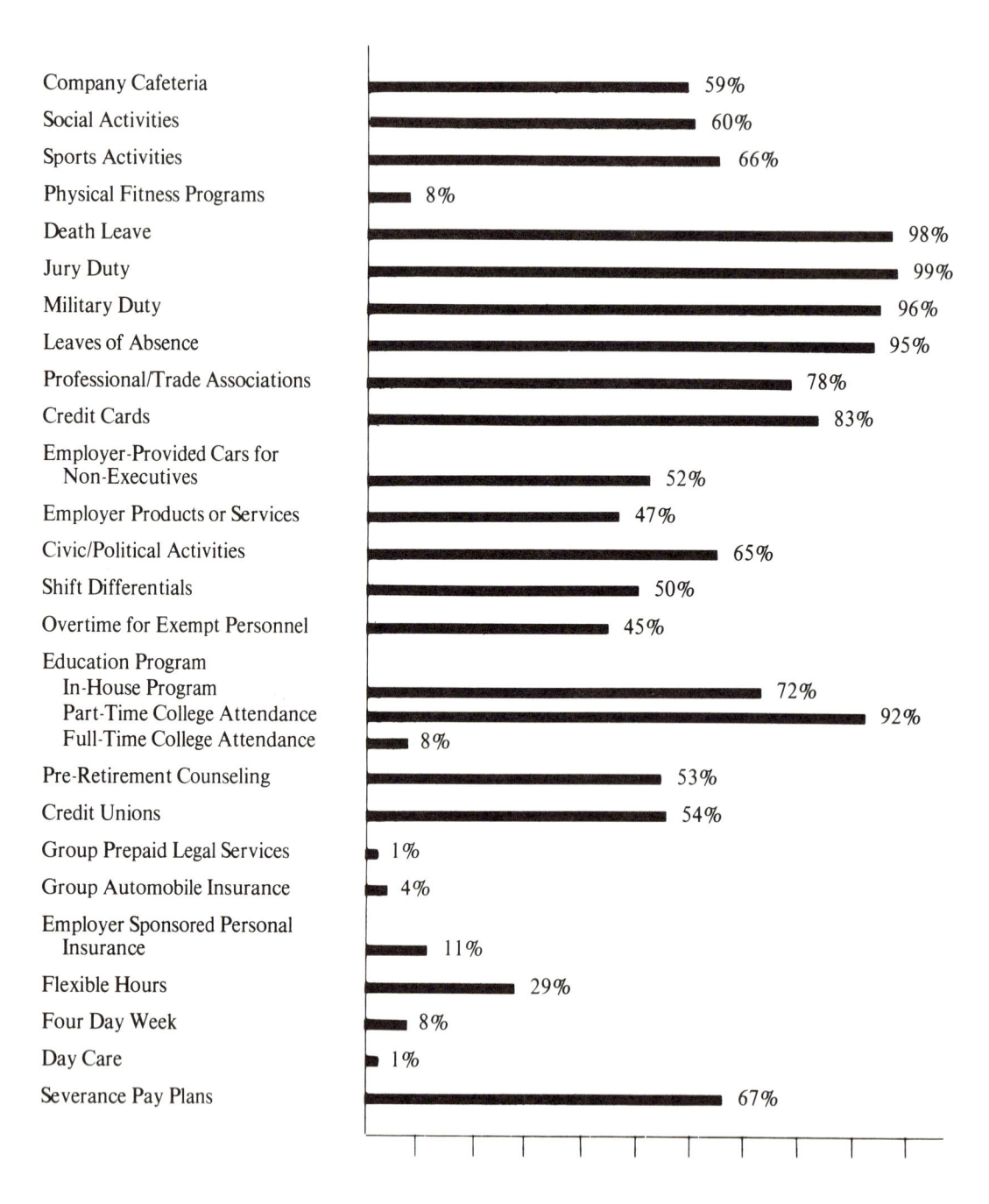

Benefit	Percentage
Company Cafeteria	59%
Social Activities	60%
Sports Activities	66%
Physical Fitness Programs	8%
Death Leave	98%
Jury Duty	99%
Military Duty	96%
Leaves of Absence	95%
Professional/Trade Associations	78%
Credit Cards	83%
Employer-Provided Cars for Non-Executives	52%
Employer Products or Services	47%
Civic/Political Activities	65%
Shift Differentials	50%
Overtime for Exempt Personnel	45%
Education Program — In-House Program	72%
Education Program — Part-Time College Attendance	92%
Education Program — Full-Time College Attendance	8%
Pre-Retirement Counseling	53%
Credit Unions	54%
Group Prepaid Legal Services	1%
Group Automobile Insurance	4%
Employer Sponsored Personal Insurance	11%
Flexible Hours	29%
Four Day Week	8%
Day Care	1%
Severance Pay Plans	67%

Source: Hay/Huggins

them the requirement of paying unemployment compensation or workers' compensation or Social Security.

I happen to represent one of the larger groups in our area, the grocery stores in northern Wisconsin and northern Minnesota. From time to time in our negotiations—and I am sure this is true across the whole United States in the spectrum of negotiations—settlements can be made because an employer has been willing to make a contribution to a pension or profit-sharing plan that does not carry the additional burden of Social Security, workers' compensation and unemployment compensation. So the taxation of employee benefits—the extent and manner in which they're taxed—obviously will make a significant difference over the long run in the collective bargaining process. Employers may find themselves unable to use that particular method for settling contracts if these fringes are going to be subject to taxation; if these benefits are going to be treated as compensation and if they are going to carry with them employer liability for workers' compensation, unemployment compensation and Social Security, it will make it more difficult for the employers to accept this approach.

In addition to the above considerations, costs for medical, pension, profit-sharing and other benefits have been steadily increasing. As those costs have gone up, it has meant that more dollars of contribution have not been subject to taxation. This has also increased the concern recently about the whole area of other benefits and their taxation. The concern on the part of the Internal Revenue Service is that if retirees, for example, are to receive various types of benefits without paying a tax on the benefit received, this continues the practice of not taxing employer dollars that are contributed to these benefit plans.

Government Involvement

A Growing Interest

The federal government has been concerned, particularly during the last several years, with this whole area of benefits received which are not subject to taxation. As a result, they have begun an active investigation and prosecution in several related areas.

Some may think that trying to collect money from independent contractors is not directly related to taxation of employee benefits. But I would suggest that the Internal Revenue Service's action in these areas is similar in nature to the move they are making with respect to taxation of employee benefits. One area they have chosen to look at has been the matter of independent contractors. The question has been whether or not a person who has been working for another person is an employee or an independent contractor. The Internal Revenue Service has taken the position, in a number of industries with which I am actively involved including the trucking and the timber industry, that in many instances these people are employees and the employers, as the IRS uses that term, are required to make payments of taxes which have not been properly withheld.

During the last several years, the Internal Revenue Service has become more actively involved and concerned about the whole matter of barter. This is where you and I agree, e.g., that if you fix my car I will provide legal services for you. Neither one of us will show the exchange as income, and the result is that there is no tax to be paid. The Internal Revenue Service has become concerned about the whole area of barter, and the concerns they have expressed with respect to this evidences to me, at least, the increasing trend on their part to want to tax *any* type of activity where an employee or individual is receiving a benefit but paying no tax.

Are Some Benefits 'More Taxable' Than Others?

I would point out that there is a difference between fringe benefits exempted by statute and those exempted by regulation or ruling.

There is also an indication by Mr. Cohen of the Internal Revenue Service that he would differentiate between various fringe benefits and he would tax some or deny deductibility to them (or would do both). Now keep in mind that when you deny the deductibility of a particular contribution to the employer, the employer becomes more reluctant to make that contribution because they are not able to deduct it as a business expense.

I took the time to go back through some materials published by BNA in their *Pension Reporter* because I found it enlightening to me. I hope it will be helpful to you in understanding what has gone on just during the past year or so with respect to this matter of taxation of employee benefits.

On September 10, 1979, BNA reported that the Senate voted on September 5th to extend Congress' self-imposed deadline for action on taxing certain employee fringe benefits from the end of that year (1979) until the end of September 1980. Then on September 24, 1979, an article appeared entitled, "Fringe Benefits—Senate Finance Panel hears testimony from Treasury Department in opposition to moratorium." The Treasury Department sees two problem areas in fringe benefits, Lubick (the author) said. The first is with payment made to employees in the employer's product, receiving a product at less than its full value. The second is in reimbursement for certain job-related expenses.

Then the November 5th *Pension Reporter* reported that Ullman had introduced a tax bill aimed at reducing the spiral in health care costs. And what did Representative Ullman propose? He proposed a bill that would place a ceiling on the tax-free amount that an employer can contribute to an employee health insurance plan. The plan that Ullman had proposed was basically to limit the amount of deductible employer contributions for health and welfare plans to $120.00 a month. I don't know where you are on your individual plans, but most of the health and welfare plans in northern Wisconsin and northern Minnesota are now at either $100 per month or *over* $100 per month in terms of contributions. So our concern about taxation of fringe benefits now takes on flesh and becomes very real.

Then, on December 17, 1979, the Internal Revenue Service's new chief counsel commented on the fringe benefit area. In response to a question as to which fringe benefits are more likely to be taxed, Mr. Cohen said it depends upon the starting point, and the starting point is that benefits not taxed in the past should not be taxed now. The benefits that will be taxed are the "new" fringe benefits. He cited a survey stating that last year, for the first time, fringe benefits became the greater part of the employment package. "It is definitely an area that we need to be looking at and not totally prevented from addressing at the national level," said Cohen. In addition to those fringe benefits which have been exempted from taxation by published rulings and those which are statutorily exempted, fringe benefits which would not be at the top of Cohen's list for taxation include those which are directly work-related, such as an employee parking lot. I don't think anybody in their wildest imagination had ever really thought that somebody was going to be saying that because you had free parking in the employer parking lot, that was income to you for the value of the parking space that you had. But I now bring to your attention the fact that the Internal Revenue Service has looked at and is specifically considering that matter.

Cohen stated that further up the list would be fringe benefits which are more tangible, such as an employees' health club, and then ones which are even *more* tangible, such as "sumptuous health clubs only for top pure management."

Cohen stated, "What the real priority [would be], if we were in a position to do something, would be [to] give agents some guidance of how they ought to value the benefits." In other words, not only exclude some of them; but how do you determine what the value is that the employees have received? "So that you don't have agents just proposing different adjustments in different parts of the country," he said, "underlying all of the fringe benefit questions is the question of valuation." That was December 17, 1979.

Then, on October 30, 1980, BNA published another article, "Push to resolve fringe benefit taxation issue seen in Congress." 'Mounting concern in Congress on the lack of uniformity in the tax administration of fringe benefits may provide a push in the early stages of the 97th Congress to resolve the issue, rather than again postpone further action,' according to Don Rickett, Assistant Chief of Staff on the Joint Committee on Taxation." Stressing that there is pressure to resolve the fringe benefit issue, Rickett said it would be unlikely that Congress would allow the moratorium to expire without taking any action, and noted that postponing the action on the issue by extending the moratorium another year or two leaves unresolved the problem of lack of uniformity in application of the law.

Don Alexander, former IRS Commissioner, who also addressed a group, called the current situation on fringe benefits unsatisfactory. Alexander emphasized the need for a uniform and administrable set of regulations on fringe benefits and said to forget about several of what he termed "inconsequential benefits," such as subsidized cafeterias or parking.

Now I would invite your attention to the fact that the whole long list that you find in the Table includes a number of things that you are involved in which the Internal Revenue Service is *not* terming "inconsequential." There are all kinds of benefits that now exist in various organizations that the employer provides through the collective bargaining process or otherwise, which are of direct benefit to the employees but are not reported as taxable income; items on which no withholding is made and on which the employee pays no tax and the employer makes no contributions for Social Security, workers' compensation or unemployment compensation.

I invite your attention to the question, what do they mean when they say "new" fringe benefits? This is an area that is going to be closely scrutinized. You can be certain that the Internal Revenue Service will be asking for all possible things to be included as taxable income. They are looking at barter as being a form of receipt of income. They are certainly going to be looking at some of these fringe benefits as representing areas that should be taxed.

State Laws May Apply

I would also suggest, when you are considering taxation of employee benefits, that you be sure to check as to the possible effect of your own state laws. In the State of Minnesota, for example, the taxation of employee benefits, and how you receive your pension fund money, or your profit-sharing money, or your health and welfare money, is treated differently in many instances than it is treated for federal tax purposes. I am not going to try to answer what happens in each state; I wouldn't pretend to be able to do that. But I do recommend that you consult with your own accountant or your own attorney when you are dealing with the matter of taxation of these benefits.

I would also suggest that you note the effect that taxation of these benefits is going to have ultimately on the collective bargaining process, for I think it will have a real effect.

Key Areas of Concern

In summary, let me make several remarks. First of all, as Robert Georgine indicated, there are two areas of concern you will be involved in, whether you are trustees, administrators, consultants or advisors to the funds. The two areas he mentioned were the PBGC's Multiemployer Amendment and the effect that would have, and the unions' involvement with respect to the whole matter of investment targeting of the funds contributed for pension or health and welfare programs.

Now I happen to agree that those two areas are going to be important, but I would suggest to you that two other areas will also be extremely significant during this next year, or perhaps the next two or three years, for those who are dealing with these funds and the area of fringe benefits.

The first of these is litigation. Each year, it is reported that there has been a substantial increase in litigation. I would suggest that this is going to become an area of more and more concern. What is being done with respect to appeals and litigating matters, particularly as it relates to plan administration and trustees' involvement in responsibilities and decision making, will become increasingly important.

The fourth area that I cite as one of increasing significance is this whole matter of taxation of fringe benefits. I am convinced that, within the next year or two, you will see changes in the legislation which will permit the Internal Revenue Service to tax various kinds of fringe benefits that are not presently subject to taxation. Perhaps it will mean that our health and welfare contributions are going to be subject to taxation with some type of limit; perhaps there will be non-deductibility involving the employer's contribution; perhaps the employer will be required to make withholding deductions, and treat various kinds of fringe benefits as being actual compensation received; I am not sure. The one thing I am sure of is that the Internal Revenue Service has looked too long and too hard to give up on this issue.

I am hopeful that this material will stimulate your thinking and your interest and concern. My purpose has been to give you some background in a broad general spectrum as to what is occurring, and what is likely to occur, in some of these areas involving taxation of employee benefits.

SUB Funds 1980

BY HAROLD G. KORBEE

Introduction

The conference program booklet briefly described this session as covering three general areas: (1) the *status* of SUB funds today; (2) *problems* facing these funds; and (3) *decisions* required of trustees.

Before addressing each of these specific points, let me observe that, in my experience, at least one-third of those in attendance at the Annual Conference are attending for the first time. It has also been my experience that, in contrast to pension and health and welfare sessions, there are many who attend the SUB fund session who do not presently serve as SUB fund trustees, but who are attending because they want some background information in order to determine whether or not a SUB fund is the type of employee benefit that they might want to have established for the members of their union, or the employees of their company.

For these two reasons, I think it may be helpful to review the background for this unique employee benefit.

Background

The concept of supplemental unemployment benefits evolves from the demand by organized labor for a guaranteed annual wage. When it became evident that a guaranteed annual wage was impractical in their industries, unions such as the Steel Workers and the United Auto Workers transformed their guaranteed annual wage demands into proposals to supplement existing unemployment compensation programs. These programs ultimately were adopted in several industries, including some of the building trades, in the form of SUB plans.

Historically, the purpose of SUB plans was to provide employment security regardless of the hours worked, rather than to afford additional compensation for work actually performed. From the employer's standpoint, SUB funds, like pension benefits, can help to ensure a stable work force through periods of short term layoffs and, like severance payments, may increase manage-

Mr. Korbee is a partner in the law firm of Korbee & Korbee, specializing in labor law, employee benefits and civil litigation. He is also an arbitrator for the American Arbitration Association. A member of the American, Ohio and Cincinnati Bar Associations, Mr. Korbee received his bachelor's degree from Xavier University and his J.D. degree from Salmon P. Chase College of Law. He has spoken at previous International Foundation educational meetings. His articles "Selection and Use of the Fund Attorney" and "Effects of the New Pregnancy Discrimination Amendment on Employee Benefit Programs" have appeared in the June 1977 and May 1979 editions of the Digest, *respectively.*

ment flexibility in implementing technological advances.

The essential function of SUB plans is to provide economic security for regular employees in the event they are laid off through no fault of their own. Unlike vacation funds, SUB funds cannot be compensation for work performed, for they are contingent upon the employee being thrown out of work.

Definitions

The generally accepted definition of supplemental unemployment compensation appears in Section 501(c)(17) of the Internal Revenue Code as follows:

"Supplemental unemployment compensation benefits" means only:

(1) Benefits which are paid to an employee because of his involuntary separation from the employment of the employer (whether or not such separation is temporary) resulting directly from a reduction in force, the discontinuance of a plant or operation, or other similar conditions, and

(2) Sick and accident benefits subordinate to the benefits described in clause (1).

Types of Funds

SUB funds can be set up on either an individual account basis, a pooled account basis or a combination of both.

An individual account generally ensures a participant that some benefits will be available to him, no matter how many other participants have drawn benefits from the fund before him. In tradeoff for this advantage, the individual accounts (set up like wage savings plans) usually suffer the disadvantage of having smaller benefit payments than the pooled accounts.

The pooled accounts generally afford easier administration, more flexible investment opportunities and management, and higher benefit payments.

Statutory Basis for Tax Exempt Status

Tax exempt status may be applied for and granted to a SUB fund under any one of three sections of the Internal Revenue Code:

1. Section 501(c)(5) for a labor organization;
2. Section 501(c)(9) for voluntary employees' beneficiary associations providing for the payment of life, sick, accident or *other benefits* to the members of such association or their dependents or designated beneficiaries, if no part of the net earnings of such association inures (other than through such payments) to the benefit of any private shareholder or individual;
3. Section 501(c)(17) for benefits payable because of involuntary separation from employment plus sick and accident benefits.

Types of Benefits

The section of the Code that a particular fund selects in qualifying its plan is generally determined by the size and funding mechanism of the plan and the type of benefits the fund sponsors desire to provide.

For example, a small union with a healthy treasury may want to pay a small benefit to union members alone. Under such circumstances, the union may want to attempt to qualify the plan under Section 501(c)(5) of the Internal Revenue Code.

However, most SUB plans are qualified under Sections 501(c)(9) and 501(c)(17). A SUB plan set up under Section 501(c)(9), the broadest classification, can pay out not only supplemental unemployment compensation and supplemental sickness and accident benefits, but also death benefits, jury service benefits, military leave benefits, funeral leave and severance benefits.

A plan qualified under Section 501(c)(17) can pay out only supplemental unemployment and supplemental sickness and accident benefits.

Problems and Decisions

With this background on SUB funds, let us consider some of the problems and decisions facing SUB fund trustees today.

Obviously, a threshold problem for those desiring to establish a SUB fund is the determination of whether or not the union membership desires a SUB fund badly enough to divert from the next wage increase some amount of money to fund such a plan. Assuming that the membership is willing to divert something from the wage package toward an hourly contribution for funding a SUB plan, the union negotiators must still convince the employer negotiators that such a benefit is a worthy component of the next bargaining agreement.

Rather than spend additional time on the mechanics of establishing a SUB fund, let us look at the problems and decisions affecting funds already in existence. The problems facing SUB trustees are essentially fivefold.

1. What should be the investment objectives of SUB funds? In answering this question, the first thing to remember is that investment objectives for a SUB fund differ from those of pension and health and welfare funds. While unemployment periods are cyclical, they are almost always certain. Therefore, the two principal investment objectives for a SUB fund are *safety* and *liquidity*. When the money is needed for the payment of benefits, it must be there. A participant who is out of work does not want to hear a trustee or an administrator tell him that benefits have been suspended until the fund's investment in the stock market comes back, or until a long term bond reaches maturity.

2. How does a healthy SUB fund in an area with little unemployment avoid attack by the Internal Revenue Service for accumulating unreasonable reserves or unrelated business income? For SUB funds whose participants have not suffered from the current high unemployment experience of recent years and whose assets have accumulated beyond that initially anticipated, a problem has existed in recent years in that the Internal Revenue Service may attack the fund and attempt to tax part of the investment income assets as "unrelated business income." The IRS argued frequently during the 1970s that funds were accumulating "unreasonable reserves." However, within the last year, the national office of the Internal Revenue Service has shown a tendency to diminish its attempts to tax such assets, particularly with respect to those funds qualified under Section 501(c)(9) of the Internal Revenue Code. In at least one case in the Midwest, a national office technical advice memorandum was issued by the Internal Revenue Service which provided in part as follows:

> ... Barring any unusual circumstances, where a 501(c)(9) organization has been created and is operated pursuant to a collective bargaining agreement between participating employers and labor unions representing the members of the employees' association, it will be presumed that the reserves accumulated by the 501(c)(9) organization are reasonable in *amount* and *duration.*

3. How do SUB fund trustees handle delinquent employer contributions? The problem of delinquent employer contributions is no different for SUB fund trustees than it is for pension and health and welfare fund trustees. The same techniques are applicable, including periodic audits, the posting of bonds, a specific detection and collection notice system, and the withholding of employees from the delinquent employer.

4. How can one prevent a SUB fund from being abused or misused by its participants? Over the years, employers in the construction industry frequently have expressed concern that a SUB fund would reduce productivity by encouraging employees to take "early retirement" by claiming SUB benefits for the period of time immediately prior to attaining retirement eligibility through the union pension fund, or taking extended vacations through use of the SUB fund. In order to avoid misuse of a SUB fund, three principles must be followed:

1. The trust and plan documents must be skillfully and professionally drawn to prevent misuse;
2. The pertinent provisions of the plan must be effectively communicated to the participants;
3. There must be cooperation and teamwork between the trustees, the administrator, the union financial secretary, the business manager and business agents of the union.

Over the years, SUB funds which have religiously pursued these three principles have not been the subject of any abuse. To the contrary, they have provided meaningful benefits to participants and have worked to the advantage of both the employee and the employer.

5. How should the SUB fund be administered during periods of high unemployment? During the past year, as in 1974, many funds have experienced such high unemployment among their participants that they have literally paid out all of their assets in benefits.

Many funds have a provision in their plan that benefits will be suspended if assets reach a certain minimum level. When this minimum level is reached, most plans with such a provision give the trustees the discretion to decide whether to pay out the remaining assets of the fund or continue the suspension of benefits.

If an end to the unemployment cycle is in sight, it may be prudent for the trustees to continue the suspension of benefits or scale down the payments until the cycle has ended. On the other hand, if there is no end in sight, it may be prudent to pay out the assets until the fund is completely dissipated.

Trustees who have had the experience of paying out all the assets should not be reluctant to do so, but should take solace in the fact that they have accomplished the primary purpose for which the fund was established: They have provided economic assistance to participants when it was most needed. The most important thing to remember in administering a SUB fund during high unemployment is to administer the plan *fairly* and *consistently* in order to avoid any claims of discrimination by participants who are already very agitated about being unemployed.

Having now spoken about five different problems facing trustees and the decisions required in connection with those problems, let us turn our attention to a significant court decision affecting SUB funds which occurred since the last Annual Conference.

A Significant Court Decision

Until June 10, 1980, there was never a record of any SUB fund case reaching the Supreme Court of the United States. However, on that date, the Supreme Court decided the case of *Coffy v. Republic Steel Corp.*, 100 S.Ct. 2100, 104 LRRM

2488. In this unanimous decision, the Court held that SUB benefits were perquisites of seniority to which returning veterans were entitled under the Vietnam Era Veterans Readjustment Act.

In order to understand the significance and applicability of this decision to SUB funds, it is necessary to discuss in some detail the facts of the case and some prior decisions of the Court in grappling with the seniority issue as it pertained to returning veterans.

Prior to the *Coffy* decision, the U.S. Supreme Court had decided three other employee benefit cases involving the seniority issue.

First, in the case of *Accardi v. Pennsylvania Railroad Co.,* 383 U.S. 225, 61 LRRM 2385 (1966), the Court held that *severance pay* is a perquisite of seniority.

Secondly, in 1975, the case of *Foster v. Dravo Corp.,* 420 U.S. 92, 88 LRRM 2671, held that *vacation benefits* are a form of deferred short term compensation for work actually performed and are not, therefore, a seniority right protected by the statute.

Thirdly, in 1977, the case of *Alabama Power Co. v. Davis,* 431 U.S. 581, 95 LRRM 2569, held that *pension benefits* are perquisites of seniority because they are predominantly a reward for continued employment with the same employer.

The statute under which Coffy claimed a right to benefits was the Vietnam Era Veterans Readjustment Assistance Act of 1974, which provides that any person who leaves a permanent job to enter the military service, satisfactorily completes the military service, and applies for reemployment within 90 days of being discharged from the military service must be reinstated to the former job "without loss of seniority." 38 U.S. Code Section 2021(b)(1).

Upon being honorably discharged from military service, Coffy made timely application for reinstatement with Republic Steel Corporation, his former employer. Because Republic was then in the process of laying off employees, Coffy was reinstated in "layoff status." While laid off, he received weekly payments under the supplemental unemployment benefit (SUB) plan created by the applicable steel industry collective bargaining agreement. Under the plan, an employee was entitled to receive SUB benefits *only* if he had completed two years of continuous service prior to being laid off; the amount of the weekly benefit was determined by his hourly wage rate, the number of his dependents, the amount of state unemployment compensation he was receiving, and the level of funding remaining in the plan.

The length of time during which an employee receives SUB payments under the Republic plan was determined by the number of credit units he had accumulated *before* being laid off, with one-half credit being accrued for each week in which he worked "any" hours, or was paid for "any" hours not worked (such as for vacation or jury duty) or lost "any" SUB credits, and the amount of the benefit did not increase with the length of service, as would a pension benefit. Thus, an employee who had worked continuously for two years would have met the threshold requirements and would also have accumulated 52 units of credit. He was eligible for benefits for the same length of time, and computed according to the same formula, as an employee with 20 years' seniority. According to the district court, the facts that no benefits were available to employees whose seniority is less than two years and that, after 52 credits had been accumulated, additional seniority did not lead to increased benefits, were evidence that the benefit was *not* a reward for longevity of service.

The Court of Appeals for the Sixth Circuit affirmed the decision of the district court.

However, upon appeal to the United States Supreme Court, a unanimous Court held that a benefit need not be meticulously proportioned to longevity of service in order to constitute a perquisite of seniority, as long as it performs a function akin to traditional forms of seniority. In arriving at its decision, the Supreme Court reasoned that under the Military Act, which is to be liberally construed for the returning veteran's benefit, the veteran steps back on the seniority escalator at the precise point he would have occupied had he kept his position with his employer continuously during the period of military service. *Fishgold v. Sullivan Drydock & Repair Corp.,* 328 U.S. 275, 66 S.Ct. 1105. In determining whether a particular benefit qualifies as a perquisite of seniority under the act, first, there must be a *reasonable certainty* that the benefit would have accrued if the employee had *not* gone into the military service; second, the "real nature" of the benefit must be a "reward for length of service," rather than a "form of short-term compensation for services rendered." *Alabama Power Co. v. Davis, supra.*

The Court stated that the Republic SUB plan satisfied the reasonable certainty prong of the *Alabama Power* test, since if Coffy had remained continuously employed by Republic instead of entering the military, he would have accumulated credits from the date he was hired until the date he was laid off. The plan also satisfied the second prong of the test, because supplemental unemployment benefits are not a form of deferred short term compensation but a reward for length of service closely analogous to traditional forms of seniority. The Court specifically held that the purpose and function of the steel industry SUB plan is to provide economic security during periods of layoff to employees who have been in the service of the employer for a significant period; hence, SUB benefits were perquisites of seniority to which returning veterans are entitled under the act. The Supreme Court reversed the court of appeals decision and that of the district court.

Thus, with the *Coffy* decision, trustees, administrators and advisors have now received Supreme Court guidance on how to treat military leave in connection with employee benefit plans for the fourth time.

Economic Status and Outlook

Let us now examine the status and outlook for SUB funds at this time.

On the 7th day of November, 1980, the Labor Department announced that the nation's unemployment increased to 7.6%. This percentage translates into 8 million unemployed workers, an increase of 1.7 million from October of 1979, just one year ago. In June 1980, pollster Louis Harris reported that "unemployment is beginning to take over from inflation as the voters' chief concern."

Consistent with that opinion, voters spoke loudly and clearly on November 4, expressing their dissatisfaction with the Carter Administration and apparently willing to assume whatever risks a Reagan Administration might bring. However, because we find today an economic phenomenon which includes increasing unemployment, increasing inflation and increasing interest rates, it will take nothing short of a miracle for the Reagan Administration to turn the economy around and substantially reduce unemployment.

While all of us will now wait anxiously to see if the campaign rhetoric can be turned into the miracle that the American voters have mandated, our SUB funds have two basic paths to pursue.

First, for those who enjoy full employment and healthy assets, this is an appropriate time to seriously consider utilizing the SUB fund to supplement and assist the health and welfare funds by paying disability benefits from the SUB fund rather than from the health and welfare fund. Most health and welfare funds are experiencing severe difficulties in coping with the escalating costs of health care. Some of this burden may be shouldered by SUB funds where a union or industry has both funds to utilize.

Secondly, for those SUB funds which are plagued with high unemployment and are in danger of completely dissipating their assets, there appears to be no immediate relief in sight. Such funds must again determine whether to pay out the remaining assets of the fund in the form of benefits or suspend benefits until assets can be regenerated. For these funds, perhaps the only words of wisdom are those that we hear everywhere we go in this Polynesian paradise called Hawaii—"Hang loose!"

Retiree Benefits—
Considering the Commitment

BY WILLIAM C. EARHART

Mr. Earhart is founder and president of The William C. Earhart Company, Inc., employee benefit plan administrators. As chief executive officer, he is responsible for the administration of all types of benefit plans including dental, vision, drug, vacation, apprenticeship and pension. Mr. Earhart received his A.B. degree from Princeton. A former member of the Executive Board of Directors of the Northwest Association of Health, Welfare and Pension Plans, he has been active in the employee benefits field for over 26 years. Mr. Earhart is a member and/or officer of many professional and civic organizations and has been active in International Foundation affairs since the early years of the National Conference. A frequent lecturer, he has been a member or chairman of various Foundation committees, served three terms as Director and is presently serving as a member of the CEBS Committee.

IT IS TRITE to say that providing or improving benefits for retirees carries a price tag. It is repetitious and tiresome to say that there ain't no such thing as a free lunch.

Such admonitions are hardly necessary with pension plans which, for the most part, are and have been sufficiently well funded to keep out of trouble. But the possibility of providing or improving benefits, most particularly for those who have previously retired, is still a major concern of pension plan trustees. And, in these days of high inflation, who can be insensitive to the predicament in which retired persons find themselves, which has been discussed at length by almost any politician running for office in the elections of 1980?

We have also read and heard much concerning the Social Security system and its problems, and if we have neither listened nor read any further than the deductions on our payroll stubs, we know that Social Security is costing the active employee more and more each payday, for more paydays each year, to support those drawing benefits.

Funding: Active vs. Retiree Needs?

The multiemployer pension plan which has been reasonably well funded does not have to penalize the active employees to maintain the proposed benefits. If it does attempt a cost-of-living increase for retirees, however, then the effect on the benefit level of future retirees—the presently active employees—must be considered.

But what about the welfare plans in which it has become customary to provide benefits for retirees pretty much from current cash income?

Fifteen years ago, in the landmark case known as *Kroger v. Blassie,* the Court handed down a decision that it was proper to cover retirees under the welfare plan as long as *at least one contribution had been made on behalf of that person while an active participant* in the plan; thus, the trustees could not pick up all previously retired persons when first establishing the retiree welfare plan. How much worse shape could the welfare plans and their retiree coverage be in today were it not for that decision!

Many retiree welfare programs are in trouble today, and are being evaluated by the experts and the trustees in an attempt to find answers. It appears likely that many more are in trouble but have not yet recognized the facts of life, which just now may be becoming apparent, as employment declines and the number of retirees continues to increase during this economic recession. The problems of retiree health and welfare plans range from expensive plan design which cannot be sustained, even in very healthy plans, to what may be excessive cost per active employee to support the retirees in dying industries. For example, a retiree welfare plan which offers a substantial death benefit of $2,000, $3,000, $5,000 or more to the retirees is faced with a certain loss, since every retiree is contemplated to die at some point in time.

Some Serious Questions

But let's look at a little more philosophical a base, and ask ourselves some very pointed and direct questions. The purpose of these questions is not to attempt to arrive at some predetermined answer for each fund, but rather to encourage careful, thoughtful, long term consideration of the entire retiree welfare program.

- Does the plan, the employer trustees, or the union trustees owe the retired plan participant welfare benefits for the balance of life?
- Does the plan, the employer trustees, or the union trustees owe anything to the spouse of the retired participant and to any other dependents the retiree may have who are still eligible for coverage?
- Does the plan, the employer trustees, or the union trustees owe the retired employee essentially a better coverage (when combined with Medicare) than the active employee enjoyed while raising his family and actively working in the industry?

There are plans where the contribution toward retiree welfare is in excess of $40 per active employee per month, and one plan is reported to be costing the active employee $55 per month to support the retiree health and welfare program. Both of these extreme examples are in dying industries, with ever-decreasing numbers of active employees relative to the number of retirees. However, several funds with retiree costs in the range of $10-20 per active employee per month are beginning to see the handwriting on the wall. Such possibly reasonable contributions will be insufficient in the near future—and these funds are not in dying industries.

The problems are also quite different for the normal retiree who retires at 65 and is entitled to Medicare, compared to the early retiree not yet entitled to Medicare; or to the disability retiree whose family may still be young, but who will be eligible for Medicare 24 months after receiving his first disability check from Social Security. And then we have the problem of the retiree who marries a far younger spouse who, within your present rules, may be entitled to many, many years of coverage following the death of the retiree. Remember that the last surviving spouse of a veteran of the War of 1812 died well into this 20th century!

One last question that might be considered is, how much would the retiree be willing to pay for continuation of some schedule of welfare benefits for himself? For his spouse?

Conclusion

Many plans are having sober second thoughts and are going through periods of soul-searching in an attempt to find answers that may bring long range fiscal responsibility to retiree health and welfare programs. However, these are painful decisions and solutions often have been deferred, as most alternatives seem undesirable in one respect or another.

If your retiree plan survives the economic recession of '79-'80—no comment as to '81—without encountering massive problems with the retiree health and welfare plan, it still is not too soon to take a long range look at your retiree welfare program. As the economy moves upward from the recessionary bottom, employment increases and things look brighter—however, it is certain that in the future what goes up must come down, and the problems will be back with us again.

Prepaid Legal Services Plans

BY SIDNEY GAINES

Legislative Background

In 1973, the Taft-Hartley Act was amended by Congress to permit jointly administered trusts to establish prepaid group legal services plans. As is the case with all jointly administered trusts, the law requires each trustee to act prudently and for the exclusive benefit of the members. However, despite the amendment, the IRS refused to rule on whether the contributions and benefits under such a plan constituted taxable income to the covered employee. Because of the uncertainty created by this silence on the part of the IRS, relatively few prepaid legal services plans were actually formed prior to 1976.

Finally, the Tax Reform Act of 1976 was enacted, amending the Internal Revenue Code to exclude from the gross income of an employee, spouse or dependent both the amounts contributed by an employer to a qualified group legal services plan on behalf of a covered employee, spouse or dependent and the value of the legal services provided to such employee, spouse or dependent under such a qualified plan. The 1976 Tax Reform Act provisions relating to qualified legal services plans are limited to five years and, unless extended, will expire December 31, 1981. However, the content and pendency of proposed final regulations, dated April 29, 1980, leave little doubt that the five year experiment will become permanent.

Legal Requirements

These tax exclusions are set forth in Code Section 120(c), and they provide that to be qualified a group legal services plan must meet the following criteria.

1. *Written Plan:* A separate written plan must be established. The plan must specify the benefits, consisting of personal legal services, which will be furnished through prepayment of, or advance provisions for, all or part of the legal fees incurred. As with all other jointly administered trusts, the trustees are required to promulgate rules relating to eligibility, administration, coverage, etc.

2. *Exclusive Benefit Rule:* The plan must be for the exclusive benefit of the employer's employees, their spouses, or their dependents.

Mr. Gaines has been a senior partner in the New York law firm of Friedlander, Gaines, Cohen, Rosenthal & Rosenberg since 1955. For nine years, Mr. Gaines was principal attorney for the New York State Insurance Department, and also was chief assistant special counsel of the New York State Welfare Fund inquiry in 1954. Active in professional and civic circles, he has become an authority in insurance law, serving as an executive and counsel with insurance organizations as well as with a substantial number of jointly trusteed welfare, pension and annuity funds in both New York and New Jersey. A graduate of New York University and the NYU Law School, Mr. Gaines has spoken at previous Foundation meetings.

3. *Antidiscrimination Test:* Contributions or benefits provided under the plan must not discriminate in favor of highly compensated employees or employees who are also corporate officers or shareholders.

4. *Contribution Limitations:* No more than 25% of the amount contributed during the plan year may be provided for a class comprising the owners (or their spouses or dependents) of the employer. An owner is any person who, on any day during the year, owns more than 5% of the stock of the employer, or an interest greater than 5% in the capital or profits of the employer.

5. *Notification:* To secure qualified status, employers or plan administrators for group legal services plans must notify their key district director that they are applying for recognition of the plan's

qualified status by filing Form 1024, Application for Recognition of Exemption under Code Section 501(a) or for Determination under Code Section 120, accompanied by Schedule L. The application for recognition of exemption of a prepaid group legal fund requires the submission of the following documents to the Internal Revenue Service:

a. A copy of the trust agreement establishing the fund
b. A copy of the legal plan itself
c. A copy of any retainer agreements with the attorneys administering benefits under the fund
d. A summary plan description for the fund, if available at the time of filing
e. A copy of the lease, if the fund has entered into any rental arrangement.

An application also requires disclosure as to the fund's affiliation with any organizations, i.e., unions, employer groups, affiliated welfare funds.

6. *Funding:* The plan may be funded only by direct payments to providers of legal services, insurance funding, and/or employer contributions to an organization exempt from tax under Code Section 501(c) that pays or credits contributions it receives to another separate and distinct organization or a trust tax exempt under Code Section 501(c)(20). As of this date, the use of insurance companies has been limited.

7. *Separate Trust:* An organization or trust must be created or organized for the exclusive function of funding all or part of a qualified group legal services plan or plans. IRC §501(c)(20), also enacted in 1976, provides exemptions for organizations or trusts "the exclusive function of which is to form part of a qualified legal services plan or plans under the meaning of Code Section 120."

Key Questions

Questions which are frequently raised are whether legal services benefits may be paid from an existing welfare benefit trust fund, and whether separate contributions are needed to fund benefits. The answers to these questions are as follows.

First, benefits cannot be provided by an existing welfare fund since, as noted earlier, a qualified plan must be a separate written plan providing personal legal services for the exclusive benefit of the employees, and must be based upon a separate trust agreement. However, a legal services plan provided by a welfare fund which became effective prior to December 31, 1976, is grandfathered by the statute.

The question relating to the need for separate contributions is somewhat more complicated. Code Section 120(c)(5) restricts any payment for service made by a qualified group legal services plan:

(5) CONTRIBUTIONS: Amounts contributed under the plan shall be paid only (A) to insurance companies, or to organizations or persons that provide personal legal services, or indemnification against the cost of personal legal services, in exchange for a prepayment or payment of a premium, (B) to organizations or trusts described in Section 501(c)(20), (C) to organizations described in Section 501(c) which are permitted by that section to receive payments from an employer for support of one or more qualified group legal services plan or plans, except that such organizations shall pay or credit the contribution to an organization or trust described in Section 501(c)(20), (D) prepayments to providers of legal services under the plan, or (E) a combination of the above. [Underscoring supplied.]

In view of the foregoing, the answer to this question seems to be that a 501(c) organization which receives contributions from employers is apparently able to funnel the contribution through to a 501(c)(20) organization.

At this point, a little history must be recounted. Prior to the Tax Reform Act of 1976, the IRS refused to rule on whether a group legal services plan could be enacted under Section 501(c)(9) as an "other benefit," in addition to the life, sick and accident benefits with which we are all familiar. As a result, Section 501(c)(20) was created to exclusively provide for prepaid qualified group legal plans, thus permitting the IRS to continue to avoid having to rule on whether such plans can be "other benefits" under Section 501(c)(9). It has been reported that the pressure was great upon IRS, and that the result was the language in Code Section 120(c)(5) quoted above which recognizes the right of a 501(c)(9) trust to *receive* the contributions, but requires the contributions to be funneled through to a 501(c)(20) trust. The most realistic view of the current status of this contribution question is that organizations which receive, or by their nature could receive, employer contributions for a legitimate purpose under Code Section 501(c) are authorized to channel money to a 501(c)(20) organization. This view also enables IRS to continue to avoid expanding the definition of "other benefits" in 501(c)(9), or under any 501(c) authority.

The currently pending proposed IRS regulations

relating to employer contributions to qualified legal services plans interpret the language of Section 120 (c)(5) without apparent change.

Restrictions on Services Provided

Before entering upon a discussion of types or kinds of services available, we should properly review the kinds of services which are *not* available for delivery under any qualified plan. Section 186 (c)(8) of 29 U.S. Code provides that no legal service may be provided under a legal services plan to:

(A) Initiate any proceeding directed (i) against any such employer or its officers or agents except in workers' compensation cases, or (ii) against such labor organization, or its parent or subordinate bodies, or their officers or agents, or (iii) against any other employer or labor organization, or their officers or agents, in any matter arising under subchapter II of this Chapter; and

(B) In any proceeding where a labor organization would be prohibited from defraying the costs of legal services by the provisions of the Labor-Management Reporting and Disclosure Act of 1959.

We noted earlier that only personal services may be provided by a qualified plan. Section 1.120-2 (c) of the proposed regulation excludes services directly pertaining to:
1. Trade or business
2. Management, conservation or preservation of property held for production of income
3. Production or collection of income. Exceptions to the foregoing are provided for:
   1. Protection or assertion of rights to property of a decedent
   2. Claims for damages other than for personal injury.

It should be noted that IRS already permits the provision of legal services in certain areas which technically "produce income" for the beneficiary, such as seeking and collecting alimony or child support, since these services are not generally considered to be of a business nature. Additionally, comments submitted on the proposed regulation recommend that permissible legal services include representation in the purchase of two- and three-family homes. Although collection of rent is, in the strict sense, income, it is nevertheless the sole means available to many purchasers by which the transaction can be effected at all, with the proceeds being applied in most cases toward amortization of the purchaser's mortgage. It should therefore not be deemed a prohibited business interest or property held for production or collection of income.

Plan Design

Types of Plans

Legal services plans are to be found in a variety of forms. The common thread running through all of them is the concept and purpose of providing quality legal services at reduced costs by reason of the purchasing power of a group.

Plan administration may be undertaken by the group itself, an insurance company or a professional outside advisor.

Plans generally are referred to as "open panel plans" or "closed panel plans." An open panel plan generally permits the member to seek the services of an attorney of his choice, who bills either the member or the plan and receives compensation pursuant to the plan's schedule of benefits and allowances. In such a plan, the fund's obligation is limited to its schedule of allowances. Any additional charges must be paid by the member. Some open panel plans limit the choice of a lawyer on a geographical basis; some do not. This is a matter for each board of trustees to determine as it deems advisable.

Several variations fall under the heading of "closed panel plans." A *fully closed plan* can take the form of a designated outside law firm which alone provides the legal services. In some instances, the firm makes its arrangement with the plan, and the members pay nothing. In other instances, the member pays a part of the cost, either by way of a deductible or a percentage of the legal fee, which is calculated according to a schedule. Some fully closed plans utilize a full-time, in-house, salaried staff of attorneys. Either way, there is no choice of attorneys available to the member under a fully closed plan. Retainer agreements between trustees of a plan and a legal firm should provide that in the event of any dispute over the quality of services rendered, the matter is to be referred to independent counsel for review.

A *partially closed plan* takes the form of a published panel of attorneys who have agreed with the plan to furnish the schedule of benefits promulgated by the plan, and who will be compensated in full by the plan or in part by the plan and in part by the member. The member's choice of attorney under this type of plan is limited to the attorneys on the panel.

No matter what kind of plan is selected, the traditional attorney-client relationship must be maintained. While statistical data may be made available to actuaries, or other general information may be released, the subject matter of each case or situation is privileged, and the lawyer's professional obligation to the participant remains the same as that due any other client.

Generally, administrative costs for closed panel plans should prove to be lower than in the case of open panel plans, and such arrangements should provide more qualitative and financial controls for the plan in connection with the services rendered.

How Are Benefits Determined?

Numerous factors are involved in determining the appropriate benefits to be provided to participants: e.g., location of the participants (large city, small city, rural or urban), and the socioeconomic status of participants, etc. For example, in a plan serviced by our firm, the majority of the participants reside in the New York metropolitan area, primarily within the city itself, and earn less than $12,000 per year. Most of our clients to date have been under 50 years of age, and many have families.

In view of these characteristics, the plan provides a wide variety of services geared to this type of individual. To begin with, an important benefit is representation in landlord-tenant matters, since in New York City most residents are renters.

Our plan members often purchase goods and services on time or with credit. As a result, debts accrue, consumer problems arise, and lawsuits for collection of amounts claimed to be due are commenced against the member. The plan represents members in almost all litigated matters in all courts except the small claims court.

Many of the plan members are from ethnic minorities, and the need arises to furnish representation in immigration proceedings involving members, spouses and dependents.

Experience has shown that coverage of all aspects of family law is essential to the plan members. Consequently, benefits include representation in divorce, separations, annulments and all family court proceedings (adoption, support, family offenses, paternity, child abuse and neglect and juvenile delinquency). Although members do not have large estates, it is important that they learn their rights and obligations in this regard, and the plan provides for consultation and preparation of wills, codicils and all related decedent's estate problems. Representation is also provided so that a member can obtain a legal change of name, petition for personal bankruptcy, and purchase or sell a home.

Virtually the only personal service excluded from our plan is representation in felony cases, although the plan does allow for an initial consultation. In addition, the plan attempts to refer the participant to a competent and reasonably priced criminal attorney. In this regard, it becomes important to install an emergency telephone, which permits contact with a staff attorney on a round-the-clock basis.

Since this is a new fringe benefit, it is important that all steps be taken to educate the membership on its value and to encourage utilization. To this end, the fund we represent has prepared and distributed to all members a detailed summary plan description as required by law. Periodic flyers are sent to keep the concept ongoing. Articles have been written for the union newspaper, and fund representatives and attorneys from our firm have attended and spoken at union meetings.

Costs

Costs are very difficult to discuss in a presentation such as this, since they are based on such variables as the extent of the benefit schedule; use of deductibles; and application of maximum allowances per benefit, or per covered member per year, etc. In addition, the basis for compensating participating attorneys can vary from a fee-for-service concept to a charge per capita per month based upon the number of all eligible employees. If the latter method is used, prudence requires that there should be a provision for the rendering of periodic experience and utilization statements, with a return to the plan if utilization is less than anticipated. This would be similar to an experience dividend from an insurance company on a group case.

There is no typical or average plan, and a board of trustees, working with its counsel, should therefore be able to design a plan to fit its budget.

Conclusion

To date, our experience has been exciting. The members of the plan we service are very enthusiastic. They have received competent professional advice where they had never previously been able to afford such advice. We are convinced prepaid legal services is a major new fringe benefit, and will in time prove itself to be as important as the other fringe benefits being provided by welfare funds.

Prepaid Legal Plans— A Growing Benefit

BY STANLEY HOWITT

THROUGHOUT THE United States there are approximately 2,500 various types of prepaid legal plans covering 5 million people, at an average annual cost of $50 per member. It is a fairly new fringe benefit and consumer service that is now a $250 million industry. These figures reportedly include collectively bargained plans as well as consumer group plans.

Applicable Laws

Enabling Legislation

Prepaid legal plans may be the subject of mandatory collective bargaining under Section 302(c) of the Taft-Hartley Act. As a fringe benefit, the prepaid legal services are not taxable to the employee and the employer contributions are not taxable to the employer under the Tax Reform Act of 1976, which amended Section 120 of the Internal Revenue Code and also added prepaid legal plans as an exempt organization under Section 501(c)(20) of the Internal Revenue Code (IRC).

The Tax Reform Act of 1976 extended the exemption for prepaid legal plans until December 31, 1981. Congress will in all probability extend the exemption and, in fact, IRS has recently issued proposed regulations[1] concerning legal plans under Section 120. Congress may also be guided in their renewal of legal plans by the study of the effectiveness of the plans called for under the Tax Reform Act of 1976. The United States Department of Labor selected the National Resource Center for Consumers of Legal Services to conduct the survey of 350 legal plans throughout the U.S. The survey will provide information on the benefits provided, funding, methods of delivery and plan participants

Mr. Howitt is supervising attorney for the Alaska Electrical Legal Fund, a prepaid legal plan for the statewide IBEW Local Union 1547. He set up the administration of the legal plan, supervises all plan and non-plan attorneys providing legal services, and reviews all legal fee billings. In addition, Mr. Howitt is full-time general counsel for the fund's pension, health and welfare, and apprenticeship and training trusts. He received his B.A. degree in political science from Brooklyn College and his J.D. degree from the New York University School of Law. A member of the New York and Alaska Bars, Mr. Howitt is vice president of the Anchorage Bar Association.

covered, and should add to our knowledge of the plans.

A collectively bargained prepaid legal plan is under ERISA and Section 514, the preemption provision, is applicable.

Prepaid legal plans usually contain language that acknowledges the Canons of Professional Ethics as binding the attorneys who provide legal services to the plan's participants.

Qualification Requirements

Qualification requirements for a prepaid legal plan under Section 403 of ERISA and under the proposed IRS regulations are basically similar to those for other employee benefit plans:

1. There must be a trust agreement setting

---

1. Proposed IRS Regulations of Prepaid Legal Plans, Section 1.120-1 and 1.120-2 (proposed April 29, 1980, 45 FR 28360). The proposed regulations would be effective beginning after December 31, 1976, through and ending before January 1, 1982.

forth the usual fiduciary obligations of the trustees and the authority to create and operate a legal plan.
2. A separate written plan that provides benefits that are limited to personal legal services must be drafted. Non-legal benefits, such as medical or pension benefits, cannot be provided.
3. The funds of the trust must be used for the sole purpose of providing legal services for the plan's participants.
4. The plan must be for the exclusive benefit of employee participants, and must prohibit any diversion of funds.
5. The usual non-discrimination rule applies. That is, the plan cannot discriminate in favor of officers, shareholders or the highly paid employees.

The above qualification requirements must also be generally met if a *health and welfare trust* under Section 501(c)(9) of the IRC wishes to provide legal services as part of its health care package.

Under newly issued regulations[2] concerning Section 501(c)(9) health and welfare trusts, such a collectively bargained trust by reason of Section 302(c)(5) of the Labor-Management Relations Act of 1947 may now *directly* provide legal service benefits. The IRS has also stated under the regulation that a Section 501(c)(9) health and welfare trust can include legal services as "other benefits" similar to life, sick, or accident benefits and therefore it can provide personal legal services benefits which consists of payments or credits to a Section 501(c)(20) prepaid legal service trust.[3]

Many health and welfare fund administrators and trustees had previously considered legal care as a part of a health and welfare program but were utilizing the method of paying over a small portion of their funds to a separate Section 501(c)(20) prepaid legal trust and plan, hoping that the IRS would approve the method under prior regulations that were in need of interpretation. It now appears that IRS has liberalized and given the go-ahead to the direct method of providing legal services benefits under the Section 501(c)(9) health and welfare trust or by the indirect method of payment over to a Section 501(c)(20) prepaid legal services trust. If the Section 501(c)(9) health and welfare trust is selected to provide the legal services benefit, the trust language should be reviewed to see if it is broad enough to cover this employee benefit or amended accordingly, as should the plan itself. The bargaining agreement should also permit the legal services benefit.

The prepaid legal plan must also apply for qualification as a group legal services plan under Section 501(a) or determination under Section 120 of the Internal Revenue Code. Form 1024 is submitted with Schedule L, which includes information on group legal services plans such as the plan name, initial qualification request, description of legal services to be offered, manner of funding, and information as to whether a trust or other organization has been set up for the handling of the contributions.

Now that we have set out briefly some of the applicable laws dealing with a qualified legal plan, we will attempt to outline some of the areas in detail which we believe the sponsors of legal plans must review.

Plan Organization, Administration and Design

Permitted Coverage and Exclusions

Exclusions. The legal plan must exclude certain actions under law and must provide only *personal legal services* to plan participants. In preparing the coverage under the legal service plan, it is necessary to keep in mind that certain exclusions are necessary for plan qualification. For example, legal services cannot be provided in a case where a labor organization would be prohibited from deferring the costs of legal services by the provisions of the Labor-Management Reporting and Disclosure Act of 1959. Plans usually do not allow the participant to sue either the union or a contributing employer to the trust, and they usually do not allow any suits directly against the trust fund itself, or any defense if the trust fund should be suing the participant for any reason. The only exception insofar as the employer is concerned is in workers' compensation cases.

Personal Services. The most important concept to understand regarding legal services is that the plan will cover only personal services to the participant. Business ventures are excluded under the Tax Reform Act of 1976. The proposed Internal Revenue Service Regulations discuss and define personal services. Finalization has been predicted for sometime during late January or February 1981.

Proposed IRS Regulation Section 1.120-2(c) states that benefits must consist of personal legal services specified in the plan. Personal legal services are then defined as services which are not directly connected with or pertaining to the trade

---

2. *See* Section 1.501(c)(9) of 26 CFR Part 1, 46 FR (Vol. No. 4) 1719-1725 (January 7, 1981).
3. *Id.* at p. 1723, Section 1.501-3(d).

or business of the employee, spouse or dependent; or the management, conservation or preservation of property held by the employee, spouse or dependent for the production of income; or the production or collection of income by the employee, spouse or dependent. Certain personal legal services which *can* be provided although they include the prohibited categories are: securing, increasing or collecting alimony under a divorce decree or redivision of community property under a community property state; legal services provided to a participant as heir or legatee of a decedent, or as beneficiary under a testamentary trust protecting or asserting rights to the property; or claims for damages other than compensatory damages for personal injury.

As can be expected, there are many comments to this particular proposed regulation. The main criticism is that there may be many incidental activities which involve the trade or business of the participant which are intermixed with his own personal rights: for example, a personal will that leaves the business or a share of the business to heirs; a personal bankruptcy that involves all the assets, including business, of the participant; sales of personal residences where rental of the old residence temporarily may be necessary; or the sale or purchase of a duplex which is part residence and in part rental unit.

The provision regarding production or collection of income is criticized in that there are matters such as wage garnishment, unemployment, or discrimination matters which are directly connected with employment but should probably be covered as personal legal services. The limitations on income-producing activities such as the collection of professional fees, commercial debts, and other activities that produce income are generally acceptable to most commentators on the proposed regulations.

Consultative Services. Within the framework of coverage by a legal plan, consultative services rank high since they are utilized by attorneys to determine if a matter is covered and also to see if a problem exists so that preventive law action can resolve the matter before it gets out of hand. Unfortunately, the IRS has proposed a regulation which would limit consultative services to four times a year or four hours a year.[4] Furthermore, the initial consultation cannot include document preparation, document review or representation of the participant.

In discussions with IRS staff as well as with others, it would appear that the main purpose of this regulation is to ensure that a legal plan would not be covering business matters. In fact, the IRS has taken somewhat of a hard line concerning consultations which might involve business matters, initially disqualifying a plan for providing consultative services on business matters.[5] The plan responded that the purpose for allowing the one consultation, which may deal with a business matter, is to avoid penalizing the client who is uncertain whether his matter is or is not business-related. The IRS accepted this explanation, and went on to qualify the plan.

At the present writing, it is not certain whether this regulation will be retained, since there has been much criticism of it at the hearings. Suggestions have been made that there should be unlimited initial consultations with the review of documents permitted, and that no further payment would be made after it was determined by the attorney that the matter was not covered and did not constitute personal legal services. It should be noted that this probably is what most plans presently do.

Other Areas. Some of the other areas of coverage and possible utilization are as follows. The utilization frequency is a factor to consider for funding

Document preparation, such as wills, deeds and powers of attorney, constitute a major source of personal service and in fact in many plans may be the highest category of personal legal services provided. In our particular plan, the Alaska Electrical Legal Plan, document preparation accounts for 19.1% of legal services provided. *Civil litigation,* which includes general types of defendant, plaintiff and family law actions, including divorce, child support, adoption and custody, and probate actions, runs a good second at 15.5% of services provided.

Criminal and juvenile litigation, including felony cases or misdemeanor cases and juvenile court proceedings, constitutes about 11.6% in our particular plan. To this might be added provisions you can include for coverage of bail bonds, legal research, representation at the trial, etc. Your plan should specify whether you will allow appeals, or whether the legal services will be limited to just the trial court. There are plans that will limit themselves only to civil litigation because of the fear that contributions could not cover both civil and criminal matters. Of course, limitation to one criminal matter a year, or to just misdemeanors (minor offenses), is also possible. The coverage of a plan can be very flexible to accommodate its funding and participants.

Investigative services are also an assistance device for attorneys, and the plan should specify that

---

4. Proposed Regulation Section 1.120-2(c)(4).

5. *See* IRS Letter Ruling on Group Legal Services Plans, 311 BPR J-1 (10-6-80).

the investigative services are performed under the supervision of an attorney. The IRS Proposed Regulation will allow investigative services such as assistance by an accountant or investigator. The plan also needs to determine what *costs* and *out-of-pocket expenses* will be paid, such as court costs and expenses for items such as long distance calls, photography exhibits, or other photographic, scientific or technical assistance. A good rule of thumb is to limit the investigative services and out-of-pocket expenses and see how the plan develops on utilization. For example, our plan trustees wished to make certain that frivolous actions would not be filed. Therefore, court filing fees were not paid by the plan. After review of the cases for a number of years, the plan in 1980 now pays court filing fees, since it found that participants were not filing frivolous actions but, instead, substantial cases.

Some plans allow the preparation of *income tax returns*; in my opinion this should be considered incorrect, and really only the function of accountants. On the other hand, the handling of an income tax audit by the plan would be perfectly proper, as would the handling of any administrative proceeding.

Funding

At this writing, there has been very little entry into the employee benefit prepaid legal plan field by insurance companies, and therefore most legal plans are self-funded. Additionally, Proposed IRS Regulation Section 1.120(e)(3) would limit contributions to those of the employer only. No employee contributions could be made, although upon separation, a former employee could make contributions and self-pay for one year after his separation from the plan.

Costs and Plan Design. The design of any plan is going to be based on the funding. From preliminary research, it would appear that the usual prepaid plan contributions can run approximately 3-15¢ an hour.

The plan sponsors should consider whether a plan should pay 100% of legal services or less than the total billing. For example, many medical plans pay only 80% or 90% of coverage, and a legal plan can do the same. Some control on the filing of plaintiff actions does result by having the member pay some percentage, since the participant watches the plan expenses and monitors them because he has a monetary share in the fees and costs besides the litigation itself.

Eligibility group requirements can be another way to raise some prefunding, before a plan is put into effect. For example, there can be a pre-eligibility requirement of 1,000 or 500 hours, which would build up a fund to cover the anticipated legal benefit costs. To cope with the fear of most plan sponsors, initially start on a smaller benefit scale and keep a statistical study, so that you not only can know the number of cases but also can begin to get an experience rating of different legal matters, as is usual in the health and welfare field.

Utilization. Probably one of the principal factors that has prevented legal plans from becoming more numerous around the states—excluding the factor of the present inflation—is the fear of *excessive plan usage* and payments that could result in plan fund deficiency. If a survey was made, I believe most plan administrators would report, surprisingly, that there hasn't been the plan abuse as was the case in the health and welfare field. However, it will take at least ten years of plan operations to gather experience and to understand the entire prepaid legal plan area.

Legal plans do operate under the insurance principle of spreading risk among all the members. Only a certain percentage of participants will need legal services. This can range from a figure of 10% to 30% of plan participants in a given plan year.[6] A utilization rate formula which is based on the number of claims is computed as follows:

> Utilization rate = number of claims of plan benefits during a given year divided by the total plan membership that year (times 100). To get a true picture, multiple claims should be included.

Most health and welfare plans' administrative costs are lower than those for the running of a legal plan. Legal plan administrative costs have been estimated to run from approximately 10% to 30% of the total fund contributions. As more control factors are made known and cost-cutting features are developed, this high cost should eventually be reduced.

Managing the Plan

The Supervising Attorney. There are control factors which the plan sponsor should note which make operating a legal plan different. Because there is not the experience rating and normal use of an insurance carrier, there is a need for expertise in the plan's product—legal matters; therefore, a

---

6. The utilization rate increases as the plan becomes better known to the participants. For example, first year utilization may be about 10%. After four years of operation, the Alaska Electrical Legal Plan had a utilization rate of 26% for the first six months of 1980. This figure includes the claims of a participant's spouse and dependent children to age 19.

supervising attorney should be selected to manage the plan or to review attorney billings.

The supervising attorney's function is to monitor the attorneys providing legal services to the plan participants. It would appear that under ERISA the fiduciary obligation of the trustees and their delegation of responsibility in a prudent manner would mean that an attorney needs to be selected for this function. Not only is he knowledgeable on legal jargon, but he also can inform you that there are methods within the legal profession to handle cases of abuse. Every state has adopted various types of canons of professional ethics which cover the conduct of attorneys in the handling of legal matters. There are also arbitration committees set up in various state jurisdictions to handle cases of fee disputes. In short, there are control points.

Recordkeeping Controls. Most important is the legal benefit claim recordkeeping. It is suggested that time records be secured on all participant cases which include the date, a brief description of what was done on the matter (e.g., a court appearance, or research), and the amount of time in six-minute intervals, which is the normal billing procedure of the legal profession. A rule can be laid down by the plan trustees that no legal services billing can be paid without these time records attached to the attorney's statement. This is what we have basically done in our plan, and it has worked very well. The records make it easy to show the plan participant the exact amount of work that has been done on his case by the attorney and, should it be incorrect, the participant will readily inform you of the fact.

The attorneys providing legal services to the plan should know and understand that they are operating under an employee benefit plan that is subject to ERISA, and therefore their records may be audited by the Department of Labor or IRS at any time. The Department of Labor has taken action previously against the trustees as well as the plan attorney of a prepaid plan where excessive billings were discovered.[7]

Delivery of Legal Services

Attorney Providers. After discussing the record keeping and administration of the plan, we can briefly touch on the delivery of legal services. There are three basic methods that are usually utilized.

An *open panel* can be used, which means that any attorney can be chosen by a plan member, or an attorney can be used who agrees to participate on a panel open to all attorneys in the area. Should the open panel approach be utilized, it is necessary to make certain that the terms of the authorization with the plan are specific and the fees agreed upon prior to legal services being provided, if possible. The consensus among many administrators at this point seems to be that there may be some difficulty in controlling costs and having uniform billings should an open panel be utilized. Even in the case of the Shreveport Plan, an open plan, the majority of participants, because there was so little information about lawyers and selection (at least 83% of the general public would not even know how to select an attorney) eventually utilized the union attorney. Therefore, there has been an opting for a *closed panel* by many of the employee benefit legal service plans. Services in this case are provided by an individual attorney or law firm or several law firms which are selected by the plan. It has usually been considered as permitting quality control and consistency in billings. There is also the matter of preferential treatment and better treatment because of the volume of cases.

Many plans, even if they do select a closed panel of attorneys, still permit non-plan attorneys in given situations such as a conflict of interest by a participant with a plan attorney, or where there has been a family attorney used by the participant over a long period of time. There is also another instance whereby a non-plan attorney can be permitted, and that is where there is a basic inability by the participant to have confidence in the plan attorney. The basis of this particular permission is really lodged in the Canons of Professional Ethics, which state very clearly that an attorney-client relationship must be changed if there is inability to have confidence in the attorney.

Plan sponsors and trustees could also consider a *staff panel.* This can really be utilized primarily where there is a high volume in a given area or, sometimes, under circumstances which appear to be quite the reverse: should there be a wide area of jurisdiction and very few attorneys in the area, then the trustees may consider a partial staff panel. Of course, a staff panel does provide the best control, but the large membership or unique circumstances may not be.

Fees and Reimbursements. As far as the payment of legal fees, we have mentioned that time records are a must. Fees should be paid on an hourly basis, unless there is such a volume of work that in cases such as a simple will or power of attorney, a flat rate can be justified. A reasonable fee can be determined that will be satisfactory to both parties.

---

7. See *New Directions, Action Line,* Vol. 4, No. 2 February 1979, at page 1. Publication of National Resource Center for Consumer of Legal Services.

Some plans pay a monthly retainer; in this case, the details of what is included in the monthly retainer should be stated. For example, the monthly retainer may be paid for giving advice without charging individual members fees; it could include telephone consultations; and/or it could mean that an attorney is available for the participants on a steady basis during office hours, and even after office hours.

Some plans have made payments of attorneys' fees on a per capita basis, and this can lead to abuse unless there is an adjustment to make certain that the fee was actually earned. For example, a flat fee of $100 per person per year times 2,000 participants would mean a fee of $200,000. This per capita amount needs to be audited to make certain that $200,000 worth of legal services on an hourly basis were actually delivered. There is room for abuse here, and careful accounting and auditing procedures should be utilized.

Finally, the agreement between the plan and servicing attorneys should be reduced to writing, with an audit and review procedure which includes situations in which the attorney's fee or legal work is contested by the participant or plan.

Review Procedure

As with any employee benefit plan, it is necessary to have within the summary plan description a complete review procedure covering cases under which legal service benefits are being denied to the participant.

Sources of Assistance and Information

There are two non-profit organizations that can supply very good information and assistance on prepaid legal plans. These are:

A. American Prepaid Legal Services Institute
1155 East 60th Street
Chicago, Illinois 60637
Tel. (312) 947-3661

B. National Resource Center for Consumers of Legal Services
1302 18th Street, N.W.
Washington, D.C. 20036
Tel. (202) 659-8514

It is expected that within the next five years there will be a tremendous increase in the number of employee benefit prepaid legal plans. From the various information which has been gathered, it would appear that there has not been the abusive factor which seems to have created an impression or fear that the legal plans would not serve the purposes for which they were intended, but which would, instead, only benefit the legal service attorney providers.

There seems, instead, a very strong indication that prepaid legal plans will be considered a necessary employee benefit that will allow part of the 70% of middle America which does not presently have legal care to feel there is someone in their corner to protect and assist them in obtaining their legal rights.

CHAPTER 6

Health Care Benefits and Cost Containment Techniques

Steven E. Schanes, Ph.D.

President
Schanes Associates
San Diego, California

Richard A. Berman

Director, New York State Office of
Health Systems Management
Albany, New York

Ben D. Ward, Sr.

President and Chairman of the Board
Ben D. Ward & Associates, Inc.
Phoenix, Arizona

Eugene G. McCarthy, M.D., M.P.H.

Clinical Professor of Public Health
Cornell University Medical College
New York, New York

George A. Frank

President
Building Trades Employers Association;
Executive Vice President
Builders Institute of Westchester
and Putnam Counties
White Plains, New York

Hirsch S. Ruchlin, Ph.D.

Professor of Economics in Public Health
Cornell University Medical College
New York, New York

Madelon Lubin Finkel, Ph.D.

Research Associate in Public Health
Cornell University Medical College
New York, New York

Kenneth A. Tannenbaum, D.D.S.

President and Senior Research Analyst
Health Systems Group, Inc.
Ann Arbor, Michigan

Carlton R. Sherman

President
Carlton Sherman & Associates
Chicago, Illinois

Douglas F. Matook

Vice President of Benefit Operations
Kelly & Associates, Inc.
Chicago, Illinois

Bernard Handel

President
The Handel Group, Inc.
Poughkeepsie, New York

Future Trends in Benefits: Wellness Intervention

BY STEVEN E. SCHANES, Ph.D.

The Cost of Illness

All these years—since 1952, in my case—we have been crying about the rising cost of medicine (meaning the whole business—hospitals, doctors, everything). When a hospital-day cost $20, those of us who had indemnity insurance coverage complained that we had to pay $5 per day, after the "disincentive" of the $50 deductible. Those who had service contracts (primarily Blue Cross) began to face the constant headache of annual increases in rates. And, those of us who lacked coverage paid the full bill and called for national health insurance.

Growing Debate

An ample discussion of the techniques and arguments which developed concerning the cost issue could take a full volume. Much too briefly and glibly: The indemnity carriers argued that the special rates the Blues had negotiated produced a higher charge for everybody else. On the other hand, they assured us that by various disincentives—e.g., larger deductibles, coinsurance—and by their vigorous audit, review and other control mechanisms, they offered the best cost containment approach. Insurance rates could remain constant from year to year—but individual out-of-pocket expenditures kept going up. The Blues offered more complete user satisfaction, but their insurance rates began going up 10-15% per year. Arguments developed among covered groups on the issue of community vs. experience rating. The concept of self-insurance was being examined as a possible way of offsetting insurance company expenses. Attempts were begun to control and limit duplication of facilities and equipment, and to eliminate overlapping insurance coverages. Meanwhile, the provider system—the doctors, medical researchers and other personnel, hospitals and other institutions, drug and equipment companies, etc.—con-

Dr. Schanes is president of Schanes Associates, advisors on employee benefit policy, with offices in San Diego, California. From 1974 to February 1976, Dr. Schanes served as the first Executive Director of the Pension Benefit Guaranty Corporation. Between 1969 and 1974, he held various positions in the U.S. Department of Commerce, including Special Assistant to the Secretary for Policy Development. In this period he represented the Department of Commerce in the development of ERISA and national health insurance. From 1958 to 1969, Dr. Schanes was vice president of the Martin E. Segal Company, consultants to public and private pension and welfare funds. He also held the positions of academic dean, professor of political science and chairman of the Division of Economics and Business Administration of the University of San Diego from 1966 to 1969. From 1952 to 1958, he served as the first director of the New Jersey State Division of Pensions. He holds a Ph.D. in International and Constitutional Law from Cornell University and is on the labor-management panel of the American Arbitration Association. He has held offices in various professional organizations, including president, National Association of State Social Security Administrators, and vice president, National Association of State Retirement Administrators. He currently serves on the International Foundation's Government/Industry Relations Committee. Dr. Schanes has lectured extensively on employee benefits, and was the recipient of Pension World's *1976 Employee Benefits Award of the Year.*

tinued to do "its thing," better and more expensively. And, of course, inflation played its major role.

Over the years, some institutional and programmatic changes have come about. Among these is the spread of health maintenance organizations, which have really been another attempt to reduce costs and/or expand the range of medical services without much of a change in the practice of medicine. Lower cost institutions and procedures have grown up as alternatives to the use of hospitals, in certain cases. Home health care and hospice programs are providing needed services, again outside of traditional and much more expensive hospitalization. But the lessons of power politics show clearly that it is not possible for any group or agency, including the federal government, to control the overall fantastic rise in health care costs.

The message seems clear enough: As a nation, we cannot afford to get sick. We have to stay healthy. For those who are ill, the system offers little financial or health consolation. Despite insurance coverage (and we still have over 10% of the population uninsured or underinsured), the expenses to the individual are very high. Too often, one operation leads to something else. Hospital stays and drugs prescribed for one cause are too often producing other illnesses. For all of us, the cost of paying close to 10% of the GNP for the present-day type of "health care" is just too much.

Breaking the Pattern

How, then, can we break this pattern? Certainly not by relying upon the existing mainstream structure and programs. Most doctors see little reason for change. The hospitals must, due to institutional loyalty and financial considerations, continue to treat sick people. HMOs concentrate on providing traditional medicine, with incentives to the doctor to reduce the number of hospital-days. (This is said without getting into the argument about the pros and cons of HMOs as care providers or as cost reduction mechanisms.) The other professionals—nurses, therapists, etc.,—are trained in longstanding standard ways and work under the direction of doctors and hospital policies. The drug companies, the developers of new mechanical or electronic devices, and other suppliers to the health care structure are—correctly, from a marketplace standpoint—producing better products for the practitioners. But where does this leave the rest of us, the recipients of all this care and cost?

Prescription for Change

At least one viable alternative is receiving recognition in many parts of the country. Studies and individual experience have now demonstrated that it is possible in many instances to avoid all or most of the above. Put in its most simplistic form, the answer is: *Stay or get healthy.* This is not as easy as it sounds. It requires a degree of personal dedication to the idea that living a full, productive, long life is important to you.

There is no one simple formula. People are different in a medical sense, they have different heredity, their work and home environments have different degrees of stress and other harmful elements, their lifestyles—whether by background or current social environment—vary greatly. Yet there seems to be good evidence that some common denominators can go into a program of good health—or wellness—maintenance. These include:

1. *Diet.* Avoid fat (almost all meat!), salt and sugar; limit calories and protein. Read food labels.
2. *Exercise.* Walk, walk, walk. Or, if you're like me and millions of others, move into jogging (with care). There are other good, enjoyable exercise activities, such as bike riding and swimming. The essential element is a degree of constant activity which raises the heart rate (pulse).
3. *Good health management.* Learn and practice techniques ranging from proper breathing to stress management. Cut out smoking and other unhealthy practices—e.g., too much caffeine and alcohol.

Each of these requires a full discussion. In fact, there are books on each one, and articles on their "subsections." All that one can do here is to identify them. The health areas in which experience demonstrates good results include coronary heart disease, high blood pressure, emphysema and obesity. The results in terms of enjoyment of life are immeasurable.

There are some institutions which specialize in those techniques and which have documented results. Noted examples of organizations specifically treating people with health problems are the Pritikin Longevity Center in Santa Monica, California, and the Continental Health Evaluation Center near Boulder, Colorado. I do not include so-called fat farms. A number of large employers have installed exercise facilities and have encouraged good health practices. In a few instances, dollar bonuses are paid to individual employees who demonstrate improved personal health. (I question the long term gains produced by these incentives.) Also, hospitals, HMOs, Ys and other organizations are beginning to establish wellness programs.

This change in our living habits is no small step. It would seem to require a corps of skilled practitioners, including doctors, to guide and assist us. I contend that this corps will arise as the public turns toward good health. The cost-effectiveness of avoiding coronary bypass surgery or a lifetime of medical treatment and drugs should interest employee health benefit plans. Both employers and unions want individuals to be healthy and productive, physically and mentally, at lower cost. The shift in public automobile and energy utilization lifestyles, and the industry reaction, in light of the oil situation, lead me to believe that a similar change will be seen nationwide in health care. In fact, it is already underway.

Prescription Drug Plans— A Cost-Effective Benefit

BY BEN D. WARD, SR.

Introduction

"Miracle Drug Cures Cancer"? No, that headline hasn't been written yet, but it will be. It's just a matter of time! With all of the extensive research and the recent exciting discoveries, we have reason to be hopeful that the time for such a headline is near.

Prescription drugs—where would we be without them? Virtually all families in the United States, healthy or not, incur expenses for prescription drugs during the course of a year. Prescription drugs will account for more claims than all the other coverages of health care combined, yet most health and welfare trusts give little or no special thought to this very important area of coverage. Why? Probably because the average prescription is relatively inexpensive. However, if the true importance of prescription drugs is brought clearly into focus, prescription drug coverage will surely receive the attention it deserves.

That's what we are going to talk about, the importance of drugs.

A Modern Miracle

I started off talking about that miracle drug we hope will be discovered, but we already have a number of miracle drugs that most of us take for granted. Miracle drugs are saving the lives of millions of people, and saving us millions of health care dollars. Today we hear a lot of negative talk about drugs and the cost of prescriptions, but in reality prescription drugs are the best health care buy we have. In spite of all the criticism leveled at pharmaceutical manufacturers, they have done a pretty remarkable job. Their drug products save thousands of health care dollars for each $1.00 of drug costs.

Let's just review some of the miracle drugs and see how they save our health care dollars. Let's go back to just before World War II when 25 out of every 100 pneumonia victims died. Yes, one out of four! Then, in the 1940s, sulfa drugs came

Mr. Ward is president and chairman of the board of Ben D. Ward & Associates, an employee benefit organization located in Phoenix, Arizona. He is also currently president of National Optical Services, Inc., and National Pharmacy Services, Inc. Active in the employee benefits field for over 26 years, Mr. Ward founded PCS, Pharmaceutical Card System, and served as its president for ten years. He also served as vice president of McKesson & Robbins Drug Company. Mr. Ward is founder, past chairman and currently a trustee of the National Council for Prescription Drug Programs.

into wide use and the death rate from pneumonia plunged to less than 1%.

Without such drugs today, think how much more money we would spend just in hospital charges alone. I know you'll agree that it has to be in the millions.

Cortisone—another miracle drug! Cortisone is used effectively in treating more different diseases than any other substance. Its cost today is only a fraction of what it used to be. Cortisone improves the quality of life for millions of people and, yes, saves us millions of health care dollars. How about tranquilizers? Another miracle drug that came along in the '50s. Thanks to tranquilizers, the patient population in our mental institutions has been reduced dramatically. No question about it, tranquilizers are widely used—and abused. We hear a lot of talk about that abuse today, and it's a serious concern. However, let us not forget that, used correctly, tranquilizers are saving a lot of health care dollars.

I'm sure everybody has met someone with Parkinson's disease. Their hands and arms shake with palsy and their feet must take short, shuffling little steps in order to walk. Well, not too many years ago, along came another miracle drug, called L-dopa. What a godsend to many people with Parkinson's disease! Virtually overnight their shaking and palsy stopped. And, let's not forget polio—virtually eliminated by a miracle drug, and that vaccine saves us over $2 billion each year. Cimetidine—that's a very recent drug. You may recognize it by its brand name—Tagamet. It's truly a miracle drug for people who suffer from ulcers. Since the introduction of the drug a few years ago, hospital admissions and surgery for ulcers has dropped dramatically. This new drug alone has already saved us over $1 billion.

Let's not forget all the miracle drugs that are fighting tuberculosis, typhoid, measles and many other diseases.

All of these drugs are saving us a staggering amount of money.

Now imagine, if you will, how many antibiotic prescriptions are written each month for your members and their families. Each antibiotic prescription is potentially preventing a hospital admission. Death is postponed for nearly 1 million people each year, thanks to antibiotics. If just one of your members elects, for financial reasons, not to purchase the antibiotic prescribed and as a result ends up in the hospital, it might cost more than the extra cost of a quality prescription drug plan. Prescription drugs are a very important part of the benefit package. Special prescription drug coverage is something to seriously consider.

What about the cost of prescription drugs? The average prescription today costs about $8.50. Ten years ago, the average cost was $5.00. That's an increase of $3.50, which is substantial. However, remember that many things have doubled or tripled in the last ten years. Drugs really are a good buy — both from the standpoint of price and particularly in what they can save your trust fund in other areas of health cost.

The Major Medical Approach— Some Flaws

A fact too often overlooked is that many people in this country, living on a tight budget, find it increasingly difficult to make ends meet and simply don't have the extra money to purchase needed prescriptions. This is true for many who supposedly have coverage for prescription drugs under a major medical program. For example: A member's wife is ill and goes to the doctor; the doctor prescribes an antibiotic. The wife takes the prescription to the drug store—and is shocked to find out the cost is $25.00. She doesn't have an extra $25.00. The trust fund's major medical policy does provide coverage for prescriptions, but the drug store won't accept an assignment of benefits, so she must reach into her pocketbook and pay the $25.00 before she can get reimbursement by the plan. After she pays the rent, groceries and other necessary things, she simply doesn't have $25.00 to spare—so she does one of several things. She may leave the prescription at the pharmacy but not pick it up; she may decide to delay picking up the prescription until next payday; or she may not leave it at all. All three of those choices are poor. Her financial inability to purchase the prescription could lead to serious complications—even hospital admission.

What I have just described happens in this country many times every day.

Estimates on the number of prescriptions written by physicians for which the medication was never obtained range as high as 30%. This factor alone means that there can be a serious breakdown in therapy. There seems to be no reliable estimate on the number of prescriptions that are filled initially but not refilled to the extent necessary to achieve optimum therapeutic results. This is believed to be a serious problem.

Also, we must consider that the average price of $8.50 per prescription obscures the fact that an individual patient may be written three prescriptions representing an average total cost outlay of over $25.00, which does become significant. Further, the average cost of $8.50 fails to reflect the higher costs of some of the newer drugs used for acute conditions, particularly antibiotics. Prescription drugs are a financial burden for many even when some form of prescription drug coverage is available. A well-designed plan can eliminate this financial burden.

When we examine the ineffective major medical shoe box approach for covering prescription drugs, it becomes abundantly clear that there is a need for a special and separate plan to cover prescriptions. We call major medical the shoe box approach because many people will save their prescription receipts in a shoe box, and then turn them in at the end of the calendar year if they have satisfied their deductible. Most major medical plans incorporate a $50, $100 or higher deductible which must be satisfied prior to paying for prescription drugs. Such a deductible serves as a financial deterrent. Yet the objective should be just the opposite: that is, to remove all barriers possible so that beneficiaries do obtain their prescribed drugs, thus potentially saving the fund thousands of dollars of unnecessary expense in other areas.

With major medical drug coverage, there isn't any cost control to speak of, because most insurance carriers or administrators simply pay 80% (or the appropriate percentage) of the total receipts in the shoe box, assuming the deductible has been satisfied. Would you believe that a few bottles of Cutty Sark are paid for from time to time using the shoe box approach? It is simply too costly to verify each receipt.

A well-designed plan makes it *easy* for the beneficiaries to obtain their prescriptions and incorporates the theory that prescription drugs are a lot less expensive than hospital admissions! A good plan, a well-designed plan, is not only cost-effective, but ensures the trustees that money is going for authorized prescription drugs only—not for Cutty Sark.

Types of Drug Plans

Let's explore the different types of special prescription drug plans that are available.

The Discount Plan

This is where the trust fund negotiates a special price with one or more pharmacies. There are many variations to the discount plan. For example, the pharmacy may charge a small annual amount to the trust fund for each member covered. This can range from $1-5 depending upon the prescription prices offered and the convenience of locations. In most of these plans, the beneficiaries pay for the prescriptions out of their pocket and later submit a claim for payment under a major medical program if their deductible is satisfied for that year. Some pharmacies operating discount plans will actually bill the trust fund for all of the charges less the per prescription deductible amount established by the trustees. However, if the pharmacy doesn't bill the trust, usually the member must initially pay out of pocket.

Usually, the lack of a sufficient number of locations hinders the success of this approach since it is inconvenient and costly to drive a long way to have prescriptions filled.

Caution should be exercised prior to entering into any agreement providing a discount plan. Just remember, if a pharmacy doubles the price and gives a 50% discount, you're back to ground zero. It is far better to have the pharmacy give the fund a guaranteed published price for the top 200 prescribed drugs than to express their prices as a given percentage discount. Look at the bottom line—not the percentage stated as discount.

The Closed Panel Plan

With this type of plan, the fund will usually enter into an agreement with a chain or a number of independents; or, an HMO may have its own pharmacy. Some of these plans have worked reasonably well. However, many families in this country still prefer to go to their neighborhood corner drug store, and this approach doesn't allow for freedom of choice—and *may not* provide convenience of location. Usually, a very favorable price basis can be obtained with the closed panel approach.

The Service Delivered Plan or Card System

The service plan unquestionably provides the best type of prescription drug coverage available. A service plan is separate from the major medical and, consequently, does not require a sizable deductible to be satisfied prior to coverage. Service plans usually establish a $1.00, $2.00 or $3.00 per prescription deductible which is paid at the time the prescription is obtained. Of significant importance is the fact that the beneficiary knows in advance exactly how much any prescription will cost out of pocket—i.e., $1.00, $2.00, etc., per prescription. This feature virtually eliminates the financial barrier; as a result, more members will receive the needed medication, thus potentially saving your trust fund money in other areas such as hospital admissions, physicians' visits and surgery.

The service plan usually boasts of a large number of participating pharmacies available in each coverage area, thus eliminating the need to drive long distances for prescriptions. Your own corner drug store is probably participating in several service plans. The plastic card usually issued by a service plan provides positive eligibility by guaranteeing payment to the pharmacy. With a service plan, no claim form need be submitted. The patient simply pays the $1.00 deductible, fills in a couple of boxes, signs the Universal Claim Form and walks out with the prescription. The *pharmacist* has the responsibility to submit the claim.

The larger service plans employ sophisticated computer auditing techniques which quite rapidly expose any pharmacy inclined toward cheating. And—the service plan won't be paying for any Scotch!

The service plan will usually pay for a 34 day supply of the medication, and allows unlimited refills if authorized by the physician. Very few prescriptions written go unfilled with a service plan, and certainly *none* should go unfilled for financial reasons.

Mail Order

Mail order certainly has a place in the overall prescription drug delivery system, and it's becoming quite popular. Quite obviously, mail order doesn't work at all for acute medication. When someone is sick they need the medication now—not several days later when the postman arrives. However, for long term and maintenance drugs, mail order can be quite convenient and can save both the plan participants and the trust fund a considerable amount of money on each prescription.

Let's see how it works. Let's use a service plan that requires a $1.00 per prescription deductible and allows up to a 34 day supply of the medication. The patient is taking Inderal—a maintenance drug for heart disease. Three per day are being taken. The average wholesale price per 100 is about $9.50. Since the service plan is limited to a 34 day supply or 100 unit doses, the patient must have this prescription refilled each month and pay a $1.00 deductible each time.

Let's see how the numbers compare using a service plan versus mail order, by extending the figures for one year. Under the service plan, let's assume a *dispensing fee* or markup of $3.00 over the $9.50 ingredient cost. So for 100 tabs, or a month's supply, at three per day, the cost of the original prescription and each refill would be $12.50; the plan pays $11.50, and the patient pays the $1.00 per prescription deductible. At the end of one year, the plan has paid $138.00 and the member has paid $12.00. The total cost was $150.00.

Now, comparing the example to mail order, we will assume that the physician has authorized a six month supply, or 600 tablets. This means the prescription is only refilled once during the first year. Because of the larger quantity, the ingredient cost would be only $9.00 per 100, or $54.00 for a six months' supply. Add a $3.00 dispensing fee, and you have $57.00 for six months or $114.00 for the year, compared to $150.00 for the service plan. For the year, then, the trust pays the mail order plan $112.00 compared to $138.00. The member pays only $2.00 for the year instead of $12.00. The overall savings is a very dramatic 24%. And, let's not forget that the member also saves 12 trips to the pharmacy!

I think it's apparent that mail order does have a place and can save both the plan and beneficiaries substantial dollars. The savings are even more dramatic if the cost of the ingredients is higher.

A Combination Approach

For *short term acute medication,* no plan is better than the service plan. It's simple, there are no claim forms, and the member doesn't have to lay out any cash and wait for reimbursement. It removes the financial barrier. For *maintenance medication,* mail order works very well and saves both the plan and plan participants a lot of dollars.

One conclusion is obvious: the best approach is to adopt both a service plan and a mail order program. Such an approach will save your fund and your members a considerable amount of money. A number of trust funds and other groups have already adopted this dual approach, and I see it as the predominant approach of the future. Service plans simply can't continue to offer *only* a 34 day supply or 100 unit dose—the members and trust funds can't afford it! So, the service plans and mail order houses should be challenged by you to bring this combined product to your members under a single agreement concept.

The service plans can no longer afford to ignore the needs of your members by refusing to administer plans that offer a six months' supply of medication. I understand that service plans need to keep their participating pharmacies happy and, as a businessman, I can certainly appreciate why pharmacies don't want to dispense a six months' supply of medication for *one* dispensing fee when they are now getting *six* dispensing fees under the 34 day supply limitation. But, they don't have to; mail order exists, it works, it saves money—and the service plans must be innovative and arrange for this type of coverage. A well-designed, quality service plan combined with an innovative mail order program is a lot less expensive than a service plan without mail order, and can go hand-in-hand in effectively, and reasonably, meeting the drug needs of your members, while saving your trust fund a lot of those shrinking dollars!

Final Comments

When reviewing your benefit package remember:
- The cost of three or four prescriptions can be substantial!
- Drug benefits are not assigned.
- Some of your members or their families may not be receiving their drugs because they don't have the ready cash.
- Drugs are important to your members and their families.

In conclusion: Cover all the prescription drugs you can—you can't afford not to.

Assisting the Troubled Employee: Alcoholism and Counseling Programs as a Plan Benefit

BY GEORGE A. FRANK

AT THE OUTSET, let me say that I am speaking as a "non-professional" management trustee of a number of collectively bargained benefit funds in Westchester County (New York). By non-professional, I mean that my primary job is not directly related to the administration or structuring of benefits, or funding of industry plans. I am an executive officer of a number of management associations which have collective bargaining agreements with various building trade unions. These agreements relate, in part, to fringe benefits for employees, hence my involvement with the funds themselves.

My subject relates to health benefit funds (more commonly called welfare funds) in the construction industry, and how these plans, in our region, are responding to an increasingly common illness—alcoholism. We can say—in Westchester County, at least—that we have gotten the problem, the illness, out of the closet and have taken the steps to respond to alcoholism in a direct and open manner. We now view alcoholism as a treatable disease. From the point of view of, perhaps, a typical management trustee, I would like to describe what has been done in our region, where we stand today, where we expect to go, and the possible applicability of our experience to other benefit funds.

Recognizing the Problem

For many years, the benefit funds on which I serve did not consider alcoholism a disease; as a consequence there was no schedule of benefits relating to alcoholism. And, I don't remember trustees ever thinking much about it. I must assume that, during that time, those alcoholics who required hospitalization or other treatment were diagnosed as having any number of other illnesses. They apparently were being treated; the funds paid the benefit; and more likely than not, they were soon back in the hospital or required some

Mr. Frank is president of the Building Trades Employers Association; executive vice president of the Builders Institute of Westchester and Putnam Counties; and executive vice president of the Apartment Owners Advisory Council. He presently serves as a trustee for a number of construction industry fringe benefit funds, including Carpenters, Building Laborers and Trowel Trades. Mr. Frank is secretary of both the New York State and the Westchester County Carpenters Apprenticeship Committees. In 1976, the Governor of New York appointed Mr. Frank to serve on the state's Apprenticeship and Training Council. Mr. Frank received his B.S. degree in journalism, magna cum laude, from Boston University.

other kind of medical treatment. We now know that many were alcoholics, but we were treating them for a host of other illnesses, such as hepatitis, gastrointestinal ailments, nervous disorders and pneumonia.

We don't really know how many men were treated in this manner; we don't really know how much it cost the funds; but we do know that alcoholics make up about 7% of the population—probably higher in the construction industry—and we do know that the illness and accident rate is substantially higher among alcoholics than in the population as a whole. We now conclude that alcoholism was costing the funds a great deal of money, not to mention the appalling human cost to the individual and his or her family.

As a result of our growing interest in the field, in 1974 we began inserting in our collective bargaining agreements the clause: "Alcoholism is a disease and should be treated as such." It is difficult to conceive now, but there was some resistance to the inclusion of this clause in the agreements. It was as though we were admitting something that was better left unsaid.

EAP— Developing a Program That Works

Gaining Support

Sometime in 1976, the Construction Industry Foundation—a management organization supported by industry advancement funds—assigned its director, Virginia Monahan, to look into the possibility of federal funding for a program that would aid troubled employees. In 1978, the National Institute on Alcohol Abuse and Alcoholism did approve funding for the Joint Labor/Management Board Employee Assistance Program of Building, Construction, and Realty Industries with a demonstration project grant of $250,000 for a three year period. The program provided for a director, two field coordinators—in our case, both members of building trade unions—and a part-time data coordinator. The federal funding was supplemented by approximately $40,000 per year "in-kind" support coming principally from employer associations.

Since its inception, 290 alcohol-related referrals (called clients) have come through the Employee Assistance Program, as well as 199 non-alcohol-related cases (non-alcohol-related referrals are classified as drug, emotional, marital, financial, and so on). The principal referral sources are work supervisors, family and the client himself. Current treatment resources utilized by the program include Alcoholics Anonymous, Al-Anon/Alateen, detoxification and mental health services, private psychological counseling and hospitals.

To give you a better idea of the purpose and functions of the EAP, I would like to read from an evaluation report of the EAP prepared by Dr. Walter Reichman and filed recently with NIAAA as part of the application for a three year extension grant. I quote:

> The Employee Assistance Program of the Westchester Foundation is a unique demonstration project that is proving successful. The EAP is striving to demonstrate that an industry-wide program in the building trades can operate effectively to serve the needs of a significant proportion of the working population that could not otherwise be serviced. With the cooperation of management and unions the program has reached into an industry composed of a multitude of jobs and job sites that hold little permanence for the worker. It is an industry in which drinking is accepted, alcoholism problems are common and alcoholism is protected. The construction industry is one of the first to feel the effects of any change in the economy. There is a constant expansion and contraction of jobs, and a continuous fluctuation in the number of union members, the number of people on the job and the number unemployed.
>
> The results of our examination of the data collected by the EAP indicates that they are developing a procedure to reach this special group of workers. We anticipate that by the end of the grant period they will have developed a model program that will be useful for similar industries throughout the country.

At the outset, the originator of the EAP began an informal relationship with a number of construction industry health benefit plans. Each fund was asked to contribute $500—more as a gesture and their first small involvement with the EAP. During the first year of the program, the advisory committee and its director spent considerable time talking to key employers and union leaders. Through seminars and meetings featuring well-known recovered alcoholics, and widespread press coverage, the concept of the program was accepted and referrals began to come in. The extent of the problem—alcoholism—began to take form. And the form it took—based on the substantial number of clients—was clearly recognized as a major industry health problem. With this kind of information, it was not long before the trustees of the health benefit funds began to see the obvious implications for their health benefit funds.

A Cost-Effective Benefit

Based on a great deal of interest and the widespread feeling that the program was working, it became apparent that alcoholism treatment could reduce the cost of basic medical services, in addition to meeting the typical objective back-up estimates by the National Institute on Alcohol Abuse and Alcoholism that alcoholic employees have an accident rate more than 3½ times higher than that of other employees.

Other studies which go further in supporting the effectiveness of treatment are cited in an excellent paper by Kenneth P. Camisa, senior vice president of Martin E. Segal Company. Quoting from Mr. Camisa's paper:

- A study by General Motors showed that the health insurance benefits paid to rehabilitated employees were 42% lower after treatment.
- The Kennecott Copper Company estimated that the weekly accident and sickness benefit cost for alcoholic employees was five times greater than that of non-alcoholics. Hospital, medical and surgical costs were three times greater.
- A health maintenance organization in Rochester, N.Y., found its members who were suffering from alcoholism required 12 times more hospitalization than non-alcoholics.

Based on our experience with the EAP there is no doubt that it has reduced the cost of basic medical services that normally would have been paid by the health benefit funds. Admittedly, this is difficult to prove on a scientific basis, particularly in the construction industry. But we know the number of "clients" that are in the program. Within the constraints of confidentiality, we know their present health condition and we know whether they are productive workers. We know the national statistics concerning the relationship between alcoholism and medical costs. And we—as well as our fund advisors—have concluded that the program is working to reduce overall health costs. This has been accomplished at little expense to the funds. From the point of financial impact on the health benefit funds we have been fortunate because the program, as I described earlier, is being funded by a demonstration grant by NIAAA and supplemented by funds from employer associations. The source of employer contributions is the collectively bargained industry advancement funds, as I have noted.

Having provided the groundwork, we already have begun to meet with fund trustees to convince them to provide coverage for the treatment of alcoholism. We understand the previous reluctance to provide the benefit based on the difficulty of predicting risks, the cost of the treatment, and the numbers which might be involved—although we suspect that the reluctance was also based on the conservative nature of fund advisors, and their hesitancy to break new ground into a field such as alcoholism.

Selection of Services

While I am not prepared to talk technically about specific alcoholism treatment programs and their cost impact on health benefit funds, there are some areas which we are considering. One, which already has been adopted by a number of funds (both insured and self-insured), is the inclusion of registered alcoholism treatment and rehabilitation facilities in the benefit payment schedule. By paying for these facilities, the funds are recognizing the need for specialized rehabilitation treatment programs for alcoholics. This represents an important first step. Incidentally, we have one case in point in which a building trade health fund saved $10,000 by sending the patient to an alcoholism treatment facility rather than a local hospital, on the basis of a 28 day rehabilitation program: the local hospital would have charged $11,200; the treatment facility actually cost $700.

We are also considering payment for more outpatient services specifically designed to treat alcoholics. Various community centers, including mental health and service agencies, would fall into this category. The charge, probably minimal, should be paid by the fund as a normal benefit.

With regard to psychiatric and counseling services, we are also considering the possibility of this benefit. However, we are giving consideration to the costs involved. On this issue, we require further information and expect to be discussing the matter with actuaries and consultants.

In summary, we have made substantial progress in the identification as well as the treatment of the alcoholism problem in the building construction industry in our area. As I have noted, we are fortunate in having a successful Employee Assistance Program which has worked closely with the various benefit funds. However, we think we can—and should—do more in ensuring that the health benefit plans themselves provide the requisite benefits that will serve employees with a comprehensive alcoholism treatment program.

Prepaid Dental Care Plans

BY KENNETH A. TANNENBAUM, D.D.S.

FIRST, I would like to clarify my goals in this discussion. One is to provide you with considerations in designing a dental benefit plan, whether or not you have one now. Second, is how you can make your existing dental benefit plan more efficient and more cost-effective; basically, how to get more benefits for your dollars. In order to achieve these goals, we are going to look at what kind of benefits one might want to consider providing, how to purchase them and where to purchase them.

To begin with, I would like to set out three assumptions for you:
1. Regardless of what kind of a dental benefit program you have, you want it to be hassle free—for yourselves, your members, your employees, for whomever.
2. You want the best buy for your dollar.
3. You want good dental care for your people.

Types of Benefits

There are four primary categories of dental benefits:
1. Preventive
2. Basic restorative
3. Complex restorative
4. Orthodontics.

The *preventive services* that we normally see in a dental benefit plan are such things as examinations, x-rays, emergency treatment, cleaning, and space maintainers for children. The rationale for this category of benefits is that they are needed by essentially all people. Therefore, they should be easy to get, and consequently we see many dental benefit plans that pay 100% of the cost of these basic preventive services. Frequently, they will pay on the basis of twice a year for exams and cleaning. The intent of these benefits is to try to avoid problems, prevent problems, and also have people get into the dentist's office as early as possible without any kind of financial barrier. These benefits also encourage patient education with regard to routine dental care.

The second category is what we call *basic restorative*. This includes such things as fillings,

As president and senior research analyst for Health Systems Group, Inc., Ann Arbor, Michigan, Dr. Tannenbaum served as project director for a nationwide study evaluating cost and quality methodologies used by third-party payers of dental benefits, and directed a study of the cost containment activities of state insurance commissioners and their potential interrelationship with the health planning process. He is also the senior consultant of Health Systems Group, Inc., and has been involved in a variety of consulting projects with hospitals, HMOs, Blue Cross and Blue Shield plans, state insurance departments and substance abuse coordinating agencies. Dr. Tannenbaum formerly served as president of Health Benefits Administrators, Inc., and, prior to that, as deputy insurance commissioner for health care, State of Michigan. He attended Haverford College, Haverford, Pennsylvania, earned his D.D.S. at the University of Pennsylvania School of Dental Medicine, Philadelphia, and received his M.P.H. at the University of Michigan School of Public Health, Ann Arbor. Dr. Tannenbaum has lectured before many professional groups and has written numerous articles on dental and health care.

extractions, root canal therapy and gum conditions. The rationale behind this category is that these services are not needed, as the preventive services are, by basically everyone, but *are* needed by a significant portion of the population. These benefits are necessary in order to correct common problems that exist. Therefore, they should be fairly easy to get. With this rationale in mind, there is frequently a deductible applied to these kinds of services, with payment usually at about an 80% level. The rationale for a deductible here is that because these services are more costly than preventive services, persons who are utilizing these services should have some investment, but not a major investment, in the services themselves. The intent is that if people have an investment in the cost of their services, they will take better care of their mouths. We are not sure that this is true, but at least that is what the rationale is.

The third category of dental benefits is what we call *complex restorative*. This includes such things as crowns or caps, bridges, and plates or dentures, either partial dentures or full dentures. This category of care is generally quite expensive. It is needed by fewer people. For the most part, these services may be optional. Because of the cost and because of the optional aspect, it is thought that most people, when they use these services, should pay a greater portion than they would for the preventive or basic restorative services. Thus, these services are frequently available at a 50% copay, usually with a deductible as well. Again, the investment by the participant is increased in this category of services.

The fourth category of dental benefits, one which is not found in all programs, is *orthodontics,* the straightening of teeth. This is needed by even fewer people. So, if you look at the spectrum of dental needs, you go from those services that are needed by almost everyone to those that are needed by very few. Orthodontics is in the last category. These benefits are almost always optional, and frequently they are of a cosmetic nature only. Therefore, again, the investment by the participant is increased. We often see a separate deductible and a separate copay for coverage of orthodontic benefits.

Cost Control and Plan Design

Depending on the kind of program that exists, you can have a dental benefit program for as little as $3 or $4 per member per month or as much as $28-30 per member per month. My point simply is that the choice available in terms of dental benefit programs is very wide, and you can select a number of things within that general framework and range.

The cost of a program is also dependent on the projected use or utilization of the group. I would like to list a number of assumptions that I would share with you as to projected utilization:
1. The more educated the group, the greater the use of dental benefits.
2. The more families in the group, the greater the use of dental benefits.
3. The more women and children, the greater the use of dental benefits.
4. The higher the income of the group, the greater the utilization. For example, a teachers' group, which is both educated and nowadays fairly highly paid, would have greater use.
5. The younger the group, the more you can expect use of preventive services.
6. The older the group, the more you can expect surgery and denture services.
7. The greater the probability of layoff, the greater the use will be. People who are projecting that they may be laid off will use the services that are available fairly heavily before they are laid off and their benefits end.
8. Groups with high turnover have, in general, a very high dental benefit use. We find that new members of a program—new employees, or new members covered by a fund—have a very high use.
9. Hourly employees have a tendency to use more dentures and surgical services; salaried employees, a tendency to use more bridges, preventive and orthodontic services.
10. The further in advance that the announcement is made of a dental benefit program, the greater the use when the program actually comes into effect. I am sure this comes as no surprise, but I wanted to mention it for the sake of completeness. You should also keep in mind that most dental care is postponeable. There is very little in the dental field that actually has to be done today; it could be done tomorrow, next week, next month or even next year. Thus, the further in advance that you announce the benefits, the more people will postpone those services until they have coverage.

Eligibility and Payment Structure

Benefits Phase-In. You can modify the effect of some of these demographic factors by including certain restrictions in your program. For example, if you have a high turnover you may want to consider a delayed eligibility for dental programs. Let's say you are going to announce that in six months or a year you are planning to put a dental benefit program into effect. What you might want to do is to modify the program so that in year one or year two there are lower maximums, and then expand that maximum in year three. Do keep in mind, as I am sure most of you are aware, that during the first year or two of a dental benefit program, the use is going to be very high. We can expect the stabilization of that use probably by the third year, and almost certainly by the fourth year.

Deductibles and Maximums. You can also modify the program costs by using a deductible and a maximum. Many dental benefit programs, as I have indicated, have no deductibles for certain preventive services but do have a deductible for all other services.

We find that if you have a $25 deductible and you decrease that deductible to zero, the cost of your overall dental benefit program is going to increase by 25%. The rationale here is that the average dental claim is only in the $20-25 range. On the other hand, if you take that $25 deductible and increase that to a $50 per person deductible, you will find approximately a 20% decrease in your benefit costs. If you take that $25 deductible and increase it to a $100 deductible, you find approximately a 30% decrease in the cost of your program. So, if you assume a monthly premium of $20, and you reduce your deductible to zero, you can expect that monthly premium to increase to somewhere around $25. If, on the other hand, you increase your deductible to $50, you can expect the monthly cost to go from $20 down to $16; if you increase your deductible from $25 to $100, you can expect your total monthly premium to drop down to $14. Obviously, these figures are not rigid, since many other factors must be taken into consideration, but I just wanted to give you some idea of the impact on program costs of changing the deductible.

With regard to maximums or caps—and most programs have some kind of an annual cap that they apply to a dental program—we find that if you increase the annual maximum from $500 to $1,000, you will have approximately a 7% increase in your benefit costs. If you increase that maximum to $2,000 per person, you can expect approximately another 8% increase in your benefit costs. Generally, expanding the maximum means that those few people who are now using expensive services will use more services. One study has shown, for example, that 5% of the enrolled population was responsible for 48% of the claims costs. So, if you do increase your maximum, keep in mind that only a limited few will take advantage of that increase.

Incentives and Reviews

There are several additional assumptions I would now like to share with you with regard to program design:

1. That you have only a limited amount of dollars
2. That in traditional programs, dentists have an economic incentive to provide more services. That is, the more services they provide on a fee-for-service basis, the greater their income. I think that's a realistic assumption in traditional programs.
3. In general, third-party payers do a very effective job of monitoring charges made and in monitoring eligibility for benefits. In general, however, third-party payers do not do a very effective job with regard to the necessity of services or the appropriateness of care.

Therefore, in accord with these assumptions, I would propose that dental benefit plans contain some or all of the following provisions:

1. That the costs for examinations be permitted no more than twice a year
2. That the payment for x-rays be limited only to those x-rays that are necessary. We have found that dentists are very good at taking advantage of what the benefits of the plan are. If the system pays for all x-rays, the dentist will take all x-rays; if the system pays for limited x-rays, they will take only limited x-rays. I do not practice dentistry anymore, nor have I practiced for a number of years, so I can afford to talk candidly about what dentists do or do not do. With regard to x-rays, most plans pay for what is called a full set of x-rays once every three years. I would recommend that plan design pay for a full set of x-rays no more than once every five years, and then only when necessary. There is no such thing as a routine x-ray. Frankly, we have seen in this country far too much radiation. I think that the dental profession has been particularly guilty of this. It is a wonderful way to generate income for them, but I am not sure it is good dental care. With regard to x-rays other than full mouth x-rays, it is my judgment professionally and from a cost standpoint that x-rays ought to be permitted only in association with some other procedure, whether it be an extraction or root canal therapy or an examination.
3. Oral hygiene instruction should not be a covered benefit. "Oral hygiene instruction" is a euphemism developed by the dental profession over the last few years, particularly with the advent of dental insurance, for teaching people how to brush their teeth better. It has always gone on in dental offices, it has always been included as part of the cleaning of the teeth; and there is no reason to pay a separate extra charge for it

just because someone else is footing the bill.
4. Caps, crowns or bridges should be done only when necessary. Consideration should be given, particularly for bridges, to have prior approval by your third-party administrator on all bridgework.
5. Prior authorization is something that should be included in your basic program design for costs of more than $150. There are two reasons for this:
   a. So that you know whether the services are necessary. You can have a dental consultant review the claim to see whether those services are needed.
   b. So that the member or employee can have an idea, in advance, as to exactly what his or her coverage will be.

We have found that effective prior authorization will save the plan 3-5% in benefit costs.
6. Similarly, there should be some type of a post-treatment review system. The system could be reviewing x-rays taken at six month recall visits. The system could be doing statistical analyses. Or, it could be responding to member complaints. Post-treatment review savings run around 5-8%. Both pre-treatment and post-treatment reviews are very important in terms of savings.
7. All group dental benefit plans should have coordination of benefits with other group dental plans.
8. Ideally, there should be language in your plan that allows for alternative treatment to permit the use of the least costly effective procedure. Keep in mind that dentistry, unlike medicine, is unique in that there are frequently a number of choices as to what can be done, given a certain diagnosis. If the dentist can make that choice, more often than not he or she will make the more costly choice because that is the incentive he has for his own income. If there is alternate treatment language built into your benefits program, it will give your claims processors and your dental consultant the ability to look at whether that particular service is necessary or whether something else might be as effective but less costly. Keep in mind that I am not advocating denying benefits to members, or cutting benefits to members, or putting members in the middle. What I am saying is that it is necessary to monitor the dental benefit program because of the unique nature of dental care. Our experience has been, quite frankly, that dentists know and understand the programs that their patients have, and that they will do what the traffic will bear.

Purchase of Services

There are a number of ways that you can consider the purchase of dental benefits. You can go with a commercial carrier like Aetna or Connecticut General. You can go with a dental service plan like Delta. You can go with the Blues or an HMO. Or, you might want to consider self-funding a program. I would like to touch briefly on some of the pros and cons of these various options.

Insurance Programs

The commercial carriers and the Blues generally offer a package of health care benefits, so that it may be easier for you as purchasers to consider buying all your health benefits from one source. Whether it be life insurance, disability, dental or medical, the commercial carriers most always, and the Blues, frequently, offer a package of benefits. Both the commercial carriers and the Blues generally provide freedom of choice as to dentist. Cost-wise, we have found that the commercials and the Blues are comparable.

The Delta plans are generally only dental in nature, so that there is no package of benefits. I think that there is one Delta plan that offers something other than dental benefits. This is neither good, nor bad, nor a pitch for Delta. The point is that sometimes people find it easier to buy all their benefits from one carrier. The Delta plans are generally run by dentists, so the benefits may be much more favorable to the dentists.

Delta plans may be limited only to participating dentists. This is not necessarily a problem; for example, I understand that in Hawaii, the Hawaii Dental Service has participating agreements with some 95% or 98% of all the dentists. Thus, from the standpoint of freedom of choice, there is no problem in Hawaii in having your members go to basically any dentist and getting the benefits that you negotiated. On the other hand, there are some areas—parts of Ohio, for example—where the number of participating dentists hovers around 40% or 45%. So if you negotiate with Delta for dental benefit programs in certain areas, your members can only obtain services at a participating dentist to get paid-in-full benefits. This may be a problem.

Some of the Delta plans have very good quality review programs. From a cost standpoint, the Deltas are generally comparable to the commercial carriers and to the Blues.

HMOs

HMOs are somewhat of an option; I am not sure how much of an option in your area, but for the sake of completeness I would mention it. They may or may not offer a package of benefits. The choice of dentists in the program may be limited. I do not know that that is necessarily bad, it is just a factor.

Our knowledge is that HMOs in general have had less experience in managing dental programs than the Deltas have, for example. They frequently have fewer members, and I think that, in general, you may find that your costs of a dental benefit program with an HMO may be a little greater than what they would be with Delta, or the Blues or a commercial carrier.

Self-Funding

The last option for purchasing services in the traditional way is the self-funded approach. I will not dwell on that. I do want to mention that basically with a self-funded approach your members can have freedom of choice as to their dentists. Self-funded programs are otherwise pretty similar to those of the commercial carriers and the Blues. In a self-funded program you can expect your administrative expenses to be of the 8-10% magnitude, less than they would be if you bought them from a commercial carrier. Frankly, self-funded programs should be considered if you have more than 500 members. If you do go self-funded or if you are considering self-funding, I would suggest strongly that you make sure that your claims processing staff is well trained. I would also recommend using a dental consultant. Let me point out that it is not particularly difficult to do dental claims, as long as you have got your system in place.

There are two other options in terms of the purchasing of dental benefits, which I will discuss later. One of them is having your own facility; the other is what we call a capitation program.

Considerations and Caveats

Several points in selecting a carrier:
1. Do not look only at the price of the benefit or the experience that is projected. I would strongly suggest that you look also at administrative costs and keep in mind that you get what you pay for.
2. Do not hesitate to use a consultant. There are a number of consultants available through brokers and elsewhere. I would suggest that if you are going to use a consultant, if possible you should use someone on a non-commission basis, to make sure that your fund or your company gets an unbiased view as to which is the best dental benefit program for you.

Claims Handling. There are a number of expectations I think you should rightfully have from your dental benefit carrier or administrator, whether you do it yourself or you buy the services. I think that you should expect no more than a 10-15 day *turnaround* from the time the carrier receives the claim until the time the benefits are paid. The only exception to this is that if you are self-funded and pay the claims yourselves, you may want to consider a policy decision to pay your dental benefits once a month and that way pick up a 30 day float on the monies that you otherwise would have paid out.

In terms of further expectations, the claims system should be able to pick up *duplicate services.* Unfortunately, many carriers do not do this real well, which is particularly surprising to me since there are only 32 teeth in the mouth. Almost all dental claims that are received are listed by tooth number, so it's very easy to pick up duplicate services if you want to look for them. Again, I have talked about *pre-authorization;* I think you should expect that there be a pre-authorization for more than $150 of services.

The Dental Consultant: Quality Review. I think there ought to be a procedure for using a dental consultant. Let me give you some reasons why using a dental consultant is necessary.

Data indicate that some 60% of the population over 35 has serious gum problems. Yet only 10% of that population gets treatment. The problem here is that we frequently see that dentists will treat patients and do extensive restorative work—you may spend $500, $600, $700, $800 or more on a bridge or a partial denture—when there is a serious gum problem that may require those teeth to be removed in six months. Frankly, I do not think it is a particularly good investment to go ahead and spend a fair amount of money and then have those teeth removed in six months because the basic underlying gum problems were not taken care of in the first place. A dental consultant can help with that.

Our experience, by the way, has been good in pointing out to practicing dentists where they have missed a problem. We write the dentists after receiving a claim and say, "Hey, Doctor, did you notice that there is a gum problem here?" You need to do this carefully and tactfully, of course. But dentists have been very receptive to the fact that they may have missed something. Then they go back and do what is necessary, or they may discuss it. I think that in terms of the long term benefits for your own program, as well as for your members' benefits, such a mode of communication should be considered.

Another reason to use consultants is with regard to wisdom teeth. Approximately 50% of all wisdom tooth extractions are not necessary. Now, obviously, if the tooth already has been removed there is no choice but to pay for it. But you might want to consider, in your benefit design, putting in the requirement that except for emergencies, wisdom tooth extractions need to be pre-authorized. Again, some 50% of those wisdom tooth extractions at an average of $80-100 per tooth, are not necessary.

The third reason for using a dental consultant is with regard to bridges. Some 35% or so of all dental claims are for bridges. (A bridge, for those of you who do not know, is a fixed unit to replace a missing tooth, as opposed to a partial plate, which is a removable appliance.) Some 35% of all claims are for bridges, yet several studies have shown that approximately one-half of the bridges, particularly in the back part of the mouth, are not necessary. What I would like to point out is that we are not dealing with *ideal* dental care, but *necessary* dental care. I would characterize this as the difference between Cadillac dental programs and Chevrolet dental programs.

Communication of Benefits. The last expectation I think you should have from your third-party payer is that the benefit booklets that are issued, as well as the explanation of benefits paid and explanation of benefits denied, should be very clear. Our experience has been that most lay people really do not understand their benefits. I think if you are going to give someone a dental benefit program, whichever way you work that out and negotiate it, you ought to let them know what it is you have done, what you have paid for and what you have not paid for. It is good business and good public relations to do so. Unfortunately, the communications that come from third-party payers are not always as clear as they could be.

Two Other Options

I would like to turn now to several options that I had mentioned earlier—options which do not transfer the cost from the fund or the insurance carrier to your member. I do not regard the latter approaches as options! Briefly, one possible alternative is owning your own facility and having dentists on salary; another option is entering into a capitation program.

Should You Own Your Own Facility?

If you are going to own your own facility, in my judgment you will need a minimum of 1,500-2,000 participants who will use the facility, plus their families. If you are going to have your own facility, it is critical that you have good management. If you are intending to hire salaried dentists, do not expect those salaried dentists, whether fresh out of school or seasoned practitioners, to be able to do a particularly effective job in managing a facility. It is our experience, frankly, that most dentists do not have a very good handle on business practices and personnel practices. And so I would suggest strongly that if you are going to have your own dental facility in-house or at a remote location, you make sure that you have good management. As with anything else, this is the key to making something work.

It should be possible to deliver a good comprehensive dental program in a facility you own yourself for under $9 a month per family. That may sound like heresy, but it is true. If you do not have enough people on your own, you may want to consider joining forces with another fund or some other employers with the idea of pooling your resources and then building your own facility.

I think that owning your own facility, using good management, is a viable and attractive option. Do keep in mind, however, that if you are going to own your own facility you will have some start-up costs—you will have to equip the facility, probably do some leasehold improvements, pay rent, and so on. You can expect the costs for start-up to run anywhere from $10,000-25,000 per dental treatment unit; that would be inclusive of all your leasehold improvements. Of course, it depends on what needs to be done. But when you consider that you are amortizing these costs—and let us say we are talking about a 10-chair unit at a cost of $250,000 over a seven year period, and then dividing that by 2,000 or 3,000 family units who will use that facility—you are not talking about a great deal of money spread out over that period of time, particularly when you compare it to what you will have to pay if you buy these services from a third-party payer.

I should also point out that if you have your own facility, with your own dentists and good management, you increase the amount of control that you have over the way services are provided. I am not suggesting that you get in the business of telling dentists how to practice. On the other hand, dentists are receptive to direction. I think that having that kind of control ensures you of keeping your costs down. I can assure you that having your own facility can be totally hassle free. I would also see having your own facility as the way of getting the maximum benefits for your dollars.

Capitation Programs

The other alternative in terms of getting more benefits for your benefit dollars is what we call capitation programs. While this is a relatively new and growing thing, a number of programs have had some experience in Minnesota, California, Ohio, Michigan, Illinois, Wisconsin and New York, to name but a few areas. At present, some 10% of the population with dental benefit programs are covered by capitation, and we expect to see that rise to as high as 40% over the next four or five years. So it is clearly a growing phenomenon.

Restructuring Incentives. Basically what capitation programs are is that you pay a dental group *x* dollars a month and in return the group is obligated to provide all necessary services. Essentially, the dentists are put at risk. This is as opposed to a traditional insurance program, where you are at risk or the carrier is at risk. If the carrier pays the bills, the incentive the dentist has in the traditional program is to provide maximum services, which will maximize his income. You are totally at risk because you are paying the bill, bottom line. On the other hand, in a capitation program, the dentist gets a fixed dollar amount for treating all these people, doing all the services that are necessary, and *he* is totally at risk. With capitation—and the reason that it works—the dentist's incentive is to provide maximum preventive services, and only those services that are necessary. If we go back to some of my earlier comments, some care is not really needed or can be done at a lower, but equally acceptable, cost level. By putting the dentist at risk, you can be assured that only those services that are necessary are going to be provided. And, to the extent that the necessary services are provided to the population as soon as possible, that is the way the dentists will make a profit. To the extent that needed services are *deferred,* and people keep coming back for the traditional care with the dentist, he is not going to make a profit.

In our experience, we have had no difficulty finding dentists who are willing to participate in this program. In order to make it work, however, you need to have very careful selection of the dentists who participate to make sure that they do not take advantage of the fact that nobody is looking over their shoulder. For this reason, we prefer group practices. At the same time, there needs to be ongoing monitoring of the kinds of services provided. Again, the risk is not with the carrier, as it may be if you are insured; it is not with the fund, as it is if you are on an experience-rated basis; it is not with the member, by having maximum out-of-pocket costs. Rather, it is with the dentist—which, frankly, I think is where it belongs, since with dentistry all the services that are provided are decided by the dentist. And the dentist will decide those services based on some very simple notions, the primary one of which is his own pocketbook. Another way of looking at capitation programs is that dentists are paid to keep people healthy.

How It Works. I would like to tell you a little about a capitation dental program that we have had going in Toledo, Ohio, for the last 2½ years in conjunction with the Teamster Health and Welfare Fund. The fund owns the equipment itself and leases the space. Our company has had a contract to manage its dental care center. We are at risk, and we provide all necessary dental services to some 2,500 families—about 8,000 people. There is no deductible in the program. There is no maximum. There are limited copayments based on actual laboratory charges for certain procedures like crowns, bridges or dentures. Other than that, there are no other charges. We get a fixed amount each month. In return, we have to pay for all supplies, all of our laboratory costs, and salaries for all of our personnel. We have about 24 people working in the clinic. We get a little less than $9 a month on a capitation basis to manage the program, pay all the expenses and make a profit. And I can assure you that we have made a profit.

I can also assure you that the quality of care we have is excellent. All treatment planning is done on a group basis, as is problem solving. We call this ongoing peer review. This process ensures that nothing is missed, that all periodontal or gum work, as I had mentioned before, is taken care of. Only necessary bridges and crowns are done. This kind of good quality care results in extremely reasonable costs—somewhere around one-third of what you might expect from a comparable insured benefit program.

Because the above facility is owned by the Teamsters fund, its use is limited to Teamsters. What we have done is expand this capitation concept in privately owned facilities in order to offer these same kinds of benefits to other labor unions, trust funds and employers. We find that we can offer the same kind of program as the Teamsters have, with privately owned facilities, for less than $13 per family per month. This is for comprehensive preventive care with no deductibles, no maximum, and only very limited copayments for certain services. I would commend this notion to your attention.

In summary, for this capitation program, the dentists are at risk, which is the key to this concept, and only necessary care is done. The program is monitored in two ways to prevent undertreatment:
1. We are very careful in selecting who comes into the program by looking at the kind of care that the dentist provides.
2. We review their treatment records to see whether they have provided good care (follow-up care and the like) and then do ongoing monitoring by reviewing records and keeping statistics of the kinds of services that were done.

This concept is now being looked at, interestingly, by a number of major carriers as an alternative to their traditional program.

The Bottom Line

There is not the same freedom of choice if you own your own facility or if you have a capitation program as compared to more traditional approaches. It has been our experience that to the extent that a member is able to look at the bottom line, where those out-of-pocket costs are coming from, if he can see a program with good care and no out-of-pocket costs, he is going to make the decision to seek his care on that basis. The freedom of choice issue has not been the factor at all. The other way that we have dealt with this, frankly, is by offering this program on a dual choice basis, so that the member can make the decision to come into the closed panel program or stay on the open panel program. There is a benefit differential, because if he is on the open panel he may have a similar scope of benefits but he will also have a considerably greater amount of out-of-pocket costs.

Conclusion

That is basically what I would like to share with you. I hope it has not been too elementary for those of you who have had dental programs for some time—I hope you can understand my rationale in going through the different kinds of benefits and basic concepts. It is my feeling that with this kind of knowledge, we can make better decisions about the kind of dental benefit programs that we have and enable them to be more effective, more efficient, and certainly more cost-effective.

COB, Subrogation and Hospital Audits: A Means to Cost Control

BY DOUGLAS F. MATOOK

Introduction

The cost of health care has been escalating at a very rapid pace. Since 1965, the national expenditures for health care have increased by $167.1 billion (1965 expenditures of $38.9 billion vs. 1979 expenditures of $206 billion).

Cost control or cost containment refers to the reduction of volume and use of services or facilities from the medical care economy. To have an impact on the nation's health care economy, cost control efforts will require government legislation to regulate and restrict the health care system as it exists today. This is not likely to occur in the near future.

However, there are steps that each of us can take to ensure that cost controls are being utilized for the benefit of our plans. The methods and concepts which are described herein provide you with information on cost containment considerations for your plan. If these methods and concepts are implemented and administered aggressively, the result will be of benefit to your participants and plan.

Coordination of Benefits

Coordination of benefits (COB) is a method of determining the amount payable when a claimant is covered under two or more group health plans. The objective of the coordination of benefits provision is to pay benefits with the result that the claimant is not confronted with any "out-of-pocket" expense for his allowable medical expenses. The present COB guidelines used by most insurance carriers and self-insured or self-funded plans are derived from the advent of non-duplication of benefit provisions which were applied to major medical coverages. Non-duplication of benefits worked similar to the present coordination of benefits provision. However, non-duplication was not standardized throughout the industry, and had a number of drawbacks.

Mr. Matook is vice president of benefit operations, Kelly & Associates, Inc., in Chicago. He is responsible for the firm's benefit processing systems, including formulation and implementation of all procedures and documentation of administrative policy. Formerly, he was national account representative for the National Association of Blue Shield Plans. Mr. Matook received his B.A. degree from Southern Illinois University, has taken selected business courses at Northwestern University and Triton College, and has completed courses of both the Health Insurance Association of America (HIAA) and Life Offices Management Association (LOMA) programs. Mr. Matook has spoken at previous Foundation educational programs.

The present coordination of benefits provisions which almost all plans have implemented resulted from insurance companies getting together with the National Association of Insurance Commissioners to establish guidelines in the early and late '60s. The cost incentive for COB was to eliminate overutilization of group health benefits, with the realization that increasingly both husband and wife were employed and both were obtaining coverage through their employment. Additionally, the increased benefits available through union-negotiated plans provided increased benefit allowances that could encourage claimants to profiteer by overutilization of their plans when two or more group plans were involved. Another reason for the adoption and standardization of the coordination of benefits provisions by insurance carriers was to contain costs for their clients, and yet be fair in the administration of benefits. Unnecessary utilization caused premium increases which disturbed state insurance commissioners.

Coordination of benefits does not usually apply to individual plans. The reason is that with individual policies, it is very difficult to obtain the information necessary to coordinate benefits. This causes unnecessary delays in the processing of those claims. Also, most state insurance commissioners disapproved of COB between group and individual plans.

Most union-negotiated plans, though at one time derived by and through insurance companies, were reluctant to adopt a COB provision, since the purpose of their insurance was to provide maximum coverage for their members and not to restrict coverage or to play insurance company "games." However, as time progressed, inflationary factors and increased medical costs necessitated cost containment in their health plans. This had to be realized due to the obvious financial impact that these plans were encountering. If a limitation or cost containment provision such as coordination of benefits were in effect, these plans would in fact have saved a great deal of money.

Definitions of Commonly Used COB Terms

Some definitions which are used in the coordination of benefits provision in the typical plan description are listed below.
1. *Plan:* The term "plan" is defined as "all types of group health coverage." Also, the term "plan" may include Part A and Part B of Medicare, which are the hospital and surgical benefit coverages of Medicare. (The definition of plan may also include dental and vision coverages.)
2. *This plan:* As used specifically, refers to the hospital and medical expense benefit provided under the basic and major medical coverage (includes dental and vision coverage) of a plan that provides the benefits subject to coordination of benefits.
3. *Benefit credit:* This is the amount of benefits *not* paid by the secondary carrier which is placed in reserve for the claimant for possible use on a later claim during a calendar year (or specified period as shown in the plan).
4. *Claim determination period:* A period of time such as a calendar year (beginning January 1 and ending at midnight December 31 of the same calendar year) or benefit period as may be defined in the plan.
5. *Primary carrier:* This is the plan which pays its full normal benefit first without regard to any other coverage.
6. *Secondary carrier:* This is the plan which may reduce its normal amount payable so that the total paid by both plans will not exceed 100% of the claimant's total allowable medical expense incurred.
7. *Normal benefits:* This is the total amount payable under the terms of a plan in the absence of a coordination of benefits provision.
8. *Allowable expense:* This is any necessary, usual and reasonable item of expense which is covered in whole or in part by at least one of the plans covering the claimant.

Order of Benefit Determination— Primary vs. Secondary Carrier

The following rules are used in determining which carrier or plan is "primary" (pays its normal benefits) and which is "secondary" (pays balance of allowable expense incurred) when both (or all) plans contain coordination of benefits.
1. The plan covering the claimant as an employee of the employer is the primary carrier, while the plan covering the claimant as a dependent of a covered employee is the secondary carrier.
2. The plan covering the dependent children of a male employee is the primary carrier when the claim is on the dependent child.
3. If the above rules fail to determine the primary carrier, then the plan which has covered the claimant for the longest period of time will be the primary carrier. In determining the length of time an employee has been covered under a plan, the effective date of coverage is the first day an employee and his dependents are entitled to benefit consideration through the eligibility rules of the plan.
   Note:
   a. In determining the length of time an individual has been covered under a given plan, two successive plans of a given group shall be deemed to be one continuous plan, so long as the claimant concerned was eligible for coverage within 24 hours after the prior plan terminated. Thus, neither a change in

the amount or scope of benefits provided by a plan, a change in the carrier insuring the plan, nor a change from one type of plan to another (e.g., single employer to multiple employer plan, or vice versa, or single employer to a Taft-Hartley welfare plan) would constitute the start of a new plan for purposes of this guideline.

b. If a claimant's effective date of coverage under a given plan is subsequent to the date the carrier first contracted to provide the plan for the group concerned, then in the absence of specific information to the contrary, the plan shall assume, for purposes of this guideline, that the claimant's length of time covered under the plan shall be measured from the claimant's effective date of coverage.

If a claimant's effective date of coverage under a given plan is the same as the date the carrier first contracted to provide the plan for the group, then the carrier shall request the group concerned to furnish the date the claimant first became covered under the earliest of any prior plans the group may have had. If such date is not readily available, the date the claimant first became a member of the group shall be used as the date from which to determine the length of time his coverage under the plan has been in force.

Note: If the other plan or plans involved do not have a coordination of benefits or similar provision, they are automatically the primary plan in every claim situation.

Examples in Determining Primary and Secondary Carrier

The following are four examples which explain the preceding rules for the determination of primary and secondary carrier. These plans contain coordination of benefits provisions.

Example 1. Male employee covered under a welfare trust fund, whose spouse is employed by ABC Manufacturing Company.

Claim on male employee:
   Primary—Welfare Trust Fund
   Secondary—ABC Manufacturing Company
Claim on wife:
   Primary—ABC Manufacturing Company
   Secondary—Welfare Trust Fund
Claim on dependent child:
   Primary—Welfare Trust Fund
   Secondary—ABC Manufacturing Company.

Example 2. Female employee covered under a welfare trust fund, whose spouse is employed by ABC Manufacturing Company.

Claim on female employee:
   Primary—Welfare Trust Fund
   Secondary—ABC Manufacturing Company
Claim on husband:
   Primary—ABC Manufacturing Company
   Secondary—Welfare Trust Fund
Claim on dependent child:
   Primary—ABC Manufacturing Company
   Secondary—Welfare Trust Fund.

Example 3. Male employee covered simultaneously under two plans, Welfare Trust Fund A and Welfare Fund B, whose spouse is not covered under any other group plan. Effective date of Welfare Trust Fund A is July 1, 1977. Effective date of Welfare Fund B is March 1, 1978. Claim is incurred in May 1978. Since the effective date of Welfare Trust Fund A predates Welfare Fund B's effective date, the Welfare Trust Fund A is the primary carrier while Welfare Fund B is the secondary carrier.

Claim on male employee:
   Primary—Welfare Trust Fund A
   Secondary—Welfare Fund B
Claim on wife:
   Primary—Welfare Trust Fund A
   Secondary—Welfare Fund B
Claim on dependent child:
   Primary—Welfare Trust Fund A
   Secondary—Welfare Fund B.

If the effective dates were reversed, Welfare Fund B would be primary and Welfare Trust Fund A would be secondary.

Example 4. Male employee covered simultaneously under Welfare Trust Fund A and another fund, Welfare Fund B; spouse is employed by ABC Manufacturing Company. Effective date of Welfare Trust Fund A is July 1, 1977. Effective date of Welfare Fund B is March 1, 1978. Claim is incurred in May 1978. Since the effective date of Welfare Trust Fund A predates Welfare Fund B's effective date, Welfare Trust Fund A is the primary carrier while Welfare Fund B is the secondary carrier.

Claim on male employee:
   Primary—Welfare Trust Fund A
   Secondary—Welfare Fund B
   Tertiary—ABC Manufacturing Company
Claim on wife:
   Primary—ABC Manufacturing Company
   Secondary—Welfare Trust Fund A
   Tertiary—Welfare Fund B

Claim on dependent child:
> Primary—Welfare Trust Fund A
> Secondary—Welfare Fund B
> Tertiary—ABC Manufacturing Company.

If the effective dates were reversed, the positions of Welfare Trust Fund A and Welfare Fund B would be reversed.

Other Considerations

Benefit Credits. This is the amount of normal benefits *not* paid by the secondary carrier, which is placed in a benefit credit bank for the claimant. If the regular benefits of both plans do not equal 100% of the allowable expense for a later claim which is incurred in the same calendar year (or benefit period), the secondary carrier can make up the difference by withdrawing the amount needed to equal 100% of the allowable expenses from the claimant's COB credit bank. COB benefit credits are determined by the expenses incurred on a calendar year basis, and can be used only for expenses incurred during the same calendar year. Thus, on January 1 of every calendar year the claimant's benefit credit returns to zero, regardless of how much the benefit credit was on December 31.

Obtaining Information Concerning Other Coverage. When it becomes necessary to contact another plan for information concerning other coverage, a duplicate coverage inquiry is forwarded to the other plan or carrier. Most insurance companies and other plans will provide information concerning COB without a written authorization from the claimant. However, sometimes the other plan or carrier cannot release these data without a written authorization. When this happens, the "authorization to release," a part of their claim form which is signed by the employee and claimant, is photocopied and sent to the other plan or carrier, along with a completed duplicate coverage inquiry.

Right of Recovery. If an overpayment has been made under the COB provision, the plan or carrier has the right to attempt to recover the overpayment from any person to whom the payments were made, or from any insurance company or organization which owes benefits.

Administrative Processing of COB Claims

Is There Other Coverage? The following indicates some of the areas which the claims office should check to determine if there is a possibility of other group coverage.

1. The claim form is checked to see if any other coverage is indicated by the claimant or the attending physician. If so, a duplicate coverage inquiry is sent to the other plan (*see* Appendix B).
2. If the claim form indicates that the spouse is employed, but no other coverage is indicated, the claims office should contact the spouse's employer for insurance information. If there is no other coverage, the claim may be processed in the normal manner. If there is other coverage, the duplicate coverage inquiry is sent to the other plan.
3. If the claim form does not indicate that the spouse is employed, but prior claims history does so indicate or other indications in the claim submitted reflect a possibility of other coverage, a spouse letter asking for information on the other member should be submitted.
4. In addition to the regular claim form, the hospital admission form is checked for an indication of other group coverage.

Whenever feasible, attempts should be made to obtain the coordination of benefits information by phone in order to speed processing of the claim.

In addition to the obvious answers shown on the claim form, there are several other ways in which a claims office may become aware of other group coverage. The following are examples.

1. *Large hospital bills for which benefits are not assigned to the hospital.* Most hospitals require either full payment of the bill or an assignment of benefits before the patient is released. Few people can pay large hospital bills in full. The lack of an assignment of benefits may indicate that an assignment was taken on benefits from another plan. Also, most hospitals now indicate the name of the patient's insurance plan on the bill. If a name other than your plan is listed, the possibility of other group coverage should be investigated by the claims department.
2. *Duplicate copies of the medical expense bill.* Duplicate copies of the medical bills can be an indication that the originals are being submitted to another carrier or plan. A letter should be sent to the member asking for the originals; return of the copies will be made once the originals are received.

Payment of Claims. When a duplicate coverage inquiry is returned to the claims office with all the necessary information, the amount of benefits due under the plan can be determined. If there is no other group coverage or if your plan is the primary carrier, payment is made in the normal manner. However, if your plan is the secondary carrier, the benefits payable are determined in the following manner:

1. The total allowable medical expense is computed. This is the reasonable charge for all necessary medical services and supplies which are covered under your plan or the other plan.
2. The amount paid by the other plan is subtracted from the amount of total allowable expense. The amount remaining represents the maximum payable by your plan.
3. The normal benefits provided under your plan should be computed as though no other coverage is involved.
4. If the amount remaining in Step 2 is less than the regular benefits payable under your plan (Step 3), the amount remaining is paid. The excess of the normal benefits then is applied to the benefit credit bank.
5. If the amount remaining in Step 2 is greater than the normal benefits of your plan, the difference can be taken from the benefit credit bank, if a credit exists. If no credit exists, the maximum payable is the normal benefit payable under the plan.

How COB Works

The following is an example of a claim submitted which will reflect different COB situations.

Synopsis of Charges

From September 1, 1979, through September 3, 1979.

St. Elizabeth Hospital	
3 days in-hospital room and board	$ 390.00
In-hospital miscellaneous expense	345.00
Total in-hospital bill	735.00
North Suburban Surgeons	
Surgery performed on September 1, 1979	300.00
Anesthesiology Associates	
Anesthesiologist fee during surgery	190.00
Total charges	$1,225.00

Note: Refer to the first Exhibit in Appendix A, which reflects a duplicate coverage inquiry being sent to the ABC Manufacturing Company.

Example 1: Assume the Plan A Trust Fund is the secondary carrier and ABC Manufacturing Company is the primary carrier. (Refer to Exhibit 2, Appendix A.)

Total amount of allowable expense	$1,225.00
ABC Manufacturing Company as primary carrier paid	745.00
Plan A Trust Fund normal benefits	935.00

Payment under Plan A Trust Fund would be as follows (Exhibits 3 and 4, Appendix A):

Allowable expense	$1,225.00
Paid by ABC Manufacturing Company	745.00
Amount payable by Plan A Trust Fund	480.00

Thus the amount paid by ABC Manufacturing and Plan A Trust Fund will be 100% of the expense incurred by this claim. To determine the amount of benefit credit, the following is calculated (Exhibits 3 and 4).

Plan A Trust Fund benefits	$935.00
Amount payable by Plan A Trust Fund after COB	480.00
Amount of benefit credit	$455.00

Example 2: When the Plan A Trust Fund is the primary carrier, benefits will be paid in a normal manner without any reference to COB. However, what if the amount paid by both carriers does not equal 100% of the total allowable expense? Here, Plan A is the secondary carrier. (Refer to Exhibits 5, 6 and 7.)

Total amount of allowable expense	$1,225.00
ABC Manufacturing as primary carrier paid	200.00
Plan A Trust Fund normal benefits	935.00
Result:	
Paid by ABC Manufacturing Company	$ 200.00
Paid by Plan A Trust Fund	935.00
Total amount payable does not equal 100% of expense incurred	$1,135.00

Note: The result is that $90.00 of incurred expense is not covered, which the member must assume.

If an unpaid amount of allowable expenses does not exist after coordination between two or more carriers, then the following rules would apply:

Rule I: If there are no benefit credits available, Plan A Trust Fund only pays up to its normal benefits, as if there was no other coverage.

Rule II: If there are benefit credits available, the Plan A Trust Fund will use whatever is available up to an amount that will equal 100% of the unreimbursed total allowable expense.

Result (refer to Exhibits 8 and 9):	
Paid by ABC Manufacturing Company	$ 200.00
Payable under Plan A's normal benefits	935.00
Amount taken from benefit credits	90.00
(Taken from basic benefit credits first.)	
100% of allowable expense	$1,225.00

Example of Actual COB Claims Payments

The following five examples of actual claims paid during the past year involve coordination of benefits. Three of these claims involved coordinating benefits with other welfare funds. One claim involves coordinating benefits with Medicare Part A, and the last example coordinates benefits with a single employer plan.

The examples also illustrate what would happen if a plan did not have a coordination of benefits provision: a plan without a COB provision would be the primary carrier in all cases, while the other plan would automatically be the secondary carrier. The exception to this is the example of the Medicare claim.

Case 1. A male employee initially became eligible under the Plan A Welfare Trust Fund on July 1, 1978. He also was covered under the Plan B Health and Welfare Fund. The claim was incurred in January 1978 on a dependent child. Since the employee was covered longer under Plan B, that fund was primary carrier while our Plan A Welfare Trust Fund was the secondary carrier. The claim was paid as follows:

Total amount of allowable expense	$19,261.35
Plan A Welfare Fund's normal benefit	18,980.15
Plan B Welfare Fund paid as primary carrier	16,920.08
Plan A Welfare Fund paid as secondary carrier	2,341.27
Total paid	$19,261.35
Plan A Fund's COB savings:	16,638.88

Without COB on Plan A, Plan A Welfare Trust Fund would have been the primary carrier and Plan B Welfare Fund would have been the secondary carrier. The claim then would have been paid as follows:

Total amount of allowable expense	$19,261.35
Plan A Welfare Trust Fund would have paid as primary carrier	18,980.15
Plan B Fund would have paid as secondary carrier	281.20
Total paid:	19,261.35
Plan A Fund's COB savings	0.00

Without a COB provision, our Plan A Welfare Trust Fund would have paid $16,638.88 more of a claim which should have been the responsibility of the Plan B Fund. In either case, the employee collects only 100% of the allowable expense, or $19,261.35.

Case 2. A male employee became eligible under Plan A Welfare Trust Fund on January 1, 1977. He also was covered under the Plan C Health and Welfare Fund since April 1975. The claim was incurred in June 1977 on a dependent child. Since the employee was covered longer under Plan C Welfare Fund, that fund was primary carrier while Plan A Welfare Fund was secondary carrier. The claim was paid as follows:

Total amount of allowable expense	$6,090.32
Plan A Welfare Fund's normal benefits	5,975.13
Plan C Fund paid as primary carrier	5,575.93
Plan A Welfare Fund paid as secondary carrier	514.39
Total paid:	$6,090.32
Plan A Fund's COB savings:	$5,460.74

Without COB, Plan A Welfare Trust Fund would have been the primary carrier and the Plan C Welfare Fund would have been the secondary carrier. The claim would have been paid as follows:

Total amount of allowable expense	$6,090.32
Plan A Welfare Trust Fund would have paid as primary carrier	5,975.13
Plan C Fund would have paid as secondary carrier	115.19
Total paid	$6,090.32
Plan A Fund's COB savings:	0.00

Without a COB provision, Plan A Welfare Trust Fund would have paid $5,460.74 more of a claim which should have been the responsibility of the Plan C Fund. In either case, the employee collects only 100% of the allowable expense, or $6,090.32.

Case 3. A female employee is covered under our Plan A Welfare Trust Fund. Her spouse is an ironworker covered under the Ironworkers St. Louis District Welfare Fund. The claim is on the husband. The Ironworkers Fund is primary carrier while our Plan A Welfare Trust Fund is the secondary carrier.

Total amount of allowable expense	$3,442.45
Plan A Welfare Fund's normal benefits	3,383.50
Ironworkers plan paid as primary carrier	3,303.50
Plan A Welfare Fund paid as secondary carrier	138.95
Total paid:	3,442.45
Plan A Fund's COB savings:	3,244.55

Without COB, Plan A Welfare Trust Fund would have been the primary carrier while the Ironworkers Fund would have been the secondary carrier. The claim would have been paid as follows:

Total amount of allowable expense	$3,442.45
Plan A Welfare Trust Fund would have paid as primary carrier	3,383.50
Ironworkers Fund would have paid as secondary carrier	58.95
Total paid:	3,442.45
Plan A Fund's COB savings:	0.00

Without COB, Plan A Welfare Trust Fund would have paid $3,244.55 more of a claim which should have been the responsibility of the Ironworkers Fund. In either case, the employee collected 100% of the allowable expense of $3,442.45.

Case 4. A male employee is covered under Plan A Welfare Trust Fund. His spouse is over 65 and covered under Medicare. Our Plan A coordinates benefits with Part A of Medicare only.

Total amount of allowable expense	$13,781.30
Plan A Welfare Fund's normal benefits	13,403.30
Medicare paid as primary carrier	12,604.90
Plan A Welfare Fund paid as secondary carrier	2,521.12
Total paid:	$15,126.02
Plan A Fund's COB savings:	10,882.18

Since our Plan A does not coordinate with Part B of Medicare, the employee received $1,344.72 more than the total expense. Without a COB provision with Part A of Medicare, this fund would pay in addition to Medicare:

Total amount of allowable expense	$13,781.30
Plan A Welfare Trust Fund would have paid as primary carrier	13,403.30
Medicare would have paid as secondary carrier	12,604.98
Total paid:	26,008.28
Plan A Fund's COB savings:	0.00

Without a COB provision with Part A of Medicare, the employee would have collected $26,008.28, which represents a "profit" of $12,226.98.

Case 5. A male employee is covered under Plan A Welfare Trust Fund. He has a working spouse covered under Sears' group plan. Since the claim is on the spouse, the Sears plan is primary while Plan A Welfare Trust Fund is secondary. The claim was paid as follows:

Total amount of allowable expense	$3,568.65
Plan A Welfare Fund's normal benefits	3,561.25
Sears plan as primary carrier	3,337.52
Plan A Welfare Fund paid as secondary carrier	231.13
Total paid:	3,568.65
Plan A Fund's COB savings:	3,330.12

Without COB, Plan A Welfare Trust Fund would have been primary carrier, while the Sears plan would have been secondary carrier. The claim would have been paid as follows:

Total amount of allowable expense	$3,568.65
Plan A Welfare Trust Fund would have paid as primary carrier	3,561.25
Sears would have paid as secondary carrier	7.40
Total paid:	3,568.65
Plan A Fund's COB savings:	0.00

Without COB, Plan A Welfare Trust Fund would have paid $3,330.12 more of a claim which should have been the responsibility of Sears' group plan. In either case, the employee collects 100% of the allowable expense, or $3,568.65.

Delays Encountered in COB Administration

Most of the delays that are encountered in the administration of COB are the result of misunderstandings and lack of communication between the employee and the fund office, or between insurance companies and the fund office. Some of the principal reasons for delays are listed below.

1. Insurance companies, and in particular Blue Cross/Blue Shield, are slow in responding to the duplicate coverage inquiries which are sent to them by the fund office. In many instances, it is necessary to followup with insurance companies a number of times in order to obtain the necessary information to complete processing the claim. It is important that a good pending system be developed and maintained for follow-up.
2. Many employees fail to furnish the claims office the required information on the claim form concerning the place of employment of their spouse, or they fail to answer the questions concerning the other group coverage. When this information is not received by the claims office, it may be necessary to write the employee several times before this information is obtained.
3. Many employees deliberately refuse to tell the claims office of other group coverage in the expectation of collecting all benefits from both plans in order to make a "profit." The claims office typically learns that there is other group coverage from either the hospital records or information submitted by the attending physician. Occasionally, the hospital returns a benefit check to the claims office with an accompanying letter which states that another insurance company or Blue Cross has already paid the bill.

Coordination of Benefits With Medicare

The procedure followed in administering coordination of benefits when Medicare is involved is as follows:

1. Medicare will always be in the primary position.
2. Our plan will always be in the secondary position.
3. Though the same procedure of coordinating expenses incurred will be followed, there will not be a benefit credit established.
4. The term applied to this method of coordinating benefits with Medicare is "carve out."

There are two methods of administering the carve-out approach. Method A is most commonly used and provides the least benefit to persons entitled to Medicare.

Example A:
- The allowable expense is determined.
- The plan's benefit allowance is determined.
- The Medicare benefit allowance is determined.
- The plan carves out its benefit allowance from the Medicare allowance.

Allowable surgical charge	$400.00
Medicare benefit allowance	300.00
Plan's benefit allowance	300.00

Since the Medicare benefit allowance is the same or more than the plan's allowance, nothing further is payable by the plan.

Carve-out Method B is a more liberal approach and provides more benefits to persons entitled to Medicare.

Example B:
- The allowable expense is determined.
- The plan's benefit allowance is determined.

- The Medicare benefit allowance is determined.
- The plan carves out the Medicare benefit allowance from the allowable expense.
- The remainder is considered up to the plan's benefit allowance.

Allowable surgical charge	$400.00
Medicare benefit allowance	300.00
Unpaid allowable expense	100.00*
Plan's benefit allowance	$300.00

*Unpaid expense is $100.00 paid by plan.

Note: Rule 3 still applies—No benefit credit is established even though a savings exists.

Revised Order of Benefit Determination

What has been stated previously is the standard approach utilized by most insurance carriers and plans since the adoption in the 1960s of a standard coordination of benefits procedure. In recent years, there have been some modifications to the COB procedure, based on the disintegration of the family structure through an increase of separations and divorces. The State of California, in their Ruling #197, provides some specifics relevant to certain changes which affected the order of benefit determination under coordination of benefits administration.

Those changes in California, which first became effective January 1, 1975, stated:
1. Mother/father—When the father and mother are legally separated or divorced, benefits of the plan which insures the children as dependents of the mother are payable before the benefits of the plan which insures the children as dependents of the father, unless evidence is submitted showing that the father has legal custody of the dependent children.
2. Stepfather/natural father—When the father and mother are divorced and the mother has remarried, benefits of the plan which insures the children as dependents of the stepfather are payable before benefits of the plan which insures the children as dependents of the natural father, unless evidence is submitted showing the natural father has legal custody of the dependent children.

The following year in California and effective February 6, 1976, the ruling included the following:

Mother/stepfather/natural father—When the father and mother are divorced, mother having legal custody of the children, mother is remarried, and the mother, stepfather and the natural father are being insured as employees, and they all have children covered as dependents, benefits of the plan insuring children as dependents of the mother are payable first, stepfather second and the natural father third.

Several years later in the State of California, namely June 1, 1978, a ruling by the California Insurance Commissioner amending Ruling #197 included the following:

When the father and mother are divorced, father having legal custody of the children, both mother and father are remarried, and the father, mother, stepfather and stepmother are insured as employees and they all have the children covered as dependents, benefits of the plan insuring the children as dependents of the father are payable first, stepmother second, natural mother third and stepfather fourth.

The logic behind this legislation which occurred first in California has been receiving acceptance in several other states by both insurance carriers and self-funded plans alike. The revised procedure for order of benefit determination, based on the California Insurance Commissioner's ruling, resulted in the following:
1. The plan covering the child as a dependent of the father will be primary and the plan covering the child as a dependent of the mother will be secondary. *Note:* This is the normal order of benefit determination under the standard approach to coordination of benefits, and was not altered from its original intent.
2. If the parents are divorced or legally separated and there is a court decree which establishes financial responsibility for medical, dental or other health care expenses for the child, the plan covering the parent who has that responsibility will be primary, and the plan covering the other parent will be secondary. *Note:* This revised procedure does not indicate a female or male designation, but only reflects on which parent has the responsibility.
3. In the absence of a court decree, the plan covering the parent who has custody of the

child will be primary, and the plan covering the other parent will be secondary. *Note:* Once again, there is no male/female gender approach—only the fact that the parent has custody.
4. In the absence of such a court decree, where the parent with custody of the child has remarried, the order of benefit determination is:
   A. The plan covering the parent who has custody,
   B. The plan of the spouse of the parent who has custody (i.e., the stepparent of the child), and
   C. The plan covering the parent without custody.

This revised procedure for order of benefit determination is by all intents and purposes a twist from the standard approach that has been used for many years. It is obvious that, based on the number of divorces and separations and the problems encountered with pursuing the natural father in the standard approach to the order of benefit determination, an ease of administration can be encountered by this approach. Once the determinations are made as to who is primary and secondary, the examples as to the administration and calculation of benefits are the same as was indicated in the standard approaches to coordination of benefits.

Summation

Based on the information and examples in this report relevant to the actual administration of coordination of benefits, it is obvious that the standardization of guidelines for coordinating benefits has proven to be advantageous to claims administrators by:
1. Facilitating the COB claims determination of payments
2. Preventing overutilization of plan benefits
3. Upgrading total plan coverage without a noticeable cost impact.

Some plans, as I have shown, have altered their COB administration methods, but the basic framework of the standard COB guidelines allows for this flexibility and still provides the advantages listed above. A key factor in obtaining the positive results of COB, in addition to avoiding the negative factor of claims processing delays (however the guidelines are modified), is to clearly convey the COB guidelines to the claims administrating unit. When the claims units are provided with easily understood methods as to following the guidelines, the administrator can be ensured that the COB guidelines will be implemented properly.

An example of providing these methods follows this summation. It is in the form of a procedural manual (Appendix B), which can be readily and easily referred to by the claims unit.

Subrogation

In a never-ending exploration to achieve more cost control, new ideas have come to light. The newest of these is subrogation.

Subrogation, as we know it, is a term primarily used by casualty companies which insure our automobiles and property. These casualty companies use subrogation to recoup expenses they have paid to their insureds when the accident causing the disability and medical expenses is the fault of another individual. The idea of subrogation for medical care plans has started to take hold due to the present health care economics and the expenditures each of us has experienced in administering these plans. Subrogation, unlike coordination of benefits, does not have a determination of who is in the primary or secondary position. If the liability for causing injury or illness can be identified, then subrogation can be applied to possibly recoup benefits paid.

Subrogation is a cost transference method. The definition of subrogation is, "to put in the place of another or to substitute." When it is adopted into the design of a plan, the procedures and screening to identify those types of claims for possible subrogation are very simple. Claims which involve accidental injuries due to third-party involvement, such as an automobile accident where an individual is hit by another individual; an injury, such as a fall, occurring on the property of a neighbor or business; or situations such as food poisoning due to dining in a restaurant, are very likely candidates for application of the subrogation provisions.

A claim, after being submitted and identified as a possible subrogation case, will require letters to be written to the participant, advising him of the subrogation provision as being part of the plan. A subrogation agreement, an example of which appears in Appendix C, must be signed and notarized by the participant and resubmitted to the claims office.

Upon resubmission of the subrogation agreement by the participant detailing how, when and where the accident occurred, the claim can be processed in the normal manner. Once the claim has been processed and benefits paid, all pertinent information (including the subrogation agreement, medical and/or disability worksheets and claims statement, etc.) should be copied and submitted to the fund's counsel for review and determination as to whether or not the plan can subrogate the benefits it has already paid. Fund counsel can usually determine after a very brief investigation whether or not subrogation will be utilized on each individual case.

Recoveries, which are in most cases very slow, should be handled by fund counsel in the name of the fund. The first year of the subrogation being integrated into a number of our plans, out of 5,000 claims, 82 were subrogated, and may have recoveries from third-party liabilities exceeding six figures. Actual claims where immediate recovery was made and/or benefits need not be processed (which we have experienced on four claims) saved the fund over $9,000 to date.

Subrogation is another entity that plans can take and utilize to their advantage. Other than coordination of benefits, subrogation will realize more benefit savings to a plan than the other methods previously considered.

It should be remembered that through subrogation we are recovering possible benefits already paid. Assuredness to the participants who receive benefits considerations will still be made on a timely basis. Subrogation does not interfere with the dollars and/or determinations of what our benefits are. This method will provide, in most cases, for the participant receiving not less than 100% of what the plan would normally have paid in the absence of such a provision.

Auditing of Hospital Bills

The alarming statistics documenting the rapid increase in the cost of health care are too well known to us. However, it is of interest to focus on the dollar expenditures for hospital care alone as a separate cost factor. A significant part of the nation's $206 billion health care expenditures in 1979 went to pay hospital bills. Expenditures for hospital care, including both inpatient and outpatient care in public and private hospitals, represents 40% of the total health care expenditures. This is an increase of 14% over 1978.

To measure the skyrocketing increase in hospital care costs, one can look at the base period of 1965. In that year, hospital care costs represented 34% of all national health care spending. This increase of 6% in the total health care expenditures devoted to hospital care is dramatized more clearly when one considers that in 1965 the total cost of hospital care was $13.6 billion compared to $82.4 billion in 1979.

Community hospitals account for 82% of the dollars spent for hospital care.

It should be noted that though the amount of inpatient stay costs increased by a total of 22% between 1966 and 1979, the average number of hospital stay days has declined since 1968. The paradox of decreasing hospital stay days and rapidly increasing hospitalization costs is explained by two factors. One is the drop of bed utilization—from an occupancy rate of 79% in 1969 to 74% in 1979, thus increasing overhead costs. The other factor is the tremendous growth in the "resource" applied to each day of the hospital stay. It is estimated that 42% of the increase in dollar costs in hospital stays is attributable to this factor, often referred to as "intensity" charges. These charges include, among other things, increased use of x-rays, laboratory tests, and other new and expensive kinds of services such as the CAT scan and other computerized equipment. It is this development of higher intensity charges that the hospital bill audit system seeks to monitor.

Everyone involved in the administration of providing hospital and medical care coverage has been searching for and experimenting with various methods of containing these costs. Yet, there is a simple and direct cost controlling measure: on-site audits of hospitals' bills.

The Audit: What It Is and What It is Not

On-site hospital bill audits are not performed for the purpose of determining whether or not the medical treatment was medically needed, proper or correct. No questions with respect to the surgical or medical procedures, type or amount of medication, tests, validity of diagnosis and success of treatment are raised.

The simple purpose of these audits is to determine if the insured actually received the services and products for which charges are being made. Secondly, the audit will show whether or not the insured's physician actually utilized the x-rays and lab tests performed in the patient's treatment. Thirdly, on combination workers' compensation and non-work-related cases, those bills can be broken down, so each party knows exactly what they are liable for. For example, a patient may enter the hospital with a WC injury—a broken leg—and while he is in the hospital, some other longstanding medical problem is attended to.

Why Audit Hospital Bills?

Most people hesitate to question their physician about the accuracy of his diagnosis and treatment of their ills and many people, even those involved in the business of operating health and welfare funds, carry this blind faith over into the area of the operation of the hospital in which the doctor works. We tend to think of the hospital staff and facilities as an extension of the doctor.

The fact is that audits of hospital bills over some time have shown that the average discrepancy or error in hospital billing, as compared to actual delivery of services and products, is about 5¼%. With an error rate of that magnitude in the total amount of hospital charges, one can readily see the dollars involved. Obviously, the numbers we are talking about are in the millions. It is apparent, that trustees of plans, acting in their fiduciary capacity, must take any necessary steps to prevent needless utilization of their plan assets where areas of overutilization can be identified. They owe it to their participants, as well as themselves, to determine if a program of hospital bill audits should be instituted.

What Causes Hospital Bill Errors?

The basic reason for the rate of error in hospital bills is not that hospital management is dishonest in any sense of the word, but that billing and accounting practices used in most hospitals lend themselves to billing errors.

The primary reason for the accumulation of errors is the practice of setting up charges on the patient bill at the point of issue of services and products, rather than at the point of use. In addition, most hospital accounting practices do not include a mechanism for crediting returns of unused products or services ordered, but not administered or performed. For example, a surgeon orders five units of matching blood product as a precaution for a surgical procedure and uses only two units. Since a charge is put through before the blood leaves the blood bank, the odds are very high that the bill will contain charges for the full five units.

Key Areas for Review. The greatest area of billing error is in the operation of the hospital pharmacy. Most pharmacies send several days' supply of ordered drugs and medications to the nursing station servicing the patient. Drugs are usually not sent out on a day by day basis. Frequent overcharges result. The doctor may change the medication or decrease dosage, or the patient may be discharged before he uses the entire supply sent to the floor for him. But the original charge for the supply sent from the pharmacy will, in most cases, appear on the bill.

Another area of common billing errors is in the hospital therapy departments such as inhalation therapy. Again, the problem is that charges for these services are made when the doctor orders them—not as they are administered. Again, it is not uncommon for the doctor to cancel these orders or discharge the patient before all the services are provided.

Lab tests and x-rays are yet another fertile field for error. In addition to the error-causing factors cited above, there is also the question of whether the attending doctor actually uses the x-rays and test results. For example, an x-ray or lab test may be performed in the afternoon of one day and the patient discharged by the doctor the following morning, without the doctor having seen these test results. In this situation there exists some confusion because, in many cases, these test results are read to the doctor by hospital staff over the telephone. The general rule is that if these items are not entered in the medical record, most hospitals will accept a ruling of discrepancy and agree they are not chargeable.

The Case of the Unused Filters. How hospital bill audits can work to save meaningful sums of money is exemplified in the case of the unused kidney dialysis machine filters. One of the major commercial carriers sent Republic Service Bureau to Anchorage, Alaska, to audit a very large hospital bill. The auditor found, among other errors, that the hospital had ordered a large supply of very expensive experimental filters to be used in the treatment of the claimant. However, the patient died after using only one of the filters. The billing, of course, included charges for the entire supply of filters, amounting to $5,000. When this was pointed out to the hospital, they gave a credit for the entire amount.

How Does It Work?

The audit is performed in the hospital where the billings originated.

First, the auditor lists each item charged on the bill which you sent him on audit worksheets, separating areas of charge by department (*see* Appendix D): He will have a separate audit sheet for pharmacy, another for the laboratory, and so forth.

Second, the auditor obtains a copy of the patient's medical record from the medical records department. Keep in mind that this record includes the floor chart in which every service provided to the patient is noted, including drugs, therapies, doctor visits and just about everything that happens to the patient during his stay. The auditor, at this step, compares the items listed on his audit sheets with the items shown on the medical records. This is the crux of the audit, and it is in this step that the discrepancies, with respect to services and products charged for and those actually received, will become apparent.

Third, the auditor proceeds to each department in the hospital which serves as a source of charges—the pharmacy, radiology, lab and so forth. The purpose of these visits is to obtain correct price information for each of the goods or services which have shown up as discrepancies and, of course, to be able to arrive at a dollar amount of the error.

Finally, the auditor takes the audit sheets to the patient accounts department and reviews his findings with the patient accounts manager. He leaves a copy of his audit with this department, and then mails a copy of his audit sheets with a summary of findings to you.

It is standard practice for the hospital patient accounts department to have 60 days in which to protest the auditor's findings. If the hospital contests any item (or all of the findings), they must provide documentation demonstrating that the discrepancies did not exist. Since a plan is liable only for payment of services and goods *actually used* by the claimant, the practice is to pay the hospital bill based on the audit. If the hospital is able to document further charges, they are paid later.

The cost savings possible are shown by the results we obtained for the year 1979. The hospital bills audited for that year averaged $16,000. The average discrepancy or error found by the audits averaged $738.00 per case. The average audit cost was $250.00 This resulted in a net average savings to the plan of $488.00 per case, or close to a 3:1 benefit/cost ratio. It can readily be seen that these average net savings can produce significant cost reductions in your hospital expense coverage.

Summation

This cost control method can result in a benefit to every plan, because it provides a claim control program which will reduce costly hospital billing errors and, hopefully, result in appreciable reduction of claims costs. Additionally, it is another means to control costs of your plan in an otherwise uncontrollable health care environment.

Appendix D provides sample forms and an actual case history of a claims audit which resulted in a definite savings to our plan.

Appendix A

Coordination of Benefits

Exhibit 1

INITIAL [X] SUBSEQUENT [ ]	MEDICAL EXPENSE INSURANCE DUPLICATE COVERAGE INQUIRY

THIS IDENTIFICATION SECTION MUST BE FULLY COMPLETED

NAME OF PATIENT: Mary	AGE: 30 — RELATIONSHIP TO OUR INSURED: Spouse

FROM: KELLY & ASSOCS., INC.

NAME AND ADDRESS OF OUR INSURED
NAME: John Doe   Zip – 60666
ADDRESS: 555 Arlington Ave., Glenview, IL

NAME AND ADDRESS OF OUR GROUP POLICYHOLDER OR INDIVIDUAL POLICY NUMBER:
RETAIL MEAT CUTTERS WELFARE FUND
P.O. BOX 11102
CHICAGO, ILLINOIS 60611

TO:
ABC Manufacturing
Employee Benefit
Claim Office

NAME OF YOUR INSURED	RELATIONSHIP TO PATIENT
Mary Doe	Self

NAME AND ADDRESS OF YOUR GROUP POLICYHOLDER OR INDIVIDUAL POLICY NUMBER
Mary Doe SS# 987-65-4321

NOTE TO RESPONDING COMPANY: Complete this form for (1) Group Only [X] (2) Group or Individual [ ] RETURN WITHIN ONE WEEK

INQUIRER	PLAN	RESPONDER
Basic [X] Supplemental Major Medical [X] Comprehensive Major Medical [ ] None [ ]	Coverage Identification	Basic [ ] Supplemental Major Medical [ ] Comprehensive Major Medical [ ] None [ ]
Group [X] Individual [ ] Other ___		Group [ ] Individual [ ] Other ___
Effective 1/1 19 79	DATE OF PATIENT'S COVERAGE	Effective ___ 19 ___
Basic [X] Supplemental Major Medical [X] Comprehensive Major Medical [ ] None [ ]	Coordination of Benefits Provision is in:	Basic [ ] Supplemental Major Medical [ ] Comprehensive Major Medical [ ] None [ ]
Calendar Year [X] Dates ___	Claim Determination Period	Calendar Year [ ] Dates ___
Order of Benefit Determination [X] Proration [ ] As a secondary carrier, retain deductible & coinsurance [ ]	Administer Coordination of Benefits By:	Order of Benefit Determination [ ] Proration [ ] As a secondary carrier, retain deductible & coinsurance [ ]

NOTE TO RESPONDING COMPANY: If you are secondary, complete the following only for that part of your coverage (1) which has no Coordination of Benefits, or (2) under which Coordination of Benefits is administered by proration (See Instructions No. 3 on reverse side)

(Show for all bills received)		(In absence of C.O.B.)		TYPE OF SERVICE	(Indicate by "x" if applicable)			(In absence of C.O.B.)	
Inclusive Dates	Amount Charged	Basic Benefits	Covered under Major Medical		Add'l Bills	No Bills Received	Not Covered	Basic Benefits	Covered under Major Medical
9/1–9/4	$390.00	$90.00	$300.00	Hospital R & B				$	$
9/1–9/4	345.00		345.00	Hospital Misc.					
9/1/79	300.00	60.00	240.00	Surgeon					
				Ass't Surgeon					
9/1/79	190.00	25.00	165.00	Anesthesiologist					
				Physician – Home					
				Office					
				Hospital					
				Ambulance					
				Nursing					
				Drugs					
	1,225.00								

CERTIFICATION—Were benefits certified to Hospital? YES [ ] NO [ ]
ASSIGNMENTS—Indicate with * in benefits column above and show amount paid.
Amount Paid ___ Type Service ___
$___
$___

TOTAL $175.00
TOTAL $1050.00
LESS: Deductible 100.00
     950.00
Coinsurance 80 %
         20 %
MAJOR MEDICAL PAYABLE $760.00

CERTIFICATION—Were benefits certified to Hospital? YES [ ] NO [ ]
ASSIGNMENTS—Indicate with * in benefits column above and show amount paid.
Amount Paid ___ Type Service ___
$___
$___

TOTAL $___
TOTAL $___
LESS: Deductible ___
Coinsurance ___ %
       ___ %
MAJOR MEDICAL PAYABLE $___

INQUIRING COMPANY (please print)
By ___
KELLY & ASSOCS., INC.
CLAIM DEPARTMENT
233 E. ERIE STREET
CHICAGO, ILLINOIS 60611
Date ___ Tel. 649-1200 Ext. ___

BASIC BENEFITS PAID $ Pending
MAJOR MEDICAL PAID $ Pending

RESPONDING COMPANY (please print)
By ___
Address (if different from that given at top left): ___
Date ___ Tel. ___

BASIC BENEFITS PAID $___
MAJOR MEDICAL PAID $___
IF PRORATE, PAYMENT BASED ON INQUIRER'S EXPENSES IS $___

GL-45256 REV. 11-72 PRINTED IN U.S.A. (DUP-1, 1968)   *Please read instructions on reverse side before completing this form*

(reverse side of Medical Expense Insurance Duplicate Coverage inquiry)

INSTRUCTIONS FOR THE INQUIRING COMPANY

1. Indicate if this is the Initial or a Subsequent inquiry by checking the appropriate box in the upper left corner (A Subsequent inquiry is used when additional bills or information are received. Do not check "Subsequent" if you are simply sending a follow-up on an Initial inquiry.)

2. Be sure to check the "Group Only" block in the "Note to Responding Company" if your Plan's Coordination of Benefits provision applies only to other Group coverages. This can save both you and the Responder much time. Check the "Group or Individual" block if your provision applies to both Group and Individual coverages.

3. Use the "TO" block to enter Responding Company's name and address. Then complete all identification in the upper right blocks. DO NOT SEND THE INQUIRY IF YOU DON'T KNOW THE OTHER POLICY-HOLDER'S FULL NAME AND LOCATION. The Responding Company can't help you if they can't fully identify their insured.

4. Complete all "INQUIRER'S" entries. You must fill out both your plan description and dollar amount entries, even if you believe you are secondary. (On a Subsequent inquiry, list only new expenses.) Be sure to complete the Inquiring Company identification block before mailing.

5. Send the original and one copy to the Responding Company, and keep one copy for your file.

REMARKS: Include any notes you feel may have a bearing on the claim, such as names of other insurers known, and any additional information for which there was insufficient room.

INSTRUCTIONS FOR THE RESPONDING COMPANY

Here are some time-savers:

1. If you have no coverage on the patient, check the "NONE" block as your Coverage Identification and return to Inquirer.

2. If the "Group Only" block is checked and you have only individual coverage, check the "Individual" block as your Coverage Identification, and return to Inquirer.

3. If you are the secondary carrier and have Coordination of Benefits on all your coverage for the patient, complete only the Responder's plan description section, and return to Inquirer.

4. If you can't identify the coverage for the patient, return to Inquirer and advise him of further identification needed.

5. If you haven't received a claim on the patient, hold the form for a period of no longer than one week. If you still don't have a claim by then, complete the Responder's plan description and the "No Bills Received" column, and return to Inquirer. BE SURE TO ADVISE THE INQUIRER IF YOU DO RECEIVE A CLAIM AT A LATER DATE.

REMARKS: Include any notes you feel may have a bearing on the claim, such as names of other insurers known, discrepancies between bills you have noted, and any additional information for which there was insufficient room.

PLEASE REMEMBER

When NONE of the time-savers apply, complete all applicable entries on the RESPONDER'S side of the form. ALWAYS complete the RESPONDING COMPANY identification at the bottom of the form before returning it to the Inquirer. (You do not need to repeat your address UNLESS it is different from the address appearing in the "TO" block at upper left.)

IF BILLS HAVE BEEN RECEIVED WHICH THE INQUIRING COMPANY HAS NOT SHOWN ON THE FORM, indicate by an "x" in the ADDITIONAL BILLS column and list below:

Type of Service	(Show all additional bills)		(In absence of C.O.B.)	
	Inclusive Dates	Amount Charged	Basic Benefits	Covered under Major Medical
		$	$	$

SPECIAL NOTES FOR INQUIRER AND RESPONDER

I. Show full pay or "first dollar" Comprehensive benefits as "Basic Benefits," and coinsured Comprehensive expenses as "Covered under Major Medical."

II. "Certification — were benefits certified to hospital" refers to certification on a HAP-4 or by any means a hospital considers to be a guarantee of benefits.

III. The phrase "Coordination of Benefits" (C.O.B.) refers not only to the Model Group Anti-Duplication provision, but also all other non-duplication contract provisions in use.

IV. Always include a prepaid return envelope with an inquiry.

V. Types of Service not preprinted in the column for that purpose, should always be typed or written in where space is provided.

GI-45256 (BACK)

Exhibit 2

MEDICAL EXPENSE INSURANCE DUPLICATE COVERAGE INQUIRY

INITIAL [X] SUBSEQUENT [ ]

THIS IDENTIFICATION SECTION MUST BE FULLY COMPLETED

FROM: KELLY & ASSOCS., INC.

NAME OF PATIENT	AGE	RELATIONSHIP TO OUR INSURED
Mary	30	Spouse

NAME AND ADDRESS OF OUR INSURED
NAME: John Doe   Zip - 60666
ADDRESS: 555 Arlington Ave., Glenview, IL

NAME AND ADDRESS OF OUR GROUP POLICYHOLDER OR INDIVIDUAL POLICY NUMBER

RETAIL MEAT CUTTERS WELFARE FUND
P.O. BOX 11102
CHICAGO, ILLINOIS 60611

TO:
ABC Manufacturing
Employee Benefit
Claim Office

NAME OF YOUR INSURED	RELATIONSHIP TO PATIENT
Mary Doe	Self

NAME AND ADDRESS OF YOUR GROUP POLICYHOLDER OR INDIVIDUAL POLICY NUMBER

Mary Doe SS# 987-65-4321

NOTE TO RESPONDING COMPANY: Complete this form for (1) Group Only [X] (2) Group or Individual [ ] RETURN WITHIN ONE WEEK

INQUIRER | PLAN | RESPONDER

Coverage Identification
- Inquirer: Basic [X] Supplemental Major Medical [X] Comprehensive Major Medical [ ] None [ ]
- Group [X] Individual [ ] Other ____
- Effective 1/1 19 79
- Responder: Basic [X] Supplemental Major Medical [ ] Comprehensive Major Medical [ ] None [ ]
- Group [X] Individual [ ] Other ____
- Effective 12/1 19 78

DATE OF PATIENT'S COVERAGE

Coordination of Benefits Provision is in:
- Inquirer: Basic [X] Supplemental Major Medical [X] Comprehensive Major Medical [ ] None [ ]
- Responder: Basic [X] Supplemental Major Medical [ ] Comprehensive Major Medical [ ] None [ ]

Claim Determination Period
- Inquirer: Calendar Year [X] Dates ____
- Responder: Calendar Year [X] Dates ____

Administer Coordination of Benefits By:
- Order of Benefit Determination [X] Proration [ ]
- As a secondary carrier, retain deductible & coinsurance [ ]
- Order of Benefit Determination [X] Proration [ ]
- As a secondary carrier, retain deductible & coinsurance [ ]

NOTE TO RESPONDING COMPANY: If you are secondary, complete the following only for that part of your coverage (1) which has no Coordination of Benefits, or (2) under which Coordination of Benefits is administered by proration (See Instructions No. 3 on reverse side)

Inclusive Dates	Amount Charged	Basic Benefits	Covered under Major Medical	TYPE OF SERVICE	Add'l Bills	No Bills Received	Not Covered	Basic Benefits	Covered under Major Medical
9/1-9/4	$390.00	$90.00	$300.00	Hospital R & B				$300.00	$
9/1-9/4	345.00		345.00	Hospital Misc.				345.00	
9/1/79	300.00	60.00	240.00	Surgeon				80.00	
				Ass't Surgeon					
9/1/79	190.00	25.00	165.00	Anesthesiologist				20.00	
				Physician – Home					
				Office					
				Hospital					
				Ambulance					
				Nursing					
				Drugs					
	1225.00								

CERTIFICATION – Were benefits certified to Hospital? YES [ ] NO [ ]

ASSIGNMENTS – Indicate with * in benefits column above and show amount paid.

Amount Paid	Type Service
$____	____
$____	____
$____	____

TOTAL $175.00   TOTAL $1050.00
LESS: Deductible 100.00
                  950.00
Coinsurance 80 %
             20 %
MAJOR MEDICAL PAYABLE $760.00

CERTIFICATION – Were benefits certified to Hospital? YES [ ] NO [ ]

ASSIGNMENTS – Indicate with * in benefits column above and show amount paid.

Amount Paid	Type Service
$645.00	Hospital
$80.00	Surgeon
$20.00	Anesth.

TOTAL $745.00   TOTAL $____
LESS: Deductible ____
Coinsurance ____ %
            ____ %
MAJOR MEDICAL PAYABLE $____

INQUIRING COMPANY (please print)
By ____
KELLY & ASSOCS., INC.
CLAIM DEPARTMENT
233 E. ERIE STREET
CHICAGO, ILLINOIS 60611
Date ____ Tel. 649-1200 Ext. ____

BASIC BENEFITS PAID $ Pending
MAJOR MEDICAL PAID $ Pending

RESPONDING COMPANY (please print)
By ____
Address (if different from that given at top left): ____
Date ____ Tel. ____

BASIC BENEFITS PAID $745.00
MAJOR MEDICAL PAID $____
IF PRORATE, PAYMENT BASED ON INQUIRER'S EXPENSES IS $____

GI-4525F REV. 11-72 PRINTED IN U.S.A. (DUP-1, 1968)

Please read instructions on reverse side before completing this form

Exhibit 3

COORDINATION OF BENEFITS
CALCULATION SHEET

Patient __Mary Doe__
Member __John Doe__
Group __Retail Meat Cutter__

Initial Payment ☒
Subsequent Payment ☐

Claim Determination Period __Calendar Year__

PART A — ALLOWABLE EXPENSE LESS PRIMARY BENEFITS

(1) Allowable Expenses not previously paid
(Line 10 previous calculation sheet for this Claim Det. Period) .... $ – 0 –

(2) Total Allowable Expense for this transaction .... $ 1225.00

(3) Total Allowable Expenses
(1) plus (2) .... $ 1225.00

(4) Primary Benefits paid or payable by other carrier .... $ 745.00

(5) Remainder (allowable expense less primary)
(3) minus (4) .... $ 480.00

PART B — SECONDARY BENEFITS

(6) Health & Welfare normal benefit
(for coverage which includes non-duplication provision) .... $ 935.00

(7) Benefit Credits from previous transactions
(Line 13 previous calculation sheet for this Claim Det. Period) .... $ – 0 –

(8) Total Health & Welfare benefit now available
(6) plus (7) .... $ 935.00

(9) Health & Welfare actual benefit (for coverage which includes non-duplication provision)
Lesser of (5) or (8) .... $ 480.00

(10) Allowable Expense not paid
(5) minus (9) .... $ – 0 –

PART C — BENEFIT CREDIT ACCUMULATION

(11) Benefit Credits from previous transactions .... $ – 0 –

(12) Benefit Credits from current transaction
(6) minus (9) .... $ 455.00

(13) Total Benefit Credits now available .... $ 455.00

Pay to: __Hospital, Surgeon, and Anesthesiologist__ .... $ 480.00

Remarks

Calculated by .... Checked .... Date ....

12R10/77

Exhibit 4

Retail meat cutter unions and employers joint Health and Welfare Fund for the Chicago area

Claim Base / Major Medical Worksheet

PREF.	SOCIAL SECURITY	DATE OF LOSS MO. DAY. YEAR	CLAIMANT NAME	CLMT CODE	AGE	CAUSE CODE	LOCAL UNION	N OR C	PLAN CODE	CONTROL NO.
R	123-45-6789	9/1/79	Mary	02	30	02	123	N	A	07799

EMPLOYEE NAME: John Doe ADDRESS: 555 Arlington Ave CITY: Glenview, STATE: Illinois ZIP: 60666

DRAFT AMT.	PAYEE I.D. #	Patient Code	DRAFT AMT.	PAYEE I.D. #	Patient Code
$ 90.00	St. Elizabeth Hospital		$ 220.00	No. Suburban Surgeons	

DRAFT AMT.	PAYEE I.D. #	Patient Code	DRAFT AMT.	PAYEE I.D. #	Patient Code
$ 170.00	Anesthesiology Assoc.		$		

Total Payable This Claim: $480.00

Type of Expense	Inclusive Dates	Benefit Code	Amount Charged	Basic Benefits	MM	Eligible MM Expense	Expenses Not Covered	See Comment # on Reverse
Hospital R & B 3 days	9/1-9/4	30	$390.00	$90.00		$300.00		
Hospital Misc.		31	345.00			345.00		
Hospital R & B days		30						
Hospital Misc.		31						
Surgery	9/1	50	300.00	60.00		240.00		
Surgery		50						
Anesthetist	9/1		190.00	25.00		165.00		
Dr.								
Dr.								
Rx Drugs		45						
Diagnostic X-Ray & Lab.		45						
TOTALS		TOTAL	$1225.00	$175.00		$1050.00		

Remarks

Major Medical Accumulations

PREVIOUSLY AVAILABLE	100.00	Deductible 1979
	950.00	Subtotal
	.80	Co. Ins. %
THIS TRANSACTION	760.00	M. M. Benefit
	935.00	Total Basic + M. M. BOX 1 PLUS BOX 2
BALANCE AVAILABLE	-455.00	C.O.B. Adj.
	480.00	Total Payable

Date MO / DAY / YEAR   CALC BY   W.S #

ROUTE COMPLETED FORM TO - D.P. COPY

104R8/78

Exhibit 5

MEDICAL EXPENSE INSURANCE DUPLICATE COVERAGE INQUIRY

INITIAL [X] SUBSEQUENT [ ]

THIS IDENTIFICATION SECTION MUST BE FULLY COMPLETED

FROM: **KELLY & ASSOCS., INC.**

NAME OF PATIENT: Mary | AGE: 30 | RELATIONSHIP TO OUR INSURED: Spouse

NAME AND ADDRESS OF OUR INSURED:
NAME: John Doe Zip - 60666
ADDRESS: 555 Arlington Ave., Glenview, IL

TO:
ABC Manufacturing
Employee Benefit
Claim Office

NAME AND ADDRESS OF OUR GROUP POLICYHOLDER OR INDIVIDUAL POLICY NUMBER:
RETAIL MEAT CUTTERS WELFARE FUND
P.O. BOX 11102
CHICAGO, ILLINOIS 60611

NAME OF YOUR INSURED: Mary | RELATIONSHIP TO PATIENT: Self

NAME AND ADDRESS OF YOUR GROUP POLICYHOLDER OR INDIVIDUAL POLICY NUMBER:
Mary Doe SS# 987-65-4321

NOTE TO RESPONDING COMPANY: Complete this form for (1) Group Only [ ] (2) Group or Individual [ ] RETURN WITHIN ONE WEEK

INQUIRER	PLAN	RESPONDER
Coverage Identification: Basic [X] Supplemental Major Medical [X] Comprehensive Major Medical [ ] None [ ] Group [X] Individual [ ] Other ___ Effective 1/1 19 79	Coverage Identification	Basic [X] Supplemental Major Medical [ ] Comprehensive Major Medical [ ] None [ ] Group [X] Individual [ ] Other ___ Effective 12/1 1978
Basic [X] Supplemental Major Medical [X] Comprehensive Major Medical [ ] None [ ] Calendar Year [X] Dates ___	DATE OF PATIENT'S COVERAGE / Coordination of Benefits Provision is in: / Claim Determination Period	Basic [X] Supplemental Major Medical [ ] Comprehensive Major Medical [ ] None [ ] Calendar Year [X] Dates ___
Order of Benefit Determination [X] Proration [ ] As a secondary carrier, retain deductible & coinsurance [ ]	Administer Coordination of Benefits By:	Order of Benefit Determination [X] Proration [ ] As a secondary carrier, retain deductible & coinsurance [ ]

NOTE TO RESPONDING COMPANY: If you are secondary, complete the following only for that part of your coverage (1) which has no Coordination of Benefits, or (2) under which Coordination of Benefits is administered by proration (See Instructions No. 3 on reverse side)

(Show for all bills received)		(In absence of C.O.B.)	TYPE OF SERVICE	(Indicate by "x" if applicable)			(In absence of C.O.B.)	
Inclusive Dates	Amount Charged	Basic Benefits	Covered under Major Medical		Add'l Bills	No Bills Received	Not Covered	Basic Benefits	Covered under Major Medical
9/1–9/4/79	$390.00	$90.00	$300.00	Hospital R & B				$50.00	
	345.00		345.00	Hospital Misc.				50.00	
9/1/79	300.00	60.00	240.00	Surgeon				75.00	
				Ass't Surgeon					
9/1/79	190.00	25.00	165.00	Anesthesiologist				25.00	
				Physician – Home					
				Office					
				Hospital					
				Ambulance					
				Nursing					
				Drugs					
	1225.00								

CERTIFICATION—Were benefits certified to Hospital? YES [ ] NO [ ]
ASSIGNMENTS—Indicate with * in benefits column above and show amount paid.
Amount Paid | Type Service
$___
$___
$___

TOTAL $175.00 | TOTAL $1050.00
LESS: Deductible 100.00
           950.00
Coinsurance 80 %
                 20 %
MAJOR MEDICAL PAYABLE $760.00
BASIC BENEFITS PAID $ Pending
MAJOR MEDICAL PAID $ Pending

INQUIRING COMPANY (please print)
By ___
KELLY & ASSOCS., INC.
CLAIM DEPARTMENT
233 E. ERIE STREET
CHICAGO, ILLINOIS 60611
Date ___ Tel. 649-1200
Ext. ___

CERTIFICATION—Were benefits certified to Hospital? YES [X] NO [ ]
ASSIGNMENTS—Indicate with * in benefits column above and show amount paid.
Amount Paid | Type Service
$100.00 | Hospital
  75.00 | Surgeon
  25.00 | Anesth.

TOTAL $200.00 | TOTAL $___
LESS: Deductible ___
Coinsurance ___ %
                       ___ %
MAJOR MEDICAL PAYABLE $___

RESPONDING COMPANY (please print)
By ___
Address (if different from that given at top left): ___
Date ___ Tel. ___

BASIC BENEFITS PAID $200.00
MAJOR MEDICAL PAID $___
IF PRORATE, PAYMENT BASED ON INQUIRER'S EXPENSES IS $___

Please read instructions on reverse side before completing this form

Exhibit 6

(*) NO BENEFIT CREDITS AVAILABLE

COORDINATION OF BENEFITS
CALCULATION SHEET

Patient __Mary Doe__
Member __John Doe__
Group __Retail Meat Cutters__
Claim Determination Period __Calendar Year__

Initial Payment [X]
Subsequent Payment [ ]

PART A — ALLOWABLE EXPENSE LESS PRIMARY BENEFITS

(1) Allowable Expenses not previously paid
(Line 10 previous calculation sheet for this Claim Det. Period) .... $ 0

(2) Total Allowable Expense for this transaction .... $ 1,225.00

(3) Total Allowable Expenses
(1) plus (2) .... $ 1,225.00

(4) Primary Benefits paid or payable by other carrier .... $ 200.00

(5) Remainder (allowable expense less primary)
(3) minus (4) .... $ 1,025.00

PART B — SECONDARY BENEFITS

(6) Health & Welfare normal benefit
(for coverage which includes non-duplication provision) .... $ 935.00

* (7) Benefit Credits from previous transactions
(Line 13 previous calculation sheet for this Claim Det. Period) .... $ 0

(8) Total Health & Welfare benefit now available
(6) plus (7) .... $ 935.00

(9) Health & Welfare actual benefit (for coverage which includes non-duplication provision)
Lesser of (5) or (8) .... $ 935.00

(10) Allowable Expense not paid
(5) minus (9) .... $ 90.00

PART C — BENEFIT CREDIT ACCUMULATION

(11) Benefit Credits from previous transactions .... $ 0

(12) Benefit Credits from current transaction
(6) minus (9) .... $ 0

(13) Total Benefit Credits now available .... $ 0

Pay to: __Hospital, Surgeon and Anesthesiologist__ $ 935.00

Remarks
Please Note: There is a balance of $90.00 due to the Anesthesiologist Associates which you must pay.

Calculated by .... Checked .... Date ....

64L12/77

Exhibit 7

Claim Base / Major Medical Worksheet

PREF	SOCIAL SECURITY	DATE OF LOSS MO. DAY / YEAR	CLAIMANT NAME	CLMT. CODE	AGE	CAUSE CODE	LOCAL UNION	N° OR 'C'	PLAN CODE	CONTROL NO.
R	123-45-6789	9/1/79	Mary	02	30	02	123	N	A	07800

EMPLOYEE NAME: John Doe
ADDRESS: 555 Arlington Avenue
CITY: Glenview, STATE: Illinois ZIP: 60666

DRAFT AMT	PAYEE I.D. #	Patient Code		DRAFT AMT	PAYEE I.D. #	Patient Code
$635.00	St. Elizabeth Hospital			$225.00	No. Suburban Surgeons	

DRAFT AMT	PAYEE I.D. #	Patient Code		DRAFT AMT	PAYEE I.D. #	Patient Code
$75.00	Anesthesiology Assoc.					

Total Payable This Claim: $935.00

Type of Expense	Inclusive Dates	Benefit Code	Amount Charged	Basic Benefits	MM EX	Eligible MM Expense	Expenses Not Covered
Hospital R & B 3 days	9/1-9/4	30	390.00	90.00		300.00	
Hospital Misc.		31	345.00			345.00	
Hospital R & B days		30					
Hospital Misc.		31					
Surgery	9/1	50	300.00	60.00		240.00	
Surgery		50					
Anesthetist	9/1		190.00	25.00		165.00	
Dr.							
Dr.							
Rx Drugs		45					
Diagnostic X-Ray & Lab.		45					

TOTALS TOTAL $1225.00   175.00   1050.00

Major Medical Accumulations

PREVIOUSLY AVAILABLE	100.00	Deductible 1979
	950.00	Subtotal
	80%	Co. Ins. %
THIS TRANSACTION	760.00	M. M. Benefit
	935.00	Total Basic + M. M. BOX 1 PLUS BOX 2
BALANCE AVAILABLE	0	C.O.B. Adj.
	935.00	Total Payable

Date: MO / DAY / YEAR   CALC BY   W.S.#

ROUTE COMPLETED FORM TO - D.P. COPY

Exhibit 8

(*) BENEFIT CREDITS AVAILABLE

**COORDINATION OF BENEFITS
CALCULATION SHEET**

Patient __Mary Doe__
Member __John Doe__
Group __Retail Meat Cutters__
Claim Determination Period __Calendar Year__

Initial Payment ☐
Subsequent Payment ☒

PART A — ALLOWABLE EXPENSE LESS PRIMARY BENEFITS

(1) Allowable Expenses not previously paid
(Line 10 previous calculation sheet for this Claim Det. Period) .... $ 0

(2) Total Allowable Expense for this transaction .... $ 1,225.00

(3) Total Allowable Expenses
(1) plus (2) .... $ 1,225.00

(4) Primary Benefits paid or payable by other carrier .... $ 200.00

(5) Remainder (allowable expense less primary)
(3) minus (4) .... $ 1,025.00

PART B — SECONDARY BENEFITS

(6) Health & Welfare normal benefit
(for coverage which includes non-duplication provision) .... $ 935.00

* (7) Benefit Credits from previous transactions
(Line 13 previous calculation sheet for this Claim Det. Period) .... $ 300.00

(8) Total Health & Welfare benefit now available
(6) plus (7) .... $ 1,235.00

(9) Health & Welfare actual benefit (for coverage which includes non-duplication provision)
Lesser of (5) or (8) .... $ 1,025.00

(10) Allowable Expense not paid
(5) minus (9) .... $ 0

PART C — BENEFIT CREDIT ACCUMULATION

(11) Benefit Credits from previous transactions .... $ 300.00

(12) Benefit Credits from current transaction
(6) minus (9) .... $ 90.00

(13) Total Benefit Credits now available .... $ 210.00

Pay to: __Hospital, Surgeon and Anesthesiologist__ .... $ 1,025.00
Remarks ....

Calculated by .... Checked .... Date ....

64L12/77

Exhibit 9

Claim Base / Major Medical Worksheet

PREF.	SOCIAL SECURITY	DATE OF LOSS MO. DAY YEAR	CLAIMANT NAME	CLMT CODE	AGE	CAUSE CODE	LOCAL UNION	N OR C	PLAN CODE	CONTROL NO.
R	123-45-6789	9/1/79	Mary	02	30	02	123	N	A	07801

EMPLOYEE NAME	ADDRESS	CITY	STATE	ZIP
John Doe	555 Arlington Ave.	Glenview, Illinois		60666

DRAFT AMT.	PAYEE I.D. #	Patient Code	DRAFT AMT.	PAYEE I.D. #	Patient Code
$635.00	St. Elizabeth Hospital		$225.00	North Suburban Surgeons	

DRAFT AMT.	PAYEE I.D. #	Patient Code	DRAFT AMT.	PAYEE I.D. #	Patient Code
$165.00	Anesthesiology Assoc.		$		

Total Payable This Claim: $1025.00

Type of Expense	Inclusive Dates	Benefit Code	Amount Charged	Basic Benefits	MMEX	Eligible MM Expense	Expenses Not Covered
Hospital R & B 3 days	9/1-9/4	30	390.00	90.00		300.00	
Hospital Misc.		31	345.00			345.00	
Hospital R & B days		30					
Hospital Misc.		31					
Surgery	9-1	50	300.00	60.00		240.00	
Surgery		50					
Anesthetist	9-1		190.00	25.00		165.00	
Dr.							
Dr.							
Rx Drugs		45					
Diagnostic X-Ray & Lab.		45					
TOTALS		**TOTAL**	1,225.00	175.00		1,050.00	

Major Medical Accumulations

PREVIOUSLY AVAILABLE	100.00	Deductible 1979
	950.00	Subtotal
	80	Co Ins %
THIS TRANSACTION	760.00	M. M. Benefit
	935.00	Total Basic + M.M. BOX 1 PLUS BOX 2
BALANCE AVAILABLE	+90.00	C.O.B. Adj.
	1,025.00	Total Payable

Date MO / DAY / YEAR CALC BY W.S. #

ROUTE COMPLETED FORM TO - D.P. COPY

Appendix B

Plan of Benefits Manual

CHAPTER 7 COORDINATION OF BENEFITS	PAGE: 1
	DATE: JANUARY 1, 1976

702.00 **COORDINATION OF BENEFITS**

The plan contains a coordination of benefits provision. This is a method of determining the amount payable under the plan so that the total amount paid by two or more group carriers, for the same claimant under a group plan will not exceed 100% of the total medical expense incurred.

One carrier, the primary carrier, will pay the normal benefits as provided in its plan, while the other carrier, referred to as the secondary carrier, will usually pay less than its regular plan benefits and only up to 100% of the total allowable expense incurred. The amount not paid by the secondary carrier will be applied to a benefit credit bank (See section 702.05) for possible use on later claims in the same calendar year.

702.0A   Order of Benefit Determination—Primary Versus Secondary Carrier

The following rules are to be used in determining which carrier is primary (pays its normal benefits) and which is secondary (pays balance of allowable expense incurred).

(1) If one plan does not have any coordination of benefits or double coverage exclusion, then that plan will always be the primary carrier, regardless of which covers the claimant as an individual.

(2) The plan covering the claimant as an individual is the primary carrier, while the plan covering the claimant as a dependent, is the secondary carrier.

(3) The plan covering the dependent children of a male employee is the primary carrier when the claim is on the dependent child.

(4) If all of these fail to determine the primary carrier, then the plan which has covered the claimant for the longest period (i.e., the earliest effective date) will be the primary carrier.

If the adjuster is still unable to determine the primary carrier, then the claim should be referred to the claim manager for evaluation.

Note: In determining the length of time an individual has been covered under a given plan, two successive plans of a given "group" shall be deemed to be one continuous plan so long as claimant became eligible for coverage within 24 hours after the prior plan terminated.

For instance, if we took over a group from another carrier, then the effective date for coordination of benefits purposes would be the date of the claimant's effective date under the previous carrier.

©Copyright, **KELLY & ASSOCIATES, INC.**

The only exception to the above noted rules would be for step-children. When a child is covered by the natural father and the step-father, it has been the industry practice to assume that the liability as primary carrier will rest with the natural father's insurer.

702.01　Definition of Coordination of Benefits Terms

Following are some general definitions which are used in the coordination of benefits provision. These definitions are only brief explanations to acquaint the adjuster with the terms. For a more in depth handling of these definitions, refer to the coordination of benefits provision in the plan.

(1) Plan: The term "plan" is defined as all types of group health insurance. Under no circumstances, will coordination of benefits be permitted with insurance purchased on an individual basis.

The term may also include franchise insurance which refers to health insurance issued under individual contracts to the employees of a common employer or association who agrees to collect and submit premiums to the insuring company.

In addition, the plan provides for coordination of benefits with government plans.

(2) This plan: The term specifically refers to the medical expense benefits provided by both basic and major medical under the plan.

(3) Benefit credit: This is the amount of plan benefits not paid by the secondary carrier and which is placed in reserve for possible use on a later claim.

(4) Claim determination period: This period begins on January 1, and ends at midnight on December 31. Thus, it is based on a calendar year. Any exception will be outlined in the plan.

(5) Primary carrier: This is the carrier which pays its normal benefits first and makes settlement without regard to any other group coverage.

(6) Secondary carrier: This is the carrier which may reduce its amount payable so that the total paid by both carriers will not exceed 100% of the claimant's total allowable medical expense incurred.

702.02　Definition of Normal Benefits

This is the total amount payable under the terms of a given plan in the absence of an anti-duplication or coordination of benefits clause.

702.03　Definition of Allowable Expense

This is any necessary, reasonable and customary item of expense, which is covered in whole or in part by at least one of the "plans" covering the claimant.

702.04　Determining Allowable Expense for Coordination of Benefits

Normally, allowable expense for coordination of benefits is determined on the same basis that reasonable charges are determined for the "usual and customary" and major medical plan. However, this creates an inequitable situation on smaller charges.

The following rules will apply in determining "allowable expense for coordination of benefits" only when there is a secondary carrier.

(1) Determine the "usual and customary" allowance by multiplying the applicable CRVS units by the appropriate area conversion factor.

(2) If this determination does not meet the charge, apply the following formula (but not to exceed the amount charged).

   (a) For reasonable charges up to and including $300.00, add $25.00 or 25% of the reasonable charge, whichever is greater.

   (b) For reasonable charges in excess of $300.00, add $75.00 or 10% of the reasonable charge, whichever is greater.

(3) If this determination still does not meet the charge, then it will be necessary to use the determination of "usual and customary" limit of the most liberal company.

The amount of allowable expense as secondary carrier should never exceed the amount determined by using the above noted formula.

702.05   Benefit Credit

The amount of normal benefits not paid by the secondary carrier is placed in a benefit credit bank for the claimant. If on a later claim, for expense incurred in the same calendar year, the regular plan benefits of both carriers do not equal 100% of the allowable expense, then the secondary carrier can make up the difference by withdrawing the amount needed to equal 100% of the allowable expense from the claimant's coordination of benefits credit bank.

Coordination of benefits credits are determined by the expenses incurred on a calendar year basis and can only be used for expense incurred during the same calendar year. Thus, on January 1 of every calendar year, the claimant's benefit credit returns to zero ($0), regardless of how much the benefit credit was on December 31.

702.06   Obtaining Information Concerning Other Coverage

When it becomes necessary to contact another carrier for information concerning other coverage, a duplicate coverage inquiry should be forwarded to the other carrier. If the information is not received from the other carrier in two weeks, a new form should be sent out.

(See section 703.06 for instructions on completing the duplicate coverage inquiry and section 703.03 for streamline procedures on handling coordination of benefits claims.)

Most insurance companies will provide information concerning coordination of benefits without a written authorization from the claimant. However, if the other plan cannot release this data without a written authorization then the following steps should be taken:

(1) Photocopy the "authorization to release" signed by the member and claimant on the front of the claim form.

(2) Attach this photocopy to a completed duplicate coverage inquiry form and forward to the other carrier.

(3) Based on the answer received, process the claim accordingly.

702.07 Facility of Payment

Whenever payments which should have been made under this plan in accordance with this provision have been made under any other plans, the Trustees shall have the right, exercisable alone and in its sole discretion, to pay over to any organizations making such other payments any amounts they shall determine to be warranted in order to satisfy the intent of this provision and amounts so paid shall be deemed to be benefits paid under this plan and, to the extent of such payments, the Trustees shall be fully discharged from liability under this plan.

702.08 Right of Recovery

Whenever payments have been made by the Trustees with respect to allowable expenses in a total amount, at any time in excess of the maximum amount of payment necessary at that time to satisfy the intent of this provision, the Trustees shall have the right to recover such payments, to the extent of such excess, from among one or more of the following, as the Trustees shall determine: any persons to or for or with respect to whom such payments were made, any insurance companies, any other organizations.

703.00 Administrative Processing of Coordination of Benefits Claims

Indicated below are some of the areas which the adjuster should check to determine if there is a possibility of other group coverage.

(1) Check the claim form to see if any other coverage is indicated by the claimant, the employer, or the attending physician. If so, then a duplicate coverage inquiry should be sent to the other carrier.

(2) If the claim form indicates that the spouse is employed, but no other coverage is indicated, it will be necessary to contact the spouse's employers. This is especially important when our member is a married female and the claim is for her husband or dependent children. The adjuster should send out an insurance inquiry to the husband's employer to determine if there is other coverage.

If there is no other coverage, then the claim may be processed in a normal manner. If there is other coverage, then a duplicate coverage inquiry should be sent to the other carrier.

(3) In addition to the regular claim form, the hospital admission form should be checked for an indication of other coverage.

Whenever feasible, an attempt should be made to obtain the coordination of benefits information by phone in order to speed processing of the claim.

703.01 Possible Indications of Other Insurance

In addition to the spaces provided on the claim form, there are a few other ways in which it can be determined whether there might be other group coverage. Following are a few examples of these "tip offs."

(1) Large hospital bills which are unassigned

Most hospitals require either full payment of the bill or an assignment of benefits before the patient is released. Few people can pay large hospital bills in full. The lack of an assignment may indicate that an assignment was taken on benefits from another carrier.

(2) Duplicate copies of medical expense bills

This may indicate that the original bills were submitted to another carrier.

(3) Other insurance indicated on a hospital bill

Many hospitals now indicate the name of the patient's insurance company on the bill. If a name other than the Fund's is listed, the possibility of other group coverage should be investigated.

These are just a few indications of other group coverage which the adjuster should be aware of. If there is a legitimate doubt as to the possibility of other coverage, a thorough check should be made before paying any benefit.

703.02 Payment of a Claim When Coordination of Benefits Is Involved

When the duplicate coverage inquiry is returned with all the necessary information, the amount of benefits due under the plan can then be determined. If there is no other group coverage or if the Fund is the primary carrier according to the order of determination rule, (See section 702.0A) then payment should be made as a normal claim.

However, if the Fund is the secondary carrier, benefits payable can be determined by using the coordination of benefits form. (See section 703.07 for instructions on completing this form.) The following steps should be used in determining the amount payable as the secondary carrier.

(1) Compute the normal benefits payable under the plan as though there were no other coverage involved.

(2) Next compute the total allowable expense. (That is the reasonable charge for all necessary medical service and supplies.)

(3) Then subtract the amount paid by the other carrier from the amount of total allowable expense.

(4) If the amount remaining is less than the regular benefits payable under the plan, then that amount remaining would be paid, with any excess of normal benefits applied to the "benefits credit."

(5) If the amount remaining at step number 4 is greater than the normal benefit payable, then the difference should then be taken from the benefit credit reserve if available. If no reserve exists, then the maximum payable would be the normal benefits payable under the plan.

703.03 Streamline Coordination of Benefits Procedures

The following procedures are to be used on claims involving other coverage when the total expense is less than $100.00.

(1) If other coverage is indicated, contact the other carrier immediately. If the other car-

rier is in the local area, every effort should be made to obtain the coordination of benefits information by phone. (For prolonged attempts, see section 703.04.)

(2) If no other coverage is indicated, but there is a strong possibility that there is other coverage, the adjuster should pay benefits and then send out inquiries to determine the possibility of other coverage.

If an attempt to obtain information concerning coordination of benefits extends for more than three weeks, the adjuster should follow the procedures outlined in section 703.04.

703.04   Prolonged Attempts in Obtaining Coordination of Benefits Information

Claims involving other insurance should never be held for more than three weeks. If at the end of that period it cannot be determined who is the primary and secondary carrier, the following procedures are to be used:

(1) Every attempt should be made to obtain the information by phone, even if it involves making long distance calls.

(2) Process the claim in the normal manner if it is on our member or a dependent child of our male member, unless it is known that the other carrier does not normally use coordination of benefits in their plans.

(3) If the claim is on a dependent spouse or dependent child of our female member, or if it is known that the other carrier does not normally use coordination of benefits in their contracts, assume that we are secondary and calculate benefits payable on the following basis:

   (a) Assume that the other plan is a comprehensive major medical policy with a $100 deductible and 80% reimbursement.

   (b) Determine the benefits that they would have paid based on (a).

   (c) Use the coordination of benefits form to determine our liability.

   (d) Notify the claimant as to how benefits have been determined and advise him that if the computation is not correct we will re-compute the claim upon submission of proof of the amount paid by the other carrier.

Any questions concerning the determination of benefits in this matter should be directed to the claim manager.

703.05   Assignments

If the Fund is the primary carrier, then all assignments must be honored in the normal manner.

If the Fund is the secondary carrier, then all assigned benefits must be honored up to the unreimbursed amount that the primary carrier did not pay.

703.06   Duplicate Coverage Inquiry

Following is a sample duplicate coverage inquiry which is to be used in requesting information concerning other group coverage. The form is self-explanatory.

703.07   Coordination of Benefits Form

Following is a sample form which we are presently using to determine the amount of benefits payable when the Fund is the secondary carrier. This form is self-explanatory and therefore step by step instructions appear unnecessary.

For settlement purposes, this form is to be made out in duplicate, with the original made part of the permanent claim file and the duplicate to the member.

703.08   Indicating Coordination of Benefits Deduction on an Explanation of Benefits Sheet

When deducting coordination of benefits from a payment sheet, code 90 should be used as indicated on the following example where the space is provided for coordination of benefits basic and coordination of benefits major medical in the payment "draft" column.

When adding an amount from the benefit credit reserve, code 91 is to be used in the same spaces as provided for deducting coordination of benefits.

703.09   Example of how Coordination of Benefits Works

As an example of how coordination of benefits works, let us assume that the Fund is the secondary carrier and Company X is the primary carrier.

Total Amount of Allowable Expense	$1,225.00
Company X as primary carrier paid	945.00
Fund's normal benefits	735.00

Payment under our plan would be as follows:

Allowable expense	$1,225.00
Paid by company X	- 945.00
Amount payable by the Fund	$ 280.00

Thus, the amount paid by company X and the Fund will be 100% of the expense incurred for this transaction. To determine the amount applied to the benefit credits, the following should be calculated:

Fund's normal benefits	$ 735.00
Amount payable by the Fund after COB	- 280.00
Amount to be applied to the benefit credits	$ 455.00

This is a simplified explanation of determining coordination of benefits payable as the secondary carrier.

When the Fund is the primary carrier, then benefits will be paid in a normal manner without any reference to coordination of benefits. (See section 702.0A for the rules determining primary and secondary carrier.)

When the amount paid by both carriers does not equal 100% of the total allowable expense, the following rules apply:

Total amount of allowable expense	$1,225.00
Company X as primary carrier paid	300.00
Fund's normal benefits	735.00

Thus,

Paid by company X	$ 300.00
Payable by the Fund	+ 735.00
Total amount payable does not equal 100% of expense incurred	$1,035.00

Rule I: If there are no benefit credits available, then the Fund will only pay up to its normal benefits as if there was no other insurance.

Rule II: If there are benefit credits available, then the Fund will use whatever is available up to an amount that will equal 100% of the unreimbursed total allowable expense.

Thus,

Paid by company X	$ 300.00
Payable under the Fund's normal benefits	735.00
Amount taken from benefit credits	+ 190.00
	$1,225.00

Any questions concerning the handling of coordination of benefits or double coverage should be directed to the claim manager.

Appendix C

Subrogation

Effective January 1, 1980, a subrogation provision has been added to the Plan. The subrogation provision provides that if the Fund makes payment for any expenses, and full or partial payment is made by any other source for those same expenses, the Fund is entitled to reimbursement of the monies that it has paid. This recovery by the Fund, however, cannot exceed the amount paid by the other source. The term "other source" includes, but is not limited to, other benefit plans, insurance company settlements, Workmen's Compensation payments or any other third party.

If legal action is instituted against the other source, the Fund is entitled to intervene and participate in that action. If a person fails, or refuses, to institute legal action, the Fund is entitled to do so in the name of the employee or the dependent.

Subrogation Agreement

A. To the extent that the Retail Meat Cutters Unions and Employers Joint Health and Welfare Fund for the Chicago Area ("Trust") shall have paid any money to or on behalf of an Employee, pursuant to the provisions of the Plan of Benefits provided by the Trust, because of loss of damage for which the employee may have a cause of action against a third party who caused this loss or damage, this Trust shall be subrogated to the extent of such payment to any and all recovery by the Employee, and such right shall be assigned to the Trust by the Employee as a condition of the payment of such money by the Trust.

B. In consideration of the payment, the undersigned Employee does hereby assign and subrogate to the Retail Meat Cutters Union and Employers Joint Health and Welfare Fund for the Chicago Area ("Trust") all of the rights, claims, interests, choses or things in action and action at law, to the extent of the amount paid by the Trust which the undersigned may have against any party, person, firm, or corporation, private or public, who may be liable, or may hereafter be adjudged liable, for the loss, and the undersigned authorizes and empowers the Retail Meat Cutters and Unions and Employers Joint Health and Welfare Fund for the Chicago Area ("Trust") to sue, compromise, or settle in the name of the undersigned or of the beneficiary of the undersigned, and said Retail Meat Cutters Union and Employers Health Joint Health and Welfare Fund for the Chicago Area ("Trust") is hereby fully substituted in the place of the undersigned and subrogated to all of the rights of the undersigned in the premises to the amount paid by the Trust.

The undersigned further agrees that the undersigned will execute any and all appeal bonds or other instruments in writing pertaining to any litigation arising out of losses herein above referred to, at the request of the Trust's representatives.

_____   Witnessed _____
Signature   Signature

_____
Social Security Number

_____
Date

Dear

The information which the Health and Welfare Fund has received together with your hospital and doctor bills, indicates that your injuries may have been caused by a third party against whom you may have a cause of action.

Your Health and Welfare Fund was created to provide you with medical care and to relieve you of the burden of paying for it. However, the cost for providing hospitalization and doctor care has risen so drastically that your Board of Trustees have adopted a policy requiring a third person who has caused you to incur medical expenses to reimburse the Health and Welfare Fund for the medical costs which it paid on your behalf.

The Health and Welfare Fund is not interested in depriving you of any rights you may have against such a third party and it is prepared to cooperate with you and any attorney you may retain in enforcing your claim.

However, it is necessary to carry out the rules of your plan of benefits and we request that you execute and return the enclosed subrogation agreement as well as the accident report in the envelope provided for your convenience. Upon receipt of the executed subrogation agreement and accident report, the Fund Office will proceed to process your claim for payment.

Obviously, if it should develop that you have no claim against a third person or that the claim cannot be enforced against the third party, for any reason, no effort will be made to seek reimbursement from you.

                              Very truly yours,

TO BE COMPLETED BY INSURED MEMBER

Answer all questions. Unanswered questions will delay benefit consideration until the missing information is obtained.

Member's Full Name: _____ Sex _____

Home Address: _____ City _____ State _____ Zip _____

Social Security Number: _____ Date of Birth _____

Member's Marital Status: ____ Single   ____ Divorced
                         ____ Married   ____ Widowed
                         ____ Separated

Employed by: _____ Occupation _____

Date of Employment: _____

Home telephone number: _____

Claim is made for: ____ Self ____ Spouse ____ Child

_____
Name of Disabled Person   Sex   D.O.B.

IF CLAIMANT WAS INJURED:

Date accident occurred: _____ Time _____

Was claimant at work when accident occurred ____ Yes ____ No

Name of claimant's employer _____

Detailed description of accident (use reverse side and tell how, when and where it occurred)

Type of insurance: Home ☐ Auto ☐

Policy # _____ Other _____

Your Insurance Carrier: _____

Other Party Liability Insurance Carrier: _____

Have you hired an attorney to represent you in this matter? ____ Yes ____ No

If yes, His (Her) name _____

    Telephone Number _____

If you have lost time from work, describe disability and indicate whether you have claimed or are claiming disability benefits.

_____

Retail meat cutter unions and employers joint Health and Welfare Fund for the Chicago area

SUBROGATION

CALCULATION SHEET

Patient __Christopher Doe__

Member __John Doe__

Group __RMC__

Initial Payment [X]
Subsequent Payment [ ]

Claim Determination Period __1980__

PART A — ALLOWABLE EXPENSE LESS PRIMARY BENEFITS

(1) Allowable Expenses not previously paid
(Line 10 previous calculation sheet for this Claim Det. Period) .... $ __-0-__

(2) Total Allowable Expense for this transaction .... $ __1598.44__

(3) Total Allowable Expenses
(1) plus (2) .... $ __1598.44__

(4) Primary Benefits paid or payable by other carrier .... $ __588.77__

(5) Remainder (allowable expense less primary)
(3) minus (4) .... $ __1009.67__

PART B — SECONDARY BENEFITS

(6) Health & Welfare normal benefit
(for coverage which includes non-duplication provision) .... $ __1404.75__

(7) Benefit Credits from previous transactions
(Line 13 previous calculation sheet for this Claim Det. Period) .... $ __-0-__

(8) Total Health & Welfare benefit now available
(6) plus (7) .... $ __1404.75__

(9) Health & Welfare actual benefit (for coverage which includes non-duplication provision)
Lesser of (5) or (8) .... $ __1009.67__

(10) Allowable Expense not paid
(5) minus (9) .... $ __-0-__

PART C — BENEFIT CREDIT ACCUMULATION

(11) Benefit Credits from previous transactions .... $ __-0-__

(12) Benefit Credits from current transaction
(6) minus (9) .... $ __395.08__

(13) Total Benefit Credits now available .... $ __395.08__

Pay to: $80.00 North Shore Medical Services $ __1009.67__
Remarks $95.04 American International Hospital
              $716.51 Victory Memorial Hospital
              $118.12 Florian R. Nykiel, M.D.

Calculated by __SCB__   Checked _____   Date __10/22/80__

12R

1980 Annual Conference 287

Retail meat cutter unions and employers joint Health and Welfare Fund for the Chicago area

Claim Base / Major Medical Worksheet

P. O. BOX 11102 • CHICAGO, ILLINOIS 60611 • (312) 649-1200

PREF	SOCIAL SECURITY	DATE OF LOSS MO/DAY/YEAR	CLAIMANT NAME	CLMT. CODE	AGE	CAUSE CODE	LOCAL UNION	N' OR 'C'	PLAN CODE	CONTROL NO.
R	123-45-6789	7/24/80	Christopher	03	16	01	546	N	M	22444

EMPLOYEE NAME: John Doe   ADDRESS: 321 E. Lane   CITY: Townville,   STATE: Illinois   ZIP: 60623

DRAFT AMT.	PAYEE I.D. #	Patient Code	DRAFT AMT.	PAYEE I.D. #	Patient Code
$80.00 FROM TO	North Shore Medical Services 1020 Glen Flora-Suite #103 Waukegan, Illinois 60085		$716.51 FROM 7 28 80 TO 7 30 80	Victory Memorial Hospital 1324 N. Sheridan Road Waukegan, Illinois 60085	
CD DAYS AMT	CODE AMT 60 128.00	CODE AMT 93 -48.00	CD DAYS AMT 30 2 260.00	CODE AMT 31 304.96	CODE AMT 60 151.55
$95.04 FROM TO	American International Hosp. Shiloh Boulevard Zion, Illinois 60099		$118.12 FROM TO	Nykiel, Florian R., M.D. 600 Greenwood Avenue Waukegan, Illinois 60085	
CD DAYS AMT	CODE AMT 31 95.04	CODE AMT	CD DAYS AMT 50 20.00	CODE AMT 40 150.00 60 295.20	CODE AMT 93 -347.08

Total Payable This Claim: **$1009.67**

Type of Expense	Inclusive Dates	Benefit Code	Amount Charged	Basic Benefits	M/K	Eligible MM Expense	Expenses Not Covered
Hospital R & B days		30					
Hospital Misc. E.R.	7/24/80	31	95.04	95.04			
Hospital R & B 2 days	7/28-7/30	30	260.00	260.00			
Hospital Misc.	7/28-7/30	31	544.40	304.96		239.44	
Surgery	7/29/80	50	435.00	20.00		265.00	
Surgery	"	50	"	150.00			
Anesthetist	7/29/80		160.00			160.00	
Dr. Nykiel	7/28-7/29		80.00			80.00	
Dr. Shih	7/28/80		18.00			18.00	
Rx Drugs		65					
Diagnostic X-Ray & Lab.		45					
No. Ill. Rad. Ass.	7/28/80		6.00			6.00	

TOTALS — TOTAL 1598.44 830.00 768.44

Major Medical Accumulations

PREVIOUSLY AVAILABLE: 100,000.00
THIS TRANSACTION: 179.67
BALANCE AVAILABLE: 99,820.33

50.00	Deductible 1980
718.44	Subtotal
80%	Co./Inc. % 20%
574.75	M. M. Benefit
1404.75	Total Basic + M. M. (BOX 1 PLUS BOX 2)
-395.08	Subrogation
1009.67	Total Payable

Date: 10/22/80   CALC. BY: SCB   W.S. # 1

ROUTE COMPLETED FORM TO - D.P. COPY

104R

Synopsis

Total amount of allowable expense $1,598.44
Casualty company payment 588.77
The plan's normal benefit 1,404.75

Payment made by the plan would be as follows:
    Allowable expense $1,598.44
    Casualty company payment 588.77
    Amount payable by the plan 1,009.67

Thus the amount paid by the casualty company and the plan will be 100% of the expense incurred for this claim.

To determine the amount of benefit credit, the following is calculated:
    The plan's normal benefit $1,404.75
    The amount payable after the casualty company payment 1,009.67
    Amount of benefit credit 395.08

Appendix D

Audit of Hospital Bill

Benefits

- Hospital audits on a systematic basis within your claim control program will reduce costly hospital billing errors. This results in an appreciable reduction in claims costs.
- Systematic audits of hospital bills place hospitals on notice to improve their billing systems and the accuracy of such bills will improve.
- You can substantiate that you are doing something positive to help control the double digit inflation in hospital care.
- This can result in a savings by uncovering discrepancies in Medicare credit reported.

Recommendations
(Situations to Investigate)

Experience has provided us with improved methods of determining likely prospects for audit.

A. We suggest use of this service on bills of $5,000 or more, and when room and board charges are 50% or less of the total bill.
B. High volume hospitals (when many bills are paid) should be audited every six months for control purposes.
C. Drug charges can be audited, however, ordinarily the time and expense involved in checking drug charges will not result in a net gain. There are certain instances where audit of drugs should be considered: for example, when the itemized bill shows drug charges for a single day amount to $50 or more. This is known as "case-lot buying" by hospital personnel. It allows the patient to buy all his drugs on one day, and to sell back the portion he does not use.
D. It is recommended that you screen the bill for laboratory charges before requesting an audit. For example, there are certain lab tests such as complete blood count, complete urinalysis, SMA-12/60s, and sodium potassium levels that are rarely given any more frequently than once every 24 hours.
E. Occupational therapy can be screened in the same manner. A patient seldom receives more than one episode of occupational physical therapy a day while in the hospital.
F. A high number of charges for whole blood, and blood derivatives, should be offset in most cases by some credits. Most patients have some means of replacing blood and these should show up as a credit on the itemized bill. If no credits, you may regard the blood category as suspect.

LIMITED POINTED CLAIM (14)	Equifax	Acct.
(Audit of Hospital Bill)	INQUIRY	
CHARGE: Hourly Rate		

File Identification _Give Claim, Policy No. or other File Identification_ Date Mailed

Name of CLAIMANT _____ Date of birth or age _____

Residence Address _____

Name & City of Hospital _____ Dates Confined _____

Nature of Treatment or Operation _____

Total charge for current claim $ _____

SAMPLE

Form 1418—11-75 Equifax Inc. U.S.A.

REQUESTOR _____ ;

1. Attach itemized copy of Hospital Bill along with an authorization for release of medical information.
2. Check block(s) below to specify type & extent of handling.
3. Mail completed form to Equifax Office controlling city where hospital is located.

BRANCH OFFICE: If in correspondent area, return inquiry to customer. Explain that facilities for making this audit are not available, but that if they wish to authorize the additional cost (give estimate), a full-time Field Representative will be sent to obtain the report.

If any questions, refer to Field Release of December, 1971 on "Claims-Professionalizing the Service," filed in Claim Director Manual binder.

FIELD REPRESENTATIVE:

1. Go directly to the medical records department, present authorization and personally review the claimant's medical record. If explanation necessary, explain your company makes audits of claims for a number of different companies and you have been asked specifically by (give name of requesting company) to make an audit of (give claimant's name) claim.
2. If Problem Hospital, go to the Business Office and explain your mission. Ask for help of the Business Manager in obtaining a personal review of the medical record. If unable to personally review the medical record, close and explain.
3. COMPARING BILL TO FINDINGS IN THE MEDICAL RECORD: Your objective is to relate the charge on the bill to corresponding results or proof in the <u>medical record</u> of the patient to assure that the service was in fact administered. Check the medical records to see if there is a record for the service charged. If there is a record, just draw a line through the charge on the hospital bill as it has been verified. If you do NOT find a result for the charge in the medical record, CIRCLE the service, charge, etc., not accounted for in the actual medical record. At the same time, use lined paper and make notes of the discrepancies as you go along to make it easier for you in writing up your finished report. CAUTION: You may note in handling some audits that the billing date does not always correspond with the date in the medical record that the service was actually performed. In such instances, you should be able to justify the charges by determining how many x-rays, for example, were taken during the entire hospital stay and how many times an x-ray was charged.
4. LIMIT YOUR HANDLING TO THE POINT(S) CHECKED BELOW:
   A. ☐ **Laboratory Tests.** Check all result slips in the medical record.
   B. ☐ **X-Rays.** Check all x-ray reports in the medical record. Reports should mention the specific number of views taken. If charged for portable equipment, check record to insure use of same.
   C. ☐ **Blood.** Check all blood stickers or slips in the medical record to ascertain total number of units (pints) given patient. Check to determine if any blood was replaced by patient's family, etc. If so, what credit, if any, did hospital make toward the bill? Also be sure to check both the front and back of the blood slips which should be in the medical record for items such as "returned," "not hung," etc., and consequently not actually used, but billed. If any doubt, an additional check of the nurse's notes, operative report or fluid list should be made to see if the billed pints were actually administered.
   D. ☐ **Inhalation Therapy.** This is usually recorded on a separate sheet maintained by the Inhalation Technician showing dates and periods of time the patient actually received treatment. If any discrepancies between bill and what was actually administered, it is usually best to obtain a photocopy of this sheet or copy by hand.
   E. ☐ **EKG—Electrocardiogram.** Is there a tracing or report in medical record for each one billed?
   F. ☐ **EEG—Electroencephalogram.** Is there a tracing or report in medical record for each one billed?
   G. ☐ **General Information:**
      1. Any other insurance indicated by the hospital records? If so, identify.
      2. Do hospital records indicate cause of accident or illness may be related to occupation? If yes, describe.
      3. Do hospital records indicate if 3rd party liability is involved in this case? If so, explain.
      4. Do the hospital records indicate that the patient received treatment for this same ailment prior to the current disability? If so, when?
      5. Were private duty nursing services prescribed by the attending physician? If not, by whom?
      6. How many visits were made by the attending physician during this patient's confinement? How many other physicians attended the patient? Who?
   H. ☐ **Other:** (Requestor: Specify other items requiring special attention; indicate any specific photocopies required, etc.)

Form 1418—12-71

WRITING UP REPORT: Report in narrative on Form 87. Be sure to explain all discrepancies in billings. Return bill to customer.

	Chicago Area Hospital Admission Program			GROUP HOSPITAL INSURANCE REPORT			Date of Report
1	Patient Name: (Last) (First) Catherine (Init.)		Patient No. 135370 01	MALE ☐ FEMALE XX	Age 19	Prev. Admin. Past 6 Mos? ☐ YES ☐ NO (IF yes, where?)	
	Name & Address of Insured (Last, First, Init.) Richard	Married? ☐ YES ☐ NO	S.S. No. of Insured	Relationship to Pt. Father		Date & Time Admitted 7 6 80 4:00pm	
			Phone No. of Insured 672-8325	Occupation of Insured		Date & Time Discharged	
2	Name & Address of Group Policy Holder			Group Policy No.		Phone No. 649-1200	
				Name of Insurance Co. Retail Meat Cutters		Empl. Clock or Badge No.	
3	Name of Insured's Spouse	Is Spouse Employed? ☐ YES ☐ NO	OTHER GROUP HOSPITAL COVERAGE? (INCLUDES SECOND OCCUPATION OF INSURED)	Yes ☐	No X	(IF 'YES' COMPLETE THIS SECTION)	
	Name of Spouse's Employer		Name of Person Insured (Last, First, Init.)			Relationship to Patient	
	Occupation of Spouse	Employer's Tel. No.	Blue Cross Group and Subscriber No. OR Name of Commercial Insurer			Group Policy No.	
4	Send to the Insurance Company Claim Office OR where applicable, the Group Policy Holder. Original Insurance Assignment and one copy of the Itemized Bill.	Kelly & Assoc. P.O. Box 11102 Chicago, Ill. 60611		Hospital (Name, Address & Phone No.) PRESBYTERIAN ST. LUKE'S HOSPITAL ID-36-217-4823-N			
	Eligibility Confirmed By: Bertha		Date 7-7-80	Benefits Quoted By: Bertha		Phone ☐	Ins. Form ☐
5	Final Diagnosis from Records (If injury give date, time & place of accident)						
	IS CONDITION DUE TO INJURY OR SICKNESS ARISING FROM PATIENT'S EMPLOYMENT?			Yes ☐	No X	Unknown ☐	
	Operations or Obstetrical Procedures Performed (Nature & Date)						

FINAL DIAGNOSIS: Portal Hypertension Esophageal Varices.

NAME SURGICAL PROCEDURES, INSTRUMENTATION, CAST, ETC.:

ACCIDENT AND INJURY DATA: Is This A Workmen's Compensation Case? ☐ NO ☐ YES ☐ UNKNOWN. If No or Unknown, Give:
Date of Accident _____ Happened at: ☐ Home ☐ Work ☐ Auto ☐ Other. Patient's Occupation: _____
Describe How and Where Happened: _____
Was The Patient Still Hospitalized Beyond This Billing Period? ☐ NO ☐ YES
If Late Discharge (after check-out hour) did Doctor Authorize? ☐ NO ☐ YES
If Patient Expired, Please Give Date: _____
Name of Attending Physician _____ NO. 222696
Report Completed by _____ Date _____
Patient's Name Catherine Hospital Pa. No. 353755-01 7-6 7-19

Retail meat cutter unions and employers joint Health and Welfare Fund for the Chicago area

Claim Base / Major Medical Worksheet

P. O. BOX 11102 • CHICAGO, ILLINOIS 60611 • (312) 649-1200

PREF.	SOCIAL SECURITY	DATE OF LOSS MO./DAY/YEAR	CLAIMANT NAME	CLMT. CODE	AGE	CAUSE CODE	LOCAL UNION	N' OR C	PLAN CODE	CONTROL NO.
R	555-11-2222	7 4 80	Catherine	03	19	02	1	C	M	28772

EMPLOYEE NAME: Ki, Richard
ADDRESS: 1100 N. Beaver Creek, Chicago, Illinois 60022
STATE / ZIP

DRAFT AMT: $3,915.00
PAYEE I.D. # 25-1063712 **Patient Code** 02426440
Presbyterian St. Lukes
1111 West Second Street
Chicago, Illinois 60612
FROM: 7 6 80 TO: 7 20 80
CD DAYS AMT: 3 15 3915.00

DRAFT AMT: $132.00
PAYEE I.D. # Other
Affiliated Radiologists
120 West Rison
Chicago, Illinois 60612
CODE AMT: 60 132.00

Type of Expense	Inclusive Dates	Benefit Code	Amount Charged	Basic Benefits	M/M/K	Eligible MM Expense	Expenses Not Covered	See Comment # on Reverse
Hospital R & B 15 days	7/6-7/20/80	30	3975.00	3915.00			60.00	2
Hospital Misc.	" "	31	11,296.10	Paid		Pending		21
Hospital R & B days		30						
Hospital Misc. Radio.	" "	31	165.00		60	165.00		
Surgery		50						
Surgery		50						
Anesthetist								
Dr.								
Dr.								
Rx Drugs		65						
Diagnostic X-Ray & Lab.		45						
TOTALS		TOTAL		3915.00		165.00		

Remarks:

Major Medical Accumulations

PREVIOUSLY AVAILABLE	—	◀ Deductible
97,540.21	165.00	◀ Subtotal
THIS TRANSACTION	80%	◀ Co./Ins. %
−132.00	132.00	◀ M. M. Benefit
BALANCE AVAILABLE	4,047.00	◀ Total Basic + M. M. BOX 1 PLUS BOX 2
97,408.21	—	◀ C.O.B. Adj.
	4,047.00	◀ Total Payable

Date: 8 / 26 / 80   CALC BY: SCB   W.S. #: 3

ROUTE COMPLETED FORM TO - D.P. COPY

104R

**HOSPITAL BILL AUDIT
REQUEST FORM**

REPUBLIC SERVICE BUREAU, INC.
P.O. BOX 219
PARK FOREST, ILLINOIS 60466
312/747-2105

DATE __8/26/80__ CITY __Chicago__ STATE __Illinois__ ACCT. NO. __I 683__

DEPT. __Retail Meat Cutters__ CLAIMS NO. __Retail Meat Cutters__

Report on _____ If Dependent, Insured Name __Catherine__

Res. Add. _____ Date of Birth __6/7/61__

Employer __Local No. 1__

Name and address of Hospital __Presbyterian St. Lukes Hospital__

__1111 West Second Street, Chicago, Illinois 60612__

Dates Confined From __7/6/80__ To __6/20/80__ From _____ To _____

Diagnosis __Portal Hypertension Esophageal Varices__

Amount of Hospital Bill __$15,271.10__

Please attach copy or original hospital bill (all original bills will be returned to you with completed report) and medical authorization with this request. All areas of the bill will automatically be audited, however if you desire special attention paid to a particular area of the bill, so indicate and explain under Special Instructions:

- [ ] DRUGS
- [ ] X-RAYS
- [ ] OPERATING ROOM
- [ ] OTHER (Please Explain Below)
- [ ] LAB
- [ ] BLOOD
- [ ] OPERATING ROOM
- [ ] INHALATION THERAPY

If bill is to be broken down to determine your liability for a particular diagnosis please indicate below under Special Instructions and explain which diagnosis you are liable for.

SPECIAL INSTRUCTIONS: _____

Requestor _____ Tele. No. __333-10000__ Dept. __X111__

REPUBLIC SERVICE BUREAU

Acct. No. __683__
__9-3-80__

Dept. __Claims Dept.__
Claim # __Retail Meat Cutters__
Reg: _____

Patients Name: _____
Address: __Emp: Local # 1__

DELAY MEMO

CONFIDENTIAL

TYPE REPORT __Audit__   DATE OF BIRTH __6/7/61__

DELAY MEMO IS BEING SUBMITTED AT THIS TIME:

- [X] We are in receipt of the audit request on the above insured and anticipate completing the audit by the below indicated date.

- [ ] The hospital has not been able to locate the medical record for us to review. We are tracing the hospital daily and will begin the audit as soon as the record becomes available.

- [ ] We have completed the audit, however, are awaiting the drug prices from the hospital at this time. We expect to receive these drug prices and have a final report to you by the below indicated date.

- [ ] We have found the medical record to be only partially complete. The hospital is now searching for the remainder of the medical record and as soon as this information is located, we will continue with the audit.

- [ ] The medical authorization submitted with the audit request is not acceptable to the hospital. Therefore, we are obtaining a medical release from the patient, or next of kin, at which time we will audit this bill.

- [ ] The hospital has advised us that the medical record is now available and we are beginning the audit immediately. We hope to have the final audit to you by the below indicated date.

- [ ] The hospital involved does not normally allow a personal review of the medical record. However, we are handling through the administration department to obtain authorization to review this record and complete the audit.

OTHER REASONS FOR DELAY _____

DATE FOLLOW-UP REPORT TO BE EXPECTED __9-19-80__

NAME OF INSPECTOR AND OFFICE __DAS__

REPUBLIC SERVICE BUREAU

DEPT. Claim Dept.

Claim # Retail Meat
Cutters Union
Emp: Local #1
Req:

Acct. No. 666
9-15-80

CONFIDENTIAL

Type of Report Audit of Hospital Bill   Date of Birth   6-7-61

NOTE: Confined to the Presbyterian St. Lukes Hospital from 7-6-80 to 7-20-80, with a total billing of $15,271.10. Requested to audit this bill by the claim department, Kelly & Associates, Chicago, Illinois.

Be advised the hospital charged a $3.00 fee to review the medical record.

DRUGS: Attached is the itemization sheet for this area of the bill. (Discrepancy in this area of $483.38).

LABORATORY: Attached is the itemization sheet for this area of the bill. (Discrepancy in this area of $226.75).

X-RAYS: Attached is the itemization sheet for this area of the bill. (No discrepancy found in this area).

Be advised that we audited all other areas of the bill and found no other discrepancy.

Therefore, we have a total discrepancy in this billing of $710.13. We have submitted a copy of the audit to JoAnne Swallows, patient finance department. She is aware she may contest this audit within 60 days.

DAS

SEP 18 1980

REPUBLIC SERVICE BUREAU, INC.

HOSPITAL BILL AUDIT WORKSHEET
(Laboratory, X-rays, EKG's, etc.)

K1   Page 1

| DESCRIPTION | \multicolumn{4}{c}{IF ITEMIZED BILL} | \multicolumn{3}{c}{IF NO ITEMIZED BILL} |

DESCRIPTION	NO. ON BILL	COST	NO. IN MEDICAL RECORD	AMOUNT OF DISCREPANCY	NO. IN MEDICAL RECORD	PRICE PER UNIT	TOTAL PRICE
SMA 6	7	12.00	10	-36.00			
Calcium	8	6.00	6	12.00			
Electrolyte	2	28.00	1	28.00			
Bilirubin	2	6.00	1	6.00			
Glucose	2	6.25	2				
Albumin	2	7.50	1	7.50			
T.P.	1	9.00	1				
Uric Acid	1	6.00	1				
Phosphorus	5	5.00	4	5.00			
SGOT	2	9.00	1	9.00			
SGPT	2	9.00	1	9.00			
CPK	1	10.00	1				
Urinalysis	4	7.00	5	-7.00			
CBC	1	10.00	1				
Hgb-HCT	2	7.00	2				
PTT	6	8.00	6				
Pro Time	6	8.00	6				
Coag. Profile	2	5.00	2				
RPR	1	7.00	1				
Rout. Culture	4	18.00	4		SEP 18 1980		
Ammonia	1	37.85	1				
LAP	1	19.00	1				
Thyroid Batt.	1	62.00	0	62.00			
SMA 18	1	29.00	1				
Magnesium	2	6.00	1	6.00			
Alk. Phos.	2	6.25	1	6.25			
Amylase	2	9.00	1	9.00			
Creat. Clear	1	12.50	1				
Misc. Culture	1	27.00	1				
SMA 12	3	17.00	0	51.00			
Blood Culture	2	25.00	0	50.00			

DISCREPANCY - $226.75

REPUBLIC SERVICE BUREAU, INC.

HOSPITAL BILL AUDIT WORKSHEET
(Drugs)

K1

DRUG NAME	AMOUNT AND HOW ADMINISTERED	NO. OF DOSES GIVEN PER MEDICAL RECORD	PRICE PER DOSE	TOTAL PRICE	COMMENT
Demerol	50mg Im	35	3.00	105.00	
Visteril	50mg Im	29	4.00	116.00	
Visteril	25mg Im	1	4.00	4.00	
Atropine	0.4mg Im	2	4.00	8.00	
Valium	10mg Im	1	4.00	4.00	
IV'S	—	29	18.00	522.00	
KCL	20meq Iv	17	4.00	68.00	
KCL	40meq Iv	4	8.00	32.00	
Prostigmine	5mg Iv	1	4.00	4.00	
Cimetidine	300mg Iv	34	24.50	833.00	
Ancef	1 Gm Iv	3	6.10	18.30	
Vit C	500mg Iv	4	4.00	16.00	
Ca. Gluconate	1 Amp Iv	3	4.00	12.00	
Mag. Sulfate	1 Amp Iv	1	4.00	4.00	
MVI	1 Amp Iv	1	4.00	4.00	
Vit K	10mg Im	3	4.00	12.00	
Compazine	5mg Im	1	4.00	4.00	
Dalmane	15mg Po	1	50	50	
Cimetidine	300mg Po	7	50	3.50	
Tylenol #3	1 Tab Po	12	1.00	12.00	
Glycerine	Supp	1	1.25	1.25	

Billed - $2,266.93   Audited - $1,783.55   SEP 18 1981

Discrepancy - $483.38

REPUBLIC SERVICE BUREAU, INC.

HOSPITAL BILL AUDIT WORKSHEET
(Laboratory, X-rays, EKG's, etc.)

K1

DESCRIPTION	IF ITEMIZED BILL				IF NO ITEMIZED BILL		
	NO. ON BILL	COST	NO. IN MEDICAL RECORD	AMOUNT OF DISCREPANCY	NO. IN MEDICAL RECORD	PRICE PER UNIT	TOTAL PRICE
Hepa-Bil Scan	1	325.00	1				
Chest PAL	1	48.00	1				
KUB Angiogram	1	760.00	1				
Port. Chest	3	54.00	3				
EKG	1	32.25	1				

SEP 18 1980

Retail meat cutter unions and employers joint Health and Welfare Fund for the Chicago area

Claim Base / Major Medical Worksheet

P.O. BOX 11102 • CHICAGO ILLINOIS 60611 • (312) 649-1200

PREF.	SOCIAL SECURITY	DATE OF LOSS MO DAY YEAR	CLAIMANT NAME	CLMT. CODE	AGE	CAUSE CODE	LOCAL UNION	N' OR C	PLAN CODE	CONTROL NO
R	555-11-2222	7 4 80	Catherine	03	19	02	1	C	M	28770

EMPLOYEE NAME: Ki, Richard
ADDRESS: 1100 N. Beaver Creek, Chicago, Illinois 60022

DRAFT AMT	PAYEE I.D. # 25-1063712	Patient Code 02426440
$ 8,208.78	Presbyterian St. Lukes	
FROM	1111 West Second Street	
TO	Chicago, Illinois 60612	
CD DAYS AMT	CODE AMT	
	60 8208.78	

Type of Expense	Inclusive Dates	Benefit Code	Amount Charged	Basic Benefits	M M E X	Eligible MM Expense	Expenses Not Covered
Hospital R & B days		30					
Hospital Misc.	7/6-7/20/80	31	10,971.10		60	10,260.97	710.13
Hospital R & B days		30					
Hospital Misc.		31					
Surgery		50					
Surgery		50					
Anesthetist							
Dr.							
Dr.							
Rx Drugs		65					
Diagnostic X-Ray & Lab.		45					

TOTALS — TOTAL — 10,260.97

Major Medical Accumulations

PREVIOUSLY AVAILABLE		
96,950.61	10,260.97	◄ Subtotal
THIS TRANSACTION	80%	◄ Co./Ins. %
−8,208.78	8,200.70	◄ M.M. Benefit
	8,208.78	◄ Total Basic + M.M. BOX 1 PLUS BOX 2
BALANCE AVAILABLE	—	◄ C.O.B. Adj.
88,741.83	8,208.78	◄ Total Payable

Date: 10 / 3 / 80   CALC BY: L.K.   W.S. #: 5

ROUTE COMPLETED FORM TO - D.P. COPY

Retail meat cutter unions and employers joint Health and Welfare Fund for the Chicago area

Claim Base / Major Medical Worksheet
P.O. BOX 11102 • CHICAGO, ILLINOIS 60611 • (312) 649-1200

PREF.	SOCIAL SECURITY	DATE OF LOSS MO. DAY YEAR	CLAIMANT NAME	CLMT. CODE	AGE	CAUSE CODE	LOCAL UNION	N' OR C'	PLAN CODE	CONTROL NO.
R	555-11-2222	10 3 80	Catherine	03	19	02	1	N	M	28771

EMPLOYEE NAME: Ki, Richard
ADDRESS: 1100 N. Beaver Creek, Chicago, Illinois 60022

DRAFT AMT: $243.00
PAYEE I.D. #: Other
Republic Service Bureau
P. O. Box 219
Park Forest, Ill 60466
CODE 49 AMT 243.00

Type of Expense	Inclusive Dates	Benefit Code	Amount Charged	Basic Benefits	MME	Eligible MM Expense	Expenses Not Covered
Hospital R & B days		30					
Hospital Misc.		31					
Hospital R & B days		30					
Hospital Misc.		31					
Surgery		50					
Surgery		50					
Anesthetist							
Dr.							
Dr.							
Rx Drugs		65					
Diagnostic X-Ray & Lab.		45					
Audit	10/3/80	49	243.00	243.00			
TOTALS		TOTAL		243.00			

Major Medical Accumulations

PREVIOUSLY AVAILABLE		Deductible
		Subtotal
		Co./Ins. %
THIS TRANSACTION	2.	M. M. Benefit
		Total Basic + M. M. BOX 1 PLUS BOX 2
BALANCE AVAILABLE		C.O.B. Adj.
	243.00	Total Payable

Date: MO 10 / DAY 3 / YEAR 80   CALC. BY L.K.   W.S. #

ROUTE COMPLETED FORM TO - D P COPY

104R

HOSPITAL BILL AUDIT REQUEST FORM

REPUBLIC SERVICE BUREAU, INC.
P.O. BOX 219
PARK FOREST, ILLINOIS 60466
312/747-2105

DATE ___/___/80   CITY Chicago   STATE Illinois   ACCT. NO. 683

DEPT. _____   CLAIMS NO. Retail Meat Cutters

Report on _____   If Dependent, Insured Name Catherine

Res. Add. _____   Date of Birth 6/7/61

Employer Local No. 1

Name and address of Hospital Presbyterian St. Lukes Hospital

1111 West Second Street, Chicago, Illinois 60612

Dates Confined From 7/6/80 To 7/20/80   From _____ To _____

Diagnosis Portal Hypertension Esophageal Varices

Amount of Hospital Bill $15,271.10

Please attach copy or original hospital bill (all original bills will be returned to you with completed report) and medical authorization with this request. All areas of the bill will automatically be audited, however if you desire special attention paid to a particular area of the bill, so indicate and explain under Special Instructions:

- [ ] DRUGS
- [ ] X-RAYS   *Dick*
- [ ] OPERATING ROOM
- [ ] OTHER (Please Explain Below)
- [ ] LAB   *SECURE AUTHORIZATION*
- [ ] BLOOD
- [ ] OPERATING ROOM
- [ ] INHALATION THERAPY

If bill is to be broken down to determine your liability for a particular diagnosis please indicate below under Special Instructions and explain which diagnosis you are liable for.

SPECIAL INSTRUCTIONS: _____

$243.00

Requestor Lesia Kirk   Tele. No. _____   Dept. X269

October 6, 1980

Presbyterian St. Luke's
1111 West Second Street
Chicago, Illinois 60612

Attention: Joanne Lows

RE: Patient Number: 02426440-01
    Admission Date: July 6, 1980

Dear Ms. Lows:

We have recently processed the claim of the above named who was a patient at St. Luke's Hospital from July 6, 1980 to July 20, 1980. The entire hospital charges incurred were audited by an independent agency representing the Retail Meat Cutters Health and Welfare Fund. Attached you will find a copy of the audit report reflecting a discrepancy in your billing in the amount of $710.13. This discrepancy has been deducted from the overall miscellaneous charges and benefit considerations provided in accordance with the plan.

Should you have any questions relevant to our payment and/or the audit we would appreciate your telephoning our office immediately.

                      Sincerely,

                      RETAIL MEAT CUTTERS

                      Douglas F. Matook
                      Fund Office

October 6, 1980

RE: Claimant: Catherine
 Disability of: July 6-July 20, 1980
 Hospital: Presbyterian St. Luke's
 Amount of Discrepancy: $710.13

Dear

This letter is to notify you that your hospital bill for the time period stated above, at the above named hospital, has been audited by an independent agency. A discrepancy has been found in the bill.

Please be advised that you should withhold payment of the disputed charges, until such time the hospital contests the audit and provides proper proof of these charges

Should you have any questions regarding this matter contact the claim office.

Sincerely,

RETAIL MEAT CUTTERS

Fund Office

Coping With Hospital Costs— The New York Approach

BY RICHARD A. BERMAN

A PART of my job is ensuring that rising health care costs don't bankrupt the State of New York. We do, in many respects, share similar goals and concerns. I want to make sure that hospital care is available—in the right amounts, in the right places, at the right time and at a reasonable cost—to all the residents of New York. You want to make sure that the same scope of services is available to the members of your benefit plans at a cost the plans can bear.

The topic at hand today—coping with hospital costs—is not a new one, nor is it one for which a hard and fast solution has been found. But, we in New York have made significant inroads into containing the *growth* of hospital costs to a reasonable and affordable level. Perhaps a good place to start would be with a brief history of New York's experience.

A Close Encounter

I'm sure you all remember quite vividly New York State's close encounter with fiscal insolvency in 1975. Hugh L. Carey had just been elected Governor, and found he had inherited the worst state fiscal crisis since the 1930s. One of the major contributors to this crisis situation was a health care budget that for several years had been growing at an alarming rate. Not only were spiraling health care costs turning health care into a luxury which fewer and fewer New Yorkers could afford, but runaway costs in this single sector of our economy were a major contributing factor to the high cost of living in New York, the high cost of doing business in New York, the high cost of obtaining insurance in New York and to New York's high (in comparison to many other states) taxes. In essence, New York's ability to attract and keep business and industry was deteriorating, and all indicators suggested health care costs were a primary culprit.

Mounting a Defense Against Runaway Costs

Immediate steps were taken by the new Governor and his cabinet to pull in the reins on runaway

As director of the State Office of Health Systems Management, a cabinet-level position, Mr. Berman administers state health care financing and reimbursement programs, development of the state's health planning activities, and the preparation, implementation and enforcement of health care standards for all licensed New York State health facilities. Prior to joining Governor Carey's health care team, he was an assistant dean and associate hospital director of the New York Hospital-Cornell Medical Center in New York City. Mr. Berman also served as a senior program consultant to the Robert Wood Johnson Foundation and as director of its municipal health services program. In the area of national health financing and public policy, Mr. Berman acted as a special assistant to the Secretary of Health, Department of Health, Education and Welfare, as well as director of health policy development for the U.S. Economic Stabilization Program. He received his master's degrees in both business administration and hospital administration from the University of Michigan, and has written numerous papers on varied health care topics.

health care costs. One of these steps was a major reorganization of the state health department to strengthen accountability for and management of New York's disparate health care responsibilities. At the Governor's direction, an Office of Public Health was formed to manage traditional public health programs such as immunization, epidemiology, laboratories and research. Responsibility for managing New York's troubled institutional health care systems was vested in the new, cabinet-level Office of Health Systems Management.

The Office of Health Systems Management was officially established by November 1977 as the focal point for three major areas of health regulation: the coordination and management of all programs related to the development and enforcement of health care standards; the administration of health care financing programs, including reimbursement rate setting; and the stewardship of health care planning and resource management activities, particularly with regard to the determination of need for building and expanding health facilities and services. Final authority for these statutory responsibilities was delegated to me as the first Director of the Office of Health Systems Management by the State Health Commissioner.

New York now had the administrative and statutory structure in place to start dealing with runaway health care costs, and a more than ample portion of motivation to carry them out.

Four Major Principles

We formulated our approach to coping with hospital and health care costs around four major principles. *First*, cost containment measures could not adversely affect actual patient care programs. *Second*, we insisted on paying only for care that is provided efficiently. *Third*, unnecessary services and, consequently, wasteful expenditures would have to be eliminated, or at the very least sharply reduced. And *fourth*, fiscal realities had to be balanced by human concerns.

The resulting cost containment program coordinates standards of efficient operation that hospitals are expected to live up to, controls on unnecessary utilization, incentives for closure of unneeded hospitals and merger of redundant facilities, and regionalization of specialized, tertiary care services. Further, through the exercise of control over all major third-party payers (except Medicare) and, since 1978, control over increases in charges to private paying patients, New York has succeeded in keeping its annual growth in health care costs over the past five years to approximately 9%—well below average national cost increases.

Of course, all hospitals were not as pleased with this success as were we. Hospital budgets have had to be tightly constructed and, in all candor, less-than efficient hospitals in some cases have encountered serious financial difficulties. For the most part, however, hospital losses derive not from our cost containment program but from the burden of providing free or below-cost care to medically indigent patients, or from sheer fiscal imprudence.

Don't let me mislead you into believing that hospital care is now easily affordable in New York—on the contrary, it is still quite dear. New York State government has, rather, succeeded in putting on the brakes; now we are trying to structure a system that will perpetuate cost efficiencies and minimize inflationary increases in health care costs so that future New Yorkers will have access to needed health services.

One way this is being done is by fostering and encouraging alternatives to institutional care. A hospital is about the *most expensive* place you could pick to go for care. Primary care services provided at a cost or charge of $50-100 in a hospital emergency room or outpatient department in most instances can be provided for $20 or $30 in a private physician's office. Through an innovative experimental program, the Office of Health Systems Management is working vigorously to expand community health resources which provide comprehensive primary care for families—care which we believe will obviate in many instances the need for crisis or emergency care and redirect care seekers for primary services away from hospitals.

Needed: A Cooperative Effort

Government, of course, has a central responsibility for helping others cope with hospital costs. We do this by continuously refining our systems for financing hospital care in order to enhance incentives for efficiency. New York has taken the lead among states in this effort, and currently has the most progressive and innovative prospective hospital reimbursement system in the country. Also, we have initiated several reimbursement experiments in our state which are seriously testing alternative reimbursement systems that offer promise for future statewide implementation. But government can't do it all alone. Government needs the cooperation of business, industry, civic organizations and everyday people to go farther than just "coping" with hospital costs. New York has welcomed the support and cooperation of business and industry in our cost containment program.

Cost Control Legislation. A most notable achievement in this respect was the passage in 1978 of New York's hospital charge control legislation. In May 1978, the New York State Court of Appeals ruled that hospitals could legally withdraw from Blue Cross contracts and charge Blue Cross subscribers and beneficiaries at any rate they desired. In essence, the ruling opened the door for hospitals to circumvent New York's cost control program and, in effect, confronted New York's 13 million Blue Cross subscribers with potential substantial out-of-pocket costs. Governor Carey swiftly submitted legislation to bring hospital charges under the state's protective cost control umbrella, and received the support of labor unions, private third-party health insurers and a major industry organization, Associated Industries, for the legislation. The bill became law, as they say, and charges to private patients and Blue Cross subscribers are now subject to increase limitations.

The Rochester Program. New York is also a partner with insurers and industry in a promising reimbursement experiment now being conducted in Rochester, New York. Rochester is a unique community with two major employers: IBM and Kodak. Concern among hospitals and government over rising health care costs was deeply shared by corporate leaders, who understood the drain on the corporate coffers of providing comprehensive health benefits to employees. With the direct involvement of corporate leaders, hospital officials, state and federal government officials and Blue Cross, a strikingly innovative reimbursement experiment was developed for the Rochester area. The experiment includes eight Rochester-area hospitals and is administered locally by a not-for-profit organization called the Rochester Area Hospital Corporation, or RAHC, which includes representatives from each of the hospitals, as well as community leaders. In its most basic terms, the project offers a single total revenue cap for the participating institutions. Out of the total revenue cap, dollars are allocated by the RAHC to the participating hospitals on the basis of utilization. Within the total cap, the RAHC must decide how the dollars can be spent best—i.e., should services be shared, centralized or realigned to meet community needs. It is truly a test of whether, given a limited number of dollars, choices which affect a community's hospital care can be made locally, and whether such local administration of limited health resources results in greater economies, improved service delivery and maintenance of high quality-of-care standards.

The project is completing its first full year, and is slated to run at least another two years. We on the state level are eagerly looking forward to results of the project, and believe the strong partnership of government, hospitals and industry in the project offers every chance of success.

I don't want to mislead you into thinking that there is a strong constituency in New York among industry, labor and the hospitals themselves for cost containment and prudent fiscal planning for health dollars. Rather, support and coordinated efforts are at this time on a single issue basis. Corporate leaders across the state have not, to my knowledge, established as one of their goals active lobbying on behalf of restricting inflationary health care increases. Such a goal would, I assure you, be most welcome and meaningful in our fight against the shrinking dollar.

Reimbursement as a Cost Containment Tool: Achieving Uniformity

I mentioned briefly New York's approach to hospital cost containment. The elemental feature of this approach is our reimbursement methodology. The key to achieving a meaningful halt in health care cost inflation lies with uniformity in how hospitals are paid. In New York, we use a prospective, average cost methodology for Medicaid, Blue Cross, Workers' Compensation and no-fault insurance reimbursement to hospitals. This methodology incorporates incentives for reduction of unnecessary utilization, peer standards of efficiency, and inflation expectations. However, a major portion of hospital income—i.e., Medicare—falls outside this protective methodology and even injects perverse incentives for cost growth.

New York has been attempting for almost two years to reverse the dichotomies in reimbursement and establish a uniform system across all payers. Our objectives are to enhance predictability of revenue for hospitals so they can plan and budget better; to allow hospital managers the administrative flexibility to use dollars as their judgment sees fit within an overall revenue cap; and to reduce the disparity between rates of payment by government-regulated payers and private insurers/private paying patients.

These concepts are embodied in the Medicare waiver proposal which we submitted, first in 1979 and in an amended fashion during the summer of 1980, to the federal Health Care Financing Administration. Also included in this proposal are additional funds to offset bad debt and charity care losses, and a discretionary fund for hospital managers. These principles are mirrored in the report recently submitted to the Governor and legislative leaders by the Council on Health Care Financing, a council established by New York State statute in 1978 to study hospital financing and to recommend a uniform system of reimbursement. Under the proposal, the major third-party payers—Blue Cross, Medicaid and Medicare—would reimburse on a prospective, average cost basis. The incentives for better management and use of resources would, therefore, be consistent. This uniformity is extremely important because, as long as hospitals can maximize revenue from uncontrolled sources, they are not compelled to budget and manage as effectively as they would were they able to project their total expected revenue for any given year. Indeed, the disparity or differential between controlled payer rates and private carrier charges has been estimated to be as high as 45%.

Employee benefit plans have a tremendous stake in what happens to hospital costs in New York and across the nation. The benefit plans have an opportunity in New York to affect their own costs and bring down that differential in payment by working with the state to secure uniformity among hospital payers.

Conclusion: How to Win Instead of Cope

When a person shops for a dress or a suit, when a business stocks its inventory, when an industry seeks raw materials, they're shopping primarily for one thing: acceptable quality at an affordable price. That, too, is what people, business and industry should be doing when they "shop" for health care.

Granted, different market forces are at play in the health field. Medicine is an esoteric field, and we must all rely on the professionalism of our physicians. But how many of us are willing to ask our physician how much our treatment is going to cost, whether our insurance is sufficient to cover it or whether we will be incurring substantial out-of-pocket costs, and what alternatives there are to being hospitalized? How many of us are willing to contact our local hospitals and ask them what their charges will approximate for the type of service we are told we need? How many people are willing and eager to submit to a second opinion when surgery is advised?

The answers here are obvious. Most of us still personally shy away from getting to the nuts and bolts discussions of cost with our local hospitals. Most of us are too stunned when told we need surgery to ask about alternatives or second opinions. But ask we must, if we intend to make prudent decisions about our own health care.

The assertive, cost-conscious attitude is even more important for organizations such as employee benefit plans, which are indeed the "buyers" of health services for around 20 million people. The plan benefits you provide—or, in other words, the services for which the benefit plans will pay—actually shape the service users' consumption of medical services. Plans that provide full coverage for hospitalization but only partial or no coverage for ambulatory surgery force penny-conscious plan beneficiaries to opt for the more expensive hospitalization to obtain treatment. Similarly, plans which do not provide coverage for health maintenance (ambulatory care services) do not encourage wellness among their beneficiaries. Plans might consider systematic, careful reviews of their present benefits with an eye to escaping from this traditional insurance trap of providing in-hospital benefits. Such careful reviews might result in expanded coverage for ambulatory services and revamping of benefit objectives to ones which seek to promote sound health status rather than financial assistance for crisis care.

Community, business and industry leaders also have a tremendous investment in their local health care services. The quality and scope of services available within the community can be a major bonus in corporate recruiting efforts. The cost of the same services may put a substantial dent in the business's profits. These leaders have an obligation to be involved—to seek appointment to hospital governing boards, to work on local health councils, to know state cost containment programs and the officials whose job it is to administer them.

Community, business and industry leaders can also promote lifestyles and health awareness programs which enhance good health and safety on the job. Identifying potential health problems before they become acute is a leading weapon in the battle against high health care costs. Offering a second opinion program as a health benefit may encourage employees to apply the same prudent buyer concepts to their health care that they apply to the purchase of a car, a home or any other major purchase.

These are only a few suggestions of ways in which we all can do our part to see that health care does not become a luxury affordable only to a few. New York State will continue to do its part; we look forward to the support of the benefit plans in this endeavor.

Second Surgical Opinion Programs— A Cost/Benefit Study

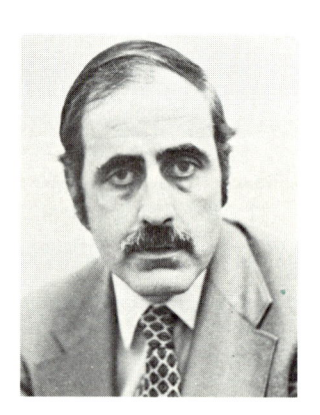

BY EUGENE G. McCARTHY, M.D., M.P.H. and
HIRSCH S. RUCHLIN, Ph.D.

Dr. McCarthy received his A.B. degree from Boston College, his M.D. degree from Yale University School of Medicine, and his M.P.H. from Johns Hopkins University School of Public Health. He served as U.S. Chief Health Advisor to the government of Paraguay, and director of the Paraguayan Health Services. He was assistant professor of administrative medicine at Columbia University School of Public Health and Administrative Medicine, and has acted as consultant in health affairs to a number of state and federal agencies and large hospitals. At the present time, he is medical advisor to several health and welfare funds, and is clinical professor of public health at Cornell University Medical College.

Dr. Ruchlin is professor of economics in public health at Cornell University Medical College, engaged in medical care research. Previously, he was a professor, Department of Health Care Administration, Baruch College—Mount Sinai School of Medicine, City University of New York. Dr. Ruchlin received his B.A. degree from Yeshiva College and his M.A. and Ph.D. degrees from Columbia University.

Introduction

The rising costs of health care services have been a source of major concern during the last decade. Various factors have contributed to this unwelcome development, one being the dramatic increase in the number and rate of surgical procedures. The number of surgical procedures rose from a level of 14.7 million in 1965 to 20.7 million in 1978, an increase of 40.8%. Adjusted for population growth,

The research reported in this paper was supported by Contract No. 600-75-0175 from the Health Care Financing Administration, U.S. Department of Health and Human Services.

the rate of surgery rose from a level of 7,735 surgeries per 100,000 population in 1965 to 9,704 surgeries per 100,000 population in 1978, a 25.5% increase.

The increasing rate of surgery has been a source of concern on two fronts. First, questions have been raised as to whether all the surgery that is currently being performed is medically justified. Questions such as, is surgery required, and are alternate medical procedures available, are being heard with increasing frequency. Second, the major consumption of health-related resources that accompany surgery has led to higher medical and hospital bills and, in turn, to higher premiums for medical care coverage.

The growth of surgery and its concomitant costs have given rise to a variety of second opinion consultation programs which provide some mechanism for reviewing the necessity of recommended elective surgery *before* the surgical procedure is performed. One of the first programs in this area was established in New York City in 1972, when the trustees of two Taft-Hartley security welfare funds and state and local government employee welfare funds approached Cornell University for assistance in studying the possibility of surplus surgery among their membership. The Cornell-New York Hospital program, developed by Dr. Eugene G. McCarthy, has been adopted by over 15 funds in the New York area representing approximately 682,000 individuals, and has served as a model for countless second opinion programs adopted throughout the country.

Since the inception of the Cornell-New York Hospital second opinion program, over 11,000 second opinion consultations have been rendered to health fund members and their covered dependents by board certified panel consultants. Findings consistently have shown that about one-third of those voluntarily seeking a second opinion consultation and 18% of those who were required to seek a second opinion consultation received a non confirmation: that is, their need for surgery was not confirmed. Patient follow-up studies conducted one year after the anniversary date of the second opinion consultation have indicated that 70% of the people receiving non-confirmations have not had surgery.

Recognizing the medical efficacy of second opinion consultation programs, one is then led to ask whether such programs lead to demonstrable cost savings. We have contended in the past that the answer to this question is in the affirmative. We recently completed a comprehensive economic evaluation of our largest second opinion program. The results which we are presenting here provide firm evidence for our contention that mandatory second opinion programs return substantial economic dividends. Before discussing the nature of our evaluation and our findings, a brief digression on the nature of the second opinion program that was evaluated and the population covered is in order.

Nature of the Program and Population Covered

The program selected as the basis for the economic evaluation is the largest *mandatory* program within the constellation of the Cornell-New York Hospital second opinion programs. The program is administered by the Service Employees International Union, Local 32B-32J Taft-Hartley Welfare Fund, which provides health coverage for 120,000 members and dependents. Under this program, a patient is required to seek a consultation in order to have health fund basic hospitalization and physician coverage for an elective surgical procedure. (The health fund is self-insured for surgical-medical expenses and purchases hospitalization coverage from Blue Cross.)

The health fund maintains a list of board certified physicians willing to serve as consultants, and directly arranges a consultation for the member or dependent at a day and time that is convenient for the patient. The cost of the consultation and any required tests is paid by the fund. The mandatory program provides for one "forgiveness" for each member and dependent: that is, benefits will be paid if the surgery is performed without a consultation first having been arranged. However, if the same individual undergoes elective surgery again and fails to have a second opinion consultation, benefits will not be paid.[1]

Once a consultation has been obtained, the patient is free to elect surgery and will be entitled to full health fund coverage even if the need for surgery was not confirmed by the consultant physician. The thrust of the program is to provide the member/dependent with more *information* about the need for surgery and possible alternatives to surgery. The ultimate choice of whether to undergo surgery is still the patient's.

The economic evaluation is based on the experience of members/dependents who were told that they required elective surgery during the two year period January 1, 1977-December 31, 1978. During this period, 2,284 covered individuals were told that they required elective surgery. Of this number, 366 (16%) did not receive a confirmation of their need for surgery by a consultant physician. In order to ascertain the economic benefit of a consultation, it was decided to randomly select individuals whose need for surgery was confirmed and compare the experience of each non-confirmed individual with that of another individual whose need for surgery was confirmed. Twenty-four not-confirmed individuals were excluded from the study due to lack of data, resulting in a study population of 684 individuals: 342 not confirmed and 342 confirmed cases.

The following sociodemographic data provide a perspective on the type of person included in this study. Fifty-three percent of the study participants were in the 45-64 age category and 37% were in

---

1. The individual is warned in writing and in a telephone conversation that a second opinion consultation must be scheduled in the future.

the 25-44 age category. Fifty-two percent of the study participants were male, and 75% were married at the time of the study. Sixty-eight percent of the participants were employed and 25% were housewives. The average study participant had not completed high school and had a gross weekly wage, exclusive of overtime, in the $200-299 range.

Program Evaluation: A Cost/Benefit Perspective

The primary focus of the cost/benefit analysis is to ascertain the cost containment potential of a second opinion consultation program. Consequently, the following rule was adopted in the evaluation design: Any recommendation emanating from the consultation process that could potentially lead to reduced health care expenditures was considered to be a non-confirmation of the original need for surgery. This is the case even if the new recommendation results in a modified surgical regimen or if the initial recommendation for surgery is ultimately accepted after a recommended medical treatment has been tried.

As a result of receiving a second opinion consultation, individuals are classified into one of two categories: confirmed or not-confirmed. The evaluation focus thus is centered on ascertaining whether the receipt of a second opinion consultation generates economic savings. These savings should materialize through the election of less surgery.[2]

Cost/benefit analysis was used to evaluate the economic efficacy of the second opinion consultation program. To conduct a cost/benefit analysis, one first must estimate the magnitude of the *savings attributed to a program*. Concomitantly, one must derive an estimate of the *costs incurred to provide the program*. The final step in the analysis entails dividing the estimate of program benefit by the estimate of program cost to obtain a benefit/cost (B/C) ratio. A benefit/cost ratio greater than one indicates that the value of accrued benefits exceeds the incurred costs and that, as a result, the program has a definite economic payback. If the benefit/cost ratio is less than one, implying that costs exceed benefits, the program is deemed to lack economic merit.

---

2. One should not expect every "not-confirmed" individual to decide not to have surgery. Similarly, not every "confirmed" individual will elect to have surgery. However, one expects that the majority of individuals in each group will follow the consultant's recommendation. For the current study population, 89% of the confirmed individuals elected surgery, while 85.1% of the not-confirmed group followed the recommendation of the second opinion consultant.

Table I

Cost/Benefit Analysis Framework

Benefit/Cost Ratio

$$= \frac{\text{Program Savings (Benefit)}}{\text{Program Cost}}$$

$$= \frac{\begin{array}{c}\text{Medical expenditures plus productivity}\\\text{losses incurred by the confirmed group}\\\text{minus medical expenditures plus}\\\text{productivity losses incurred by the}\\\text{not-confirmed group}\end{array}}{\text{Program Cost}}$$

Benefits (Savings)

    Medical
        Physician Fees
        Surgical Fees
        Anesthesiology Fees
        Hospitalization Costs
        Diagnostics and Laboratory Costs
        Therapies and Nursing Costs
        Drug and Prosthesis Costs

    Productivity
        Work Loss Days
        Homemaker Loss and Restricted
          Activity Days
        Other

Costs

    Administrative Costs
    Medical Costs
    Member/Dependent Out-of-Pocket Costs

The avoidance of surgery due to the additional information obtained from a second opinion consultation can result in two types of benefits that have clear economic value: (1) reduced medical care utilization and cost, and (2) reduced productivity losses. Productivity losses result primarily from a person's inability to work due to his/her illness. Thus, for the purpose of the current study, program benefit is defined as the difference in medical care utilization and productivity-loss patterns exhibited by the not-confirmed group compared with those exhibited by the confirmed group. For example, if the confirmed group incurred medical care costs and productivity losses valued at $100,000 and the not-confirmed group sus-

Table II

Program Benefit Resulting From
Reduced Medical Care Utilization

Category	Total Expenses Incurred Confirmed	Total Expenses Incurred Not-Confirmed	Savings
Physician Fees	$ 30,994	$ 27,856	$ 3,138
Surgical Fees	215,718	115,383	100,335
Anesthesiology Fees	54,124	24,665	29,459
Hospitalization Costs	461,816	243,297	218,519
Diagnostics and Laboratory Costs	10,413	5,370	5,043
Therapies and Nursing Costs	7,443	1,356	6,087
Drug and Prosthesis Costs	6,787	7,661	(-874)
TOTAL	$787,295	$425,588	$361,707

Number of Observations: 342 Confirmed and 342 Not-Confirmed Individuals

Table III

Program Benefit Resulting From
Reduced Productivity Losses

Category	Productivity Loss Value Confirmed	Productivity Loss Value Not-Confirmed	Savings
Work Loss	$260,949	$121,416	$139,533
Homemaker Loss and Restricted Activity Days	66,882	44,340	22,542
Other*	20,825	9,961	10,864
TOTAL	$348,656	$175,717	$172,939

Number of Observations: 342 Confirmed and 342 Not-Confirmed Individuals

*Relative work loss, outside household help, travel and time cost to obtain medical care

tained medical expenses and productivity losses valued at $25,000, program benefit would be $75,000 ($100,000-$25,000).

Program benefit was estimated for ten specific categories, seven representing various aspects of medical care utilization and three depicting types of productivity losses. These categories are enumerated in Table I together with the three component categories established to estimate the total cost of the second opinion consultation program.

Patient Profiles

Utilizing data from medical claim forms submitted to the health fund and responses to detailed questionnaires administered via telephone interviews, we developed detailed profiles for the 342 confirmed and 342 not-confirmed cases. These profiles indicated all medical expenses generated and productivity losses sustained within a 12 month period following the receipt of the second opinion consultation.[3]

Savings resulting from reduced medical care utilization are profiled in Table II. Over the one year follow-up period, the total confirmed group incurred medical expenses of $787,295, compared with $425,588 for the not-confirmed group, result-

---
3. All cost data presented in this study are reported in constant (1977) dollars. Costs incurred in the post-1977 period were discounted, utilizing a 10% discount rate.

Table IV

Program Cost

Category	Total Cost	Percent
Administrative Cost	$ 78,700	38.7
Medical Cost	101,520	49.9
Out-of-Pocket Cost	23,080	11.4
TOTAL	$203,300	100.0

Total Cost Per Second Opinion Consultation Arranged

Total Cost $\quad \dfrac{\$203{,}300}{2{,}308^*} = \$88.08$

Administrative Cost $\quad \dfrac{\$\ 78{,}700}{2{,}308^*} = \$34.10$

Medical Cost $\quad \dfrac{\$101{,}520}{2{,}308^*} = \$43.98$

Out-of-Pocket Cost $\quad \dfrac{\$\ 23{,}080}{2{,}308^*} = \$10.00$

*During the two year study period, 2,284 individuals obtained a second opinion consultation and 24 individuals obtained an additional (i.e., third) opinion.

ing in a savings of $361,707. With the exception of drug and prosthesis costs, the confirmed group incurred greater expenses for all medical care utilization categories than the not-confirmed group. As expected, the avoidance of surgery resulted in major savings in the area of surgical fees ($100,335) and hospitalization costs ($218,519).

By following the treatment regimen suggested by the consultant physician, the not-confirmed group sustained fewer productivity losses, as can be seen from the data presented in Table III. Total productivity losses sustained by the not-confirmed group equaled $175,717 compared with an estimated loss of $348,656 sustained by the confirmed group, resulting in an estimated productivity savings of $172,939.[4] Of this estimated productivity savings, 80.6% ($139,533) resulted from a lower work-loss profile sustained by the not-confirmed group.

---

4. Work loss was valued at the individual person's hourly wage. The prevailing minimum wage was used to value restricted activity time. Housewife time loss was valued at the market cost of household services performed by housewives. For a discussion of this technique, see Will. Brody, "Economic Value of a Housewife," *Research and Statistics Note 9-1975*. DHEW Publication No. (SSA) 75-11701, August 28, 1975.

Program Costs

Program cost is profiled in Table IV. Over the two year study period, the administrative cost of the second opinion consultation program equaled $78,750. Consultation (i.e., medical) fees and costs of required diagnostic procedures equaled $101,520. Travel costs incurred by the member/dependent to obtain a second opinion and time costs associated with obtaining the second opinion consultation were estimated at $23,080. The sum of these cost components yields a total program cost estimate of $203,300. On a per consultation basis, total cost is estimated at $88: $34 being incurred for administrative costs, $44 for medical costs, and $10 for out-of-pocket costs.

Annual expenses incurred to administer the second opinion consultation program are presented in Table V. (These data pertain to the first year of the two year study period.) Labor costs account for 75% of the total estimated cost. Imputed rental costs account for 72% of all non-labor costs.

One can now assess the economic efficacy of the second opinion consultation program by noting whether estimated benefits offset program cost. For the current program, this is indeed the case, as can

Table V

Administrative Cost, 1977

Category

Personnel
  1.5 FTE Intake Officers,
    at $10,000 per FTE $15,000
  Fringe Benefits (29% of salary)   4,350
  Medical Advisor (1 day/wk.)   10,000
                        Subtotal $29,350

Supplies, Forms, Brochures   1,600

Telephone—2 trunk lines,
  at $600/line   1,200

Rent, Utilities, Maintenance
  (imputed)*   7,200
                        TOTAL $39,350

---

*The second opinion intake office occupies one room (20' × 20'). The average cost for space rental in Manhattan, including utilities, maintenance and insurance was $18/sq. foot.

Table VI

Benefit/Cost Ratio
Cornell-New York Hospital Second Opinion
Consultation Program

Benefits

  Total $534,646
    Medical   361,707 (67.7%)
    Productivity   172,939 (32.3%)

Cost $203,300

Benefit/Cost Ratio

$$B/C = \frac{\$534,646}{\$203,300} = 2.6$$

be seen from the data presented in Table VI. Total program benefits were estimated to be $534,646. Of this total, 68% of the benefits resulted from reduced medical care utilization and 32% from lower productivity losses. Program costs were only $203,300, yielding a benefit/cost ratio of 2.6: that is, for every $1 in program cost incurred, $2.60 of benefits were realized.

If one wishes to overlook benefits and costs that do not impinge directly on a health fund, a benefit/cost ratio greater than one is still obtained. Dividing the $361,707 benefit estimate resulting from a reduced level of medical care utilization by $180,220 (total program cost minus out-of-pocket expenses) yields a benefit/cost ratio of 2.0. Thus, for every $1 expended by a health fund on the second opinion consultation program, a $2 reduction in medical care expenditures was realized.

Conclusions and Comments

In an era when medical care costs are rising and health funds are confronting the escalating costs of medical benefits, it is incumbent upon health fund trustees and administrators to seek out ways of containing cost. The data presented in this study indicate that a mandatory second opinion consultation program for elective surgery is a very effective way of containing medical benefit costs. Consequently, second opinion programs merit serious consideration by all health funds and medical insurance carriers.

There is reason to believe that the total program benefits would be greater if the population under study was drawn from a higher paying occupation. Median hourly earnings for building service employees are in the $5-8 range. Had the covered employees commanded an hourly wage in the $13-16 range, as is the case for carpenters, teamsters and other members of the skilled crafts, productivity savings would have been much higher.

In establishing a second opinion program, health funds are well advised to incur the extra costs associated with an appointment desk. If patients are entrusted to make their own appointment for a second opinion consultation, experience indicates that one out of every three will not do so. By making the appointment for the member/dependent, one can significantly increase the "adherence" rate and thereby ensure that all the potential program benefits are reaped.

A Second Opinion Podiatry Program

BY MADELON LUBIN FINKEL, Ph.D.,
EUGENE G. McCARTHY, M.D., M.P.H. and DAN MILLER

Dr. Finkel, as research associate in public health at the Cornell University Medical College, is primarily responsible for conducting statistical analyses and evaluation research of several research projects, supervising the research staff at Cornell and acting as liaison with personnel at participating Taft-Hartley welfare funds. Her research focuses on second opinion programs, disability reviews, alcoholism and pregnancy disability; she also serves on the faculty in the Department of Public Health. Dr. Finkel earned her B.A. degree at University College, New York University, Bronx, New York, and her M.P.A. and Ph.D. degrees at the Graduate School of Public Administration, New York University, New York City.

Dr. McCarthy received his A.B. degree from Boston College, his M.D. degree from Yale University School of Medicine, and his M.P.H. from Johns Hopkins University School of Public Health. He served as U.S. Chief Health Advisor to the government of Paraguay, and director of the Paraguayan Health Services. He was assistant professor of administrative medicine at Columbia University School of Public Health and Administrative Medicine, and has acted as consultant in health affairs to a number of state and federal agencies and large hospitals. At the present time, he is medical advisor to several health and welfare funds, and is clinical professor of public health at Cornell University Medical College.

Introduction

The foot is probably the most used and the most neglected part of the human body. The average person walks roughly eight miles a day, and with each step subjects the foot to a minimal degree of trauma. The advent of hard, unyielding walking surfaces and the wearing of shoes has hindered the foot's ability to function naturally. Not surprisingly, the current popularity of jogging and marathon running also has created a sudden surge of complaints of foot, ankle and knee problems. Approximately 15-20% of industrial trauma, sports injuries and office practice involves the foot and ankle. The majority of Americans suffer foot problems, yet many bear them without complaint. For the others, however, abuses to their feet create a constant source of annoyance, discomfort, pain and/or disability.

A survey of foot problems in the continental U.S. conducted in 1978-79 found that 74 million Americans—40% of the population—have foot problems. Those most prone to foot trouble are women, the elderly, those with incomes below $5,000, non-whites and people in the South. The most commonly treated problems are ingrown toenails, calluses, corns and plantar warts. It has been

---

Dan Miller is a master's candidate at Columbia University School of Public Health and served as a public health intern at the Building Service Employees Local 32B-J Health Fund.

estimated that 23 million individuals have had surgery performed on one or both feet, and that 13.5 million others have had medical treatment for their condition. Simple arithmetic shows that 37.5 million people with foot problems have not had treatment or surgery.

Podiatric Surgery

Most surgery on the foot is elective (non-emergency) and is performed to correct deformity, relieve pain, improve function or prevent future disability. Conditions most frequently encountered for which surgery is indicated are hammertoes, corns, overlapping or underlapping toes, bunions, bone spurs and cysts/tumors. Bunions, in particular, are the most common affliction of the normal adult foot. They are more common in women than in men for a good reason: high heeled shoes. A shoe that pinches the toes will add to the valgus strain on the big toe and aggravate the condition. There has rarely been a fashion in women's shoes—or men's shoes, for that matter—that has been designed to protect the toes. In comparison, however, men's footwear tends to be much more accommodative.

The increase in the rate of specific podiatric surgical procedures clearly reflects the difficulty people are having with their feet. From 1971 to 1978, there was a 558.8% increase in the rate of foot surgery in which the bones of the foot were cut. There was a 103.9% increase in the rate of joint surgery performed on the foot or toe during the same period. In comparison, the rate of all orthopedic surgery increased 36.3% from 1971 to 1978 and the rate of all operations increased 24.3% during this period.

Foot problems are handled either by an orthopedic surgeon or a podiatrist. While the former is a surgeon who specializes in treating the musculoskeletal system of the body, the podiatrist is concerned with the diagnosis and treatment of the foot and ankle. Disorders of the toenail, for example, are probably diagnosed and treated more often by podiatrists than by any other medical specialty. Podiatrists are allowed by law to deal only with the foot; however, in six states they are permitted to treat up to the knee and in another six states they may work on the foot and tendons of the leg. Most podiatrists still confine themselves to work on the foot, however. The situation is analogous to that of a non-surgical physician who is technically licensed to set a broken bone, but is unlikely to do so.

Podiatrists have considerable patient acceptance in the U.S. Roughly 7,500 podiatrists engaged in patient care of some 35 million visits in 1978, a 40% increase since 1970. Although the demand is increasing, the supply of podiatrists is relatively small. While there is one medical doctor for every 670 people and one dentist for every 2,000 individuals, there is only one podiatrist for every 25,000 persons.

The cost of foot care is staggering, not surprisingly. The provision of foot care (excluding home treatment using over-the-counter remedies) costs over $1 billion a year, with office visits and hospital stays accounting for $450 million each. The remainder is accounted for by surgeons' fees, emergency room care and outpatient clinics. Foot-related office visits account for about 2% of all payments to direct providers of health care, and foot-related hospital stays account for roughly 1% of all hospital expenditures. The concern over the rising cost of health care in general and surgical care in particular should not be limited to physician and dental care; cost containment programs have ignored podiatric services even though over $1 billion is spent on foot care each year. In an attempt to contain costs related to foot care, an innovative program was established at the health fund of Local 32B-J, the Building Service Employees union.

The Second Opinion Podiatry Program

Study Population

The Service Employees International Union Local 32B-J represents workers of both sexes who are employed in the maintenance, operation and upkeep of all private and public buildings (residential and commercial) in boroughs of the City of New York, except the Bronx. Specifically excluded are those employed as superintendents working in loft and office buildings, exterminators and window cleaners. The local is chartered by the Service Employees International Union under the American Federation of Labor Congress of Industrial Organizations. The union covers 600,000 members and dependents. The local is composed of 120,000 members and dependents and serves as the exclusive bargaining representative for its members, assisting them in obtaining adequate compensation for their labor and promoting their welfare.

Members work as elevator operators, doormen, porters and office cleaners in over 6,000 scattered worksites. Sixty percent work the night shifts, particularly the women who work as cleaning ladies, usually without supervision. Since the tasks of maintaining and servicing buildings requires that the individuals be on their feet much of the time, it is not surprising that there is a high incidence of foot problems among the membership.

Mandatory Consultation

From 1979 to 1980, the Building Service Local 32B-J Health Fund paid over $162,000 for podiatric surgery and related care. Almost $60,000 was paid for in-hospital surgery and $17,870 was paid for surgery performed in the physician/podiatrist's office. The majority of in-hospital claims were for bunion removal, while 44% of the office surgery was for removal of ingrown toenails. It was decided to require a second opinion consultation for podiatric conditions in an attempt to contain the costs of such surgery and, hopefully, to enhance the quality of care.

The second opinion program for podiatric problems was established in the fall of 1979. Each member and his or her dependents are required to have a second opinion consultation scheduled for all non-emergency foot surgery recommended by a podiatrist that costs over $100. Whether the surgery is to be performed on an inpatient or outpatient basis is immaterial. Although the program tried to refer half of the individuals to a podiatrist and half to an orthopedist for the second opinion consultation, it became quite obvious that most orthopedic surgeons refuse to see patients with common podiatric problems such as ingrown toenails, corns, warts and other minor conditions. The consultant (podiatrist or orthopedist) is paid $50 for the consultation and the fund pays the costs of any ancillary tests performed by the consultant.

The objective of the program was to contain costs and enhance the quality of care rendered. The findings, however, suggest that in order to achieve these goals more effectively the program design should be restructured.

Findings

Demographic Profile. Of the 244 individuals who had a second opinion for initially recommended foot surgery, 61.9% were females. Two-thirds of the sample were between the ages 45-64 (37.6% were between 45-54 years and 29.3% were between the ages 55-64). The plurality of males and females were between the ages 45-54 (32.6% and 40.7%, respectively).

Among the males in the study, 22.6% were porters and 16.1% were doormen and handymen, respectively. Among the females in the study, 44.4% were cleaning ladies and 35.1% were covered dependents for whom an occupation status was not known. The remaining individuals of both sexes were either building superintendents, elevator operators or security guards.

Consultant's Recommendation. Approximately one-fifth (22.5%) of those initially recommended for podiatric surgery were seen by an orthopedic surgeon (board certified) and 77.5% were seen by a podiatrist. Almost 84% of the study population was confirmed for surgery. However, a closer inspection of the data shows that the confirmation rate among those seeing a podiatrist was 92.6% as compared to a confirmation rate of 52.7% among those who were seen by an orthopedist. That is, whereas the podiatrists did not confirm the need for surgery in 7.4% of the cases, the orthopedists did not confirm the need for surgery in 47.3% of the cases. Data presented in Table I show that with the exception of those initially recommended for surgery to correct a heel spur, the majority within each podiatric diagnostic category were confirmed for surgery.

Table I

Podiatric Conditions Analyzed by Confirmed/Not-Confirmed Status

Condition	Confirmed N	Confirmed %	Not-Confirmed N	Not-Confirmed %	Total N	Total %
Bunion	61	82.4	13	17.6	74	100.0
Corn	14	87.5	2	12.5	16	100.0
Hammertoe	55	91.7	5	8.3	60	100.0
Heel Spur	5	38.5	8	61.5	13	100.0
Ingrown Toenail	41	100.0	0	0	41	100.0
Neuroma	5	83.3	1	16.7	6	100.0
Osteoarthritis	6	85.7	1	14.3	7	100.0
Other	14	58.3	10	41.7	24	100.0
Total	201	83.4	40	16.6	240	100.0

When we analyzed the data by the second opinion consultant's specialty, dramatic differences were apparent. Table II shows the confirmed/not-confirmed status of the podiatric conditions screened by the podiatrists. For every condition, the podiatrists overwhelmingly confirmed the need for surgery. Conversely, Table III shows that the orthopedic second opinion consultant was less likely to confirm the need for surgery. Whereas the podiatrists confirmed the need for a bunionectomy in 94.5% of the cases, the orthopedists confirmed 52.3% of the potential bunionectomies. Whereas the podiatrists confirmed the need for surgery in 93.8% of the cases with hammertoes, the orthopedists' confirmation rate for hammertoes was 83.3%.

Differences were also apparent in reasons for non-confirmation. In general, the orthopedist consultants were more conservative in their recommendation for surgery. In nine out of ten cases, it was the orthopedist who suggested that corrective footwear was preferable to surgery. In three out of four cases, the orthopedist felt that the surgical procedure was contraindicated, and in two out of three cases, the orthopedist felt that the symptoms were not severe enough to warrant surgery. As was shown earlier, the podiatrists were more likely to confirm the need for surgery.

Table II

Confirmed/Not-Confirmed Status Analyzed by
Podiatric Conditions Screened by a Podiatrist

Condition	Confirmed N	Confirmed %	Not-Confirmed N	Not-Confirmed %	Total N	Total %
Bunion	52	94.5	3	5.5	55	100.0
Corn	9	90.0	1	10.0	10	100.0
Hammertoe	45	93.8	3	6.2	48	100.0
Heel Spur	5	62.5	3	37.5	8	100.0
Ingrown Toenail	40	100.0	0	0	40	100.0
Neuroma	5	100.0	0	0	5	100.0
Osteoarthritis	6	100.0	0	0	6	100.0
Other	13	76.5	4	23.5	17	100.0
Total	175	92.6	14	7.4	189	100.0

Table III

Confirmed/Not-Confirmed Status Analyzed by
Podiatric Conditions Screened by an Orthopedist

Condition	Confirmed N	Confirmed %	Not-Confirmed N	Not-Confirmed %	Total N	Total %
Bunion	11	52.3	10	47.6	21	99.9
Corn	5	83.3	1	16.6	6	99.9
Hammertoe	10	83.3	2	16.6	12	99.9
Heel Spur	0	0	5	100.0	5	100.0
Ingrown Toenail	1	100.0	0	0	1	100.0
Neuroma	0	0	1	100.0	1	100.0
Osteoarthritis	0	0	1	100.0	1	100.0
Other	2	25.0	6	75.0	8	100.0
Total	29	52.7	26	47.3	55	100.0

The decision whether to have surgery is made by the patient regardless of the consultant's recommendation. Table IV shows that of those who were not confirmed, 82.5% did not have surgery. Conversely, of those who were confirmed for surgery, half (50.5%) did not have the operation performed. The majority of these individuals report that they had their condition for years and choose to "live with it."

The majority (79.5%) of those who did have surgery performed did so within two months from the date of their consultation. Moreover, over half (53.7%) of those who had surgery had the procedure performed in the physician/podiatrist's office. Logically, conditions such as corns, ingrown toenails, removal of warts and other minor podiatric conditions were performed on an outpatient rather than an inpatient basis. Data show that 51.9% of those seen by a podiatrist decided against surgery whereas 69.1% of those seen by an orthopedist decided against surgery.

In general, the podiatrists ordered more ancillary tests than did the orthopedists. Each patient was instructed to bring x-rays with him to the second opinion consultation; however, of the 55 potential bunionectomies seen by the podiatrists, 24 (43.6%) had additional x-rays taken. Conversely, of the 21 cases of potential bunionectomies seen by the orthopedists, none needed additional x-rays taken.

Of the 48 individuals with hammertoes seen by the podiatrists, 24 (50%) had additional x-rays taken. Conversely, only one of the 12 individuals with hammertoes seen by the orthopedists needed additional x-rays taken. Of the eight individuals with a heel spur seen by the podiatrists, six (75%) had additional x-rays taken, as compared to one of the five individuals with a heel spur seen by the orthopedists. Of ten individuals with corns seen by the podiatrists, three (30%) had x-rays taken as part of the second opinion examination. The cost of the additional x-rays taken by the podiatrists totaled $2,850.00.

Economic Considerations. The surgical bill for the major podiatric conditions* totaled $74,689; the mean cost of the surgeon's bill was $678.99. The total cost for all of the conditions was $83,524, and the mean cost was $780.60. Table V shows the cost for the major podiatric conditions. The surgeons' bills for bunionectomy totaled $46,542, with a mean of $1,034.27 and a range of $300-3,091. Removal of corns averaged $325 and removal of ingrown toenails averaged $141. There was not a large range in bills for these procedures. The surgeons' bills for correction of hammertoes totaled $18,746, with a mean of $1,041.44 and a range of

---

*Bunions, removal of corns, hammertoes, heel spurs, and ingrown toenails.

Table IV

Confirmed/Not-Confirmed Status Analyzed by Surgical Status

	Yes Surgery N	Yes Surgery %	No Surgery N	No Surgery %	Total N	Total %
Confirmed	101	49.5	103	50.5	204	100.0
Not-Confirmed	7	17.5	33	82.5	40	100.0
Total	108	44.2	136	55.7	244	99.9

Table V

Surgical Bills for Specific Podiatric Conditions

Condition	Total Bill	Average Bill	Range Low	Range High
Bunion	$46,542	$1,034.27	$300	$3,091
Corn	2,275	325.00	300	350
Hammertoe	18,746	1,041.44	250	2,650
Heel Spur	3,601	720.00	410	1,285
Ingrown Toenail	3,525	141.00	55	260
Total	$74,689	$678.99		

$250-2,650. The surgeons' bills to correct a heel spur totaled $3,601.00, with a mean of $720 and a range of $410-1,285.

One explanation for the large range in bills for specific procedures is that in some individuals a bilateral bunionectomy was performed or several toes were corrected. Also in a few individuals, several procedures were performed at one time but were counted as one procedure (e.g., bunionectomy, osteotomy, tendon lengthening and capsulotomy performed at one time). Some individuals, too, suffered complications which served to inflate the surgeon's bill.

Since the fund pays "reasonable and customary" costs, it is likely that the patient would have to pay the difference between what is charged by the surgeon and what is paid or reimbursed by the fund. We found that the podiatrists, in particular, were charging in excess of the reasonable and customary costs but were more than likely to accept the amount paid by the fund. Specifically, the podiatrists billed a total of $28,090 for in-office surgery but accepted payments totaling $17,870. The podiatrists billed a total of $124,630 for in-hospital surgery but accepted $56,354—less than half of what they billed!

The cost of the consultations totaled $12,250, the reimbursement of the surgeries performed totaled $83,524 and reimbursement of ancillary tests totaled $3,600, for a grand total of $99,374. If one were to assume that the 136 individuals who reported not having surgery "saved" the fund $92,342.64 in surgical bills foregone (136 people x $678.99 per surgical bill), the net cost of the program becomes $7,031.36. Quite obviously, if a second opinion consultation is not required for removal of corns, warts and ingrown toenails, the program in all probability would be cost-effective.

Discussion and Conclusion

The findings from the 32B-J podiatry second opinion program clearly show the predilection among podiatrists to confirm podiatric surgery and to order an excessive amount of ancillary tests both prior to and after surgery. Analysis of the program's first year has made it crystal clear that thousands of dollars are being spent unnecessarily. Specifically, claims for ingrown toenails have cost the fund $3,265 in nine months. Since the orthopedic consultants refused to examine ingrown toenails and since almost all second opinion podiatrists confirmed the need for toenail removal, it seems economically unsound for the fund to require a second opinion for this procedure. This uncomplicated procedure is always done in the podiatrist's office.

Corn removal, too, is almost always confirmed by the podiatrist and is performed in the podiatrist's office. There is no compelling reason to require a second opinion for corn removal. Indeed, it would be more economical just to pay the surgical claims rather than pay the consultant's fee and the surgical fee. Also, such an arrangement would eliminate the need for the member to take time off to get a second opinion, a process which is costly and time-consuming.

Regarding the more complicated podiatric conditions (bunionectomies, hammertoes, heel spurs), a second opinion consultation definitely should be required. It's our opinion that the consultant should be an orthopedic surgeon. These procedures are almost always performed in the hospital and have high rates of non-confirmation. They also are the most costly procedures, and substantial savings could be realized if a second opinion consultation was required.

Although foot surgery is not as "glamorous" as other surgical subspecialties such as eye or gynecological surgery, the statistics do show that a lot of people are having their feet operated upon and millions of dollars are being spent to relieve foot pain or discomfort. It is also clear that the podiatrists in this study tended to take advantage of a situation and were not only charging excessive fees, but probably were performing many procedures unnecessarily.

Therefore, it seems quite sensible from an economic as well as a medical standpoint to encourage or to require a second opinion consultation with an orthopedist for the commonly performed podiatric surgical conditions.

HMOs and Multiemployer Funds—Do They Mix?

BY CARLTON R. SHERMAN

Introduction

To paraphrase Mark Antony—who apparently failed to carry out his fiduciary responsibilities to Caesar and probably engaged in a prohibited transaction with Cleopatra—I come neither to bury HMOs nor to praise them. Our purpose here is to examine the practical administrative and policy questions which arise when a Taft-Hartley fund chooses to offer a health maintenance organization to its participants.

Perhaps a little background may be helpful. The total national outlay for medical care in 1979 was over $212 billion, and the projections for the future are horrendous. Everyone is looking for some method of controlling this voracious monster.

There is a great national debate going on as to the best way to accomplish this. Basically, the debate is between those who believe in regulation and those who believe competition is the way to go. However, both sides agree, generally, that HMOs are a viable, efficient and cost-effective method of medical care delivery.

Yet, Taft-Hartley multiemployer funds are not, for the most part, strong buyers of HMO care. There is a fair amount of fund participation in HMOs on the West Coast and some in New York, but not much elsewhere. For example, in Minneapolis-St. Paul, with six HMOs and about 14% market penetration, there is only one Taft-Hartley fund which offers an HMO option. (Please note that I am differentiating Taft-Hartley multiemployer funds from single employer collectively bargained benefits, such as those commonly found in the auto and steel industries.)

So, the question is, why has there been such a slow development of fund participation in the HMO movement?

Types of HMOs

Let's take a moment to review the basic structure of HMOs. There are two distinct kinds of HMOs. The independent practice association, or IPA, can be called an "HMO without walls." Fre-

Mr. Sherman is a contract administrator to health and welfare plans, as well as a consultant on labor relations, contract negotiations, grievance processing and arbitration. Mr. Sherman is the executive director of the Janitors Union Local No. 1 Welfare and Pension Funds (Chicago). He was appointed an arbitrator for the American Arbitration Association panels in 1965 and a labor arbitrator for the Federal Mediation and Conciliation Service in 1966. Mr. Sherman has been a guest lecturer at Northwestern University on problems in collective bargaining and has conducted a course at the University of Chicago, Labor Education Division, on collective bargaining and contract administration. He received a B.A. degree with a major in labor economics from the University of Wisconsin. Mr. Sherman has spoken at previous International Foundation educational meetings. He is a member of the Educational Program Committee and chairman of the Administrators Committee.

quently organized by doctors as an answer to the threat they perceive in the growth of the HMO movement, the IPA is generally an organization based on the voluntary participation of doctors in an area, practicing in their own offices. The IPA pays the doctors either a fixed monthly per capita fee for each enrolled member who chooses him as his physician, or pays on a negotiated fee schedule. Some IPAs include financial incentives for the doctors to curtail hospital utilization.

There is also a variation of the IPA model which results in a sort of "hybrid" structure, generally called a "network" IPA. Under this system, the IPA, usually organized and marketed by an insurance company, contracts with a network of doctors practicing as groups which are not themselves staff HMOs, to service enrollees in the IPA. These groups run fee-for-service practices side by side with the prepaid HMO-type practice. An example of this model is Intergroup, owned and operated by CNA Insurance Company, marketed in the Chicago area and now expanding into Tucson and Wisconsin.

The other basic type is the staff or group model. In this situation, the doctors practice in the same physical facility and are either directly employed by the HMO or are partners in a corporation or partnership from which the HMO buys physician services.

Evaluation of these two modalities could be the subject of another paper.

A Cost Paradox

There is a paradox of cost in the HMO, generally speaking. In many cases, the monthly premium (capitation) is higher than the monthly indemnity insurance plan premium. This is true because HMOs give more services than the insurance plans. There are usually no deductibles or copayments. On the other hand, the total cost of treating a specific case or illness is usually lower with an HMO. In other words, when the monthly premium of an insurance plan is added to the out-of-pocket cost to the patient, the total medical care expense will usually be higher under the insured arrangement.

So, it generally comes down to the question of cost allocation: Who is going to pay the difference in the HMO premium and how is it to be collected?

HMO Act Requirements

Much like ERISA, the HMO Act of 1973 was written without attention to the unique characteristics of multiemployer funds. Section 1310 of the act, which appears in the Appendix, mandates employers to offer federally qualified HMOs as an option providing (a) the employer is subject to the Fair Labor Standards Act; (b) 25 or more employees live in the area served by the HMO; (c) the HMO's approach is timely; and (d) the union approves the HMO.

It is important for our discussion to note that the act mandates that the employer contribute only the same amount to the HMO as he is paying for the standard insurance plan.

Since the act itself is silent on the question of multiemployer funds, the question arises—Is the fund—the trustees—in the same position with respect to this legal requirement as a single employer? To my knowledge, this question has never been tested in the courts. It is generally assumed, however, that the trustees stand in the shoes of the contributing employers. The HMO regulations speak of "employer designees" who may be approached by the HMO—but do not specifically mention Taft-Hartley trustees as designees.

There are, it seems to me, some areas of conflict between the HMO Act and ERISA. On the one hand, the HMO Act, as we have seen, mandates offering an HMO option. On the other hand, ERISA imposes strict fiduciary standards on the trustees. So, the question arises—Can the trustees pay a higher premium for those who choose an HMO than the cost of the indemnity plan? This differential can be quite substantial, particularly in the case of self-insured plans.

Again, this is a grey area. I have spoken to a number of attorneys and others and have found no consistent opinion, and the question has, to my knowledge, not been tested in the courts. But, do the trustees want to expose themselves to a possible challenge by a participant, for example, who does not live in the area serviced by the HMO? This could be the case with respect to some building trade locals or public utility workers whose membership is domiciled over a large geographical area, including rural and semirural areas.

It is interesting to see how some funds with HMO options handle the problem. One fund on the west coast is paying the higher premium for those participants who opted for the HMO on the theory of de minimis—the differential is only $15.00 per month. Another fund in the New York area, where the differential is $42.00 per month, requires advance payment of six months from those participants who enrolled in the HMO. You may know of other arrangements.

Section 1310(B)(2) provides, in effect, that if the employees are represented by a union, the union has the right to reject or "veto" the offering of the HMO. In many situations, the union trustees are the same individuals who are the "collective bargaining representative(s)" as stated in the regulations. I would think that the union trustees should exercise some care with respect to their actions in this area. If the decision to reject the HMO is made, it probably should be made by the "collective bargaining representative," not by the union trustees acting in their capacity as trustees.

It is noteworthy that the HMO Act confers this

right to reject on the union without qualification. The union is not required to explain or justify its decision.

Implementing the Decision

Choosing an HMO—Or Two?

Assuming the trustees have solved the problems we have discussed and have made the decision to include an HMO option in the plan of benefits, what are some of the questions that should be raised before entering into an agreement with the HMO?

First, you will notice that this part of our discussion is headed, "Choosing an HMO—or two?" The "two" refers to two aspects of this question. First, the HMO Act requires that an employer offer both a staff model HMO and an IPA HMO, if a timely approach is made by each of them. It is not necessary for the trustees to solicit one or the other, however, to comply with this requirement. Second, those folks who believe competition is the best way to moderate medical care costs argue that more than one of the same type of HMO, either staff model or IPA, should be offered.

Regardless of which type you are dealing with, there are some basic questions you should ask, particularly of a staff model HMO.

Quality of Care. What is the general quality of the medical staff? Are the doctors board certified or eligible for board certification in their various specialties? With what hospitals are the doctors affiliated? A word of caution here—it is not necessary for all the doctors, particularly the primary care doctors, to practice in the most "prestigious" (also most costly) hospitals. Most medical care can be provided just as well in smaller community hospitals, and it is not necessary to bed most medical patients in hospitals which perform "high risk" surgery or are prestigious teaching centers.

It would, in my opinion, be worthwhile to investigate the normal daily operation of the HMO in some detail. How long is the waiting period for appointments? How long is the waiting period to see the doctor? Are there adequate provisions to care for "drop-ins" or unscheduled patients? How are emergencies handled? Who are the consulting specialists such as neurologists, oncologists, neurosurgeons, cardiologists, etc.?

It might be worthwhile to employ a medical consultant for the task of evaluating the medical staff and quality of service of the HMO.

The next large area of concern is the *financial stability* of the HMO. Who are the sponsors? How is it organized? Has enrollment been increasing? Are other funds participating? What employers are offering the HMO to employees, and what has their experience been? What are the utilization rates of enrolled groups? Most importantly, what is the HMO's ratio of debt to working capital? How much are the unallocated reserves?

The record shows that the HMOs which have failed have done so because of a lack of good management. One of the most pressing problems HMOs face is the lack of qualified financial and management personnel. Contrary to what many people believe, there is no serious lack of doctors willing to work in an HMO environment. Medical directors, however, are another problem. There are too few qualified physicians who also have management skills necessary to run a quality yet cost-effective medical service. The dearth of qualified management people is so acute that the Group Health Association and other groups are now running a special seven month course of training, funded by the government, for such positions.

I cannot overemphasize the importance of making sure the HMO is financially stable.

Access to Services. It is important to determine if the HMO will, in fact, be accessible to your membership in terms of geography. I would suggest you run a zip code analysis to see how many of your participants live within the service area of the HMO. Does the HMO have satellite locations in the suburbs to provide service to your people?

What are the provisions for emergency service and out-of-area coverage? If a participant is stricken while on vacation, for example, what is the coverage? Some HMOs have adopted agreements which provide medical care for members of other HMOs on a reciprocal basis. This development of "reciprocity agreements" is growing.

Contract Negotiation

Having satisfied yourself on all of these points, it is time to negotiate a contract. First, of course, the services to be provided must be addressed. The HMO Act mandates the basic services to be provided by a federally qualified HMO. There are supplemental services which many HMOs offer, and you should be sure that these are costed out separately.

Periodic utilization reports are essential in order to measure not only the frequency of use, but the cost-effectiveness of the HMO plan. A cost equivalence analysis, where you equate the cost of services provided by the HMO with the usual and customary allowances of the standard insurance plan for the same services, would tell you if you are getting your money's worth on a gross dollar basis.

Bear in mind that, with some narrow exceptions having to do with establishing a composite rate, HMOs are required to charge community rates, generally after they have been qualified for a period of 48 months. Thus enrollment can have an important impact on the HMO premiums, if the enrolled population of an HMO is particularly adverse. In fact, there are some critics who accuse HMOs of "skimming"—that is, of only going after the most medically desirable risks. You may want to establish some method of checking the enrollment activities of the HMO to monitor this question.

You will want to know how hospital claims are handled. Is hospitalization insured or reinsured? How are claims processed? Are they paid within time limits which conform to reasonable industry standards? Is coordination of benefits enforced?

Certainly, your contract should include a "hold harmless" clause which will protect the trustees against malpractice claims as well as claims arising in the unhappy event of the HMO's financial failure. What happens to hospital bills or current hospital confinements? What provisions are made for continuing care of participants whose treatment has not been completed? These are all areas of legitimate concern, and should be covered in the contract.

Enrollment of Participants

Once the contract has been negotiated, the next step is enrollment of participants. This may not be as simple a task as it sounds. Generally, the HMO regulations state that the employer must give the HMO equal access to the employees as he gives to the insurance plan. Remember, we are in a dual choice situation. First, the fund administrator should review the literature, brochures or other offering material the HMO proposes to use to make sure the claims and statements made conform with the contract. Secondly, a decision must be reached on how the material will be distributed. Since most funds will not want to release their mailing lists, the offering will probably be mailed by the fund.

You may want to include a setup whereby participants can ask for more information, including a home visit, by the HMO marketing people. Incidentally, the HMO Act does authorize the employer to pay such administrative costs without counting them toward the payment of equal premiums relative to the HMO and the standard insurance plan; thus the fund can, if so desired, pay the cost of the mailings and other administrative costs. Other means available to explain the options to the participants are the union meetings and union publications.

The important point here, I believe, is that the administrator is to be neutral in the participants' selection process, and is to act merely as a funnel for information.

In addition to an initial enrollment period, it is necessary to have annual enrollment periods, so that participants can switch from the HMO to the insurance plan and vice versa. It is equally important not to permit switching back and forth during the year to prevent participants using both plans to their advantage, at an increased cost to the fund.

Appeals Procedure

Another area of concern is the question of the appeals procedure. As you know, ERISA requires a very structured, documented appeals procedure, including the right of third-party representation. I believe you should make sure the HMO's appeals procedure meets the requirements of ERISA, and you may want to play some role in the appeals procedure, if only as an observer.

The Future Role

I said earlier that the participation of Taft-Hartley funds in HMOs is relatively small and, as you can see from our discussion, the administrative burdens as well as policy problems imposed by such participation probably go a long way to explain why that is the case. From the HMOs' viewpoint, Taft-Hartley funds generally have not been considered choice marketing prospects for basically the same reasons, looked at from the other side of the coin. Most HMOs, at this point, probably find it much easier to deal with large single employers because the employees are available for interviews under one roof and usually during working hours and, of course, checkoff of the premium differential from wages is generally provided.

However, there is a consensus that, as the HMOs continue to expand and increase market penetration among the available single employers in their service areas, and with the growing number of HMOs competing with each other, the time will come soon when HMOs will turn their attention in a concentrated way to multiemployer funds.

Furthermore, I am of the opinion that within a comparatively short time the monthly premium differentials between HMOs and standard insurance plans will disappear. Indeed, with the continuing rise in hospital costs, which seem to be accelerating in the last few months, the day may come soon where HMOs will charge *less* than the insurance plans. The reason this may occur is that lower hospital use is the major single cost-savings attribute of the HMOs. Generally, HMOs use half the hospital days per thousand population as the number used by the general insured population.

Despite the fact that the HMO Act comes up for Congressional review in October 1981 and there probably will be an attack on the mandate provisions of Section 1310 as well as on government funding, the consensus is that HMOs are here to stay. It is likely that the Reagan Administration will come down heavily in favor of the competition approach to medical care, and this will stimulate the private sector involvement in HMOs. There is already an increasing amount of private capital, particularly insurance companies', entering the field, and these entrepreneurial entities have the resources to finance determined, large-scale marketing efforts. Indeed, the attraction for HMOs to be federally qualified may diminish considerably with the infusion of private capital in the development and organization of HMOs, particularly if Section 1310 is weakened. There are obvious advantages to an HMO in not being required to community rate, to have the ability to offer more flexible service packages and to have better control of open enrollment policies.

From the funds' point of view, there is the consideration that HMOs do have a favorable impact on the total costs of medical care. In Minneapolis-St. Paul, for example, where there is a flourishing HMO movement, medical costs overall have not increased at the same rate as the national figures.

So, in conclusion, I think it is fair to say that, if it has not already happened, you will be hearing from an HMO or two in the not too distant future and that, despite the problems involved, you ought to give them a fair chance to show their stuff.

Appendix
HMO Act of 1973, excerpt

Sec. 1310(a)(1) In accordance with regulations which the Secretary shall prescribe:

(A) each employer—

(i) which is now or hereafter required during any calendar quarter to pay its employees the minimum wage prescribed by section 6 of the Fair Labor Standards Act of 1938 (or would be required to pay its employees such wage but for section 13(a) of such Act), and

(ii) which during such calendar quarter employed an average number of employees of not less than 25, shall include in any health benefits plan, and

(B) any State and each political subdivision thereof which during any calendar quarter employed an average number of employees of not less than 25, as a condition of payment to the State of funds under section 314(d), 317, 318, 1002, 1525, or 1613, shall include in any health benefits plan, offered to such employees in the calendar year beginning after such calendar quarter the option of membership in qualified health maintenance organizations which are engaged in the provision of basic health services in health maintenance organization service areas in which at least 25 of such employees reside.

(2) If any of the employees of an employer or State or political subdivision thereof described in paragraph (1) are represented by a collective bargaining representative or other employee representative designated or selected under any law, offer of membership in a qualified health maintenance organization required by paragraph (1) to be made in a health benefits plan offered to such employees (A) shall first be made to such collective bargaining representative or other employee representative, and (B) if such offer is accepted by such representative, shall then be made to each such employee.

(b) If there is more than one qualified health maintenance organization which is engaged in the provision of basic and supplemental health services in the area in which the employees of an employer subject to subsection (a) reside and if—

(1) one or more of such organizations provides basic health services through physicians or other health professionals who are members of the staff of the organization or a medical group (or groups), and

(2) one or more of such organizations provides basic health services through (A) an individual practice association (or associations), or (B) a combination of such association (or associations), medical group (or groups), staff, and individual physicians and other health professionals under contract with the organization, then of the qualified health maintenance organizations included in a health benefits plan of such employer pursuant to subsection (a) at least one shall be an organization which provides basic health services as described in clause (1) and at least one shall be an organization which provides basic health services as described in clause (2).

(c) No employer shall be required to pay more for health benefits as a result of the application of this section than would otherwise be required by any prevailing collective bargaining agreement or other legally enforceable contract for the provision of health benefits between the employer and its employees. Each employer which provides payroll deductions as a means of paying employees' contributions for health benefits or which provide a health benefits plan to which an employee contribution is not required and which is required by subsection (a) to offer his employees the option of membership in a qualified health maintenance organization shall, upon request of an employee who exercises such option, arrange for the employee's contribution for such membership to be paid through payroll deductions.

(d) For purposes of this section, the term "qualified health maintenance organization" means (1) a health maintenance organization which has provided assurances satisfactory to the Secretary that it provides basic and supplemental health services to its members in the manner prescribed by section 1301(c), and (2) an entity which proposes to become a health maintenance organization and which the Secretary determines will when it becomes operational provide basic and supplemental health services to its members in the manner prescribed by section 1301(b) and will be organized and operated in the manner prescribed by section 1301(c).

(e)(1) Any employer who knowingly does not comply with one or more of the requirements of subsection (a) shall be subject to a civil penalty of not more than $10,000. If such noncompliance continues, a civil penalty may be assessed and collected under this subsection for each thirty-day period such noncompliance continues. Such penalty may be assessed by the Secretary and collected in a civil action brought by the United States in a United States district court.

(2) In any proceeding by the Secretary to assess a civil penalty under this subsection, no penalty shall be assessed until the employer charged shall have been given notice and an opportunity to present its views on such charge. In determining the amount of the penalty, or the amount agreed upon in compromise, the Secretary shall consider the gravity of the noncompliance and the demonstrated good faith of the employer charged in attempting to achieve rapid compliance after notification by the Secretary of a noncompliance.

(3) In any civil action brought to review the assessment of a civil penalty assessed under this subsection, the court shall, at the request of any party to such action, hold a trial de novo on the assessment of such civil penalty unless in a prior civil action to review the assessment of such penalty the court held a trial de novo on such assessment.

(f) For purposes of this section, the term "employer" does not include (1) the Government of the United States, the government of the District of Columbia or any territory or possession of the United States, a State or any political subdivision thereof, or any agency or instrumentality (including the United States Postal Service and Postal Rate Commission) of any of the foregoing; or (2) a church, convention, or association of churches, or any organization operated, supervised or controlled by a church, convention or association of churches which organization (A) is an organization described in section 501(c)(3) of the Internal Revenue Code of 1954, and (B) does not discriminate (i) in the employment, compensation, promotion, or termination of employment of any personnel, or (ii) in the extension of staff or other privileges to any physician or other health personnel, because such persons seek to obtain or obtained health care, through a health maintenance organization.

(g) If the Secretary, after reasonable notice and opportunity for hearing to a State, finds that it or any of its political subdivisions has failed to comply with one or more of the requirements of subsection (a), the Secretary shall terminate payments to such State under sections 314(d), 317, 318, 1002, 1525, and 1613 and notify the Governor of such State that further payments under such sections will not be made to the State until the Secretary is satisfied that there will no longer be any such failure to comply.

Health Systems Agencies: Health Planning and Interaction With Welfare Plans

BY BERNARD HANDEL

HEALTH PLANNING should be a major activity in the operation of all employee welfare benefit plans, whether insured or self-insured. Participation by plan trustees, administrators and covered individuals in local and regional health systems agencies and education can represent a significant step toward a national partnership for health. This joint effort including employee benefit plans, consumers, industry and government can achieve substantial beneficial action in increasing the availability of quality health care at reasonable and competitive costs.

Rising Costs

Chart 1 (*following page*) indicates that national health spending increased from an annual expense of $43 billion in 1965, before Medicare, to over $192 billion in 1978. As Chart 2 indicates, personal health spending in 1978 can be broken down as follows:

Hospitalization	45%
Practitioners' Services	30%
Drugs and Prescriptions	10%
Eyeglass and Optical Care	2%
Nursing Home Care	10%
Other	3%
	100%

In 1979, the nation spent an estimated $212 billion for health care, approximately 9% of our Gross National Product, representing approximately $932 per person. Estimates put the per capita cost at $1,078 in 1980 and almost triple that figure—$3,057—by 1990. In 1980, health care costs for a family of five approximated $5,400, rising to $15,300 in 1990.

Poor health planning is a major reason for these escalating costs, which are passed on to the consumer in the form of high medical bills and insurance rates. Unfortunately, the constantly escalating per capita and overall national health care bill is

Mr. Handel is president of The Handel Group, Inc., an actuarial, consulting and administrative firm specializing in jointly managed trust funds, corporate and public employee plans. A graduate of City University of New York and a certified public accountant, he has over 27 years' experience in the joint trust field. Mr. Handel is a member of the New York State Society of Certified Public Accountants, and has served on several of their committees; a member of the American Pension Conference; and a member of the board of directors of the federally established Hudson Valley Health Systems Agency. He also serves on the New York State Hospital Review and Planning Council which regulates hospitals, health costs, nursing homes, etc. Mr. Handel has spoken at numerous Foundation and other educational meetings and has written many articles in the employee benefit field, some of which have appeared in the Digest *and* Employee Benefits Journal. *He is chairman of the International Foundation's Consultants and Health Services Planning Committees, and a member of the Educational Program Committee.*

not always measured in terms of quality care for all Americans. Despite these high costs, many persons do not receive reasonably effective treatment, and there is limited accessibility to such care in many areas of the country.

International Foundation Annual Conference 1980 327

Chart 1

**RISING HEALTH CARE COSTS
NATIONAL AND PERSONAL HEALTH
CARE EXPENDITURES—
1965-1978**

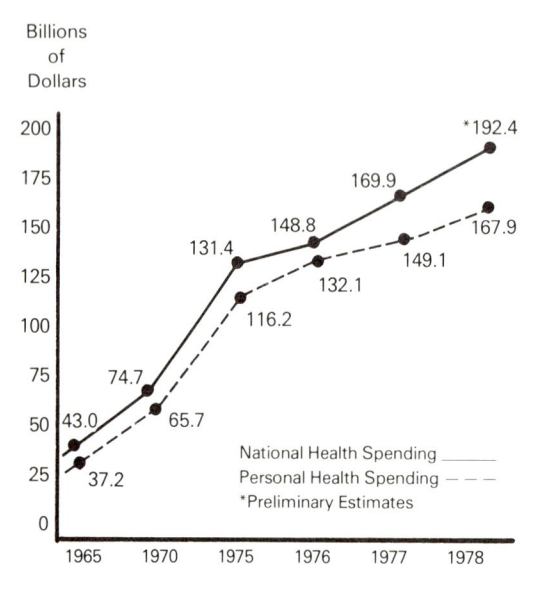

Year	National Health Spending	Personal Health Spending
1965	43.0	37.2
1970	74.7	65.7
1975	131.4	116.2
1976	148.8	132.1
1977	169.9	149.1
1978	*192.4	167.9

*Preliminary Estimates (Billions of Dollars)

Source: Division of National Cost Estimates, Office of Financial and Actuarial Analysis, Health Care Financing Administration, HEW.

Note: All expenditures are reflective of calendar years rather than federal fiscal years. This is a new reporting method of HFCA, HEW.

Cost, Quality Paradoxes

About 5 million people are employed in health services, making it one of the largest industries in America. Many independent appraisals indicate that this huge system is disjointed, uncoordinated, sometimes managerially inefficient and singularly not subject to overall regulation. This is substantiated by our high per capita costs, which exceed similar costs for any other nation.

A major factor is that over 75% of our total health care cost is paid by government and third-party payers. The small direct cost to individual families may contribute to consumers' lack of undue concern in the total health bill.

Despite this gigantic expenditure and the size of the health industry, there is no question that many people suffer from inadequate health care. This is particularly true in rural areas, in low income sections of larger cities, and for older people. Our educational system has failed to provide sufficient health care manpower, despite an apparent oversupply of doctors. This shortage may be most significant with respect to paramedical assistants, nurses and health technicians.

Problems of Distribution and Access

Another contributing factor has been the maldistribution of manpower and facilities on a geographic basis. An analysis of health care facilities and supporting professionals indicates major duplication and excess facilities in some areas, and a paradoxical unavailability or limited availability in other areas. Government statistics relating to hospital beds, for example, indicate that the number of beds available per thousand population varies from about 3.5 in some states to over five in others. Hospital occupancy rates also vary from a low of 50-60% in Alaska to a high of 90% in the Northeast. The average length of stay varies from under seven days in the West and South to over nine days in some Eastern hospitals.

New hospital construction costs average over $100,000 per bed. More significantly, the daily expense to maintain a bed is well over $150, or more than $60,000 a year. If the entire country includes about 100,000 unnecessary beds at $60,000 each per year, the estimated annual waste is $6 billion.

Our rate of increase in physicians is growing substantially faster than the population, due to expansion of medical schools, increased admissions, and an increased number of foreign-trained physicians who permanently practice in the United States. It is estimated that there will be about 50% more physicians practicing in 1990 than at the present time. Doctors are concentrated on the Northeast seaboard from Washington, D.C., to Boston, and on the West Coast. The distribution weighs heavily toward metropolitan areas, which average close to 200 doctors per 100,000 population, compared to only 40 per 100,000 population in rural and less populated areas. A large percentage of these doctors are in specialty fields, with a shortage of general or family practitioners and those involved in geriatric care.

Without cost containment, it is estimated that the price tag for health will continue to rise astronomically. It is significant that the 1979 statistics, as bad as they are, were reduced by the fact that many unemployed people had lost their health insurance and deferred medical treatment.

National Health Planning Efforts

In view of these statistics and the financial cost of Medicaid and Medicare, it became clear to Congress that a planned, orderly approach was required

Chart 2

HOW HEALTH CARE MONEY WAS SPENT IN 1978

National Health Expenditures
1978
(000,000 omitted)

Type	Total
Personal Health Care	$167,911
Prepayment and Administration	$ 10,022
Public Health Activities	$ 5,073
Research	$ 4,267
Construction	$ 5,154
	$192,448

Personal Health Expenditures
1978
(000,000 omitted)

Type	Total
Hospital	$ 76,025
Physicians	$ 32,250
Dental	$ 13,300
Other Professional Services	$ 4,275
Drugs and Drug Sundries	$ 15,098
Eyeglasses and Appliances	$ 3,879
Nursing Home Care	$ 15,751
Other Health Services	$ 4,333
	$167,911

to correct the situation. This approach required solutions on a long term economically sound basis. New developments called for a review of our financing and delivery system, including: the development of alternative and new reimbursement methods; expansion of ambulatory and emergency care; new training and educational techniques; and development of peer review mechanisms and regulation by a myriad of federal and state agencies. In addition, a new examination was required of economic supply and demand relationships in health care and the lack of competitive alternates to traditional providers.

The National Health Planning and Resources Development Acts of 1974 and 1979 combined all prior planning programs with extensive federal funding. The law is based on several concepts. Planning requires participation by local people, consumers as well as providers. It must be financed by the government and have sufficient funds. Planning requires strong implementation techniques, with authority and funding. Planning includes review of necessity of continuing existing facilities. Finally, health care planning cannot be limited to medical care alone, and must expand into financing and into all phases of the health care system, including transportation, ecology, occupational hazards, disasters, etc.

The act required development of a national health planning policy; mandated health service areas and health system agencies throughout the country; governed federal funding; coordinated HHS and state planning agencies; created statewide health coordinating councils; established a national health planning information center; revised the certificate of need procedure for medical facilities construction; and authorized grants, loans and guarantees for construction, modernization and conversion of new health services.

HSAs Established

Health service areas were designated throughout the country. Each area is geared to include a geographically correlated area with a population of 500,000 to a maximum of 3 million. This area is to include at least one center for specialized health services with available health resources to furnish all necessary services. Wherever possible, the area was to be coordinated with the geographic area of professional standards review organizations (PSROs) and state planning areas.

Approximately 200 agencies, known as HSAs, were established.[*]

Among the major responsibilities of the HSA is the gathering and analysis of data relating to health care services and needs in an area; development of

---
[*] A 1980 listing of health systems agencies nationwide is available from the Foundation's Information Services.

a health systems plan with long term goals and objectives to be integrated into a statewide health plan; developing an annual implementation plan with respect to the local health plan; taking measures to increase the accessibility, acceptability and continuity of health services, as well as increasing quality; and, significantly, to restrain increases in cost and prevent unnecessary duplication of services. Its duties include coordination with peer standards review organizations and other state and federal agencies in connection with review of health care performance.

Governing Board Membership

Basically, an HSA is governed by a board of from ten to 30 members. If a larger governing body is created, an executive committee must be established. The majority of the board must be consumers. A *provider* is a person whose current activity is primarily related to provision of health care to individuals, or the administration of facilities or institutions, including outpatient facilities. An *indirect provider* would include one who holds a fiduciary position in an entity engaged in providing health care, research or instruction, or who receives directly or through a spouse more than one-tenth of his annual income from entities engaged in providing health care or health insurance. Thus, fiduciaries involved in the administration of employee benefit welfare plans would probably find themselves in the position of being an indirect provider.

The category of board membership in an HSA is significant since the majority of the board must be consumers. While all providers are, in effect, consumers, an individual's occupation (or that of the spouse) would determine each membership category.

The members of the governing board should be residents of the area (providers who practice in the region are an exception) and should include elected officials and government representatives. In a typical HSA including a number of counties, with local sub-area councils, the sub-area units might nominate regional board members. The law provides, however, that the overall governing board of an HSA must be broadly representative of the social, economic, racial, linguistic and age composition of the population, of the geographic portions of the area, and of the major purchasers of health care (industry, labor unions, etc.). Thus, a mix is required of directors from throughout the area and from all aspects of the health industry, to meet the approximate proportions by the factors mentioned. As a result, the minority provider portion of the governing board is not dominated by any particular segment of the health care industry. A typical regional HSA would be represented among its provider directors by a small number of physicians, hospital administrators, HMO representatives, dentists, health care insurers, nurses, nursing home administrators, mental health representatives, medical school directors, Veterans Administration heads and other health professionals.

The HSA nominates delegates to statewide planning coordinating councils, the members of which would be designated by the governor of the state.

An HSA engages a full-time staff paid from federal funding. The staff would normally include health planners, administrators, economists, data analysts, specialists, consultants, etc.

Local Participation

A mainstay of the area-wide health planning concept is local participation. When a local sub-area council exists, its function is to assist and advise the HSA, designate HSA board members and fill committees and task forces of the area HSA; in addition, it advises the HSA as to project review in its local area, can initiate local plans for financial assistance, and assists in development of the local health plan and needs assessment. A typical sub-area council would include a large number of consumer and provider members in the area. Generally, any person seeking membership can join a local council, limited only to avoid an excess of providers over consumers. The basis of local participation varies throughout the country with each HSA. Consumer roles may be designated with respect to urban-rural residence, ethnic background, language, economically disadvantaged status, sex and age.

Throughout the country, providers have cooperated in joining local area sub-councils and HSAs. There have been difficulties in obtaining consumer participation. Local agencies as well as towns and cities were generally given the right to name directors to the local sub-area council. In rare instances, unions were granted such rights. It does not appear that union members have aggressively sought membership in local sub-area councils. It would appear that administrators of employee benefit plans should strongly recommend that union members and trustees become members of a local sub-area council.

The regional HSA operates through committees for specific purposes. Committees typically include administrative functions; project review of construction applications; plan development and task forces for major health services; and community education and training committees. In recent years, greater attention has been devoted to mental health, and to developing concepts such as medical technology, hospices, etc.

Cost Containment Strategies

Setting Goals and Priorities

In actual practice, the law stresses specific national health priorities which include primary care services in underserved areas, multi-institutional coordination and consolidation, group medical practice development, increased utilization of physician assistants and nurses, emphasis on ambulatory care, multi-institutional sharing of services, improvement in quality of care, coordination with PSROs, geographically integrated care, preventive care and health education, uniform cost accounting, and simplified reimbursement and reporting methodology.

Assessing Needs

A major function of an HSA is its "certificate of need" role in approving and reviewing applications for construction, modernization and conversion of health care facilities, in coordination with state agencies. The priorities involved in furnishing such approval include consideration as to whether population changes warrant improvement; need determination; emphasis on serving rural areas and areas with small financial resources; modernization of facilities serving densely populated areas; new outpatient facilities; elimination or prevention of safety hazards; assurance of compliance with state licensing and accreditation standards; and medical facilities providing comprehensive health care (including preventive care), such as health maintenance organizations, as well as character and competency of the provider.

A recent innovation in this connection is the "batching" methodology, in which similar proposed capital expenditures are grouped together for purposes of intelligent evaluation in light of the entire regional needs for such facilities.

HSAs have also taken over a significant role in appropriateness review, in which regional and state criteria are established to determine the continued need fulfillment of each type of medical component with substantial cost implication. In New York, for example, such reviews are now being conducted with respect to therapeutic radiology, burn treatment, cardiac catheterization, and open heart surgery.

The HSAs' functions in connection with construction and elimination of facilities may be of particular significance to multiemployer funds in the building and hospital service industries. While the trustees, administrators and participants of such plans are vitally concerned with cost containment and overall economies in the health care system, their views may frequently conflict with the interest of the building trades in acquiring job opportunities. Similarly, unions involved in hospital employment will be affected by the loss of jobs on a permanent basis due to elimination of services or the prevention of the opening of certain facilities.

The federal law requires that expenditures by hospitals for substantial equipment such as C.T. scanners are subject to HSA review. However, several states have proposed similar legislation to govern the acquisition of such equipment in doctors' offices. Obviously, if a hospital is unable to buy a C.T. scanner because of the substantial capital expenditure plus the $300,000-plus annual expense to operate such machinery, while a local doctor can do so, then little is gained in overall cost economy in that particular area.

Examining Alternatives

In developing regional health plans, HSAs are reviewing many possible cost containment strategies. HSAs are now involved in possible elimination of excess beds and facilities and reducing unnecessary duplication of services in each area. Such reviews incorporate evaluation of existing facilities by per capita cost, average length of stay, and efficiency and quality of service. Alternatives are explored, such as ambulatory surgical centers, expansion of home health care and outpatient care instead of long term nursing home care, and encouragement of group practice and health maintenance organizations. Consideration may be given to link reimbursement by government (Medicaid and Medicare) to all third-party payers.

A major concern is the modification of present consumer and provider attitudes toward health care, including improved preventive health habits, and changes in lifestyle, behavior and exposure to environmental and ecological conditions. At open hearings, members have recommended stronger controls on diagnostic tests for hospital inpatients, mandatory second opinions for elective surgery, and election of hospital board members by public vote.

In the 1979 amendments to the law, HSA board composition requirements were tightened to specifically emphasize labor and purchasers of health care. A stronger antitrust protection was extended to planning organizations. Health system plans were established on a three year basis, and greater input was extended with respect to new resources, loans and grants.

Mutual Goals

Local health planning is dependent upon participation in each area. Industry, labor, health and welfare funds and private corporate plans have a vital opportunity under this law to participate in the operations of local sub-area councils and regional HSAs.

Administrators, trustees and advisors to employee benefit plans have a unique contribution to offer to HSAs. They have the know-how, background and experience to lend inestimable assistance. The strength of the entire HSA program is in its consumer participation. Fiduciaries of jointly managed trust funds have a long background of organizational know-how and the ability to use the combined voice of many participants. These characteristics are often lacking in the interested consumers now participating in HSAs.

Employers and employer associations have understood the necessity to participate. They have always been involved in management of local hospitals and public facilities. They have aggressively been active in HSA formation and activity as consumer members.

Health planning shares mutual goals with welfare plans in its commitment to cost containment and maintenance of quality of care—despite frequent difficulties in attaining both goals simultaneously. HSAs attempt to eliminate needless facilities through regionalization and centralization, and emphasize the community hospital as a primary treatment center. Tertiary hospitals in each regional area are designated for more complex, highly technical and complicated treatment. It is hoped that these concepts will result in long term reduction in the cost of hospital care. Other techniques include encouragement of sharing of facilities, reimbursement mechanisms which emphasize penalties, coordination with other agencies, uniformity of reimbursement rates, ambulatory outpatient emphasis (even including "nursing homes without walls") and encouragement of competition.

In many parts of the country, labor and industry groups have already formed joint organizations and task forces to work in similar programs, generally in collaboration with HSAs. These labor-management groups seek to lower costs by administrative control, plan design and modification of provider charges.

With respect to *administrative controls,* the emphasis is on detailed, specific claims review, coordination of benefits, pre-authorization of treatment, second surgical opinions, consideration of closed panels, self-insurance and ambulatory outpatient alternatives.

With respect to *plan design,* the emphasis is on incentives to participants by sharing costs and by emphasizing alternative services with lower costs. A major trend could result in larger plans seeking to furnish medical and other health care services directly to their participants. Certainly, many industrial plants are now more actively seeking to utilize existing group medical practice facilities, on-site facilities and even to develop health maintenance organizations of their own.

With respect to the *charges of providers,* many plans have successfully negotiated reduced charges by hospitals and practitioners, often linking hospitalization reimbursement to state and federal reimbursement methodology. Despite FTC problems with medical and dental associations, plans have been successful in many areas in establishing negotiated fee ranges with closed and open panels. Some groups are considering using peer review facilities for their own self-insured plans.

Conclusion

Planning and new approaches to traditional health care are in their infancy. There are many skeptics with vested interest in the health care field who are anxious to see the joint consumer-provider effort fail. Many of these traditional die-hards react equally negatively toward any type of government regulation or intervention or industry and labor efforts to modify consumer and provider attitudes and lifestyles. It is incumbent on employee benefit plans, industry and unions to take an active role in planning and health education efforts.

The International Foundation recently innovated a Health Services Planning Committee, with representation on the committee by high-ranking officials from the American Medical Association, American Dental Association, American Hospital Association, American Comprehensive Health Planning Association, Group Health Insurance Association, insurance carriers and HMOs. This joint committee will work toward a Foundation goal of health care education and cost containment and an active role for all employee benefit plans in such efforts. We look forward to the success of the committee.

We who are involved in such health care plans can either be spectators or join the players. I urge all persons to encourage their company and/or their plan to seize the opportunities provided by law and become involved.

CHAPTER 7

Topics in Plan Administration

Lee F. Jost

Executive Vice President
Tolley International Corporation
Milwaukee, Wisconsin

Robert A. Bohrer

Partner
Ekman & Bohrer
Seattle, Washington

Howard S. Susskind

Partner
Kaplan, Sicking, Hessen,
Sugarman, Rosenthal & DeCastro
Miami, Florida

Marc Gertner

Partner
Shumaker, Loop & Kendrick
Toledo, Ohio

Walter J. Butler

International Vice President
Service Employees International Union
Syracuse, New York

Joseph Eichenholz

Director of Health Policy Analysis
Connecticut General Life Insurance Company
Hartford, Connecticut

Sheldon P. Lewis

Senior Partner
Lewis, Mattes, Connelly & Higgins
President
Benefit Administration Corporation
Fresno, California

Jonathan F. Haber

Audit Partner
Ernst & Whinney
Detroit, Michigan

Lawrence N. Bader

Vice President and Actuary
William M. Mercer, Inc.
New York, New York

Robert A. Semenza

Audit Partner
Main Hurdman & Cranstoun
New York, New York

Robert D. Cooper, Ph.D.

Director of Research
International Foundation of
Employee Benefit Plans
Brookfield, Wisconsin

Effects of a Recessionary Economy on Plan Administration

BY LEE F. JOST

Introduction

The purpose of this discussion is to present the potential effects of a recessionary economy on employee benefit plan administration so that trustees, administrative staff, and other advisors are alert to the issues and activity and are prepared to make changes, if necessary. Including this topic on the program does not imply that prior consideration of the issues was lacking. In fact, the design and practices of most plans include many of the concerns we are going to review. In light of the current economy, the uncertainty of its duration and its effect in specific plans, it is timely to review possible effects to plans' and procedures' ability to weather a sustained economic decline. While many of us have experienced one or more of the effects of earlier recessions on plan administration, we now have an opportunity to refresh our memories, exchange experiences and strengthen our short range planning.

The parts of plan administration which can be affected by a recession include employer accounts, employee accounts, benefits experience in health care and pension plans, plan finances, plan operating costs and other management controls. The potential effects are not only multifaceted insofar as which part(s) of the operation may be affected, but the causes also are multiple and include the employers, participants, trustees and administrative personnel functioning within a depressed economy. Since administrative managers consult legal counsel, we may not have primary responsibility in each of these named areas as trustees do; but we can contribute to and participate with the trustees more meaningfully in their decision making if thought has been given these matters.

Employer Accounts

During national economic declines reaching the proportions of a recession or worse and during economic declines affecting an industry in a given area, money is in shorter supply, credit tightens and em-

Mr. Jost is executive vice president of Tolley International Corporation, Milwaukee. He is an administrative manager and consultant to trust funds for the construction, retail clerks and meat cutters industries. He received his M.A. degree from and served on the Marquette University faculty for two years. He became associated with his present firm in 1960. Mr. Jost has addressed sessions of the Practising Law Institute, Society of Professional Benefit Administrators, and American Society of Pension Actuaries. He served as a member of the Pension Benefit Guaranty Corporation work force on changes to ERISA, Title IV, for multiemployer pension plans. Active in the Foundation for many years, Mr. Jost is a former member of the Board of Directors and several committees, and is currently a member of the Administrative Cost Study and Employer Liability Committees. He has written articles for the Foundation's monthly Digest, *and is co-author of the* Guide to Professional Benefit Plan Management and Administration *published by the Foundation.*

ployers' products and services are paid for more slowly. This forces employers with insufficient capital to delay paying their obligations and, in some cases, causes even those employers with adequate capital to meet obligations a bit later than usual. As a result, trustees, administrative managers and other advisors can reasonably expect:
- The timeliness of employer payments of contributions, liquidated damages, interest

and installment payments on earlier delinquencies to be affected
- An increase in the amount of uncollectible delinquencies
- The frequency and size of employer reporting and payment errors to increase
- Payroll audit costs to increase
- Collection costs to increase, both because the delinquencies may increase and/or because individual delinquencies involving lawsuits may be prolonged, with additional and more intensive effects.

What measures are taken by employers who are unable or unwilling to pay the contractually required contributions to employee benefit plans in good times? They try to gain time with or without services of an attorney; they refuse to respond to correspondence and personal contact; they hide; they pay less than the full amount due the plans because of their personal interpretations of the labor agreements, or other reasons; and in severe circumstances they abandon the business with substantial liabilities. Under the 1980 ERISA Amendments regarding multiemployer pension plans, we can expect larger amounts of uncollected employer withdrawal liabilities.

In light of these possibilities, it is necessary that we examine the effectiveness of trustee policy, administrative and payroll audit procedures, and legal procedures on delinquencies and on collectibles. As you know, ERISA identifies a delinquency of any amount or duration as a prohibited transaction; the Labor Department Class Exemption 76-1 provides that a delinquency shall not be considered to be a prohibited transaction *if* the trustees have a uniform policy which is diligently applied with respect to identifying and pursuing delinquent employers. Many plans have codified their procedures in this regard, and many have as part of such policies established automatic dates to ensure uniform progress in the pursuit of delinquencies. The deadlines were undoubtedly adopted as reasonably diligent under then-existing circumstances. It may be dangerous now to rely on procedures and deadlines adopted under more favorable economic circumstances. We ought to review the policies and procedures to protect the plans against potential loss in a recession, and adjust them as needed.

Employee Accounts

A recession or regional or industry economic decline reduces employment in the jurisdiction of our plans and we, of course, can expect fewer credits to employee accounts. The results will differ depending on the nature of the plan and its eligibility rules.

Health and Welfare Plans

Trustees and staff of health care plans can anticipate
- More participants will be unable to meet the minimum requirements for eligibility; such participants will use the "banked eligibility" or other extension provisions of the plan more intensively.
- More self-payments will be required to maintain eligibility, involving
  — More notices
  — More telephone calls and
  — More appeals on the timeliness of self-payments.

Where these results are experienced, there is greater demand on administrative staff's time and effort to provide the additional service required.

Under the eligibility rules of many multiemployer health care plans, employees are able to accumulate "future earned eligibility" or "banked eligibility," as it is often referred to. Such a feature is particularly important in industries subject to seasonal unemployment, such as the construction trades. As you know, under such provisions the participant's eligibility is continued although contributions are no longer received in his behalf for either (1) a specified number of months; or (2) until the cumulative total in the most recent one, two, three or four quarters drops below the minimum requirements for continued eligibility. Further, in most such plans, it is customary to provide employees who have exhausted "banked eligibility" with the opportunity to continue coverage by making self-payments. Often, the amount of the self-payments required is intended to assist (to subsidize) the unemployed or partially employed participant because the self-payment amount required is less than the cost of providing benefits.

Both the "banked eligibility" and the subsidized self-payment amounts are purposely adopted by trustees, and in good times are used by a certain *average* number of participants yearly. The cost for providing such eligibility extensions is part of the overall plan cost, and a plan can be easily designed to support such costs. In some cases, the contingent liabilities created by the eligibility extensions are funded; in other cases, they are either partially or totally unfunded. Where more than the usual number of participants needs to use eligibility extensions, the plan which has only partially funded for the extensions (or has not funded the extensions at all) may find itself in financial difficulties. In serious cases, it may face the prospect of being unable to live up to participant expectancies, and be unable to give the eligibility required under the bank and under subsidized self-payments.

To anticipate such potential difficulties, it is necessary to examine the appropriateness of each plan's "banked eligibility" in financial and human terms. If the results of the financial analysis discussed below are positive, trustees may find it is possible to further reduce the self-pay amount required from participants to assist them through economically difficult times; and, of course, if the results of the analysis are negative, the trustees can prepare to take one of a number of remedial steps. (Conversely, the impact of this factor should be included in the overall review of fund finances.)

One additional thought is appropriate in closing these comments on a recession's potential effect on employee welfare fund accounts: Welfare plans which credit unpaid contributions worked for delinquent employers need to be particularly alert to cost changes if delinquencies increase.

Pension Plans

With respect to the effect on employee pension accounts, trustees and staff can anticipate more interruptions in continuous service, under plan provisions adopted to comply with minimum break-in-service requirements; under the Schedule SSA Regulations; and under DOL proposed regulations for individual benefit statements. To the extent that this effect is experienced for vested participants, the result is a longer list of names on Schedule SSA for the annual filings, and notices to more terminated vested participants.

The need for pension plans to credit hours worked for delinquent employers is treated later.

Benefits Experience and Claims Activity

Health and Welfare Plans

Increased Utilization. Trustees and staff of pension, health care and vacation funds can anticipate greater claims activity during a recession and the resultant lower full-time employment. Past experience demonstrates that benefits available under health care plans are used more intensively during economic declines because (1) people have the time to take care of elective medical, surgical, hospital and dental needs; (2) they choose to have the necessary care while they remain covered with future earned eligibility and have the opportunity of obtaining weekly loss-of-time benefits instead of losing income completely; (3) the stress created by the uncertainties of economic decline may also increase claims utilization; and (4) more persons claim all of the legitimate reimbursements to which they are entitled. The latter observation is particularly true with respect to major medical coverages. Many covered charges unfortunately are not submitted to health care plans during good economic times because people forget about some of the smaller coverages to which they are legitimately entitled. The reverse is true during hard times, when families are searching for ways to conserve resources. This prompting, when misdirected, can also lead to an increased potential for fraudulent claims.

"Bending" the Rules. Discussing fraud is not popular in our industry, but fraud is practiced and we need to focus on it and, with our awareness, take reasonable measures to protect against it. Trustees and advisory staff should be alert to the increased potential for fraudulent claims with respect to coordination of benefits, subrogation and false claims. Recent news articles discuss this potential result, and also discuss increased thefts and expected increases in fidelity bond premiums.

Economic pressures may distort some people's sense of right and wrong. When applied to plan administration, it is possible that when family income is curtailed due to reduced employment or unemployment, it may be easier for participants to ignore or falsify information on the claims form; for example, information about other group coverage. Trustees of many plans have exercised their subrogation rights in recent years (and under such rights have regained substantial sums from third parties and their insurance companies for medical, surgical and hospital expenses originally covered by the plan). Such plans also require information on the claims form with respect to possible third-party liability; during economic declines, they can expect resistance from claimants in furnishing this necessary information. It may also occur that, even as some participants may be prompted to try to obtain a payment or an amount to which they are not entitled, a fund employee, knowing of a family's financial hardship, will go beyond plan terms to help the family by ignoring COB or subrogation provisions.

With regard to loss of time, it is evident from a review of claims experience that when less work is available, the frequency and length of the periods for which this benefit is paid increase. There appear to be three influences at work. The first is related to the earlier observation about participants getting the elective work done while eligible and while loss of time is payable. The second is related to the fact that some physical conditions—e.g., a certain amount of pain—are tolerated by participants when work and full pay are available; but these same people seek medical relief when full-time employment is unavailable. The third influence is related to participants being more willing to follow their physician's recommendations for rest or length of recuperation when work is unavailable, but loss-of-time benefits are; and, physicians may be more apt to recommend longer courses of treatment and convalescence knowing the patient is apt and able to follow the recommendations.

The increased claims volume will also increase the number of claims denied in whole or in part, and the number of appeals. The administrative manager of a fund paying its own health care claims might in his or her claims audits specifically watch that sympathy is not playing an improper role in his claims examiner's administration of COB; and trustees must be prepared to take appropriate action to have the plan made whole when plan benefits were paid with fraudulent information.

Falsified Claims. The third area in which trustees and staff need to be alert with respect to fraudulent claims involves false claims, in the sense that a period of disability is falsely renewed, charges are falsely increased for services or supplies actually received, or a fictitious service provider and/or patient is named. Unfortunately, a number of plans have experienced losses through such practices.

With respect to falsely renewed periods of disability, many health care plans provide that a period of disability is renewed in the event the employee is able to return to gainful employment. Sometimes "return to gainful employment or occupation" is not defined, and the requirement might be satisfied with an hour's work. Other times, the terminology is defined or additional standards have been imposed to require a return for a full day or a full week before a period of disability is renewed. There are certainly legitimate reasons for a period of disability to be renewed after only a few hours' return to the job, but such occurrences should be reviewed carefully by claims personnel and discussed by the trustees. It is certainly difficult to determine if a physician's discharge of a patient, the patient's return to work for several hours and immediate subsequent care by the same physician for the same or related condition is honestly a recurrence, or whether it indicates a dishonest statement on the part of both the physician and the employee. Another version involves the employer and employee: the physician has not discharged the patient from care, but an employer sends in enough contributions (with or without the work being performed) to establish a renewed disability period. The difficulty of determining whether a dishonest act is involved should not blind us to the fact that it may occur, especially with regard to renewal of disability periods for loss-of-time benefits.

Today's accessibility to photocopy machines and the practice of some providers of using photocopies of subsequent billings creates an increased risk that legitimate providers' invoices can be "doctored" by altering the fee, especially when the service may cover a range of severity, with a parallel range of usual, customary and reasonable fees. In one such case, the participant had not executed an assignment of benefits and the perpetrator was in a trusted fund position.

The false claim, for a fictitious service or by a fictitious provider, may involve invoices stolen from a legitimate provider's office and supplies stolen from the fund office (claims forms or benefit checks). Claims forms, however obtained, and stolen invoices from providers have been used to submit fictitious claims and it doesn't require much imagination to visualize how dishonest fund employees, participants, former participants or others intent on theft might proceed with the script.

These comments are intended to merely reawaken an awareness of fraud potential and relate it to an economic climate. Now let's get on with a more positive aspect of claims experience: i.e., that which pension plans might experience.

Pension Plans

Trustees and staff of pension plans can anticipate increased numbers of early and normal benefit applications; disability applications from more participants who may not meet the definition of "disabled" or "permanently and totally disabled"; and more instances in which trustees are not notified of a retiree's death and in which efforts are made to cash the deceased retiree's benefit checks.

Increased Applications. Certainly during times of reduced full-time employment, persons unable to find work who are also eligible for pension benefits will retire early and apply for early retirement benefits, or will change their plans to work beyond normal retirement age and apply for normal retirement benefits. There are also many more participant inquiries on the benefit amount payable and how to protect their accounts, as well as requests for just general information about the plan and individual accounts. Anticipating an increase in the volume of applications and calls will help the administrative manager maintain the necessary personnel to keep up a high level of service to the applicants.

With respect to disability benefit applications, the point can be made that unemployment may cause participants to take a different view of an injury or illness than at a time when they are fully employed. The bricklayer, truck driver or warehouse employee may be able to tolerate the low back pain when fully employed because he has other priorities, whereas when employment is unavailable, the priorities are rearranged for him and it becomes easier to do what his doctor may have told him to do some time ago: namely, to retire or stop doing the job that aggravated the pain. As the number of applications increases, more personnel time is required; and if increased volume is accompanied with questions of whether the condition satisfies the plan definition of "disability," additional time is needed to check diagnoses and judge the merits of the application. This checking may involve more assistance from and costs of the fund medical examiner.

Potential for Fraud. Now let's examine some areas of potential loss to pension plans resulting from behavior which might be triggered under financial duress. As the effects of a recession add to the pressures created by inflation upon fixed incomes, pension plans' staffs may see more situations in which surviving spouses or others illegally endorse a deceased retiree's benefit checks because they "misunderstood" the nature of the benefit.

Another area in which pension plans may be subject to greater loss through fraudulent acts is that of death benefits. When a retiree dies in a remote place or in a nursing home without friends or family, persons aware of the deceased's monthly benefit payments may attempt to negotiate monthly checks, or produce fraudulent documentation designating them as the beneficiary of death benefits. Where the beneficiary has not been designated well in advance or is not a member of the immediate family, appropriate steps to verify the designation should be taken, and those steps should be adopted by the trustees in conjunction with the administrative manager and fund counsel.

Finally, I believe we can expect that the number of disputes over death benefit payments will increase and the disputants will be more tenacious during a recession. This can occur more easily in cases where a retiree has not designated a beneficiary, or the beneficiary predeceased the retiree and the plan does not provide for an automatic distribution to survivors in priority. The disputes will generally involve confrontations such as the former and the current spouse, a parent and a former spouse or a natural child and a stepchild.

Vacation Plans

Before moving on to the impact of a recession on employee benefit plan finances, we should note that vacation plans, too, can anticipate increased administrative activity, especially in those vacation plans which limit payouts to requested vacation periods and holidays except in financial emergencies. Obviously, more people will encounter financial emergencies during a recession than at other times, and the plan's response will be to satisfy more individuals' requests with individually written checks.

Finances of Health and Welfare Plans

One of the most significant steps prudent trustees and advisory staff of health care plans can take is to determine the potential effect of a recession on cash flow reserves and investments. A primary objective of such financial analysis is to determine if a problem exists or if one can be anticipated, and the point at which it may occur. The issues are broader and more complex for health care plans using balanced hours in eligibility rules, and my examples use cost-plus plans.

As part of this analysis, the potential cumulative effect of several factors on income, liabilities and reserves should be examined for various future periods. The study of a financially healthy plan might incorporate the projected impact of a 20%, 30% or 40% decline in employment on the fund's contribution income, interest income, cash flow and reserves. It should also project the impact of subsidies made to persons retaining eligibility through self-payments and, perhaps, the impact of a 15-20% increase in claims utilization.

For insured plans, the objectives of the analysis are to anticipate premium action by the carrier; help determine if existing or expected increased premiums will create a cash flow problem; determine how much of a premium increase the fund's reserves can absorb, and for how long; estimate the extent to which reserves may have to be rebuilt at a later date; and consider contingency plans if projections indicate a cash flow and/or reserve problem.

For self-funded plans, the objectives of the analysis are similar, because it helps (1) determine if existing claims or increased claims experience will create a cash flow problem; (2) determine how much of a claims utilization increase plan reserves can absorb, and for how long; (3) review the degree of protection the plan's stop-loss maximum creates; (4) estimate the extent to which reserves may have to be rebuilt at a later date; and (5) enable trustees and advisors to consider contingency plans if projections indicate a cash flow and/or reserve problem.

Exhibit 1: Reserves and Income

With the assistance of the Exhibits which follow this text, we can visualize the extent to which a non-insured health care plan's contribution income, dollar reserve and reserve position are affected by reduced employment created in a recession. The dollar amounts below the column furthest to the right captioned "100% (150 hours)" represent results under more or less full employment with 150 hours worked by the average number of eligible participants per month. With a 20% reduction in hours, contribution income will fall to 80% of its previous levels, and those figures are shown in the center column. As a result of a 20% reduction in contribution income and assuming operating expenses remain constant (despite increased demand on staff), the deficit spending contemplated by the trustees increases to $1,351,850, leaving a fund balance of $1,314,650, net of reserves for incurred and unreported claims. Since no reserve was established for future earned eligibility in this example, the fund balance is equivalent to 3.4 months of benefits and operating expenses only. This relatively small amount would be called upon for increased claims experience as well as increased demand on subsidies that may be inherent in the self-payment formula.

The lower half of Exhibit 1 demonstrates the effect on the fund if the reductions in contribution income continue through a second plan year. The examples do not incorporate any offset of deficit spending from interest earnings because of today's volatile interest rates. However, the footnote assumes that if 15% were earned on average in the plan year ending May 1, 1981, interest earned would have ranged from $237,000-360,000; and if the same 15% were earned on the reduced income and reserves in the plan year ending May 1, 1982, the interest earnings would have dropped dramatically to a range of $37,000-240,000.

Exhibit 2: Costs and Expenses

Next, analyze the potential impact of a recession on benefit costs. Exhibit 2 does not reflect any increased costs or increased claims as we considered were possible in a recession. The Exhibit demonstrates how the total of paid benefits and expenses varies when expressed as a per hour cost at an average of 90, 120 or 150 hours per month. As you can see, the total of benefits plus administrative and operating expenses of the plan in this illustration is $4,480,150 a year. That amount during good times amounts to 65.5¢ per hour, but in a deep recession where employment is reduced by 40%, the hourly cost is $1.09. The lower half of Exhibit 2 demonstrates what the same plan of benefits is expected to cost a year later assuming continued trends and inflation under the same circumstances.

This type of analysis makes it possible for trustees to determine whether a financial problem exists and its extent, or to anticipate an emerging problem. With this information, trustees are able to request necessary additional information with which to monitor the plan's response to an economic decline. Trustees may wish, for example, to have a cash flow analysis prepared for a six or twelve month period, or for a longer period of time. If a cash flow problem is indicated, it is necessary to examine the fund's liquidity position and double check maturity dates of investments. If time permits, strengthen the plan's liquidity position from cash flow and matured investments, and select the most desirable candidates for liquidation prior to maturity. Where investments are to be redeemed prior to maturity, calculate the loss potential from early redemption and make it part of the financial analysis.

Trustees' Alternatives

In the event the financial analysis and cash flow indicate potential problems, before any corrective action is taken, trustees should determine if there is any mitigating or intensifying factor known or anticipated strongly enough to affect the projections. When action is required, recall that the following are among the trustees' interim and longer term alternatives:

1. Modification of eligibility rules by adjusting minimum requirements for continuation of eligibility, self-payment amounts and/or limiting the use of future earned eligibility
2. Modification of benefits for active employees and/or retirees and survivors
3. Planned use of reserves allocated for incurred but unreported claims and/or future earned eligibility
4. Reduction of operating budget by cutting back on personnel, equipment, facilities and/or services
5. Borrowing from outside sources
6. Review of income sources: improve cash management, collect delinquencies, recommend an increased contribution rate and/or collect costs shared with others and paid in advance by this plan.

Pension Plan Concerns

Trustees and staff of pension plans can anticipate reduced contribution income and increased retirements; thus, increased benefit payments. However, it should be noted at the outset of these remarks that a recession usually does not create serious financial problems for pension funds that are not already in trouble, though it does increase administrative activity. Some results which can be anticipated include the following:

1. Reduced income means less credit for participants and less plan liability; or, reduced income may mean giving the same credit for less hours, in which case less assets accumulate to fund the same or similar liabilities.
2. More retirees mean more benefits paid from reduced contribution income, and some reduction in the amount available for current investments.
3. Reduced opportunity for employment means fewer younger employees entering the plan, influencing the group's average age.
4. More earlier retirements may reduce the average retirement age somewhat.
5. Less employment opportunity causes more one year breaks in service and, if it affects non-vested participants, may influence plan turnover somewhat.

Pursuant to ERISA, pension plans must credit covered employment even though employer contributions may not be received. If, despite trustees' and staff's intensified efforts, the amount of uncollectible contributions increases, plan costs increase to some extent because participants must be credited for vesting and accrual purposes. In certain industries, if employers are faced with far less work and attempt to keep good journeymen employed in some capacity albeit not at their trade, we may find some increased use of vesting credits from contiguous non-covered employment. Contributions from more employers may cease, and it must be determined if employer withdrawal has occurred as described in the 1980 ERISA Amendments for multiemployer pension plans.

Results will vary from plan to plan, depending on a number of factors including plan design, average age of the group, whether actuarial assumptions are realistic and the strength of the benefit security ratio.

Summary

Obviously, none of these concerns are new. However, with the opportunity to focus on each of them and to see the relationship of one concern to the other, we may be able to adjust our priorities so that these matters receive adequate consideration for the plans with which we are associated.

Exhibit 1

HEALTH CARE PLAN PROJECTED RESERVE STUDY

May 1, 1980 — May 1, 1981

	Reduced Employment		
	60% (90 hrs)	80% (120 hrs)	100% (150 hrs)
I. Contribution Income	$ 2,462,400	$ 3,283,200	$ 4,104,000
Expenses	4,635,050	4,635,050	4,635,050
Change in Reserve	(2,172,650)	(1,351,850)	(531,050)
Estimated Reserve at 5/1/80 (net of o/u only)	2,666,500	2,666,500	2,666,500
Balance	$ 493,850	$ 1,314,650	$ 2,135,450
Reserve Position Equivalent at 5/1/81	1.28 Mo.	3.40 Mo.	5.53 Mo.

— — — — — — — — — —

May 1, 1981 — May 1, 1982

II. Contribution Income	$ 2,462,400	$ 3,283,200	$ 4,104,000
Expenses	5,103,300	5,103,300	5,103,300
Change in Reserve	(2,640,900)	(1,820,100)	(999,300)
Estimated Reserves at 5/1/81 (net of o/u only)	493,850	1,314,650	2,135,450
Balance	Nil	Nil	$ 1,136,150
Reserve Position Equivalent at 5/1/82	-0-	-0-	2.8 Mo.

Cal. Yr. 1979 = $250,000 or 0.65 month reserve in period I;
                        0.59 month reserve in period II.

5/1/80 - 5/1/81   15% on average balance = range $237,000 to $360,000
5/1/81 - 5/1/82   15% on average balance = range $ 37,000 to $240,000

Prepared by Technical Services Department-Tolley International Corporation

Exhibit 2

PROJECTED EXPENSES STUDY

May 1, 1980 to May 1, 1981
Active Eligibles

		Reduced Employment		
		60%	80%	100%
		Hourly Equivalents		
		90	120	150
Death, AD&D and Casualty Claims	$4,215,750	$1.0272	$0.7704	$0.6163
Cost Factor	87,500	0.0214	0.0160	0.0128
Total Benefits Expense	4,303,250	1.0486	0.7864	0.6291
Administrative, Operating and Other Expenses	176,900	0.0431	0.0323	0.0259
Total Benefits, Administrative and Operating Expenses	$4,480,150	$1.0917	$0.8187	$0.6550

--- --- --- --- --- --- --- ---

May 1, 1981 to May 1, 1982

Death, AD&D and Casualty Claims	$4,639,100	$1.1304	$0.8478	$0.6782
Cost Factor	96,200	0.0234	0.0176	0.0141
Total Benefits Expense	$4,735,300	$1.1538	$0.8654	$0.6923
Administrative, Operating and Other Expenses	194,500	0.0474	0.0355	0.0284
Total Benefits, Administrative and Operating Expenses	$4,929,800	$1.2012	$0.9009	$0.7207

Prepared by Technical Services Department-Tolley International Corporation

Trustee Responsibilities: Communications to Participants

BY ROBERT A. BOHRER

COMMUNICATION at its best informs participants of benefits which are available and gives participants peace of mind and security concerning future health and pension benefits. Effective communication also lays a foundation which encourages full utilization of available benefits because the participants know and understand the benefits for which application can be made. Good communications also encourage the participant to communicate with the plan trustees, e.g., to express appreciation and to make recommendations for areas of plan improvement.

This article concentrates on four aspects of communication to plan participants. First, we will briefly review the ERISA requirements of plan communications to participants. In the second and third aspects, we will focus on trustee liability for communication failure and techniques for minimizing that liability, such as through the use of booklet disclaimers. Finally, we will review pending communication requirements in the Department of Labor's proposed regulations on individual benefit statements for pension plans.

Mr. Bohrer is a partner in the Seattle, Washington, law firm of Ekman & Bohrer, which is primarily devoted to work in employee benefit plan law and in the area of delinquent contributions for joint funds. Before returning to private practice, Mr. Bohrer was manager of client services for United Administrators, Inc., in Seattle and, prior to that, practiced with the Seattle law firm of Donaldson & Kiel. Mr. Bohrer received his B.A. in economics from the University of Washington and his J.D. degree from Indiana University. He is a member of the American Bar Association Section on Labor Law and has spoken at previous Foundation educational meetings.

Three Basic Principles

When working on any communications problem, you should keep in mind three underlying principles of communication. These are like building blocks, which together support each other for effective communication to plan participants.

The first building block for a plan communication program is good *recordkeeping*, and the ability to extract needed information from the trust records. The plan cannot communicate meaningfully if it can't put its hands on information which is relevant to the participants! Information should be organized in the trust office so that accurate information on a member's eligibility status can be retrieved promptly. A delay in responding to participants' requests for information, or inaccurate or incomplete advice to them, amounts to a failure to communicate.

The second building block of a communications program is *compliance* on an ongoing basis with the statutory and regulatory requirements of the Employee Retirement Income Security Act of 1974 (ERISA). Plan trustees certainly can design a sophisticated communications program which exceeds the minimum requirements of ERISA and its regulations. Nevertheless, trustees should regularly undertake to assure themselves that their plans are in compliance with the minimum ERISA disclosure requirements.

The third building block of effective communication is *publication* of relevant information to the individual participant in an understandable and meaningful format. Information presented in a confusing or unreadable format is as much a hindrance to effective communication as is a direct failure to comply with the statutory requirements, or an inability to obtain relevant information in the plan records. In a recent case dealing with plan communications, the court looked to the legislative history of ERISA and quoted from the House Committee on Education and Labor as follows:

> An important issue relates to the effectiveness of communication of plan contents to employees. Descriptions of plans furnished to employees should be presented in a manner that an average and reasonable worker participant can understand intelligently. *Allen v. Atlantic Richfield Retirement Plan,* 480 F.Supp. 848, 272 BNA BPR D-17, (D.C. E.D. Pa. 1979) *aff'd w/o opinion* __F.2d__, 313 BNA BPR A-23 (3rd Cir. 1980).

This quotation expresses a foundation principle in communicating effectively with plan participants.

Technical Requirements

Policy and History

The concept of required disclosure of plan information to participants is not new to ERISA. The Welfare and Pension Plans Disclosure Act required certain basic disclosures to participants. In 1972, the Department of Labor proposed new regulations under that act which required the disclosure of more pertinent information to employees. Those proposed regulations essentially required a comprehensive description of a plan in simple, nontechnical language and a description of the circumstances under which benefits might be lost by a participant. Final regulations were published in 1973 which incorporated these basic concepts.

In its preparation of ERISA, as shown by the earlier quotation from some of the legislative history, Congress recognized a need to have plan information described to participants in a clear and understandable fashion. Congressman Dent of Pennsylvania, in remarking on the importance of the summary plan description, said that the summary plan description "Will provide participants with a much better understanding of how their plans operate. It is clearly unfair to hold an employee accountable for acts which disqualify him from benefits if he had no knowledge of these acts, or if these conditions were stated in a misleading or incomprehensible manner in plan documents." The policy reflected in this statement runs throughout ERISA's legislative history, and is an element of all disclosure-related issues with which trustees are confronted.

The requirements of disclosure are, consequently, among the primary responsibilities imposed on trustees of employee benefit plans. It is the trustees' duty to comply with this policy by adhering to the specific requirements of ERISA and the various regulations issued by the Internal Revenue Service and the Department of Labor. Moreover, a failure to disclose pertinent information can be deemed a breach of fiduciary duty, which amplifies the liability of the trustees who fail to disclose the required information. This is a new element introduced by ERISA which was not present in earlier law. Under the Welfare and Pension Plans Disclosure Act which preceded ERISA, a participant's only remedy against trustees who failed to disclose the required summary of the annual report was to sue the trustees for a statutory penalty.

ERISA Requirements

There are three forms of ERISA-required plan disclosures. First, there is the disclosure material which must be distributed to all participants and beneficiaries at specific times of the year and when special events occur. Examples are the summary plan description, summary annual report, and summary of material modifications. Second, there is the information and material which must be furnished upon request, such as statements of eligibility and accrued benefits. Finally, there is the material which must be maintained and available for participants' inspection. Examples are the availability of plan documents, the annual report Form 5500, the applicable labor agreements and the annual audit.

The specific disclosure provisions of ERISA are found mostly in Title I under Sections 101, 102, 104 and 105. Regulations are issued pursuant to these sections.

Plan Booklet. For the majority of plan members, the primary contact and point of communication will be through the descriptive booklet. We should note here that what we know as the plan descriptive booklet may not necessarily comply with the regulations covering publication of a summary plan description. The summary plan description is a relatively technical recitation of plan information in a required format. Usually this listing is found in a plan's descriptive booklet; however, we should be clear that when we speak of the summary plan description we are talking about the summary of plan information specifically required under ERISA. The descriptive booklet generally is a more complete outline of procedures and information which sometimes even includes a complete copy of the benefit plan.

Communications Checklist. It is often helpful to see required procedures listed out in a checklist format in order to grasp the totality of the responsibility. In the material at the end of this text (*see* Appendix B) is a Communications Checklist which will help you to understand the basic outline of the communication responsibility. Note that it is not a complete listing of all communication functions and that you should review particular cases with your own plan counsel.

The Communications Checklist is broken down into two sections. The first section contains the formal disclosure items, which generally fall into one of our three ERISA disclosure categories. The second part of the checklist generally covers the processing of inquiries and claims for benefits. During our discussion on recordkeeping at last year's Annual Conference, I encouraged trustees to acquaint themselves with the duties of their plan advisors so that the trustees are familiar with the operation of the plan and are satisfied that basic functions are being performed. [*See* Robert Bohrer, "Trustee Responsibilities: Recordkeeping Policies and Techniques," *Textbook for Employee Benefit Plan Trustees, Administrators and Advisors,* Volume 21 (1980), p. 305.] I would encourage you also to ask your plan advisors for a description of the various communication functions that your plans are carrying out. You can use this Communication Checklist as your own informal guide to learn more about your plan's communication activities.

You are probably familiar with most of the items listed on the checklist. One area that frequently is overlooked, however, is the sixth item dealing with responsibility of advising participants and beneficiaries of *material modifications to the plan.* What is a material modification? Generally, a material modification is an amendment to the benefit plan or a change in plan information which is important or significant to an individual plan participant's understanding of his rights under the plan and his ability to enforce those rights. So, for example, obvious material modifications of which participants should be advised are changes in the name and address of the plan administrator, the method of filing benefit claims, and changes in eligibility rules. The Department of Labor goes even further, however, and indicates that it considers changes in the methods of accumulating assets, changes in service providers to the plan (such as plan administrator, consultant or attorney), and changes in the trustees' appointments to be material. A summary of material modifications needs to be published only when such a change occurs and then only once a year, seven months after the end of the plan year. You might note that this roughly coincides with the time for publication of the plan's summary annual report, and you might be able to consolidate the two reports or, at least, distribute them together.

The checklist also includes the *updated five year summary plan description* which is specifically required by ERISA [Section 104(a)(1)(B)]. *If* a plan has adopted amendments or events have occurred which amount to material modification, an updated SPD is required five years after the last publication. Many health and welfare plans published a new plan booklet around 1976. If you have had material modifications in your plan since that time, you will need to publish an updated five year SPD sometime during 1981. Most pension plans did not publish a booklet until after they received an IRS letter of determination. In the event of a material modification to your pension plan, you will need to publish an updated five year summary plan description within five years from the date of your last booklet.

I also want to draw your attention to the ninth item on the checklist, the *inspection of pertinent trust documents.* A simple way to comply with this requirement is to maintain at the administrative or union offices a general disclosure file in which copies of the summary plan descriptions, summary annual reports, annual report Form 5500, trust agreement and similar plan documents are maintained on a current basis for inspection upon request by a participant or beneficiary. In this way, simple maintenance of the file will document compliance with this requirement.

Multiemployer Act Requirements

Not included in the checklist material are communication items under the Multiemployer Pension Plan Amendments Act of 1980. This statute was signed into law on September 26, 1980, by President Carter and basically amends those portions of ERISA which cover withdrawal of employers from pension plans. Under that act, special notices to participants are required in different circumstances. Here again you will want to review with your own trust counsel the requirements which may pertain in a given situation.

Many of the various notices which are required under the Multiemployer Act apply to the withdrawing or the remaining employers. Four special disclosure items, however, must go to participants and beneficiaries. These are (1) a notice of reorganization, where the plan is not terminated but is maintained through an increase in contributions; (2) a notice of reduction of accrued benefits, where a pension plan is amended to reduce benefits during reorganization of a plan; (3) a notice of insolvency, where a plan determines that it may become insolvent, and finally, (4) a notice of resource benefit level. The resource benefit level is a technical term under the act which is the highest level of monthly benefits which a troubled pension plan is able to pay out of its available resources.

These four notices are very technical disclosure items. If you are involved with a plan reorganization or insolvency, you should consult with your professional advisors to ensure compliance with these requirements.

Extra-ERISA Disclosure

Remember that under ERISA there are three basic forms of required disclosure: (1) material which must be distributed to all participants and beneficiaries at specific times or if certain events occur, (2) material and information furnished to individual participants and beneficiaries upon their request and (3) material which is available to participants and beneficiaries for their inspection. These can be generally viewed as the *minimum* communication requirements. Three recent court cases have explored the question of whether trustees are required to make disclosure efforts which exceed the statutory and regulatory minimums.

In *Castello v. Gamacho* 593 F.2d 358 (8th Cir. 1979) [District Court Opinion at 457 F.Supp. 310 (E.D. Mo. 1978)], the sister of a deceased participant insured under a group life insurance policy of a welfare trust sought death benefits as the beneficiary of the life insurance policy. Upon application the sister discovered that coverage had lapsed due to the participant's layoff, and that the participant had not taken the opportunity to convert to an individual policy while she was alive. The court of appeals held that the trustees had no duty to advise the participant that her status had changed due to her layoff from work and that the trustees had no duty to advise that she could convert to an individual policy under the provision of the plan. In this case we see that plan trustees generally need not (1) individually advise participants of their changed status under a plan nor (2) make an extraordinary effort to advise individual participants of particular provisions of a plan which may pertain.

These principles were followed in the case of *Allen v. Atlantic Richfield Retirement Plan, supra*. In this case, the surviving wife of the deceased participant sued to recover death benefits under the company's retirement plan. Mr. Allen was ill for a considerable period of time due to serious coronary problems. His fellow employees and supervisors were aware of this fact, and a company representative advised him to make application for lump sum benefits for his wife in the event of his death. The plan eligibility rules required a 30 day waiting period before the benefits became effective. Mr. Allen died six days after executing the application forms. The federal district court held that the plan was not required to make an extra effort to warn employees of special provisions such as the 30 day waiting provision. In effect, the participant assumes the burden of being sufficiently familiar with the plan to be alert to special provisions that may apply in an individual case.

Contrast the *Castello* and *Allen* cases, both of which dealt with applications for death benefits, with the 1980 decision of the 6th Circuit Court of Appeals in *Hodgins v. Central States Southeast and Southwest Areas Pension Plan*, 624 F.2d 760 (6th Cir. 1980). In this case, a pension fund unilaterally changed the status of a pension participant from employee to supervisor based upon information which the plan received from the participant's employer. The effect of the change in status was to make Mr. Hodgins ineligible for a pension benefit. The participating employer secured a refund of the contributions after notifying the fund of Mr. Hodgins' change of status. The appellate court required the plan to pay a pension benefit to Mr. Hodgins because he had no notice of his change of status and no opportunity to appeal the adverse determination. The court held that the plan should have advised Mr. Hodgins of his change in status and the effect it would have on his eligibility for pension benefits. The court said that the plan took affirmative action to unilaterally change the status of a participant. In effect, the court upheld the principle that plan fiduciaries must accord what amounts to fundamental due process to a participant in making a decision as to his status under the plan. [See *Sturgill v. Lewis*, __F.Supp.__, 62 L.R.R.M. 2034 (D.C. D.C. 1966) for fundamental due process elements required of benefit plans.]

The general rule which we find in the *Castello*, *Allen* and *Hodgins* cases is that a plan does not need to advise individual participants of the effect of plan rules where participants change their *own* situation or status under the plan. On the other hand, where the *trustees* change some aspects of the plan or facts which affect individual participants, they must make extra efforts to communicate the change to the affected individuals and give them an opportunity to appeal.

Failure to Communicate

Of all the different factual circumstances in which participants have contact with their benefit trust funds, there are basically three types of communication breakdown. There has been a failure of communication if (1) a participant has not received relevant information; (2) a participant has received incorrect information; or (3) a participant has received ambiguous or unclear information.

The member's most frequent contact with his or her benefit plan is through the receipt of the plan's descriptive booklet, telephone contact with the trust office, and contact with union office personnel. It is not a coincidence, then, that the court cases which have dealt with disclosure problems have arisen out of factual situations involving these three basic points of contact.

Which Controls: Benefit Plan or Plan Booklet?

The plan booklet is usually the first place that a participant will turn for information regarding available benefits and procedures. The Department of Labor views the summary plan description as the single most important element in the disclosure process required by ERISA because the SPD is the only document which is distributed to all participants, including new participants, and filed with the Department of Labor. This attitude toward the plan booklet by participants and the Department of Labor raises two obvious questions: (1) To what degree should plan participants be permitted to rely upon the printed summaries of plan benefits? and (2) When will a trustee be held liable for misunderstandings which arise out of booklet language? Several recent cases give us guidance in answering these important questions.

Court Cases. In *Adams v. Hercules* 265 S.E.2d 781 (Ga. 1980), a disabled employee sued his employer for benefits under a supplemental payment plan alleging that he was not aware of the eligibility rules and therefore could not take steps to become eligible. The plan booklet, described by the Georgia Supreme Court as a well-organized and readable plan summary, specifically stated that the plans presented in the booklet were in a very brief form and that fuller details could be obtained from the employee's foreman, personnel office, or supervisor. The court sided with the employer in this case, holding that the language of the booklet specifically put the employee on notice that there existed a master agreement which the employee could consult and should have investigated to become familiar with the detailed rules of the plan. The court said that the language in the booklet would alert an ordinarily prudent person, and that the employer was not bound by the language in the booklet. The employer is bound only by the terms and provisions of the benefit plan.

The identical issue was presented in *Trombly v. Marshall,* __F.Supp.__, 290 BNA BPR D-1 (D.C. D.C. 1980), which involved the eligibility rules of the plan and a written disclaimer contained in the summary booklet which read as follows:

> This booklet is not a part of and does not modify or constitute any provision of the plan described herein, nor does it alter or affect in any way the rights of any participant under the plan. The plan and all descriptions and outlines thereof are governed by the formal plan document. A copy of this plan is on file at the office of the company and may be inspected upon request, during normal business hours of any regular working day.

On the face of it, this appears to be a good example of well-written disclaimer language. Nevertheless, its use was challenged.

The plaintiff was the beneficiary of a pension plan in which her husband had been a participant. The plan administrator had determined that because her husband lacked sufficient credited service, Mrs. Trombly was not eligible for survivors' benefits under the plan's rules. She sued not only the plan but, significantly, she also sued the Secretary of Labor to enjoin the use of and reliance on such disclaimers. Mrs. Trombly claimed that the use of booklet disclaimers constitutes an attempt by fiduciaries to relieve themselves from responsibility or liability, and that the disclaimer violates the statutory requirement that a summary plan description, in the words of Section 102, be "sufficiently accurate and comprehensive to reasonably apprise such participants and beneficiaries of their rights and obligations under the plan." ERISA Section 102(a)(1).

The *Trombly* case is significant inasmuch as the Department of Labor joined with the defendant in moving for dismissal of the plaintiff's case. In a narrow holding, the court found that Mrs. Trombly was not a bona fide "beneficiary" as defined by ERISA, and therefore had no standing to bring the suit. The question as to the validity of disclaimers was not answered in the court's opinion. However, the fact that the Department of Labor joined in the motion for dismissal appears to indicate that the Department is not generally opposed to the use of disclaimers, although we should be cautious in taking this case to be a blanket approval of booklet disclaimers. In preparing the final regulations on summary plan descriptions, the Department of Labor specifically omitted any reference, direction or guidance on the use of disclaimers. The Department elected to deal with the issue of disclaimers on a case by case basis.

Acceptable, Effective Disclaimers. Based upon these two cases, it appears that the courts are presently willing to uphold disclaimer language where there is a clear, obvious and unambiguous statement in the plan booklet that the booklet is a summary only and that further information can be obtained from another identified source. Generally, under current law, disclaimers are an acceptable method whereby plans can alert plan participants that more complete and detailed information is available from sources other than the booklet summary.

Great care should be taken, however, in designing the language and format of a disclaimer notice. Put yourselves in the place of the participant. Does the booklet language clearly tell you where to go for complete information, or are you more confused after reading the booklet? In designing a disclaimer notice, it should (1) be prominently displayed inside the front booklet cover or in the first few pages of the booklet; (2) be simply written in a short, boldly printed paragraph; and (3) prominently display the name, address and telephone number of the plan administrator. These are three commonsense rules, but when you sit down to write one of these paragraphs it is easy to get all wound up trying to cover all your bases. As shown by the *Hercules* and *Trombly* cases, the courts will generally uphold simple disclaimers that refer participants to the actual plan document; however, you can expect self-serving and ambiguous statements to be fair game for invalidation.

Note, also, that there are different kinds of disclaimers. We have been talking about *booklet* disclaimers; however, some plan documents contain disclaimers as to the responsibility for continued funding and future payment of benefits. A disclaimer which seeks to limit a sponsor's overall funding liability was invalidated in the United States Supreme Court case of *Nachman v. PBGC,* __U.S.__, 291 BNA BPR D-1 (1980). See also *Thurnhorst v. Janes,* 310 BNA BPR A-9 (unpub. opinion, Wis. Ct. App. 1980).

Statements by Plan Personnel

In addition to relying on the language in plan booklets, participants frequently rely on affirmative statements made by plan personnel regarding a participant's eligibility or benefits. The courts have been much less willing to penalize the participant where the participant has received misinformation from plan representatives. An excellent example of this is the recent case of *Nevada Public Employee Retirement Board v. Byrne,* 607 P.2d 1351 (Nev. 1980), in which the participant specifically inquired as to his anticipated pension benefits and, over a period of four years, corresponded with the plan on this subject. In the early correspondence, the plan computed his monthly benefits to be approximately $725, and it was in reliance upon this advice that Mr. Byrne resigned his position as county assessor, sold his personal residence and purchased a retirement home. Subsequent to all these transactions, however, the board informed Mr. Byrne that they had recomputed his monthly benefits to be a mere $86.78.

The Nevada Supreme Court's decision is a classic in its application of the legal doctrine of equitable estoppel. This doctrine essentially holds a person responsible for statements of misinformation where another party has relied upon those statements and changed his or her position in reliance on those statements. The plan was required to pay the benefit based upon the misinformation from a plan representative. Although this is a pension case, its principle should be equally applicable to statements made on behalf of a health and welfare plan, such as where a participant asks for pre-authorization of anticipated dental claims or surgical procedures.

Statements by Third Persons

Plan participants also frequently rely on statements by individuals who are not official representatives of a health and welfare or pension plan. In *Allen v. Atlantic Richfield,* discussed earlier, one of the plaintiff's main arguments was that a company vice president had gratuitously undertaken to advise Mr. Allen by encouraging him to make application for the death benefits. The court refused to hold the plan responsible based upon the statements of the company representative. The court held that the company representative was merely acting in a private capacity and there was no policy of individual counseling. It is significant that the court also emphasized that the summary booklet clearly placed employees on notice of certain application deadlines and the existence of a master benefit contract.

Is there a general rule which we can follow in these situations? First, we should recognize that there is definite potential liability to a health and welfare or pension plan where individuals, who ostensibly have some connection and knowledge of plan affairs but who are not acting in an official capacity, make statements which are construed by participants to be reliable. Business agents are in a particularly sensitive position, because they are frequently asked about the application of plan rules and how certain factual circumstances might be handled by the plan office. Labor and management trustees are in an even more sensitive position, because their statements are easily perceived to be official judgments made on behalf of the plan. It is not easy to identify a general rule in these cases, since the courts' decisions, generally, turn on the facts and circumstances of each case. You can expect courts to carefully investigate questions such as (1) Who made the statement? (2) Did the person hold a unique position with the plan in the eyes of the member? (3) How was the statement relied upon? (4) Was it reasonable to rely on such information, in the context of all other plan communication material? Cases involving statements by third persons must be judged on a case by case basis. [See also *Dorward v. ILWU-PMA Pension Plan,* 452 P.2d 258, 70 L.R.R.M. 3401 (Wash. 1969) and *Dohrer v. Wakeman,* 14 Wash. App. 157, 539 P.2d 91 (1975).]

Disclaimers which we put in our booklets should not only be obvious and simple to understand, but also should contain a clear declaration that statements covering eligibility or benefit matters made by anyone other than plan office personnel, including the statements of plan trustees, are not binding on the plan. Moreover, business agents, employers and plan trustees should be instructed to refer all technical questions to the plan office for response. Such a disclaimer will help trustees in controlling the overall liability and integrity of the benefit plan.

Trustee Liability

Beyond liability for the amount of a participant's claim, trustees can be personally liable for failing to properly communicate with participants. Under the Welfare and Pension Plans Disclosure Act, the only remedy for a plan's failure to disclose required information was for a participant to sue the trustees to recover a statutory penalty which could be awarded at a court's discretion. Under ERISA, there are broad remedies in both criminal and civil liability for failure to comply with the various disclosure requirements.

Criminal Penalties

ERISA and other related laws impose substantial criminal sanctions for willful violation of disclosure requirements. Under Section 501 of ERISA, a penalty of $5,000 or one year in prison or both can be imposed. If the defendant is not an individual, a fine can be levied up to $100,000.

The availability of criminal penalties was brought home in the filing of the 1979 indictment in the federal district court for Nebraska in the case of *United States v. Douchey,* 245 BNA BPR A-23. In that case, the individual who served as the plan administrator of the Omaha Dressed Beef Company Profit-Sharing Plan was charged with failing to furnish copies of summary plan descriptions, copies of summary annual reports and statements of accrued benefits to two individuals. While this case may involve the extreme in refusal to disclose required information, it underscores the seriousness of the disclosure requirements and the substantial penalties which can be imposed for failure to comply.

Another federal criminal statute which is not specifically contained in ERISA is Section 1027 of Title XVIII, which is part of the Federal Criminal Code. This statute imposes a fine of $10,000 or imprisonment of five years or both against any person who files false statements or conceals any facts in relation to material required by ERISA. The language is broad enough to include any person connected with employee benefit plans. *United States v. Tolkow,* __F.2d__, 92 L.R.R.M. 3027 (2nd Cir. 1976). To those of us who are frequently involved in collection of delinquent contributions on behalf of trust funds, this statute is of particular interest because it appears to cover even contributing employers who knowingly file false or incomplete information with the plan administrator by submitting incorrect (or failing to submit) monthly employer report forms.

Civil Liability

In addition to these substantial criminal penalties, ERISA established a comprehensive framework of civil liability for a person's failure to comply with ERISA's disclosure requirements. Under Section 502 of ERISA, civil actions can be brought (1) to enforce any participant rights under a benefit plan; (2) for violation of Section 409, which covers breach of fiduciary responsibility; and (3) for a violation of Section 105, which essentially covers the reporting of participants' benefits and plan rights. Section 502 expands the traditional remedy of a money judgment by authorizing use of injunctions and other appropriate relief. These remedies are generally available to the Secretary of Labor and any participant or beneficiary.

Section 502(c) provides a significant penalty for failing to respond within 30 days to a request for any information from a participant or beneficiary. This section imposes a personal fine against the plan administrator in favor of the participant or beneficiary of up to $100 per day from the date of the failure to respond, and other appropriate relief as a court may deem proper. The cases which have construed the meaning of "other appropriate relief" have included the appointment of a receiver and a special court master to take over the affairs of a plan, and the processing of a case under the procedure known as a declaratory judgment. The courts have broad remedial powers when they are presented with a consistent pattern of lack of compliance under ERISA.

The news, however, is not all bad. Simply because these various remedies exist does not mean that they will be imposed if a plan does not automatically distribute required documents or respond to requests for information. The cases which were brought under the Welfare and Pension Plans Disclosure Act focused on the facts of each case and the good faith of the plan officials involved in the failure to disclose. Under ERISA, courts still retain the discretion to fashion the appropriate relief on a case by case basis. *Pollock v. Castrovinci,* 476 F. Supp. 606 (D.C. D.N.Y., 1979).

You should also note that trustees' obligations in communication programs with participants are covered by the general umbrella of fiduciary responsibility to the participants. Consequently, the ultimate liability of a trustee in failing to communicate properly with participants or beneficiaries is to defend a claim of breach of fiduciary duty, which can include monetary damages and removal as a trustee. It must be stressed, again, that in dealing with participants and beneficiaries, a plan must accord fundamental due process to participants. Just as in the *Hodgins* case, a trustee's failure to accord basic notice and disclosure to participants of changes in the eligibility rules or structure of a benefit plan can be deemed unreasonable and, therefore, constitute a breach of fiduciary duty.

Individual Benefit Statement and Recordkeeping Regulations

During the last two years, pension plans have been faced with a tidal wave of burdensome disclosure requirements. First, detailed and comprehensive regulations were finalized on issuance of statements covering status and benefits to terminated vested participants. Those of us who have been intimately involved with administrative details of pension plans found that these regulations required extensive retooling of data processing programs to achieve simple compliance.

Pension plans are now faced with a second substantial disclosure requirement under the recently proposed regulations covering individual benefit statements and recordkeeping. In 1979, the Department of Labor issued proposed regulations on individual benefit statements which triggered negative comments from throughout the employee benefits industry. The initial regulations were thereupon withdrawn and separate regulations were proposed covering single employer plans and multiemployer plans. These two sets of proposed regulations are essentially the same, with minor differences.

It is easy to complain that the Department of Labor has proposed overbroad and unreasonable regulations; however, we must recognize that it is the statutory language of ERISA that requires pension plans to make these extraordinary efforts to report status and benefit information to plan participants and beneficiaries. Although the reproposed regulations present significant communication and recordkeeping difficulties, they are a vast improvement over the initial draft. Included at the end of this text (*see* Appendix A) is an outline of these proposed regulations. This is a simple outline which may not cover all points applicable to your situation, and you will want to consult with your own plan advisors in determining to what extent the regulations would apply to the provisions of your pension plan.

Individual Benefit Statements

Contents and Format. Generally, the proposed regulations require publication of a statement of accrued pension benefits upon request and upon termination or after a one year break in service. The outline lists the general contents of the required benefit statement. Defined benefit plans must report the total accrued benefit and accrued vested benefit in the form of a straight life annuity payable at retirement age, or in the normal form of benefit available under the plan. The statement also must show the percent of accrued vested benefit. A plan is permitted to project benefits which would be payable assuming the participant continues to work until normal retirement age. Care must be taken that the participant is not misled by such a projection.

Contributory plans must separately show the respective amounts of the accrued benefits derived from the employer and employee contributions, or at least the percentage attributable to each. Plans which include an offset for Social Security benefits must state the accrued benefit after reduction by the applicable amount of the Social Security benefit. Assumptions may be used to make this calculation; however, a statement must be included that the amounts are approximate.

The outline also lists several other statements of a general nature which must be included in the statement of benefits. The underlying policy is full disclosure of a participant's benefit calculation and notice of where additional information can be obtained. This is consistent with all the other disclosure requirements.

The outline includes other general requirements covering these benefit statements. The information must be based on the data of the immediately preceding plan year, and not any earlier data. Just like a summary plan description, the individual benefit statement must be written in a manner calculated to be understood by the average plan participant and must not be misleading in any way. Moreover, procedures for filing requests for benefit statements may have to be published in a foreign language where certain percentages of plan participants are literate only in a non-English language. (Note that the statement itself does not need to be in the foreign language, but must contain a simple notice in the foreign language that assistance can be obtained in understanding the benefit statement.) The statements must be distributed by first class mail or personal delivery.

Alternatives and Options. Basically, a benefit statement must be issued within the later of 60 days after receipt of a request by a participant or 120 days after the end of the immediately preceding plan year. For example, for a pension plan which operates on a calendar year basis, a request that is received on January 1 need not be answered until April 30, which is 120 days after the end of the preceding plan year. On the other hand, a request for a benefit statement which is received on June 1 of a plan year must be answered by August 1, since that is 60 days after the date of the receipt.

As an alternative, the proposed regulations permit a plan to issue an annual benefit statement to all participants within 180 days after the end of the plan year. Although many plans in the construction trades already issue annual benefit statements, the format would have to be substantially changed to comply with these proposed regulations.

As an additional alternative, the proposed regulations also permit a *nonvested* participant to receive a simple statement of nonvested status which can be published in a standardized form, advising that he has no nonforfeitable benefits under the plan and that he can obtain a personalized benefit statement on his accrued benefits upon request. This is a separate notice from the alternative permitting annual benefit statements.

Pension plans must still provide an individual statement of deferred vested benefits to *terminated vested* plan participants pursuant to the Internal Revenue Service final regulations. Under the proposed Department of Labor regulations, however, the benefit statement requirement can be met if the IRS-required notice to terminated vested participants is provided within the Department of Labor time limit: that is, within 180 days after the end of the plan year in which a break in service occurred.

The timing alternatives and the format alternatives should provide pension plans with sufficient options to structure a meaningful communications program under these proposed regulations.

Recordkeeping

A separate section of the proposed regulations covers the recordkeeping requirements imposed on sponsoring employers and the benefit plans. These requirements are also summarized in the outline. Basically, records for computing benefit information must be maintained as long as they are relevant to the determination of benefits of a participant or beneficiary. Information must include address, age and marital status of each participant and, where information is missing, the plan must make reasonable efforts to obtain it. In addition, any other information necessary to determine benefits must be obtained from employers and maintained in the plan records, e.g., data on contiguous non-covered service and credited past service. It is interesting to note that the regulations specifically control the reporting activity of participating employers by requiring that written service reports contain all relevant information regarding their covered employees.

Plan records must be generally available for inspection by plan participants within ten working days following a request.

Comments and Criticisms

These are detailed and extensive regulations covering a pension plan's obligation to communicate with plan participants. As indicated earlier, these reproposed regulations are a vast improvement over the initial draft, and are more directly based upon the statutory requirements enacted by Congress. Nevertheless, there are several aspects which will impose substantial cost burdens on both plan administration and the participating employers.

First, the proposed regulations require the maintenance of addresses, age and marital status for all participating pension participants. Many plans already maintain this to the best of their ability; however, in many industries this information has not been traditionally maintained and may even be impossible to obtain. This requirement of obtaining and maintaining accurate information on address, age and marital status will impose a tremendous recordkeeping cost for many plans.

Second, the proposed regulations would also require a participating employer to report an employee's credited past service. This information is generally unknown to participating employers, and indeed is usually unknown to the majority of participants. Administrative agents spend a substantial amount of time in investigating and verifying credited past service. This is not information which can be simply included on a service report submitted by participating employers. The computation of credited past service under most plans is a complicated and time-consuming procedure, and usually requires verification from third sources such as an international union and the Social Security Administration.

Finally, the proposed regulations would require an employer to continue to report non-covered service by a former plan participant with the employer subsequent to leaving active participant status with the plan. This is the contiguous non-covered service aspect of an employee's service which must be credited by a plan for vesting purposes. It is unreasonable to require a participating employer to continue to report such non-covered service to a plan, since all reporting obligations are geared to written agreements specifically detailing the type of covered service for which an employer is obligated to report. The proper time for obtaining accurate and reliable information on contiguous non-covered service is at the time of a formal status inquiry or application for pension benefits, when an employee can directly supply his entire work experience to a plan so that the pension claims adjuster can review all aspects of a participant's employment. Maintaining a record of contiguous non-covered service on a current basis is not an easy recordkeeping matter. An employer's personnel department cannot automatically add this information to the monthly service reports. If this portion of the proposed regulations is included in the final regulations, plan administrators and employers will suffer an increased recordkeeping burden with little or no real gain in the value of the information furnished to the participant.

Conclusion

We have only highlighted some of the most important areas and recent developments dealing with communications with your plan participants. One area which we do not have time to explore is the important area of techniques for language simplification to achieve more effective communication. Understanding the social and psychological aspects of face-to-face and printed communications with participants can be just as important a part of your communication program as understanding and complying with the legal requirements. To those of you who are interested in designing a more understandable and sophisticated communication program for your participants, I highly recommend the International Foundation publication entitled *Communication Dynamics for Employee Benefit Plans,* by Dr. Hideya Kumata.

Appendix A

Summary of Proposed Regulations on Individual Benefit Reporting and Recordkeeping
(Proposed August 8, 1980 45 FR 52782)

I. Individual Benefit Reporting (Proposed regulations: §2520.105-3)

   A. Statutory basis: ERISA §102(a) and (c), §209(a)(1), and §505

   B. "Benefit Statement" to participants and beneficiaries

      1. Upon written request—once a year, within the later of 60 days of receipt of request or 120 days of end of immediately preceding plan year.

      2. *Alternative:* Annual Benefit Statement—within 180 days of end of plan year.

      3. Upon one year break in service—within 180 days of end of plan year.

      4. *Alternative:* Statement of Nonvested Status—within 180 days of end of plan year in which break in service occurred—No benefit information required unless participant later requests such information, in which case benefit statement must be distributed within 60 days of request or 180 days after end of plan year, whichever is later.

      5. *Alternative:* Statement of Deferred Vested Status—Statement under IRC §6057 will be sufficient for statement to separated vested participants.

   C. Contents of Statement

      1. Amount of total accrued benefit—in straight life annuity or normal form of benefit (must separately state amounts based on employee contributions).

      2. Percent of accrued vested benefit (i.e., nonforfeitable percentage) as defined by ERISA §203 and IRC §411(a).

      3. Amount of accrued nonforfeitable (vested) benefit—in straight life annuity or normal form of benefit.

      4. If Social Security offset, must state net plan benefit.

      5. Statement to the effect, "Election of options under plan might affect amount of accrued benefits."

      6. Statement to the effect, "Refer to summary plan description for more information on available options."

      7. If accrued benefits are *not* stated in joint and survivor annuity form, statement to the effect, "The periodic benefit the participant will receive at retirement may be reduced on account of survivor benefits."

      8. Statement to the effect, "Refer to summary plan description for information on circumstances which may result in reduction or elimination of accrued or nonforfeitable benefits."

9. If there are no nonforfeitable benefits, statement as to earliest date on which any benefits will become vested.

10. Statement to the effect, "Records which form basis of benefit computation are available for inspection upon request." Must include name, address and phone for participant's contact.

11. Statement to the effect, "Participant urged to bring promptly to attention of plan administrator items which may be incorrect."

12. The date as of which benefit information is reported.

13. The participant's or beneficiary's Social Security number.

14. If records are incomplete, must so state and invite participant to furnish information.

D. General Requirements

1. Information must be based on data of immediately preceding plan year.

2. Plan may prescribe procedures for submission of participant's benefit statement requests. May use SPD or SAR for publication.

3. Benefit statement must be written in manner calculated to be understood by the average participant.

4. Response to request for statement must be made within 60 days of receipt of request or 120 days after end of preceding plan year.

5. Annual Benefit Statement alternative must be distributed within 180 days of end of preceding plan year.

6. Must provide duplicate statement upon request.

7. Participant must be given opportunity to furnish information regarding benefit entitlements.

8. May need to communicate in non-English languages if participant groups justify (defined in proposed regulations).

E. Distribution

1. Must distribute to all participants and beneficiaries EXCEPT participants and beneficiaries currently receiving benefits, those with fully guaranteed benefits, those who have received all benefits, beneficiaries of participants entitled to receive statement, separated vested participants entitled to receive statement of deferred vested benefits or who have incurred a one year break in service and who have not returned to the plan.

2. By first class mail to last known address or personal delivery.

II. Recordkeeping (Proposed regulations §2520.209-3)

   A. Statutory Basis: ERISA §209(a)(2)

   B. "Sponsoring Employer's" Obligations

      1. Must furnish written Service Reports no less frequently than once a quarter.

      2. Service Report must contain all information regarding covered employee's service relevant to a determination of benefits.

      3. Include employees who have met plan's eligibility requirements even though employee may not currently perform service in job classification covered by plan (i.e., contiguous non-covered service).

      4. Include employees who perform services in a job classification covered by the plan even though employee may not have satisfied plan's eligibility requirements.

      5. "Sponsoring employer" includes any party required to make contributions to the plan; does not include another plan contributing pursuant to reciprocity arrangement.

   C. Plan's Obligations

      1. Must maintain name and address of each participant and information sufficient to determine benefits.

      2. Plan administrator must make reasonable effort to obtain complete and accurate information from all sponsoring employers.

      3. Plan may prescribe rules regarding reporting format, manner and information.

      4. Must maintain records for as long as possibility exists information might be needed for determination of benefits.

      5. Must permit access to records for inspection and copying.

III. Penalty for non-compliance—ERISA §209(b):

   If any person who is required, under subsection (a) to furnish information or maintain records for any plan year fails to comply with such requirement, he shall pay to the Secretary a civil penalty of $10 for each employee with respect to whom such failure occurs, unless it is shown that such failure is due to reasonable cause.

Appendix B

Communications Checklist

This list includes many of the communication and disclosure subjects for which trustees are generally responsible to participants. (It does not include notices or filings required by the various government agencies.) You can use this as a checklist for review of your trust funds; however, it is not an exhaustive listing and you should review your specific trust requirements with your own trust counsel.

I. Formal Disclosure Communications to Participants:

—Notice to Interested Parties of Filing Application for Tax Exempt Status—Posted notice to participants in conjunction with application to Internal Revenue Service for tax exempt status (posting required at least seven days prior to filing of application).

—Summary Plan Description (SPD)—A summary of pertinent plan information in format prescribed by regulations distributed to all plan participants including all beneficiaries and separated vested participants. Some trusts publish special SPDs for separated vested participants, retirees, and beneficiaries (within 120 days of plan becoming subject to ERISA and within 90 days of employee becoming a participant).

—Updated Five Year SPD—Updated summary incorporating all changes, if any, in plan adopted or occurring since prior SPD publication (within five years of prior SPD publication and distribution).

—Updated Ten Year SPD—Redistribution of SPD or updated SPD regardless of whether plan modifications have occurred (within ten years of prior SPD distribution).

—Notice of Apprenticeship/Training Trust—Special notice to eligible participants regarding availability and nature of program (ongoing requirement with no deadline).

—Summary of Material Modifications (SMM)—Summary of significant changes in the plan, such as changes in trustees, eligibility rules, agent for service of process, etc. (within 210 days of end of plan year in which modification or change adopted).

—Summary Annual Report (SAR)—Summary of financial information from annual report Form 5500 (within nine months after end of each plan year).

—Notice to Separated Vested Participants (also called Statement of Accrued Vested Benefits)—Notice to inactive vested participants must include the nature, amount and form of benefit, and other pertinent information to enable inactive participants to file claim (within seven months after end of plan year in which participant incurred second of two consecutive one year breaks in service).

—Inspection of Pertinent Trust Documents—Upon written request, must furnish by mail or permit examination at trust office or other locations, of SPD, SAR, plan description, annual report Form 5500, bargaining agreements, trust agreements, benefit plan, insurance contracts, etc. (within 30 days of written request for mailing, and within ten days for examination).

—Form 1099R—IRS form stating amount of total lump sum or death benefit disbursement to beneficiary (by January 31 of following year).

—Form W-2P—IRS form stating amount of periodic benefits paid to beneficiary during calendar year (by January 31 of following year).

II. Benefits and Claims Communications:

—Statement of Accrued Benefits—Report of accrued pension benefits to date (within later of 60 days of written request or 120 days after end of preceding plan year).

—Method of Filing Claim—Included in SPD.

—Statement of Reasons for Claim Denial—(Within 90 days of application for benefits).

—Statement of Reasons for Decision to Deny Appeal of Claim—(Within 60 days of plan's receipt of request for review).

—Notice of Opportunity to Elect Early Survivor Annuity (if not automatic)—General description of early survivor annuity, availability of election, and explanation of relative financial effect on participant's annuity (90 days before latest date for beginning the election period under early retirement option).

—Notice of Opportunity to Reject Joint and Survivor Annuity Option—General description of joint and survivor annuity, availability of election out of automatic joint and survivor annuity benefit, and explanation of relative financial effect on participant's annuity, assuming joint and survivor annuity is automatic form at early retirement age (nine months before participant attains early retirement age).

—Statement of Joint and Survivor Option Financial Effect—Written explanation to participant of terms and conditions of joint and survivor annuity and its specific financial effect on such participant's annuity (on receipt of participant's request).

Trustees' Responsibility for Collection of Employer Contributions

BY HOWARD S. SUSSKIND

ALL TOO often, a meeting of the board of trustees is preoccupied with the consideration of collection of fringe benefits from employers, as opposed to providing benefits for the employees. We all understand that the purpose of any employee benefit fund is to provide the best possible benefits to the beneficiaries and participants of the fund but, of course, those benefits must be funded by and from some source. Employer contributions for the purposes of those funds are funded directly from those contributions or from deductions from employees' pay.

Mr. Susskind is a partner with the law firm of Kaplan, Sicking, Hessen, Sugarman, Rosenthal & DeCastro in Miami, Florida. He serves as counsel to more than 60 Taft-Hartley trust funds, specializing in the establishment of collection procedures for delinquent contributions and the collection and litigation of fringe benefit cases. Mr. Susskind received his J.D. degree from the University of Miami School of Law. He is a member of the American Federation of Trial Lawyers; the Dade County Bar Association; and the Labor Law Section of both the Florida and American Bar Associations.

The CBA: The Need for Proper Tools

The responsibility for collections, though contained within ERISA, codified by case law as part of the Taft-Hartley Act, and incumbent upon the trustees through the various declarations and agreements of trust and the plans that accompany those trust agreements, really has its source within the collective bargaining agreement that the union has with the employer. There are certain tools which the collective bargaining agreement can provide to the board of trustees which will enable them to handle the job of collections far more efficiently. Though the trustees, as trustees, do not take part in the collective bargaining process, I am sure that the individual union and management trustees who are sitting on the board do take part in those negotiations, and there are certain considerations which they might want to take into account when they get into collective bargaining negotiations.

Initially, the fringe benefit amount should be set forth specifically in the collective bargaining agreement. Whether the amount is a certain percentage of the pay that is received by the employee, or whether it is a contribution based on the number of hours worked, it should be set forth specifically in the agreement. The contribution due date should also be set forth specifically, because this sets forth when an employer can be considered delinquent.

Various funds throughout the country utilize a system whereby the fringe benefits are paid weekly, others will have provisions where they are paid monthly or bimonthly; there are any number of combinations, and many times it will depend on the industry involved to make the determination of when the contribution is due.

In line with the statement of when the contribution is due, there should also be a provision stating at what point an employer becomes delinquent. Very often, collective bargaining agreements may provide that fringe benefit contributions are paid, or are to be payable, on a weekly basis, but they may allow an additional seven or ten days before a contractor or an employer is considered to be delinquent. It's very important to spell that out in detail, so that not only does the employer know when he is delinquent, but the trustees, the administrator for the fund and the attorney for the fund also know this information, as well as any other professionals that you may utilize.

Audits

Audits—there's no God-given right to audit an employer's books and records. You have got to include that within the collective bargaining agreement. Just to say that an employer shall be audited is not enough; the agreement must set forth specifically the terms under which you can audit an employer (for example: "When an employer becomes delinquent, he is subject to an audit by either the board of trustees or by the union"). Another provision would be that the employer shall always make available its payroll books and records for the purposes of an audit at the request of the board of trustees or the union—thus making it incumbent upon the signatory employer to make those records available, whether or not there has been any complaint or a reason to believe that the employer is delinquent.

Contractors' Responsibility

Two clauses which have particular reference to the construction industry are subcontracting clauses and general contractors' responsibility clauses. Without delving a great deal into the legal ramifications of the subcontractors' clause under Section 8(e) of the act, a subcontractors' clause is a valuable tool for the trustees. This type of clause would provide that, should the employer utilize a subcontractor who fails to abide by the union's area standards and pay the fringe benefits, then the signatory employer becomes responsible for the payment of damages based upon the hours worked by his employees. This would also be available for use by the trustees where an employer may hire persons, but not pay them directly as employees, but rather consider them as contract labor or day labor.

General contractors' responsibility clauses are synonymous in a sense with subcontracting clauses because they would put the burden on the general contractor to pay the delinquent fringe benefit contributions of a subcontractor who does have a collective bargaining agreement with the union. The only caveat there is that the employer should be notified in writing and, because of some problems and interpretations of the National Labor Relations Act and recent decisions of the National Labor Relations Board, it should be provided that in any subcontracting situation the union is not allowed to use self-help, strikes or picketing in order to enforce these provisions of the collective bargaining agreement. That would be up to the trustees to enforce, if there is a situation presented where these contributions can't be collected.

Bonds

Bonds are another provision which again must be specifically set forth in the collective bargaining agreement. As with audits, there are a variety of ways that you can describe under what circumstances a bond must be posted by an employer. It could be a blanket provision stating that the employer must post a bond when he becomes signatory to the collective bargaining agreement or, alternatively, it could provide that the employer only needs to provide a bond if he becomes delinquent in the payment of his contributions to the funds. Again, the delinquency date, as defined in the collective bargaining agreement, has a significance. Bonds can also be required in order to allow an employer to take advantage of peculiar reporting situations; for example, where a collective bargaining agreement provides for weekly contributions, you could require the employers to post a bond in order to permit them to pay on a monthly basis.

Employer Liability for Claims

Employer responsibility for payment of health claims really is not a matter that comes too much within the realm of the trustees. It merely provides an extra method whereby, if an employer is delinquent in the payment of contributions to the fund and if an employee loses his health and welfare coverage, then he would be entitled (or the fund in his name would be entitled) to seek payment of those health claims directly from the employer, without excusing the employer's liability for actually paying the fringe benefit contributions on that employee's behalf. Though some may consider that to be a double payment, it's really not, because it is enforcement of the collective bargaining agreement and various methods and damages which flow from the breach of the collective bargaining agreement, and not a penalty.

Reporting Forms

Reporting forms are really a vehicle. They are a communication device whereby an employer notifies the fund of the names of its employees, the number of hours worked and the contributions made. It's a method by which the fund obtains information. The fund or the union should not consider a reporting form as an alternative to a collective bargaining agreement and believe that by merely having an employer sign a reporting form, he then becomes bound to the collective bargaining agreement. Unfortunately, there have been too many cases which have been decided against this issue, despite having all sorts of self-protecting language on the reporting form. I would avoid the use of reporting forms as consideration for an employer being bound to an agreement.

Trust Agreement

The trust agreement and plan for any of the various employee benefit plans should be specifically incorporated by reference in a collective bargaining agreement. The employer acknowledges that there is a health and welfare trust agreement, pension trust agreement, vacation, annuity, whatever form of benefit you may want to provide. He specifically authorizes the board of trustees to act in his behalf. He agrees to any amendments which the board of trustees may, from time to time, out of the requirements of law or other considerations, need to place within the trust agreement or the plan. This also may become important because situations may arise where the collective bargaining agreement cannot be negotiated to provide the trustees with enough tools to go out and collect delinquent contributions. It's conceivable that if the trust agreement is incorporated within the collective bargaining agreement, amendments can be made to the trust agreement to provide these tools to the trustees, which they can't get through collective bargaining. However, the far better method is to have these tools provided for you within the collective bargaining agreement.

The Collection Procedure

Legal parameters which govern trustees' responsibility for collection of delinquencies are contained in the collective bargaining agreement, the trust agreements and plans, codified in case law and within the Employee Retirement Income Security Act of 1974, as amended in 1980. In addition to those things, there are various interpretative bulletins which are published by the Department of Labor and the Internal Revenue Service, and various regulations which are issued by those agencies, which deal directly with the responsibility for collection of delinquent fringe benefit contributions.

PTE 76-1

The scripture for collection of delinquencies is contained within Prohibited Transaction Exemption 76-1. PTE 76-1 relieves the trustees of certain obligations for the collection of delinquent fringe benefit contributions provided that certain stipulations are met. The trustees have the ability to settle a delinquent account without collecting all of the contributions which are due and owing—76-1 makes that clear. However, a caveat in any situation where that is done is to fully document the minutes of your trust meeting as to the reasons why the full amount is not being collected from the employer. As an example, if the cost of collection—the amount that you have to pay an attorney to collect a delinquency—is far in excess of that delinquency, and it appears likely that you may not collect in full, you are permitted to resolve the case on a reasonable basis pursuant to the prudent man rule, in order to accomplish the settlement. Perhaps the most difficult questions facing any board of trustees are in those types of situations where collections cannot be made in full.

PTE 76-1 also states that the trustees must establish a reasonable, diligent and ongoing collection procedure in order to monitor and collect fringe benefit delinquencies. This procedure should be contained in the form of a resolution at the trustees' meeting or should be specifically documented in the minutes of the trust meeting so that if anybody, such as the Department of Labor, should inquire as to whether or not the trustees have a collection procedure, you can produce it in writing.

The Delinquency Subcommittee

The best way to foster this collection policy, as set out within the prohibited transaction exemption, is to set up a delinquency subcommittee. It is a very useful tool because it allows a small group of the trustees, as designated by the board, to sit with the attorney and the administrator and take whatever time is necessary in order to review all the information to determine whether or not an employer is delinquent and what action should be taken. It's far easier to accomplish this task with two or three trustees, as opposed to having the whole board of trustees present, because inadvertently the discussion on delinquencies becomes sidetracked and it's necessary to devote a specific amount of time in order to get this work accomplished. A caveat to the delinquency subcommittee would be that they would report directly to the board of trustees as to recommended action, especially in those situations where there are audits or lawsuits to be filed. The delinquency subcommittee probably should not take it upon itself to authorize the attorney or any other party to engage in that type of specific action without advising the entire board of trustees because, even though some decisions may be delegated to the delinquency subcommittee, the responsibility of accomplishing certain tasks, the ultimate responsibility falls on the trustees. The subcommittee should report regularly, as it meets, to the full board of trustees.

Teamwork and Communication

Division of responsibility is also very important, and it can take its form within the collection subcommittee or it can take its form outside of such a subcommittee. It should be established within the delinquency collection procedure: Who is responsible for what, and when?

When an employer becomes delinquent, the procedure could provide that one of the union representatives shall contact the employer by calling him or visiting his shop, or the administrator shall automatically send out a notification to any employer when a report is submitted and received late by the administrator. The attorney could immediately write a letter when advised by the board of trustees or the administrator that an employer is delinquent. All of this should be spelled out. Each party who is involved with the delinquency subcommittee should know what their area of responsibility is and communicate with the other members of the subcommittee to ensure that the job is being done. All too often, when one party is charged with the responsibility of contacting a delinquent employer and for some reason that person gets sidetracked and the work is not done, the subcommittee and the board of trustees may not know about it until months later. Meanwhile, a much larger delinquency may have accrued.

Trustees must be diligent in the collection procedure. You've got to communicate with all the parties who are involved with the collection. The communication should also come from those professionals whom you are hiring, in the form of reports: an attorney's collection report, an administrator's delinquency report, a union delinquency report. All of these reports should be in writing and should be submitted to the trustees at their regular meeting. If the fund does not meet monthly or bimonthly, but rather quarterly, the professionals should mail out these reports to you so that you are involved and knowledgeable about what's going on.

The Role of Audits

Provision for auditing delinquent employers' records or any employers' records has been a subject of controversy for quite a while. Number one, the question is presented, are payroll audits mandated by the provisions of ERISA? At this point and, of course, this is my opinion, they are not mandated by ERISA; it is not required that trustees audit every single employer who is party to a collective bargaining agreement with the union, or those who contribute to the fund. However, it may be that in the very near future, such a provision will be incumbent upon the board of trustees, that every employer be audited during the term of the collective bargaining agreement.

Audits can take a variety of forms. One form in connection with the provision as it is contained within your agreement is to have a random audit procedure. Alphabetically, all the employers are audited during the collective bargaining period.

As part of litigation, in any situation where you are suing an employer for delinquent fringe benefit contributions, you've got to know the amount that's owed and, of course, the best way to determine that is to get in a qualified certified public accountant to audit the books and records and determine the amount which is due and owing. There's a certain aura about certified public accountants; when they get to court, they are considered as expert witnesses. They carry with them all the years of study and education to present to the court. The accountant would present the audit in the form of a booklet of some kind, showing the names of the employees, the Social Security numbers, the delinquent hours or, if it is a percentage of wages, that amount. Have it set out and typed to look very nice and easy to read so that the judge understands it.

Another reason to audit would be upon a complaint from an individual participant that he didn't receive credit for his contributions. He may discover this in a number of ways. If your fund, through its administrator, publishes a run or log that is distributed to the employees on a quarterly or semiannual basis, the employee can very readily see if he's being given credit. One thing about employees, they are very diligent. They keep their check stubs and if the man doesn't do it, his wife makes him, and if the wife doesn't do it, the husband makes her. They go through all those check stubs and they go through the log and see if there are any hours missing. If there are, you know that they are going to be contacting somebody, whether it is a union representative, the board of trustees directly, or the administrator or sometimes the attorney. In those situations, it is pretty much incumbent upon the board of trustees to go ahead and audit, because your fiduciary responsibility to collect all delinquencies and all contributions has been triggered by this complaint. However, merely because an employee makes a complaint does not automatically make his employer delinquent. An investigation should be undertaken by the board of trustees checking through the employee's pay stubs, reviewing all the contributions that were made by the employer, and taking whatever other steps are necessary to determine whether or not they should proceed with an audit. That's part of the diligent, ongoing process which the trustees must use in proceedings with delinquencies.

There are special situations where the employer goes bankrupt. As a result of recent amendments to the Bankruptcy Act, fringe benefits have been given a new and high priority, so there is a great likelihood that if there's any money in the bankruptcy estate, the trustees will receive payment of health and welfare, pension, vacation, and any other type of benefits which are due to the funds as a secured creditor; they are now given a priority similar to wages, but just below. You are also allowed to recover your costs of collection within the bankruptcy court as part of administrative expenses.

Another situation where an audit might be advisable is where a collective bargaining agreement expires and an employer has posted a bond and wishes that the bond be canceled, or the bond expires by its terms. Before the trustees release the bond, a final audit should be done of the employer's records, again utilizing a prior investigation to determine whether or not the cost is justified. Once that bonding company is released from liability, you cannot go back later and try to collect the delinquency from them. You are left to your own devices with a delinquent employer, so it's always a good idea to audit before the expiration of a bond.

An Ongoing Effort

Of all the people who are involved with the collection of delinquencies and the monitoring of delinquencies, first and foremost are the trustees. They've got the responsibility; they've got to make sure that the procedure works. The administrator is part of that team, and the attorney, the union, the employer associations and the employees themselves. All of these parties become an integral part of the collection procedure, as you develop it to work for your fund.

There may be some very fortunate funds that have very few delinquencies, and I commend all of the trustees who sit on those funds for doing a job above and beyond the call of duty, because that is the minority of cases. There are funds, though, that have serious collection problems, and there are some that historically have a traditional collection problem. All the individuals who compose the professional advisors and the board of trustees should blend themselves in the best way possible to accomplish the goal of the trust fund and meet the responsibility of the trustees to collect all of the delinquencies.

There are certain checks and balances which you can use. Audits are one. You can also have your administrator or that person who is in charge of receiving the benefits publish a log, weekly, monthly or bimonthly, showing the names of all contributing employers, the date that his last contribution was received and the date that it was due. By reviewing this log, you can see very clearly in easily identifiable and readable material when an employer's last contribution was made and whether or not he was delinquent. That will then trigger the procedures which you have established, whether they are automatic or discretionary, in order to collect delinquencies.

Stewards' reports are another way of obtaining information, but unfortunately they are not as reliable as the trustees need. There are always problems coming up on a job which may prevent a steward from keeping accurate records of the number of employees, the names of the employees, the number of hours which they worked on the job. But stewards' reports can be used in those situations where the trustees need corroboration.

Bonds provide a fund of money for the trustees in the event that they run into a situation where the employer cannot pay the amount which he owes to the fund. The fund is then entitled to make a claim on the employer's bond. To be effective in collections, where an employer is required to post a bond, once that employer becomes delinquent the bonding company, if it is a surety company, should be notified immediately. Bonds are underwritten, just like insurance policies are underwritten, and bonding companies hate to have claims made against them. It is a useful leverage device because many of those employers may have other forms of insurance with the same company, particularly in the construction industry. They may be required to have performance and payment bonds for certain public works projects, or even private projects, so an employer really hates to have his bond account upset and the bonding company hates to handle them. It's a useful tool that the trustees have available to them.

Wage reports apply more specifically to government work where an employer is required to submit wage reports listing the name of the employee, the type of work that he performs and the number of hours that he worked, so that he can use this in obtaining his payment for the work performed. If the trustees know of any delinquent employers who are working on projects which require wage reports, these wage reports are public records, and they can and should be obtained as a cross-check on whether or not the employer is reporting properly.

How to Collect

Once you determine that an employer is delinquent, what is the best method calculated to collect the delinquencies? It could be a variety of things, and many times it's going to depend on the type of fund that you have and the type of employer that you have. It could take the form of letters or phone calls or individual meetings, but whatever the procedure is, it should be set forth within that written document that you have entitled "collection procedure."

Delinquency letters are a commonly used item. The administrator or the attorney will automatically send a letter out to a delinquent employer. If he fails to respond, a second letter is sent out and at that point, if there is no response, you can be pretty much assured that further letters are not going to make any difference. So you've got to be a little innovative, you've got to change your procedure to accomplish the task. If you've got to go and make a phone call, if you've got to go and visit the employer's shop, if you've got to try to arrange a meeting, then that should be done. There's nothing that says that you have to follow the exact letter of your collection procedure *if* you can come up with a better way of collecting the delinquency. The collection procedure merely provides the framework to go out and collect the delinquencies.

Strikes are a tool which is used in order to collect delinquencies. However, the board of trustees does not have any power to require the union to take economic sanctions against any delinquent employer. As much as the trustees may feel that it will be extremely helpful to them in collecting the delinquencies, they don't have the power to require the union to do that. That's solely within the realm of the union, and the union makes the decision. But the trustees are the sole party responsible for the collection of any delinquent amounts. The trustees must take charge of the delinquency situation and handle it. If that involves giving responsibility to union representatives, giving responsibility to the administrator or the attorney, make sure that they do the job. Attorneys and administrators charge the trust funds for the work that they do. If they are charging the trust funds, make sure that they are doing their job.

Litigation or Arbitration?

The last resort is lawsuits. If all else fails, go to court. Issues have recently arisen concerning the applicability of arbitration as opposed to going to court. There are certain advantages and disadvantages of each.

As far as lawsuits are concerned, the advantages are that all issues can be decided in front of the court. Once you obtain your judgment against the employer, you are immediately entitled, subject to the rules of procedure of that court, to collect the amount through execution or garnishment or any other post-judgment collection procedure. Also available in court actions are discovery proceedings. Discovery allows you to investigate, through the court rules, the records of the employer by asking him to produce records whether or not there is an audit provision in the collective bargaining agreement. It allows the attorney for your fund to interview and depose witnesses and to gather all this information in preparation for winning the suit.

The disadvantage with the courts usually is time. Although it could, in some instances, be as short as three months, it could be as long as three years before a case is decided.

The advantage with arbitration is that it could be made to work quicker. You don't have available the discovery techniques, and if the employer doesn't pay the arbitrator's award, then you've got to go back into court and seek enforcement, which causes delay. Usually, though, the outstanding advantage of arbitration is the time factor involved. One of the disadvantages of arbitration is that it could be very expensive. Arbitrators charge anywhere from $150-400 a day. If it's a significantly long presentation, you will have a couple of days, then add into it the court reporter's fees, add in the amount of time that the arbitrator has to spend in reviewing the case and writing up his opinion—you could be looking at a substantially large bill for the arbitration. In many cases, the use of courts might be cheaper. It would depend, though, on certain provisions in the collective bargaining agreement as to who pays the costs.

Costs are an interesting aspect as far as litigation is concerned under the new amendments to the Pension Reform Act. The act specifically provides, number one, that the obligation to collect contributions is now an ERISA obligation. Number two, if you go into court, if you litigate, and if you are successful, then you are entitled to receive the court costs, you are entitled to receive professional fees, accountants' fees and attorneys' fees, you are also mandatorily entitled to receive either 20% of the delinquency, as a liquidated damage, or interest.

It is important to have provisions within the collective bargaining agreement for the collection of costs. The law only provides for reimbursement of these costs *if you go to court*. If you want to impose the costs of collection on the delinquent employer, where they rightfully should be, then it should be spelled out in the agreement that the employer agrees to pay all reasonable costs of collection acquired by the trustees in order to collect any delinquent amount. The advantage of this, of course, is to reimburse the funds for the use of any professionals which they may need to utilize. If the fund is collecting a certain amount of money, if they are required to deduct from that amount of money the amount that they've got to pay to the professionals, then the employees' benefits become diluted to the extent that you've got to subtract your costs of collection.

What About Partial Payments?

Settlements

Settling cases provides one of the most difficult areas that the trustees must address. Number one, you've got to know your responsibility—your responsibility under the law to collect the contributions and to have the knowledge that you can settle cases under Prohibited Transaction Exemption 76-1.

Utilize all the professional advice you can obtain. A new method is to utilize the services of private investigators to find out what kind of work an employer is doing, how many employees he has, to dig out asset reports and provide that information to the board of trustees. A typical situation would be where an employer has unfortunately accumulated a debt of $10,000 to the trust funds. He says to the trustees, I can't possibly pay $10,000, I don't have the money, but I can give you 50¢ on the dollar, and we'll call it even, and in the future I will make all of my contributions to the fund in full. What do the trustees do? The attorneys have to give advice to the trustees. The investigative report could also be significant, because if this employer has half a million dollars in assets and he only owes $10,000 to the fund, then I would question the trustees' prudence in going ahead with this type of settlement agreement since the employer does have sufficient assets. So, verifying the information that you get is very important, especially in situations where less than payment in full is made.

Pension Credit

What do you do with the money once you have it if it doesn't cover all of the delinquencies accrued by the employer? Well, the way that the IRS is now interpreting ERISA is that the trustees must give credit to all employees for hours worked for pension purposes, whether it's for benefit accrual or vesting accrual. You cannot decline to give an employee credit merely because you failed to collect the delinquent contributions. Thus, you know right off the bat that if you have a pension fund and the employer is delinquent, pension credit must be given whether you collect the money or not.

There are tools available to the trustees for purposes of notifying the employer that he is delinquent and limiting the fund's responsibility. This should be taken up with your attorney because it may depend, to a great degree, upon the type of industry that you are involved in. The bottom line is that you are responsible for crediting those benefits; if you've got to credit them, the money must come from somewhere, and that's within the trust corpus.

Health and Welfare Eligibility

How about health and welfare funds not receiving payment in full? You come to the end of an eligibility period and a number of employees won't have sufficient hours paid in order to be covered by health and welfare benefits, if you need to cover employees for health and welfare and the only way that you can accumulate hours in the fund is to have them actually paid. There is a difference as far as the law is concerned: under health and welfare there is no mandated responsibility for crediting those hours that were not worked. Vacation funds are another problem, where insufficient contributions are received from the employer and the employees are expecting a payout at some point in the year, usually around Christmas time; the employee knows how many hours he worked—if he gets his vacation fund payment and it's half what he expected, well, he's knocking on somebody's door and complaining.

The whole question is whether the trustees in the exercise of their diligent and prudent approach to fringe benefits can credit on a discriminatory basis. Ideally, you don't have to, because you would collect all of the money that is due and owing. However, under certain limited circumstances you may need to do this. In any situation where you are crediting benefits but they are not to be done in full, it should be set out within the minutes of the trustees' meetings, so that if the Department of Labor or anybody else who has access to records wants to know why you did something, it's spelled out in detail as to why and how you did it. The more difficult problem is where you don't have enough money to go through the entire list of employees or even one type of benefit, and that's going to require you to discriminate. There might be enough money to go from A to S, but then the people at the end of the alphabet don't have their benefits credited, because there is not enough money. The way some funds handle that is they will credit the employees on an hour-for-hour basis, starting with the oldest hours first, and just taking it as long as it goes; when the money runs out, that's it. Another provision, though something on which the trustees should seek *specific advice from their attorneys,* is whether the fund will cover an employee in full for delinquent hours when the fund has not received all the contributions due. A lot of times that will depend on the financial stability of your fund. If you have a significant delinquency problem and you are covering everybody, you are going to see your reserves wiped out very quickly.

Installment Payments

Installment payments are a useful tool in obtaining payment from an employer who can't pay all of its delinquencies in full. The installment payment schedule should be in writing in the form of a promissory note, should be signed by the employer. It should include a reasonable rate of interest to cover the time period over which the employer is making these delinquent contributions to the fund. It should also have a provision whereby the employer acknowledges that, should he become delinquent in the payment of his current contributions to the fund, the trustees are entitled to cancel and rescind the installment payment schedule and proceed against the employer for the full amount that is due and owing.

Many times it is advisable to try to isolate the delinquency period. For example, if an employer is delinquent the months of June, July and August, and you are now into September, isolate June, July and August. Say, O.K., this is the period of time for which he owes the fund the money. Set up a payment schedule; but require that he must now pay his current contributions to the fund. Again, you have a variety of choices, and a lot will depend on whether you have to meet current needs as far as eligibility for health and welfare purposes, or whether you want to go ahead and instruct your administrator to honor claims of employees, though they may be terminated as a result of failure of payments on a point-of-claim basis until enough monies are collected.

Making It Work

I think the most important thing about any procedure that trustees decide to come up with is making it work. You can become complacent and too comfortable once you have established a procedure. You must be diligent and follow through. Don't let the procedure operate by itself. The procedure only operates as well as the people who are running it. So be diligent about it, make it work, make your professionals work for you.

Most of all, be imaginative and innovative in a situation. This is the way that you can get things done. For example, the United States Supreme Court said that a trust fund could collect from a general contractor a subcontractor's delinquencies under a public works bond, under the Miller Act. A lawsuit was initiated by somebody who was imaginative enough to try to seek the collection of the delinquent contributions for a subcontractor from the general contractor. He was successful. Well, the same thing can be used in your individual states if they also have a provision for public bonding. Check with your attorney to see if such a law exists and, if it does, make a claim on the general contractor and its bonding company for delinquent fringe benefits that are owed from a subcontractor.

So, there's a great tool that can be utilized and, once it's established within your jurisdiction, that's a vehicle for collection. You won't have to get involved in very many lawsuits because the word gets out quickly. The bonding companies have their own way of communicating with each other and, if they know they're going to be responsible, they are not going to fight with you. Rather, they are going to take steps to protect themselves to make sure they have sufficient monies to pay your claims. Many times, however, it will be necessary to comply with certain state requirements as to notification of the bonding company or the general contractor within specified time limits. That also is the situation with liens. Many states do have provisions which provide for the collection of fringe benefits through the filing of liens. Again, in bond claims and with liens, most of this does apply to the construction trades, but just because the law may not exactly say what you think it should say, don't give up, go ahead; don't spend a million dollars trying the case but, if you've got a good case to make and if it will provide another tool for you to collect delinquencies, then, by all means, utilize it.

Developing a Welfare Plan Reserve Model and Level

BY MARC GERTNER

ONE OF THE most common, most quoted and most accurate of all of the Mark Twain sayings is his comment on the weather: Everybody talks about it, but nobody does anything about it. If there is an application of this truism to the Taft-Hartley welfare industry, it is in the area of establishing welfare plan reserves; everybody talks about it, and a lot, but few have done anything—at least anything worthwhile—about it. You can't go to an IF Annual Conference, read the literature or attend many trustees' meetings without hearing the trite and often unthought-out generalizations— one year's expenses, nine months' contributions, enough to produce sufficient investment income to defray administrative expenses, or all of the above. These glib generalities are worth the study that went into them—nothing.

Last year I had the opportunity to be involved in the question in a real life, serious way. As fund counsel to a multiemployer, multiunion, area-wide health and welfare plan, I sat through hours of discussions and a series of deadlocked motions. The union trustees argued with force and logic that the current fund balance or reserve was excessive— beyond the amount prudently needed—and that benefits should be increased without new contributions. The employer trustees argued with equivalent articulate reason that the reserves were inadequate and, therefore, no benefits could be expanded or added without new contributions to cover their cost, plus a kicker to expand the reserves.

After the umpteenth deadlocked vote, the chairman asked for an opinion on what alternatives were available to the trustees. Essentially, there were two. The first, go to arbitration to resolve the deadlock. This was not, in my opinion, particularly satisfactory. It would be time-consuming, expensive, adversary and would permit an unknowledgeable stranger to resolve a basic issue that only the trustees were qualified to resolve. The second was to allow the team of advisors (the consultant, the administrative manager, the auditor and the

Mr. Gertner is a partner in the Toledo law firm of Shumaker, Loop & Kendrick. He is the responsible partner for all Taft-Hartley trust clients. Admitted to the bar in 1957, he is a member of the Toledo, Ohio and American Bar Associations and has been a lecturer on law at Toledo University Law School. He is a graduate of Harvard College and received his law degree from Ohio State University College of Law. Mr. Gertner has spoken before American Bar Association Annual and Sectional Conferences; Pacific Coast, Arizona and Midwestern Labor Law Conferences; and national and regional conferences of the Financial Analysts Federation Practicing Law Institute. He is co-author of the book The Prudent Man. *Long active in Foundation activities, Mr. Gertner has been a frequent speaker or panelist at educational meetings, and has contributed to the IF Digest. He is a former member of the Foundation's Board of Directors, Attorneys Committee and Employer Liability Study Committee, and currently is a member of the Constitution and By-Laws Committee, which he formerly chaired. He also served on the special committee that prepared the* Investment Policy Guidebook for Trustees.

fund counsel) to provide the trustees with more input on the basic question which was at the heart of the deadlock: What was the appropriate level of reserves for *this plan at this point in time?* The trustees opted for the latter; and I'd like to share with you what I deem one of the most interesting and productive experiences I've had.

The first place we looked was to the trust agreement. As the source of all trustee authority, it seemed like a logical starting point. In Appendix A, I've reproduced the applicable provisions of the plan's trust agreement, which are fairly standard.

Tax Considerations

A second preliminary area of inquiry was that of tax or IRS considerations. The trust is exempt from taxation under IRC Section 501(c)(9), which is integral to the continued operation of the plan. To maintain the tax exempt status, it is necessary that the reserves not be unreasonably large, or the danger exists that the excess portion and the earnings will lose their tax exempt status. Recently, the IRS revised its viewpoint and rules, easing the burden on welfare plan trustees concerning the tax aspects of reserves.

As I have previously noted, the unreasonable accumulation of reserves by a Section 501(c)(9) organization is inconsistent with proposed regulations promulgated under the Code. First, unlike a retirement plan, for example, the purpose of a welfare plan qualified under Section 501(c)(9) is the "current" provision of benefits. Second, the Internal Revenue Service has indicated in proposed regulations that while passive investment income (e.g., interest, dividends, etc.) is not taxable when it is properly set aside to provide for the payment of life, sick, accident or other benefits and reasonable administrative expenses in connection therewith, such income would become taxable if the amount of such income or period of time during which such income accumulated was unreasonable.

> Although set aside income may be accumulated, any accumulation which is unreasonable in amount or duration is evidence that the income was not accumulated for the purposes set forth in subdivision (iii) of this subparagraph. However, income which has been set aside may be invested temporarily, pending the action contemplated by the set aside, without being regarded as having been used for other purposes. Prop. Treas. Reg. §1.512(a)-3(c)(3).

I have continually counseled the trustees that, from a practical standpoint, the amount of reserves which is reasonable for a particular fund depends on such factors as the nature of the fund's extended eligibility rules, the frequency of strikes and the employment cycle in the particular trade. Until recently, however, there has been no concrete guidance on the subject.

In June 1980, the Internal Revenue Service released Technical Advice Memorandum (hereinafter referred to as the "TAM") Ref. No. 8024187 (March 1980). While this written determination letter has no binding precedential authority, it is nevertheless instructive. The TAM involved a collectively bargained, jointly trusteed health and welfare plan providing a broad range of hospital, medical and surgical benefits via insurance policies and/or on a self-funded basis. The plan had investment income from its reserves of $263,920 in 1977; $359,733 in 1976; and $444,289 in 1975.

After reviewing the several applicable provisions of the Code [Sections 501(c)(9), 511, 512(a)(3)(A) and 512(a)(3)(B)], the TAM summarizes the rationale of the law as follows:

> The legislative history of section 512(a)(3)(E) of the Code indicates that investment income is an integral part of the exempt insurance function of an organization exempt from federal income tax under section 501(c)(9). Section 512(a)(3)(B) serves to remove from the unrelated business income tax an organization's investment income where that income is committed to provide for the payment of life, sick, accident, or other benefits within section 501(c)(9).

The TAM then discusses the extent to which investment income must, in the case of a Section 501(c)(9) health and welfare plan, be "set aside" for the purposes of the exempt functions of the entity. While stating that, generally, set aside income must be specifically earmarked as such or placed in a separate account, in the case of a health and welfare plan which by its governing instrument (trust agreement) must use its net income for benefits under its plan of benefits, the income and assets of the plan can be considered as committed to purposes within Section 512(a)(3)(B) of the Code without additional action by the trustees. Further action, such as the annual exempt function income regulations, would merely make explicit the existing fact. The TAM concludes:

> Accordingly, in the case of a voluntary employees' beneficiary association which by the terms of its governing instrument uses its net investment income for life, sick, accident, or other benefits, net investment income need not be otherwise designated by the organization to be considered properly set aside.

Next, the TAM addresses the question of the reasonableness or unreasonableness of the accumulation of reserves, and states the alternatives as follows:

> In the case of 501(c)(9) organizations, accumulations which are reasonably necessary for the purpose of providing life, sick, accident, or other benefits to members, are not unreasonable even though such accumulations may be quite large and the time between the date of receipt by the organization of such amounts and the date of payment of the benefits is quite long. On the other hand, if an accumulation has become unreasonable in amount or duration, through continual additions to it over a period of years, it would no longer be reasonably necessary to set aside additional amounts to be added to the accumulated reserve.

The TAM notes that there is no specific statutory language or published precedent concerning the reasonableness of reserves, and that in each case it is a question of fact, depending on the circumstances of each plan at the time. The TAM enumerates the many valid purposes for which a health and welfare plan may accumulate reserves and notes the virtual dependence of a Section 501(c)(9) plan upon employer contributions for its funding:

> The existence of reserves allows such an organization to conduct its activities without interruption during financially adverse periods, such as, for example, strikes, lock-outs, and economic recessions. Normally, as is the case here, a voluntary employees' beneficiary association is almost totally dependent on employer contributions for its funds. Therefore, it would of necessity be forced to suspend or substantially reduce its operations if those employer contributions were to be totally cut off or substantially reduced unless it retained a reasonably large reserve fund.

Based upon the foregoing, the TAM concludes:

> Many 501(c)(9) organizations are created and operated pursuant to a collective bargaining agreement between participating employers and labor unions representing the members of the employees' association. In these cases, the specific financial details of the employees' association's operations, including the amount of the employer contributions, the amount of the benefits to be paid to the members, and the amount of reserves the employees' association may accumulate, have been determined as a result of arm's-length negotiations between adversary parties. In this manner, the collective bargaining process acts as a control against the unreasonable accumulation of funds.
>
> *Accordingly, barring any unusual circumstances, where a 501(c)(9) organization has been created and is operated pursuant to a collective bargaining agreement between participating employers and labor unions representing the members of the employees' association, it will be presumed that the reserves accumulated by the 501(c)(9) organization are reasonable in amount and duration.* [Emphasis added.]

The "unusual circumstances" preventing application of the aforesaid general rules would include evidence that "the agreement was reached by other than arm's-length negotiations between adversary parties."

This opinion, though lacking binding precedential authority, is strong evidence of the thinking of the Internal Revenue Service. To meet the parameters of the TAM, we recommend that:

1. If the trustees have not already done so, they should adopt at year end a final exempt function income regulation tracking this TAM to "make explicit the existing fact that the income and assets of the organization are already committed to purposes in Sections 501(c)(9) and 512(a)(3)(B)."
2. The trustees continue to monitor the amount of the reserves themselves by means of a reserve model or the consultant's analysis and opinion, to avoid "any unusual circumstances" when the reserve "has become unreasonable in amount or duration."

ERISA Guidelines

Next we look to ERISA for some insights or guidelines. There are no provisions of ERISA which deal directly with the concept of reserves for health and welfare plans. However, any ERISA consideration of this type would undoubtedly come within the provisions of ERISA Section

404(a)(I)(A) and (B):

> Subject to Sections 403(c) and (d), 4042, and 4044, a fiduciary shall discharge his duties with respect to a plan solely in the interest of the participants and beneficiaries and—
> (A) for the exclusive purpose of:
> (i) providing benefits to participants and their beneficiaries; and
> (ii) defraying reasonable expenses of administering the plan;
> (B) with the care, skill, prudence, and diligence under the circumstances then prevailing that a prudent man acting in a like capacity and familiar with such matters would use in the conduct of an enterprise of a like character and with like aims;

The points to be made are threefold. First, the trustees are to act for the exclusive benefit of the plan participants. While a management trustee may want to minimize benefit increases and to maximize reserves to protect employers from future increased contributions to sustain the plan of benefits; and while a union trustee may want to continually offer new and more expanded benefits to boost his personal strength within his union and to assist in organizational efforts; the only legal test is, what is in the exclusive best interests of the participants.

Second, the purpose of the plan is to provide benefits. That is, all trust monies are to be used for benefits, or to defray the reasonable and necessary expenses of administration. The plan exists only to provide benefits, and for no other purpose. Hence, the first and omnipresent question is and must be, can the plan provide new or improved benefits? Finally, the trustees must do so as prudent men. To expend every dollar with no reserves would not be prudent; nor would the accumulation and maintenance of enormous reserves to meet any and all conceivable contingencies. What is required is a balance. The trustees must determine proximate and foreseeable contingencies, fluctuations in income and expense, and reserve sufficient monies to continue to fund the plan operation during their occurrence; they must devote the remaining monies, if any, to benefits.

Precedents and Authorities

Our next inquiry was for precedent authorities on reserves. We were unable to locate any reported cases on the issue of the appropriate size of health and welfare reserves. One recent arbitration decision does reflect what we perceive to be appropriate. In *In re Trustees of the National Benefit Fund for Hospital and Health Care Employees,* 77-1 CCH Arb. 8201 (Arb. Morris Glushien, 1977), an arbitrator decided that:

> ...the benefits being provided by a very large health and welfare fund (90,000 participants) had to be reduced substantially, due to adverse claims experience and other factors. The evidence indicated that the reserves of the fund, including the reserves for incurred but unpaid claims, were largely depleted. The arbitrator ordered that the trustees should meet and consider specific benefit reductions with the proviso that, if they could not agree, he would determine the reductions. The trustees were unable to agree and, accordingly, the arbitrator conducted further hearings and then issued a supplementary award directing specific benefit reductions. *See* 77-1 CCH Arb. 8299 (1977). Before all of the reductions were implemented, however, the collective bargaining agreement was changed to require additional employer contributions and this had the effect of generating additional funds to offset the necessity for certain of the reductions. Upon application by the union trustees, the arbitrator then conducted additional hearings as a result of which he issued a second supplementary award, restoring the prior level of benefits.

There have been numerous speeches given and articles written on the subject (*see* Appendix B). Although none of these authorities resolved the problem for the trustees, we believed that some of the comments of the writers would be helpful in the deliberations of the trustees. Yet, a review of materials points up the weakness in the treatment to date of the issue of health and welfare plan reserves; we find glittering generalities with no specific guidelines. While each health and welfare plan is unique and *sui generis,* the approaches glibly proffered were similar for each.

Developing a Reserve Model

Reference Points

It is suggested that the weakness in prior treatments is a failure to specify the reference points to be analyzed and considered. The following are the reference points which we deemed relevant.

1. *Stability of Work Force.* This requires a consideration going back over several years and projected into the future concerning how many persons will be contributed on and how many will become eligible for benefits. The former goes to income stream and the latter to predictability of future claims. While a volatile work force may lend to contributions without eligibility and thus represent a plus for the plan, it also makes future financial projections more speculative and suggests a need for higher reserve levels.

2. *Stability of Economy.* This is a variation of the prior topic and relates to projections of future work levels and, hence, future contributions and eligibility. Since claims tend to increase in periods of short term unemployment (e.g., increases in elective surgery, routine medical and dental and increased income disability claims), this has a short-run impact on claims. Another aspect is the impact of inflation on health care costs. Some judgments must be made on this topic, and this must be factored into reserves.

3. *Stability of Collective Bargaining Agreement.* If a new collective bargaining agreement has just been signed, economic work stoppages are less likely to occur and more predictability of income is present; hence, the reduced need for reserves. As the plan sponsors approach collective bargaining, the converse occurs.

4. *Patterns of Income and Expense.* This relates to the prior items, and is generally reflected in projected income and expense statements for a year or two in the future. These will indicate profitable or deficit operations and suggest the need for reduced or increased reserves.

Purpose of Reserves

Next, we discussed with the trustees the specific items for which reserves are established.

1. *Reported but Unpaid Claims.* Not all claims can or are processed and paid the day they are received. Generally, patterns develop as to the amount of unpaid claims in process at any time. Clearly, this is a liability for which reserves must be made.

2. *Incurred but Unreported Claims.* At any point in time claims have been incurred, but the claims have not yet been reported (filed). Again, patterns develop for a given plan. The pattern should be traced and a reserve increment set aside for such claims.

3. *Extended Eligibility.* In all plans there is a period during which a member need not work (and hence no contributions are made), but during which he remains eligible (and hence claims will be paid). This varies from one month in most Teamster plans to three months in many plans, up to two years in plans with hour banks. The actual amount of extended coverage and its anticipated cost must be qualified; this then must be factored by inflationary trends in costs, and the resultant amount reserved.

4. *Expenses.* There should be a reserve increment for further expenses of operation without income.

Financial Data—Plan A

In order to place the topic in a factual context, in response to questions from the trustees, the advisors compiled the data on the plan.

A. Cash Reserves at July 31, 1979
  1. Invested for trustees by investment manager $4,363,036
  2. Incurred but unreported claims reserve held and invested by insurance company at 8½% to secure payment of claims incurred during the current policy period, but reported and paid thereafter 2,344,999
  3. Total $5,597,033
B. Fund Balance—Excluding Reserves for Incurred but Unreported Claims:
  1. May 31, 1977 — ($751,826)
  2. May 31, 1978 — $653,370
  3. May 31, 1979 — $2,122,899
C. Current Data
  1. Paid claims (1/1/79-8/31/79)—$2,750,000, or an average of $343,750 per month.
  2. Contribution income (exclusive of investment income) (1/1/79-8/31/79)—$3,720,596, or an average of $465,074.50 per month.
  3. Payments to insurance company if plan had not adopted split funding (1/1/79-8/31/79)—$3,041,000, or an average of $380,125 per month.
D. Hours Worked
  1. Per administrative manager, calendar year—field hours only:
     a. 1977 — 4,185,898
     b. 1978 — 4,794,030
     c. N.B. — field hours up by 600,000 but total hours, in-

cluding self-contributions and office, up only 450,000 for 1978 over 1977.
2. Per consultant, total hours on a plan year basis:
   a. 6/1/76-5/31/77 — 4,792,000
   b. 6/1/77-5/31/78 — 5,119,000

Considerations and Recommendations

The advisors then identified the elements and considerations relevant to the specific plan-client.

1. *Pending Claims.* The plan office has excellent turnaround time in the processing and payment of claims. Nonetheless, there are always claims on the adjusters' desks, awaiting further data and generally in the system. This amount (or the average amount of pending bills) must be included as a component in the reserve.

2. *Incurred but Unreported Claims Reserve.* At any moment in time, insurance contracts contain commitments which are liabilities to be paid (incurred) but have not yet been paid or reported to the fund. In the event of contract termination, funds must be available to pay these claims.

Under the split-funded contract, this reserve has been released to the trustees, but remains under the insurance company's control. It is also known as the "deposit fund" or the "side fund." The trustees will earn 8½% on this reserve for 1979 from the insurer.

This reserve can increase or decrease at renewal time depending on the level of insureds' claim experience for the previous 12 months and expected medical inflation. This is one factor in determining the premium and required cents per hour to fund the plan. The level that must be maintained under the split-funded contract is no less than 115% nor more than 150% of expected incurred claims. The level is determined by the insurance company's actuarial people and is subject to review and evaluation by plan advisors. In the event of a significant increase in this requirement, it usually may be funded over several months.

It was the recommendation of the advisors that the incurred claims reserve be computed annually as in the past, and that the amount determined be added to the overall reserve calculation.

3. *Reserve for Accumulated Eligibility—Active Participants.* At any moment in time the fund has collected contributions which, under the rules of eligibility, are to provide insurance eligibility several months down the road. At accounting statement date May 31, qualified employees, for hours worked through May 31, are entitled to coverage for June, July, August, September and October, or five months. In addition, high hour employees are entitled to November, December and January, or a total of eight months after the statement date. There are a very few who may be entitled to three months beyond the January month, for a total of 11 months after the statement date.

The certified public accountants determine the amount of reserves necessary to cover this liability by multiplying the premium rate times the number of insureds as determined by computer analysis. If the hours and insureds go up and/or the premium rate increases, this calculation will result in an increase in the level of reserves needed to fund the liability, and is a factor in the cents per hour needed to maintain the plan.

In addition, consideration should be given to the provision that an amount equal to 10% of the accumulated eligibility reserve figure be added to the reserve figure. The logic of the recommendation is severalfold. The history of health care costs is one of annual escalation. The claims will be paid in the future and, therefore, may be subject to higher costs. Also, if there are any increases from the insurance company, they will be put in force at the beginning of each policy year or renewal date; hence, the possibility of an increase in cost when they are paid. There is little doubt, based upon the experience of recent years, that when a member earns eligibility in the past and is granted coverage for claims in the future, the claims cost will be higher when the claims are, in fact, processed and paid in the future. Therefore, we believe it is prudent to add a factor to approximate such an increase in constructing the reserve model.

4. *Extended Eligibility—Retirees.* There was a lengthy discussion at a recent trustees' meeting on the amount of future coverage to be extended to a retiree for medical benefits. It was the opinion of the advisors that the legal and prudent coverage to be afforded in the event of a plan termination is the same period of extended medical benefits and coverages as is provided for actives. An examination of law supports certain opinions expressed during the trustees' discussions that "lifetime coverage" for retirees vis-a-vis "limited coverage" for actives in this area would be imprudent. Accordingly, the advisors recommended that a calculation be made for retirees paralleling that suggested at No. 3 above for actives.

5. *Death Benefit.* The advisors discussed this problem in depth and concluded with the recommendation that the retiree death benefit (except in the case of a retiree of a union which withdraws as plan sponsor and plan participant, which has already been addressed by the trustees) be treated as

a fixed obligation. Further, the advisors recommended that this be self-funded. The consultant would compile the data on all current retirees and would calculate the present value of the future death benefits to be paid to all retirees. This amount would be sequestered in a separate reserve account, but would still be a part of the overall reserves. If all retirees expire at their actuarial time, the initial deposit plus the earnings thereon would fund the expense of the benefit. As new retirees are added to the rolls, an amount calculated by the consultant would be added to the account; and as a retiree expired, the benefit would be paid from the account. The overall reserve would be reviewed periodically. Therefore, this initial cost would be set up as a component in the reserve model and thereafter adjusted as necessary to keep it actuarially sound.

6. *Administrative Expenses.* Even if the plan were to be terminated, it would take up to six months to conclude all administrative activity. Hence, a reserve of six months' administrative expenses, based upon current levels of administrative expenses, was recommended and approved.

7. *Economic Reserves.* All of the commentators on the subject of reserves recommend an economic or special situation reserve. The function of this reserve component is to cover short term contingencies. This would include such items as temporary cessation of employer contributions due to a strike or other work stoppage; short-run reductions in contributions because of adverse weather conditions; short term claim fluctuations as a result of an epidemic; short term increases in expenses due to a change in administrative procedures or compliance with new statutory provisions; etc.

There are no fixed guidelines to the quantification of this figure. We discussed a fixed figure ($x); or a formula relating to monthly premiums (i.e., number of actives times current monthly premium times three), a formula relating to eligibility hours versus projected hours (i.e., 1,600 less 1,200 times monthly contribution times number of actives divided by two). This is a matter to be talked out to determine a logical figure or formula, which should then be added as the final component to the reserve model.

Trigger Events

Having created a reserve model, initially and at quarterly intervals thereafter actual figures would be inserted and the reserve levels determined versus actual dollars in reserve. Thus, every three months, the trustees would have a report on the desired reserves pursuant to the model versus the actual dollar reserves.

Downside Warning. The advisors recommended that the trustees adopt two separate definitions of trigger events: if the economic reserve is 50% of projected reserve and/or if the plan has operated at a cash deficit for six consecutive months. When a trigger event occurs, the trustees shall:

a. Seek increased contributions, and/or
b. Reduce benefits;

unless, in their opinion, the trigger event is an aberration due to an unusual and non-recurring condition.

Further, there should be two stated early warning events: if the economic reserve is 66% of the projected reserve level and/or if the plan has operated at a cash deficit for three consecutive months. The purpose of the early warning signals is to alert the trustees and their advisors and plan participants that a potential problem exists, and unless it is reversed, the trigger events will be reached in 90 days and more money will be requested or benefits reduced. The procedure is subject always to the ability of the trustees to prudently suspend the trigger event response.

Upside Trigger Event. Conversely, if the economic reserves exceed the projected reserves by a stated percentage for more than four consecutive months, the upside trigger event occurs and the trust must increase benefits without new money, *unless* the trustees in the exercise of their prudent fiduciary discretion determine this condition to be the result of a temporary phenomenon which will not continue.

Having put this information together, we realized we were closing in on an answer; so we invited the executive committee to meet with us. We talked out the components and the figures and came up rather easily and rather quickly with a reserve model we all felt comfortable with.

Reserve Model and Policy—Plan A

1. The trustees of the plan shall establish a reserve model as soon as possible.

2. The plan's reserve model shall consist of the following components:

a. Reserve for Incurred but Unreported and for Pending Claims. Currently, the insurance company computes this figure annually and certifies it to the administrative manager. The figure as established by the insurance company shall be used as the amount necessary to fund this component.

b. Adjusted Extended Eligibility for Active Members. This component shall be computed quarterly by the administrative manager using an actual calculation and determination of the aggregate number of months of earned extended eligibility for participation by all then-current active members. To determine the amount necessary to fund this component, the number of actual months of eligibility shall be multiplied by the current insurance company monthly premium rate and shall be adjusted upward for inflation by an amount equal to 1% per month for each month from the inception of the new insurance company policy year.

c. Extended Eligibility for Retirees—Medical Only. The administrative manager shall compute the amount of this component by multiplying the number of retirees at the end of the quarter times the current insurance company retiree premium rate times six. This contemplates action by the trustees in the event that the plan were ever totally terminated, by providing six months' extended medical coverages.

d. Retiree Death Benefit. Whether the trustees continue to insure this benefit or hereafter determine to self-fund it is a decision beyond the scope of the advisors and this report. However, for purposes of creating and funding a reserve model, it is recommended that a component be established and that it be calculated at the rate of $700 times the number of retirees at any computation date. This contemplates trustee action, in the event of total plan termination, of buying each retiree a paid-up $1,000 life insurance policy.

e. Administrative Expenses. The reserve model should include a component for ongoing administrative expenses. This should be calculated at the then-current monthly average of total administrative expenses times six (months).

f. Economic Reserves. This component, which is essential to a prudent reserve model, is also the most subjective and difficult to quantify. After extended discussion of the concept and numerous alternate formulae, the advisors recommended a calculation of the funding of this component at the number of current active participants times the current insurance company rate times three (months).

3. The administrative manager shall calculate the projected reserve needs of the plan quarterly, based upon the above model, and report to the trustees the projected reserve needs and the total fund balance.

4. The matter of a trigger system was tabled for further study.

The recommendation was then taken to the trustees, discussed and approved. Then, after approval of the concepts, the consultant put numbers with the words:

A. Reserves Needed
1. Incurred but Unreported and Pending Claims $1,233,999
2. Extended Eligibility—Actives—Adjusted 3%   2,354,137
3. Extended Eligibility—Retirees—Medical   83,228
4. Retirees—Death Benefit   271,000
5. Expenses   118,104
6. Economic Reserve   1,050,000

Total Reserves Needed $5,110,468

B. Total Fund Reserves   5,597,000

C. Surplus $ 486,532

Under this recommendation, 91.31%, or $5,110,468, of the total plan reserves of $5,597,000 are committed to plan obligations; and 8.69%, or $468,532, represents uncommitted reserves.

At this point, the trustees turned back to the issue that caused the deadlock and gave rise to the study. The dispute was resolved. The appropriate level of reserves for this plan at this time was $5,110,468. This was almost $500,000 less than the total plan reserves. Hence, a modest increase in benefits was approved without new money.

The administrative manager does the computations quarterly. As the needed reserve level grew slightly and the actual reserve level grew dramatically, recently more benefit improvements were made—without new money, without prolonged debate and without a deadlock.

Financial Data—Plan B

When the news of the success in the prior plan got around, another client wanted to go through the exercise. Their data appear below.

A. Reserve for Incurred but Unreported Claims and Extended Eligibility
1. December 31, 1979 $1,441,473
2. December 31, 1978   1,221,217

3. December 31, 1977   1,011,000
4. December 31, 1976   1,314,000
5. 1979 Breakdown
   a. Incurred but unreported claims reserve $ 450,450
   b. Extended eligibility reserve   991,023

B. Fund Balance
1. December 31, 1979   ($715,503)
2. December 31, 1978   ($398,458)
3. December 31, 1977   ($243,568)
4. December 31, 1976   ($488,000)

C. Current Data—1979
1. Contributions income $1,927,737
2. All other income   266,253
3. Administrative expenses   62,718
4. Premiums and benefits paid   2,060,469

D. Miscellaneous Data
1. Liquid assets at 12/31/79 $ 725,970
2. Number of retirees   188
3. Retiree coverage annual cost
   a. Medical $182,125.87
   b. Life   11,152.20
   c. Prescription   19,196.69
   d. Total $212,834.76
   e. Total Without Life $201,322.55
      (i) Per Month $ 16,776.88

Reserve Model and Policy—Plan B

This board, or more accurately its subcommittee and the advisors, approached the problem on two different bases: the terminated plan method and the ongoing plan method. The former proceeds from the assumption that termination of the plan is a significant possibility and, therefore, there shall be sufficient assets in the trust reserves to fund the benefits and expenses of a plan termination. The ongoing plan theory assumes that the plan will continue on as a benefit provider to the participants and beneficiaries indefinitely. However, the plan may at any time and from time to time suffer economic setbacks, and the trust reserves must be sufficient at such times to maintain the coverages provided.

With the background data and with the legal, tax and ERISA considerations discussed previously, the subcommittee and advisors hammered out a three-pronged recommendation, which is set forth below.

1. The trustees of the plan shall establish a reserve model as soon as possible. In fact, the recommendation was that the trustees establish a reserve model goal based upon the ongoing plan theory and an interim reserve model to be attained between the present time and June 30, 1982, the expiration of the current collective bargaining agreement. Finally, it was recommended that the trustees acknowledge what their reserve needs would be on a terminated plan basis.

2. The plan's reserve model shall consist of the following components:

   a. Reserve for Incurred but Unreported Claims and for Pending Claims. Currently, the consultant computes this figure annually and certifies it to the administrative manager and certified public accountant. The figure as established by the consultant shall be used as the amount necessary to fund this component. This computation shall be used in the short term reserve model and the long term optimum model, as well as for the terminated plan reserve model.

   b. Adjusted Extended Eligibility for Active Members. This component shall be computed quarterly for the administrative manager by an actual calculation and determination of the aggregate number of months of earned extended eligibility for participation by all then-current active members. To determine the amount necessary to fund this component, the number of actual months of eligibility shall be multiplied by the current average monthly claim cost per participant and shall be adjusted upward for inflation by an amount equal to 1% per month for each month from the inception of the new claim cost per participant calculation. The same calculation would be made for purposes of a terminated plan basis reserve model. For purposes of the short term reserve model, calculated on the ongoing plan basis, it is recommended that only 75% of this liability be included in the model.

   c. Extended Eligibility for Retirees—Medical Only. The administrative manager shall compute the amount of this component by multiplying the number of retirees at the end of the quarter times the current average retiree claim cost per month, times the number of months for which extended coverage is desired.

   (i) For the short term ongoing reserve

model, it is recommended that one month's extended eligibility be used.

(ii) For the long term model, it is recommended that three months' extended eligibility be used.

(iii) For the terminated plan model, it is recommended that six months' extended eligibility be used.

d. Retiree Death Benefit. Since the ongoing plan theory is being utilized, no reserve is necessary for either the short term or long range reserve models. However, for purposes of creating and funding a terminated plan theory reserve model, it is recommended that a component be established and that it be calculated at the rate of $700 times the number of retirees at any computation date. This contemplates trustee action, in the event of total plan termination, of buying each retiree a paid-up $1,000 life insurance policy.

e. Administrative Expenses. The reserve model should include a component for ongoing administrative expenses. This should be calculated at the then-current monthly average of total administrative expenses.

(i) For the short term ongoing theory reserve model, it is recommended that one month's reserve be used.

(ii) For the long term ongoing theory reserve model, it is recommended that three months' reserve be used.

(iii) For the terminated plan theory reserve model, it is recommended that three months' reserve be used.

f. Economic Reserves. This component, which is essential to a prudent reserve model, is also the most subjective and difficult to quantify. For preliminary discussion purposes only, it is recommended that the calculation of the funding of this component be the average monthly total benefit expense.

(i) For the short term ongoing reserve model, it is recommended that one months' total expenses be used.

(ii) For the long term ongoing reserve model, it is recommended that three months' total expenses be used.

(iii) For the terminated plan theory, it is recommended that three months' total expenses be used.

3. The administrative manager shall calculate the projected reserve needs of the plan based upon the above model quarterly and report to the trustees the projected reserve needs and the total fund balance.

Three Projections

The subcommittee and advisors then quantified the three reserve models with current figures. The calculation of projected needed reserves and the amount available for reserves for the *long term, ongoing theory reserve model* appears below.

A. Reserves Needed

1.	Incurred but Unreported and Pending Claims	$ 450,450
2.	Extended Eligibility—Actives—(Without Adjustment)	991,023
3.	Extended Eligibility—Retirees—Medical	50,331
4.	Retirees—Death Benefit	-0-
5.	Expenses	15,679
6.	Economic Reserve	515,117
	Total Reserves Needed	$2,022,600

B. Total Fund Reserves   725,970
C. Surplus (Deficit)   ($1,296,630)

Under the approach of first establishing a *short term reserve model using the ongoing plan theory* the following computation is proper:

A. Reserves Needed

1.	Incurred but Unreported and Pending Claims	$ 450,450
2.	Extended Eligibility—Actives—(Without Adjustment)	743,267
3.	Extended Eligibility—Retirees—Medical	16,777
4.	Retirees—Death Benefit	-0-
5.	Expenses	5,226
6.	Economic Reserve	171,705
	Total Reserves Needed	$1,387,425

B. Total Fund Reserves   725,970
C. Surplus (Deficit) $ 661,455

For purposes of a benchmark *if plan termination were to be considered,* it was recommended that the following model be considered.

A. Reserves Needed

1.	Incurred but Unreported and Pending Claims	$ 450,450
2.	Extended Eligibility—Actives—(Without Adjustment)	991,023

	3.	Extended Eligibility —Retirees— Medical	100,662
	4.	Retirees—Death Benefit	131,600
	5.	Expenses	31,659
	6.	Economic Reserve	515,117
		Total Reserves Needed	$2,220,211
B.		Total Fund Reserves	725,970
C.		Surplus (Deficit)	($1,494,241)

I wish I could report that the trustees adopted the recommendations and lived happily ever after —but they didn't. They sent the committee back for more study; in the meantime, they took $.10 per hour from some floating money and the total fund reserve went up to $1,400,000 in a matter of months. The recommendations were then adopted with only minor adjustment.

The Bottom Line

What's the bottom line on all of this? It's simple. As trustees you have a legal duty, a legal obligation under ERISA, under the Internal Revenue Code, and under your trust agreements to establish a reserve level for your health and welfare plan. Second, you can do it one of two ways. You can grab a glib generalization, a trite rule of thumb and retire to the bar. Alternatively, you can go through the exercise of establishing a reserve model based upon the specifics of your specific plan. You can isolate your turnaround time to determine what, if any, money you may need in the sock for pending claims. You can get your consultant and/or your carrier to quantify your needed reserve for incurred but unreported claims—not a textbook formula or percentage, but yours. You can ask your administrative manager to push the pencil and tell you now and from time to time in the future the actual number of months of extended eligibility for the actual members of your actual plan and the cost of this exposure. You can face up to what, if anything, you must do, can do or should do for retirees. And, you can decide on the appropriate money to have available for continued administrative expenses and for unknown contingencies.

If you do all this, put it on paper and adopt it, you will have a reserve model. Then at any time you want, you plug in the numbers and you know if you're overreserved, underreserved or on the mark. If you do, you'll have a basis for a highly scientific, highly accurate trend line.

If you do all of the above you will have fulfilled your fiduciary duty. You will be able to protect your plan from an IRS unreasonable reserve attack —an attack which, if successful, could cost you your tax exempt status. You'll be able to explain to your members why you need an extra nickel, even with $1 million in reserve. You will know when you can increase benefits unless you get new money. Best of all, you can do all these great and wondrous things without prolonged debates and without deadlocks. That's a godfather offer if I ever heard one.

Appendix A

Provisions of Trust Agreement

A. Article II, Section 1

The Trust and Fund are hereby created for the purpose of maintaining, through policies or certificates of insurance issued by a licensed insurance company or companies or by self-funding or a combination thereof for the benefit of eligible Employees, health and welfare benefits, as are now or hereafter permitted by law and as the Trustees may determine in such amounts, of such types and with such coverages as the Trustees in their sole discretion shall determine. The Fund shall not be used to provide pension or retirement benefits.

B. Article II, Section 8

The Trust Fund is and shall constitute an irrevocable trust created pursuant to the provisions of Section 302(c) of the Labor-Management Relations Act of 1947 as amended for the benefit of the Employees and to provide the following types of benefits:

(a) Death benefits providing for payment to the beneficiaries named by the Employee in the event of death;

(b) Accidental death and dismemberment benefits providing for payments in the event of nonoccupational death or dismemberment;

(c) Accident and health insurance providing for benefits to the Employee for limited periods of time when injury or illness prevents work;

(d) Hospital benefits providing for payment of hospital bills; payment of surgical bills and payment of physicians' bills (arising from nonoccupational sources);

(e) Such other benefits as the Trustees of the Health and Welfare Plan may agree upon subject to the provisions of any applicable statutes;

for Employees who meet the qualifications as to age, length of service with contributing Employers, length of payment by the Employer of contributions and such other provisions, limitations and conditions as may be established by the Trustees under the authority granted to the Trustees.

It is the intention of this Agreement and Declaration of Trust that the Trustees, within their discretion, shall provide the maximum amount of benefits that the Trust Fund shall from time to time provide after taking into consideration the reasonable reserves to be established. The benefits to be provided shall be determined by the Trustees and based upon actuarial methods and assumptions which, in the aggregate, are reasonable and which take into account the experience of the Plan and its reasonable expectations. The Trustees shall have the authority to increase or decrease the various types of benefits which in their judgment can best be procured and purchased with the monies in the Trust Fund available and to amend the Plan of Benefits accordingly.

It is the intention of all parties that the benefits are limited to those which can be financed from the proceeds of the Trust Fund. It is expressly understood and agreed that there is no liability upon the Union, any Employers or the Trustees for the furnishing of any specific type or amount of benefits, except as otherwise expressly provided in any Collective Bargaining Agreement.

* * *

[Emphasis supplied.]

C. Article IV, Section 6(d)

Any and all funds received by the Trustees in the form of contributions, income, dividends on policies of insurance, interest on bonds or bank deposits, gain or yield on stocks or bonds or otherwise, shall be received by them as part of the Trust Fund to be administered and disposed of for the following purposes:

* * *

(d) *To establish and accumulate as part of the Trust Fund such reasonable reserves as the Trustees shall determine advisable to carry out the purposes of the Health and Welfare Plan, including but not limited to reserves left with the insurance company or companies pursuant to the terms and conditions agreed upon between the Trustees and the insurance company or companies.*

* * *

[Emphasis supplied.]

D. Article IV, Section 8(c)

Subject to the stated purposes of the Trust Fund and the provisions of this Agreement and Declaration of Trust and subject to the terms and conditions of any policy or policies of insurance obtained as herein provided, the Trustees shall have full and exclusive authority to determine all questions of coverage and eligibility, methods of providing and arranging for benefits and all other related matters. They shall have full power to construe the provisions in this Agreement and Declaration of Trust and the terms used herein. Any such determination and any such construction adopted by the Trustees in good faith shall be binding upon all of the parties hereto and the beneficiaries hereof. The Trustees shall be free to use their own judgment and discretion in all things pertaining to the affairs of the Trust Fund and shall not be personally liable for any action done or omitted to be done when acting in good faith and in the exercise of their best judgment; and the fact that such action or omission, based upon advice of counsel employed by the Trustees, shall be conclusive evidence of such good faith and best judgment. No matter respecting the foregoing or any difference arising thereunder or any matter involved in this Agreement and Declaration of Trust shall be subject to the grievance procedure established in any Collective Bargaining Agreement between any contributing Employer and the Union.

Without limiting the generality of the foregoing, the Trustees in their administration of the Trust Fund for the stated purposes thereof and consistent with the provisions of this Agreement and Declaration of Trust shall have the power and authority to:

* * *

(c) Make such uniform rules and regulations as are consistent with and necessary for effectuating the provisions of this Agreement and Declaration of Trust, including but not being limited to the following:

(i) To prescribe rules and procedures governing the application for benefits by Employees and beneficiaries, and an appeals claims procedure for appeals by parties aggrieved by the action of any said application.

(ii) Subject to the provisions of any applicable policy or policies of insurance, to make determinations which may be made final and binding upon all parties as to the rights of any Employee or any beneficiary to benefits, including any rights any individual may have to request a hearing with respect to any such determination.

(iii) To obtain and evaluate all statistical data which may be reasonably required with respect to the administration of the Health and Welfare Plan.

(iv) *To make such other rules and regulations as may be necessary for the administration of the Health and Welfare Plan which are not inconsistent with the purposes of this Agreement and Declaration of Trust.*

* * *

[Emphasis supplied.]

E. Article IV, Section 26

* * *

If at any time the Trust Fund shall not be sufficient to carry out the purposes of this Agreement and Declaration of Trust, the Trustees may take such action as may be necessary or advisable in connection with the reduction of the then existing benefits in order that the cost of the benefits shall not be greater than that which, in the judgment of the Trustees, can or should be paid from the Trust Fund. [Emphasis supplied.]

F. Article IX, Section 29

All actions taken by the Trustees in accordance with this Agreement shall be taken with the care, skill, prudence and diligence under the circumstances then prevailing that a prudent man acting in a like capacity and familiar with such matters would use in the conduct of an enterprise of like character and with like aim; in accordance with the documents and instruments governing the Plan, to the extent such documents and instruments are consistent with the law; and in accordance with the Act and the Code.

Appendix B

Selected Readings

In Kordus, *Trustees Handbook,* "ERISA Issues for Self-Funded Plans," International Foundation of Employee Benefit Plans (1977), it is stated:

The importance of reserves in the context of welfare plans is diminished by the fact that such plans have as their sole legitimate purpose the current delivery of the maximum amount of benefits possible to those eligible to receive them. The time orientation of a welfare plan is to the present and the short term, in contrast to a pension plan's concern with the future and long term security. By the very nature of the benefits provided by the usual welfare plan, a rapid turnover of assets is unavoidable, with the consequence that in the plan's administration of its assets the emphasis must be on liquidity. While, as a result of this emphasis, welfare plans need not be as concerned with developing a sophisticated investment policy as pension plans, the issue of the amount of plan assets that may be voted to investment will become increasingly significant.

The determination of the proper amount of plan assets to be held for investment . . . and the amount to be maintained for the payment of current and anticipated claims . . . is related to the type and level of benefits offered by the plan, the level of plan contributions, and the plan's claims experience.

* * *

In my opinion, ERISA's effect in the area of prudence in plan administration will be twofold: the maintenance of total reserves in an amount sufficient to pay all benefit claims as due, and the prevention of the accumulation of excessive investment reserves to the detriment of a plan's potential to provide an increase in the types or levels of benefits.

* * *

The second problem area I alluded to involves fiduciary prudence in the accumulation of investment reserves. Under ERISA there is no provision comparable to the pre-1969 provision of Section 501(c)(9) of the Internal Revenue Code giving the precious tax-exempt status only to employee benefit trusts that derived 15% or less of their income from interest earnings or investments. The absence of an ERISA-imposed ceiling on income derived from investment reserves could be interpreted as a Congressional intent to encourage welfare plans to accumulate investment reserves, since as the interest income and invested reserves increase, benefit levels could be increased.

However, in view of the purposes of welfare plans, i.e., to presently provide the maximum amount of benefits possible, I feel that as a matter of fiduciary prudence the amount of investment reserves accumulated should be limited. Thus, should the fiduciaries of any welfare plan find their investment reserves ballooning, either because a large percentage of plan contributions are being allocated to investment reserves rather than liquid reserves or because of tremendous earnings on the investment reserves, I believe that they are obliged as a matter of prudence to remedy the situation by transferring some portion of the investment reserves to the plan's liquid reserves and to take action to increase the benefit package offered by the plan correspondingly. If such a situation is a recurring phenomenon, of course, the plan managers should take steps to amend their funding policy accordingly so as to reduce the allocation of contributions to investment reserves.

This area is one which I foresee as fertile ground for litigation by plan participants to compel a plan to offer more benefits on the ground that a welfare plan's accumulation of large investment reserves is in contravention of the fiduciary obligation of the plan managers to act in the best interests of the plan participants, which interests, it will be alleged, require the payment of the maximum level of benefits within the plan's capacities. I feel that such a claim is arguably encompassed in ERISA's unique, and at present nebulous, concept of the responsibility owed by plan fiduciaries to plan participants, and has a reasonable chance of prevailing in court.

In Levin, *ERISA and Labor-Management Benefit Funds,* 2nd Ed., Practising Law Institute, the author (a noted lawyer in the field) stated:

> Trustees must determine how much of a reserve they will build for future contingencies. I know of no clear-cut, authoritative formula which decrees that a welfare fund should have a certain number of months' expenditures in reserve and no more or less. On the contrary, there cannot be such a definitive formula, since the true answer depends on so many variables as to make it an individual matter to be determined by a particular fund.

In Heusinkueld, "Reserves for Cents-Per-Hour Welfare Plan," *Annual Conference Proceedings,* National Foundation of Employee Benefit Plans (1965), the author submitted the following chart and conclusions:

RESERVES FOR CENTS-PER-HOUR WELFARE PLAN

Reserves	Amounts
1. Reduced Income	
A. Economic	6 to 9 months excess income
B. Work stoppage	3 to 4 months expenses
2. Extended Coverage	3 to 6 months expenses
3. Rising Expenses	3 to 6 months medical claims
4. Claim Fluctuations	6 to 12 months claims
Total	14 to 24 months contributions

> To sum it up, I would say the trustees have the responsibility to manage the finances of their plan so that it will have reserves adequate to maintain benefits through all misfortunes that can reasonably be expected to occur. Circumstances vary considerably from one plan to another, so I have indicated a pretty wide range in the amount of reserves required. However, I think it is safe to say that any plan with reserves in the maximum end of the range would be considered as operating prudently according to almost any standard.

Insurance vs. Self-Insurance: A Case Study

BY WALTER J. BUTLER

Introduction

I am going to discuss the actual case history of our welfare funds, which have been in existence for many years and have utilized virtually every means of financing the provision of benefits to members and their dependents. Many of the views that I will express may contradict certain popular beliefs with respect to the funding of jointly managed welfare trust funds. However, the Foundation requested me to speak as a representative of plans which have elected to retain the services of insurance carriers. In outlining the considerations which influenced our boards of trustees, my remarks will hopefully omit the technical language and statutory references so beloved by our professional advisors.

The SEIU Welfare Plans

Our funds cover more than 8,000 employees stretched over the wide geographical area of the State of New York, roughly including the entire state with the exception of the New York City metropolitan area. Primarily, the employees are employed by medium and small-sized businesses engaged in industrial and institutional cleaning, maintenance and auxiliary medical services. To a great extent, our members are in the lower income brackets and are involved in industries which traditionally have reflected a high rate of employee turnover as well as a relatively high degree of employer change. Many of the employers work on a contractual basis for leading business and non-profit institutions, and their existence is subject to the continuation of their contracts.

Our industry is not conducive to negotiating high rates of employer contributions to either welfare or pension plans. When contracts are negotiated for lower income employees in relatively unskilled occupations, it is difficult to establish reasonable rates of employer contributions to fringe benefit plans, since such amounts may diminish available monies needed by members to maintain their standard of living. Therefore, many of our views on provision of welfare benefits are related to the particular pertinent characteristics of our workers and the industry.

Another consideration has been the organizational nature of the union. Over the past 20 years, our related unions have enjoyed an enormous

As the president and chief officer of Local 200 of the Service Employees International Union, Mr. Butler supervises the activities of the 13,000-plus member local union throughout the entire upstate New York area. Active in the joint trust field for over 25 years, he has also served as chairman of five SEIU pension and welfare funds. He serves as international vice president (and member of the International Executive Board) and as secretary-treasurer of the New York State Service Employees Council and the SEIU Eastern Conference, with assignments and duties covering the 16 states on the Eastern seaboard. Additionally, Mr. Butler serves as secretary-treasurer of the Florida State SEIU Council. He received his education at Cornell University, and has testified before the United States Senate and House of Representatives as well as the New York State and other legislative bodies on behalf of social and labor legislation. In addition to serving in executive capacities for several other labor councils, Mr. Butler is a member of the advisory board for the New York State Labor Relations School, Cornell University.

growth rate due to vast organizational efforts. During this period, the union has grown from insignificant figures to membership in excess of 14,000. Negotiation of fringe benefit plans has played a vital role in this organizational effort. Continuous growth has also caused great pressure on fund administration, with heavy burdens on staff personnel and our ability to provide meaningful benefits to our workers. This growth and organizational emphasis have also played significant roles with respect to the financing of our funds.

In our early years, our welfare plans were completely insured by insurance carriers utilizing traditional group insurance contracts. It was easier, in the 1950s and 1960s, to arrange a relatively small amount of employer contributions, which would enable the welfare plan to provide minimal amounts of life insurance, hospitalization and medical benefits. Health care costs were relatively low, and death benefits generally served to cover burial expenses.

In those early years, we were limited in negotiating welfare fund contributions by the emphasis on raising wage standards. Since collective bargaining efforts generally provided relatively small differentials above the basic costs of providing minimal benefits, we were not in a position to accumulate vast reserves or to fund benefits out of previously established assets. An excellent year would be one in which we were able to allocate 10% of net receipts (after expenses) into our reserve fund.

As medical costs began to rise, particularly after 1966, our boards of trustees faced an annual problem in financing a continuation of health care benefits. This was hardly unusual and was probably typical of most service industry welfare funds in the country. In our case, financing was even more difficult, since our operating methods did not serve to accumulate reserves to fund cost increases. Therefore, we engaged in very strenuous competitive bidding, almost annually, in order to maintain our insurance costs at the lowest possible level; we held administrative expenses to a minimum, and survived from year to year. It was desirable from both an employer and union viewpoint to negotiate collective bargaining agreements for a longer period than one year. However, our tenuous financial situation prevented us from arranging long term commitments with respect to rates and plans with the carriers. As a result, we continued for a number of years in a fully insured status, with an occasional change of carrier as a result of competitive bidding, in a continuous battle to maintain our costs at the lowest possible level in the best interest of employees.

The Move to Self-Insurance

Eventually we reached a stage where the trustees had accumulated a reasonably safe level of reserves. At this point, we were able to consider some form of self-insurance as an alternative to constant rate adjustment requests by insurance carriers. While we were able to allocate portions of gross employer contributions and investment income to reserve fund accumulation, the constant growth in number of participants prevented us from establishing a stable per capita amount of reserve fund. Even though aggregate dollar reserves grew dramatically, the constant increase in the number of covered participants served to prevent accumulation of a high per capita reserve fund.

Our growth was matched by required increases in administrative costs to handle the vastly increasing number of employers in contractual relationship. However, strengthened by growth in reserves and stabilized income, we entered into self-insurance for a number of years for most of the benefits from our plan.

Self-insurance was basically a satisfactory method of operating while providing conservative benefits to employees. However, we encountered certain problems with respect to public relations, pressures on the fund office and trustees from many of our unsophisticated members, organizational difficulties, and collective bargaining difficulties with respect to self-insurance. I will discuss some of these problems subsequently.

At the same time, our self-insurance program was affected by the nationwide increase in health care costs as well as the exposure under individual claims. By maintaining a fully self-insured plan, we soon found ourselves in the position of being unable to risk exposure to large claims. Our alternatives were to maintain benefits at reasonable levels within our financial range—thus depriving our members of true protection for complex medical treatment—or to expose the fund to the risk of large individual claims. At an early stage of self-insurance, we were faced with the necessity of improving our major medical maximum benefits to achieve a more equitable relationship to actual prospective costs for large claims, which required either expanded exposure or acquisition of excess insurance.

Change in Method

After detailed review and examination of all of the facets of self-insurance, we made a significant change a number of years ago. This major step basically contradicted the trend in welfare funds in the jointly managed multiemployer field. We changed to a combination of insurance and self-insurance, and have been basically satisfied with the results.

Our dental plan is fully insured by a non-profit insurance carrier, operating under a competitively established low-retention arrangement. This program features a wide panel of participating dentists who accept dental allowances in full payment in most parts of the state. On the other hand, our vision care plan is completely self-insured and is arranged by direct contracts with a number of optical providers throughout the state.

With respect to health care, we use two methods. In certain parts of the state where hospital costs are extremely high, it is financially more attractive to utilize a non-profit service benefit carrier strictly for basic hospitalization. Studies indicated that this method in these areas would produce economies which could not be equaled by negotiation of reduced reimbursement rates from hospitals.

In the larger geographical areas of our funds, for the overwhelming majority of participants, we combine basic hospitalization, medical-surgical, major medical and disability insurance under an "administrative services only" contract with an insurance carrier. Under this method, referred to in many areas as "ASO," we utilize the carrier as a service facility. The "insurer" pays claims directly through local facilities. Our premium represents the amount of claims actually paid by the carrier, augmented by a competitively established handling charge to cover the carrier's expenses. Since we are required to maintain reserves in the event of plan termination for the protection of employees and to meet state statutory requirements, we have deposited certain sums of money with the insurance company, on which they credit our funds with monthly investment income. Such monthly interest is applied in reduction of the carrier's handling charge each month.

The handling charge of the carrier is resolved annually by negotiation between the trustees and insurer, in the same manner as the amount of reserve deposit and interest to be credited. Our contractual arrangement provides that the residue of reserves will be returned to the fund upon termination of the service contract, after the carrier has met its obligations for claims. As an alternative, the trustees have the option of paying claims directly after termination, holding the carrier harmless and recovering the reserves in full. In any event, our true costs will be actual claims paid after termination.

With respect to life insurance, accidental death and high-level major medical insurance, such coverages are fully insured through the carrier by monthly premium payments. Overall, the trustees are self-insuring their basic health care plan (with some minor exceptions) and fully insuring the high risk features of the program through competitively established premium rates. This method achieves relatively low-cost pure insurance protection for what we consider the high risk portion of our program. In view of our relatively low per capita accumulation of reserves (although the total dollar amount of our welfare fund reserves is considerable), we believe we gain the economies of self-insurance plus the risk protection which enables us to provide broad comprehensive benefits.

We generally have been satisfied with this method. The combined form of funding enables us to basically budget our benefit costs each year, limits our exposure to unusual or major claims, and facilitates the extension of broader plans of pure protection to our participants and their covered family members.

The negotiated service fee of the carrier is reasonable to cover their expenses, profits and risk charge with respect to the purely insured portion of the program. Excluding the direct costs of payment of claims, the carrier's charges have been in the neighborhood of 4%, before credit for interest on reserves. This compares favorably to our insured plans with non-profit carriers, where there is a somewhat higher overall carrier retention, offset to a certain degree by the savings inherent in provision of service benefits in hospitals, and the advantages to our members through the participating dental provider arrangement.

Results of Change

Costs and Expenses

From a financial point of view, our approach results in a reasonably understandable statement of income and expenses for trustees, union officials, union members and employers. We have been able to budget the estimated self-insured cost of our program with considerable accuracy over the years, based upon past history, trends and adjustment for inflation. Premiums for the insured portion are readily determinable, since they are fixed for at least one year and, in actual experience, for a number of years. Our income statement facilitates comparison to other funds and is simplified by exclusion of certain expense items which are absorbed by the insurance carrier. For example, the cost of printing booklets and certificates for each employee is not reflected in our financial statement, since it is included in the handling charge of the insurance carriers. Such items are transferred from operating administrative expenses to direct benefits provided to participants in the form of premiums.

Direct claims processing costs are an element of the insurance benefit cost under this method, and are not reflected as administrative expenses to our fund. Other expenses are included in the overall benefit cost under the joint ASO and insured approach. Therefore, our financial statement reflects basically gross income received from employers and investment income earned, reduced by pure administrative expenses related to the operation of the fund and collection of employer contributions.

As a result of this arrangement, we are able to separately determine the annual per capita cost of pure benefits and the cost of administration of our plan. This becomes invaluable to our union agents in their organizational and negotiating functions. They are reasonably able to determine the per capita cost in each vital form of welfare fund operation for the purpose of establishing employer contributions.

From our experience with the collective bargaining negotiation process, we believe it is easier to present benefit costs and administrative costs as separate factors, without administrative costs swollen to include expenditure items which are more properly within the area of health care benefits. We are proud of the fact that we collect millions of dollars every year from employers at a relatively minimal cost of administration. By segregating the cost applicable to provision of benefits in the direct benefit category, and isolating the direct administrative expenses of collection and general operation, our figures more accurately reflect true allocation of employer contributions for purposes of collective bargaining and organization.

I am aware that the International Foundation administrative cost study combines all administrative and carrier expenses of a plan into one figure for purposes of statistical comparison. I do not disagree with that contention. By aggregating the ASO handling charge, insurance retention and operating expenses actually paid from the fund, our overall costs compare most favorably with welfare funds of our size throughout the country. For our purposes, however, it is extremely helpful to transfer all of the cost of providing benefits to the direct benefit category rather than including it in the "administrative" cost figure. When New York State conducted its own welfare fund bureau and performed examinations of welfare funds prior to preemption by ERISA, our funds fared better in a fully insured status than while it was self-insured.

Under self-insurance, our financial statements reflected a higher per capita figure for administrative costs than in earlier examination during our insured era. We had difficulty explaining to the state insurance department the inaccuracy of such a comparison when insurance premiums included a good percentage of administrative expenses. Self-insurance, at least in the pre-ERISA days, was not helpful to all funds with respect to statistical data released by governmental agencies with respect to administrative costs.

Communication of Benefits

The needs of our participants were the most significant factors to our board of trustees in changing from self-insurance, per se, to the hybrid form of combined self-insurance and risk protection currently in use. In a union setting in which organization is of major significance, it is extremely helpful to provide employees with detailed booklets and insurance policies describing their benefits. These communications also serve to provide the reassurance of an established carrier to fund benefits.

In organizational efforts, workers may be skeptical as to the ability of the union to furnish benefits which will be negotiated. Self-insured funds may serve a great purpose for large unions in which organization is not a major problem. In our case, however, our prime objectives were to sell employees on the advantage of becoming affiliated with our local unions and encouraging them to ask their employers to recognize us for collective bargaining purposes. We deal basically with lower income, less-sophisticated workers who do not enjoy the advantages of being able to obtain financial counseling to any reasonable extent. Any assurance we can give to such employees is helpful in achieving our joint aims. The physical role of the insurance carrier, reinforced by documented summaries of benefits, is helpful in satisfying new prospective members as to the solvency of the union and its funds, and its actual performance in attaining the goals sought.

Conversion and Coverage Issues

The turnover of participants was another factor in influencing us to change from the purely self-insured method. Lower income persons in transient industries tend to be mobile, and high turnover is a natural result. During our self-insurance period, conversion upon termination of employment was a major problem. We became a clearinghouse for terminating employees who would apply for extended benefits under the welfare fund, wherever possible, and thereafter obtain conversion data (although in many instances they were not able to finance the cost of conversion).

We were faced with a constant problem on a self-insured basis of attempting to provide coverage under our eligibility rules for employees who were no longer working for participating employers and, in many instances, were no longer members of the union. By not utilizing an insurance carrier, we were not in a position to provide benefits during the interim period following an employee's termination of coverage and the date when he was able to obtain new employment and insurance protection. In many instances, the new employer would not be in contractual relationship with an affiliated union. We tried to help such employees, but soon found ourselves in the position of maintaining welfare fund coverage for a large number of workers who were no longer members of affiliated unions and had little likelihood of continued relationship. No matter how altruistic our intentions, we could hardly place ourselves in the position of endangering the financial stability of our fund by furnishing long term coverage under our self-insured plan for laid-off or terminated employees who did not reinstate within a reasonable period. (I will not even go into the problem of ERISA and the extent to which we would be able to legally maintain such coverage for an indefinite period of time for employees who were no longer participants in the plan.)

Conversion presents a problem to any self-insured welfare fund with a high rate of employee turnover. Obviously, we could have taken the extreme position of denying any protection at all to terminating employees, since they were no longer covered by the plan. However, that would have violated our conscious desire to be of assistance to the lower income worker and our overall policy in this connection. Our present hybrid insured and self-insured approach enables us to provide full statutory conversion opportunities to terminating participants.

Provider Relationships. Another problem during our self-insurance period was service benefits and participating providers. Our funds expanded over a large geographical area. In many local communities, we had comparatively small numbers of covered employees working for participating employers. It was not always practical (on a self-insured basis) to arrange provider relations in many of these rural and less-populated areas of the state. In addition, we faced continual antagonism in such areas from medical and dental providers with respect to negotiation of fees.

By using non-profit carriers with participating providers who had agreed to accept benefit payments in full, we were able to furnish to our membership the names of local medical and dental practitioners willing to extend treatment and accept our allowances in payment for their charges. If participants chose to use other health care providers, identical benefit allowances would be paid. This method served to broaden the benefits of our program in such isolated areas. Our local groups report that they are reasonably satisfied with this method, and are able to achieve a level of quality care with the assurance of little or no charge beyond the allowances under the plan.

Premium Waivers. "Waiver of premium" under life insurance programs also became an element of concern to us in self-insurance. We resolved this problem by continuing the coverage of employees who met the waiver requirements in the event of permanent disability. However, this solution was compounded by the requirements to establish long term actuarial reserves to fund such claims. We considered the possibility of acquiring single premium insurance to dispose of such waiver claims. Before we finalized action on the purchase of single premium insurance for such employees, we changed to the insured method and arranged for coverage for such individuals. However, in the absence of such an arrangement, we believe that waiver of premium presents an unattractive aspect of self-insurance. Although it can be handled, it does cause complications. In many instances, self-insured plans do not provide waiver, which may lead to unfortunate results for disabled employees and lessen the attraction of the entire program for participants and employers.

Employer and Employee Attitudes

Self-insurance tended to make the trustees more conservative with respect to improvement of benefits. Certainly, it was difficult to provide extensive major medical benefits for large claims. The trustees, with good reason, questioned the ability of welfare funds with limited per capita reserves to provide broad major medical benefits, despite the desire to keep pace with the growing use of more esoteric and complicated means of providing life-sustaining health care. Under the ASO and partially insured approach, that particular problem has been solved, and we have been able to provide extensive benefits for employees. There is great gratification and satisfaction when a trustee knows that the benefits of the plan have enabled a low income person to obtain major life-sustaining medical procedures that might not otherwise have been available. From the standpoint of the trustees, the ability to provide for major health problems must take precedence over the desirability of restricting benefits in the interest of conservatism. Under our present method of funding benefits, we are able to provide extensive protection in the instance when such medical care is required.

By changing from self-insurance, we increased employee confidence in our program. We also reacquired the role of the outside third-party insurance carrier as an independent buffer between the participant and the trustees. To a great extent, the trustees are reinstated as a helpful force to the employee in obtaining the maximum benefits available under the plan, rather than being viewed as an antagonist. Thus participants are more enthusiastic about the beneficial scope of their welfare fund. This has reflected itself in increased employee assistance with respect to collection of delinquent contributions from employers, and cooperation relating to claims cost controls and claims appeals.

Cost Controls. Cost control is a vital function of welfare fund operation. After we changed from complete self-insurance, we became more involved in cost control than in the past. Under self-insurance, our organizational and membership goals to a degree conflicted with our attempts to employ maximum cost control methods. Under our present funding approach, reinforced by greater participant enthusiasm, we have introduced a series of cost control measures. These steps have served to reduce claim costs and also achieved cooperation and assistance from our membership. In this respect, we utilize a very tight coordination of benefits provision with other group plans which may involve our employees and/or their spouses. We use predetermination for major dental claims, encourage second surgical opinions and review of doctors' charges, actually audit hospital charges, and are involved in other cost control efforts.

Needless to say, there is considerably reduced pressure on our fund office when claim payments are processed directly by representatives of the insurance carriers. While we still have claim appeals and requests for more information, the pressure is reduced and is on a higher level. In many respects, the position of the board of trustees is changed. During self-insurance, the trustees were placed in the role of defending policies with respect to claim appeals. Under the present arrangement, the trustees are deemed to be the ally of the claimant seeking to obtain from the insurance carriers a full explanation for inability to pay greater benefits to the insured. It is a subtle change in attitude, but one highly beneficial to the success of welfare funds.

Employer Confidence. We have found it easier to live with our employers with respect to negotiation of welfare fund contributions under our present arrangement than under the self-insured method. The employers have more confidence that our premium costs are in line with comparative competitive costs. We are able to isolate the per capita costs of direct benefits and administration, demonstrating that our funds operate as inexpensively as possible, and that the vast majority of contributions are allocated to direct benefits to employees.

Employers have confidence in reputable insurance carriers. The presence of the insurer with improved guaranteed benefit levels has offset employer fears that the welfare fund will be overexposed with respect to benefits, thus requiring additional employer contributions in the future strictly to bail out the funds. The employers are reassured as to the stability of the fund by the availability of budgeted costs, and assurance that major claims will not exhaust the fund.

Internal Operations

With respect to internal operations, our welfare fund administration and union operational offices have enough problems from an administrative point of view without becoming further involved in welfare fund claims, benefits, medical providers, certificates, booklets and all the other related problems of claims payment. The fund office assists in cost control, which is primarily handled by our consultant and carriers. We were able to reduce costs by eliminating personnel and procedures which were linked to the self-insurance features of our plan. We eliminated the need for medical and dental consultants directly employed by the fund, by utilizing practitioners who are in contractual relationship with the insurers. In a period of constantly increasing office and administrative costs, we have been able to concentrate our computer facilities and our personnel in the major problem areas of collecting employer contributions and servicing workers, with a reduction in expenditures for office space, personnel and office equipment.

I have referred to the change in employer attitude. That change also extends to employer trustees, who are more comfortable with the partially insured approach, particularly with respect to exposure to larger claims. They are satisfied that administrative costs are maintained at the lowest practicable levels, and can concentrate on administering the fund and supervising the investment program without maximum emphasis on benefit payments.

Under our present method, printing expenses are substantially reduced in that publication of certificates, booklets, claim drafts, etc., are paid by the insurance carriers. Our accountants are no longer as involved in auditing individual claim payments and bank reconciliations for claim bank accounts. There have been similar reductions in actuarial consulting, computer and legal costs. Our lawyers are less likely to be involved in claim problems, with a resultant reduction in their charges. We are basically satisfied with the hospital and practitioner/provider arrangements of the insurers. Our internal control is considerably improved, since we no longer have to be concerned with the physical location of claim drafts, signatures on such benefit payments, disappearance of drafts, accidental loss of claim records, etc.

Overall, our trustees feel that they have enough unpaid work with respect to operating these funds. Most of them have never sought the dubious distinction of becoming insurance company executives or assuming responsibilities of the insurance carrier. Frankly, I have great sympathy for employer trustees in this connection. They serve without pay, put in a considerable period of time reviewing financial statements, make policy decisions, review investments, and work for the sole best interests of participants. To be able to reduce their work load, by eliminating decision making with respect to claims and claims procedures and other aspects of self-insurance, is a service to employer trustees.

COB. I note that employer trustees were not happy about being involved in coordination of benefits problems, particularly when such matters involved their own employees. Constant battles over whether self-insured benefits should be paid when the spouse of a working employee enjoyed coverage elsewhere were not in the best interest of good employer-employee relations, in their opinion. At the present time, these matters are handled in the very technical, administrative computerized method of one insurance company dealing with another. Our fund office and employers are just as pleased not to be involved in such sometimes technical and thorny situations. We also encountered problems when other insured plans refused to honor our self-insured plan's claims to coordination of benefits. Other insurers attempted to unload their claims on our self-insured program. The present arrangement does avoid this type of dispute.

The change from self-insurance has produced some ancillary benefits. We have some cash flow advantages in sometimes not being required to reimburse the insurance carrier as quickly as they might like, which furnishes us with additional investment income on our employer contributions and reserves. We also have gained greater budgetary control and internal control over our accounting for claims costs.

Premium Taxes. Certain states do lessen the economies which may be gained under the ASO method by charging premium taxes. To the extent that we use non-profit carriers, we have eliminated a portion of that problem. Our method may include a limited tax which is included in the handling fee negotiated by competitive bidding.

The premium tax matter has not been of overwhelming significance with respect to our overall determination as to the advisability of our present vehicle for funding benefits, based on comparison shopping. In this connection, trustees should not rush into self-insurance just to save premium taxes before they make a viable determination as to whether the savings in that particular area will offset some of the disadvantages of the self-insurance method, which have been discussed.

The Carrier as Intermediary. It is important to emphasize the intermediary role of the carrier and its importance to fund operations. Large insurance carriers, whether of the profit-making or non-profit variety, have great capability in the claims control area, with proper monitoring by fund trustees. If insurers process claims and are reimbursed on a claims handling basis, it is an obvious objection to state that the carrier may gain by inflating claims. In this connection, we employ a very strict monitoring system and have not had any problems in this connection. In actuality, we use a third-party claims administrator to pay claims so that we do gain the advantage of the administrator verifying to us that claims are paid properly and without excess "churning" on behalf of the carrier. In reviewing our appeal and claim procedure during the past few years, we have been pleased with the fact that the carriers are defending the great majority of the questions which are based on technical interpretation of benefit provisions and insuring conditions. We certainly prefer them in that role rather than the boards of trustees.

A minor gain from our method is that we obtain an insurance buffer which will absorb the criticisms of insurance departments and governmental agencies with respect to benefit wording and printed material. While we are still responsible for those documents, basically we have relied upon the legal departments of the carriers and our consultants to provide us with protection in this area.

Reserves. With respect to claim reserves, the claim costs under our methods are going to be the same as under self-insurance, with the exception of truly insured excess major medical claims. We still maintain reserves for the estimated liabilities to be incurred in the future for existing and unreported claims. Part of our problem is solved by the carrier's annual calculation of the insurance reserve with respect to insured benefits for which we have deposited matching assets. We calculate our own independent reserves for continued self-insured benefits. Our balance sheet and statement of income and expense properly reflect the benefit charges for the year, and aggregate liabilities.

Some funds using the ASO approach have used a different method of providing reserves to the carrier. Rather than our method of providing certificates of deposit or direct cash deposits earning interest, other funds have deposited securities on which they retain equitable title. The important factor is for the fund to earn investment income on reserves, or to clearly negotiate that investment income is being applied toward reduction of specific charges by the carrier. (In some states, insurance regulations do not permit the transfer of securities to the carrier, with title retained by the trust fund.)

Overall Gains

We solved the problem of internal control and accounting for direct claims payment by eliminating self-insurance, with the exception of optical and certain other coverages. Our bonding costs were also reduced, since we no longer were required to bond claims processors.

As a result of our change, we reduced the fiduciary responsibility of our trustees to an extent. We also gained some independence. We continue to utilize actuarial consultants, who represent the trustees in their negotiation with the carriers. We gain an additional advisor in the form of the insurance carrier with respect to their recommendations on claims control, underwriting, etc. By leaving the self-insured method, we did not increase our costs by any appreciable amount. We gained some reduced amount of fiduciary responsibility, at least with respect to direct responsibility for each claim payment. We gained considerably in public relations and confidence by our members in the credibility of our plan.

With respect to waiver of premium and conversion, we were able to furnish highly improved methods of benefit protection. However, by ceasing to be self-insured, we eliminated our ability to avoid certain state mandates with respect to benefits. From a practical point of view, however, from a competitive organizational viewpoint, it is hardly in our best interests for our welfare plans not to offer the maximum possible benefits within our financial ability. If a state mandates a particular coverage, no matter what our feelings may be with respect thereto, we certainly want to be able to tell our present and future members that our plan provides all the minimum benefits of any other insurance plan. Therefore, we do not feel that state-mandated benefits are a particular major concern to us as cost items.

Overall, we believe that our combined method of self-insurance for basic coverages and risk protection for major benefits is an excellent, practical method to facilitate the provision of health care security to our members. This method gives us regional flexibility in being insured for service benefits in certain areas, and self-insured in others under the ASO approach. Administrative costs are properly identified and segregated from the cost of furnishing direct benefits. The involvement of health care insurers further assists us in claims control. Our plan is more widely accepted by members and employers. Communication and service have been facilitated by the intermediary roles of providers and participating practitioners. The insurance carriers serve as another helpful buffer between the trustees and participants on appeals and other difficulties encountered in claims.

Conclusion

It is important that, in any type of combined arrangement, the trustees must be prepared to enter into competitive bidding and to review costs regularly to determine whether they are achieving the lowest possible level of benefit costs consistent with their method of operation. It is certainly conceivable that if insurance operating costs increase beyond the point at which it becomes financially feasible to continue this arrangement, we will be prepared to enter into a self-insurance arrangement again.

Our approach has been a reverse from the tendency of jointly managed welfare funds to self-insure all or the great majority of the benefits. In our particular circumstances, we believe that our local needs and the circumstances of our particular employee group are best served by our method. We now have accumulated many millions of dollars in our fund as the result of the growth of our plans and the number of employees and employers in contractual relationship with affiliated unions. We are able to furnish a far greater variety of benefits than in past years. Our combined methodology has worked well in our funds.

A word of caution to all trustees: Do not rush into self-insurance as a panacea which will solve all your fund problems. In our experience, self-insurance may produce as many new problems as the number solved. The allure of huge interest on your reserves is a transitory type of thing. After the first year under self-insurance, you have utilized the cash flow advantage in the run-off by the insurance carrier, and the trust fund has to establish its own reserves. In the long run, you may or may not be able to earn substantially higher interest on your reserves in excess of the amount which may be guaranteed by a carrier. Indeed, in a falling interest rate era, a guarantee by an insurance carrier for a certain period of time may become extremely valuable. Welfare funds can negotiate with an insurer as to investment income on reserves within reasonable ranges of long term rates. You cannot adjust the interest rate monthly or every 60 days. On an annual or semiannual basis, it is possible to arrange a method under which interest on reserves will be adjusted to be generally commensurate with prevailing market rates for interest. Like premium tax "savings," interest alone should not be a reason for adopting self-insurance, particularly for funds which do not enjoy large amounts of reserves.

You may perform a disservice to your members by self-insuring at too early a stage. Conservatism resulting from self-insurance may result in lessened benefit levels or preclude expansion into new areas of medical care, which will prevent your participants from obtaining the maximum security they are entitled to under a welfare fund.

Before a fund makes a change in its funding method, a careful preliminary study by its consultants should be authorized. The report should be reviewed in detail. Whatever decision is made as to the method of providing benefits, the methodology should be monitored carefully and reviewed periodically. One of the great obligations of trustees in a health care welfare fund is to carefully monitor and follow up on the method used to fund and furnish benefits. It is the bottom line that counts. But that bottom line includes not only financial aspects, but the goal of providing maximum service and protection to participants in the plan.

Funding Arrangements

BY JOSEPH EICHENHOLZ

Introduction

I am pleased to have the opportunity here to do what an economist does best, which is to use the gifts bestowed upon him or her by the Lord—two hands, on the one and on the other. Thankfully, today my job is not to provide answers but to raise questions. I hope I will be able to do that for you in a meaningful way. I used to work in the federal government, and they tell a story about the world's biggest lies; I somehow get a sense that it applies to insurance company representatives the same way. Of course, the first one is: "The check is in the mail." The second biggest lie is: "I've been meaning to call you." The last biggest lie is always: "I am an insurance man; I am here to help you." I will not sell you anything today. I frankly am not licensed to sell anything except a bill of goods.

But really, our topic should be, "Everything you always wanted to know about alternatives to traditional funding; or, there is no free lunch." Just remember that. There is no free lunch. By the way, that one statement got me through graduate school in economics. I learned that, and everything else was safe. After that, I was a free marketeer, and I could handle anything that my professors threw at me. Really, there is no free lunch, and if you think that by playing around with one coverage product or another, or by trafficking with the evil folks in the third-party administration world or the insurance companies, you are doing something else, you are mistaken. It all comes out in the wash. As an economist, when we set up our little models and our algebraic functions, we have to account for everything. It's like matter and energy. What goes in, comes out—one way or another.

At the same time, however, there is an awful lot of room for innovation and meeting each other's needs in such a way that the entire system is served better. In this presentation, I hope to avoid stating any of my biases about what's good for what kind of fund or what's not good for certain kinds of clients. Let me just say on this whole subject that as economists, we study each person, each firm, each individual. Each has what we call a utility function, and my perception of value and risk will

Mr. Eichenholz is director of health policy analysis for the Connecticut General Life Insurance Company. He is responsible for economic, legislative and political analysis of health issues; application of external environment in company activities; and education of external (public and private) policymakers in the aspects of insurance impacting on their decisions. Previously, Mr. Eichenholz was director of economic analysis and policy planning in the office of the assistant secretary for health with the U.S. Department of Health, Education and Welfare. He received his B.S. from the State University of New York and his M.A. in economics from Brown University. Mr. Eichenholz is a member of the health care management committee of the Health Insurance Association of America and the liaison between the commercial insurance industry and the U.S. Department of Health and Human Services on technology assessment.

be different—will be unique—from that of any other person, fund or organization. I hope that as I talk about the issues and alternatives to traditional funding, and then work out some numerical examples with a hypothetical case, you will not only think about what I'm saying, but also think about what is important to *your* funds, and what's not important to your funds.

You will hear some things and say, "That's not relevant." It may not be relevant to you, but there might be someone else who instead of having 1,000 insureds has 500 insureds or 5,000 insureds and the issue is different. Keep that in mind, because what I hope you will get out of this discussion is a better sense of the structure within which you ought to be making your own decisions about what is best for your fund and your insureds.

Cash Flow Products

Objectives

Cash flow products is a generic title that has come to describe a large variety of different alternatives to traditional funding (perhaps more alternatives than you really have a sense of at the moment). *Objectives*—first, you are trying to *reduce the expenses against an experience-rated plan.* Remember, the benefits are the benefits. By and large, somebody has to pay for them, whether it is you directly or whether it is you through premiums paid to a carrier or an administrator of some sort. The benefits are going to be the benefits. What you are talking about is the difference in how you pay, and in what additional factors or services you pay for.

You want to *improve your cash flow.* Time is money, and dollars invested today are worth more tomorrow than dollars that haven't been invested. The value of cash is going up and up and up, and fluctuations in the interest rates and the money markets have been such that we all, whether it is our personal money or fund money, have to be much more aware of what is happening. We have more investment instruments available to us, just starting very simply with liquid asset funds. We have to be cognizant of the price we pay for leaving money, for example, in a checking account or with an insurance carrier.

There is also a desire to *control the level of benefits* and avoid state minimum benefit laws; in particular one may use administrative services only (ASO) contract arrangements. A number of states have enacted legislation in the areas of mental health, hospice care, home health care, optometrists, vision services, chiropractic services, etc.,—they are called mandated state benefits, and one of the advantages of self-insurance is that you may not be subject to many of those laws. At the same time, you can *control cash flow.*

A Growing Interest

How did everybody come to worry about all these alternatives? First of all, *inflation,* starting really in the early '70s, has driven up medical prices tremendously. Everybody began to see premium increases in the 10%, 20% and then 30% range during parts of this past decade. Everybody became more aware of the fact that insurance was getting expensive. In addition, there has been a growing awareness of *the cost of money,* particularly in this last year. There was also *pressure for new benefits*—for example, dental coverage. In the last few years, coverage for dental services has grown to 70 million people, and we project that by the end of this decade there will be about 130 million people covered for dental services. It's a new benefit. It is something that has to compete with the dollars of employer contributions for other benefits. Where can you save a penny? Where can you save a nickel?

When you think of the corporate arena, as opposed to funds themselves, the control of the health insurance decision, the benefits decision, has also, in many instances, been *transferred from the personnel to the financial departments.* Now, we're also in a much more cutthroat business, and the margins—maybe I shouldn't use the word margins, because that is a term of art—but the potential cash associated with a tiny change in your policy can be considered much more important to the financial person who is responsible for the overall cash flow needs of a company than it would be to a personnel staffer. Further, *national broker acquisition of smaller operations,* the big alphabet soup brokerage houses, the big consulting firms, has had an effect. They had to do something innovative to obtain more business. There was a need for *greater sales volume* to justify their own existence and keep them growing. There were *pressures for new product lines,* and for innovation in products. All this contributed to the trend of the 1970s, particularly the last few years, being prime time for new products.

On the other side, the policyholder and the broker, acting as the policyholder's representative, were interested in cash flow products because, first, you can *reduce premiums in advance.* Retrospective premium agreements allow for cutting down on the cash flow up front. The insurance company does not get the cash; the fund keeps that money. With some of the more esoteric and comprehensive of the cash flow alternatives, you can *recapture claim reserves,* particularly when you have deferred premium, minimum premium and ASO arrangements. You can hold onto those claim reserves to some extent, as opposed to the insurance company having a larger margin. And then again, the *retention can be reduced.*

You can reduce or eliminate *premium taxes.* This one area is held up very frequently as a factor in pushing people toward self-insurance. Minimum premium and ASO contracts are the two key ways of reducing the premium tax cost. I might add, by the way, someone asked me yesterday whether premium taxes are 2% all across the country. They are not. They range up to 4%, but by and large they are 2% and there are state laws that allow for differential taxation based on the home state of the insurance carrier doing business. So, for example, if Virginia charges 2¾% to companies doing business in Virginia, then Connecticut would charge 2¾% instead of 2% to a Virginia-licensed company that wants to do business in Connecticut. So you have to think about that as well.

The public policy issues also have been important. At the time cash flow products were first developed, *the role of the carrier in cost containment* was not yet very well developed. Many companies didn't understand what services the insurance carrier could provide. In particular, cost containment is one service where, through the use of data networks, uniform claims processing and utilization review, the carrier could provide a service to the insured that would be difficult for the company or the fund to do on its own.

There is something else that doesn't normally get written up in the textbooks but is important, particularly if you are a labor trustee. If you are running your own benefit program and somebody has a gripe, where will they go to complain? They are going to come to you. That has financial implications and it has precedent-setting implications, if you make a decision a certain way because somebody is really giving you a hard time about a particular benefit. One advantage of having a third-party administrator or a carrier involved in one form or another is that you keep the transaction about use of benefits and reimbursement for benefits at arm's length. Then you and the fund member can remain good friends—or at least less bad enemies—if you are negotiating about other benefits and wages as well. So there really is some value here that people may not understand fully.

They also didn't understand the price that was paid to the carrier for *risk-taking*. This is a funny concept, but this is really where the flea market comes into play. The insurance company takes a risk for underwriting your benefits. They could get stuck with three terrible burn cases in one 500 member group: three people driving from one job to another; car accident; all three are burned very badly. That could completely deplete the reserves of a small group. You'd run up a bill of $50,000, $60,000, $70,000 each very quickly. That's a risk. It's not likely to happen, but it happens every once in a while. You pay for that risk with insurance, and some people haven't understood what they were getting and what they were paying. We are now becoming much more sophisticated both as carriers, explaining our risk charges, and as insureds, demanding those explanations.

Finally, ERISA preemption. You have heard about the confusion caused by ERISA preemption and state-mandated benefits and the benefits of self-insurance, and that's all going to shake out in the next few years. But this, too, has been a factor in the growth in cash flow products.

The Bottom Line

The Value of Cash. What this all boils down to is the value of cash. *How are you going to use the money that you save?* To determine the value of any cash flow alternative, you must look at the *returns available* from other short term investments. You're surely not going to leave that cash in a checking account at no interest. That doesn't earn you anything. What can you earn from it? What's the *earnings position* of the fund, basically your income position, or the earnings position of an employer? What's the *tax position*? Do you have transactions where tax losses have been deferred to this year or next year, or you know you are going to have a runout and you don't have to worry about it?

What's your *credit rating*? Basically, if you need cash, what are you going to have to pay for it? Think about when gold shot up to $800 an ounce and you saw all these numbers in the newspapers about what it was worth. That's what you'd have to pay if you wanted to buy it. But go into one of those places and say, I've got gold to sell. You don't get the $800. You get $700, $750, $600. Take a look at the exchange rates anywhere in Europe—it's a different rate to buy and sell. Buying versus selling. Your credit rating. What could you need money for, and what would you have to pay for it?

Availability of funds from other sources: Are you going to use this money that you save on a cash flow alternative in place of short term borrowing or long term borrowing?; or is it just going to be added to your war chest, in which case are you going to invest it short term or are you going to invest it long term? Remember, what you do to your cash affects the reserves you can touch in certain contingencies. These are the kinds of questions that you have to ask yourself, and the answers are going to be different depending upon your fund, your size and your situation.

How much are you going to need in the way of liquid assets? Can you be or are you a 501(c)(9) trust? I might add, by the way, that with the publication of the "new proposed regulations" in July that whole world has become much more uncertain. All these things have to come into play in your own individual decision on how you want to fund *each* particular benefit; and it doesn't have to be the package, it can be split.

Summary. Let's summarize so far. The value of cash flow, the risk charge and state-mandated benefits. Consider:

- *Premium taxes.* The premium tax ranges from 0-4%. They are assessed state by state on funds held by an insurance carrier to pay expenses or claims. ASO or minimum premium, in particular, can reduce them.
- The *cash flow* comes in from reduced premiums, particularly retrospective premium rather than an advanced margin. That basically says, as you do with your homeowner's insurance, "stretch out the payment period." My policies divide up into two payments. They charge me a 50¢ loading factor. That's a good deal any way you look at it.
- *Recapturing claim reserves.* Again, here it's transferring of liability, through basically ASO and some minimum premium plans; delaying payment under a deferred or supplemental premium.

All these terms are ones that you'll be hearing from brokers and consultants and companies. Think about these alternatives next time you have a decision to make. It isn't all fully insured or ASO.

Let's talk for a moment about sources of funds. First, the risk charge. This is where you get into a funny situation sometimes. Basically, the risk charge is for the uncovered, unrecovered, deficits on experience-rated contracts. It's the runout claims. It's the fact that the customer can stop paying premiums yesterday. Remember, we've got grace periods and deferred premiums, and the carrier is stuck doing business. I do know of one case where John Hancock Life Insurance Company was stuck paying claims on a policy beyond its standard runout provisions because the courts in Massachusetts felt that they had a responsibility to the insureds that ran beyond the provisions of the contract.

Companies are going to have to keep some money. They want money up front to hold against the day when you as a fund might decide you can get a better deal down the street. And, finally, there's a little bit of profit in there. Face it. Nobody's going to go into business for love. Only the federal government does that, and you see what happens there. We've got to make some money out of this deal. We're making a lot less than we used to, and still smiling about it—because if we didn't take what we get, we'd be out of business altogether. There is leverage that you guys have, and we know it, and we're changing. But, the times are changing and we all have to adapt. We're going to make a profit; we're not going to do this for nothing. But, depending upon how well you understand how this mechanism operates, you can be a more effective negotiator.

When you go ASO, you go self-insurance. You've got to recognize you're taking on a big risk, and you may have to think about reinsuring some of that so it all becomes a cash flow transaction. Finally, state-mandated benefits. As I said, there are a number of minimum benefits laws proliferating, particularly in long term care, home health and mental health areas, and self-insured plans may be able to circumvent these laws. I am not an attorney, and my counsel would not want me to advocate evading any state laws, but there are ways in which you can set up your organization so that you can avoid a number of legal requirements.

Contract Alternatives

Retrospective premium, deferred premium, cost plus or *flexible funding, minimum premium* and *ASO,* administrative services only—those are key examples of the kinds of products that you have available. Again, think about each one of them in relation to your fund, its size, individual products, and the value associated with taking risks and different degrees of risk.

Retrospective Premium

Under retrospective premium, you can reduce or eliminate the margins in the advance rates. Basically, we're allowing you to hold off a small part of your monthly claims. The carrier may recover, up to a fixed limit, any excess of incurred claims and expenses over the premium that was collected at the end of the policy year. Generally, it's a simple administrative agreement, with no bureaucracy involved. The size of the case that can benefit from it tends to be small—this is different from some of the other alternatives. In the $100,000 range, for some insurance companies, they will sell you this kind of a product; administratively, it's simple to handle.

Deferred Premium

A deferred premium is a little bit more formal a mechanism. It reduces the reserves held on incurred but unreported claims. Remember, every time I go to the doctor, it takes awhile for the physician to bill me and then for me to turn the claim in because these days, you know, who's a participating physician anymore? Those of you who deal with Blue Cross/Blue Shield are probably finding out that those numbers are shrinking. The premium payments can be delayed for 30-60 days beyond the normal grace period; that depends on the amount of the reserve, the situation with the client and how long you've been with the insurance company. It's all these intangibles that make you a good customer and the company a good partner.

Now, here's the kicker: The companies may charge for loss of investment income. As I said at the outset, there's no free lunch, and if you think Connecticut General is going to give $400 million or $500 million worth of extra 30 or 60 day units for nothing, you've got to be kidding. We're going to charge you for it. What you've got to try to find out is *how much* we are charging you, and whether it is the lowest price you can get. Here's where we get to a special concept in economics. The concept is that of "rent," which, to an economist, means a price that is paid over and above the minimum price necessary to purchase a good. If you want to be aggressive fund managers, go after the companies there. What are they charging you for the loss of investment income? That's how we make our money. Go after that final line item: What is the minimum price you have to pay? It really makes a difference.

This mechanism also can be handled administratively by letter. It doesn't require new policy filings, which get into real problems with some of the state governments.

With deferred premium, the benefits recur. This is not a one-time savings, because every year you are stretching out your payments, so every year you've got a saving based on what you could earn with that money. The amount of savings will differ depending upon where you are going to invest your money, and when. Just remember that. Also remember that the deferred premium falls immediately due at cancellation, and you've got to pay it. This is where we get into some problems with some customers—how long it takes to get that money, and whether what's done has to be done in an acrimonious manner. But at the same time, the insurance company liability for runout claims is not affected. It is not altered by a deferred premium situation.

Cost Plus or Flexible Funding

Cost plus or some form of flexible funding comes next. Different companies call it different things and run it differently. It has had isolated demand, more in the life insurance area than in the health and welfare areas. It has been in existence for several years in health insurance, although it is still not common in many areas of the country. In Texas, I gather, cost plus in casualty coverage is a major alternative in particular areas.

What you do here is try to limit the policyholder's monthly cost to the sum of actual claims paid plus an expense factor. That's where the "cost plus" comes in. It commonly includes a maximum monthly payment so that if you have, for example, very low claims in December (after all, nobody wants to be in the hospital around Christmas time) you will pay the actual claims in December. You can pay less than actual claims in January, and it will even itself out over the course of the year.

Eventually, remember, the carrier always gets its money. One way or another, we get paid. Normal contract, experience-rating and administrative practices are employed, so you are not changing the basic way you've been doing business with your carrier. You can improve your cash flow and retain the benefits of the insurance contract. You save some of the money. This is not one of the favorite alternatives offered by the larger carriers. If you are interested in playing this game, you may have to push a bit. You may have to find yourself a smaller carrier, but it's there.

Minimum Premium

Minimum premium is a concept that people are beginning to understand a little bit better. You assume, as the policyholder, direct legal liability for claims up to a specified level, with the carrier responsible for claims in excess of that level. Let's say you are a $1 million case. You buy a policy with a $900,000 deductible. You are responsible for the first $900,000 in claims; the carrier pays anything above that and the carrier is legally responsible for catastrophic expenses, which provides you with the safeguards of an insurance policy. This limits premium taxes, because premium taxes are assessed only against insurance company reserves. You also retain the use of the money on the first $900,000 until the claims are actually submitted and require payment.

The financial advantages of this mechanism are questionable for small cases. You've got to be a little bit more sophisticated to play this game. The tax avoidance issues are also not completely resolved at this point in time. There is both a state and an ERISA question, which I don't want to go into here. You should be talking to your own tax counsel about them. There are some benefits, and there are some risks; there are still some open cases in the courts and some conflicting precedents. Basically, what we've done here is gone from a

Figure 1

CASH FLOW ALTERNATIVES

			Insured Products		Uninsured
		Retros	Deferred Premium	Minimum Premium	ASO
$ .10	Margin	✓		✓	✓
.10	Expenses			✓	✓
.80 { Reserves .25			✓	✓	✓
Paid Claims .55					✓

$1.00

very simple delay in payment for a standard insurance contract to approaching the financial arrangements available under ASO, while retaining most of the insurance benefits.

Administrative Services Only (ASO)

Finally, ASO. Here, the policyholder is legally responsible for all claims. The carrier would perform only claims payment and administrative functions. Benefits paid are uninsured. This can be a problem if you've got, for example, multicraft trusts and some small, potentially more tenuous, employers. Who knows what's going to happen to some of those employers, and what's going to happen to their contributions to the fund? With ASO, you eliminate the advance margins. You capture the reserves. You retain the funds until the claims are paid. You don't have any premium taxes. You can avoid some mandated benefits laws at the state level.

You can have what we call a stop-loss arrangement. That's to minimize the annual cash outflow and to control, at least at the top level, the risk that the employer or the fund would assume. It does not insure the employees' benefits in any way. Remember that. And don't forget the administrative charge. You're paying for something. The insurance company will attempt to recover as much as possible of the carrier's foregone revenues. Basically, you go to an insurance company, you say, "Let's do ASO." They are going to charge you for the administrative services—but they are also going to throw in a factor because that $1 million that they are administering would have produced for them a certain amount of income if they had had it as a standard insurance contract; so they are going to try and get as much of that money as possible in their fee. Remember that, and go after it if you can. That's the jugular—what you are going to have to pay for them to give up their favorite product, which is traditional insurance.

What Are the Real Savings?

If I haven't put you all to sleep, confused you or driven you crazy, let's go to some arithmetic. I'm going to give you a couple of simple examples to give you an idea of how much you can save under each one of these alternatives. Each line item that you'll see represents a financial decision that you have to make in your own case. We'll discuss traditional funding, retrospective premium, deferred premium, retro and deferred in combination, minimum premium and ASO. These are the key examples of the options that you have available.

Figure 1 presents a little summary as to which aspect of the price of coverage is affected by which kind of cash flow alternative. Down the vertical side you've got the standard premium dollar. Ten percent of every dollar—10¢—is the insurance company's margin. That's profit and risk charge. Of course, I work for an insurance company; I always list that item first. The next 10% is the basic expense that you would expect to have involved with administering a group contract. Reserves and paid claims amount to roughly 80%. Together, this accounts for each $1 of premium income.

Let's review the options briefly. Retrospective premium—remember, that's holding off until the end or stretching out payment and making up a lump sum at the end. It affects the margin that the insurance company has. It doesn't really affect most of the other factors. Deferred premium—by deferring your premium liability, you reduce the reserves that must be kept against losses each month. Minimum premium starts to impact on more. It impacts on the margin, it impacts on expenses, it impacts on reserves. Remember, you've still got to pay the claims. ASO affects everything. There is no money that is put aside in advance for claims. Now that's an advantage to the fund or employer that wants total control over payments. It's a risk to the employees or to the beneficiaries.

Let's make some assumptions and set up a very simple example (Figure 2). Let's assume a $1 million case. Going back to those percentages on Figure 1, incurred claims—$800,000; expenses—$100,000; margin—$100,000; previously accumulated reserves—$250,000. Let's assume the value of money is 10%. When I made up this figure a number of weeks ago, that was a pretty close approximation of the prevailing interest rate. Well, it has changed. This illustrates why you've got to keep reevaluating this decision. This factor is important—the value of money. I can't emphasize it strongly enough. That's what's going to make or break many decisions—the *value of the money against the risk of the alternative* that you select. You've got to be more sophisticated about this analysis than in the past, because otherwise you won't get the potential benefits—you have every right to expect them. The considerations are timing of payment and return, the size of the payment and return, and the risk.

We can start off with a very simple example—*traditional funding* (Figure 3). You may delay your monthly premium by 30 days. Remember, nobody is going to cancel your coverage until after 31 days. Take your average monthly payment times your 10% interest rate. You can save $8,333 or 0.8% compounded just by saying, "The check is in the mail." Until day 31, no company will ques-

Figure 2

ASSUMPTIONS

- Premium $1,000,000
- Incurred Claims   800,000
- Expenses   100,000
- Margin   100,000
- Accumulated Reserves   250,000
- Value of Money   10%

Figure 3

TRADITIONAL FUNDING

Grace Period: $83,333 × 10% = $8,333

                                    0.8%

Figure 4

RETROSPECTIVE PREMIUM

Grace Period: $75,000 × 10% = $ 7,500
Margins: 50,000 × 10% =   5,000
                                 $12,500

                                    1.3%

tion you. A 0.8% saving by doing nothing, just as long as you get your bookkeeper to handle the mail properly. At a minimum, you can keep your money in a liquid asset fund as opposed to a standard checking account.

With *retrospective premium* (Figure 4), you're talking about a lump sum or extra payment made at the end of the year. The grace period monthly payment is not going to be $83,000 as in the previous example; it's going to be $75,000 over the course of the year, because some of that doesn't come due until the end of the period. So you save $7,500, which is your own 10% of your monthly premium using the grace period; you also save a little bit on the margin, because now you've got $50,000 that you've cut out of the margin by having the extra payment at the end of the year. Total savings are $12,500, or 1.3%. Notice that by holding money off until the end of the year the insurance company doesn't have to keep your reserves; you don't have to keep your reserves; you don't have to pay taxes on it up front. That's where that 10% comes in.

Figure 5

DEFERRED PREMIUM

Grace Period:	$83,333 × 10% =	$ 8,333
Additional Deferral:	166,667 × 10% =	16,667
		$25,000
Charge for Deferral:	166,667 × 8%	(13,333)
		$11,667
		1.2%

Figure 6

RETRO & DEFERRED PREMIUM

Grace Period:	$ 75,000 × 10% =	$ 7,500
Additional Deferral:	150,000 × 10% =	15,000
Margins:	50,000 × 10% =	5,000
		$27,500
Charge for Deferral:	150,000 × 8% =	(12,000)
		$15,500
		1.6%

Figure 7

MINIMUM PREMIUM
(90/10 Split)

Premium Tax:	$900,000 × 2% =	$18,000
Margins:	50,000 × 10% =	5,000
Reserves:	250,000 × 10% =	25,000
Grace Period:	8,333 × 10% =	833
		$48,833
Charge for Reserves:	166,667 × 8% =	(13,333)
Minimum Premium Expenses:		(5,000)
		$30,500
		3.1%

With *deferred premium,* the situation gets a little bit more complicated (Figure 5). You save on the grace period and you save through an additional, let's say 60 day, deferral—two months' premium. You run it out into 15 months, or 14 months plus the grace period. You save $25,000 in just delaying payment in one form or another. Here's the kicker. We charge you for this privilege. Let's assume this charge is 8%. This item was not listed before. I wanted it to be a little pleasant surprise for you. Here's where the insurance companies start to get it back. They charge you for the fact that this $166,000 was deferred, and it ends up that you've got to pay an extra $13,000 in this case. So the savings are only 1.2%, as opposed to some greater amount. Still, it's better than paying your bills on the first of the month.

Now put the two together—*retrospective premium and deferred premium* (Figure 6). First, you've got the grace period savings of $7,500, then you've got the additional deferral on a drawn down monthly premium. Remember, by doing retrospective premium your basic premium is not $83,000 but $75,000. You've got that factor here and then the deferral on two months' worth of premium. Both at 10% gives you $22,500 in savings. Now, because you've used deferred premium, you can save something on the margin, for a total saving of $27,500. If you remember in the last example, the deferral charge was 8% on $167,000. Now it's going to be 8% on $150,000, because of the retro factor. So now your charge for deferral is only $12,000, leaving you a net savings of $15,500 in this example, or .6%.

The savings get better, but it gets a little bit more complicated. As a fund, you've got to decide whether or not the added hassle of this arrangement, negotiating it, monitoring it, updating it, is worth the extra .4%. That's how you have to make those decisions.

Now it gets to be fun—*minimum premium* (Figure 7). Let's assume a 90/10 split. First of all, on that first 90%, or $900,000, you are saving, for example, a 2% premium tax. That's to begin with. You are saving on the margin, just as in all the other examples. You are saving that $5,000. The reserves—you've recovered most of those reserves, $250,000. You've got the use of that money, worth 10%. You've also got the grace period. Your annual premium is now $100,000, not $1 million. The monthly premium that you saved through the grace period is $8,000 times 10% compounded, or $833. When you get down to minimum premium, the numbers really can get very small. But $833 in your pocket is better for you than that same amount in the insurance company's pocket. The total savings are $48,833.

Remember, we also charge for reserves. We gave you money back, we want to be paid for the fact

Figure 8

ASO

Premium Tax:	$1,000,000 × 2% = $20,000
Margins:	50,000 × 10% = 5,000
Reserves:	250,000 × 10% = 25,000
Risk Charge:	1,000,000 × 1% = 10,000
State Benefits:	900,000 × 0.5% = 4,500
	$64,500
Charge for Reserves:	166,667 × 8% = (13,333)
ASO Expenses:	(5,000)
	$46,167
	4.6%

Figure 9

NET VALUE OF CASH FLOW ALTERNATIVES

- Traditional Funding   0.8%
- Retrospective Premium   1.3
- Deferred Premium   1.2
- Retro & Deferred Premium   1.6
- Minimum Premium   3.1
- ASO   4.6

that we gave it to you. Remember, there is no free lunch. This 8% is what we'd like. It might be 10%. It might be 12% in reality, depending upon market conditions. But it's there, and we want it; however, if we really want your business, we'll negotiate. Let me stop here for a moment and tell you who negotiates all these items. You've got the broker, the consultant; in the insurance company you've got the salesperson, who wants that case at any price. You've got the underwriters who say, "Who needs it at any price?" You've got to come to a meeting of the minds and pencils, and it's in that 8% that everybody does all the fighting, and that's where it comes out. Finally, you've got the fact that we will charge you for expenses, something to run the case. Let's say we charge you $5,000. In this case, the net savings would be $30,000, or 3.1%. So minimum premium gives you more saving—and more hassle in getting it underway.

Finally, comes the big case—*ASO* (Figure 8). First, premium tax, which you probably would not be paying. That's 2% of $1 million, or $20,000. Margins are no longer there. You save it, with a use value of 10%. Today, I'd borrow anything I could at 10%. You get your reserves of $250,000 back, and you can start investing them and earn your 10%. You also don't have to pay the risk charge that would normally be put in there, a 1% factor, for example. State-mandated benefits may also be involved, which on average might be about 0.5% of the $900,000 of expected plan benefits. As we said before, the charge for the reserves, if you have an insurance carrier, would be the average monthly reserve that the carrier would have over the course of an annual contract. This item includes what the insurance company would be earning if it had those reserves. We're going to try and charge you $13,333 because of the fact that we no longer have those reserves to invest, and then we add the ASO expenses to run the case. There is a net saving of $46,167 or 4.6%. With ASO, the savings are greatest; however, benefits are not insured. There is no arm's length transaction between the fund and the insured, and you have to consider that risk.

Figure 9 summarizes the net value of the different cash flow alternatives. First, traditional funding might save 0.8%. Retrospective and deferred premium or a combination might save 1.2-1.6%. In these options, you are in essence playing around with the mail, the grace period and trying to delay paying your bills a little bit. Minimum premium yields a big jump in potential savings, to 3.1%, but you've got to do a lot more by yourself. It becomes more complicated, and you've got to be more sophisticated. Finally, under ASO, you achieve the greatest savings—4.6%—but also bear the greatest risk.

With that figure, I close. I hope that this presentation has raised some questions for you, and will help you be more informed and aggressive purchasers in the future.

An Analysis of the Senate Report on Labor Union Insurance

BY MARC GERTNER

The Senate Report

In October and November of 1977, the Permanent Subcommittee on Investigations (the "Subcommittee") of the Committee on Governmental Affairs of the United States Senate (the "Committee") held hearings with regard to labor union insurance activities. On November 26, 1979, the Committee by its Subcommittee published a report (the "Report") of its findings together with recommendations. The Report generated a fair amount of discussion in the industry, because of the magnitude of the scams revealed and the scope of the recommendations. Although the Department of Labor generally disavowed the recommendations of the Subcommittee, many of the items are appearing on the checklist of the DOL compliance officers for field audits of plans. The Report clearly warrants serious consideration and, in some cases, in my personal opinion, action by the trustees.

The first part of the Report deals with the Findings and Conclusions of the Subcommittee. These findings and conclusions have been summarized in the Appendix to this article. After presenting its findings and conclusions, the Report sets forth a series of recommendations, which are summarized below.

Specific Recommendations

ERISA

The Report starts out by noting that all union members in the country are entitled to demand the highest standards of professionalism and care from those entrusted with the responsibility for the administration of their health and welfare plans. The Report then traces the problems pre-ERISA and the Congressional intent that, with the enactment of ERISA, the interests of participants in these plans and their beneficiaries would be protected by the establishment of standards of conduct, responsibility and obligations for plan fiduciaries, and

Mr. Gertner is a partner in the Toledo law firm of Shumaker, Loop & Kendrick. He is the responsible partner for all Taft-Hartley trust clients. Admitted to the bar in 1957, he is a member of the Toledo, Ohio and American Bar Associations and has been a lecturer on law at Toledo University Law School. He is a graduate of Harvard College and received his law degree from Ohio State University College of Law. Mr. Gertner has spoken before American Bar Association Annual and Sectional Conferences; Pacific Coast, Arizona and Midwestern Labor Law Conferences; and national and regional conferences of the Financial Analysts Federation Practicing Law Institute. He is co-author of the book The Prudent Man. *Long active in Foundation activities, Mr. Gertner has been a frequent speaker or panelist at educational meetings and has contributed to the IF Digest. He is a former member of the Foundation's Board of Directors, Attorneys Committee and Employer Liability Study Committee, and currently is a member of the Constitution and By Laws Committee, which he formerly chaired. He also served on the special committee that prepared the* Investment Policy Guidebook for Trustees.

by providing for appropriate remedies, sanctions and access to the federal courts.

Notwithstanding the fact that ERISA was in effect during most of the period of Hauser's activities, the frauds were perpetrated, primarily by

Hauser's cultivation of influence through payments and other inducements and exploitation of plan fiduciaries and businessmen. The Subcommittee states its belief that this kind of conduct can be deterred by improved disclosure which would permit the detection of such payments; clarification as to what persons serving employee benefit plans are fiduciaries under ERISA, and the nature of the responsibilities of plan fiduciaries; strengthening of sanctions and remedies for misconduct; and improved enforcement procedures by the DOL. These are addressed in more detail below.

Insurance Regulation

Historically, the licensing of insurance companies and regulating of insurance business has been reserved to the states. This means that there are 50 sets of laws and regulations governing the industry throughout the country, with wide variations in their legal requirements. These variations were manipulated by Hauser to perpetrate his fraud. Further, in the opinion of the Subcommittee, the present state insurance regulatory network does not provide adequate protection to employee benefit plans. Significant differences exist in state laws and regulations pertaining to reinsurance agreements, particularly the fronting agreements used by Old Security and the Hauser companies.

ERISA preempted state regulation of employee benefit plans and reflects the basic policy of the McCarran-Ferguson Act, leaving the regulation of insurance to the states despite the fact that insurance contracts are a major investment medium for employee benefit plans. The Report suggests that it is of paramount importance to the national policy of protection of employee benefit plans that they deal only with financially responsible companies with regulated patterns of payments. With this in mind, the Committee Report makes the following specific recommendations:

1. Minimum Standards for Insurance Companies Doing Business With Employee Benefit Plans

The Subcommittee recommends that Congress enact legislation amending ERISA which would direct the Secretary of Labor to establish minimum standards that insurance companies would be required to meet before an employee benefit plan could deal with such companies. These standards should cover licensing, capitalization, reserving and other fundamental requirements. These standards would prohibit the use of "fronting" reinsurance arrangements while allowing room for legitimate reinsuring arrangements. The legislation should require that an insurance company doing business with an employee benefit plan certify that it has met each of the minimum standards, with criminal penalties for a willful miscertification or misstatement.

It is suggested that this proposal is consistent with ERISA's basic purpose of protecting employee benefit plans by imposing standards of conduct on persons who control the disposition of plan assets. This suggestion is intended to create only a "minimum standard" and is not designed to relieve plan fiduciaries of their responsibilities to evaluate specific proposals.

2. Disclosure of Fees and Payments

The Subcommittee recommends that Congress pass legislation which would direct the Secretary of Labor to adopt regulations which: (1) would require insurance companies which offer to sell insurance contracts to employee benefit plans to disclose all commissions, finder's fees and other payments made or proposed to be made in connection with such sale, and (2) require insurance companies to make and keep accurate records of all payments and commissions in connection with such sales.

This legislation should also make it a crime to willfully make false or misleading statements or otherwise violate the regulations, as well as providing for appropriate civil remedies. The Committee suggests that this recommendation would provide employee plan fiduciaries with the information which would enable them to discharge their duty to prevent plans from incurring costs reflecting payments made in connection with the sale to plans of insurance which is of little or no economic value to the plan; and would permit the fiduciaries to determine whether any payments are being made to parties in interest.

3. Financial Statements and Reporting by Insurance Companies

The Subcommittee finds that there are inadequate reporting provisions and/or exemptions under the Securities Exchange Act of 1934 covering reporting to the SEC by insurance companies. *The Subcommittee recommends that Section 12(g)(2)(G) of the Securities Exchange Act of 1934 be amended to impose the independent audit and periodic reporting of financial information by insurance companies to the SEC.* The SEC would also become the repository for audited insurance company statements under state reporting laws.

4. State Regulation

*The Subcommittee recommends that the several

states take steps to strengthen their respective insurance laws and regulations relating to licensing, capitalization, reserve requirements and reinsurance; and that the investigatory and enforcement powers of their department be increased.

5. Interstate Cooperation

The Subcommittee recommends that states enter into interstate compacts which would enable them to obtain prompt enforcement of their subpoenas, injunctions and orders relating to domestic insurers doing business in other jurisdictions, and which would require the exchange of data obtained in investigations among states.

6. Federal-State Cooperation

The Subcommittee recommends that the Departments of Labor and Justice and the SEC establish procedures which provide for the prompt reporting to the appropriate state insurance authorities of information evidencing possible violations of state laws and regulations, and conversely so.

Fiduciaries Under ERISA

The Subcommittee notes that ERISA sets forth the basic rules governing the fiduciary's employee benefit plan and defines the term "fiduciary." It finds, however, some uncertainty as to whether certain individuals dealing with such plans are, in fact, fiduciaries. Therefore, the following specific recommendations are made:

1. Insurance Consultants

The Subcommittee notes the uncertainty as to whether insurance consultants are fiduciaries under ERISA. It notes that the interests of employee benefit plans cannot be protected when plan trustees make decisions in substantial reliance upon expert evaluations by insurance consultants who fail to conform their conduct to the fiduciary standards of ERISA. The Subcommittee notes that, because of their special expertise, independent insurance consultants have considerable influence on plan decisions and therefore in effect exercise discretionary control within the meaning of ERISA. Accordingly, the *Subcommittee recommends that the DOL issue interpretative regulations which would specify that consultants selected by employee benefit plans to evaluate insurance matters are fiduciaries under ERISA whenever they render advice or related services that will be relied upon by the plan, or that will otherwise be a significant factor in any decision or action by the plan.*

2. Conflict of Interest

The Committee Report notes the prohibitions under ERISA from a fiduciary receiving consideration for his own account from any party dealing with a plan—but also the DOL administrative exemption which permits a pension consultant to receive a sales commission from an insurance company in connection with purchases of insurance contracts with plan assets, if certain conditions are met. The Committee Report notes that although this method of compensation appears to be common in the insurance industry, it significantly impairs the independence of insurance consultants, and in a practical sense permits insurance companies rather than plan trustees to set the amount of compensation of consultants. The Report, as noted above, is negative to the percentage-of-premium payment of the consultant, and feels that the time and difficulty involved in the assignment should govern the amount of the commission. The *Subcommittee believes that the exemption noted above* (Prohibited Transactions Exemption 77-9, 42 Fed. Reg. 32395, June 24, 1977, and 44 Fed. Reg. 1479, January 5, 1979) *is inconsistent with the objective of ERISA to ensure that persons serving a plan in a fiduciary capacity discharge their duties to the plan solely in the interest of plan participants and beneficiaries and for the exclusive purpose of providing benefits to them. The Subcommittee believes that the practice noted above constitutes an irreconcilable conflict of interest and, therefore, recommends that the DOL repeal the exemption from the Prohibited Transactions Provisions of ERISA for the receipt by an insurance consultant to an employee benefit plan of compensation from insurance companies, in connection with the purchase of an insurance contract with plan assets.*

3. Guidelines for Determining Who Are Fiduciaries

Noting that four years have gone by since the enactment of ERISA, during which time the DOL should have gained experience with regard to the role of professionals serving employee benefit plans and their trustees, the Subcommittee *recommends that the Secretary of Labor issue interpretative guidelines which identify with greater specificity the circumstances under which persons providing professional or other specialized services to employee benefit plans are fiduciaries under ERISA.* Such guidelines would serve to alert persons dealing with the benefit plans as to when their activities make them fiduciaries, and of their obligations to conform their conduct to the ERISA standards.

Prohibited Self-Dealing and Conflict of Interest Transactions Under ERISA

The Report notes that as a result of the Subcommittee investigation, questions have been raised concerning the adequacy of the prohibited transactions provisions of ERISA which are designed to obviate conflicts of interest in the administration of plans. Therefore, the Report makes certain specific recommendations.

1. Relatives of Union Officials as Parties in Interest

After reviewing the statutory definitions of "party in interest" and "relative," the Report notes that relatives of union officers who are not trustees or otherwise fiduciaries of a plan are not considered parties in interest and, therefore, are not subject to the prohibited transactions provisions. The record in the Hauser investigation shows how this loophole was utilized to perpetrate a fraud. In view of the substantial influence that relatives of union officials may potentially wield over union-related employee benefit plans, the Subcommittee *recommends that Congress consider amending ERISA to include relatives of non-fiduciary union officers as parties in interest with respect to any employee benefit plan which covers members of the union.*

2. Receipt of Compensation by Parties in Interest

The Report reviews the relationship of the attorney to Hauser and the payment of fees by Hauser to the attorney for assisting him in his Florida activities. Based upon the testimony and evidence adduced, the Subcommittee *recommends that the DOL adopt interpretative regulations making it clear that so-called introduction fees paid to parties in interest, including counsel to the plan and other non-fiduciary parties in interest, constitute a prohibited transaction. Further, the Subcommittee recommends that ERISA be amended to make it clear that a non-fiduciary party in interest who knows or should know that he has engaged in a prohibited transaction is also a proper subject of an action seeking injunctive or other relief.*

The Subcommittee notes that ERISA does not impose a specific duty on the part of either fiduciaries or parties in interest to disclose to a plan that they are engaging in transactions that are or may be in violation of ERISA. The Subcommittee *recommends that Congress amend ERISA to impose on parties in interest a specific duty to disclose to plan administrators their financial interests in any party dealing with the plan and any arrangement whereby such party in interest will receive compensation or other payments, including loans, for his own account from a party dealing with the plan.* These disclosure arrangements should be patterned after the LMRDA provisions. The information disclosed pursuant to the proposed regulations should be filed with the DOL and included in the annual reports of the plans provided for under ERISA. Violations of the disclosure requirements should subject the parties to criminal as well as civil sanctions.

In addition to the proposed new disclosure regulations designed to facilitate detection of questionable, improper and prohibited transactions, the Subcommittee *also recommends that Congress amend ERISA to require the Department of Labor to adopt rules requiring fiduciaries of employee benefit plans to obtain written, certified disclosures from parties dealing with the plan, prior to entering into any material transaction with the dealing party.* The disclosure should cover any payments made or to be made in connection with the proposed transactions to any fiduciary or other party in interest, and any financial interest which any fiduciary or other party in interest may have in the dealing party. The legislation should provide for criminal sanctions for its violation.

Jointly Managed Trust Funds

The Subcommittee notes its concern that the present structure of Taft-Hartley plans does not adequately protect against potential conflicts of interest. The Subcommittee notes with particular concern the evidence adduced at its hearings dealing with union domination of these plans. To minimize this potential conflict of interest in Taft-Hartley funds, the Subcommittee *recommends that Congress amend the Taft-Hartley Act to require the inclusion of independent neutral trustees. The Subcommittee further recommends that Congress extend the "sunshine" or open meeting principles to jointly trusteed plans by requiring that all meetings of the trustees be open to participants in the fund. It also recommends that a verbatim record be kept of the proceedings and made available for review by any plan participant and members of the public,* similar to the LMRDA requirement.

Sanctions and Remedies Against Union and Plan Officials Who Abuse Their Positions

As a result of the evidence adduced at the hearings concerning the Council President's continued service as a trustee to the plans after conviction of criminal violations, the Subcommittee recommends certain specific sanctions and remedies.

1. Forfeitures of Positions

A union or employee benefit plan official who is convicted of racketeering violations involving embezzlement of plan assets or other misconduct affecting these entities should not be permitted to exercise control over the plan. *The Subcommittee recommends legislation which would suspend such an individual from his position with the plan during the pendency of an appeal following a conviction.*

2. Disqualification

Both LMRDA and ERISA prohibit a convicted felon from serving as a trustee or other official of an employee benefit plan, but the disqualification does not take effect until judgment is sustained on appeal. *The Subcommittee believes that a union or plan official who is convicted by a trial court of a crime involving a breach of his position of trust with a union or with a plan should be suspended from performing any official function pending appeal. The Subcommittee further recommends that an existing loophole be closed by extending the disqualification provisions to corporations and other entities controlled by disqualified persons or which employ disqualified persons.*

3. Preconviction Remedies

After noting that the disqualification provisions of LMRDA and ERISA apply only after conviction of the specified crimes, the *Subcommittee recommends that the criminal statutes involved be amended to authorize the Department of Justice to seek appropriate preconviction restraints on union and plan officials under indictment for crimes involving misuse of union or employee benefit plan assets.*

4. Civil Remedies Against Union Officials

The Subcommittee recommends that LMRDA be amended to contain the same broad language, "equitable and other remedial relief," as is now found in Section 409 of ERISA.

"Prudent Man" Guidelines Under ERISA

The Subcommittee recommends that the Department of Labor formulate and issue appropriate interpretative regulations setting forth the "prudent man" standards under ERISA based upon its experience to date with the enforcement of ERISA. The proposed regulations should specify the steps trustees should take to investigate the backgrounds of persons furnishing services to the plan in order to determine their reliability, any potential conflicts of interest they may have, and their status as fiduciaries. Such inquiry should adduce information which would permit plan trustees to determine whether to retain the services of consultants or other persons who have special expertise. The proposed regulations should also require trustees to make inquiries into bidding insurance companies in order to determine the reputation and financial responsibility of such companies.

The proposed regulations should further require plan trustees to adopt written procedures designed to prevent and detect overreaching, fraud, and breaches of fiduciary duty and prohibited transactions. Procedures should set forth the details of the plan's internal control and accountability system and provide for documentation and audit of compliance with plan procedures. The regulations should also require the adoption of competitive bidding procedures for the purchase of insurance or other appropriate transactions, and emphasize the need for plan trustees to be watchful for deviations from the established procedures and other irregularities.

Improvement in the DOL's Enforcement Program

The Subcommittee makes certain recommendations dealing with the Department of Labor filling its remaining positions and continuing its commitment to support the organized crime program. Further, the Subcommittee recommends that the DOL reassess its position that it has no responsibility to detect and investigate violations of criminal law relating to employee benefit plans and to generally act in accordance with the GAO recommendations.

Insurance Company Standards. The DOL, in a statement released in March 1980, generally whitewashed and disavowed the Senate Report and its recommendations. For example, the DOL said that there was no need to establish standards for insurance companies seeking to do business with employee benefit plans because ERISA already imposes a variety of substantive obligations on plan fiduciaries. Under ERISA, plan fiduciaries violating their duties may be held personally liable for any losses resulting to the plan. This, combined with the already existing disclosure provisions, provides adequate safeguards insofar as the protection of plan assets is concerned.

The DOL said that although it recognized the merits of many of the Subcommittee recommendations, it believed some of the suggestions have already been successfully carried out. Other recommendations may duplicate authority the DOL presently possesses under ERISA to prevent the abuses documented in the Report. For example, several lawsuits have already been filed by the DOL alleging improper insurance arrangements. These lawsuits indicate the DOL's support of the view that a consultant to an employee benefit plan may be a fiduciary by virtue of rendering investment advice to a plan if that consultant is retained by a plan to evaluate the plan's insurance funding needs and makes recommendations regarding proposed purchases of suitable insurance contracts. In addition, the DOL said specific disclosure and regulatory requirements exist which affect insurance companies doing business with employee benefit plans.

PTE 77-9. The DOL disagreed with the Subcommittee recommendation calling for the repeal of Class Exemption 77-9. The DOL said, "Prohibited Transaction Exemption 77-9 is a realistic approach for assuring that plans have access to necessary funding instruments and services while, at the same time, lessening the possibility of the occurrence of actual conflict of interest abuses." The class exemption, which was originally published in June 1977 and republished as amended in January 1979 (221 BPR R-19), was granted on the basis of an administrative record compiled over three years and consisting of exemption applications, interested party comments and hearing testimony. Relief under the class exemption is conditioned, in part, on disclosure to the plan's disinterested fiduciary of the sales commission to be received by the agent and the nature of the agent's affiliation or any agreement with a particular insurance company limiting the agent's ability to recommend insurance contracts.

While receipt of the disclosure required by the exemption assists fiduciaries in evaluating recommendations made by consultants or agents, the fiduciaries still must determine that the purchase of an insurance contract satisfies the general fiduciary responsibility provisions of Section 404(a)(1) of ERISA.

After examining the Subcommittee recommendation for repeal of this class exemption, the DOL concluded that it would have a detrimental effect on many plans dependent on legitimate insurance consultants for necessary and desirable support services.

Parties in Interest and Fiduciary Standards. The DOL said that it does not support the Subcommittee's recommendation to further extend the definition of parties in interest to include relatives of non-fiduciary union officers. A definition so far-reaching as to include individuals twice removed from plan assets is not necessary to protect those assets. With respect to a Subcommittee recommendation regarding "introduction fees," the DOL said that it does not have the authority to prohibit the payment of such fees by non-fiduciary third parties to non-fiduciary parties in interest simply by stating in a regulation that such payments are prohibited transactions. If a party-in-interest recipient of such fees is in a position to exercise discretionary authority or control with respect to the management of a plan or its assets and uses such fees from a party dealing with the plan in connection with a transaction involving the plan's assets as a payment for his own personal account, the DOL would consider this a prohibited transaction under Section 406 of ERISA. However, to extend such a prohibition to a party in interest who does not exercise discretionary authority would broaden ERISA to an extent that is not necessary at this time.

In response to a Subcommittee recommendation calling for the DOL to adopt rules defining minimum standards that fiduciaries must meet to comply with the prudent man rule, the DOL said that it has already issued one important regulation concerning prudence in investments. The regulation applies to any decisions made by plan fiduciaries regarding the purchase of insurance and the selection of carriers. The DOL said that other regulations in this area will be considered in the future.

Other Areas. The DOL is considering other suggestions made by the Subcommittee for legislation. If the Administration determines that legislative change is required, the DOL said that it would be willing to work out the specific details with the Subcommittee. The Secretary of Labor has delegated responsibility to the Justice Department with respect to the investigation of criminal matters arising under Sections 411 and 511 of ERISA. The Subcommittee recommended that the distinction between criminal and civil investigations be clarified so that effective enforcement could be achieved in both areas.

Having heard the Senate Subcommittee's side of the story, including its recommendations, and having heard the response of the DOL, I would like to give you my thoughts and the thoughts, suggestions and recommendations of an ERISA trust fund counsel.

Considerations and Recommendations for Trustees

While it is true that government committees hold hundreds of hearings and publish scores of reports each year (with only a limited number of legislative proposals resulting) and while the data considered by the Subcommittee were limited and biased (thereby tainting its conclusions), nonetheless, the November 26, 1979 report by the Subcommittee appears to have awakened substantial latent interest in Washington in the Report and its recommendations. Whether or not Congress ultimately enacts amendments to ERISA and other laws as recommended to it and whether or not the DOL issues any or all of the recommended interpretative regulations suggested by the Subcommittee in its Report, it is my opinion that you should seriously consider the recommendations I have made below and consider adopting your own rules and regulations in advance of and without regard to any lack of subsequent Congressional or DOL enactments.

Insurance Regulation

1. Minimum Standards for Insurance Companies Doing Business With Employee Benefit Plans

The Subcommittee recommends that Congress enact legislation amending ERISA which would direct the Secretary of Labor to establish minimum standards to be established for insurance companies desiring to deal with employee benefit plans. We do not believe that such recommendation will meet with much favor or success. The insurance industry has had great success in lobbying Congress to avoid federal regulation of the industry. Further, employee benefit plans are so different that no one set of minimum standards would suffice or be meaningful. For example, how can one set of standards be meaningful for a 1,000 member, $1.5 million per year in claims plan as well as for a 30,000 member, $40 million per year in claims plan?

I suggest that trustees respond to the recommendation, which is proper and appropriate, by their conduct rather than by legislation. That is, if trustees determine to insure one or more benefits, trustees should charge their consultant, with the assistance of their fund auditor and fund counsel, to obtain information on all prospective carriers as to capitalization, reserves and reinsurance arrangements. In addition to the factual investigation and report, the consultant should express his opinion as to the adequacy of the prospective carriers to properly insure the subject benefits. This procedure would enable trustees to comply with the intent of the Subcommittee's recommendation without relying on possible Congressional action.

2. Disclosure of Fees and Payments

The Subcommittee recommends that Congress pass legislation which would direct the Secretary of Labor to adopt regulations requiring insurance companies which sell policies to employee benefit plans to disclose all commissions, finder's fees and other payments made in connection with such sale, and to keep records on the same. I believe this is a proper recommendation, but I believe that trustees can and should implement this policy on their own and without waiting for the Department of Labor to act.

With minor exceptions, all group insurance policies can be bought without commissions. Without exception, I urge and recommend that trustees adopt and state as their policy that all of their insured benefits should be bought without commission. In those cases where by state law or otherwise a minor commission must be paid, I recommend that the commission be paid to the consultant, who shall offset this payment against its fee-for-service compensation. Finally, both the carrier and the consultant should be required to certify in writing as to the non-payment and non-receipt of commissions.

3. Miscellaneous

The Subcommittee makes certain further recommendations as to amending the Securities Exchange Act of 1934 and state insurance laws to avoid the frauds disclosed in the Subcommittee's hearings. There is nothing further for trustees to do at this time.

Fiduciaries Under ERISA

1. Insurance Consultants

The Subcommittee recommends that the DOL adopt regulations which would specify that consultants who evaluate insurance matters are fiduciaries whenever they render advice or related services which will be relied upon by the plan or otherwise be a significant factor in any decision or action by the plan. This recommendation will be strongly opposed by the consulting industry, but the existing regulations and advisory opinions and the definition of a fiduciary under Section 3(21)(A) have already reached this conclusion.

I recommend that trustees respond in two respects to comply with the spirit and intent of this recommendation.

First, trustees must be ever mindful of the fact that they are the named fiduciaries of their plans and that they, and not the consultants (nor the auditors nor counsel nor the union nor the association) are charged by law to operate and administer their plans. Trustees should seek advice and suggestions from their professionals on issues of which trustees lack knowledge and expertise. However, the trustees make the final decisions.

Second, the trustees should charge and demand that all of their advisors act as if they were fiduciaries. That is, the consultant, auditor and counsel, et al., must act solely in the interest of participants; to maximize benefits, to minimize expenses; as prudent men and in accordance with the plan documents and the law. These are the rules by which the trustees must play. These are the rules by which the trustees should insist their advisors play also—or the trustees should fire their advisors.

2. Conflict of Interest

The Subcommittee recommends that the DOL withdraw its Exemption 77-9, which allows a consultant to be compensated by an insurance company from the sale of insurance by the company to the plan which the consultant represents. Whether or not this happens, I recommended above and renew my recommendation that the trustees buy all insured benefits without commission; that if a minor commission must be paid, it should be paid to the consultant and offset against his fee-for-service compensation; and that the carrier and the consultant certify in writing that no fees, commissions or other compensation are paid by a carrier to any advisor to the plan in connection with any plan business.

3. Guidelines for Determining Who Are Fiduciaries

The Subcommittee recommends that the DOL adopt regulations which identify with greater specificity the circumstances under which persons rendering professional and specialized services to a plan shall be deemed fiduciaries. The DOL has already issued several regulations and advisory opinions on this topic, and more regulations and opinions will be issued. No series of regulations or opinions will cover each and every factual situation of each and every plan.

Pending these further promulgations, to meet this recommendation of the Subcommittee I recommend that trustees adopt the following program:
a. Direct fund counsel to continue to monitor the evolution of this aspect of the law and to keep the trustees fully advised;
b. Direct fund counsel to study the role of all professionals and other involved parties in the operation and administration of the plan, and to advise the trustees of the probable legal status of such persons; and
c. Demand that all advisors and others involved in the operation and administration of the plan act as if they were fiduciaries; i.e., act solely in the interest of plan participants and beneficiaries, to maximize benefits and minimize expenses, as prudent men in accordance with the plan documents and the law.

Prohibited Self-Dealing and Conflict of Interest Transactions

1. Relatives of Union Officials as Parties in Interest

The Subcommittee recommends that ERISA be amended to include a relative of a non-fiduciary union official as a party in interest, so as to expand the scope of persons covered by the ERISA Section 406(a) prohibited transactions. I suggest that the intent of the recommendation is excellent, but its scope is too limited. If it is improper (or potentially so) to deal with a relative of a union official, is it any less improper to deal with the relative of an association officer, or the relative of a contributing employer, or the relative of a plan professional? I think not.

Therefore, I urge trustees to act now, without regard to the recommended amendment of Section 3(15) of ERISA, and adopt rules which provide that:
a. The plan shall not deal with a relative of any non-fiduciary plan sponsor (union or association), employer or plan advisor unless and except by specific action after a full disclosure of all facts; and
b. The plan adopt procedures to enforce this rule.

2. Receipt of Compensation by Parties in Interest

In its discussion of this point, the Subcommittee made several specific recommendations:
a. Adopt regulations that provide that the payment of finder's fees or introduction fees are a prohibited transaction;
b. Expand the relief afforded by ERISA Section 409 against fiduciaries (removal, injunction, damages and other relief) to cover prohibited transactions by parties in interest;
c. Amend ERISA to require all parties in interest to disclose any personal interest they may have in any party dealing with the

plan, and any compensation they do or may receive from the party dealing with the plan;

d. Require the DOL to promulgate regulations requiring the plan to obtain certified disclosures from all parties dealing with the plan as to payments it made or is to make to any fiduciary, party in interest or other person; or financial interest any fiduciary, party in interest or other person involved with the plan has in the service provider.

Again, the DOL has adopted some regulations in this area and, in response to the Subcommittee, may adopt others. Again, I urge trustees to take action on their own, to wit:

a. As previously suggested, trustees should buy all insured benefits without commissions. Further, to meet the finder's fee issue, trustees should require *all service providers* (not only insurance companies, but also banks, investment managers and advisors) to certify in writing and under oath that they paid no such fees; and all persons involved in plan administration and operation should be required to certify that they received no such fees.

b. Trustees can implement the recommendations by refusing to do business (or to continue to do business) with any person who pays or receives payments from service providers in connection with doing business with the plan. This does not include a situation when, for example, the plan's certified public accountant is also the certified public accountant for the association and is paid his usual, customary and reasonable fee for professional services actually rendered to the association, but rather those cases where consideration is paid directly to the association to "get the plan business" for the certified public accountant.

c. All service providers of a plan (administrator, attorney, accountant, consultant, actuary, bank, insurance company, investment manager and others) should be required to certify in writing any financial interest they have in any other service provider or party involved in the plan (plan sponsor, trustees, etc.) and any monies paid to or from any other service provider or other party involved in the plan.

Jointly Trusteed Plans

The Report contains a recommendation that Taft-Hartley Section 302(c) be amended to require, in addition to the equal number of labor and management trustees, one or more neutral or impartial trustees. The reason given is the apparent dominance of the management trustees by the union trustees. I take strong exception to this recommendation. I have seen no evidence of domination of either group of trustees in any plan I represent. If dominance exists, won't the dominating parties also dominate the neutral trustees? No impartial third parties can bring to the trustees' table the knowledge of the industry and the understanding of the wants and needs of the plan participants that the labor-management representatives do. I urge you to resist any legislative attempt to carry out this recommendation.

The Subcommittee Report also recommends open, "sunshine" meetings and a taping of all discussions at all meetings. The recommendation sounds good to anyone not familiar with the operation of Taft-Hartley plans and their trustee meetings. As all trustees know, it takes several months of hard work to become a knowledgeable trustee and to understand the parties involved in the decision making process. To allow an employer or a participant to attend and hear the discussion at one meeting, without the benefit of the decisions at prior meetings and without the benefit of the reports the trustees have from their professional advisors, is to invite misunderstanding.

Although trustees have nothing to hide as to their discussions, a tape recorder or court reporter will inhibit the fully frank and unfettered discussions which lead to good decisions. Will a service provider or trustee be willing to ask a "dumb question" if he is being recorded for posterity? Will a management trustee be willing to speak for and support a "union position" if the tape is to be played to or the transcript read at an association meeting? I cannot urge you strongly enough to resist these uninformed recommendations.

Sanctions and Remedies Against Union and Plan Officials Who Abuse Their Positions

A series of recommendations are contained in the Report under this heading. For the most part, these relate to proposed changes in the LMRDA. Trustees can meet the intent of the recommendations by:

a. Removing any plan official or service provider upon conviction of any felony or misdemeanor involving moral turpitude; and

b. Urging plan sponsors to remove their appointed trustees immediately upon such a conviction.

"Prudent Man" Guidelines Under ERISA

The Subcommittee recommends that the DOL promulgate regulations setting forth prudent man standards. The regulations would specify:

a. Steps trustees should take to investigate potential (and initially existing) service providers to determine reliability, potential conflicts of interest, fiduciary status and expertise;
b. Procedures designed to prevent and detect fraud, overreaching, conflicts, breaches of fiduciary duty and prohibited transactions; and
c. Procedures for competitive bidding.

Again, I suggest that guidelines already exist and that trustees can and should adopt their own procedures now to accomplish these purposes. A thorough investigation of all new service providers and the certificates discussed previously would accomplish many of these objectives. Periodically, the auditor and/or counsel should be charged to make an investigation of plan procedures seeking to detect any such violations.

Implementing the Recommendations

I assume it will come as no surprise that I have prepared and distributed to all of my trust fund clients my report on the Senate Report and discussed it in detail with the trustees. Most of the plans have accepted my recommendations and moved forward to implement and document them.

The Exhibits following this article present examples of some of the paperwork employed by trustees to prudently protect themselves, the plan and its participants and beneficiaries from the scams reported by the Senate Subcommittee, and to anticipate the inquiries of a DOL compliance officer. Exhibit 1 is a letter from the administrative manager to the consultant seeking an opinion on the stability of the carrier to provide the contracted-for benefits, and on reinsurance arrangements. Exhibit 2 is a letter and form of affidavit to the consultant to ascertain the existence of a conflict of interest situation, as reported in the Senate Report. Exhibit 3 is a request to the fund counsel for an opinion letter on the legal status of persons dealing with the plan. Exhibit 4 is a form of letter and affidavit to be completed by all advisors to determine if any of them are receiving payments from any other parties in interest or fiduciaries, such as, for example, the introductory fees and boat scams of Hauser in Florida. Exhibit 5 is a form of trustee rules and regulations declaring the intention of the trustees to avoid the perils of Hauser. Exhibit 6 is a format for rules by the trustees to avoid the post-conviction embezzlements of the Florida union leader.

All of these forms represent one approach, for one plan to meet its specific situation. Other or further documentation may be appropriate for your plan.

Conclusions

It could be argued that since this Report is one of hundreds issued by Congressional Committees each year and since it is based on inadequate and biased data, the recommendations should be ignored, at least until legislative administrative action is initiated. I do not agree. Taft-Hartley employee benefit plans are becoming increasingly suspect. DOL and IRS enforcement is being stepped up. I, therefore, strongly urge the trustees to study and consider this Report; to make it an agenda topic for full discussion at a future trustees' meeting; and to direct the appropriate advisors to begin implementation of a program to meet the valid recommendations of the Report.

Exhibit 1

Mr. John Doe
John Doe Consultants, Inc.
One Main Street
Toledo, Ohio 43600

    Re: ABC Health and Welfare
                Plan and Trust

    Re: Fees and Commissions on
                Group Life Insurance

Dear John:

At the September 1, 1980 meeting of the Trustees of the ABC Health and Welfare Plan, the Trustees reviewed, discussed and approved the report of Shumaker, Loop & Kendrick concerning the Report of the Senate Subcommittee on Investigations regarding Labor Union Insurance. At the same meeting the Trustees adopted the recommendations set forth in Section III of the Shumaker, Loop & Kendrick report and directed Fund Counsel to assist the Trustees in implementing these recommendations.

In this regard, at the request and direction of the Trustees, would you please prepare and present to the Trustees a written report concerning the group life insurance policy funding the death benefits provided for in the Plan of Benefits and discussing in detail the following items:

1. In the opinion of John Doe Consultants, Inc., does XYZ Insurance Company meet the minimum standards appropriate for an insurance company doing business with the Plan and providing this benefit? In your response, please refer to and comment upon the licensing, capitalization, reserving and other fundamental requirements your firm deems appropriate in these circumstances.

2. Does XYZ Insurance Company use reinsurance arrangements with regard to the benefits provided to the Plan? If so, please provide the Trustees with the details of these arrangements and your opinion as to the propriety of these arrangements as they relate to the carrier and the Plan.

3. Is any commission, fee or other compensation, direct or indirect, in cash or otherwise, paid to any individual, firm or corporation by XYZ Insurance Company with regard to this coverage? If so, in your report please respond in detail to the following additional items:
   (a) To whom is it paid?
   (b) How long have such payments been made?
   (c) How long in the future will such payments be made?
   (d) How much is paid:
      (1) annually?
      (2) to date?
   (e) What designation is made for the payments (e.g., fees, commission, administrative service allowance, administrative service fee, etc.)?
   (f) If the designation shown in (e) above is "commission," what commission scale is used by the carrier?
   (g) If the designation in (e) above is "fee," what services are performed by you for the fee?
   (h) Will the insurer sell the same coverage without any commissions, fees or other compensation?

If you have any questions concerning this request, please do not hesitate to contact Fund Counsel or me.

                              Very truly yours,

                              Administrative Manager

cc: Board Chairman
       Board Secretary
       Fund Counsel

Exhibit 2

Mr. John Doe
John Doe Consultants, Inc.
One Main Street
Toledo, Ohio 43600

    Re: ABC Health and Welfare
              Plan and Trust

    Re: Conflict of Interest

Dear John:

At the September 1, 1980 meeting of the Trustees of the ABC Health and Welfare Plan, the Trustees reviewed, discussed and approved the report of Shumaker, Loop & Kendrick concerning the Report of the Senate Subcommittee on Investigations regarding Labor Union Insurance. At the same meeting the Trustees adopted the recommendations set forth in Section III of the Shumaker, Loop & Kendrick report and directed Fund Counsel to assist the Trustees in implementing these recommendations.

In this regard, at the request and direction of the Trustees, would you please prepare an Affidavit on the letterhead of John Doe Consultants, Inc. in accordance with the attached general format, have the same properly signed and notarized, and return the copies to me.

If you have any questions concerning this request, please do not hesitate to contact Fund Counsel or me.

                            Very truly yours,

                            Administrative Manager

cc: Board Chairman
      Board Secretary
      Fund Counsel

CONSULTANT LETTERHEAD

STATE OF OHIO   )
) SS:
COUNTY OF LUCAS)

I, John Doe, being first duly sworn upon oath, depose and say:

1. I am the President of John Doe Consultants, Inc.

2. John Doe Consultants, Inc. is the duly designated and acting consultant to the Board of Trustees of the ABC Health and Welfare Plan and Trust.

3. I an not now nor have I in the past five (5) years ever received any commissions, fees, payments, compensation or other consideration, direct or indirect, in cash or otherwise, from any insurance company providing coverage or benefits to the Plan [except as follows (INCLUDING THE DETAILS OF THE AMOUNT PAID, TO WHOM, BY WHOM, FOR WHAT SERVICES OR CONSIDERATION)].

4. To the best of my information, knowledge and belief based upon due diligence and proper inquiry, neither John Doe Consultants, Inc. nor any director, partner, officer, employee or agent of John Doe Consultants, Inc. has in the past five (5) years received any commissions, fees, payments, compensation or other consideration, direct or indirect, in cash or otherwise, from any insurance company providing coverage or benefits to the Plan during the time it was providing coverage [except as follows (INCLUDING THE DETAILS OF THE AMOUNT PAID, TO WHOM, BY WHOM, FOR WHAT SERVICES OR CONSIDERATION)].

_____
John Doe

Sworn to before me and subscribed in my presence this _____ day of _____, 1980.

_____
Notary Public

Exhibit 3

Marc Gertner, Esquire
Shumaker, Loop & Kendrick
811 Madison Avenue
Suite 500
Toledo, Ohio 43624

  Re: ABC Health and Welfare
    Plan and Trust

  Re: Guidelines for Determining
    Fiduciary Status

Dear Marc:

  At the September 1, 1980 meeting of the Trustees of the ABC Health and Welfare Plan and Trust, the Trustees reviewed, discussed and approved the report of Shumaker, Loop & Kendrick concerning the Report of the Senate Subcommittee on Investigations regarding Labor Union Insurance. At the same meeting the Trustees adopted the recommendations set forth in Section III of the Shumaker, Loop & Kendrick report and directed Fund Counsel to assist the Trustees in implementing these recommendations.

  In this regard, at the request and direction of the Trustees, would you please prepare and present to the Trustees a written report concerning guidelines for determining fiduciary status and discussing specifically the following points:

  1. The status of the law on who are fiduciaries of an employee benefit plan subject to ERISA and guidelines for determining who are fiduciaries of such plans.

  2. The probable legal status of the advisors to the ABC Health and Welfare Plan and Trust.

          Very truly yours,

          Administrative Manager

cc: Board Chairman
   Board Secretary

Exhibit 4

Mr. John Doe
John Doe Consultants, Inc.
One Main Street
Toledo, Ohio 43600

    Re: ABC Health and Welfare
          Plan and Trust

    Re: Receipt of Compensation
          by Parties in Interest

Dear John:

At the September 1, 1980 meeting of the Trustees of the ABC Health and Welfare Plan and Trust, the Trustees reviewed, discussed and approved the report of Shumaker, Loop & Kendrick concerning the Report of the Senate Subcommittee on Investigations regarding Labor Union Insurance. At the same meeting the Trustees adopted the recommendations set forth in Section III of the Shumaker, Loop & Kendrick report and directed Fund Counsel to assist the Trustees in implementing these recommendations.

In this regard, at the request and direction of the Board of Trustees, would you please prepare an Affidavit on the letterhead of John Doe Consultants, Inc. in accordance with the attached general format, have the same properly signed and notarized, and return two copies to me.

If you have any questions concerning this request, please do not hesitate to contact Fund Counsel or me.

                        Very truly yours,

                        Administrative Manager

cc: Board Chairman
     Board Secretary
     Fund Counsel

CONSULTANT LETTERHEAD

STATE OF OHIO)
) SS:
COUNTY OF LUCAS)

    I, John Doe, being first duly sworn upon oath, depose and say:

1. I am the President of John Doe Consultants, Inc.

2. John Doe Consultants, Inc. is the duly designated and acting consultant to the Board of Trustees of the ABC Health and Welfare Plan and Trust.

3. I am not now, nor have I within the past five (5) years, received any commissions, fees, payments, compensation or other consideration, direct or indirect, in cash or otherwise, from any provider of service(s), fiduciary or party in interest of the Plan, or any of them [except as follows (INCLUDING THE DETAILS OF THE AMOUNT PAID, TO WHOM, BY WHOM, FOR WHAT SERVICES OR CONSIDERATION)].

4. To the best of my information, knowledge and belief, based upon due diligence and proper inquiry, neither John Doe Consultants, Inc. nor any partner, director, officer, employee or agent of John Doe Consultants, Inc. has within the past five (5) years received any commissions, fees, payments, compensation or other consideration, direct or indirect, in cash or otherwise, from any provider of service(s), fiduciary or party in interest of the Plan, or any of them [except as follows (INCLUDING THE DETAILS OF THE AMOUNT PAID, TO WHOM, BY WHOM, FOR WHAT SERVICES OR CONSIDERATION)].

5. I do not now nor have I ever had a financial interest in any provider of service(s) or fiduciary or party in interest to the Plan, or any of them [except as follows _____].

6. To the best of my information, knowledge and belief, based upon due diligence and proper inquiry, neither John Doe Consultants, Inc. nor any partner, director, officer, employee or agent of John Doe Consultants, Inc. has any financial interest in any provider of service(s) or fiduciary or party in interest to the Plan, or any of them [except as follows _____].

_____
John Doe

Sworn to before me and subscribed in my presence this _____ day of _____, 1980.

_____
Notary Public

[SIMILAR AFFIDAVIT TO BE DONE FOR ALL SERVICE PROVIDERS]

Exhibit 5

Promulgation of Rules and Regulations by the Board of Trustees of the ABC Health and Welfare Plan and Trust

---

KNOW ALL MEN BY THESE PRESENTS, that

WHEREAS, the undersigned are the duly designated, qualified and acting Trustees (the "Trustees") of the ABC Health and Welfare Plan and Trust (the "Plan"); and

WHEREAS, in accordance with the terms and provisions of the Agreement and Declaration of Trust, as amended (the "Trust Agreement"), the Trustees are authorized and directed to establish the Plan, to operate and administer the Plan, and to promulgate Rules and Regulations as may be necessary thereto; and

WHEREAS, the Trustees have received, reviewed, considered and discussed a report from Fund Counsel concerning the November 26, 1979 Report of the Senate Permanent Subcommittee on Investigations of the Senate Committee on Governmental Affairs and have adopted the necessary motions and regulations directing the implementation of the report of Fund Counsel; and

WHEREAS, as the named fiduciaries of the Plan and mindful of their fiduciary obligations to the participants in the Plan and their beneficiaries, the Trustees desire to promulgate Rules and Regulations to prevent prohibited self-dealing and conflict of interest transactions as discussed in the Senate Report and the report of Fund Counsel.

NOW, THEREFORE, in consideration of these premises and by virtue of the authority granted to them in the Trust Agreement, the Trustees of the Plan do hereby promulgate the following Rules and Regulations, to wit:

1. The Trustees of the Plan and the Plan shall have no financial or prohibited transactions or dealings with any of the following persons:
    (a) the Employer Plan Sponsors;
    (b) the Union Plan Sponsor;
    (c) any Employer;
    (d) any service provider;
    (e) any relative of any of the foregoing, as defined in ERISA Section 3(15);

except by specific action of the full Board of Trustees at a regularly scheduled meeting and after a full disclosure of all of the relevant and material facts.

2. The Administrative Manager of the Plan, with the assistance of the Plan's auditor, consultant and counsel, shall establish procedures to implement these Rules and Regulations.

3. The Administrative Manager shall establish and maintain a permanent file in the Plan Office for the records of any transactions referred to herein.

4. The Trustees shall adopt such further Rules and Regulations as are necessary and proper to implement this Promulgation.

Adopted at Toledo, Ohio this _____ day of _____, 1980.

UNION TRUSTEES	EMPLOYER TRUSTEES
_____	_____
_____	_____
_____	_____

Exhibit 6

Promulgation of Rules and Regulations by the Board of Trustees of the ABC Health and Welfare Plan and Trust

KNOW ALL MEN BY THESE PRESENTS, that

WHEREAS, the undersigned are the duly designated, qualified and acting Trustees (the "Trustees") of the ABC Health and Welfare Plan and Trust (the "Plan"); and

WHEREAS, in accordance with the terms and provisions of the Agreement and Declaration of Trust, as amended (the "Trust Agreement"), the Trustees are authorized and directed to establish the Plan, to operate and administer the Plan, and to promulgate Rules and Regulations as may be necessary thereto; and

WHEREAS, the Trustees have received, reviewed, considered and discussed a report from Fund Counsel concerning the November 26, 1979 Report of the Senate Permanent Subcommittee on Investigations of the Senate Committee on Governmental Affairs and have adopted the necessary motions and regulations directing implementation of the report of Fund Counsel; and

WHEREAS, as the named fiduciaries of the Plan and mindful of their fiduciary obligations to the participants in the Plan and their beneficiaries, the Trustees desire to promulgate Rules and Regulations to prevent employer association officials, union officials, Plan employees and providers of services to the Plan from abusing their positions of trust.

NOW, THEREFORE, in consideration of these premises and by virtue of the authority granted to them in the Trust Agreement, the Trustees of the Plan do hereby promulgate the following Rules and Regulations, to wit:

1. The Trustees do hereby declare their intention to discharge forthwith any employee of the Plan and/or provider of services to the Plan who is convicted of any felony or any misdemeanor involving moral turpitude.

2. The Trustees do hereby urge that the employer and union Plan sponsors declare a policy to remove any Trustees appointed by them, or either of them, who is convicted of any felony or any misdemeanor involving moral turpitude.

3. The Administrative Manager is hereby directed to provide a copy of this Promulgation to all Plan employees, to all providers of services to the Plan, and to the Plan sponsors.

Dated at Toledo, Ohio this _____ day of _____, 1980.

UNION TRUSTEES	EMPLOYER TRUSTEES
_____	_____
_____	_____
_____	_____

Appendix

The Senate Report on Labor Union Insurance: Summary, Findings and Conclusions

A. General

The Report notes that few things are more important to the well-being and financial security of millions of union members and their families throughout the country than the proper administration of their employee benefit plans, both pension and welfare. The employee welfare benefit plans finance health care, disability benefits, death benefits and other programs to help union members and their dependents.

The Report is the result of detailed and lengthy inquiry into the sale of life, health, accident and other insurance programs to 20 jointly trusteed welfare programs throughout the country during the period 1973-1976. The insurance contracts which were the subject of the investigation were solicited and obtained by companies controlled by or associated with Joseph Hauser. The investigation showed that of some $39 million in premiums paid to the Hauser companies, $11 million was diverted to other firms in the form of questionable commissions, commission advances, questionable investments, conversions to cash, and payment of personal expenses. The most significant victim was the Teamsters Central States Welfare Plan, which allegedly suffered a loss of some $7 million. Major losses allegedly totaling over $1 million were incurred by several Florida Laborers' Union health and welfare funds. In addition, 20,000 policyholders of Farmers National Life Insurance Company had their insurance cancelled and lost the cash surrender values of their policies or unpaid claims. After generally describing the Hauser operation, the Report analogizes it to a "Ponzi scheme." The Report then details the criminal and civil proceedings which have been commenced as a result of the findings from its prior investigation.

B. Florida

On pages 5-8 of the Report, the activities of Hauser in Florida are detailed. In October 1973, Hauser acquired a controlling interest in Farmers National Life Insurance Company, a small, financially troubled Florida insurance company, along with its dormant subsidiary, Family Provider Life Insurance Company of Phoenix, Arizona. He managed to do so in spite of information received by the Florida State Department of Insurance questioning Hauser's "integrity, competency and experience." To represent him in this acquisition, Hauser retained the law firm in which the then-current Florida State Insurance Commissioner was formerly a partner. To conceal his acquisition, Hauser created a holding company and placed shares of stocks in the name of his brother-in-law and an employee hired by him to be president of Farmers National.

Once having gained control of Farmers National and concealing his interests in the firm, Hauser set about acquiring insurance business from certain labor union trust funds in Florida, particularly the Laborers' plans. To gain access to these unions, Hauser paid a retainer of $2,500 per month to an attorney, who was counsel to most of the unions and their welfare plans. In return, the attorney introduced Hauser to important union officials, particularly the president of the Southeast Florida Laborers District Council and a trustee of a number of the plans. At the time Hauser was soliciting business from the Laborers' plans, a Hauser-controlled company leased an expensive sports car for the Council President's use and provided employment for the son of the Council President. Another Hauser company purchased an expensive pleasure boat for use by another Laborers' officer and plan trustee. Based upon this information, the Subcommittee made the following finding:

> The Subcommittee finds that the acceptance of gratuities from Hauser by [the Council President and the Plan Trustee] was incompatible with their positions as employee benefit plan fiduciaries. The Subcommittee also finds [the attorney's] acceptance of compensation from Hauser for providing access to his

---

Author's Note—The findings and conclusions which appear here represent a summary of what is contained in the Report. Please note that many of those involved dispute the factual accuracy of the presentation.

client employee benefit plans constitutes a serious conflict of interest. The record also indicates that [the Council President, the Plan Trustee and the attorney] were instrumental in the Hauser group's success in selling insurance to the funds with which they were associated.

While Hauser was soliciting insurance business from the Laborers' Union Funds, the Council President was indicted in an action in a U.S. District Court in Florida for embezzlement of $400,000 from unions and union trust funds. The Council President was allowed to remain at large, as a union official and plan trustee, following his conviction and during all of the post-conviction appeals. The evidence indicated that in the two years following his conviction, he embezzled an additional $2 million from the unions and trust funds. Based upon these facts, the Subcommittee made the following finding:

> The Subcommittee finds that the Department of Labor and the Laborers' International Union failed to act in a timely fashion to protect union and trust fund assets from further looting by [the Council President] after he had been convicted for embezzlement of approximately $400,000 from the same funds. The Court of Appeals decision to grant a stay of the District Court's order requiring [the Council President] to forfeit his union and welfare plan positions, following his conviction, appears to have been within the discretion of the court. However, the granting of the stay created a substantial risk that the union and plan's assets would not be adequately protected from repetition of the kind of conduct for which [the Council President] was convicted and indeed which occurred to a much greater extent after his conviction.

The lucrative nature of union trust fund business was illustrated by the rapid increase in premiums received by Farmers National. In 1973, the year prior to the Hauser takeover, the total premiums received by the company amounted to approximately $1 million. Under Hauser's leadership, premiums increased to more than $4.5 million in 1974, primarily because of the new business generated from Laborers' Unions and employee welfare plans in Florida, most affiliated with the Laborers and other building trade unions. One reason these premiums increased so rapidly was that the union trust funds purchased individual whole life insurance policies which cost considerably more than group term policies. The death benefit coverage was the same, although the individual whole life policies did have cash surrender values resulting in the higher premium expense. However, most of the policies lapsed in 1975 due to the high turnover in the construction industry, resulting in the loss of cash surrender value to the members. According to the Report, the high cost approximated $1 million per year.

The facts further showed that in 1974 and 1975 two of the Hauser-controlled insurance agencies were paid approximately $2.5 million in commissions and commission advances by Farmers National. The Florida Department of Insurance was unable to obtain documentation to justify these payments. In addition, Hauser and his associates withdrew more than $775,000 in cash and paid out approximately $200,000 in personal expenses from these companies.

The head of the Justice Department strike force noted that Hauser's operation in Florida was typical of labor union insurance fraud schemes encountered by the Department of Justice, all involving the same basic factors:

    a. Contracts by the insurance fraud artist with an initiator, who is usually willing in exchange for gratuities or a kickback to provide assistance in securing the approval of insurance programs by the board of trustees;

    b. The sale of high-cost, whole life policies;

    c. Exorbitant commissions;

    d. Shell companies which transfer premium payments in a maze of financial transactions which hide substantial sums of money;

    e. Lack of any method to guarantee the availability of funds to beneficiaries; and

    f. Bankruptcy and final dissolution within a short period of time.

C. Indiana

The Report traces Hauser's activities in Indiana commencing in 1975. In October 1975, Hauser obtained a contract from the Indiana State District Council of Laborers and Hod Carriers Welfare Fund for Old Security Life Insurance Company as a front for Farmers National. This was done, as in Florida, through inside contacts, primarily the grandson of the Laborers' International Union President and son of the current President. Farmers established the grandson in the insurance business as P. F. Insurance Agency, agreed to cover his salary and expenses, and paid an override on all insurance sold by Farmers National, amounting to approximately $260,000. The contact then used his Laborers' Union connections to bring about a rebidding of the fund's insurance program, leading to the award to Old Security.

The Report also discusses the relationship of Hauser to the consultant to the Indiana fund. Initially, the consultant rendered a report unfavorable to the Old Security proposal, but after an officer of the consultant company visited Farmers National in Miami and held discussions with Hauser, the consultant reversed its position and recommended favorable consideration to the Old Security proposal. Also, the consultant relied on an analysis prepared by a Hauser associate in its report. The final consultant's report concerning the reinsurance arrangements and financial condition of Old Security and Farmers National was materially incomplete and misleading. The Committee concluded as follows:

> The Subcommittee finds that the foregoing conduct by [the consultant] fell well short of the standards of independence and care an employee benefit plan should expect of its insurance consultant.

As compensation for its consulting services to the Fund, the consultant received a commission from Old Security consisting of a percentage of premiums, which arrangement was disclosed to and approved by the trustees. The Report states:

> However, the Subcommittee finds that such a compensation arrangement creates an irreconcilable conflict of interest. Since the compensation is based on a percentage of premiums, it does not necessarily bear any direct relationship to the true value of the consultant's services and creates an incentive to recommend either more insurance or higher premium cost insurance than may be appropriate. As a result, [the consultant] stood to gain a higher consulting fee if the Fund had approved its recommendation for higher premium group permanent insurance.

After noting the testimony of a representative of the consultant that this is a common practice for employee benefit plan consultants, and that the practice has been exempted from prohibited transactions under ERISA by the DOL, the Report concludes:

> The Subcommittee finds that this practice and the exemption impair the independence of insurance consultants to employee benefit plans.

D. Massachusetts

During 1975, Hauser used similar tactics to obtain an insurance contract with the Massachusetts Laborers' Health and Welfare Fund. He was assisted by a consultant which was brought in to make a study and which promoted the Hauser interest. In Massachusetts, Hauser sought out a local contact and set him up with his own insurance company. Hauser through the contact also obtained the approval of an officer of the Laborers' International Union.

When the consideration of group permanent life insurance was considered by the Massachusetts fund, a different consulting firm wrote a report critical of this form of benefit and of Old Security. One of the union representatives recommended that the Indiana consultant be brought in as an outside consultant. At the next trustees' meeting, an officer of the new consultant presented a report which was favorable to Old Security and its proposal. In his report and discussion with the Massachusetts trustees, the representative did not disclose the full facts of his involvement with Hauser and Hauser's associates, nor the fact that the consultant relied upon Hauser associates in preparing his report.

The Report also details other activities by Hauser in Massachusetts, all using the inside assistance of persons involved and the use of payments to them to secure business.

E. Arizona

The Report details Hauser's activities in Arizona and again his practice of relying on persons of influence, here trustees on two union health and welfare plans. When the plan's consultant went out to bid for one of the Arizona funds, Old Security was not on the list. At the request of the associates of Hauser, the consultant was asked to send specifications to five additional companies, including Farmers National and Old Security. At the trustees' meeting, two management trustees raised objection to the late bids and to the inadequate size of the companies to sustain the risk. Nonetheless, the trustees, led by the Hauser associates, voted to award the contract to Union Labor Life Insurance Company. After objections by the two trustees assisting Hauser, the trustees solicited new bids and later awarded the business to Old Security.

F. Teamsters Central States

The largest portion of the Findings and Conclusions is directed to the Hauser activities with regard to the Teamsters Central States Fund. The Report contains several pages of review of the evidence that was considered in the 1977 hearings and the following findings:

> The Subcommittee finds that the award of the $23 million Teamsters Fund insurance contract to Old Security was the result of several contributing factors:
> a. the questionable and undisclosed relationship between [the consultant] and the Hauser group;
> b. a failure on the part of [the consultant] and Fund trustees and other Fund officials to assure that the contract was awarded strictly on the basis of sealed, timely bids and in strict conformity with the bid specifications and procedures;
> c. a failure on the part of the Fund's trustees to heed the recommendation by the Fund's Executive Director that the contract be awarded to the Prudential Life Insurance Company;
> d. Hauser's agreement with Allen Dorfman to permit Dorfman's Amalgamated Insurance Agency to process claims under the Old Security contract and the willingness of the Fund trustees to accept Amalgamated as the claims processor; and
> e. efforts exerted by Kleindienst [former Attorney General of the United States] on behalf of the Hauser group in return for a substantial fee.

G. Reinsurance

The Subcommittee Report notes that reinsurance is a common and legitimate practice in the insurance industry whereby the company actually issuing a policy limits its exposure by reinsuring a portion of the risk with the other party to the agreement, which receives a commensurate share of any profit. Generally, reinsurance is beneficial to both the insurance industry and the consumer: that is, by enabling insurers to spread their risks, consumers are often able to purchase insurance protection that otherwise would not be available to them. However, the Hauser group abused the reinsurance concept to the detriment of the plans with which they did business.

Farmers National entered into a reinsurance agreement known in the industry as a "fronting arrangement." Under this agreement, Old Security issued the insurance policies and then reinsured 100% of the risk into Farmers National, retaining in Old Security 2% of the premiums with Farmers National receiving 98%. In Indiana and Massachusetts, Old Security used Farmers National as its reinsuring company, but with the Teamsters Central States business it used Family Provider. The Subcommittee's findings with regard to the reinsurance activities of Hauser are stated as follows:

The Subcommittee finds that Old Security failed to conduct anything approaching an adequate background investigation of Farmers National or of Family Provider prior to entering into the reinsurance agreements. There is no indication in the record that any inquiry was made either to the Florida Department of Insurance or to the Arizona State insurance authorities to ascertain the financial status or problems or the ownership of either company. Instead, Old Security relied solely on routine financial statements filed by the companies and an evaluation of the president of Farmers National based on telephone conversations with unidentified industry contacts. Despite substantial financial risks entailed in dealing with Hauser's marginal insurance companies Old Security permitted those companies to have access and control over millions of dollars of employee plan insurance premiums without safeguards to assure that adequate reserves were maintained and that expenditures were made for proper purposes.

The Hauser group's use of reinsurance fronting arrangements to obtain the union trust fund contracts raises grave questions concerning current industry reinsurance policies and practices, the adequacy of present State laws and regulations governing the insurance industry, and the effectiveness of present Federal statutes in combatting abuses of labor-management health and welfare insurance programs.

H. Department of Labor's Enforcement of Criminal and Civil Statutes Relating to Labor Organizations and Employee Benefit Plans

As a result of the 1977 hearings in the Hauser case, the Department of Labor commenced an investigation pertaining to labor organizations and employee benefit plans. On November 29, 1977, the Subcommittee asked the General Accounting Office to determine whether the DOL's present organizational structure, procedures and manpower were sufficient to carry out its responsibilities to detect and investigate violations of the applicable labor statutes. The GAO report of September 28, 1978, and the Subcommittee's additional hearings in April 1978, disclosed serious deficiencies in the DOL's criminal and civil enforcement program.

The GAO found that most of the DOL's efforts and priorities dealt with criminal violations; that most of the DOL's effort under ERISA was devoted to activities other than enforcement of the criminal or civil provisions of ERISA; and that the DOL used its national office computerized reporting process and desk audit system to achieve voluntary compliance with the law. The GAO found additional weaknesses, including lack of coordination in investigations of criminal and civil violations under both ERISA and the Labor-Management Reporting and Disclosure Act, lack of formal procedures for notifying the Justice Department of cases under investigation, little investigative effort by area offices to follow up on reasons for deficient reports submitted by unions and plans, lack of sufficient field audit work at labor organizations and benefit plans, insufficient staff to enforce both laws, and little formal training provided in the area of office investigative and audit staffs.

The GAO recommended that:

> 1. The Secretary of Labor determine the additional resources needed to effectively enforce the criminal and civil provisions of LMRDA and ERISA and provide this information to Congress.
> 2. The Secretary direct the Labor Management Services Administration (LMSA) to (a) strengthen area office audit activity by increasing the number of on-site field audits of labor organizations and employee benefit plans and assure that consistent, high-quality audits are made; (b) improve the timeliness of area offices' investigations of cases with potential for criminal violations; (c) establish procedures to require direct, continuous coordination between criminal and civil LMRDA and ERISA investigative activities at area offices; (d) establish procedures to notify the Department of Justice of its investigative activities to avoid duplicative efforts; (e) review the training of LMSA area office field staff to ensure that the auditors and compliance officers receive the training needed to carry out their duties.

The Subcommittee Report is critical of the DOL's response to these findings, and specifically finds as follows:

1. The Subcommittee finds that the Department of Labor takes an unduly narrow view of its responsibility to detect and investigate violations of Title 18 criminal provisions relating to ERISA plans.

2. In order to have an effective criminal enforcement program, it is necessary for the Department of Labor to have a comprehensive program to detect potential violations and to make appropriate preliminary inquiries prior to referring cases to the Department of Justice for further criminal investigation. Without this initial inquiry process by the Department of Labor it is inevitable that many criminal as well as civil violations will go undetected. The proper utilization of an effective audit system by the Department of Labor, as recommended by the GAO report, will go a long way to correct serious problems in the detection of potential criminal violations.

3. The Subcommittee finds that the Department of Labor's response to the GAO report fails to evidence the needed commitment to vigorous enforcement of the criminal and civil laws relating to labor unions and employee benefit plans.

Basic Concepts of Accounting for Trustees

BY SHELDON P. LEWIS

Introduction

Question: You are a trustee of a multiemployer health and welfare or pension trust and accounting is a mystery to you. Why should you make any attempt to read and evaluate the financial statements given to you?

Answer: Because if you cannot read, understand and interpret financial statements you will not be a competent, useful and prudent trustee.

Everybody knows that accounting is a necessary evil. After all, without it how could the books be audited—a legal requirement—and how could somebody prepare accurate income tax returns and that most recent glorious invention from Washington—Form 5500?

Most importantly, good accounting is the basis for the preparation of meaningful financial statements and statistical analyses which make it possible for trustees to know where the plan is, where it has been, where it is going and why. The primary purposes of this paper are to help the trustee understand what he is getting in the form of financial information, to suggest the type of questions which should be asked of the administrator or the accountant, and perhaps to encourage trustees to require in many instances meaningful supplementary information of an accounting nature.

Except for the motion to adjourn, probably the resolution requiring the least amount of time to discuss and act upon in a trustee meeting is the notation in the minutes authorizing the annual audit of the books of account and financial statements of the trust. The audit has been a necessity of prudent fiduciaries long before federal law required it. It is necessary, not a necessary evil, and frequently the management letter covering the auditor's evaluation of internal control and other procedures which supplement the audit report turns out to be of considerable value. However, it is not the audit and ancillary services which are being discussed here. Rather, it is the *current,* analytical, unaudited interim financial statements

Mr. Lewis, a C.P.A. for 31 years, is senior partner of Lewis, Mattes, Connelly & Higgins, certified public accounting firm, and president of Benefit Administration Corporation. A contract administrator for 27 years, he has fringe benefit fund experience covering a wide variety of trades, industries and programs, both private and governmental, with beneficiaries in all western states. Mr. Lewis is a graduate of the California State University, Fresno, and received an M.B.A. degree from Harvard Business School. A member of the board of directors of the Fresno Chamber of Commerce, Mr. Lewis is a past president of the Fresno Chapter of the California C.P.A.s' Society and Fresno Estate Planning Council. He has participated as a speaker, panelist or moderator at numerous International Foundation educational meetings, and is a former member of the Board of Directors, and the Accountants and Financial Review Committees. Mr. Lewis presently serves on the Administrators Committee.

which provide to the members of the board of trustees the information they need in order to act knowledgeably, promptly and in a prudent manner.

First, it will be necessary to discuss certain definitions.

Basic Definitions

Cash Basis vs. Accrual Basis

Many interim statements are presented on the cash basis. This means simply that income and expenditures actually received and actually made during the period of time are summarized and placed in financial statement form. There is no recognition, for example, of employer contributions owing but not received by the statement date. By the same token, claims expense represents only those insurance premiums paid or claims actually paid (if self-funded) during the period. Thus, cash basis financial statements do not represent the actual position in which the trust finds itself, nor the actual operating results for the period involved. They do, however, tend to represent a reasonable estimate of operating results if one assumes that the beginning contributions receivable and ending contributions receivable are not materially different. The same is true with respect to claims expense.

Audited financial statements must, in order to comply with generally accepted accounting principles, be presented on the accrual basis. This means that all income earned and expenses incurred must be taken into consideration; thus, greater credence can be given to financial statements and information prepared by the use of the accrual method.

Basic Financial Statements

Throughout the history of accounting, semanticists have continually changed the terminology used to describe financial statements which show where you are and where you have been. Currently the statement describing where you are is called, "Statement of Funds Available for Benefits," and the statement which describes where you have been is frequently entitled, "Statement of Changes in Funds Available for Benefits." There are a whole variety of other terms, such as, "Statement of Assets and Trust Fund Balance," "Statement of Cash Receipts or Disbursements," "Balance Sheet," "Statement of Income and Expenses," ad infinitum.

Whatever the title, the pieces of paper basically must describe the financial status of the trust and its operating history for the period involved.

Supplemental Information

For interim evaluation by trustees, it is most important that the administrator provide analytical information with respect to claims paid. Such information may show the type of claims paid (medical, dental, vision, drug, etc.) by month and should convert the total in each of these claims paid categories for the period involved to the amount per participant per month. Other major accounts also may be described further, either in analytical form or in the form of descriptive footnotes to the financial statements.

Comparative Statements

Here is where the greatest value occurs. It is most important to know how the current period compares to a like period of the preceding year, in terms of dollars as well as in terms of percent of total income and amount per eligible per month. If the fund administrator or accountant does not now provide periodic information on a comparative basis, it is wholeheartedly recommended that such information be requested.

Sometimes, statements of operating results will show the most current month and the year to date. Current monthly information may be useful, but there can be wide variations in operating results in a short period. A too frequent flood of numbers and words thus can water down the most useful portions of accounting information. If the writer were to have a choice between monthly financial statements and cumulative quarterly financial statements with meaningful supplementary data on a comparative basis, there is no doubt that the choice would be the latter because of the opportunity it provides the trustees to observe trends in a most useful format.

Understanding and Using Comparative Health and Welfare Statements and Supplemental Data

Now that we have reviewed pertinent definitions and the type of accounting information which should be provided trustees on an interim basis, we will discuss the reading, understanding and use of it. In this regard, we will comment first on certain major accounts and indices of the financial health of a health and welfare trust fund.

Bank of Hours Liability

Building trades plans in particular allow participants to accumulate credits toward future eligibility. Although the actual form of such accumulation may vary, we shall in this paper use the bank of hours approach as an example. The current calculation and proper evaluation of the dollar amount of this liability is vital if trustees are to make appropriate decisions relative to the financial position of the trust.

The bank of hours liability is calculated by multiplying the person-months of future eligibility earned times the premium or equivalent claims cost per month per eligible participant. The writer believes that this amount should be calculated on a consistent basis at each statement date, and compared along with the net fund balance available for benefits to the same amounts calculated for at least the immediately preceding four quarter ends (assuming quarterly statements).

Utilization of Reserves

It is inadequate for the "Statement of Net Assets Available for Benefits" to show merely a total of funds held in banks, certificates of deposit or other forms of investment. Footnote information should describe the various types of investments with the amounts, maturity dates and interest rates explained. If longer term evidences of indebtedness are held or if equity instruments are part of the portfolio of the trust, it is important that these be valued at market value, with the unrealized gain or loss shown on the operating statement supplemented by footnote information describing all pertinent facts of these investments.

Employer Contributions

Employer contributions may be affected by seasonal factors, employment conditions and collection problems. Thus, it is necessary to evaluate the dollars of contributions for given periods with like periods of the previous year. After making these comparisons, the trustees should determine the reason for trends of increased or decreased contributions during the given period of time.

Claims Expense

The evaluation of claims expense trends is of vital importance. This is especially true in the case of self-funded plans, where claims costs have an immediate effect upon the resources of the trust. If plans are self-funded and a maintenance of benefits provision has been negotiated, trends must be identified as soon as possible so that contribution increases may be implemented in a timely manner.

A major problem is the determination of whether, in fact, a trend has occurred. The first requirement is to compare the claims expense with the average for the immediately preceding like period. If the current results are grossly in excess of those for the most recent like period, it is important to evaluate the reasons for such variation, such as the number of "shock claim" payments made during this most recent period as compared to the same type of claims paid during previous comparative periods. It is also necessary to determine if the claims lag (i.e., the length of time the administration office takes to pay claims) is materially different from the claims lag at the beginning of the period under review.

All of these questions must be asked and answered in order to determine whether or not a trend has developed, or whether the bulge in the results is due to an unusual series of factors which in all probability will not occur in the same magnitude in the immediate future.

Costs of Administration

Costs of administration include all costs except actual benefits paid to participants. It is important that these costs be broken down into the various categories of expenses incurred compared to the same categories of expenses for like periods of the immediately preceding year. Frequently, the audited statements lump all costs of administration into one category, and for purposes of evaluation these statements are relatively meaningless. Commonsense comparisons allow trustees to have the opportunity to question unusual amounts and request the administrator to explain to the trustees the details behind the amounts questioned.

Self-Funded vs. Insured Plans

Plans which are self-funded are affected instantly by major changes in claims expense patterns. Here, the comparison of like periods with those of the immediately preceding year and the immediately preceding like periods is vital in order to determine whether or not a trend has developed, as discussed above. When plans are insured, the administrator should provide as supplemental information to the financial statements the actual amount of claims paid under the insurance contract, so that the trustees will be in a position to anticipate premium renewal adjustment. Although this information is not absolute, it does, nevertheless, provide valuable information which can affect the negotiation process and allow the trustees to consider the various alternative decisions open to them.

Understanding Interim Comparative Pension Statements and Supplemental Data

Employer Contributions

Actuarial assumptions are based partly upon the continued receipt of a consistent dollar amount of employer contributions into the foreseeable future. Major changes in work patterns and the resultant changes in the dollar amount of employer contributions have potentially a material effect upon the unfunded liability of the plan and the length of time necessary to amortize this liability. Although actuaries will spread out variations in employer contributions over a number of years on an averaging basis, it is incumbent upon the trustees to make such comparisons so that they may be alert to potential trouble spots in the future.

Market Value of Pension Investments

Generally accepted accounting principles require that investments be shown on the financial statements at market value, and that the unrealized gain or loss on these investments be recognized on the "Statement of Changes in Financial Position of the Pension Trust." It is the writer's point of view that if the assets involved are high quality bonds, if they are intended to be held to maturity and if there is no reason to question the ability of the entity issuing these evidences of indebtedness to pay the principal, the trustees need not be concerned as to any short term variation in their value. However, the expression on the financial statements and footnotes of both market value and maturity amount is important to allow trustees the maximum of all meaningful information.

It is difficult for accounting statements to present the market value of certain types of other investments, such as real property. Here it is important for the statements to indicate whether or not rental income is current or delinquent, and any unusual factors relating to the evaluation of this property which would affect its carrying value or basis.

It is relatively easy and quite valuable to provide in supplemental statement form the yield to maturity of bonds, the dividend yield on equity securities, as well as the yield on other investments. Trustees can then compare the income experienced to the actuary's interest assumption.

Liability for Accrued Benefits

One of the historical problems of pension trust interim financial statements is that the funds available for benefits increase at an incredible rate and it is extremely tempting to ignore the simple fact that these funds are subject to a liability which frequently does not appear on interim financial statements: namely, the liability for accrued benefits, both of a vested and nonvested nature. The writer believes the trustees should be alerted by a written statement on the face of all financial statements presented to them that without recognizing the liability for accrued benefits the statements are only partial representations of the actual position and operating experience of that trust.

The writer's final message to trustees is simple: accounting *is not* a necessary evil. Trustees must be alert to all unusual or major variances which adequate financial information allows them to observe and to evaluate. And above all, trustees should always ask *why*!

The FASB for Non-Accountants

BY JONATHAN F. HABER

Introduction

The past year, 1980, has been a very active year regarding new pronouncements in pension plan disclosures. The Financial Accounting Standards Board (FASB) issued two related statements that establish generally accepted accounting principles for defined benefit pension plans: Statement #35 issued in March 1980, and Statement #36 (May 1980), which requires new pension disclosures in financial statements of plan sponsors. It is the purpose of this presentation to give you, who are not accountants, an overall understanding of the new statements and the new disclosures required, beginning in 1981, in financial statements of defined benefit plans.

I will begin the discussion with an overview about the Financial Accounting Standards Board—what it is and what it does.

The FASB

The FASB is the best known accounting rule-making authority in the United States and, perhaps, in the entire free world. Headquartered in Stanford, Connecticut, the FASB is the principal organization for establishing financial accounting and reporting rules.

The FASB began in 1973 as the successor to the Accounting Principles Board of the American Institute of C.P.A.s. The work of defining accounting standards is carried out by a seven member board of the FASB. The board members serve on a full-time basis for five year terms. While serving on the board, they are required to separate themselves from all other business and professional associations and affiliations. Although most board members have been C.P.A.s, it also includes non-accountants. This was done to avoid the criticism that it is concerned with the preparers of financial statements rather than the users of financial reports.

There should be no misunderstanding about the authority of the FASB pronouncements. The rules of the AICPA provide that their members (C.P.A.s) must disclose departures by their clients from FASB standards. Failure to do so is a violation of professional ethics that makes the C.P.A. liable for

A C.P.A., Mr. Haber is an audit partner of Ernst & Whinney, with responsibility for audit assignments in the Detroit office. During the past 19 years he has been responsible for the annual audits of many fringe benefit plans. Mr. Haber assisted in the preparation of the AICPA Pension Fund Audit Guide exposure draft, participated on the Ernst & Whinney task force to develop a pension plan audit manual and contributed to Accounting and Auditing for Employee Benefit Plans (Warren, Gorham & Lamont). Mr. Haber is a graduate of the School of Business Administration, University of Michigan. He is a member of the American Institute of Certified Public Accountants, the Michigan Association of Certified Public Accountants, the National Association of Accountants and the Financial Analysts Society. He has spoken at previous Foundation educational programs.

disciplinary action. Since December 1973, the FASB has issued 39 standards. Two of these standards, #35 and #36, apply to accounting and reporting of employee defined benefit pension plans.

The FASB standards on accounting and reporting comprise what is referred to as generally accepted accounting principles (GAAP).

FASB Statements #35 and #36

Background and Development

The impetus to develop GAAP for employee benefit plans was the Employee Retirement Income Security Act of 1974. ERISA is the most comprehensive piece of federal legislation in the area of pension and welfare benefit plans in the history of the United States. Its requirements have had a far-reaching impact. Virtually all existing plans had to be changed to comply with ERISA. The effects of ERISA relative to accountants and their clients have been enormous.

ERISA §103 requires the accountant to perform an annual audit of any pension plan covered by the legislation. It is the accountant's responsibility, as stated in Section 103, to perform the audit in accordance with generally accepted auditing standards, and give an opinion whether the financial statements are presented fairly in conformity with generally accepted accounting principles applied on a basis consistent with the preceding year. The major issues that had to be resolved concerning accountants were:
- Accounting and reporting objectives
- Status of actuarial liabilities
- Valuation methods for investments
- Format of financial statements.

In other words, what are generally accepted accounting principles for pension plans?

In October 1975, the FASB issued a discussion memorandum entitled, "Accounting and Reporting for Employee Benefit Plans." Public hearings on the memorandum were held in 1976. The first exposure draft of a statement was issued in April 1977.

The FASB had anticipated that a final statement would be issued in 1977; however, over 700 comment letters were received. The FASB decided not to issue a final statement until the comments could be analyzed. After reviewing the responses, the FASB worked closely with the DOL and the actuarial profession in an attempt to avoid conflicts, duplication and confusion in determining meaningful financial reporting for pension plans.

As a result, the FASB decided to revise and reissue the exposure draft in July 1979, and issued the final statement in March 1980, "Accounting and Reporting by Defined Benefit Pension Plans," known as Statement #35. Statement #35 should eliminate the diversity of ways in which pension plans have provided financial information.

Also, the FASB has a longstanding project to reconsider, "Accounting for Pension Cost by Employers," that is not scheduled for completion until 1982. But the FASB believed that certain new disclosures are necessary now, and issued Statement #36 in May 1980 entitled, "Disclosure of Pension Information," which affects contributing employers of defined benefit pension plans.

FASB Statement #36 Disclosures

Statement #36 requires employers that *sponsor* defined benefit pension plans to disclose in their financial statements:
1. The actuarial present value of vested accumulated plan benefits
2. The actuarial present value of non-vested accumulated plan benefits
3. The plan's net assets available for benefits, including any excess of the employer's accrued pension liability over the plan's contributions receivable from the employer
4. The interest assumption used in determining the actuarial present values of vested and non-vested accumulated plan benefits
5. The date when the benefit information was determined.

The Statement #36 disclosures in employer financial statements should be determined in accordance with FASB Statement #35.

Statement #36 does not change APB Opinion #8 disclosures about the:
1. Nature of the plan
2. Participants covered
3. Accounting and funding policies
4. Provision for pension cost for the period, and
5. Nature and effect of significant matters affecting comparability.

Statement #36 is effective for annual financial statements of contributing employers for fiscal years beginning after December 15, 1979. Comparative financial statements for earlier years do not have to contain the new disclosures.

Applicability of Statement #35

General Requirements. Statement #35 adopts accounting and reporting requirements that are very similar to the Department of Labor (DOL) reporting and disclosure requirements. The FASB reasoned that additional administrative costs would have been incurred if unnecessary differences existed between DOL and FASB requirements. Statement #35 also applies to many defined benefit plans not currently subject to DOL requirements.

The primary accounting provisions require the accrual basis of accounting, the fair value measurement for plan investments and the reporting of participants' accumulated benefits. The primary objective of a plan's financial statements, according to the FASB, is to provide financial information that is useful in assessing the plan's ability to pay benefits when due.

Accumulated plan benefits, according to Statement #35, are measured based on employees' earnings and service prior to the benefit valuation date. Future salary increases that lead to increased pension benefits are not included in the valuation. Expected earnings on investments are used in the selection of an interest assumption to discount the accumulated benefits to present value.

Plans Covered. Statement #35 applies to annual financial statements of all defined benefit pension plans, including multiemployer plans, where there is a promise to pay participants a determinable benefit. This also includes plans not presently subject to the provisions of ERISA—for example, state and local governmental plans and church plans, as well as unfunded plans. Defined contribution plans (profit-sharing plans), welfare benefit plans, terminated plans and plans for which a decision to terminate have been made are excluded from Statement #35.

According to the Statement #35 definition of a defined benefit pension plan, it includes a plan which is funded pursuant to a collectively bargained multiemployer agreement that specifies a fixed rate of employer contributions and a prescribed scale of benefits. It is expected that employer contributions will be periodically adjusted to enable the determinable benefits to be maintained.

Statement #35 does not require plans to prepare financial statements in conformity with its requirements or to distribute the financial statements to the participants. In other words, Statement #35 is applicable only to those plans that wish to present financial statements in conformity with GAAP.

Statement #35 is effective for plan years beginning after December 15, 1980. The Statement encourages earlier application. Accounting changes necessary to conform to the Statement are to be made retroactively and disclosed in the year of change. Upon adoption of the Statement, plans must restate financial statements of prior plan years that are presented, but comparative statements are not required.

Pension Plan Financial Statement Requirements

Purpose and Contents

The objective of pension plan financial statements is defined as "to provide financial information that is useful in assessing the plan's present and future ability to pay benefits when due." The plan's financial statements should focus on the needs of plan participants because pension plans exist primarily for their benefit. A plan's financial statements also should be useful to other users of the statements, such as individuals who advise or represent participants, and government authorities. To accomplish the objective, a pension plan's financial statement should provide information about:

1. Plan resources, and how the stewardship responsibility for them has been carried out
2. The accumulated plan benefits of participants
3. The results of transactions and events that affect the information about those resources and benefits.

The following financial information, prepared on the accrual basis of accounting, is required to meet the overall objective of pension plan financial statements:

1. Statement of net assets available for benefits
2. Statement of changes in net assets available for benefits
3. Information about the actuarial present value of accumulated plan benefits as of the benefit information date
4. Information about certain significant changes in the actuarial present value of accumulated plan benefits.

The FASB did not consider it essential to resolve the issue of the accounting nature of the accumulated plan benefit obligation: that is, whether it is a liability of the plan. Statement #35 provides several alternatives for the presentation of accumulated benefits. The information may be disclosed either:

1. As separate financial statements
2. In the footnotes to the financial statements; or
3. As part of the statement of nets assets and statement of changes in net assets.

Regardless of which of the three alternatives is chosen, the plan must present the required accumulated plan benefit information in its entirety in the same location of the financial statements.

The FASB also permits disclosure of accumulated plan benefit information determined at the beginning of the plan's reporting year as long as the statement of net assets is presented as of the same date and as of the end of the current plan year in comparative form. The statement of changes in net assets would be required for both the current and prior plan years in comparative form. For example, a calendar year plan using accumulated plan benefit information determined as of the beginning of the year would have to present the following financial information for 1980 and 1981:

- Statement of net assets available for benefits as of December 31, 1981 and 1980
- Statements of changes in net assets available for benefits for the years ending December 31, 1981 and 1980
- Information regarding the actuarial present value of accumulated plan benefits as of December 31, 1980

- Information regarding significant changes in the actuarial present value of accumulated plan benefits for the year ending December 31, 1980.

In addition, if significant amendments were made during 1981, disclosure would be required that accumulated plan benefits determined as of the beginning of the plan year do not reflect those amendments in 1981.

Other Financial Statement Disclosures

The financial statements should describe all significant accounting policies, including the methods and significant assumptions used to determine:
1. The fair value of investments and value of insurance contracts
2. The actuarial present value of accumulated plan benefits and any significant changes in the method or assumptions.

The financial statements should also disclose the following, if applicable:
1. A general description of the plan agreement (May omit, if this is provided by other sources such as a summary plan description, but must refer to the other source.)
2. A description of significant plan amendments during the year
3. A description of the priority order of participants' claims to the assets of the plan upon termination (Again, many refer to other sources of this information.)
4. The funding policy
5. The policy for purchasing contracts with insurance companies, if excluded from plan assets
6. The federal income tax status of the plan
7. The identification of individual investments that represent 5% or more of the fair value of net assets available for benefits
8. Significant real estate or other transactions between related parties.

Voluntary Disclosures

Voluntary disclosures are helpful to highlight those matters expected to be of most interest and usefulness to you users of the financial statements who are not accountants. For example, information concerning investment strategy and investment performance (i.e., rates of return on existing assets) can assist you in assessing the plan's administrative money manager's performance.

Other voluntary information that would be helpful for you includes ratios to assist you in assessing trends in the plan's ability to pay benefits when they are due. Among these could be the:

- Ratio of net assets available for benefits to accumulated benefits
- Ratio of net assets available for benefits to benefits paid during the year
- Ratio of retired participants to active participants.

These ratios' comparisons should be analyzed over a period of years to fully understand their importance.

The voluntary disclosures, if made, are in *addition* to the financial statements, and could be presented as a "financial highlights" section. The C.P.A. would not give his opinion on this section of the report.

Illustrative Pension Plan Financial Statements

Appearing in the Appendix are illustrative financial statements prepared in conformity with Statement #35. These financial statements include many of the disclosure requirements I previously discussed.

I believe the format of these financial statements, when combined with the additional DOL schedule and note requirements, conforms with the financial statement requirements of Form 5500.

When the financial statements prepared in accordance with Statement #35 are used in filings with ERISA, additional information must be presented including:
1. Disclosure of tax status. Statement #35 only requires disclosure if plan has not obtained or maintained a favorable tax exemption
2. An explanation of differences, if any, between the GAAP financial statements and items 13 and 14 of Form 5500
3. A description of *any* agreements and transactions with parties in interest
4. A schedule of assets held for investment. Statement #35 only requires disclosure of investments in excess of 5% of net assets' value
5. A schedule of loans or fixed income obligations in default
6. A schedule of transactions with parties in interest
7. A schedule of leases in default
8. A schedule of transactions or series of transactions in excess of 3% of the current value of assets.

Statement #35 only requires current year financial statements. However, under DOL guidelines, plans are required to include comparative statements of assets and liabilities. I recommend that comparative financial statements be presented as shown in the Appendix.

As I previously discussed, accumulated plan benefit information may be presented in the body of the financial statements or in a note. I prefer this information in a note, as shown in the illustrative financial statements, because, in my view, the benefit obligation of a plan may be neither more nor less than the amount of its net assets. By using a note, plans may avoid conveying the impression that accumulated plan benefits are a liability of the plan. That is the position the FASB has not yet resolved.

Following the illustrative financial statements of a multiemployer defined benefit pension plan in the Appendix I have included Reference Notes to the financial statements which explain the requirements of Statement #35.

Valuation of Pension Plan Net Assets

The Statement #35 accounting requirements are very similar to the accounting requirements of DOL's Form 5500 which eliminates duplication in pension plan accounting and reporting.

Investments in Securities

Even though Statement #35 requires the accrual basis of accounting, investment transactions may be recorded on a settlement date basis if the effect is not material to the plan's financial statements. Plan investments, except for insurance contracts, would be presented at their fair value at the date of the financial statements.

Fair value is defined as the amount that the plan could reasonably expect to receive in a current sale between a willing buyer and a willing seller. This basis was selected because, in the FASB's opinion, "This basis provides the most relevant information about the economic resources of a plan consistent with the objective of the financial statements." Fair value should be measured by quoted market prices, if they exist. If no active market exists, the plan may use the selling prices of similar investments, forecasts of expected cash flows discounted at a rate commensurate with the risk involved, or the opinions of independent experts, in estimating fair value.

Statement #35 requires that plan investments be presented in the statement of net assets in sufficient detail to permit identification of their nature. This includes identification of individual investments representing 5% or more of the net assets. This disclosure is illustrated in Note D to the sample financial statements which appear in the Appendix.

Insurance Contracts

The FASB concluded that it did not have sufficient information at this time to reach definitive conclusions as to the accounting for insurance contracts. Therefore, Statement #35 requires that the recognition of those contracts as plan assets would be the same as that required by the reporting regulations of DOL. Generally, payments to insurance companies to purchase guaranteed benefits for each participant would *not* be included as plan assets. (These are generally referred to as allocated contracts.) However, disclosure of the plan's accounting policy of excluding these contracts should be made in the notes to the financial statements.

Insurance contracts where the plan participates in the investment performance of an insurance company and the assets held by the insurance company are for the benefit of all participants (generally referred to as unallocated contracts), would be included in the statement of net assets, as plan assets. This would include deposit administration and immediate participation guarantee contracts.

The FASB interprets the DOL regulations as requiring the reporting of these assets even though it "may" be conceptually more appropriate to exclude these assets from the plan's financial statements. The FASB also has adopted the DOL requirement for the measurement of the value of those insurance contracts considered plan assets. The DOL permits investments in these insurance contracts to be valued either at fair value or at contract value, which is basically the contributions made under the contracts, plus interest at the contract rate, minus funds used to purchase retirement annuities and to pay administration expenses. The Statement does not appear to require the plan to consider termination penalties in valuing insurance contracts.

Contributions Receivable

Not only should contributions receivable as of the report date include all amounts legally or contractually required to be paid to the plan by either the employer or participants, but other sources of funding also should be accrued (e.g., state subsidies or federal grants). More importantly, contributions resulting from formal commitments are to be recorded as a plan asset.

Contributions due from contributing employers should be identified separately from those due from participants. An adequate allowance should be provided for estimated uncollectible amounts.

Operating Assets

Assets employed in the operations of the plan are to be measured at historical cost, less accumulated depreciation or amortization. This is *at variance* with DOL regulations that presently require current value be used in measuring such assets in financial data filed with the DOL. This difference in valuation should not present a problem for most plans, since operating assets normally are not significant.

Operating Liabilities

Statement #35 does not specifically address plan liabilities; however, the Statement requires that the vested benefit category of the accumulated plan benefits should include those benefits due and payable as of the year end. This means that benefit payments for the month that have not been paid should not be considered as a plan liability. This differs from the DOL requirements that unpaid benefits due may be recorded as a liability of the plan.

The FASB reasoning is that all benefit information should be presented together.

Accumulated Pension Plan Benefits

Definition

Accumulated plan benefits for accounting purposes are defined by the FASB as "those future benefit payments that are attributed, under the plan's provisions, to employees' service rendered to the benefit information date." Accumulated benefits include:

1. All benefits that are vested;
2. Additional benefits earned to date based on the employees' history of pay and service that are expected to become vested; and
3. Pro-rata allocation of benefits employees are expected to become eligible for upon satisfying minimum service provisions; for example, disability benefits to which an employee is entitled upon completion of ten years of covered service.

The definition of accumulated benefits includes both the retirement benefits and the ancillary benefits provided by the plan, such as death, disability and early retirement benefits.

Once the accumulated benefit for each participant has been determined, the actuarial value of accumulated benefits according to Statement #35 will be determined on an ongoing plan assumption—a significant departure from the initial exposure draft. Previously, the FASB proposed that accumulated benefits be measured on a termination basis. The revision in Statement #35 means that the valuation should adjust the amount of accumulated benefits to reflect both the time value of money through discounting for interest *and* the probability of payment by death, disability, withdrawal or retirement between the benefit valuation date and the expected date of payment. In selecting these assumptions, the plan should reflect the best estimate of the plan's future experience solely with respect to each individual assumption.

The Statement #35 measurement of accumulated benefits is consistent with the DOL's requirements relating to the measurement of the present value of accrued benefits as defined by Schedule B to Form 5500 under ERISA. Once the actuary selects an appropriate mortality assumption to estimate the number of monthly retirement payments to be made to each participant as well as the expected timing of the pre-retirement death benefit, the actuarial valuation of accumulated benefits becomes a mathematical exercise.

Practical Problems

Negotiated Increases. Collectively bargained plans often provide benefits at a flat amount per year of covered service. In subsequent contract negotiations, the flat amount per year is renegotiated and scheduled benefit improvements become effective periodically during the term of the new contract. This presents a practical problem in applying the requirements of Statement #35.

An example will illustrate the problem.

Assume a participant has completed 20 years of covered service as of December 31, 1980. The plan's benefit formula provides that upon retirement, each participant will receive a monthly retirement benefit determined by: benefit rate in effect x the covered years of service. On September 30, 1980, the benefit rate was renegotiated from $11.50, the rate under the old contract, to higher amounts effective on:

October 1, 1980	$13.40
October 1, 1981	$14.60
October 1, 1982	$15.45

Based on these scheduled increases, the participant's accumulated plan benefits as of the following benefit valuation dates would be:

Monthly Benefit Levels

December 31	Not Anticipating Improvements	Anticipating Improvements
1980	$268 (20 years x $13.40)	$309 (20 years x $15.45)
1981	$307 (21 years x $14.60)	$324 (21 years x $15.45)
1982	$340 (22 years x $15.45)	$340 (22 years x $15.45)

Statement #35 does not specifically discuss whether collectively bargained plans of this type should anticipate negotiated benefit improvements when the effective dates of the improvements are after the measurement date of the accumulated benefits. Including negotiated benefit increases that are not effective as of the measurement date would significantly affect the level of the actuarial value of accumulated plan benefits.

I understand that the FASB staff believes all negotiated increases such as those in my example should be reflected as of the current benefit information date. However, the American Academy of Actuaries, in their Interpretation #2 states, "Increases in the level of benefits which become effective in the future need not be recognized even though they have already been adopted." Notwithstanding the FASB staff's unofficial view, some actuaries may decide not to anticipate the effect of benefit improvements that are not effective. This position by actuaries would significantly affect the comparability of the measurement to other similar plans that include the effects of the improvements that are not effective at the measurement date.

Plan Provisions. Another problem is that for pension plans providing a retirement benefit based upon the participant's final average earnings, Statement #35 provides that neither inflation nor merit increases should be projected to determine the employee's accumulated benefit earned at the current valuation date. This reflects the FASB's view that the total increase in the employee's accumulated benefit attributed to compensation earned in a future year of service is properly considered to have been earned in that future year. Accordingly, for those pension plans *only the salary earned to date* would be used in measuring accumulated benefits; however, the *actuarial* value of accumulated plan benefits would increase in each subsequent valuation as a result of inflationary increases in salary.

Conversely, the FASB requires that future increases in the accumulated benefits caused by certain plan provisions should be anticipated in calculating accumulated benefits. This means that any automatic cost-of-living increase (COLA) in retirement benefits provided in the plan, as well as any stated increase in benefits earned after a specified number of years of service, should be included in the measurement of accumulated benefits.

Summary

I hope during my discussion I have helped you as non-accountants understand what the FASB is, what its Standard #35 on financial reporting of defined benefit pension plans means, and what you should look for when reading your pension fund statements.

The illustrative financial statements with reference notes which appear in the Appendix should also be of help to you.

Appendix

Illustrative Financial Statements
in Accordance With FASB Statement #35

Statements of Net Assets Available for Benefits
Multiemployer Defined Benefit Pension Fund

		December 31 1981	December 31 1980
(1)	**ASSETS**		
(2)	Investments, at fair value—Note D:		
	United States Government securities	$ 3,888,740	$ 1,606,214
	Corporate bonds and notes	8,815,701	8,458,329
	Common stock	11,116,668	7,106,171
	Common trust fund	2,500,000	2,450,000
	Insurance company separate account	2,450,000	2,600,000
		28,771,109	22,220,714
(3)	Unallocated insurance contract, at contract value—Note E	5,050,000	4,950,000
	Total investments	33,821,109	27,170,714
	Receivables:		
	Contributions receivable from Employer Companies	238,305	216,145
	Contributions receivable from employees	25,000	23,000
	Accrued income	136,202	171,295
	Total receivables	399,507	410,440
	Cash	232,028	136,674
	Total assets	34,452,644	27,717,828
	LIABILITIES		
	Accounts payable and accrued expenses	99,145	67,968
	Employer guarantee deposits and related interest	42,765	39,254
	Unclaimed pension benefits	1,824	1,607
		143,734	108,829
	NET ASSETS AVAILABLE FOR BENEFITS	$34,308,910	$27,608,999

See notes to financial statements

Statements of Changes in Net Assets Available for Benefits
Multiemployer Defined Benefit Pension Fund

		Year Ended December 31	
		1981	1980
	ADDITIONS		
	Investment income:		
	Interest	$ 955,100	$ 929,832
	Dividends	602,012	467,175
		1,557,112	1,397,007
(4)	Contributions:		
	Employer Companies	4,700,000	3,900,000
	Employees	209,855	144,264
		6,466,967	5,441,271
	DEDUCTIONS		
	Benefits paid directly to participants	1,395,821	1,122,467
	Administrative expenses	215,972	174,558
		1,611,793	1,297,025
		4,855,174	4,144,246
(5)	Net realized and unrealized appreciation (depreciation) in fair value of investments—Note D	1,844,737	(1,363,363)
	NET INCREASES	6,699,911	2,780,883
	Net assets available for benefits at beginning of year	27,608,999	24,828,116
	NET ASSETS AVAILABLE FOR BENEFITS AT END OF YEAR	$34,308,910	$27,608,999

See notes to financial statements

Notes to Financial Statements
Multiemployer Defined Benefit Pension Fund
December 31, 1981

NOTE A—SIGNIFICANT ACCOUNTING POLICIES

Valuation of Investments: Marketable securities are stated at fair value. Securities traded on a national securities exchange are valued at the last reported sales price on the last business day of the plan year; investments traded in the over-the-counter market and listed securities for which no sale was reported on that date are valued at the average of the last reported bid and ask prices.

For certain investments consisting of corporate bonds and notes that do not have an established fair value, the joint Board of Trustees Pension Administration Committee has established a fair value based on yields currently available on comparable securities of issuers with similar credit ratings.

The fair value of the participation units owned by the Fund in the common trust fund and separate account were based on quoted redemption value on the last business day of the Fund year.

The unallocated insurance contract is valued at contract value as estimated by the insurance company (insurer). Contract value represents contributions made under the contract, plus interest at the contract rate, less funds used to pay retirement benefits and to pay for the insurance company's administrative expenses.

Actuarial Present Value of Accumulated Plan Benefits: Accumulated plan benefits (see Note C) are those estimated future periodic payments, including lump-sum distributions, that are attributable under the Plan's provisions to services rendered by the employees to the valuation date. Accumulated plan benefits include benefits expected to be paid to (a) retired or terminated employees or their beneficiaries, and (b) present employees or their beneficiaries. Benefits for retired or terminated employees or their beneficiaries are based on employees' compensation during their last five years of credited service. The accumulated plan benefits for active employees are based on their average compensation during the five years preceding the valuation date. Benefits payable under all circumstances—retirement, death, disability, and termination of employment—are included, to the extent they are deemed attributable to employee service rendered to the valuation date.

NOTE B—DESCRIPTION OF THE PLAN

The pension fund for union workers was established pursuant to a contributory defined benefit plan that covers substantially all eligible union employees as a result of a collective bargaining agreement, to provide for retirement, death and disability benefits. Covered employees may contribute 2% of their annual compensation. Present employees' accumulated contributions are $3,420,000 and $3,147,000 as of December 31, 1981 and 1980, respectively, including interest at 8% compounded annually.

The Fund is financed entirely by employer contributions as specified in the collective bargaining agreement to provide assets sufficient to meet the benefits to be paid to participants. The Fund has met the ERISA minimum funding requirements.

(6) Should the Plan terminate at some future time, the Fund's net assets will generally not be available on a pro-rata basis to provide participants' benefits. Whether a particular participant's accumulated plan benefits will be paid depends on both the priority of those benefits and the level of benefits guaranteed by the Pension Benefit Guaranty Corporation (PBGC) at that time. Some benefits may be fully or partially provided for by the then existing assets and the PBGC's benefit guarantee, while other benefits may not be provided for at all.

(7) Information about the Plan agreement, the vesting and benefit provisions, and the PBGC's benefit guarantee is contained in the pamphlet <u>Description of Employee Benefits.</u> Copies of this pamphlet are available from the Pension Administrator.

NOTE C—ACCUMULATED PLAN BENEFITS

(8) An actuary from the AAA Company estimates the actuarial present value of accumulated plan benefits, which is the amount that results from applying actuarial assumptions to adjust the accumulated plan benefits earned by the participants to reflect the time value of money (through discounts for interest) and the probability of payment (by means of decrements such as for death, disability, withdrawal or retirement) between the valuation date and the expected date of payment.

(9) The accumulated plan benefit information as of the end of each plan year is as follows:

	December 31	
	1981	1980
Actuarial present value of accumulated plan benefits:		
Vested benefits:		
(10) Participants currently receiving payments	$ 4,960,414	$ 4,108,207
Other participants	19,790,421	19,542,036
	24,750,835	23,650,243
Non-vested benefits	7,351,800	6,925,400
	$32,102,635	$30,575,643

(11) The actuarial present value of accumulated plan benefits was $28,816,421 as of December 31, 1979. There were no factors significantly affecting the comparability of accumulated plan benefits during the two years ended December 31, 1981.

Significant assumptions underlying the actuarial computations are:

Assumed rate of return on investments	8%, including a reduction of 0.2% to reflect anticipated administrative expenses associated with providing benefits
Retirement	At normal retirement age (65)

These actuarial assumptions are based on the presumption that the Plan will continue. Were the Plan to terminate, different actuarial assumptions and other factors might be applicable in determining the actuarial present value of accumulated plan benefits.

NOTE D—INVESTMENTS

The Fund's investments are held by a bank-administered trust fund, except for its separate account and unallocated insurance contract with The Insurance Company (see Note E). During 1981 and 1980 the Fund's investments (including investments bought, sold, as well as held during the year) appreciated (depreciated) in fair value by $1,844,737 and ($1,363,363), as follows:

	Net Appreciation (Depreciation) in Fair Value During Year	Fair Value at End of Year
Year ended December 31, 1981:		
Fair value as determined by quoted market price:		
United States Government securities	$ 97,000	$ 3,888,740
Corporate bonds and notes	12,413	7,814,826
Common stock	1,341,174	11,116,668
Common trust fund	275,000	2,500,000
Insurance company separate account	236,150	2,450,000
	1,961,737	27,770,234
Fair value estimated by the Pension Administration Committee:		
Corporate bonds and notes	(117,000)	1,000,875
	$1,844,737	$28,771,109
Year ended December 31, 1980:		
Fair value as determined by quoted market price:		
United States Government securities	$ 28,000	$ 1,606,214
Corporate bonds and notes	207,586	7,475,000
Common stock	(1,535,000)	7,106,171
Common trust fund	(35,000)	2,450,000
Insurance company separate account	(41,949)	2,600,000
	(1,376,363)	21,237,385
Fair value estimated by the Pension Administration Committee:		
Corporate bonds and notes	13,000	983,329
	$(1,363,363)	$22,220,714

The fair value of individual investments that represent 5% or more of the Fund's net assets are as follows:

	December 31 1981	1980
ABC Company, 8% debenture due 1995 ($2,500,000 face amount)	$1,950,000	$2,000,000
XYZ Company common stock (30,000 shares)	1,875,000	1,925,000
Example Corporation common stock (25,000 shares in 1981 and 24,500 shares in 1980)	2,125,000	1,860,000
Another Company common stock (15,000 shares)	1,775,000	1,498,000
First City Bank Fixed-Income Common Trust Fund (27,000 in 1981 and 26,000 units in 1980)	2,500,000	2,450,000
The Insurance Company Pooled Separate Account No. 1 (24,000 in 1981 and 25,000 units in 1980)	2,450,000	2,600,000

NOTE E—CONTRACT WITH INSURANCE COMPANY

In 1979, the Fund entered into an insurance contract with The Insurance Company under which the Fund deposits a minimum of $100,000 a year. The Insurer maintains the Fund's deposits in an account to which it adds interest at a rate of 7% per annum. The interest rate is guaranteed through 1983 but is subject to change for each succeeding five-year period. When changed, the new rate applies only to funds deposited from the date of change. At the direction of the Fund's administrator, a portion of the account can be used to purchase units in The Insurance Company Pooled Separate Account. The Separate Account's portfolio is primarily invested in high-grade corporate bonds and notes. The Insurer does not guarantee the monies invested in the Separate Account as to principal or income. Benefit payments to participants or their beneficiaries are made directly by the Insurer from the funds accumulated under the contract.

(12) NOTE F—INCOME TAX STATUS

The Internal Revenue Service has ruled (January 15, 1978) that the Fund qualifies under Section 401(a) of the Internal Revenue Code (IRC) and is, therefore, not subject to tax under present income tax law. Once qualified, the Fund is required to operate in conformity with the IRC to maintain its qualifications. The Joint Board of Trustees is not aware of any course of action or series of events that have occurred that might adversely affect the Fund's qualified status.

(13) NOTE G—TRANSACTIONS WITH PARTIES IN INTEREST

Fees paid during 1981 for legal, accounting and other services rendered by parties in interest were based on customary and reasonable rates for such services.

Reference Notes to Illustrative Financial Statements
Multiemployer Defined Benefit Pension Fund

GENERAL: —FASB Statement No. 35 is effective for all defined benefit pension plans for years beginning after December 15, 1980 (i.e., Calendar 1981). Earlier application is encouraged.

—A multiemployer plan which specifies a fixed rate of employer contributions may be a defined benefit plan subject to the Statement, if a scale of benefits is prescribed and it is expected that the level of contributions will be periodically adjusted to maintain such stated benefits.

—FASB Statement No. 35 recommends supplementing the financial statements with voluntary disclosures of matters deemed important, including a summary of financial information.

—The format of financial statements prepared in accordance with Statement No. 35 need not conform to item 13 of Form 5500, however significant differences which are not readily apparent, in the presentation of net assets, should be explained in a note to the financial statements.

1. The financial statements for 1980 are not required by Statement No. 35 because the accumulated plan benefit information is presented at the end of the year. However, under DOL guidelines, plans are required to include comparative statements of assets and liabilities.

   When the accumulated plan benefit information is presented as of the end of the year, it is recommended that plans present comparative financial statements for years subsequent to the initial adoption of the Statement. This will facilitate including the financial statements in the filing under ERISA, as well as assisting users in assessing trends.

2. Investments, except for insurance contracts, must be presented at their fair value (or current market value). Because it also applies to bonds, mortgages and other fixed-term investments, the fair value requirement is particularly significant. Even if the plan has the ability and intention to hold such investments to maturity, it must establish a fair value as of the reporting date.

   Disclosure of historical cost is permitted, but not required.

3. The Statement requires that insurance contracts be treated in accordance with the instructions to Form 5500. Under these instructions, allocated insurance contracts are not included in plan assets and unallocated insurance contracts are included in plan assets.

   Under an allocated contract, the insurance company provides specified benefits to designated participants, without future premiums from the plan.

   In addition to excluding the asset, plans should exclude the benefits provided by the allocated contract from the actuarial value of accumulated plan benefits.

   The current instructions to Form 5500 permit the plan to value unallocated contracts at either contract value or fair value when the underlying investments are commingled with the insurance company's general investment assets. Because determining contract value is generally easier, we expect many plans to use this method of valuation. Plans should disclose the method used.

4. Contributions should be stated separately according to their source. Non-cash contributions should be stated separately, recorded at fair value, and described either parenthetically or in a note. Refunds of employee contributions may be netted against contributions received, or included in benefits paid.

5. Several alternatives for presenting appreciation or depreciation of investments are acceptable. I have presented it as the last item, while Statement No. 35 presents it as the first item under investment income. Item 14 of Form 5500 segregates "realized" from "unrealized," and includes realized gains or losses separately in the income section and unrealized appreciation or depreciation as the last item. If realized gains and losses are presented separately, the method of determining cost (e.g., specific identification or average) should be disclosed.

6. The Statement requires a brief description of the priority order of participants' claims to the assets of the Fund upon plan termination (first, employee contributions; second, vested benefits of retired participants; etc.) and benefits guaranteed by the PBGC. If material providing this information is otherwise published and made available to participants, the descriptions required by this paragraph may be omitted provided that (1) reference to such other source is made and (2) disclosure similar to the wording in the illustrative footnote (taken from the Statement) is made.

7. The Statement requires a brief, general description of the plan agreement, including—but not limited to—vesting and benefit provisions. Plans may omit this information if it is provided in other published sources, such as a summary plan description, but they must then refer to the other source.

8. Even though not required by the Statement, the FASB's illustrative financial statements identify the actuarial firm. Considering the extensive participation of the plan's actuary, I believe this disclosure is desirable.

9. Accumulated plan benefit information may be disclosed on the face of the statements, in separate statements, or in the notes to the financial statements. I prefer for plans to present this information in a note.

    Information should be included about the actuarial present value of accumulated plan benefits, measured either as of the beginning or end of the plan year, and significant changes therein. If measured as of the beginning of the year, statements of net assets available for benefits and changes in net assets should be presented for the prior year as well as the current year.

    The Board encourages plans to use end of the current year benefit information. To help plans prepare timely year-end benefit information, plans may use interim service-related data projected to year-end in estimating benefit information, provided the results are substantially the same as using year-end data.

10. The "participants currently receiving payments" category includes benefits payable as of the benefit information date (e.g., retirement payments due for the last month of the plan's year that have not been at year-end).

    Benefit payments due and unpaid may be recorded as a plan liability under DOL but should be reflected in the actuarial value of accumulated plan benefits under Statement No. 35.

    For most plans, the effects of these differences will not be material to the financial statements. However, when the effects are material, the GAAP financial statements would differ from those reported in Items 13 and 14 of Form 5500. This would require a description of the reasons for the difference in a note to the GAAP financial statements submitted with the Form.

11. The Statement provides two alternatives for disclosing changes in accumulated plan benefits: a reconciliation format that accounts for the changes between the two valuation dates, or a narrative format. Under either presentation style, the minimum required disclosures should include the significant effects of (1) plan amendments that retroactively increase accumulated benefits earned, (2) changes in the nature of the plan that affect comparability (e.g., plan spin-off or merger) and (3) changes in actuarial assumptions. Disclosure of the actuarial value of accumulated plan benefits as of the preceding benefit valuation date also is required under either presentation style.

Other recurring changes may be, but are not required to be, separately disclosed, including increases caused by the passage of time, such as interest accretion and additional benefits accrued, and decreases caused by payment of benefits.

12. This note would be required under GAAP only when the plan has not obtained or maintained a favorable letter of determination from the IRS. I have included this disclosure in this illustration because disclosure of the plan's current tax status is required in financial statements submitted to DOL.

    A letter of determination is based on facts submitted as of a specific date and, therefore, does not protect a plan if it is not operated in conformity with the statutory and IRS administrative rules. Furthermore, a new determination letter generally should be requested when the plan is materially amended.

13. This note is required under ERISA in the notes to the financial statements even though the Plan may be exempt from reporting the transactions on the schedule of transactions involving parties in interest. Under GAAP, similar disclosure in the notes to the financial statements only is required when such transactions are related party transactions as defined by Statement on Auditing Standards No. 6, "Related Party Transactions."

Understanding Unfunded Liabilities

BY LAWRENCE N. BADER

Introduction

In this presentation, what we'll be talking about is not a passive acceptance of unfunded liabilities, but some ways to understand and to actively manage them. We'll begin with a look at some history to see what the fuss is all about. How have we come to be so concerned with unfunded liabilities? How does the financial community look at them, and why is that view critical to trustees and contributing employers? Then we'll explore just what is meant by unfunded liability. It's not a single unique measure of a plan's obligation but, as we'll see, at least five different measures, each with its own method of calculation and its own significance. We'll then discuss how to look into the future to see where your unfunded liabilities may be heading. Finally, and most important, we'll consider what can be done to control unfunded liabilities.

A New Importance

Fifteen years ago, unfunded liabilities were one of the more obscure topics in the pension field; even a specialized meeting like this might have ignored them. The numbers weren't particularly frightening, and therefore not of much interest to the media. The occasional interesting exception, like the notorious Studebaker closing, only showed that companies could in fact walk away from their "liabilities."

Times have changed. Pension funding obligations have skyrocketed, due to a familiar litany of causes:

1. Benefit improvements—
   - Benefits at age 65 have become richer in relation to pay
   - Early retirement reductions have been reduced or eliminated
   - Disability and survivors' pensions have been introduced and improved
   - Vesting now benefits many more people
2. The erratic investment climate—
   - Unsatisfactory returns and wild swings in the stock market
   - No safe harbor in the bond market

Mr. Bader is a vice president and actuary with William M. Mercer, Inc., in New York City. He is manager of the New York consulting group and serves as an actuarial consultant to a number of large corporate and multiemployer plans. An enrolled actuary, Mr. Bader is a fellow of the Society of Actuaries and a member of the American Academy of Actuaries, New York Actuaries Club and the International Association of Consulting Actuaries. He has published numerous articles on pension plan design and funding. He received his B.A. degree, magna cum laude, Phi Beta Kappa, from Yale University and attended Gonville and Caius College at Cambridge University, England.

3. Inflation creating the need for benefit increases just to keep up, not really improve
4. Decline of employment in certain industries or geographical areas (not so much increasing unfunded liabilities as spreading them over declining numbers of active plan members).

Accompanying this growth in unfunded liabilities has been a growth in the attention paid to them. Since 1968, single-employer plan sponsors have been required by Accounting Principles Opinion #8 to show their unfunded vested liability in a footnote to the corporate annual report. This did not directly affect multiemployer plans, but it did start raising consciousness. The reporting requirements have been expanded further by Financial Accounting Standards #35 and #36, and the accounting issues remain under study by the FASB. Meanwhile, the footnotes have been showing larger and larger liabilities, and financial analysts have been wondering whether they really belonged in a footnote—should they, in fact, be right up in the balance sheet itself? For example, in 1978, Moody's published a pension funding survey reviewing how companies' balance sheets would be affected by including pension liabilities—not the first such survey, but a significant event to which we'll return shortly.

For evidence that concern with unfunded liabilities has reached the darkest and most distant corners of the land, the last bastions of ignorance and apathy, we can note that even Congress became aware of the danger that the unfunded liabilities of several multiemployer plans posed to the solvency of the Pension Benefit Guaranty Corporation. Congress became sufficiently aroused to legislate four consecutive postponements of the applicable ERISA provisions before finally passing the Multiemployer Pension Plan Amendments Act of 1980.

This brings us to a final reason for the attention now focused on unfunded liabilities: ERISA and the Multiemployer Act have changed their nature. An unfunded liability is no longer something you can walk away from, or eliminate by adjusting benefits. Because of legal obligations retroactively imposed by these acts, unfunded liabilities have now acquired an inevitability which has changed the way they are viewed by the financial community and by contributing employers.

The question alluded to before is a pressing one: Are these unfunded liabilities true accounting liabilities which belong right on the balance sheet, not just in the footnotes? Current accounting rules say no, but many investors think otherwise. In increasing numbers, they are working with adjusted balance sheets which reflect pension liabilities. You can see this in the Moody's Bond Survey that I mentioned, or in a number of other studies by financial analysts. These studies recompute the ratios that security analysts use, e.g., debt-to-equity ratios, after adding the unfunded pension liability to the balance sheet. So for practical purposes it may not much matter whether the FASB decides to put pension liabilities on the "official" balance sheet sooner, or later, or not at all. They are there already in the minds of many influential users of the balance sheet. A company's cost of financing, and indeed its access to financing, is therefore affected by any unfunded liability it has or shares, a condition which must be recognized in running pension plans. And, while FASB #36 says that an employer need not report his share of multiemployer plan liabilities which are not determinable, we can expect the omission of such liabilities from employer financial statements to gradually end.

Types of Unfunded Liabilities

Despite all the attention and concern lavished on unfunded liabilities, they remain poorly understood—partly because of the peculiar terminology we use, partly because pension obligations are in fact elusive things to measure. Are you talking about the long or short range? Continuation in the plan, withdrawal, or termination? We'll now look at five different concepts gathered loosely under the title "unfunded liability" and detailed on the chart immediately following this text.

Unfunded Liability

The first type I have called simply the *unfunded liability*; it goes under a variety of alternative names, including *unfunded accrued liability, unfunded frozen initial liability* and *unfunded supplemental present value*. At any rate, it's the liability the actuary uses in setting the long range funding schedule for the plan. It therefore may include provision for benefits not yet earned, and it depends on the funding method used by the actuary. There are many different funding methods in use. To understand why, an analogy to life insurance may be helpful. A person seeking $10,000 of life insurance can find several ways to pay for it:

- He may buy a renewable term insurance policy. The premium would start out low, but would rise each time the policy is renewed.
- He may instead choose whole life insurance. The premium would be much higher at the start, but would remain level for his lifetime.

Each of these and many other policies provides the desired coverage with a different cost incidence, and the buyer must decide which fits his financial situation best.

A similar choice confronts a plan sponsor in financing pension benefits. The funding method governs the rate of asset build-up by setting a funding target each year—the amount of assets the plan *should* have on hand. The unfunded liability, then, is the amount by which the actual assets fall short of that asset target. If a plan uses a cost method with low costs in the early years, like the term insurance concept, it will have a low asset target today and a low unfunded liability. If it uses a level cost method, it will have a higher current asset target and a higher unfunded liability. So the unfunded liability depends only partly on the health of the plan, and partly on the target set under the plan's actuarial cost method. In fact, there is one cost method—the aggregate method—under which the target is automatically equal to the assets, so the unfunded liability is always zero.

What, then, is the significance of this unfunded liability? Only that the actuary uses it to determine costs. The past service cost, representing ten to 40 year funding of the unfunded liability, is added to the cost for future service—the normal cost—and that gives the necessary annual contributions for sound long range funding. The unfunded liability is based on assumptions chosen for the long range—a 6% interest assumption, for example, and some artificial asset valuation method designed to remove short term fluctuations. The unfunded liability is generally of no use in comparing plans or assessing liabilities upon withdrawal from or termination of the plan.

Unfunded Value of Accumulated Benefits

Our next unfunded liability is the unfunded value of accumulated benefits, a creation of Financial Accounting Standards #35 and #36. Actually, those standards ask separately for the assets and the value of accumulated benefits, but people will naturally be putting the two together and looking at the unfunded amount. How is that unfunded amount different from the unfunded liability we just discussed?

Though we're talking about the same pool of assets, the target against which we're measuring to figure the shortfall is different. For the unfunded value of accumulated benefits, the target is the sum of money needed today to provide all benefits earned to date. That might have nothing to do with the target set by the actuary for the long range funding of the plan, which is used to determine the unfunded liability. The actuary might well set as the funding target the amount needed to provide all accumulated benefits; but he might instead set some higher level to provide a cushion against future cost increases as the plan membership ages.

Another difference between the unfunded liability and the unfunded value of accumulated benefits is in the assumptions. The unfunded liability is based on a long range interest assumption, reflecting the rates at which money received 20 years from now may be invested. A typical choice is 6%. The unfunded value of accumulated benefits, though, measures the plan's current status. It answers the question, "How much more money would you have to invest *today* to fully fund accumulated benefits, keeping in mind that the money could be invested at 10+%?" So it might well be based on 10% interest, while the long range funding, and the unfunded liability, are based on 6%.

Because of the focus on today's values, the unfunded value of accumulated benefits is based on the market value of assets. For long range funding, on the other hand, the actuary may try to avoid having costs reflect short term fluctuations in market value by using an asset valuation method which smooths out such fluctuations.

Unfunded Value of Vested Benefits

The unfunded value of vested benefits is a simple modification of the unfunded value of accumulated benefits. When FAS #35 and #36 call for a presentation of the value of accumulated benefits, they specify a breakdown: benefits to retirees, other vested benefits, and non-vested benefits. To develop the unfunded value of vested benefits, merely remove the non-vested benefits before comparing the figure with assets. That is, consider the benefits already in pay status, plus the vested benefits earned by members who have not yet retired. Ignore those benefits for which members can qualify only by continuing to work until completing ten years (or whatever vesting requirement the plan imposes).

The unfunded value of vested benefits is, by the way, the original unfunded liability disclosure called for by Accounting Opinion #8, before its 1980 modification by FAS #36.

Withdrawal Liability

The unfunded value of vested benefits leads readily to the withdrawal liability. Withdrawal liability is the amount owed under the Multiemployer Act to a multiemployer plan by a contributing employer who withdraws from that plan. While the law offers a plan several methods for computing withdrawal liability, the basic idea behind all the methods is the same: the total unfunded value of vested benefits for the plan is determined and then allocated in some fashion among the contributing employers. For this calculation of unfunded vested benefits, the plan may use either its own assumptions or assumptions developed for this purpose by the PBGC. Upon withdrawal from the plan, an employer's share of the unfunded vested benefits becomes his withdrawal liability. It is paid off over a period of up to 20 years, at an annual rate based on his highest three year average rate of contributions during the preceding ten years.

Termination Liability

Our fifth and final unfunded liability is the termination liability. This is the amount an employer owes upon plan termination. As defined in the law, the employer's obligation on termination is simply to go on contributing at his highest rate of the preceding five years, until the plan is fully funded. A slightly different view is to regard the plan as having an overall termination liability. That is like the unfunded value of vested benefits, except that certain benefit decreases, down to PBGC-guaranteed levels, may take place on plan termination. The PBGC does not guarantee any benefits arising from plan amendments less than five years old, and it guarantees only a limited percentage of the older benefits. So benefit cutbacks on termination can reduce liabilities substantially.

There are a few other adjustments on termination: actuarial assumptions may be different, and liabilities of previously withdrawn employers may be adjusted. The adjusted total then is spread among the remaining employers in proportion to their highest contribution rates during the preceding five years. They pay it off through annual payments at those rates until the reduced benefits are fully funded.

Summary

Here, then, is our family of unfunded liabilities:
- The *unfunded liability*, related to the long range funding target set by the actuary in determining contribution rates
- The *unfunded value of accumulated benefits*, showing in the annual report to participants and the government the current security of benefits earned to date
- The *unfunded value of vested benefits*, similar to the unfunded value of accumulated benefits, but excluding those which are nonvested
- The *withdrawal liability*, each employer's allocated share of the unfunded value of vested benefits, which remains an obligation upon his withdrawal from the fund
- The *termination liability*, each employer's share of the unfunded value of vested benefits, reduced to reflect benefits only up to PBGC-guaranteed levels. This remains an obligation upon plan termination.

It is not critical for a trustee to be able to distinguish readily among these terms, but he must be able to ask the right questions in a discussion about "the" unfunded liability. What benefits are included? What actuarial assumptions are being used, and why? What value of assets? Is the employer continuing in the plan, withdrawing from it, or is it terminating? Get that part right, and the rest of the discussion will be much more useful.

Forecasting Unfunded Liabilities

Let's turn now to the forecasting of unfunded liabilities. Once the plan is underway, all the unfunded liabilities change similarly through the years; let's consider the unfunded value of vested benefits. One year's liability changes to the next year's in the following manner:
- *Plus,* the value of additional vested benefits earned by increasing age or service
- *Plus,* increases due to plan amendments
- *Plus (or minus),* increases due to actuarial losses (or gains)—for instance, if the fund earns more than the interest assumption, the unfunded liability drops; if retirees live longer than expected, the liability rises
- *Plus,* interest—if $100,000 is needed to fully fund the plan this year on a 6% interest assumption, next year $106,000 will be needed to catch up to where the plan would have been if it had been funded this year
- *Minus,* contributions to the fund
- *Plus (or minus),* change in size of membership—this doesn't necessarily affect the unfunded liability, but does affect the contribution base over which it is spread. A loss of nonvested members, for example, does not change the unfunded vested liability directly, but can strain the plan by increasing the per employee charge for unfunded benefits.
- *Plus (or minus),* the effect of mergers or withdrawals—the funding status of any new groups brought into the plan, and the impact of departures.

Knowing these factors, you can sit down with your actuary, discuss some questions about where the plan might be going in terms of future membership and benefit changes, and give him enough information to prepare a rough sketch of how the unfunded liabilities might be expected to change over the next few years.

There are also some formal forecasting techniques, commonly used by large corporations but rare among multiemployer plans. These techniques use detailed assumptions about future plan provisions, changes in membership and actuarial experience to give comprehensive five to ten year forecasts of the costs and unfunded liabilities of the plans. These forecasts are expensive to prepare and quite time-consuming because of the assumptions which must be agreed upon, including not only the traditional actuarial assumptions but economic forecasts, hiring patterns, result of future negotiations, business failures and so forth. Nonetheless, they are useful educational and planning tools, and I expect we'll be seeing their use grow among multiemployer plans in the future.

Controlling Unfunded Liabilities

We've covered what unfunded liabilities are and how to prepare either a back-of-the-envelope guess or a sophisticated forecast of where they might be going. We come now to the big question: What can be done to control them? We'll go once again through the factors affecting unfunded liabilities, this time considering which of those factors are at least partially under the control of the trustees.

Plan Amendments and Benefit Increases

The additional benefits earned by members' getting older and accruing additional service are not really controllable, but the additional benefits created by plan amendments can be controlled. A plan can give a large increase in credits for future service only, or a smaller increase for both past and future service. The two increases might carry the same cost, but only the past service increase adds to unfunded liabilities. Of course, there are good reasons to give increases in past service benefits, despite the accompanying unfunded liabilities, and plans certainly should not rule out such increases. What is important is that trustees considering a benefit increase must look not only at its annual cost, as they've been doing all along; they also must pay attention to the resulting unfunded liability, as they've likely *not* been doing. If the benefit increase is justified, it should be adopted, but only after considering the effect that the additional unfunded liability will have on current and prospective contributing employers.

Changes in Actuarial Assumptions

Changes in actuarial assumptions are somewhat controllable by the trustees. According to ERISA, the actuary controls the assumptions, but most actuaries have encountered clients like the one who told me, "I know you get to choose the assumptions but don't forget that I get to choose the actuary." But I'm not talking now about twisting your actuary's arm or finding another actuary whose assumptions you like better. What I mean is that changes in assumptions can be the direct result of how the plan is managed. For example, suppose a plan's interest assumption is 5%, and an erratic performance history in the stock market makes a higher rate inappropriate. A well thought-out change in investment strategy, perhaps to insurance company guaranteed interest contracts or the new immunized funds which some banks are offering, would ensure an improved return and justify a change in the interest assumption. The policy change must not be just cosmetic but must represent a serious, documented shift in direction; otherwise, the increase in the interest rate will merely result in underfunding, permit withdrawing employers to escape with less than their true liability and saddle remaining employers with future actuarial losses.

Plan Experience—Actuarial Gains and Losses

This brings us to the next controllable item, actuarial gains and losses. The assumptions, what we think will happen, are somewhat controllable by the trustees; can they also control the plan experience itself, what actually does happen? In some areas, clearly not. For example, the trustees can adopt an early retirement provision, but they cannot control how many members will take advantage of it, or how long they will live. But there *are* some things they can control.

Disability retirements should be properly reviewed, both as to initial qualification and continuing eligibility.

Contribution audits are, of course, a long recognized responsibility of a well-run fund, to make sure that the plan collects everything it's entitled to.

Benefit Payment Audits. Trustees cannot control how long pensioners will live. But they *can* see that benefit checks don't go on being paid after the demise of the intended recipients, by conducting periodic audits to see that the payees of the pension checks are, in fact, alive.

Investment Performance. This is a very complicated area, but here are three simple rules which trustees ought to follow:
- First, establish objectives, which will form the basis of agreement with the investment manager.
- Second, measure progress against the objectives.
- Third, demand results.

Setting objectives sounds easy, but is surprisingly rarely done. Many funds skip this task and instead follow the common practice of letting their investment manager set his own objectives, unilaterally and *after* the event.

Most trustees have seen this one: A new money manager makes an impressive presentation and is hired. A year later, he delivers his performance report. If he earned 10% and the Dow is up 15%, he talks about meeting the interest assumption. If he *lost* 10% and the Dow is *down* 15%, he talks about beating the Dow. If he's down and everything else is up, he talks about the economy. If a trustee is impolite enough to ask about his performance, he says that can't really be measured over less than five years. So in fairness to the fund, as well as to the money manager, trustees should set objectives, short term or long, put them in writing to the investment manager, and learn how he intends to meet them.

The second rule is to measure progress. If the objectives and the methods for meeting them have been well defined, this should be a straightforward, orderly process. Trustees should look at the numbers they said they would look at, see whether the manager did what he said he would do when they last met, and whether it worked the way they thought it would work. Then they should jointly write out the plans for the next few months—and there is the agenda for the next review.

Third and last, "Demand results." Trustees must take charge, seek explanations, make decisions and act—just like any other management function.

Contributions to the Fund

The next of our controllable elements is contributions to the fund. The progress of the unfunded liability depends importantly on the number of years over which the contributions are set to fund those liabilities—from ten years on the most rapid tax deductible schedule to 30 or 40 years under the minimum funding requirements of ERISA and the Multiemployer Act.

I feel strongly that the funding periods used by most plans, with the approval of their actuaries and of ERISA, are too long. Thirty years is satisfactory for the unfunded liability at the start of a plan. Setting up a plan incurs a debt which might be likened to the mortgage on a home, and an extended period for payment seems reasonable. The routine increases to keep up with inflation, though, happen every one to three years. Taking 30 years to fund debts which are incurred every three years is like getting 30 year payment terms on a car purchase: a person able to get such terms would eventually find himself paying for ten cars at once—plus all of that interest.

This just sounds like common sense, so it's natural to ask why 30 year funding is so commonly used. The problem is that most corporate pension plans are pay-related, while multiemployer plans generally are not. So in a corporate plan, benefits rise automatically as pay increases; the actuarial funding schedule anticipates the increases and starts funding them as soon as the plan is adopted. In a typical multiemployer plan, benefit increases occur only through plan amendment, and IRS rules forbid prefunding future plan amendments on a tax deductible basis. This means that multiemployer plans are always trying to catch up, starting to fund new plan amendments before they've made a dent in earlier ones. It's surprising how far behind they get.

Take a simple example of a plan amended each year to increase benefits for active members by 7%, a rather modest rate these days. If the plan uses 30 year funding, its funding ratio will settle at just 32%; that is, the active members' benefits will never be better than one-third funded (assuming also a 7% interest assumption and a stationary population). That's because, even after 30 years, the plan will still be working off 29 separate benefit increases, and as fast as it gets rid of one, another comes along. In this example, pensioners would be fully funded; but if the plan gives pensioner increases, that too can come undone. Remember, this is less than one-third funding, forever. So trustees should not take comfort from the fact that they are within the law and within the standards used for corporate plans, which are prefunding future benefit increases. They should have their actuary do a simple projection, and they may find themselves thinking about more rapid funding, at least for future plan changes.

Membership, Mergers and Withdrawals

Our last two controllable elements are changes in the size of the membership, and mergers and withdrawals. They are obviously connected, so we'll consider them together. The economic benefits of increasing membership are obvious: lessening the dependence of the fund on the fortunes of a few employers, increasing the economies of operation and spreading the unfunded liability charges over a larger group. The possible negatives are equally apparent, if the new groups are in poorer shape than the current plan, or if the new employers may fail or withdraw soon, saddling the plan with additional liabilities. The Multiemployer Act makes mergers fairly easy—from a legal viewpoint, that is. Its withdrawal liability provisions, however, should mean much greater attention to the actuarial aspects. Employers on each side of a merger previously were concerned only with their contribution rates. Now they will be more concerned with the unfunded liabilities on the other side: their size, how they will be allocated and perhaps how they will be collected.

The result of this concern is that trustees will need to think rather hard about their plans' *general policy* toward mergers, not merely handle each possible merger as it comes. As discussed earlier, the Multiemployer Act offers several ways for a plan to allocate withdrawal liability among employers. A plan can use rules which are quite attractive to new employers, freeing them from existing unfunded liabilities; or it can use rules under which new employers rapidly inherit the liabilities which predate their participation. The plan can make things attractive or unattractive for small employers compared to large ones, or for temporary employers compared to long term contributors. The decisions will be difficult, because you can only favor one class of employers at the expense of another. But trustees should decide how much they want to attract various types of employers; they should not let the Multiemployer Act's automatic rules apply unless they have decided they're the right ones.

Defined Contribution Plans: A New Attraction

A final thought on controlling unfunded liabilities is something I think will be an important result of the Multiemployer Act, something not intended by the framers of that act: a growth in multiemployer defined contribution plans. Under a true defined contribution plan, employers contribute on some fixed basis, say 50¢ per hour for each employee, just as under a regular defined benefit plan. But the cents contributed with respect to a particular member are all credited to an individual account for him. His account shares the fund's overall investment return. When he leaves or retires, he gets whatever is in his account (to the extent vested), either in a lump sum or, if the plan so provides, some optional form of payment. This is a plan which participants can readily understand and appreciate, since each sees his own account build up from year to year, rather than hearing repeated promises of some distant reward.

A major disadvantage of this type of plan is that it does little for people close to retirement, since there is not enough time for their accounts to build up. This disadvantage, though, can be overcome with creative plan design; for example, by grading up contribution rates for older employees. The big advantage, especially in the wake of the Multiemployer Act, is that there is no unfunded liability. An employer's obligation is to contribute the contract rate. The employee's benefit is whatever results, and there is no promise beyond that to create additional liability. When the contract is over, so is the employer's obligation to contribute. If this sounds simple and familiar, maybe it's because this funding obligation is about what existed before ERISA.

I do not foresee plans of this type replacing the current defined benefit plans, but I do expect to see them coming in as supplements, in lieu of part or all of the increases that otherwise would occur in the existing plans. I believe a union operating such a plan would have an extremely attractive vehicle for recruiting new contributing employers who are frightened, duly or unduly, by ERISA and the Multiemployer Act. This plan design has been increasingly common since ERISA among single-employer plans, where it has been clear that the employer could not walk away from his unfunded liability. Now that the Multiemployer Act has placed employers in the same position regarding multiemployer plans, a similar trend may develop here.

Conclusion

This completes our actuarial look at unfunded liabilities—why people are concerned about them, what they mean and, most important, how they can be controlled. The task is not simple. Only through a great deal of study, thought, questioning, labor-management cooperation and very hard choices can the growth in pension liabilities be controlled and orderly. The alternative to a planned and orderly growth is all too clear.

Table

Unfunded Liabilities for Multiemployer Plans

	Unfunded Liability	Unfunded Value of Accumulated Benefits	Unfunded Value of Vested Benefits	Withdrawal Liability	Termination Liability
What is it?	Costs assigned to past years under the actuarial cost method used by the plan, less the plan assets.	Value of benefits attributable to past service, less the plan assets.	Value of vested benefits attributable to past service, less the plan assets.	Employer's share of unfunded value of vested benefits, subject to various adjustments.	Employer's share of unfunded value of vested benefits guaranteed by PBGC.
Where is this information available? —Financial Statements of Plan*	Form 5500 Schedule B, Line 8(a)-8(b). (No disclosure under certain actuarial methods.)	Form 5500 Schedule B, Line 6(d) + 6(e)-6(c).	Form 5500 Schedule B, Line 6(d)-6(c).	Not published.	Not published.
What is its significance?	The annual contribution includes the amount required to fund the unfunded liability over ten to 40 years. No significance on withdrawal or termination.	A measure of the plan's current ability to pay benefits already earned.	A measure of the plan's current ability to pay benefits already earned and vested. Used to determine if plan is in "reorganization," giving it the right to reduce benefits and altering the funding requirements.	This amount is the continuing obligation of an employer who withdraws from a plan and must be paid in annual installments over as much as 20 years.	This amount is the continuing obligation of an employer after plan termination and must be paid until the liability is funded.

How is it calculated?					
—Benefits recognized	Some portion of all benefits.	Benefits based on service to date, whether or not vested.	Vested benefits.	Vested benefits.	PBGC-insured vested benefits.
—Actuarial Cost Method	Six methods recognized under ERISA.	Unit credit method.	Unit credit method.	Unit credit method.	Unit credit method.
—Actuarial Assumptions	Actuary's best estimate of anticipated long-range experience. A typical interest assumption is 6%.	Similar to unfunded liability, but interest assumption must reflect rate expected on assets held by fund during period for which benefit payment is deferred. Insurance company annuity rates are acceptable.		Plan may use its own rates or rates developed by PBGC for this purpose.	PBGC rates.
—Valuation of Assets	Any reasonable method reflecting market value, usually adjusted to reduce fluctuations. A typical method is five year average of market value.	Market value.	Market value.	Market value.	Market value.
—Other notes				Allocated among employers paying at highest rate of last five years. native formulas in MPPAA. Annual payment based on highest three consecutive plan years in last ten.	Each employer continues paying at highest rate of last five years.

*With respect to the financial statements of the contributing company, as distinct from those of the plan, companies are required to disclose the first three unfunded liabilities in SEC filings or a footnote to the annual report, with respect to single employer plans which they sponsor. They are not required to disclose their share of unfunded liabilities in multiemployer plans to which they contribute if the amounts are not determinable.

Reporting and Disclosure of Unfunded Liabilities

BY ROBERT A. SEMENZA

THE PREVIOUS ARTICLE discussed liabilities from the actuarial point of view. I am going to talk about them from the accountant's point of view. Basically, I will review them from two vantage points, namely their impact on plan financial statements and their effect on the financial statements of the contributing employer or plan sponsor.

Who Sets the Standards?

Let's start off by discussing some of the different professional bodies to which I will be referring. What professional groups are interested in unfunded liabilities, and what role do they play in this area? First of all, there is a group called the Accounting Principles Board, referred to as the APB. The APB was composed of members of the American Institute of Certified Public Accountants and, until 1973, established generally accepted accounting principles (GAAP). Many believed this was somewhat self-serving, especially Congress, and in 1973 a separate, independent group was established in its place, known as the Financial Accounting Standards Board—the FASB. The FASB is made up of seven full-time members from within and outside of the accounting profession. The board members who came from accounting firms had to sever their relationships with their firms so as to be completely independent. The Financial Accounting Standards Board now sets accounting principles and, if the principles used to prepare financial statements differ from what the FASB has promulgated, the accountant is required to disclose these differences.

There is also a body referred to as Audboard; although the FASB sets accounting principles, the American Institute of Certified Public Accountants still sets generally accepted auditing standards (GAAS); these standards are issued by the auditing standards board of the AICPA, or Audboard.

The government is, of course, also interested in employee benefit plans. There is the Securities and

Mr. Semenza, an audit partner in the New York office of Main Hurdman & Cranstoun, has developed considerable expertise over the years in the reporting and auditing requirements for employee benefit plans. He is chairman of his firm's ERISA Committee and Employee Benefit Plans Committee, and serves on several committees and task forces of the American Institute of Certified Public Accountants relating to employee benefit plans. Mr. Semenza has written and addressed a variety of audiences on various aspects of employee benefit plans, and gave expert testimony before Joint Congressional Committees proposing ERISA legislation. He also serves on his firm's committee on not-for-profit organizations and has primary responsibility for several major publicly held clients and for a diversified Fortune 500 company. In addition to his experience in the public accounting sector, he served for several years as a financial executive for a publicly held international engineering firm. Mr. Semenza is a member of the American Institute of Certified Public Accountants and the National Association of Accountants, and served as national director of the latter organization.

Exchange Commission, and I do not think I have to explain what the SEC is. Basically, they establish the financial reporting standards for public companies. And last but not least, there is the Department of Labor and the Internal Revenue Service, and they establish reporting and other requirements under ERISA.

Employee Benefit Plan Issues

Let's briefly review the roles these various groups have played in the employee benefit field. The APB attempted to establish accounting principles for pension plans back in 1973, right before it was disbanded. They issued an exposure draft of a proposed audit guide which discussed what the financial statements of a plan should contain and how they should be audited. There was a lot of controversy over this draft, mainly because of the liability issue. No one could quite agree upon whether or not there was a liability, whose liability it was, how it should be calculated and how it should be audited. As a result, the draft was never finalized, thus written accounting principles and auditing standards were not set.

In the meantime, the government came along in 1974 and passed ERISA, and ERISA was quite clear. It required that plans had to file certain financial statements with the government; plans with over 100 participants would have to be examined by an independent accountant who would have to follow generally accepted auditing standards (GAAS) and report upon whether the financial statements were in accordance with generally accepted accounting principles (GAAP). As we all now know, the problem was that there *were* no GAAS and GAAP. No published GAAS or GAAP, that is. As a result, the Department of Labor issued a series of exemptions in the regulations which permitted plans to deviate from generally accepted accounting principles in preparing financial statements—as long as they disclosed the differences—and allowed administrators to eliminate certain auditing standards which auditors would follow. These limited exemptions are still in use by many plans.

FAS #35

The FASB still recognized, of course, that they had to get about the business of setting accounting principles for plans so, following their usual due process, they issued a very lengthy discussion memorandum in October 1975 on the pros and cons of different issues related to employee benefit plans. This was followed by a two day public hearing and, in April 1977, by a first exposure draft. The FASB issues exposure drafts and then, based on the comments received, will either issue a final standard, modified where necessary, or withdraw the proposal. The board received over 700 letters of comment on the exposure draft on pension plans. That's more letters than they have ever received on any other issue, including major topics such as lease accounting and foreign currency translations. Many of the responses came from the actuarial profession, and the actuaries and many other respondents were not pleased with that first exposure draft, primarily because of the manner in which plan "liabilities" were to be calculated.

The FASB restudied the proposal and issued a revised exposure draft in July 1978 and finally, in March 1980, issued a final standard, Financial Accounting Standard #35. Although FAS #35 only relates to defined benefit pension plans, it does apply to multiemployer plans. The FAS #35 discusses the fact that:

> Even though a plan may be funded pursuant to periodic agreements that specify a fixed rate of employer contributions (for example, a collectively bargained multiemployer plan), such a plan may nevertheless be a defined benefit pension plan as that term is used in this Statement. For example, if the plan prescribes a scale of benefits and experience indicates or it is expected that employer contributions are or will be periodically adjusted to enable such stated benefits to be maintained, this statement considers such a plan to be a defined benefit pension plan.

Briefly, the standard requires that investments be reported in the financial statements, in most cases, at fair value; that is, their current market value or some other measure of fair value. The statements are to be presented on the accrual basis, as compared to only reporting cash transactions. FAS #35 is effective for plan years beginning after December 15, 1980.

With respect to plan "liabilities," FAS #35 requires that financial statements issued for a defined benefit pension plan include information concerning accumulated benefits at the determination date and information about certain changes in these benefits. The information must be based on an annual evaluation and, although there is provision in the standard for a triennial evaluation, that would generally only apply to small, stable plans. The accumulated benefit information is not going to be based on the funding method followed by plans, and will differ from the "unfunded past service liabilities" developed under these funding methods. It is a different measure of liability which is to be based on the benefits earned to date.

In essence, what the FASB requires is a set of financial statements where you can compare, at a point in time, the fair value of the investments with the benefits that have accumulated under the plan. It generally does not consider any events that may take place after the determination date. For example, the accumulated benefits cannot take into account future salary increases. Although this does not impact multiemployer plans, many single employer plans base their pensions on a retiree's pay status during the last few years of employment. Because of this, the accumulated benefits reported generally will be significantly less than the unfunded liability under which plans are being funded and which companies have disclosed in the past. Many financial analysts, accountants and other groups feel this will be misleading, as companies may now be reporting much lower "liabilities." I will discuss this a little further on.

Accumulated benefits must also be based on certain assumptions: an interest assumption and assumptions with respect to death and employees leaving before retirement (termination and withdrawal). The interest assumption is to be based upon the assumed income to be earned on the investment portfolio of the plan, and this rate will probably be higher than the rate actuaries are using for funding purposes. A higher rate will reduce the amount of the "liability."

The FASB did not really decide the liability issue. Although they required plans to include information on accumulated benefits in financial statements, they did not say whether or not it is a liability. The information has to be included someplace in the financial statements; it can either be on the financial statements or in a footnote. The liability issue is being left to another study being conducted by the FASB, which I will mention later.

ERISA requires, as I stated earlier, that certain large plans file periodic financial statements with the government, prepared in accordance with GAAP unless filed under certain limited exemptions. Therefore, financial statements filed for plan years beginning after December 15, 1980, have to comply with FAS #35 and include this accumulated benefit information if the statements are to comply with GAAP.

That is where accounting principles stand as far as the plans are concerned. Incidentally, this standard only applies to defined benefit plans and does not apply to health and welfare plans and defined contribution plans, which are being considered separately.

Employer Disclosures: FAS #36

Now, let's turn to the liability issue and accounting principles required from an employer's standpoint. You will recall I mentioned that the APB had set accounting principles until 1973; they issued APB Opinion #8 in 1966, which in essence said how much an employer had to record as pension costs and what types of disclosures they had to make in their financial statements. The FASB merely carried over and adopted APB #8. When FAS #35 was issued, however, FASB promptly followed with FAS #36. FAS #35 relates to the *plan* financial statements, while FAS #36 relates to the *employer's* financial statements and changed the disclosure requirements of APB #8. Under APB #8, employers had to disclose "the excess of the actuarially computed value of vested benefits over the assets of the pension plan." FAS #36 requires the employer, effective in 1980, to disclose the accumulated benefit data calculated in accordance with FAS #35, including both the vested and the nonvested portions. The fair value of the plan's net assets available to meet these benefits and the assumed rate of return (that is, the interest rate used to calculate the benefits) also must be disclosed.

As I mentioned, although these standards only apply to defined benefit pension plans, most multiemployer plans are in essence defined benefit plans (although for years you may have thought they were defined contribution plans). Briefly, in a defined contribution plan, the contributor has no liability after he makes a contribution to the plan. The participant receives whatever is in his account when he leaves or retires. In any event, FAS #36 did specifically discuss the unique problems of multiemployer plans. It recognizes that employers may not be in a position to determine what their portion of the plan's accumulated benefits is. Therefore, unless the information is determinable, unless it is determined and provided by the plan, the employers would not have to disclose it as long as they disclose their situation in the report.

Withdrawal Liability

Now, what about the impact of the Multiemployer Pension Plan Amendments Act of 1980, which was enacted after FAS #36 was issued? This established another liability, "withdrawal liability"—employers will now have to share in any unfunded vested benefits if they withdraw from the plan. The question is, although FAS #36 stated that the accumulated benefit information would not have to be disclosed where it was not determinable, the withdrawal liability is, of course, determinable. The accounting profession is studying this problem right now, and my guess is that this liability will have to be disclosed when it is provided by the plans. It is a question of time. I do not think that the withdrawal liability is going to be determinable, however, until the PBGC issues regulations, since many plans probably will opt to follow the PBGC assumptions rather than use their own. There is also a question as to whether or not the plans will have to provide this information unless a particular employer is actually withdrawing from the plan. While I think ultimately this liability is going to have to be disclosed in the financial statements of the sponsor, in the meantime I think employers are only going to be required to disclose that they have this contingent liability and that the amount is not presently determinable.

As far as actually recording this liability—I have only been talking about disclosing it, up to this point—I do not think there is going to be any requirement to record this as a liability unless it appears likely that there will be a withdrawal or plan termination. There is precedent in this area. The FASB did issue an interpretation of APB #8 when ERISA was first enacted: ERISA established a termination liability for single employer plans of up to 30% of a sponsor's net worth, and the FASB interpretation said in essence that this liability did not have to be recorded on the financial statements of an employer unless there is convincing evidence that termination is eminent.

Other Issues

As I mentioned, the FASB has undertaken a project to restudy APB #8—this has not been examined in depth since ERISA and, of course, there is the Multiemployer Act of 1980 to consider. The board has issued a summary of some of the major issues that they see on the horizon, and one was the multiemployer plan problem. They mentioned that there are uncertainties as to whether or not these are defined benefit or defined contribution plans and whether an employer has a liability for any unfunded defined benefits. I think that this issue has pretty much been resolved by the Multiemployer Pension Plan Amendments Act of 1980 and, I think, although I am not a lawyer, by the courts. There was a case in California a few years ago, the *Connolly* case, where it was held that a plan which contributors thought was a defined contribution plan was deemed by the courts to be a defined benefit plan basically because individual participant accounts had not been set up to meet specific requirements of the law. My understanding is that the case went to the U.S. Supreme Court but the Supreme Court refused to hear it—I believe they refused because they wanted to wait for some further lower court decisions on the issue. I personally think the issue of defined benefit versus defined contribution plans has pretty well been resolved.

Now, what about the SEC? I mentioned that the accounting requirements had been to disclose the unfunded vested portion of the liability, which now has been changed by FAS #36. The SEC had an additional disclosure requirement: in addition to the vested benefit disclosure, they also required public companies to disclose the unfunded past service liabilities. This is the liability calculated by actuaries for funding purposes. The FASB anticipated that when FAS #35 and #36 came out, the SEC would remove the requirement to disclose the unfunded past service liability. In speeches made by the staff of the SEC, however, there was mention about the SEC continuing to require this information. (The SEC has since agreed to delete this requirement.)

Questions Remain

There is a lot of interest in the unfunded past service liability; it gets a lot of press. Every year in *Business Week* and a number of other financial publications, there is a table which shows the vested and unvested portion of this liability for some of the major corporations in America. These liabilities showed some very significant increases in 1979, and a number of the financial analysts and investors are concerned about this. We may not have heard the last of these liabilities.

As I mentioned, there are seven members of the FASB and it takes four members in order to pass a standard. Three of the seven board members dissented to the issuance of FAS #35 because of the very issue we are discussing—accumulated benefits or unfunded liabilities. The three members did not feel that it was meaningful to make the comparison of accumulated benefits to net assets. They also felt that accumulated benefit data were actuarial information which should be shown as supplemental information rather than as part of the basic financial statements.

This leads us to another problem—the auditing of these plans. As I mentioned, generally accepted auditing standards had never been issued for employee benefit plans. I am a member of the American Institute of C.P.A.s' committee that has been in the process of writing an audit guide for employee benefit plans since 1974. The committee issued an exposure draft of a guide in July 1980, and will be reviewing the responses. There are a number of key issues but, again, one of the major issues is this area of accumulated benefits and the relative responsibility of the accountant and the actuary for these data. The guide also deals with a number of other issues with which you should be concerned, including the audit of the payroll records of employers contributing to multi-employer plans. The guide deals not only with defined benefit plans but also with defined contribution and health and welfare plans.

I think you can now see that this question of "unfunded liabilities" has been debated within the accounting profession for years, and basically there are only two issues: Whose liability is it? and, how do you calculate it? I think that ERISA and Congress and the courts are deciding some of these issues and, hopefully, the FASB will resolve the remaining issues when it completes its project on the review of APB #8. I am not too optimistic, personally. I really do not think there is one answer as to whose liability it is and how it should be calculated. Maybe the answer is just more disclosure.

Administrative Costs of Pension Plans

BY ROBERT D. COOPER, Ph.D.

The Study

Our administrative cost figures are based on information collected from collectively bargained, jointly managed, multiemployer defined benefit plans—and defined benefit plans only. We selected 505 plans originally, and we received some information from 466 of those, or about 92%. We received complete financial information from over 380, or about 75% of the plans that we originally selected for study. Therefore, the response rate to our study was very good; most of the information was received through voluntary submissions from the plans themselves. The plans ranged in size from 17 to 550,000 participants and from two to 15,000 contributing employers, and they are representative of the Taft-Hartley universe.

Operations and Benefits of Taft-Hartley Trusts

Plan Size

Not only did we collect information on costs, we also collected a great deal of information on how the plans are actually operated. The general characteristics of Taft-Hartley plans are essentially unknown because the government has not seen fit to systematically collect and report those data. However, we estimate there are approximately 1,825 Taft-Hartley multiemployer pension trusts. They cover about 8.5 million workers and about 10 million total participants, including beneficiaries and retirees. The plans account for $45-50 billion in assets in the United States. The average plan, based on the median, has about 880 participants, and has about 80 contributing employers. Based on the 176,000 pension plans in the United States, the average Taft-Hartley trust is a very large plan. Plans average about $900,000 a year in total contributions. One-third of the active participants in these plans are fully vested and the ratio of actives to retirees is about 4.5:1, as compared to the Social Security figure of 3:1.

Figure 1 shows the distribution of plans by their size. We use these size categories because these categories were used by the PBGC in their study of

Mr. Cooper is currently staff research director for the International Foundation of Employee Benefit Plans. He received his B.A. (1967) from Butler University and his Ph.D. (1970) from Kent State University. He has also completed post-doctoral work at the Institute for Social Research, University of Michigan, and is a candidate in the Certified Employee Benefit Specialist program. Prior to joining the Foundation in 1977, Mr. Cooper held positions as a college professor and as a marketing representative. He has been engaged by various groups as an advisor and consultant in the areas of program evaluation and market research. Mr. Cooper is co-author of A Study of Current Collection Practices, Procedures and Problems *(1978);* Technical Report: A Study of Taft-Hartley Health and Welfare Trust Fund Operations Cost *(1979); and* Pension Fund Operations and Expenses *(1980), all published by the International Foundation.*

multiemployer funds. Figure 2 lists the industries that the funds represent. As you can see, the construction trades dominate multiemployer defined benefit plans; 55% of these plans are in the construction trades.

The funds are experiencing dramatic growth. Annual contributions and total assets increased over 30%. Operations costs increased by 23% in that same period, while the number of plan participants only increased about 1-1½%. These figures can be compared with the cost of living. Based on the Consumer Price Index, the cost of living during that same two year period increased by 15%.

Figure 1

NUMBER OF PLAN PARTICIPANTS

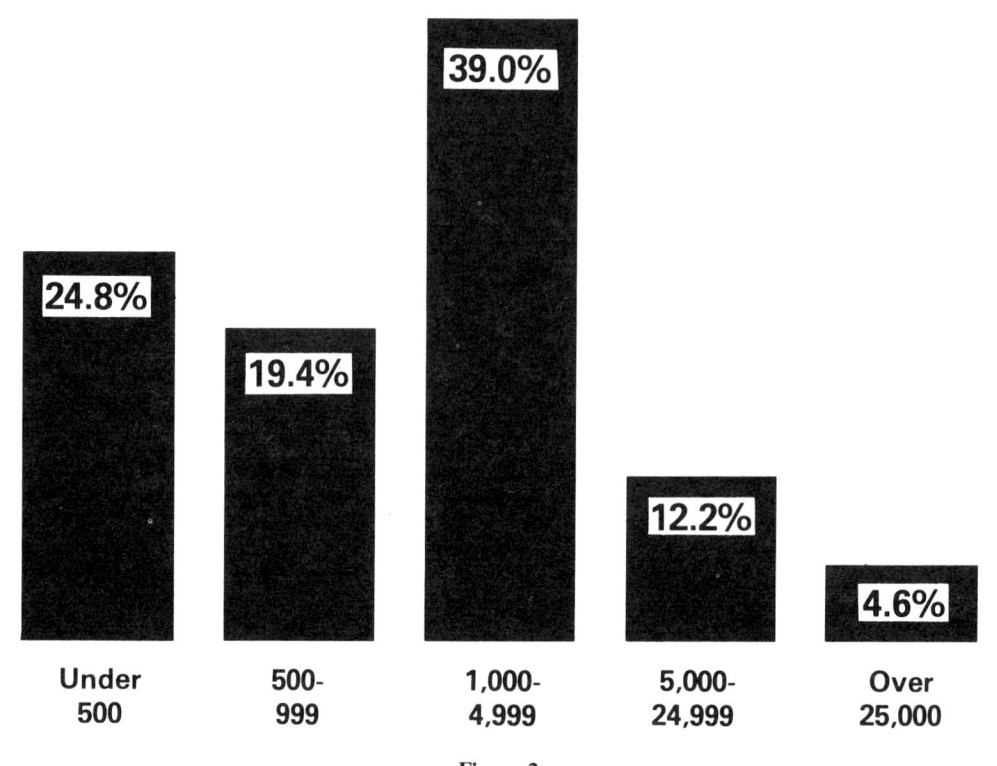

Under 500	500-999	1,000-4,999	5,000-24,999	Over 25,000
24.8%	19.4%	39.0%	12.2%	4.6%

Figure 2

TYPE OF INDUSTRY

Percentage of Funds

%	Industry
7.2%	Other
15.1%	Manufacturing and Meat Processing
3.9%	Service
8.1%	Retail & Printing
7.3%	Transportation
3.1%	Culinary
55.3%	Construction

Assets and Investment Practices

We collected substantial information on investment practices for the annual reporting year 1978. These are the best data available. In 1978, assets increased 12% over 1977. We can attribute 6.1% of that to an increase on investments. The remainder—5.8-5.9% of the increase in that year—came from increased employer contributions. Half of the funds had investment committees helping to direct investment policy. When an investment committee was used, the following were considered the most important matters the investment committee handled: (1) setting investment policy; (2) monitoring the investment manager; and (3) making buy and sell decisions.

Seventy percent (70%) of the funds used at least one outside manager, and 56% used an inside manager. However, a number of funds (about 15%) used no investment manager whatsoever. Plans with less than $5 million in assets actually averaged less than one investment manager per fund, but those with over $250 million in assets averaged about 5.5 investment managers. Only 25% of the investment managers are compensated through a salary or fee. The rest are paid as a percentage of the portfolio or on trading commissions on the buy and sell transactions. Less than half of the funds use services of an outside firm to evaluate their investment manager's performance. We found that somewhat surprising. As a matter of fact, only 25% of the funds that have less than $1 million in assets, but 75% of those that have more than $50 million in assets, use an outside firm to do the evaluation.

Benefits

The average amount of total benefits paid by pension trusts in our study was $312,000 a year. Plans averaged 100 retirees, which means that each retiree was receiving approximately $3,000 a year. Vesting provisions for benefits varied, but almost two-thirds (62%) of them have ten year cliff vesting, and only 3.3% have 100% immediate vesting. Over 90% of the plans have both an age and service requirement for normal retirement. Three-quarters of those plans use age 65, 13% use age 62, and only 5% use age 60. (Six out of ten, or 60%, use a ten year service requirement as well.) Eleven percent use a 15 year graded vesting schedule and 6% use a five year, 100% vesting schedule. There was an early retirement provision in 95% of the plans we studied. The most common age for early retirement is 55, and the most common number of years of service required is ten.

The overwhelming majority—94%—of the plans provide for disability retirement. Forty-four percent provide long term disability benefits and 97% provide death benefits. Plans are relatively homogeneous, then, except for the long term disability provision.

Collection of Contributions

Collection of contributions was another area of administration about which we collected a great deal of information. The median amount of employer contributions was $890,000 a year per fund. Only 17 of 380 plans are contributory. Taken together, the total annual contributions to Taft-Hartley funds per year is $8-10 billion.

That amount of money, with only a 1% delinquency rate, would lead to lost employer contributions in excess of $100 million annually. In fact, our study shows that the average delinquency rate is about 1.5% And, almost 80% of the funds had known delinquent employers in the 1978 plan year.

Administration

We also collected data on general administration. We found that 55% of the funds use a third-party administrative manager—a contract administrator, if you will. For those plans that tend to allocate expenses because they are cooperatively administered with a health and welfare plan, supplementary unemployment benefit plan or apprenticeship plan, an average of 40% of the total cost of operation is allocated to the pension fund as its expense portion.

Operations Cost

Definition

I want to talk now about the most important part of our study—operations cost. First, let me define it for you. It includes a number of items: the cost of the administrator, office expense, mailing expense and the rent, etc. It also includes all costs for advisors, except the investment manager; i.e., the attorney, the actuary, the consultants, the accountants, etc. Finally, any premium taxes, any administrative charge, etc., paid to an insurance company will be included in calculating total operations cost. It is a more inclusive concept than pure administrative costs. We simply don't know what pure administrative costs are.

In early deliberations of the Foundation's Ad Hoc Administrative Cost Study Committee, we tried to outline what went into administrative costs. This task proved to be overwhelming. Some have argued that administrative costs do not include

Figure 3

SAMPLE FORM

Form **5500** Department of the Treasury Internal Revenue Service / Department of Labor Pension and Welfare Benefit Programs / Pension Benefit Guaranty Corporation	**Annual Return/Report of Employee Benefit Plan (With 100 or more participants)** This form is required to be filed under sections 104 and 4065 of the Employee Retirement Income Security Act of 1974 and sections 6057(b) and 6058(a) of the Internal Revenue Code, referred to as the Code.	**1978** This Form is Open to Public Inspection
For the calendar plan year 1978 or fiscal plan year beginning	, 1978 and ending	, 19

File original of this form, including schedules and attachments, completed in ink or type.

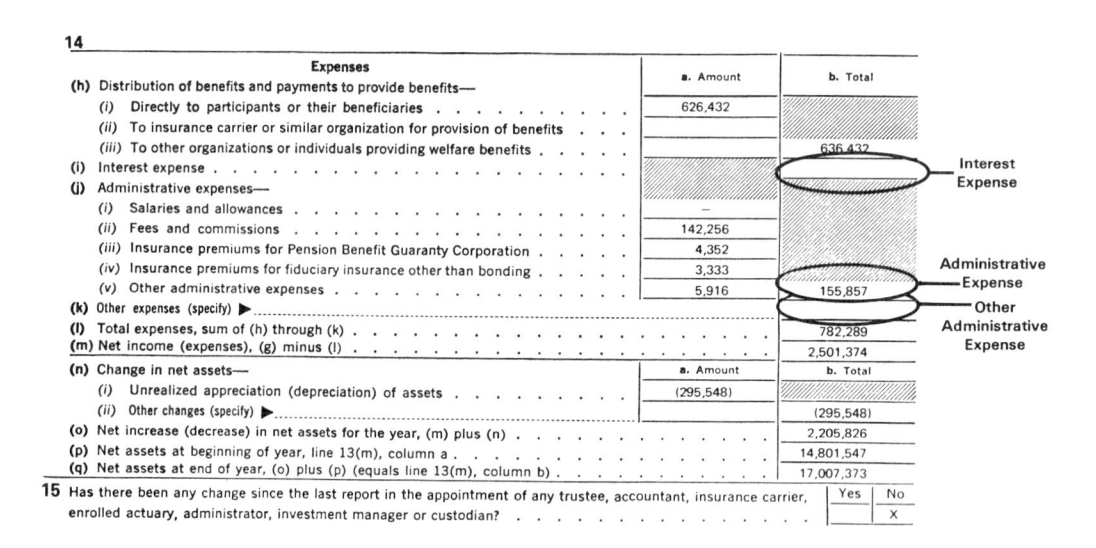

14

Expenses	a. Amount	b. Total
(h) Distribution of benefits and payments to provide benefits—		
(i) Directly to participants or their beneficiaries	626,432	
(ii) To insurance carrier or similar organization for provision of benefits		
(iii) To other organizations or individuals providing welfare benefits		636,432
(i) Interest expense		— Interest Expense
(j) Administrative expenses—		
(i) Salaries and allowances	—	
(ii) Fees and commissions	142,256	
(iii) Insurance premiums for Pension Benefit Guaranty Corporation	4,352	
(iv) Insurance premiums for fiduciary insurance other than bonding	3,333	— Administrative Expense
(v) Other administrative expenses	5,916	155,857 — Other Administrative Expense
(k) Other expenses (specify) ▶		
(l) Total expenses, sum of (h) through (k)		782,289
(m) Net income (expenses), (g) minus (l)		2,501,374
(n) Change in net assets—	a. Amount	b. Total
(i) Unrealized appreciation (depreciation) of assets	(295,548)	
(ii) Other changes (specify) ▶		(295,548)
(o) Net increase (decrease) in net assets for the year, (m) plus (n)		2,205,826
(p) Net assets at beginning of year, line 13(m), column a		14,801,547
(q) Net assets at end of year, (o) plus (p) (equals line 13(m), column b)		17,007,373

15 Has there been any change since the last report in the appointment of any trustee, accountant, insurance carrier, enrolled actuary, administrator, investment manager or custodian? Yes | No X

Figure 4

SAMPLE FORM

12 Did any person who rendered services to the plan receive, directly or indirectly, compensation from the plan in the plan year? ☐ Yes ☐ No
If "Yes," furnish the following information:

a. Name	b. Official plan position	c. Relationship to employer, employee organization or person known to be a party-in-interest	d. Gross salary or allowances paid by plan	e. Fees and commissions paid by plan	f. Nature of service code (see Instructions)
ABC International	Contract Adm.	None		79,246	13
John Doe & Assoc.	Consultant	None		4,500	11
Smith, Smythe & Joan's	Legal Counsel	None		6,370	22
ACE CPAs	Auditor	None		2,714	10
XYZ National Bank	Invest. Agent	None		41,650	21 — Investment Management Expense
John Q. Public Co.	Consultant	None		2,000	17

legal fees, for instance. However, if the attorney is out collecting fund income, then is not the attorney, or that portion of the attorney's expense, actually administrative expense? To avoid those problems, we lump all expenses together and talk about total operations expense. Operations cost, then, is the amount of money that is disbursed each year for non-benefit expense and, therefore, is unavailable for providing benefits.

We did not include investment managers' expense, and I guess I should explain why. The reason is this: Not all funds report investment management expense. One reason is, they don't know what it is. The asset pile is netted out; they are told how much they had at the beginning of the year and how much they had at the end of the year, and the actual fees paid are not necessarily known by the fund. When those fees were, in fact, reported as a separate disbursement, then we analyzed that separately. The basis for our information on operations cost is item 14 and Schedule A, Form 5500. The information regarding investment managers' fees is taken from item 12. A lot of funds simply do not report investment management fees in item 12.

Sample Plan Computations

Figure 3 is an example of an item 14 from Form 5500. It indicates all the expense items, monies paid out directly to the participants, etc. The items that are important here are three in number: the interest expense item; the total administrative expense item, which is made up of a combination of those sub-items to the left, including salaries and allowances, fees and commissions, insurance premiums paid to the PBGC, fiduciary liability insurance and other administrative expenses; and, finally, the all-encompassing "other expense (specify)."

Figure 4 shows item 12 of Form 5500. We use this item to determine if investment managers' fees are included in item 14. Investment managers' fees are coded 21 on Form 5500, item 12. In the case of our sample, we have an item marked code 21 which is for slightly over $41,000. Figure 5 is a sample insurance attachment (item 6, Schedule A, Form 5500). From this schedule, we take two items: administrative charge and "other charges." The "other charges" item and the administrative charge item from Schedule A, the three charges from item 14, Form 5500, are combined. Because some funds report their income on investments net of investment managers' fees, subtract investment managers' expense from this total for those funds in which that expense is reported in item 12. (For those not reporting investment managers' fees, do not make this subtraction.) When it is reported in item 12, subtract that amount from the total.

Figure 5

SAMPLE FORM

Funds that report in different ways can be compared following this procedure.

Going through the sample items from Figures 3-5 and completing our calculation (*see* Appendix A), there is nothing under interest expense; there is $155,000 for administrative expenses, and there is nothing under other expense on item 14. In addition, there is nothing under either of the two categories for the insurance attachment. The total of administrative expenses, then, is $155,857. From that figure, we subtract the investment managers' fee reported separately in item 12. Total operations cost (the actual operations cost as we define it) for this fund is $114,207.

Comparisons: Actual vs. Estimated Costs

Now we are going to make some assumptions about the fund. We are going to assume that this plan has 7,200 participants, $1.96 million in annual employer contributions, and assets of $14.8 million. We need these figures to enter the tables to find the average expenses for plans of a similar size. The Table is an example taken from the published *Summary Report*. This is one of 21 similar tables, and is very complex. I'm going to simplify the materials and use the overall average in this report. The numbers in Appendix B, A-G, are based on the overall averages. The published *Summary Report* is more accurate. The *Technical Report* is also more accurate, because it describes the original regression formulas.

In our example, we assumed annual employer contributions of $1.96 million. So we would refer to Appendix B, item A, under the column headed $1.2-3.5 million, and we find the average operations cost is $111,200. That's what we would expect operations costs to be for a plan that size measured by annual employer contributions. Additionally, we assumed $14.8 million in net assets, so we refer to the table at the asset range of $10-50 million. The range is large because there aren't that many funds of this size, and we have to lump the

Table

Total Operations Cost

Annual Employer Contributions

Number of Active Participants		Under $200,000	$200,100-$500,000	$501,100-$1,200,000	$1,200,100-$3,500,000	$3,500,100-$10,000,000	Over $10,000,000
250 and under	Lowest	4,300	3,300				
	Average	9,650	21,400		[b]	[b]	[b]
	Highest	43,300	123,300	31,300[a] 53,100			
251 to 500	Lowest	4,300	11,300	180,300			
	Average	16,500	32,500			[b]	[b]
	Highest	37,300	87,300		45,300[a] 97,500		
501 to 1,500	Lowest	12,300	15,300	30,300	398,300		
	Average	27,900	39,400	77,200		[b]	[b]
	Highest	65,300	376,100	725,200			
1,501 to 4,000	Lowest				28,300	54,300	
	Average	[b]	[b]	[b]	115,800	136,500	[b]
	Highest				1,297,200	231,200	
4,001 to 20,000	Lowest					88,300	65,300
	Average	[b]	[b]	[b]	[b]	271,800	466,400
	Highest					1,980,700	1,310,800
Over 20,000	Lowest						178,300
	Average	[b]	[b]	[b]	[b]	[b]	2,012,200
	Highest						22,150,200
	Overall average	13,200	37,300	72,400	111,200	241,800	1,219,300
	Number of sample funds in category	(n=62)	(n=79)	(n=87)	(n=70)	(n=41)	(n=35)

[a] Categories combined because of small sample size.
[b] No sample cases.

ranges into rather large groups to get a sufficiently large sample in each category. The average operations cost is $161,900 for plans having $10-50 million in assets at the beginning of the year. Finally, we assumed 7,200 active participants. We enter the table in the 4,000-20,000 active participants category and find the average is $312,900.

Now, we have three estimates of what the costs ought to be, compared to our actual costs of $114,000. But a better average yet—or a better guess of what it ought to be—is the average of the three. And so, our estimate of what operations costs would be for this plan is the average of the three, or $195,000. The actual operations costs is $114,000, so this plan is below the average for a plan of similar characteristics. A note of caution: Whether you are high or low may reflect where (i.e., which end of the range) you actually fell within the categories. So this isn't the end of it, it requires careful examination. But this method gives a ballpark figure for operations cost.

Cost Factors Examined

The amount of annual employer contributions is the most important factor. However, additional factors are also important. For instance, third-party administration is important. When plans are small, a third-party administrator is less expensive than salaried administration. Additionally, older plans are more expensive than newer plans. Now, how is this possible? I believe that third-party administration offers the small plan the economies of scale available only to very large plans regardless of the type of administration. That is, by accumulating a series of small plans, third-party administrators can offer economies, the use of computer facilities, etc., and in effect act as one large plan, offering substantial savings. In the case of plan age, it would seem that older plans have a record-keeping burden which is far larger than that of younger plans and, as a result, will tend to have increased costs.

The number of contributing employers has an impact: the more contributing employers, the higher the costs. Recall that the average is 80 employers. Plans that have more contributing employers, particularly for their size, will tend to have higher costs. Such plans will spend relatively more on operations.

Portability agreements increase costs. When such agreements are in effect, costs tend to be higher. When a plan is amended in a particular year, the total operation costs tend to be higher. If you have amended a plan, you might expect increased costs during the year. Finally, when the active participants as a percentage of the total number of participants is high, costs tend to be higher. Those are some additional factors that you should consider when evaluating your fund based upon its actual costs vs. its estimated costs as we measured them.

Professional Services Expense

Accounting Expense

Next, I would like to discuss professional services expenses. This is something we did not include in the health and welfare study. For our sample plan, we should refer to Form 5500, item 12 (Figure 4). The item coded with a 10 is the accounting expense. The actual accounting expense for a plan, as we measured it, is the sum of the codes 10 that are found in item 12 of Form 5500. In this sample case, the actual accounting expense is $2,714. Appendix B, item B, includes the overall averages for accounting expense. Returning to our original description of this fund, we assumed that it had $1.96 million in annual employer contributions. As before, enter this table at the category $1.2-3.5 million in contributions and find the overall average—over $5,000. Similarly, the $14.8 million in net assets plan is found in the column $10-50 million, and the average is $7,595. For a plan with 7,200 participants, we find that the average is $10,385 for the accounting expense. Again, the best estimate is the average of the three, $7,668. This figure is substantially higher than the actual accounting expense for this plan.

In examining the relationship between your actual accounting expense and our estimates, consider these additional factors. The higher the *percentage of assets in common stocks,* the higher the accounting expense tends to be. We have not yet determined what the average percent of assets in common stock is for Taft-Hartley funds, but 30% is a reasonable estimate. If common stocks exceed 30% of the assets, you may expect higher than average accounting costs. The *wage scale* in the local area where the fund is administered has an impact. In our health and welfare study, we present a great deal of information about the differences between metropolitan area wage costs. Accounting expense is the only item for which we found wage costs to be an important factor; accounting expense seems to be more dependent on the local wage scale. In *large urban areas,* we find that accounting expense is greater than average. Further, if a plan requires *employee contributions,* accounting expenses will tend to be higher.

Finally, plans *sharing auditing expenses* with

plans or funds covering the same group of participants will tend to have *lower* accounting expense. That is, when there is a health and welfare and/or supplementary plan covering the same group of participants and those expenses are shared, pension plan accounting expense tends to be slightly lower.

Actuarial Expense

Actuarial expenses are coded 11 on the Form 5500, and on our sample the actual actuarial expense for this fund was $4,500. For a plan with $1.96 million in employee contributions, the appropriate expense will be $8,375; for a fund with $14.8 million in assets, about $10,000 is the expected actuarial expense; and for a fund with 7,200 participants, the expected expense is $16,765 (*see* Appendix B, item C). Taking the average of the three, we see that we would have estimated the actuarial expense to be $11,700, while its actual expense is $4,500.

Some additional factors to consider: If the plan was *amended* in the plan year, then you can expect above average actuarial expense. If *investment activity as a percentage of the total assets is high,* expect higher actuarial expense. Finally, if there are *portability agreements* in effect, expect higher actuarial expense. I think the reasons for the impact of these three factors are obvious.

Administrative Expense

Now we examine administrative expense. In our study, administrative expense includes items coded 13, 16, 23, 24, 25 and 26. What are all those things? They are a group of services to the fund, including the administrator's fee (code 13) and several other administrative codes, including trustees' expenses and computer services. All six services are identified on the 5500 and defined in the instructions. All six are aggregated as administrative expense. In our sample case, we have only one code 13. The actual administrative expense was $79,246. Going to our charts (Appendix B, item D), we find that a fund with $1.96 million in contributions is estimated to have $20,500 in administrative expense. In the appropriate asset column, the administrative expense is estimated at $29,700, and in the appropriate participant column administrative expense is estimated to be $56,560. An overall average of the three is $35,653 vs. the actual $79,246.

For our sample, administrative expenses are high compared to the estimate. However, in this case, we find that the administrator was actually providing a number of services to both the actuary and accountant in terms of maintaining records, thereby partially offsetting the expenses of those services. Furthermore, the sample fund was administered by a third-party administrator who has paid the expenses for mailing supplies and paper, etc., which may be reported separately by other funds. Finally, while the administrative expenses were high, the *total* operating expenses were relatively low. Therefore, the administrator in this case would appear to be taking on a great deal of the burden of operating the plan—i.e., of the total operations cost—which is not being provided by others.

When you go through the process of evaluating the administrator's fee, consider these additional factors. If the fund is administered by a *third-party administrator,* it will tend to have higher administrative fees, though not necessarily higher total operating expense. In fact, small plans using a third-party administrator may tend to have lower total operating expense. Since the total administrative fee is reported in item 12 of Form 5500, the third-party administered plan will tend to have higher salaries and fees than will a self-administered plan.

Secondly, if there has been a *benefit increase* for retirees during the past year, there will tend to be greater administrative expense. Third, there will tend to be higher administrative expenses if the *percent of delinquent employers* is high. How high? Well, as I mentioned before, about 1.5% of the employers in our study were found to be delinquent. Therefore, delinquencies above that level are high. If the plan *does not share eligibility records* with other plans or other funds, then the administrative expense will tend to be higher than the expected average. Finally, administrative expense in this category also tends to increase as the *number of field audits* for employer contributions increases. Those five additional factors should be considered in evaluating administrative expense.

Consulting Expense

Consulting expense (Appendix B, item E) includes items coded as general consulting, investment advisory, valuation services and investment evaluations (codes 17, 20, 28 and 29). A caveat: some plans substitute investment advisory services (code 20) for investment managers' expense (code 21); when that was obvious from materials sent to us, including the accountant's statements, we corrected it. In our sample, we have one code for the general consulting services (code 17), an expense item of $2,000. Where the plan actuary is also the plan consultant, actuarial service and consulting service fees may be combined. If this is how plan expenses are reported, combine the two categories from the tables to get an overall average. For our sample plan, we expect a consulting fee of $10,330 based upon the amount of employer contributions, $9,415 based on the assets, and $17,400 based on the total active participants, versus our actual expense of $2,000.

In evaluating consulting fees, there are two additional factors to be considered. First, the *percentage of assets in common stocks:* as that percentage increases, consulting fees are higher. Second, if *an investment advisor and/or outside evaluation service* is employed to evaluate your manager's performance, the plan will tend to *decrease* its consulting expense. This is principally a result of the service codes available on the 5500.

Investment Management Expense

We have already identified this figure in our sample when calculating operating expense. It is code 21, and the fee is approximately $41,000. How much would we have estimated? Based on the contributions, $26,930; based on the assets, $37,910; based on the number of participants, $75,650; overall, $46,830. Our actual $41,650 is in line with what we would have expected from a plan of similar size (Appendix B, item F).

There are only two important factors affecting expenses. As *net assets increase,* the cost of investment management increases—and that is the only factor used to predict investment management fees. A second factor, the *number of investment managers,* will also tend to increase investment management expense. Those are the only two factors that need to be considered.

Legal Expense

Our actual legal expense (code 22 for our sample) is $6,370. We expected $6,540 based on the annual contributions, $9,190 based on the assets and $14,705 based on the number of active participants. The average for those three is $10,145, compared to our actual expense of $6,370 (Appendix B, item G).

Employer contributions tend to be the most important determinant of legal expenses, but some additional factors are: the percentage of delinquent employers, whether the plan is contributory, shared recordkeeping expense, and the percentage of assets in common stock. If you have *high delinquencies,* higher than 1.5%, then expect higher legal expense. Secondly, if the plan is a *contributory* one, you can expect higher costs. Third, if the *recordkeeping is shared,* you can expect higher costs. This is one case where putting fund operations together works against you. The legal expense tends to increase with the sharing of recordkeeping. And finally, for some unknown reason, when the *percentage of assets in common stocks* is high (above 30%), the legal expense is high. We have no explanation for this.

Conclusion

So what can we say about administrative costs? Two things, I believe. Only the Foundation has attempted a comprehensive study of costs of operating pension plans in the United States since 1974, and while the data are based on 1978 information, our analysis of the 1976 information suggests that estimates of plan expense based on these data will remain accurate for an unknown number of years into the future.

Interestingly enough, plan expenses have not increased as a function of the cost of living. Plan expense tends to increase with increasing employer contributions, increasing assets and an increase in the number of participants. In one sense this means that if your plan remained absolutely stable, not increasing in contributions, assets or participants, then it shouldn't cost more to operate from year to year. That sounds outrageous, I know. But plans don't remain unchanged. They do, in fact, change in terms of assets, contributions and active participants. As the plan gets larger, the per contributions dollar cost of administering it or the per participant cost of administering it tends to become smaller, thereby reducing the impact of inflation. Therefore, we believe that the data in this study will be adequate for your use for evaluating your plan's expenses until we update the study in 1983.

Appendix A

Calculating Actual Plan Expenses

A. CALCULATION OF ACTUAL OPERATIONS COST

Calculate actual *operations cost* by taking the sum of:

Form 5500	line 14i	(interest expense)
Form 5500	line 14j(b)	(total adm. expense)
Form 5500	line 14k	(other expense)
Schedule A	line 6d(ii)	(administration charge)
Schedule A	line 6d(iv)	(other charge)

Subtotal = _____

And subtract investment managers' fees:

Form 5500 item 12, code 21 and/or code 20 if clearly investment management fees − _____

Actual Operations Cost = _____

From the sample:

14

	a. Amount	b. Total
(i) Interest expense		
(j) Administrative expenses—		155,857
(k) Other expenses (specify) ▶		

6

(d) Deductions:
 (ii) Administration charge made by carrier . . . .
 (iv) Other (specify) ▶

12

| XYZ National Bank | Invest. Agent |

Subtotal = $155,857
− 41,650   Code 21
Actual Operations Cost = $114,207

B. **CALCULATION OF ACTUAL ACCOUNTING AND AUDITING EXPENSE**

Calculate actual *accounting and auditing expense* by taking the sum of all salaries and fees:

Form 5500 item 12, (code 10)

Actual Accounting Expense _____

A fund's actual accounting expense is compared with the results in Appendix B, item B.

From the sample:

12				Code
ACE CPAs	Auditor		2,714	10

Actual Accounting Expense = $2,714

C. **CALCULATION OF ACTUAL ACTUARIAL EXPENSE**

Calculate actual *actuarial expense* by taking the sum of all salaries and fees:

Form 5500 item 12, (code 11)

Actual Actuarial Expense _____

A fund's actual actuarial expense is compared with the results in Appendix B, item C.

From the sample:

12				Code
John Doe & Assoc.	Consultant		4,500	11

Actual Actuarial Expense = $4,500

D. **CALCULATION OF ACTUAL ADMINISTRATIVE EXPENSE**

Calculate actual *administrative expense* by taking the sum of all salaries and fees:

Form 5500 item 12, (codes 13, 16, 23, 24, 25 and 26)

Actual Administrative Expense _____

A fund's actual administrative expense is compared with the results in Appendix B, item D.

From the sample:

12				Code
ABC International	Contract Adm.		79,246	13

Actual Administrative Expense = $79,246

E. **CALCULATION OF ACTUAL CONSULTING EXPENSE**

Calculate actual *consulting expense* by taking the sum of all salaries and fees:

Form 5500 item 12, (codes 17, 20, 28 and 29)

Actual Consulting Expense _____

A fund's actual consulting expense is compared with the results in Appendix B, item E.

From the sample:

12

John Q. Public Co.	Consultant	2,000	Code 17

Actual Consulting Expense = $2,000

F. **CALCULATION OF ACTUAL INVESTMENT MANAGEMENT EXPENSE**

Calculate actual *investment management expense* by taking the sum of all salaries and fees:

Form 5500 item 12, (code 21 and/or code 20 if clearly investment management fees)

Actual Investment Management Expense _____

A fund's actual investment management expense is compared with the results in Appendix B, item F.

From the sample:

12

XYZ National Bank	Invest. Agent	41,650	Code 21

Actual Investment Management Expense = $41,650

G. **CALCULATION OF ACTUAL LEGAL EXPENSE**

Finally, calculate actual *legal expense* by taking the sum of all salaries and fees:

Form 5500 item 12, (code 22)

Actual Legal Expense _____

A fund's actual legal expense is compared with the results in Appendix B, item G.

From the sample:

12

Smith, Smythe & Joan's	Legal Counsel	6,370	Code 22

Actual Legal Expense = $6,370

Appendix B

Actual vs. Estimated Costs

A. Average Total Operations Cost

Annual Employer Contributions

	Under $200,000	$200,100-$500,000	$500,100-$1,200,000	$1,200,100-$3,500,000	$3,500,100-$10,000,000	Over $10,000,000
	13,200	37,300	72,400	111,200	241,800	1,219,300
Number of sample funds	(n = 62)	(n = 79)	(n = 87)	(n = 70)	(n = 41)	(n = 35)

Assets at Beginning of Year

	Under $1,000,000	$1,100,000-$2,500,000	$2,600,000-$5,000,000	$5,100,000-$10,000,000	$10,100,000-$50,000,000	$50,100,000-$250,000,000	Over $250,000,000
	14,500	31,200	48,900	87,600	161,900	673,800	4,088,100
Number of sample funds	(n = 60)	(n = 55)	(n = 76)	(n = 63)	(n = 79)	(n = 29)	(n = 12)

Number of Active Participants

	Under 250	250-500	501-1,500	1,501-4,000	4,001-20,000	Over 20,000
	12,200	29,100	54,300	117,900	312,900	2,012,200
Number of sample funds	(n = 48)	(n = 57)	(n = 98)	(n = 64)	(n = 46)	(n = 23)

$$(111{,}200 + 161{,}900 + 312{,}900) \div 3 - 195{,}300$$

Estimated Operations Cost = 195,300
Actual Operations Cost = 114,207

B. Average Accounting Expense

Annual Employer Contributions

	Under $200,000	$200,100–$500,000	$500,100–$1,200,000	$1,200,100–$3,500,000	$3,500,100–$10,000,000	Over $10,000,000
	1,160	1,810	2,745	5,025	10,310	26,800
Number of sample funds	(n = 49)	(n = 45)	(n = 61)	(n = 58)	(n = 38)	(n = 26)

Net Assets at Beginning of Year

	Under $1,000,000	$1,100,000–$2,500,000	$2,600,000–$5,000,000	$5,100,000–$10,000,000	$10,100,000–$50,000,000	$50,100,000–$250,000,000	Over $250,000,000
	1,190	1,735	2,575	3,400	7,595	16,800	68,600
Number of sample funds	(n = 43)	(n = 44)	(n = 62)	(n = 51)	(n = 67)	(n = 22)	(n = 10)

Number of Active Participants

	Under 250	250–500	501–1,500	1,501–4,000	4,001–20,000	Over 20,000
	1,195	1,990	2,260	6,025	10,385	39,100
Number of sample funds	(n = 32)	(n = 46)	(n = 83)	(n = 53)	(n = 39)	(n = 18)

$$(5{,}025 + 7{,}595 + 10{,}385) \div 3 = 7{,}668$$

Estimated Accounting Expense = 7,668
Actual Accounting Expense = 2,714

C. Average Actuarial Expense

Annual Employer Contributions

	Under $200,000	$200,100-$500,000	$ 500,100-$1,200,000	$1,200,100-$3,500,000	$ 3,500,100-$10,000,000	Over $10,000,000
	3,200	4,115	6,680	8,375	14,285	46,725
Number of sample funds	(n = 33)	(n = 37)	(n = 59)	(n = 51)	(n = 34)	(n = 21)

Net Assets at Beginning of Year

	Under $1,000,000	$1,100,000-$2,500,000	$2,600,000-$5,000,000	$ 5,100,000-$10,000,000	$10,100,000-$50,000,000	$ 50,100,000-$250,000,000	Over $250,000,000
	3,370	3,615	6,300	6,890	10,000	28,600	77,450
Number of sample funds	(n = 30)	(n = 26)	(n = 55)	(n = 36)	(n = 60)	(n = 19)	(n = 10)

Number of Active Participants

	Under 250	250-500	501-1,500	1,501-4,000	4,001-20,000	Over 20,000
	3,735	4,010	5,570	8,665	16,765	59,000
Number of sample funds	(n = 18)	(n = 37)	(n = 64)	(n = 48)	(n = 33)	(n = 16)

$$(8,375 + 10,000 + 16,765) \div 3 = 11,713$$

$$\text{Estimated Actuarial Expense} = 11,713$$
$$\text{Actual Actuarial Expense} = 4,500$$

D. Average Administrative Expense

Annual Employer Contributions

	Under $200,000	$200,100-$500,000	$500,100-$1,200,000	$1,200,100-$3,500,000	$3,500,100-$10,000,000	Over $10,000,000
	4,100	10,000	13,080	20,500	53,850	192,400
Number of sample funds	(n = 43)	(n = 45)	(n = 60)	(n = 49)	(n = 30)	(n = 25)

Net Assets at Beginning of Year

	Under $1,000,000	$1,100,000-$2,500,000	$2,600,000-$5,000,000	$5,100,000-$10,000,000	$10,100,000-$50,000,000	$50,100,000-$250,000,000	Over $250,000,000
	4,764	9,400	12,760	15,355	29,700	71,100	391,600
Number of sample funds	(n = 39)	(n = 35)	(n = 50)	(n = 44)	(n = 53)	(n = 19)	(n = 10)

Number of Active Participants

	Under 250	250-500	501-1,500	1,501-4,000	4,001-20,000	Over 20,000
	3,625	6,850	12,570	18,975	56,560	327,225
Number of sample funds	(n = 31)	(n = 34)	(n = 70)	(n = 43)	(n = 34)	(n = 17)

$$(20{,}500 + 29{,}900 + 56{,}560) \div 3 = 35{,}653$$

Estimated Administrative Expense = 35,653
Actual Administrative Expense = 79,246

E. Average Consulting Expense

Annual Employer Contributions

	Under $200,000	$200,100-$500,000	$ 500,100-$1,200,000	$1,200,100-$3,500,000	$ 3,500,100-$10,000,000	Over $10,000,000
	2,580	6,390	8,095	10,330	13,200	37,250
Number of sample funds	(n = 12)	(n = 10)	(n = 17)	(n = 36)	(n = 16)	(n = 17)

Net Assets at Beginning of Year

	Under $1,000,000	$1,100,000-$2,500,000	$2,600,000-$5,000,000	$ 5,100,000-$10,000,000	$10,100,000-$50,000,000	$ 50,100,000-$250,000,000	Over $250,000,000
	3,100	5,310	7,250	8,675	9,415	44,300	60,770
Number of sample funds	(n = 8)	(n = 10)	(n = 22)	(n = 17)	(n = 38)	(n = 13)	(n = 7)

Number of Active Participants

	Under 250	250-500	501-1,500	1,501-4,000	4,001-20,000	Over 20,000
	1,920	7,580	7,730	9,470	17,400	44,000
Number of sample funds	(n = 6)	(n = 8)	(n = 31)	(n = 31)	(n = 18)	(n = 12)

$$(10{,}330 + 9{,}415 + 17{,}400) \div 3 = 12{,}381$$

Estimated Consulting Expense = 12,381
Actual Consulting Expense = 2,000

F. Average Investment Management Expense

Annual Employer Contributions

	Under $200,000	$200,100-$500,000	$500,100-$1,200,000	$1,200,100-$3,500,000	$3,500,100-$10,000,000	Over $10,000,000
	3,400	6,300	13,700	26,930	55,160	157,160
Number of sample funds	(n = 7)	(n = 17)	(n = 21)	(n = 32)	(n = 25)	(n = 23)

Assets at Beginning of Year

	Under $1,000,000	$1,100,000-$2,500,000	$2,600,000-$5,000,000	$5,100,000-$10,000,000	$10,100,000-$50,000,000	$50,100,000-$250,000,000	Over $250,000,000
	2,410	6,715	10,600	18,950	37,910	120,090	190,600
Number of sample funds	(n = 8)	(n = 11)	(n = 18)	(n = 20)	(n = 42)	(n = 16)	(n = 10)

Number of Active Participants

	Under 250	250-500	501-1,500	1,501-4,000	4,001-20,000	Over 20,000
	2,650	8,510	10,600	26,000	75,650	193,240
Number of sample funds	(n = 5)	(n = 10)	(n = 25)	(n = 32)	(n = 28)	(n = 16)

$$(26{,}930 + 37{,}910 + 75{,}650) \div 3 = 46{,}830$$

Estimated Investment Management Expense = 46,830
Actual Investment Management Expense = 41,650

G. Average Legal Expense

Annual Employer Contributions

	Under $200,000	$200,100-$500,000	$500,100-$1,200,000	$1,200,100-$3,500,000	$3,500,100-$10,000,000	Over $10,000,000
	1,615	2,670	4,370	6,540	13,470	79,375
Number of sample funds	(n = 37)	(n = 44)	(n = 65)	(n = 57)	(n = 35)	(n = 25)

Assets at Beginning of Year

	Under $1,000,000	$1,100,000-$2,500,000	$2,600,000-$5,000,000	$5,100,000-$10,000,000	$10,100,000-$50,000,000	$50,100,000-$250,000,000	Over $250,000,000
	1,630	2,620	4,170	4,475	9,190	30,850	173,000
Number of sample funds	(n = 33)	(n = 34)	(n = 52)	(n = 49)	(n = 64)	(n = 21)	(n = 10)

Number of Active Participants

	Under 250	250-500	501-1,500	1,501-4,000	4,001-20,000	Over 20,000
	1,500	2,250	4,110	7,495	14,705	154,115
Number of sample funds	(n = 24)	(n = 35)	(n = 73)	(n = 53)	(n = 37)	(n = 18)

$$(6,540 + 9,190 + 14,705) \div 3 = 10,145$$

Estimated Legal Expense = 10,145
Actual Legal Expense = 6,370

CHAPTER 8

Computers and Data Processing

Robert A. DeCori

Vice President-Financial Operations
Kelly & Associates, Inc.
Chicago, Illinois

Robert J. Beres

Administrator
Ohio Carpenters Health and Welfare Fund
Youngstown, Ohio

Donald H. Rowcliffe, Jr.

Administrative Manager
Carpenters Welfare and Pension Funds
of Illinois
Geneva, Illinois

G. A. Mele

Vice President
TEDRO & Associates, Inc.
Chicago, Illinois

Spencer V. Bell

President
National Labor Systems, Inc.
Houston, Texas

Bennie Jones

Vice President
National Labor Systems, Inc.
Houston, Texas

Solving Administrative Problems Through EDP

BY ROBERT A. DeCORI

AS THE TITLE of this presentation implies, problems in the administration of employee benefit plans can be solved through the use of electronic data processing (EDP). What it does not imply is that administrative problems can be *created* by the improper use of electronic data processing. Before one can address the solution of administrative problems in the employee benefits industry, it is appropriate that we attempt to identify, in a general sense, the potential problems that can be impacted and solved by the proper use of data processing.

Potential Problem Areas

Elements of Recordkeeping Responsibility

The first category of problem areas can be described as the elements of recordkeeping responsibility inherent in the administration of employee benefit plans, whether handled by a third-party administrator or a salaried administrator. The relatively inclusive list of the elements would be as follows: administration/management; requirements/obligations; storage/retention; financial records; government compliance and other disclosures. Administration encompasses "subelements" of planning, organizing, guiding, directing and controlling. Management can be defined as the "subelements" of coordination, supervision and internal leadership. The above, if properly performed, will result in effective decision making and problem solving. Obviously, these identified elements are not the sole proprietorship of the employee benefit administration industry, but are evident in every well-run organization. Effective utilization of data processing will enable an organization to be better administered and better managed.

The requirements and obligations for an employee benefit plan administrator are many. In addition to normal business requirements and plan requirements, ERISA and its various amendments (e.g., the Multiemployer Pension Plan Amendments Act) and the resulting government regulations sig-

Mr. DeCori is vice president-financial operations of Kelly & Associates, Inc., and is responsible for its accounting, financial systems and data processing operations. Prior to his present position, he was manager of a computer software house specializing in financial systems. Mr. DeCori received his B.S. degree with an accounting major from Bradley University and has attended IBM and AMA seminars, including the AMA President's Association. He is a present or former member of the National Association of Accountancy, Data Processing Management Association and COMMON (National IBM Users Group). Mr. DeCori has spoken at previous Foundation educational meetings.

nificantly impact the reporting and compliance obligations of an administrator. It is safe to say that, without effective data processing, an administrator of any size will have trouble in this area.

Storage and retention includes both participant records and contributing employer records. In addition to standard enrollment information for the participant, service records for entitlement and/or eligibility must be maintained. Employer records can cover a wide area, including the labor agreement, contribution rate history, remittance history and (new) withdrawal liability information. This is not an inclusive list for storage and retention. Obviously, adequate accounting records and financial statements reflective of a plan's operation are also critical elements of an administrator's responsibility. A few of the accounting records are contribution accounting, delinquent contributions, benefit payment and trust operating expenses.

The applicable government compliance requirements are an additional area where problems can occur and, likewise, data processing can be properly utilized to help prevent same. Other disclosure requirements include summary plan descriptions, summary annual reports, benefit accruals, claim denials, statements to separated vested participants, employee benefit statements, etc.

Implementing Plan Provisions

Above we have covered elements of recordkeeping responsibility which can become potential problem areas. The actual benefit plan coverage in itself can also be a potential problem area. Plan provisions covering basic benefits, reciprocity, survivor benefits, supplemental benefits, participation/reinstatement, eligibility/vesting and the application (claim/pension) procedure are all potential areas of difficulty.

Eligibility in itself covers the full gamut from initial eligibility, continuing eligibility, termination of eligibility and the various provisions relating to the determinations. It is probably the single largest problem area for administrators of any consequential size—and therefore the most necessary area in which to have effective systems and data processing support. Reviewing the brief listing above, one can see there are major areas where problems can develop in the administration of employee benefit plans.

Application of the EDP Tools

The proper use of data processing, whether through an in-house operation, service bureau or sharing of on-line data processing facilities, can help solve many of the administrative problems that are encountered in our profession. There are many steps that need to be taken in determining the proper direction to take in deciding when and how and in what form to utilize data processing. Other than to say that the selection, feasibility, design and cost are all critical aspects of this determination, this presentation will not go into depth on this subject. Rather, this article will attempt to address the application of EDP tools in solving some of the most common administrative problems encountered.

The areas that will be addressed as to the application of the EDP tools are as follows: eligibility; claims processing; pension processing; and communications. These are obvious generic areas within an administrator's organization. Note that this is not intended to be an inclusive list, but these certainly are areas that can be impacted most favorably by effective use of data processing.

Eligibility

The starting point in determining eligibility is the receipt of contributions. The most commonly used description for this receipt of contributions is fund processing. There are several effective approaches utilizing the computer in recording contributions. Likewise, the approaches can be either batch-oriented or on-line—which, right or wrong, seems to be the consensus as to the most optimal approach. Properly designed and implemented, on-line data entry will allow the receipt of monthly contributions, an update and maintenance of eligibility credits (for a health and welfare fund) or an accumulation of service credits (for a pension fund). Various checks and balances, edits and audit trails should be an integral part of a good on-line fund processing system. Techniques such as exception crediting, alpha search and duplicate Social Security number checking, and capabilities such as multiple fund input and magnetic tape input should be "given" features of a good fund processing system.

Needless to say, particularly for a third-party administrator, flexibility in the type of contributions (monthly, weekly, hourly, etc.) is an absolute necessity in the above-described system. The system should allow extensive flexibility in determining eligibility. Differing plan needs, differing industries covered, differing styles from varied consultants, mandate the ability for a fund processing system to handle the variety of eligibility rules that permeate the industry—not the least of which are eligibility systems based on hour banks, hour averaging, lag months or lag quarters, as well as many others. A good data processing system will have the front end capability to store the applicable information in the data base, and the program modularization capabilities to use the information as applicably needed. An inherent part of the eligibility system is the ability to determine initial eligibility, continuing eligibility and loss of eligibility. It also should have the ability to provide for the handling of self-payments when loss of eligibility occurs, assuming the plan provides for same. Plans often require different eligibility provisions for different benefits: an example would be differing plan provisions for medical, dental, vision and prescription drug coverages.

One can see from the brief description above that without an effective data processing system the entire arena of fund processing and resulting eligibility could be a nightmare. It also should be noted here that improperly applied data processing tools can actually create a bigger disaster. Very thoughtful planning and design must accompany the effective implementation of a data processing system. By all means, the user must be involved throughout the process, and if at all possible your data processing professional should know your business.

Claims Processing

Claims processing is another area where the application of EDP tools can have a positive impact. The extent of the use of EDP in the claims processing area can vary considerably. The spectrum is truly wide, from fully automated on-line claim adjudication to simple, after-the-fact, batch collection of experience data. This article will address the upper half of the spectrum called, for lack of a better description, computer-assisted claims processing. This approach is in all likelihood the most applicable from the standpoint of implementation and return on investment and time.

The approach consists of manually adjudicating the claim and, in the process of same, preparing a worksheet that becomes the data entry document for the system. By proper utilization of editing and balancing within a well-designed system, the following items can be generated: the benefit check, E.O.B. statements, positive check verification and bank reconciliation magnetic tape, check register, check roster, 1099 meds., 1099 misc., experience reports and other selective analyses. By utilizing both member and provider files and, as indicated above, well thought-out editing routines, the process can be optimum in time, effort and control. This approach has two major benefits and, if designed properly, can be quite effective. It maintains the quality and flexibility that many perceive in manual adjudication, and it minimizes, if not eliminates, the non-critical, menial clerical functions that are generally regarded as inherent in a manual claims operation. Therefore, this approach optimizes the claims adjusters' time, maintains high data integrity and minimizes detail drudgery.

How Does It Work? At this point in the presentation an example of an on-line eligibility and computer-assisted claims payment system follows. One of the most significant advantages of on-line processing is instantaneous updating of an employee's eligibility. In a batch system, the balancing process can take several steps. In many cases, the report is "clerically prepped" and sent to a key-punch section or similar off-line data entry section. The data are then processed on a computer. If out of balance, the report is returned to the contribution accounting area, corrected, submitted again to data entry and subsequently computer-processed. If again not in balance, the same cycle is repeated, and it is repeated again until in balance. The eligibility is not updated until month-end, and probably is not available either in hard copy or screen until several days after the close of the month-end processing. The net effect is that eligibility determination is delayed. Members being dunned for medical bills are calling and asking why their claims have not been processed. This grief is largely eliminated in an on-line processing environment with on-line eligibility.

Continuing on the existing system as described above, an individual in the claims department upon receipt of a new claim enters the fund code and the member's Social Security number on a CRT screen. The member's master screen is displayed. The screen contains such information as the name and address, birth date, sex, marital status, effective date in the fund, local union number, termination date (if applicable), present employer, employer contribution rate, plan code and plan information, and 24 (rolling) months of eligibility. The system, whether the fund is on a monthly or an hourly basis, utilizing an hour bank or other eligibility determining mode, will do the eligibility determination and indicate same on the CRT screen.

An interesting programming technique should be noted here. If the eligibility program for each fund uses standard input and output arrays, then it is possible to develop these programs at a fraction of the normal development cost. This is done through the use of a decision table type module. The analyst enters the decision table logic from the summary plan description, which generates the given eligibility program(s). By use of the decision table, improved understanding and communications with the user are accomplished. This is a very powerful and yet low cost development tool allowing the system to handle a large variety of eligibility rules.

If there is a question as to lack of eligibility in an hourly fund, the clerk can call a second screen with an hourly breakdown supporting the eligibility determination or lack of eligibility. If the fund has self-payment provisions, the screen will indicate whether the eligibility was generated by an employer's contribution or a self-payment. Once eligibility is determined, the claim forms are notated and forwarded to a claims adjuster. In this example of on-line processing, the claim adjudication is performed by the adjuster and a worksheet is prepared. Once prepared, the worksheets are forwarded, along with a dollar control total, to the data entry section. The data entry section processes the worksheet by entering the fund code and the individual's Social Security number. A screen appears with the employee's name and address. Note: if there is any one time that a member gives his correct address, it is at the time when he expects dollar consideration; that is, a benefit check. Experience has been that at the time of eligibility determination, address updating can be handled very effectively, thereby creating a current file of member addresses.

Returning to the claim screen, the worksheet is set up to enter both payee information by payee across the top of the screen and benefit code amounts vertically on the screen. The system will crossfoot the amounts to determine if there is a calculation error. The data entry clerk cannot proceed any further until the dollars balance. Additional information is entered, such as "from and to" dates for hospitalization and loss of time. The system internally calculates the number of days for the applicable benefit amount. Several edits are performed in addition to crossfooting. First of all, the employee has to be on the employee master file, or processing stops. The benefit codes have to be acceptable as defined by the system, the date has to be within acceptable parameters, etc.

Once the above information is entered, the clerk proceeds to the next screen, where the payee I.D. numbers are entered. If it is the member himself, an "M" is entered, the system draws the Social Security number entered on the first screen, goes to the employee file and displays the name and address of the employee. The data entry clerk enters a "P" if the payee is a physician or an "H" if it is a hospital, along with the corresponding physician or hospital I.D. number. The system, utilizing the number entered, applies same against a provider file, pulling the name and address and displaying it on the screen for verification. If the provider is not on the file, the appropriate name, address and I.D. is added to eliminate the data entry effort on the next occasion. The payees are then listed on the screen as they will appear on the benefit check. Note that full audit trails are necessary for this system. The subsequent screen displays claim loss information, such as date of loss, claimant code (member or dependent), claimant age, cause code, local union number and claim status (whether it is new or continuing). An optional final screen may be invoked in order to enter "charge" data per benefit code processed.

A Total System. What is accomplished with this on-line claims data entry system? The system has edited and balanced the data and performed necessary file maintenance to the employee file and to the provider file. The benefit check(s) as well as the check register and check roster are generated. A magnetic tape can be forwarded to the bank for mechanized bank reconciliation and positive check payment verification. Additionally, the information necessary to generate claims experience reports on the first day of the following month is collected. The system has collected and stored information for 1099 meds. and 1099 misc. to be generated at year-end. Information for subsequent special analysis reports that may be requested at a later date is also stored. All of this has been accomplished in one step, again with a fraction of the effort that would be necessary to accomplish all of those steps manually or on a totally batch data processing system.

Pension Processing

Application of EDP tools in the pension processing aspect of benefit administration can have a very favorable effect. In addition to the obvious check issuance, new awards and recertification can be handled quite easily with a good systems approach.

Probably the most critical areas where data processing can have a major impact are in the application of vesting and break-in-service rules and the maintenance of applicable actuarial data bases for active and inactive members as well as pensioners. Selected computer-generated mailouts to members having missing census information and tape match-ups against data from an international union are just two tools that data processing provides to improve overall data integrity. SSA inclusions on the 5500 as well as individual member notifications are easy byproducts of an actuarial data request processed on a well-designed data processing system. Varied past service determined by local unions' participation is a manual nightmare; proper use of systems and programming can ease the effort considerably. (Note that the complexity and size of the plan determines the extent of the data processing application.)

Communications

Communications—always an important area—has been impacted tremendously by ERISA. Communications, both internal and external, can be vastly improved with appropriate data processing techniques. Internal communications generated via a data processing approach can significantly improve an administrator's service. Monitoring of cash receipts, of individual contributions reports processed, of claims volume, etc., via daily computerized status reports can inform an administrator and his staff that no processing breakdown is occurring—or, if one does occur, allow management to act expeditiously to solve the problem. This monitoring, if coupled with an on-line system, can ensure quality and consistency of administration in a multilocation environment. The monitoring can be developed further to allow exception items to be flagged and reviewed immediately.

External communications to trustees, plan advisors, government agencies, contributing employers and the participant can be improved with data processing. Whether it's a computerized delinquency report to the board of trustees, an experience analysis to a consultant, a delinquency notice to a contributing employer, a termination of eligibility notice to a participant, or one of many reports required by the IRS, DOL or PBGC, an effectively interfaced data processing system can ease the administrative burden significantly.

Summary

It is safe to state that data processing has a significant role in employee benefit plan administration. With the improved technology and price/performance ratios available, sophisticated approaches such as on-line processing are now available and, in many instances, practical. Employee benefit plan administration in the post-ERISA era has created significant demands on data processing. On-line data processing allows for these demands to be effectively met.

Employer contribution processing, eligibility determinations, benefit processing and communications can be greatly enhanced in an on-line environment. Telecommunication with or without distributed processing coupled with on-line systems can definitely improve the administration of employee benefit plans. Proper systems design with state-of-the-art hardware technology will allow effective tools to be implemented in processing health and welfare, pension and other employee benefit plans. The results will be greater data integrity, more effective work flows, minimized data entry and improved service to the covered employees. Additionally, on-line processing will give an administrator the ability to accommodate the changes that have been and continue to be generated by ERISA-related government regulations.

This presentation attempts to highlight only the areas where problems can occur, and to suggest potential areas where the use of the computer through effective systems design, implementation and operation can reduce administrative burdens, prevent bottlenecks and solve existing problems in the day-to-day administration of employee benefit plans. It should be cautioned that if the administrator is presently having problems in this area through existing systems, or is considering the implementation of a data processing system or service, he should avail himself of the information that is available in developing a new data processing system. The improper use of data processing, a poorly thought-out system design, a shortcut and/or an improper hardware/software mix can actually create additional problems. Possibly this presentation should have been entitled "Solving administrative problems through carefully thought out and judicious use of EDP, with proper system design, programming, implementation and operation."

Solving Administrative Problems Through EDP—The Positive Side

BY ROBERT J. BERES

IN THIS DISCUSSION, we will dig into the solving of administrative problems through electronic data processing. I'll be telling you about a lot of wonderful and miraculous accomplishments you can achieve through data processing, and all of my discussion will be on the positive side. I'll be followed by Don Rowcliffe, administrative manager of the Illinois Carpenters fringe benefit funds. Don will be commenting on the pitfalls, potholes and tons of trouble you can find suddenly burdening you when you mechanize.

I don't want to mislead you into thinking everything becomes beautiful and great when you carry one of these electronic wizards into your office and plug it into the wall. I point out in advance that I happen to personally agree with all of the points Don will present—I've been there.

What Can EDP Do for You?

When in Doubt, Communicate

So you want to computerize? OK, that's one big decision out of the way! It's probably the easiest one to make. The next step is to establish some goals and objectives, and to make a decision as to which way to go from there.

Should your operations be in house? Should you consider contract administration? Should you consider a service bureau? If your operations are to be in house, should you buy or lease a system? The answer is, I don't know. That is, I don't know what direction *you* should take—but you can find out.

One of your methods is by communicating. That is, communicating with those who know—those who have gone the route, and those who will be going the route with you. When you are developing a new system, take a good, long, hard look at what you have and an equally good, long, hard look at what you expect to get. Let others in your organi-

Mr. Beres, as administrator of the Ohio Carpenters Health and Welfare Fund and the Carpenters Central Collection and Administrative Agency, is responsible for managing the collections of fringe contributions and payroll deductions from 1,200 employers for 10,000 carpenters, with other duties including accounting, data processing management, delinquency controls, eligibility calculations and payments for medical, hospital, surgical, major medical and prescription claims. Active in the joint trust field for over 24 years, he previously served as manager of the Iron Workers Welfare and Pension Plans of Western Pennsylvania. Mr. Beres has been involved as a participant in International Foundation activities for many years.

zation take a look and provide their input. Then, take all of the best points and pull them together.

Take some *more* time to communicate. Talk to the people who have already done what you expect to accomplish. Somewhere among the membership of the International Foundation is a welfare/pension operation that has just gone through the misery of the project you are about to undertake. They made mistakes. I made mistakes. And, you will make mistakes. Learn and burn is a tough process to take.

The point is, though, the help is there. You can easily contact other funds similar in size and nature to your own operations. Most, including the Ohio Carpenters Health and Welfare Fund, are very proud of their accomplishments and will be happy to show them off.

Finding the Right 'Fit'

There's always a nagging question lurking in our minds when deciding how large a configuration to get. The question is whether the system will be too small, too big or just right. You'll probably never achieve the just-right point, and the worst is the too-small situation. I call this being byte bitten.

Having a central processor and files that are too small usually doesn't show up until you are well into your program development.

What do you do to head off this problem? Of course, if you're going from an existing system to a new one, your experience will help you greatly. If it's your first system, though, you have to depend on the advice of others. Various of the vendors can help you. Those who can help you more are the people who have systems up and running. Once again, go to others in your business. Ask about the size of their membership, the number of eligibles, whether companion funds are administered. Ask about the complexities of the programs in use. Then compare those operations to your own funds. Try to get more than one other organization to help you. When you do have the opportunity to "pick someone's brains," be sure to ask the question, "If you had it all to do over again, what would you do differently?"

Even after you have relative assurance of your computer needs, don't box yourself in. Talk with the vendors about upgrading possibilities and their costs. For example, if you will be getting a central processor with a quarter million bytes, find out if the memory can be upgraded without physical removal and replacement of the processor. Don't just ask about the cost of memory boards. Find out if other items are needed in conjunction with the upgrade, such as addressing.

The same advice applies to all of the peripherals. You may even find it more economical to consider later expansion needs at the time of your original purchase. I've experienced circumstances where it's more practical to overbuy at the outset.

The Talking Computer

We are now well into the swing of ERISA and have an understanding about what is legally required to be provided to the plan's participants. Even before the advent of ERISA, we had major recordkeeping problems. The plan administrators were in need of convenient ways to keep track of thousands of items of detail on thousands of participants and employers. ERISA not only increased the recordkeeping need but certainly increased the need for ways in which to disseminate the information. One of the ways is to get your computer to talk—to you, and to the members.

A computer company developed a talking computer. They wanted to test it, so people were brought in from off the street. When the first man was brought in, the computer introduced itself. It said, "Good morning sir, I am the talking computer. What is your IQ?" The man replied that his IQ is 160 and the next hour or so was spent discussing Einstein's theory of relativity. A second man was brought in and the computer went through its introduction again. "Good morning sir, I'm the talking computer. May I ask, what is your IQ?" The man replied that his IQ is about 20. The computer said, "Well, ten-four good buddy, what's your handle?"

Our own in-house system does just that. It talks to us—figuratively, that is. It can also talk to other computers in other offices. Most of our work is done on-line. We have a number of cathode ray tubes (CRTs) in the fund office. These are used extensively for the input and retrieval of data.

When we need to make an inquiry on a member's account, his name is keyed onto the screen and transmitted to the system. Within a fraction of a second, the member's complete history is displayed. Need to change an address? Add a dependent? Check if welfare coverage is in force? Find out who employed your member? All of this and more is available to you in seconds. Your turnaround is accomplished without running (or roller skating) to several different places in your office. Your effectiveness is increased many times over, and you leave your members with the good feeling that you can very capably service their needs.

Our system will soon be expanded. We have added five additional tubes which will be located in the district council offices throughout the state. The CRTs will be connected to our system via telephone lines, and will be providing the membership with services on a more localized basis. In total, we have ten terminals. The system can talk to ten different people about ten different subjects at the same time. If the need were there, it is capable enough for 70 CRTs to be attached and operate at the same time, performing 70 different functions.

But, what's that you say? You're listening to some guy from Ohio. The fund—
- Has 16,000 members on file
- Has records on 48,000 dependents
- Puts out 100,000 pieces of mail a year
- Collects contributions for 46 entities
- Covers a geographic area of 70,000 square miles.

Perhaps your fund has a few hundred or a few thousand participants, and you may feel that what I have to say about data processing doesn't, or can't, apply to you. That's not so! You never really know what you can do until you try! And, that rule also applies to data processing.

Virtually every fund operation of every size has the need (work-wise) and the ability (economically) to automate, at least in part. No fund is too small.

Conversely, too often, I have heard from programmers and analysts that this job or that job can't be accomplished. Nonsense! Don't listen to the people who say it can't be done. If you can write down a formula and demonstrate that two plus two does, in fact, equal four, then the computer can do it.

And, as you get into the mechanization of your fund, you'll be amazed at the brainstorms you get. The farther you go, the better they will get.

Specific Areas

Employer Reports and Contributions

Many fund offices operate companion plans; the welfare and pension plans frequently are administered by the same people in the same office, and on the same system. Most often, collections are also made for other funds such as vacation, apprentice, industry advancement and working assessments or dues checkoff. Getting the money in, properly recorded to the members and contractors, and then paying it out to the participating funds is probably the most complicated, time-consuming and critical area of administration facing the fund's personnel.

Many plans have more than one local or district council and they frequently have many different rates of contribution, with as many different levels. One local may have an annuity plan, while six others do not. Three locals may have supplemental unemployment contributions and others have none. One local could be contributing to the welfare and pension plans on a percentage basis while the others are on a cents-per-hour basis. Contractor reports can have errors in addition or multiplication. Rates of contribution or deduction change, yet reports come to you at the old rates. Many funds have late payment provisions, or penalties. The employers can also be required to put up cash bonds or purchase surety bonds. Some can even be required to make weekly deposits, if they do not have a good credit status. Well, how do you handle these situations—and quickly? No, you don't go to a quiet corner of the office and whimper and cry and then walk out!

Rates and their effective dates, percentages and cents per hour, and local union identification can all be stored in tables in your system to accommodate a virtually endless combination of the situations I just broached.

Employer data are keyed to the system. The date of employment and local jurisdiction are compared to the table. The percentages or cents per hour are multiplied by the system, and a comparison is made between the amounts keyed and the amounts that should be paid. The operator has the calculations displayed on the screen in a matter of seconds. If differences do appear, a decision is made as to whether they are valid. If valid, the system holds the detail, the records are ready to be written, and there is an instantaneous update of the employer's cash account, the employees' records and even the accounts receivable file. The data keyed into the CRT just one moment ago are then available for inquiry. Turnaround can be reduced from days to minutes.

My statements about processing of employer reports only took a few minutes to present. Of course, the problems are many and the techniques are very detailed. This subject, by itself, could absorb one or two days of our time.

Reciprocal Agreements

Too often, we have seen situations of members "booming" about the country; virtually never missing a day's work; devoting 30 or 40 years to a business they love; and finding at retirement the sad, sad problem of not qualifying for a pension.

Equally sad is the situation of a medical or hospital claim arising and the member finding that he or she is not covered by any health and welfare benefit program, yet the only work-time missed was during holidays, or vacations, or in traveling to the next job site.

Some employers have helped head off the problem by making dual contributions—once to the funds where the job is located, and once to the members' home funds.

The problem's resolution is, of course, to reciprocate. Just as with the decision to mechanize, the decision to reciprocate is the easiest part of solving the problem. You are next faced with the problem of *how* to reciprocate.

There are, basically, two types of reciprocal agreements. One provides for a transfer of contributions from one fund to another. It is known generally as a "money-follows-the-man" agreement. The second type, frequently used in pension plans, is the pro-rata reciprocal agreement. The pro-rata agreement calls for no transfer of contributions. It allows a combination of service in various funds to qualify for the payment of a partial pension from each of the signatory plans at the time of retirement.

Both types of agreement are easily administered with even the most simplified data processing systems. In the money-follows-the-man situation, we have tagged each member's master file with a "yes" or "no." We have also tagged the file with an identification of his or her home fund. A "yes" in the file precludes the member from obtaining coverage in our health and welfare fund. It is also our key to locating the people whose contributions we must reciprocate. We pass the files through our program on a regular basis. Those with a "yes" who have employment reported are then sorted down according to their home fund designation. Our programs write a detail record to the employees' accounts. The detail record reads, "Transferred to fund XYZ." Then, the program prepares a report to the respective reciprocating funds, showing who the employer is, the work period, the number of hours and the amount of contributions received. That report, and an accompanying check, are sent to the other funds.

The pro-rata agreement does not require an exchange of contributions. You should, however, maintain information in your system about other places where your own members have earned service. Your method of maintaining the information is similar to your methods of processing employer reports. Your member has told you he was employed in Oshkosh or Walla Walla. You should contact the other funds—I suggest a preprinted standard letter—and inquire as to the service earned. When you receive the employment record from the other fund—and you have been satisfied with the accuracy of it—set up an employer in your file. Call the employer "Carpenters of Walla Walla" or "Oshkosh" and load the employment information into your system. I caution, though, to make sure you are showing no contributions received so that you don't accidentally overstate your pension benefit accrual rate.

This approach will prevent an artificial break in service, and your member will correctly continue toward meeting your fund's vesting requirements.

Audit Trails and Registers

I constantly kid with the fund's auditors. I've told them the letters "CPA" mean "Can't Prove Anything." I emphasize, though, that I recognize these guys are needed in our fund's operations. Since we do need the auditors—and because "Uncle" says we need the auditors—we have to do some things in our operations to accommodate them and we must make sure we do them right. This includes providing adequate audit trails and registers throughout the data processing operation.

We have included the auditors in our DP planning. We have asked them to first look at our system overview (our plan of attack) and followed this up by including them in our periodic status meetings. We have looked at the accounting firm's DP specialist to provide us with input, as well as to review the internal controls we all recognize are necessary to satisfy not only the auditors, but ourselves as well. The result of our joint effort has been meaningful reports from the system, along with assurance that our processing is not running off the track. And, please remember—the auditor is your friend. That's what he keeps telling me. I keep telling him, "An auditor is the guy who comes in when the war is over and bayonets the wounded."

No-Payment Eligibility Records

Uncle says that a pension fund has to provide credit for covered employment, even if the contributions have not been paid to the fund. Strangely, the bank where I have my mortgage is not inclined to adopt the same policy. Nor have I been a success at convincing Congress to legislate that the bank adopt such a policy. In any event, recordkeeping for unpaid eligibility is a problem that extends beyond the economics of providing benefits without receiving any income.

Once again, though, your computer comes to the rescue. In cases of employer delinquency, bankruptcy and the like, you can still record employment activity in the form of hours or wages and the amounts the contributions should have been. As with the recording of employment in pro-rata reciprocal agreement situations, we can use the programs for processing of employer reports to key data to the employees' accounts. If only part or none of the contributions are paid, the differences or balances due from the employer get logged to an account receivable file for a later bad-debt transaction.

Conclusion

As I mentioned at the outset of our discussion, I have presented the positive side of "solving your administrative problems through EDP." I still wish, however, to comment about Murphy's Law. That is, "Everything costs more than you think it should. Everything takes more time than you planned. Everything that can go wrong, does!" And, my tag line: "Murphy was an optimist."

Solving EDP Problems Through Administration

BY DONALD H. ROWCLIFFE, JR.

The Computer as a Tool

As Mr. Beres suggested, I'm going to take a little different twist by discussing the solving of EDP problems through administration—or, a shot of penicillin simply doesn't do the trick. In my opinion, there has been quite a revolution in EDP installations over the last ten years, and that is that the hardware costs of an EDP installation are a far smaller part of the total EDP budget than they were as little as ten years ago. Computer hardware has gotten smaller in size, and the cost of magnetic memory devices has gotten cheaper over the years. I think back to 1970, when I was involved in the Chicago Carpenters Fund. We had a model 360/20 IBM computer with an internal memory of 8,000 bytes. If I recall correctly, we spent about $50,000 to double that capacity to 16,000 bytes of internal memory. I now have a little home computer that has 48,000 bytes of memory, and it cost only a small percentage of that conversion cost ten years ago for an additional 8,000 bytes.

There is no question but that the computer is a fantastic tool; and that's all it is—a fantastic tool! It can replace typewriters, calculators, etc., but I have yet to see one replace people. I can remember years and years ago when automated data processing came into being, it was sold on the basis that you would be able to decrease personnel. I have yet to see such results. Initially, you will add system analysts, programmers and computer operators to your staff. Eventually you may see some reduction, but primarily EDP tends to enable more work to be accomplished, more output, without addition to your staff. One thing the computer does, of course, is that it can change job assignments, responsibilities and work flow.

The major concern that I have with computers—and please, let me state up front that I am totally in favor of computers—is that it is so easy to lose sight of who is working for whom. I admonish you, make it work for you and do not become a slave to your computer. About 15 years ago, I had an oc-

Mr. Rowcliffe is administrative manager of the Carpenters Welfare & Pension Funds of Illinois. His office also provides administrative services to 18 other construction industry welfare, pension, apprentice and vacation funds. His experience encompasses 15 years in the multiemployer benefits field as an auditor, contract administrator and salaried administrator, serving welfare, pension, apprenticeship and vacation funds. He is a past president of the Fox Valley Chapter of the Illinois Society of Certified Public Accountants and a member of the American Institute of Certified Public Accountants. Mr. Rowcliffe has written articles for the International Foundation's Digest *and* Employee Benefits Journal *and has spoken at various Foundation educational meetings. He serves on the Foundation's Board of Directors and is a member of the Administrators and Educational Program Committees.*

casion to have lunch with the chairman of the board and president of a large bank in Chicago. Just before lunch we had toured their computer facilities, and he admitted to us, his clients, that he was beholden to his computer and his EDP manager. I made a vow to myself that at no time would I ever be in such a situation. Make your computer work for you. Do not become its slave.

Will your computer alleviate or increase your administrative responsibilities in employer reports and contributions? In my opinion, it increases your responsibilities. Stop and think about it. Information is no longer in a form such that you can pick up and hold it in your hand, look at it and study it. Most of the information is embedded in a magnetic form in the computer, and is only available to you through various computer programs. This is difficult for the uninitiated to understand. It's difficult for trustees to understand that it can take a considerable amount of time to develop the programs necessary to gather certain pieces of information and display them in a particular form. That's what it's all about!

Systems Design: What Are Your Goals?

It's not the computer; it's the system that makes the computer good or bad as a tool. Some of you may have heard me make this statement before, but it's one of my favorites: "You can't determine how to get there if you don't know where you're going." Think about it for a minute. Would you ever ask your secretary to prepare your itinerary for December 12 and not tell her where you're going? Of course that's impossible, but I've seen systems created in just that fashion. In developing any kind of system, you must start at the *end* of the line. You must determine the end results—the destination—what you want to accomplish and the form you want it in, and then proceed to develop the method and the means to get there— the itinerary.

A Continuing Responsibility

You, as administrative managers, are in the driver's seat and, most likely, are the only one in a position to know that. You cannot abdicate your responsibilities in the development of systems for your operation! I'm not suggesting that you become programmers, that you become systems analysts and design experts, but really, systems analysis and design is really nothing but common sense and experience. We know what's required of us under the reporting and disclosure requirements under the various acts. We know what kind of communications have to be developed. We know what kind of governmental reports have to be developed, prepared and filed.

Although I've had considerable experience in systems analysis and design, I can't get totally involved because of many other responsibilities. Therefore, I'm in a position, and you'll be in a position, to communicate your wants and needs to the people whom you have entrusted with this responsibility, whether it be your own staff or whether you've subcontracted from someone else. But you must be totally involved and you cannot abdicate that position, and it's not a one-time thing. It has to be followed through. Communication is the secret. I told my two children many years ago that the art of communication is probably the most important subject they'll ever face in their education. That's simply the ability to read, speak and write. I don't care how sharp you are, whatever your IQ, if you do not have the ability to communicate to others via the written and spoken word, your knowledge is next to useless.

How many of you have made a decision at one time or another, based on certain facts, and then discovered some time later that you made a little different decision, based on the same facts? I have. Now, one thing the computer can help with—and that's what we're doing in creating system designs— is to make the same decision each time the facts are similar. If the computer is nothing else, it is consistent—right or wrong, it is consistent!

I believe we take on additional problems with *internal controls and security* when we get involved in EDP operations, because of the invisibility of the information. We must give a lot of consideration to who makes the decision; who has the responsibility for entering information from employer reports; and what built-in checks and balances are necessary for controlling the entering of such data. Seems kind of simple, but think about it for a moment. And, your system must leave *audit trails* so that, at any future time, you can reconstruct that original entry and any subsequent adjustments to it. We're responsible for a lot of money. In my own operation, I have $40 million crossing the threshold every year, and I want to be sure that the $40 million is properly credited to one of the 120 groups I'm collecting for. Every penny must be accounted for.

Haste Makes Waste

I had an old friend, long since departed, who told me something one time that I've never forgotten: "Measure twice and saw once." Think about it! Haste makes waste in developing systems just as in any other kind of operation. Spend sufficient time in developing systems to prevent, as much as possible, major modifications—or, in some instances, total rewrites. To give you an example, just before I left Chicago we had finished developing a system for recording employer reports and subsequently maintaining and using that information. The development of the total system involved a systems analyst for one entire year. That was her total responsibility—just developing the total system. Following that, the next requirement would have been to develop the program specifications, which would take a considerable additional period of time. Only when those program specifications are created and approved can you start writing the computer programs. A long period of time. But it is well worth that kind of investment because it can, and does, prevent major modification and rewrites.

I have a bone to pick with programmers, and that is this: they are always too quick to pick up the pencil and start writing programs. All of this planning and design has to come first in order to end up with a first-class product. Any system must be for the user, not the programmer. How many times have you told your EDP person that you want this particular information, and he says it can't be done? The computer won't handle that! The only reason it can't be done is that he didn't plan to do it. The only actual programming I've done during the last year has been for my little home computer. It's like eating peanuts. Once you get started and get into something, it's hard to set it down. It's difficult to turn off the switch and come back tomorrow morning to pick it up.

It's a challenge for them, and I'm not suggesting that it should not be. They're trying to utilize the computer to do more and better things for you, and they shouldn't be discouraged. But they cannot lose sight of the overall design that has been developed. The logic of the design cannot give way to the logic of the programmer.

Employer Reporting: A Key Area

When's the last time you looked at your employer reporting form? Is it doing the job for you? Does it provide the wherewithall for all of the information you must have? Is your staff spending too much time reconciling the employers' contribution reports with the employers?

Dues Checkoff. I once saw an employer report form and, in this particular instance, the collective bargaining agreement required contributions to a welfare plan, a pension plan, a dues checkoff, an industry advancement program and an apprentice fund. It very conveniently provided an opportunity for the employer to indicate the number of hours worked that month for each employee; but it did not provide any opportunity for the employer to indicate the amount of dues checkoff for each employee. This constantly created problems with these reporting forms and the balancing of the report, especially in the amount of the dues checkoff. Here's the problem. The monthly report covered the hours worked that month, but under dues checkoff, it only covered the dues checkoff withheld from the date the authorization to make the deduction was received from the employee. It was possible that a participant would go to work the first part of the month and not make the authorization until the middle of the month; thus, the employer didn't start the dues checkoff deduction until the middle of the month. But there was no place on the employer report form for the employer to explain this. What did it take? It took telephone calls back and forth to the employer to resolve it. This could have been avoided simply by providing a column for the employer to indicate the dues checkoff for each employee.

Single vs. Multiple Checks. How many of you are still demanding individual checks for the individual funds, or do you permit the employer to use a single check to cover all of the contributions? It still appears to be about half and half. There has been controversy over the past ten or 20 years on this subject and, evidently, it still continues. We made the decision for a single check some years ago and found that it has worked well. It's very easy to program the computer to split the check and direct it to the respective funds—say, 38% to the welfare fund and the other 62% to the pension fund. But the cheese gets a little more binding when, all of a sudden, there's a welfare plan, a pension plan, a vacation plan, a dues checkoff, an apprentice program and an industry advancement fund. It's just as easy to make this multiple split, but not when the dues checkoff isn't covering every hour worked, or when an employer decides not to contribute to the industry advancement fund, etc. Thus, it's gotten to the point that I feel it's most important that, even though we still permit the individual checks, we also demand from the employer that he advise us of the amount being paid to each of the funds.

Reconciliation. Is your employer report form designed so that the employer will help you in your work by cutting down the amount of reconciliation necessary? There is another thing that computers can so easily do, and that is to assist in the reconciliation of any discrepancy. A reconciliation form can be designed that can be mailed to the employer immediately after the report has been processed. This report can set forth the various discrepancies between the employer's report and our calculations—number of employees, hours, extensions, etc. (by fund). If this information is provided quickly to the employer, it can help him assist you in the reconciliation.

Accounts Receivable. I noticed that Mr. Beres indicated that his office has created an accounts receivable for each employer. We did this many, many years ago because we found it an important tool, especially in collections. We created an accounts receivable for every employer, and any time there was a discrepancy, it appeared as a charge to the account, together with other charges for liquidated damages, audit and collection costs, or any other amount owing by the employer. We eliminated the liquidated damages approach for delinquent employers in favor of charging 1½% per month on late payments and overdue balances. This, of course, was an easy thing to do because of the computer. The calculation of interest was made and charged to the appropriate employer's account, both for late payments and monthly balances yet unpaid. After the close of each month, the statement was forwarded to each employer.

In conclusion, the employer contributions report is the key to everything that we do. It is most important, and the design of the system to receive and maintain this information is well worth the great amount of time necessary to create the best system possible. You, therefore, must be involved in its design. Do not abdicate that responsibility.

EDP: What Goes On in the Little Black Box?

BY G. A. MELE

Today's Computers

The preparation for entrance into, or continuing in, the field of electronic data processing has become much more important today than in years past. As the age of miniaturization matures, computers are becoming more and more accessible to those of us with fewer dollars to spend on large equipment. The question today is not whether I can afford a computer, but which computer I can afford.

Those of you who already have computers of one sort or another I'm sure have encountered some of the problems that will be discussed in the following presentation. For those of you who do not as yet have computers, maybe we can help you avoid making some basic mistakes that would cost you time and money.

Let's start by asking some basic questions about the "little black box"—our friends, the computers. What are they? What can they do? How can they help me? Who is going to make them work?

What Are They?

Today's computers are anything from the little calculator that you keep in your pocket to giant-size computers that send men and machines to the moon and beyond. Some of the people in the advertising industry would like us to believe that if we don't buy computers for our youngsters they will grow up to be something less than total human beings.

That may be pushing it a little bit far, but in the future, the very near future, our lives are going to be somewhat controlled by the computer. We are moving more and more toward that type of environment, and if you have ever listened to any of the industry futurists talk about where we are going in this age of computers, it sometimes is very exciting, and sometimes a little frightening: 1984 is coming closer each and every day, and the era of George Orwell may be upon us sooner than we think. The government certainly has given us our number;

Mr. Mele, as vice president of TEDRO & Associates, Inc., Chicago, is in charge of all administration and corporate sales activities of the firm. Before assuming his present position, he served as vice president and director of marketing with MICA in Chicago, where previously he was director of data processing and manager of computer operations. Mr. Mele attended the University of Illinois in Chicago and has attended various American Management Association courses. He is a member of the Foundation's Administrators Committee and has spoken at many educational programs.

they call it our Social Security number, the number by which we are primarily identified. Our employers have given us numbers; credit card companies have given us numbers; department stores have given us numbers; and maybe not too far in the future we will all have numbers instead of names.

Computers are only tools, just like hammers, nails and saws to carpenters, and pencils to administrators. Computers are tools that we use to assist us in doing a better job. They are there to provide a service, these pieces of machinery; they really as yet are not able to think, even though the people from IBM and Sperry Rand and everyone else who makes them would like us to think that they can. They are not as yet ready to do that on their own.

I am a native Chicagoan, and our Police Department has a motto painted on the outside of all their patrol cars; it says, "We serve and protect," and I equate that with the computer. It is there to "serve" the administrator, and there to "protect" the beneficiaries, participants and trustees.

What Can They Do?

The Paper Chase. What can they do? They can do many things—and they can do nothing. That may sound a little ludicrous, but it is very true. If we purchase something just to purchase it, not knowing what it can or cannot do, it will never do anything productive. If we purchase a computer, any computer, just because the guy down the block has one or so we can say that we have a computer terminal on our desk, it will produce nothing worthwhile. Computers can produce mounds of meaningless information that will bog us down, instead of concise, to-the-point information, that we need to do a better and more accurate job. Or, they can do many things if we use them prudently.

Sometimes computer products and their value are judged by how many pounds of paper they can put out in a day, or in a month. Here's a little story. Before I got into the administrative business, I worked for a large international food manufacturing firm, and we produced, on a weekly basis, a large sales report, by product and a number of other categories. This report would take something like 30 hours to run on a very high-speed computer; when it was finished it stood about five and one-half feet tall. Each Wednesday, this report was brought up to the sales director and placed on his desk; we never heard anything, good, bad or indifferent about it. So after about four months of doing this, I walked upstairs and asked him how the report was and how he was using it. He said it was just great and that he couldn't do without it because his men in the field needed it, and that it was imperative that he have this thing at 9:00 a.m. each Wednesday. It was an awful looking report. We read it for months, and I never understood what it was trying to tell him. So, I tried something. I placed not only my job but my life in jeopardy at the same time. One Wednesday, I ran about 250 pages of this report and gave him six boxes of blank paper, sent the report upstairs to his staff and waited a day, then another day; then at the end of the second day, I walked into his office and asked him if the weekly report was all right. He said, "Fine, nothing out of the ordinary." So I proceeded to walk over to the corner and give him the first 200 pages and asked him what was on the rest of the report. After he got finished ranting, raving and calling me an awful lot of unflattering names, he admitted that not everyone really used that report, because it was filled with meaningless information.

The reason I tell the story is to illustrate the results of that type of situation. After that happened, we sat down and designed a usable report—something that was not only manageable, but something that was useful, not only to the manager, but also to his people in the field. So you can't ever get hung up on how much poundage a computer puts out. Whether it is a little computer or a giant computer, it could bog you down with unnecessary information. If you are continuously looking at meaningless, cluttered information and never getting to the meat of what you need, that computer will not be worth the electricity it uses.

We used to say a long time ago that the initials IBM at times stood for "It's Better Manual," and there are times when that actually still applies. Computer applications are not for every single thing that you do. Sometimes it just doesn't make any sense to put a small job on a large computer. Something that will take you many, many weeks or hours or days or whatever to program and set up, if it is operating in a manual environment and it doesn't take a lot of time to do it, there is no real reason to change. The simple fact that you have a computer doesn't mean that what you did manually two days ago now has to be done mechanically—although many hardware salesmen and systems analysts would like you to think that. It really isn't necessary.

How Can Computers Help Me? I like to say that computers can do all kinds of *things* and people do the *thinking* for them. They can perform all the tasks that are repetitive, boring and time-consuming. A computer can add two and two a million times and always come up with four. A college instructor once told me that not even the human brain can do that.

So they can do the day-to-day repetitive tasks that get to be boring—balancing employer reports, producing notices for self-payment, etc.—those types of things that are automatic, that deal with a certain specified set of rules, where once those rules are satisfied, a product can be prepared. Computers can provide us with all types of important products. They are extremely accurate. That is one of the largest assets of the computer: their accuracy.

In today's environment, we are all looking at cost controls. Whether it be for administration, claims, pension, welfare, savings plans or any other area, we are all looking at ways to cut costs. In the welfare field, a computer can help us analyze those cost items. Everyone today talks about *comput-*

erized claims systems, and I am sure you have heard it a hundred times. Well, it is an all-encompassing term, and it can mean several things; different things to different people. There are many ways of processing claims on a computer, from a very simple application of recording some basic statistics, to the ultimate—actually having a computer adjudicate a claim. There are a lot of things between these two extremes.

It is very important today for us to see how well our plans are doing. Those people charged with the responsibility of providing employee benefits (trustees, benefit managers and employers) are concerned about providing the best type of benefits that they can to their participants. Computers can provide us with the necessary data for making intelligent decisions about benefits. For instance, they can take all the data that apply to room and board expenses, diagnostic x-ray and lab expenses, surgical expenses, etc., using reasonable and customary tables to develop our own profiles. All of those types of cost control items are very important, not only to us as administrators and trustees but, increasingly, to the government. Government regulations are continuously requiring us to retain more and more information, and for longer periods of time. Computers can constantly gather information without ever getting tired of doing it.

When we look at what we want the computer to do, I think one thought should remain in our minds: *it can retain all of the data that we give it.* What I mean by that is, whenever we want to know something about a particular benefit or an individual or a group of individuals or a group of family members, with a properly designed system we can retrieve all the information at one time. Anytime anything changes for an individual, we can alter any record, or any material, within the entire system that applies to that individual. For example: John Jones is a participant in the fund, he is an eligible employee, he lives at 123 ABC Street and he continuously moves. This week he lives on ABC Street and next week he lives on CDE Street, and he continues to move. He is considerate enough to tell us when he moves (one of the very few people to do that). But now, in our system, we have a record that tells us about this participant, we have a name and address record for him, we have a welfare record for him, we have a pension record for him, we have claims records, we have savings records, we have apprentice records and we have all kinds of things in different areas. With the proper utilization of the computer system we can take that one change and alter all of those records.

If we did this with a manual system, we would have to give the person who handles welfare records that name and address change and they would make that change to his file; and then we would have to give a pension person the change, and they would have to enter it into his pension record; and we would have to give the savings person that record, and so on. Every time we move that piece of paper from one individual to another, we have not only created an additional piece of work but we have added one more possibility of error. The more times we handle that piece of paper, the more possibility there is for error, so we can let the computer do those tasks and only do them once (or fewer times than we would do them normally depending on the sophistication of the system and the computer).

Who Is Going to Make It Work?

Who is going to make the computer work? That is probably the single most important question to anybody. As I said before, computers can't think, they can't do anything unless somebody turns that button on that says, you've got power, Mr. Computer. Getting the right people is as important, possibly more important, in a computer environment than it is in any other environment in any business. Good people today are extremely hard to find. Good computer people today are almost *impossible* to find. Someone once told me the best way to get good people is to steal them from your competitors. That is probably a good idea, but it doesn't always work.

Asking the Right Questions. There are a number of ways to secure good people. I am sure all of you run ads in the newspapers and use employment agencies. Whatever vehicle works most successfully for you in your own area is the one to pursue. The only thing that I would add is to be extremely diligent in following up on technical people from a reference standpoint. Oftentimes, this is very difficult, and you may have to make a lot of phone calls and/or write a lot of letters; but believe me, the effort that you put into the front end evaluation of that highly skilled, technical, highly compensated individual will pay off down the line. With all of our EEOC limitations on what we can ask new employees and what previous employers can tell us about the employees, it may be difficult to secure the type of information that we need. But it is extremely important, because that individual can become the hub of a wheel and if that hub does not work right, the wheel isn't going to.

Try to develop some type of test. We are in a rather unique business. The administration of employee benefit funds, the administration of any type of employee benefit program, is unto itself a little unique. It differs from working for an insurance company, it differs from working for a single employer and, because of that, we really have to develop some type of test to see if that individual who was good at programming inventory control can adapt to and understand what we are trying to do. The best test to develop is a test of your own. You are the most familiar with your own operation; therefore you can design and develop a comprehensive test that will allow you to know that this individual is capable of comprehending what you are trying to accomplish.

Most of us believe that we can go ahead and hire somebody who formerly worked for an insurance company, because if they know how an insurance company works, they know what we need. Right? Well, maybe. We certainly deal or have dealt with a lot of insurance companies. Those of us who are also involved with self-funded programs know that we deal with the same concepts, but not the same type of reporting, so be careful of the "insurance company"-oriented individual.

A Special Kind of Skill. When you talk about securing good people, you are talking about the systems analyst, the programmer and the person in the office who runs the computer. It is extremely important to choose those employees carefully from top to bottom, because even when you get to the level of a data entry clerk, that person has to have more than the typical clerical skills. They will be doing more types of work than the average clerk who opens the mail for you or records an employer report.

Those people who are dealing in data processing are dealing with all areas of benefits. They are not specializing in just the welfare, or pension, or savings or any one of the fringe benefit plans, they are in fact required to become familiar with *all* of those areas because the same person who enters the data for the welfare fund is going to enter data for the pension fund, it is not going to be someone else.

The point I am trying to get across is that by using something you are familiar with you will have the ability to judge the qualifications of any particular individual, and that is the most important element. People are the most expensive part of operating a data processing department. In the computer environments with which I have been involved, the piece of hardware you buy is a large cost item, but it's a fixed cost and when it's paid for (or once the leasing arrangements are set up), the amount is fixed. But people costs in this area keep going up and up.

Eliminating the Mystique

Eliminating the mystique of the computer in today's environment is much easier than it was a number of years ago. Almost all of us are familiar with some type of computer or electronic data processing device.

The aura of mystery that surrounded computers in the past was created by the "computer professionals" to chase away outsiders. It was a certain form of job security. If no one else knew what you were doing, you became "the indispensable person" of the department or maybe even the entire company.

There is no real mystique about a computer, or a computer department, or a computer area, or the "little black box." I have never seen a black computer, I don't know if any of you who have computers have a black one; we have blue ones, yellow ones, orange ones, brown and red ones, but I have never seen a black one. There shouldn't be any mystique about a computer. Computers really, as I mentioned before, are only pieces of machinery. But remember: they *can* do anything; the only limits we can put on them are the limits of our own imagination.

What Do You Really Need?

What we can do with the computer can be extremely profitable, not only from the standpoint of doing a good job, but from the standpoint of understanding another discipline. Many times, when we first become involved in the computer field we get confused with our egos. We want to have a machine that is just as big as the guy's down the block, or we want to have a cathode ray tube (CRT) sitting on our desk, or we want to have something that is the Cadillac of the industry instead of a Chevrolet. There is nothing wrong with that *if* you have the funds, the need, and the expertise to go into it. Go right ahead and do it.

Need is the biggest question for those of you who are starting out with computers. What do you really need, not just for today, but for years from now? When you look at a piece of hardware and you look at an application that you are now doing, you must rely on foresight for future applications. If you have a fund with 1,000 people and you see a possibility of expanding that fund from 1,000 to 2,000, or if you have a 50,000 man fund and you see that moving from 50,000 to 60,000 to 70,000, consider how many different decisions you will have to make.

Eligibility requirements make a big difference. What are my eligibility criteria? Is eligibility determined semiannually, is it annual, is it quarterly, is it weekly, is it based on an hour bank, what are the self-pay provisions, is it a simple type of eligibility or is it complex? If it is an annual eligibility and I have to record this year's hours for next year's eligibility, I will not require a great deal of sophistication. If, on the other hand, I have a weekly eligibility, I may require a high degree of sophistication, because I have to know whether participant A is eligible, if payment is made on Monday and he goes into the hospital on Thursday.

How do I do that? Well, the degrees of sophistication are certainly different. If I have a quarterly or semiannual or annual eligibility, I can pick up hours or weeks, or whatever the contribution vehicle is, and at the end of a quarter produce a report. I can produce 50 copies of that report and I can give it to anybody who wants one. If I really want to be fancy, I can place a terminal on everyone's desk. I can give all the trustees terminals in their offices and they can check on everyone they want to, at any time they wish. But is all that really necessary? I don't know of too many trustees, union or management, who sit at their desks all day and have nothing better to do than look at eligibility records, or look to see if employer ABC has paid his bill this month. I think that is what they depend on us, as administrators, to do for them.

(Almost) Anything Is Possible

You can do anything between these wide ranges of sophistication; it merely takes a little bit of thought in the beginning and asking yourself the right kinds of questions. What do I want to do now? What do I want to do six months from now? What do I hope to do two years from now? Almost anything is possible with a computer. I would like to use a little story that I heard Myron Cohen once tell that really illustrates the concept that anything can be done under the right set of circumstances.

Seems there was this little Italian immigrant who was about 70 years old and who finally decided, after being in this country for some 50 years, to get his citizenship papers. He had studied very hard. The day he was to go before the judge and get his citizenship papers, he walked up to the courthouse and looked at this gigantic edifice in front of him, saying to himself, "I don't think I will ever get-a my papers when I go in this-a place." He walked into the courthouse and into the huge courtroom and sat there for what seemed to be an eternity before the judge appeared on the bench. The judge finally appeared and called up a number of people and passed them for their citizenship. Finally, it was his turn. He was called before the judge, and if you can, picture this little five foot tall Italian immigrant walking up to the bench looking at the judge in his impressive black robes and saying to him, "You-a Honor, I love-a this country very much, I have-a been here for 50 years, I have-a nine children, all have-a become good citizens, they have-a become doctors and lawyers, and mothers and school teachers, but I no talk-a too good-a English because I never learned how to speak real-a well, but I know all about-a this country and its constitution-a, and its George Washing Machine, its-a president, Abraham Linguini," he said, "All of them-a things, I know about-a, but because I don't speak-a too good English, I no think you gonna give-a me my papers," and the judge peered down at him and after what seemed an eternity said, "Long I sit up on-a this-a bench, you gonna get-a you papers."

So you can see that under the right set of circumstances, anything is possible. The same applies to computers.

The Computer Department

What Are the Real Costs?

When we look at most computer departments, they are the largest cost centers most companies have. That really applies across the board. I don't know of any "computer department" that earns any money for its company, unless it is a service bureau and then it's *supposed* to earn money. Many computer departments do nothing but eat up money; they don't generate one cent of income. What you have to try to do is control that cost area and, at the same time, produce enough good products to help the support areas save the company money. Then you've got a good working system.

One of the biggest selling points used by computer hardware salesmen is that they are going to save you money by eliminating something. That something is usually people. I'm sure those of you who have ever purchased any type of EDP equipment have heard the argument that this or that piece of hardware is equal to 1½ or two or 2½ people. The logical conclusion, then, is that I can save people dollars by spending machine dollars. They are going to take this $250,000 computer and eliminate A, B, C and D so that you can end up with a $25,000 savings, or some similar type of savings. I don't know of an installation that has ever accomplished that.

What usually happens is that we replace 1½, two or 2½ clerical people who may be earning $10,000 per year with one or two computer people at $12,000-25,000 per year. We really wind up with fewer people—but more expense.

We usually ask ourselves at this point in our deliberation, do I really need a computer and all the headaches that go with it? The answer to the question is yes, and for a number of very practical reasons. The first is that the types of situations we deal with today—the gathering of large amounts of data—in the long run will cost you more in a manual environment. It will cost more not only because it will require more people—and remember, we said people are our largest cost item—but in addition, and far more importantly, it will cost us in the areas that can hurt us most—service and accuracy.

The average trust fund or the average medium-sized business cannot function today in a competitive environment without some type of electronic data processing system. The amount of equipment may be small, medium or large, but if you feel that you can do the same thing manually that can be done on a computer, you are not being realistic. Not over the long haul. If you have a person sitting at a desk at a salary of $10,000 a year and that person is recording all the eligibility information that you need, or that you think you will ever need, then you don't need an expensive computer, what you may require is a $15,000 computer which can utilize the talent of that person in a better manner than a manual operation will. Then you are going to be saving money.

People are also more mobile than computers, and they certainly are more temperamental than machines. In a manual environment, if the person responsible for recording eligibility decides to leave, a problem may arise until that person is replaced and the replacement is trained. In a mechanical environment, we need only pick up the slack which losing that person has created as far as processing data for the computer. Remember, the computer already knows the eligibility criteria. If we lose an employee, we still have the services of the machine. Computers don't have to be retrained. It may sound insignificant but, depending on the degree of personnel turnover you have, it can become a substantial dollar figure.

The cost of accuracy is something most of us rarely look at. But if you ever tried to analyze what an error costs you in your office, you will find that it can be very expensive. Errors in a computer environment can become exceedingly expensive.

For example, let's assume that a clerk who is responsible for entering eligibility information makes an error on Mr. John Jones' record by crediting him with 80 hours instead of eight. What happens? In a well-run data processing department, all functions are costed, because they are charged back to a specific department or unit. Let's say it costs $.02 to process an eligibility transaction through the entire "employee eligibility system." By entering an incorrect piece of information, we have in fact increased the cost of that transaction threefold: first the initial cost, second, a reversing entry, third, a new and correct entry. This transaction that normally cost $.02 has now cost $.06. This would not seem to be an amount which by itself will be considerable, but if we multiply this threefold cost many times, we can see what the bottom line will be.

In the data processing department, errors of omission are also added to errors of commission. Data processing managers must be held accountable for the performance of their people just as all other managers are.

A computer can be your biggest asset if it provides you with what you need. The key phrase, again, is "what you need." You, the user of data processing products, must receive all the information you need to carry out your job responsibilities to their highest level of accuracy. The five foot report that no one fully understands becomes a liability because it wastes precious time—the time of creative, productive human beings trying to sort out good information from a poorly designed mechanical report. These types of situations drain not only men but machines.

Department Structure

Department structure really depends on size. Large computer departments are structured in a fashion similar to the diagram, "Data Processing Organization Chart."

The most important thing to remember about this structure is that the department head should have officer status. The primary reason for this is that in many situations the data processing director must have the authority to set priorities. For instance, if the accounting vice president and the sales vice president want something at the same time and the data processing director is not on the same corporate level, he has to try to satisfy both, not the one that is most important at that time. Most companies today have realized the importance of this concept, because now the data processing officer has the same reporting responsibilities as the other officers. No longer is the chief financial officer of most companies responsible for the data processing department, as in years past. This is a change for the better because, frankly, most financial officers do not have either the time or the desire to become data processing experts.

Data Processing Organization Chart

- Director Systems & D.P.
  - Admin. Assistant
  - Systems Manager
    - Sr. Systems Analyst
  - Prog. Manager
    - Senior Programmer
      - Programmer
        - Programmer Trainee
  - Operations Manager
    - Comp. Oper. Supervisor
      - Sr. Comp. Operator
        - Jr. Comp. Operator
    - I/O Control Supervisor
      - Sr. I/O Control Clerk
    - Keypunch Supervisor
      - Sr. Keypunch Op. Operator

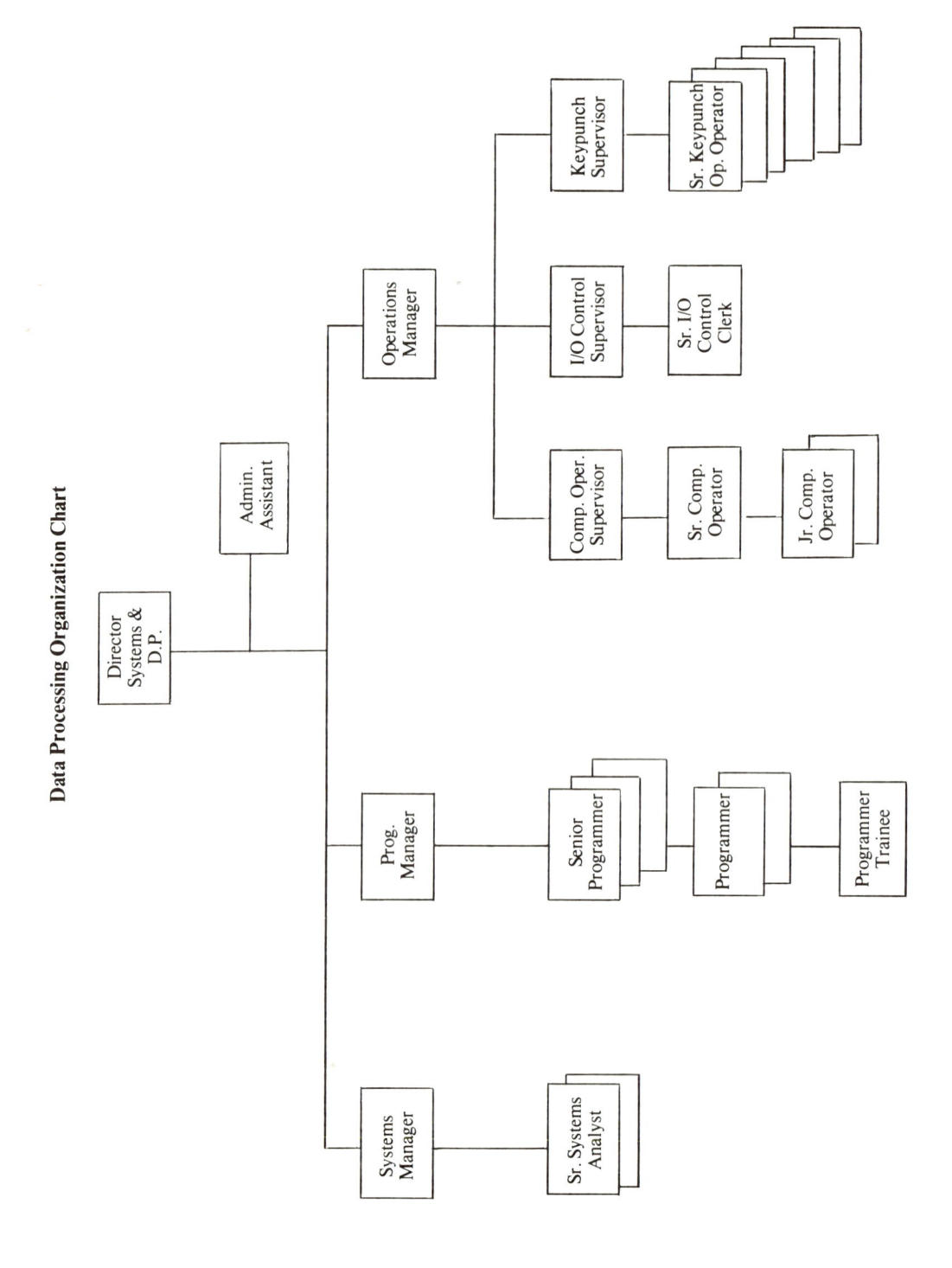

Earlier I spoke about personnel costs in data processing. In order that you might appreciate the significance of these salaries as they compare to normal clerical salaries, let's look at them in more detail. The following salary amounts are based on information gathered in October 1980 for the Chicago Metropolitan Area. They may vary slightly by geographic area, higher on the East and West Coast, lower in the North and South.

	Low	High
Director		
Data Processing	$25,000	$40,000
Systems Manager	$23,000	$30,000
Senior Systems Analyst	$17,000	$22,000
Operations Manager	$22,000	$28,000
Senior Programmer	$15,000	$20,000
Programmer	$12,000	$17,000
Programmer Trainee	$ 9,000	$13,000
Computer Operations		
Supervisor	$15,000	$21,000
In/Out Control		
Supervisor	$12,000	$15,000
Data Entry Supervisor	$12,000	$15,000
Senior Data Entry		
Operator	$10,000	$14,000
Data Entry Operator	$ 9,000	$12,000

These are all subject to change at a moment's notice. The data processing industry is very sensitive to the law of supply and demand. My suggestion is that you survey your area when looking to hire data processing personnel. A couple of telephone calls could save you a lot of time and money.

Just a small note: We have gone through elaborate procedures to secure the best people possible; now, how do we keep them? The first thing most of us think of is money. Money is certainly a motivator. However, most technical people are most interested in keeping up with the "state of the art." Continuing education and challenge are more important to these people than money. Don't be afraid to ask what types of things interest these people most.

In the small installations, several functions can be combined. The person who operates a small computer department must wear a variety of hats. He becomes the chief cook and bottle washer for the entire area. He must be the director, the systems manager, the programmer, the analyst and so on. He becomes a very valuable commodity. When that situation occurs, the best thing for us to do as managers and department heads is to make sure that those people who are primarily responsible for what is going on in the administrative areas become actively involved. The person who operates the computer in small installations can also be the systems analyst and/or programmer or the programmer-analyst. These three disciplines can be combined into a single individual because in the smaller operation, a smaller degree of specialization is required. Example: It is extremely important to employ a senior systems analyst if you are designing an on-line claims system. However, it is not necessary to have that same talent if you are dealing with a cash receipts situation.

Structuring an Effective Environment

Responsibility and Accountability

Setting Standards. By operating in a structured environment as opposed to a non-structured environment we will be able to assign specific responsibilities. All of us who have been in the data processing business for any length of time have heard this kind of exchange: "I would like to have a report that gives me the following information, when can I expect to get it?" Response: "We might be able to get it for you in six months" or "We can't do that." Most data processing people have little sense of timing and have a tendency to tell you something—anything—so that they can get you out of their hair.

An answer of this nature should no longer be acceptable, for two basic reasons. First, if a client, or our immediate supervisor, asks for a report it usually means that he/she needs the information in that report within a reasonable length of time. That length of time can be agreed upon by the requestor and the data processing individual. Once a time is set, hold them to it. Data processing personnel must be held to times and dates just as all other departments' personnel are—no special treatment, no special exceptions.

Second, the reply "We cannot do that" is not acceptable. Why? Because the computer can do anything. Remember, we said the only limitation is our own imagination. More importantly, we don't get paid for things we can't do. When someone tells us they cannot do something, they either do not want to do it or the system has some flaw in its basic design. If you do not get a satisfactory answer to "Why can't we?" you may want to start looking for someone who says "We can" and then tells you how much time and effort it will take.

This type of responsibility or accountability is necessary in every area of data processing, from systems to programming to operations to data entry to input/output control. It is just as important for each level of a data processing department to be held to standards of performance as it is for every other discipline. I repeat, no special rules for the data processing department and its personnel.

Who's Responsible? Who's responsible for getting things done? When something doesn't happen, where does the buck stop? In a claims department, when somebody pays a claim incorrectly you know exactly where to go. You may start with a junior claims examiner, and then move up to the senior and then the supervisor and, last, the department head. The same holds true for the administration department. You know exactly where to go and how to get there. Computer departments are sometimes more confusing. Everybody always seems to say, "I didn't get it from him, she didn't get it from him, they didn't give me the right information." We can't allow this to happen. They have to operate under the same rules as the other departments. If the axe falls from the top in every other department, it should fall the same way in the computer department. But it always seems that computer people live under a different set of rules.

Now, it's a little different if the data processing director said: "Well, I didn't have enough time— what you told me to do changed, and it took us three more weeks in order to do it"; or, "We were 90% finished with the project, and you came up with major changes, that's why it is not ready." If you ask the systems people to make a major change to specifications that have been previously agreed to, they have a justification for changing the due date for that system. However, the new due date should be set at the time the change is agreed to. Make sure that you receive a new target date right then, not weeks later when you expect the project to be completed. "No surprises!"

If you tell your claims supervisor that you want your backlog cleared up in a week and a half, she says, "Yes, I can do it" or "No, I can't do it" or "This is what I need to get it done." You have got to use that same discipline within the computer department, particularly when that department becomes the support area for all other departments. If you are waiting for a claims report to come out of the computer department and you have seven people sitting in the claims area waiting for a report that is late and they are sitting idle or less productive than normal, what happens? It is costing money. Or if somebody is waiting to look at a screen that tells me John is eligible because they have a hospital on the phone who wants to confirm eligibility and you can't get to it for five minutes or five hours, what happens? It's costing you money and it's reducing efficiency.

It also will start to create a morale problem.

You will hear people who are not in the computer department saying, "What is going on in there?" And, "I can't do my job anymore because they are fouling up." Then the people in another department start to say, "We can't do a good job because they are not cooperating," and you wind up having a lot of unhappy people who start to blame all their problems on the DP department.

I believe the best type of manager to look for is one who is result-oriented. A person who believes in seeing that things get done is the kind of person you want. No matter how intelligent the systems people are, or how great the programmers are, the only thing that we see, and that our clients see, is the end result. If that end result isn't any good, or isn't timely, it doesn't make any difference how smart or good your people are. If we have all that intelligence working in a systems or programming environment, and we are not getting anything out of the machine, then we stand to lose our credibility.

Communication and Support. Once we demand a high level of responsibility and standards from the data processing department, we can put the same demands on the user departments. The ideal situation is to have the lines of communication always open between the user and data processing departments. The higher the level of communication between user and supplier, the more timely and accurate the information, at the lowest possible cost.

What is required from and by the DP support areas? What is required *by* data processing is good input; good input from those people supplying data to the computer. Remember what it costs to process an error. If information comes into the data processing department in an accurate fashion, it will go out the same way. I'm sure that all of you who have computers have heard the old garbage-in/garbage-out phrase, and it does sound a little trite at times but it's very true. What you want to do is build as many safeguards into the system to identify errors before they progress too far in the processing cycle. At the same time you want to design, or have your computer people design, documents for handling input that are easily understood by the users responsible for processing the input.

Keep Your Options Open

Today's computer environment allows you to get things done fairly quickly. Systems should be designed to provide the user with a large number of product options. New, high-level operating system software can give today's user the option and capability of maneuvering data in such a manner as to provide many different analyses of the same data. The key to doing this is in the system's design. When you are putting a system together, building files and records, you want to put in as much data as you can about each participant, employer, supplier, etc. Make sure that you gather as much information as possible about each.

There are only so many things that we as administrators or trustees or managers of employee benefit departments or corporations can know about an individual *today*. Next month, however, we may need to know a little more and next year we may need to know even more, and five years from now we may require twice as much information as today. Whenever we are designing a system, we want to make sure that that system is flexible enough to handle those situations. Today, I need to know that Jerry Mele is 41 years old, lives in Arlington Heights, Illinois, works for TEDRO and Associates, has a wife and five children, one car, and owns a home. Next year, I might be required to know how large a lot the house is on, the make and model of the car, how old the children are, if they are married or single, and what his/her mother's maiden name was. Five years from now the necessary information may double.

Prior to ERISA we weren't required to maintain very detailed records. The purge criteria or the drop-out criteria or the loss criteria were such that there was no need to keep work history for 50 years. Back in 1968, the company I worked for designed a pension system that was capable of keeping 50 years of work history for any participant. We thought at the time that would suffice, but with today's new laws prohibiting mandatory retirements that 50 year segment may not be sufficient. In 1968 it was thought to be more than adequate. We laughed about it because we were certain that no one would remain in the same job or same profession for 50 years. In 1977, the government said, "Guess what, you can't arbitrarily retire someone at 65." Five years from now they may tell us we can't retire someone at 75. In the multiemployer environment, it's possible to have a person work for 50 or 55 years for two hundred different employers, still be in the same industry, have 50 different contribution levels and have 25 sets of criteria for meeting service credit rules.

Today when we design systems we must keep in mind those areas where expansion is possible. When I first entered the data processing field many years ago, I was fortunate enough to have an excellent teacher who also happened to be my boss. One of the first things he taught me was that when you ask someone a question and the response is, "That never happens," that is the first thing you should plan for. Go no further until the system is designed to handle "what never happens" because as sure as the Lord made little green apples, what someone said wasn't going to happen, will happen as soon as you press the start button. It's the nature of the beast.

Easing the Transition

If you are moving from manual to mechanical processing, the natural tendency of your employees will be to fear the change. They are afraid of what might happen to their jobs. Somebody says, "You are going to get mechanical processing," and the early reaction is generally negative. Your employees are probably no different than most of us. To begin with, no one likes change. Someone who has operated in a non-computer environment who suddenly hears "computers are coming" will no doubt recall all of the horror stories they have heard. They won't accept the computer, and may do everything in their power to avoid it.

Ideally, it should be the other way around. The approach that should be taken in that situation is to say, "We are buying a computer to assist us, but it can't assist us if it doesn't know what we are doing. The only one who really knows what you are doing is yourself, and we are going to ask you to help us as much as you can." The more involvement you receive from the non-data processing people, the more cooperation you can expect in return and the better your system will run. No systems analyst can do a competent job unless he knows and understands what has to be done.

Systems Design

How should systems be designed? Most systems, at least in our field, can be designed with the KISS principle in mind. Keep it as simple as possible. One of the biggest mistakes made today by people in the computer business is to allow systems people to "design the system." They can't do it. They don't know "the system"—your system. You can't hire a systems analyst from an insurance company and have him come in and design an eligibility system for you. Unless he understands exactly what that eligibility clerk requires to perform his or her job, or what the trustees need to make responsible decisions, he will be unable to design a good system.

The approach that should be taken is that whoever is responsible for a function says, "This is what I need." A systems analyst says at that point, "This is the most efficient way to get what you need." The problem arises when I tell a systems analyst that I need A, B, C and D and he tells me that he can only provide A, B and C. I didn't ask him what he could give me; I told him what I needed. If he comes back to me and says, I can give you A, B, C and D, but I am going to give them to you in two reports and they are going to be marked A and B, that's fine, because I am still going to receive the same information, the information I need to do my job. If it comes out on a single report, two reports, or a single piece of paper, that's fine.

Oftentimes, we allow systems people to tell us what they can give us, not what we need. It is important, extremely important, never to lose sight of the fact that *you* and *your* people know what you need. If we allow a systems analyst to dictate a system, we will end up with something that is less than desirable. The minute that systems analyst leaves our area, our company or our department, we end up with a lot of extra work. It might even mean starting from scratch. We don't want to fall into the trap of getting a faster typewriter. Let's say that you are doing a particular task and you just want to do that same identical thing, only faster; when you are changing from a slower to a faster environment, ask yourself, why not improve it? How many times have you asked somebody why they are doing something that way and they say, "Well, because we have always done it that way." We have all done that. What we want to make sure happens is that when you ask, "Why are you doing it that way?" you also ask, "How can we do it better?"; "What can we do to improve it?"

It is essential that those people who are performing the tasks be involved in the systems design. Be specific. It's like the old story about buying a dog. A father told his son to go out and buy him a dog. The son came back with a Chihuahua. The father said, "I wanted a Great Dane"; "Well, you told me to go out and buy you a dog, you didn't tell me what kind." When you design systems and instructions, be specific. When setting up an input form, don't just say, this is an eligibility transaction; we need to know it's an eligibility transaction to accomplish the following jobs, or a pension transaction to accomplish specific goals. Even when we are specific, those who hear what we are saying may not understand it the same way. Being specific may help eliminate many of the possibilities for error.

Plan Applications

What do we require of the data processing department? Two basic things: timeliness and accuracy (not necessarily in that order). Accurate data will result in timely reports. The only thing that should deter a timely report is a problem with the hardware. Timeliness and accuracy are the cornerstones of a good data processing department, and can result in good relations with all of the other departments within an organization.

Recordkeeping and Data Management

Storage and Retrieval. My peers become angry with me when I suggest that we are in a business that doesn't require complex applications. We aren't sending space craft to the moon, and we aren't building skyscrapers. We are, however, gathering an awful lot of data. Our concepts and our calculations are fairly basic.

Once the data are gathered, we can do virtually anything that we want with them. For instance, assume we know the number of days for a hospital stay for a broken leg, and it amounts to five days at x number of dollars per day, and we know that two doctors treated the patient and he required 14 x-rays. Once the information is captured by the computer, we can extract it in any manner we wish. We can analyze all of the broken legs that we have on file. We can ask the computer to tell us how many people under age 40 had broken legs and spent more than five days in the hospital. We can determine how many people had appendectomies or how many people are suffering from lung problems in a specific geographic area. Our computer can perform all types of analytical tasks, and perform them quickly. Those aren't complex tasks, but they will require us to "massage a lot of data." We will be able to look at a file that has five, ten, 20 or perhaps as many as 50,000 records.

If we attempted a similar project on a manual system, we would be required to go back to the claims department and ask for all claim files to determine how many appendectomies had been performed in the last two years. An undertaking of that nature could take years to complete. If, however, the information has been gathered and stored on a computer, we would be able to have our answer in minutes—not years.

The increased amount of data that we are required to retain since the passage of ERISA will probably continue to increase for the rest of our lives. I don't believe any of us are predicting a *decrease* in the amount of data that we are required to retain. If there is a change, it's going to be the other way: toward increased retention.

Reports and Analyses. The number of requests from trustees, benefit managers and consultants for reports that analyze special circumstances has been increasing at a steady rate for the last five years. For example, a report that reflects a comparison of charges versus benefits paid is extremely important. Example: A participant spends five days in the hospital, his room and board charges are $1,000, and the plan pays $900. The plan paid 90% of the charges—a high percentage; however, if the plan had only paid $500, or 50% of the charges, there may be a need for improving coverage in this area. This type of analysis can be produced for each line of coverage. It can provide us with valuable information about how well the plans are serving the participants.

Similar reports are available for use by administration departments.

Analyses can be provided for eligibility, contributions, number of participants who attain and retain eligibility and self pay information, to mention a few. This information can be retrieved quickly in a mechanical environment. To obtain the same results manually would not only take an unreasonable amount of time, but would not guarantee a high degree of accuracy.

Plan Ahead. One more reminder about the systems department. Don't allow someone unfamiliar with your business to control your destiny. That's what's happening if you allow a systems analyst to design your system while you stand idly by. It's imperative that you get your nose in there, even if it's contrary to your nature.

Do we design systems to solve problems, or to fit hardware? This question is more important to those of you currently entering a computer operation than those already operational. It is very important not to put the cart before the horse. Don't purchase the hardware and then decide what you are going to put on it. Decide what you are going to put on your system and then decide what type of system configuration will handle it. The former is similar to buying a car, taking it home and then deciding that you want a radio. The same thing applies to a computer. Purchasing a data processing system that fulfills only your current needs and does not have the capability to grow at a pace as fast as your plan's growth could cost time and money. Before you buy, think about your future needs.

Company officials and trustees will not be pleased if every so often they hear, "We have to buy a bigger computer again, because we have outgrown the one we have."

When you are looking to implement a computer system, always decide what you want to do first, then choose the hardware that will get the job done, now and in the foreseeable future.

Documentation

Documentation is extremely important. Documentation that is understandable is imperative. I don't mean systems flow charts and programming definitions, I mean documentation that can be understood. We need to know in plain English (or, to quote our friends in the federal government, "language understandable to the average plan administrator") what that system is going to do for you.

Most programmers and systems analysts don't like to document. With the new systems and the new software available to us, most analysts will tell you that the software generates its own instructions. That's fine for all of the analysts who are going to follow them, but I personally still require some kind of systems definitions. I want someone to tell me how the system is working and what it is doing, so that I can say to a new employee during a training period, "This is what you are going to be doing, this is what you are going to be looking for, this is what you are going to be receiving," and have that employee be able to read and understand them.

Security

Security! Seminars on data processing and computer security are legion. Security means different things to different people. Security means that no one can get to and destroy or alter my data. Security means that no one who leaves my employ under adverse circumstances can destroy or otherwise harm my data. Security means having another system available if something happens to mine. Security means no unauthorized person having access to my data. And, security means tight controls for those who handle checks, have signature authority, and do the bursting and mailing.

Systems Backup

Each of us must make a determination as to where this priority lies. If you are in an environment that can operate for a day or two without your hardware working and still catch up once repairs are made, then backup systems aren't an important factor. If, however, you are in an environment that will not allow that, determine *before purchasing a system* who has a system equivalent to yours that can be used. A reciprocal agreement can be entered into: I'll use yours when mine breaks down, and you can use mine when yours breaks down.

Conclusion

In summary, let me say that an attempt should be made to remove the mysterious "little black box" theory of computer departments. Encourage all the user involvement that you possibly can.

The more interested user departments are, the more interested you become, the better the systems are that you will have working for you. Remember, the more outside user involvement you create, the better off you will be. It may mean the difference between a smoothly operating data processing area and one that fails to do the job.

Appendix

A Short Glossary of Terms

Acknowledgement

Most of the definitions which follow were selected from the International Business Machines publication "Glossary for Information Processing," in which permission is granted for reprinting in whole or in part with the exception of those definitions credited to the American Standards Association.

In any relatively new discipline the definitions will vary from text to text. Terms in the computer field have had an ancestry traceable to several disciplines, primarily engineering and mathematics. Business too has added a number of terms to the vocabulary of the computer field. We would expect, then, that during the coming years there will be repeated attempts to develop a universal vocabulary on which scientific studies in the field can depend. In the meantime we must struggle along as best we can, sometimes limiting definitions to serve our own purposes.

absolute address: (1) an address that is permanently assigned by the machine designer to a storage location or device; (2) a pattern of characters that identifies a unique storage location or device without further modification; (3) synonymous with machine address

absolute coding: coding using absolute operators and addresses

access arm: a mechanical device on a storage unit which positions the reading and writing mechanism

access time: usually the time taken to move data from storage to some delivery point either internally (mathematical operations) or externally (printing of a report on an on-line device), conversely, reference may be to the time taken to move data from some external device into storage

accumulator: a register or section of storage in which the answer to an arithmetic, or logical arithmetic, operation is placed

addend: a quantity which is added to another quantity

address: the reference location of a register or datum in storage (The address may be actual [numeric] or symbolic [name or label]. Reference may be to the entire datum or to its leftmost or rightmost digit.)

address modification: the process of changing the address part of a machine instruction by means of coded instructions

algorithm: a set of rules for solving a problem in a finite number of operations

alphanumeric: a general term for alphabetic letters, numerical digits, and special characters which are machine-processable

analog computer: a computing device which represents data as a point in a continuum and simulates or models behavior (The common slide rule is a good example.)

argument: a variable which is independent (Generally, it serves as an address or as a reference to some other quantity.)

arithmetic operation: any of the fundamental operations of arithmetic, e.g., the binary operations of addition, subtraction, multiplication, and division, and the unary operations of negation and absolute value

arithmetic unit: that circuitry or section of a computer in which arithmetic operations are performed

array: an arrangement or pattern of items

assemble: to prepare an object language program from a symbolic language program by substituting machine operation codes for symbolic operation codes and absolute or relocatable addresses for symbolic addresses

augend: a quantity to which another quantity is added

automatic coding: the production of a machine language computer program under the guidance of a symbolic representation of the program

automatic computer: a device which performs a series of operations under the guidance of an internal program

automatic data processing: the manipulation of data by means of automatic devices

auxiliary equipment: equipment not under direct control of the central processing unit

batch processing: a systems approach to processing where a number of similar input items are grouped for processing during the same machine run

binary: generally referring to the ability to achieve one or the other of two states, e.g., on-off, light-not light, magnetic field-no magnetic field

binary coded decimal: the representation of the binary number system in some special coded form, e.g., 8-4-2-1 (Sometimes such coding will include internal accuracy checks and signs.)

bit: a computer colloquial meaning binary digit

bit density: a measure of the number of bits recorded per unit of length or area

blank character: any character or characters used to produce a character space on an output medium

block diagram: generally, the representation of a data manipulation system by graphic means; often, a diagrammatic representation of a computer program

bootstrap: a self-starting system (Usually, reference is to a few instructions which will start some kind of continuing loading procedure.)

branch: (1) to depart from the normal sequence of executing instructions in a computer—synonymous with "jump"; (2) a machine instruction that can cause a departure as in 1—synonymous with "transfer"; (3) a sequence of instructions that are executed as a result of a decision instruction

buffer: any device which operates as an intermediary between two devices operating at different speeds or using different coding media

byte: a collection of binary bits treated as a word or as a computing datum

card code: the combinations of punched holes which represent characters in a punched card

card column: one of the vertical lines of punching positions on a punched card

card field: a fixed number of consecutive card columns assigned to data of a specific nature, e.g., card columns 15-20 can be assigned to identification

card punch: a device to record information in cards by punching holes in the cards to represent letters, digits, and special characters

card reader: a device which senses and translates into internal form the holes in punched cards

card row: one of the horizontal lines of punching positions on a punched card

cell: a location

central processing unit: that part of the computer which controls the execution of instructions

chad: that piece of material removed in punching a hole in perforated tape

chaining: a system of storing records in which each record belongs to a list or group of records and has a linking field for tracing the chain

channel: (1) a path along which signals can be sent, e.g., data channel, output channel; (2) the portion of a storage medium that is accessible to a given reading station, e.g., track, band; (3) a unit which controls the operation of one or more input/output units

character: one of a set of elementary signals which may include decimal digits 0 through 9, the letters a through z, punctuation marks, and any other symbols acceptable to a computer for reading, writing, or storing

character set: a list of characters acceptable for coding to a specific computer or input/output device

clear: to convert all digit storing units of the computer to either zeros or blanks

closed routine: a routine which is not inserted as a block of instructions within a main routine but is entered by basic linkage from the main routine

COBOL (COmmon Business Oriented Language): (1) a data processing language that makes use of English-language statements; (2) pertaining to a computer program which translates a Cobol language program into a machine-language program

coded decimal: a type of notation in which each decimal digit is identified by a group of binary ones and zeros

collate: the process of merging two uniformly ordered sets of data into one unit

collating sequence: usually the arrangement of the characters in a set in some kind of sorting hierarchy

collator: generally an electro-mechanical device which performs the collating act

command: an instruction in machine language

common language: a language in machine-sensible form which is common to a group of computers and associated equipment

compile: to prepare an object-language program from a program written in another programming language by performing the usual functions of an assembler and also making use of the overall logical structure of the program for generating more than one machine instruction for each symbolic statement or both

complement: a quantity derived from a given quantity and expressed to the same base (Usually a complement represents the negative of the given quantity.)

computer program: an ordered set of instructions linked in such a way as to describe completely the operations required to solve a problem

console: the operator control and contact point of the computer system

constant: a fixed or invariable value or data item

control: generally, the automatic internal actions of the computer which handle the interpretation and sequencing of instructions

core storage: a form of high-speed storage using magnetic cores

corner cut: a corner removed from a card for orientation purposes

counter: a storage location in which a count is kept, or a set of instructions to the computer which will keep track of the number of times an operation is performed

data processing: the manipulation of data by planned means

data processing system: a network of machine components capable of accepting information, processing it according to a plan, and producing the desired results

debug: to detect, locate, and remove mistakes from a routine or malfunctions from a computer

decision box: a flow chart symbol whose interior contains the criterion for decision or branching

deck: usually a set of punched-cards which constitutes a pack

decrement: (1) the quantity by which a variable is decreased; (2) in some computers, a specific part of an instruction word; (3) to decrease the value of a number

destructive reading: a reading procedure which destroys that which is read

diagnostic: usually refers to the process by which an error or machine malfunction is located

diagnostic routine: a routine designed to locate and explain errors in a computer routine or hardware component

digit: one of the ideographic characters 0, 1 . . . 9 . . . used to designate a quantity smaller than n for a base n number system

digital: pertaining to the use of discrete integral numbers in a given base to represent all the quantities that occur in a calculation

digital computer: one which solves problems by the treatment of discrete data

disk storage: a storage device which uses magnetic recording on flat rotating disks

display: any graphic representation of data

dividend: the quantity which is divided by another quantity; also the numerator of a fraction

divisor: a quantity which is used to divide another quantity; also the denominator of a fraction

double precision: pertaining to a quantity having twice as many digits as are normally carried; e.g., a double precision number requires two machine words in a fixed-word machine

double punch: a term which usually refers to more than one numeric punch in any one column of an IBM card

drum storage: a storage device which uses magnetic recording on a rotating cylinder; a type of addressable storage associated with some computers

duplex channel: a channel providing simultaneous transmission in both directions

dynamic storage: storage such that information at a certain position is changing over time and so is not always available instantly, e.g., acoustic delay line storage

effective address: the address (absolute) which results from all prescribed manipulations specified in the instruction

electronic data processing: the manipulation of data by electronic means

end mark: a code or signal which indicates termination of a unit of information

end-around carry: a circular carry in which the leftmost digit replaces the rightmost digit and intermediate digits shift one place to the left

end-of-file mark: a code which signals the last record of a file has been read

execute: to carry out an instruction or perform a routine

exponent: a number placed at the right and above a symbol in typography to indicate the number of times that symbol is a factor, e.g., 10 to the 4 equals 10x10x10x10, or 10,000

expression: a source-language combination of one or more operations

external storage: a storage device outside the computer which can store information in a form acceptable to the computer, e.g., cards, tapes

feedback: the feeding back of part of the output of a machine, process, or system to the computer as input for another phase, especially for self-correcting or control purposes

field: usually refers to a complete datum in storage or to a column or group of columns in a punched card which records one datum

file: any labeled collection of records

file gap: usually refers to an unrecorded section of magnetic tape which marks the end of one file and the beginning of another

fixed point: refers to a system of decimal control in which the decimal point is at one end or the other of the numerals as they are internally stored

fixed point arithmetic: arithmetic using a fixed location for the decimal or binary point in each number, e.g., 2.5 plus 212.73 equals 215.23; that one of the two elements of the floating point representation of a number which is not the exponent or power of the base

fixed word length: a term which refers to computers in which data are treated in units of a fixed number of characters or bits (as contrasted with variable word length)

flag: usually a signal which marks off a data element in storage, e.g., a minus sign in the left most position of a computer word can constitute a flag marking the end of the computer word

floating point: a form of number representation in which quantities are represented by a number multiplied by the number base raised to a power, e.g., the decimal number 397 can be written as 3.97 x10 squared, or 0.397x10 third power

floating point arithmetic: arithmetic using a variable location for the decimal or binary point in each number, where the location in each number depends upon the size of the number, and its power of 10 or 2, e.g., 2.5 plus 2.1273x10 squared equals 2.1523x10 squared

flow chart: a graphical representation for the definition, analysis, or solution of a problem in which symbols are used to represent operations, data, flow, and equipment

FORTRAN (FORmula TRANslating System): (1) a data processing language that closely resembles mathematical language; (2) pertaining to a computer program which translates a Fortran language program into a machine-language program

gang-punching: to punch all or part of the information from one punched card into succeeding cards

garbage: unwanted or meaningless information carried in storage

generalized routine: a routine designed to process a large range of specific jobs within a given type of application

generator: a program which causes another program to be generated by the assembly of groups of previously prepared instructions

group mark: any indicator to signal the end of a word or other unit of data

gulp: a small group of bytes, similar to a word or instruction

hardware: the mechanical, magnetic, electrical, and electronic devices or components of a computer

hash total: a summation for checking purposes of one or more corresponding fields of a file which would ordinarily not be summed

heuristic: a process or program which is open to a variety of solutions and which requires exploration

hexadecimal number system: a number system using the equivalent of the decimal number 16 as a base

housekeeping: operations in a routine which do not contribute directly to the solution of the problem but do contribute directly to the operation of the computer

image: an exact logical duplicate stored in a different medium

immediate address: the designation of an instruction address which is used as data by the instruction of which it is a part

index register: generally a register containing a fixed datum to be added to or subtracted from an instruction operand to generate an effective address

indexing: a technique of address modification often implemented by means of index registers

initialize: to set certain counters, switches, and addresses at specified times in a computer routine

in-line processing: the processing of data in random order, not subject to preliminary editing or sorting

input area: the area of internal storage into which data is transferred from external storage

inquiry: a request for information from storage, e.g., a request for the number of available airline seats or a machine statement to initiate a search of library documents

instruction: a single element of a program which provides an operation specification and one or more addresses which may be the location of operands or may constitute special signals for control of the operation

instruction format: the allocation of bits or characters of a machine instruction to specific functions

instruction register: usually any register which contains the instruction while it is being executed

internal storage: storage within the computer from which instructions can be executed directly

interpretive routine: a routine which decodes instructions written as pseudocodes and immediately executes those instructions, as contrasted with a compiler which decodes the pseudocodes and produces a machine-language routine to be executed at a later time

interrecord gap: the unrecorded portion between records on magnetic tape

Interrupt: a break in the normal flow of a system or routine such that the flow can be resumed from that point at a later time (An interrupt is usually caused by a signal from an external source.)

iterate: to repeatedly execute a loop or series of steps, e.g., a loop in a routine

justification: the act of adjusting, arranging, or shifting digits to the left or right to fit a prescribed pattern

key punch: a device for punching holes in cards according to a predetermined mode of data representation

label: a code name that classifies or identifies a name, term, phrase, or document

leading edge: the edge of a card which first enters the machine

library routine: a checked-out routine which may be incorporated into a larger routine and is maintained in a library as an aid to programmers

linkage: the interconnections between a main routine and a closed routine, i.e., entry and exit for a closed routine from the main routine

list: to print every relevant item of input data

literal: a symbol which names itself and which is not the name of something else

loop: any series of instructions which constitute a circular process from which exit may be made only upon the achievement of some predetermined state

machine language: that computer language, usually numeric, in which operations are actually performed

MACRO instruction: in symbolic programming, a MACRO instruction is replaced by a previously written series of instructions

magnetic core: a ferrite device capable of achieving either of two possible states of magnetization

magnetic tape: any tape capable of recording and retaining a code in the form of magnetic impulses arranged in channels

mantissa: the fractional part of a logarithm, e.g., in the logarithm 2.5, 2 is the characteristic and 5 is a mantissa

manual operation: processing of data in a system by direct manual techniques

mapping: (1) a transformation from one set to another set; (2) a correspondence

mark-sense: to mark a position on a punched card with an electrically conductive pencil for later conversion to machine punching

master file: a main reference file of information

matrix: an array, items arranged in a pattern

memory: generally means internal computer storage

merge: to combine (Usual reference is to the process of combining two decks of previously ordered cards or combining the information on two or more ordered tapes.)

MICR: abbreviation of the term "magnetic ink character recognition"

microprogramming: machine-language coding in which the coder builds his own machine instructions from the primitive basic instructions built into the hardware

microsecond: one millionth of a second

minuend: the quantity from which another quantity is subtracted

mnemonic code: a technique to assist the human memory (A mnemonic code resembles the original word and is usually easy to remember, e.g., MPY for multiply and ACC for accumulator.)

modulo: a mathematic operator which yields the remainder function of division, thus, 39 modulo 6 = 3

monitor: to control the operation of several unrelated routines and machine runs so that the computer and computer time are used advantageously

Monte Carlo method: any procedure that involves statistical sampling techniques in order to obtain a probabilistic approximation to the solution of a mathematical or physical problem

multiplexing: the transmission of messages simultaneously over a single information channel

multiplicand: the quantity which is multiplied by another quantity

multiplier: the quantity which is used to multiply another quantity

multiprocessor: a machine with multiple arithmetic and logic units for simultaneous use

nanosecond: one thousand millionth of a second

nesting: including a routine or block of data within a larger routine or block of data

no-op: an abbreviation of the term "no operation" (Often, reference is to a dummy or space-filling computer command which accomplishes nothing more than the movement beyond itself to the next instruction in sequence.)

numeric coding: coding which uses digits only to represent data and instructions

object routine: the machine-language routine which is the output after translation from the source language

off-line storage: those storage devices which are not electronically connected to the computer and are not subject to its programmed control

one-for-one: a phrase often associated with an assembly routine where one source-language instruction is converted to one machine-language instruction

one-line: subject to control by the computer

operand: usually an element to be used in an arithmetic process or the address of such an element

operation code: a numeric or symbolic representation of a computer process or operation

optical scanning: a technique for machine recognition of characters by their images

optimize: to arrange the instructions or data in storage so that a minimum amount of machine time is spent for access when instructions or data are called out

output area: the area of internal storage from which data is transferred to external storage

overflow: (1) that portion of data that exceeds the capacity of the allocated unit of storage; (2) pertaining to the generation of overflow as in 1

overpunch: a second hole in a card column which is above the original one

parity bit: a redundant bit added to a group of bits so that an inaccurate retrieval of that group of bits is detected

primary storage: the main internal storage

print wheel: a single element providing the character set at one printing position of a wheel printer

printer: a device which expresses coded characters as hard copy

problem-oriented language: usually a symbolic computer language which is not directly constructed for a particular computer but is designed for convenience in solving a given class of problems (Cobol and Fortran are examples.)

program library: a set of computer programs for the solution to common classes of problems

programming: the art of reducing the plan for the solution of a problem to machine sensible instructions

quotient: the quantity which results from dividing one number by another

random access: pertaining to the process of obtaining data from, or replacing data into, storage when there is no sequential relation governing the access time to successive storage locations

random number generator: a special machine routine or hardware designed to produce a random number or series of random numbers according to specified limitations

register: any device which can store a datum such as a computer instruction or a computer instruction element

report generation: a technique for producing complete machine reports from information which describes the input file and the format and content of the output report

reproducer: a device which will duplicate, on one card, all or part of the information contained in another card

routine: a sequence of machine instructions which carry out a well-defined function

scaling: the process of changing a quantity from one notation to another

scan: sequential examination element by element

sequencing: ordering in a series or according to rank or time

serial access: access to a datum by means of movement through an ordered collection of data

shift: a data movement (Accumulators usually permit the shifting of data contained therein either to the left, or to the right with or without rounding.)

sign position: the location of the sign of a number (usually the units position of the number)

simplex channel: a channel which permits transmission in one direction only

simulate: to represent a function by some other system

skip: in terms of computers, reference is usually to the jumping of one or more instructions in sequence

source language: a language that is an input to a given translation process

statement: one instruction; one group of instructions which constitutes a process

step: (1) one instruction in a computer routine; (2) to cause a computer to execute one instruction

storage dump: to output the entire contents of an internal memory module

store: usually, to enter information into a computer or an on-line auxiliary computer memory device

stored program computer: a computer which can contain and follow a set of instructions and manipulate data or its own instructions

string: a connected sequence of characters, words, or other elements

subroutine: a routinized, generalized, set of instructions which are a subset of a larger collection

subscript: (1) a letter or symbol in typography written below a set name to identify a particular element or elements of that set; (2) an indexing notation

subtrahend: the quantity which is subtracted from another quantity

sum: the quantity which results from adding two quantities

symbolic address: any computer address which is written in characters other than those which constitute the basic numeric code of the computer

symbolic language: a pseudo-language made up of letters, characters, and numbers which are not the internal language of the computer system

table: a data collection ordered in such a way that any item therein may be located by a reference to position

tape: a linear medium for storing information which can be used as input or output to a computer, e.g., magnetic tape

tape to card: pertaining to equipment or methods which transfer information directly from tape to cards, usually off-line

terminal unit: equipment on a communication channel which may be used for either input or output

tie line: a leased communication channel

translator: a routine for changing information from one representation or language to another

truncate: to cut off at a specified spot (as contrasted with round)

unit record: historically, a card containing one complete record; currently, the punched card

unpack: to recover the original data from packed data

update: to modify a master file with current information according to a specified procedure

validity check: a check for accuracy of character representation

variable: any quantity capable of assuming a set of values

visual scanner: (1) a device that scans optically and usually generates an analog or digital signal; (2) a device that optically scans printed or written data and generates their representation

word: a set of characters which have one addressable location and are treated as one unit

word length: (1) the number of bits or characters handled as a physical unit by a computer; (2) the size of a field

zero suppression: usually refers to the process of eliminating leading or non-significant zeros in numbers

zone: the 12, 11, or 0 punches in IBM card code

zone bits: the bits other than the four used to represent the digits in a dense binary code

zone punch: an additional punch or punches in a card column for purposes of expanding the number of characters which may be represented

Mini and Microcomputers—
Data Processing for Small Funds

BY SPENCER V. BELL and
BENNIE JONES

THE TOPIC of our discussion is mini and microcomputer data processing for a small fund. A brief qualification is necessary in order to limit the subject, because it is a broad one. Mini and microcomputers, as noted in the Glossary, are more or less determined now by dollars. As the Glossary indicates, $15,000 to $150,000 (or more) defines a mini and less than $15,000 defines a micro. The difference is usually based upon the amount of peripherals that are on the system, but basically there is no technological difference between the two types of computers. The definition of a smaller fund is equally hard to pinpoint. For our purposes, we will limit and define a smaller fund as one with less than 100,000 lives. Basically, there is no difference between a smaller fund and a larger one, only the number of lives involved.

Mr. Bell will make the first part of the presentation.

Do You Need EDP?

The computer itself, whether it is a mini, micro, or maxi, can be considered the tip of an iceberg. I would like to talk about not just the tip of the iceberg, but the entire topic of data processing. Mr. Jones will give you some of the technical jargon on how a computer works, which will apply to all kinds of computers, not just minis and micros. What I want to address is the scope of the decision to go to data processing in the first place, because the iceberg underneath the computer is as important as the computer itself. I don't believe anyone is going to jump up as a result of this talk (or any other talk) and become a programmer. What you do need to know is the elements you have to consider in order to reach an intelligent decision on a topic which is unfamiliar to you in your line of work.

With that in mind, I would like to start off by asking a series of questions. The first question would be, should you go to a computer at all? or, why go to data processing? Some of the reasons could be:

Mr. Bell, as president of the firm, National Labor Systems, Inc., Houston, is responsible for the overall direction of data processing procedures involving management, technical development and consulting to trust funds. A graduate of the University of Colorado, Boulder, he has been active in data processing work for over 15 years. Mr. Bell is also a graduate of the General Electric Financial Management Program. While at G.E., he served as consultant to NASA's Mississippi test site, and implemented G.E.'s first on-line collection system in the United States.

Mr. Jones, as National Labor Systems' vice president in charge of systems and programming, is primarily responsible for the firm's data processing services including management, technical development and consulting to representatives of trust funds. Active in the joint trust field for over four years, he is a graduate of Mississippi State, Starkville, Mississippi, where he majored in computer science.

1. Your reporting system is inadequate or late. This is one of the symptoms of the need for data processing.
2. The inability to obtain information for a trustee or fund advisor on a timely basis
3. Lack of control, either of money or personnel, is a possibility
4. A backlog of work that is never done on time
5. Retraining of personnel when a valued employee of 15 or 20 years leaves. How easy is it to train someone else? Does he/she leave with all the information in his/her head?
6. Another symptom could be auditing. Has it become difficult to audit the fund?

These are just some of the symptoms I have outlined. There are probably as many different reasons for deciding to go to data processing as there are individuals in the room. You represent a large number of funds; and these funds probably have their own unique problems, all of which lead you to say, "OK, I think I should go to data processing," or, "I think it would help." By and large, if it is done right, data processing will help. It would be a great value to you now and it would be of even greater value to you in the future.

Current Needs?

But you have to ask some further questions. The first review that you need to conduct, once you have decided you need data processing, is an analysis of your present operation. If you are an administrator, you have to review the operation around your office (if you are still doing it in-house). What you need to do is to identify what you want out of data processing.

The main criterion in this industry is to define goals. I have listed here some basic fund requirements. The list is by no means definitive, but they are generally the most common funds. You may have one, two, three or four of these funds.

One of the basic funds is the health and welfare fund. You will need eligibility reports, and you will need statistics for carriers in order to make premium payments. You will need self-pay notices, letters to members, various reports. If you have a pension fund, you will need pension census information, information to fill out Form 5500 and the corresponding SSA supplement. You need to write pension checks, and you will need actuarial valuation information for your actuaries to properly evaluate the fund. You need to send out W2-Ps. If you have a vacation fund, is it a monthly fund? Is it an annual fund? What about the W2s that you send out at the end of the year? Do you need status information when a member comes to your office and withdraws money for an emergency? Where do you get the information, and how current is it?

Contribution accounting, which is probably the most important function of all, is what we call "putting the money in the bank." Probably the most important aspect of this process is getting the money into the bank on a timely basis and accounting for the hours or the dollar premium for each employee, so that you can properly account for all money and hours. We have found the biggest problem in the data processing area for labor organizations is getting the right information credited to the right Social Security number so that the employee has all the credits he has earned. Claims processing is a possibility, unless the carrier performs this function. If not, you will need to produce claims checks for participants, and produce 1099-meds at year-end for providers. You have to keep provider information current for names and addresses.

Annual statements and proper allocations of interest are some of the requirements you might encounter in an annuity fund.

This list is by no means complete, as there are hundreds of requirements for specific funds, but these represent some of the fundamentals in the labor industry, and could constitute a starting place when you begin defining what it is you want a computer to do.

Future Requirements?

While you are thinking about what you want the computer to do today, you also should consider what you want it to do tomorrow. After you get over the conversion crunch, you ought to be considering what the machine can do next year, and also five years from now. What is it that you would like to have the computer do in the future?

One of the possible functions would be dues control. This area, which has received a lot of attention recently, is one you might want the computer to handle for you. Another area is the general ledger; you can't make very accurate decisions if you don't have proper financial statements. Financial information is something you might want to put in the machine because you already have your money going into the bank from the fund. By inputting the few checks written from the fund's accounts, you have the basis for some pretty good financial information. Operating statements, balance sheets, budgeting, all of these reports could help you. You might want to include payroll if you have a large enough payroll. Even if you don't have a large payroll, it is easier to use the computer to write payroll checks in order to keep track of all the government reporting requirements.

You might want to consider doing word processing, in the form of sending out information bulletins to members, or typing up financial statements, 20, 30, 40 at a time and keeping track of each monthly statement so you can send out the same information repeatedly. You might want to include credit union processing. You might want to do payroll auditing. You could prepare auditing worksheets for the auditors and also be able to spotlight those contractors that might need a detailed payroll audit. This is a time-consuming process if done manually, but if everything is in the machine it becomes a straightforward operation.

Almost any other function deserves consideration at this stage of the decision making. What do you want the computer to do now and in the future?

What Are Your Options?

Once you decide on what you want the computer to do, what data processing options do you have? The first option is probably another fund that is similar to you in size or in locality which already has some form of data processing. They might have something available that you could piggyback. This option has been available to some funds, especially in the larger cities.

You might try a batch service bureau, where you batch the remittance forms and send them to the computer center for processing. The bureau keypunches the data and sends back an edit list and processes your data. It is usually a very efficient system. It is a little bit older style of data processing, but these bureaus have the people who defined the industry problems and developed data processing systems to where they are today.

You can tie in to an on-line system, where they perform all the necessary functions in your area. In reality, where the black box is located really doesn't make any difference anymore. You can also go to an in-house computer: get your own computer and put it in your shop. You might even use a combination of all these services, but smaller funds by and large will probably pick one option and stick with it.

The Decision Making Process

Sources of Advice

Once you have decided what options you have available, where do you go for advice? Again, other funds are an excellent source because they have gone down this path before. If you have talked to other funds' managers, you have probably heard some horror stories. You have also probably heard some success stories. These funds are a good source of information because they are in exactly the same position you are in today if you are thinking about getting a computer.

You should consult with auditing firms, especially firms that audit your funds. They can tell you what information you need, and what information they require. Auditing firms usually have professionals available to consult with you from an accounting standpoint. Plan consultants are a good source of advice. Pension and health and welfare consultants, who are in the business of designing systems for any type of company or industry, are a good source of advice. Management consultants usually charge a lot of money for their advice—but then, people usually don't pay any attention to anyone unless they charge for their advice. You can go down to the local pub and ask the bartender and he will give you all the advice in the world—but it is free, and therefore ought to be taken with a grain of salt. You should go to a professional who understands your business.

The RFP: Spelling It Out

The end result of all the topics we have discussed is a request-for-proposal, or RFP. An analogy can be drawn to an architect drawing up the plans for a building. When he is finished with the design—or in our case, the RFP—he sends it off to the consulting engineers and finally to the bid contractor. We had an attorney speak to us at the EDP Conference in October. He said the saddest thing he has ever seen was two people who were at a legal impasse. The data processor said he did exactly what he was asked to do from the computer standpoint, and it was exactly what he was told to do. On the other side of the desk was the administrator or the trustee and he said, "I'm not getting the job done." It came down to the point that they both thought they were right—and neither one of them was satisfied. They had not agreed in writing what should be done.

The RFP should contain the *scope of the job* that you have defined earlier, and it should define what you want in terms of any future modifications to your system. It should be detailed to the extent that there is no room for assumptions. I used to teach data processing, and one of the basics I used to teach my class was an analysis of the word "assume." If you break it up, it makes an ass-out-of-you-and-me, and that is about what assume does. The RFP should outline your present operation, whether it is manual or automated. It should outline what you are doing now, because that information is going to be needed in order to convert the data as they exist to the new computer system.

Do you want a turnkey operation? Are you going to go in-house, or are you going to go to a service bureau? I would suggest a shotgun approach when you construct the RFP, so it can be responded to by different organizations in all three categories. There is no sense limiting yourself to just an in-house computer when it is possible your answer lies in another area. I would make the RFP broad enough. But be specific as to what you want in terms of reports and the features of such reports. It should be detailed, so you don't have to worry when a programmer sits down to code to the system; he does not have to make any assumptions.

You need to know what *staffing* you will have to provide. Does it require one person, two people, three people? Do you have to hire different types of individuals in your operation? It will vary depending on which option you finally select. What kind of ongoing *software support* are you going to have? What happens a year from now, when things are going along well but you need to make a modification? Maybe ERISA comes out with a modification, or maybe PBGC comes along and says, "Let's have that first contractor withdrawal. What are the last five years of contributions? What is each contractor's percentage?" Who is going to do the work? How are you going to get it done? What about any future software enhancements? What happens if your contract expires, or your programmer leaves and you want to do something two years from now? Who is going to do it for you?

How is your *hardware* going to be maintained, if hardware was included in the proposal? Who is going to do it, and how close are they? What are you going to do about preconversion? How are you going to keep things going while you are going from one rock to another rock in the middle of the stream? Obviously you can't eliminate your present system, and not get wet, unless you have a firm definition in the new system. Are you going to have your regular conversion team in place? Who is going to learn the new system, and who will maintain the old one? What kind of peripheral equipment are you going to have? Are you going to have CRTs, are you going to have a computer in-house? What kind of equipment do you need, and how fast can you update it if you need to?

Finally, how much money is it going to cost you? The cost is actually the last consideration, because what you really need is to make sure the system works. There is an old saying which is trite because it is true, and that is, "Why is there never enough time to do things right the first time, but always enough time to do it over again?" Who are the prospective vendors? What is their track record? Who else have they performed similar services for?

Last, you should ask, "To whom should I send the RFP?" For that answer, you should go back to the same people you first asked for advice. Who are the prospective vendors? Did you make the RFP broad enough so you can send it to all the different organizations qualified to install your new system?

Evaluating the Responses

A period of time will pass, and you will start to get responses back. Then you will have to develop a system of evaluating the responses. The first way is try to evaluate them with some sort of formula. A comparative analysis is necessary so that you are not comparing "apples" returns with "oranges" returns—you must actually be comparing like responses. Check the references that the vendors furnished. Don't just believe them, check every reference. Go to the clients that they have listed and say, "I understand that you have this type of operation, how does it work?"

Review the context of the response to see if whoever responded to the RFP has the foggiest idea of what it is that you wanted. There was a recent talk in Dallas at a medical convention. One of the speakers said that if he ever got an RFP response which was just a "fill in the blank, checkoff list" type of response, it was thrown in the trash can immediately, because the vendor could not know the scope of the problem by a form letter response. It was obviously not what they were looking for.

The Final Selection

Once you have narrowed the field down, you need to consider other factors. You need to actually go and see, not just talk to, the people who perform the work. You need to see what it is that someone is proposing, and see if it works in the real world. See it in operation at someone's shop. See if their operation is like yours. If you are an administrator, see if their administration procedures are the same as yours, see if it is in a like industry. See it work! Be from Missouri! Bring in a professional, if you don't already have one on staff, to see if the technical specifications of the RFP are being adhered to. You are not going to be able to tell if a system works unless you are a technical programmer. Have somebody evaluate it. Get an opinion.

Check on the vendor's stability. Who owns the company, what is their financial state? There is no sense in awarding the contract to the lowest bid if that is how they are running themselves out of business. Check the ownership. Check to see if there is a conflict anywhere. Check the vendor out!

Then look at the price, see *how* you have to pay. Do they want the money all up front? Do they want it on a contract basis? What kind of performance guarantees are they going to give you? Who is going to be responsible if it doesn't work? Evaluate the experience you have had with the representatives you are negotiating with. Some vendor representatives can portray themselves very well at higher level management, but when they get down to the people who are doing the work they become abusive or overbearing. Check to see that there is going to be a good relationship on a personnel basis.

Finally, you need to determine the staffing

changes you are going to make—because there *will* be changes. It is not going to be done the same way as it was before. Alert your people so they can anticipate some of the changes that will be taking place, because they are going to affect your entire organization.

Setting Up Your In-House Computer

Physical Environment

Now that you have got to this point and you have eliminated other funds doing your work; and you have eliminated batch service bureaus as being too slow and uneconomical; and you have eliminated on-line service bureaus; and you have chosen an in-house computer, you have some further considerations. First, you have to check your physical environment. Do you have enough space to put the computer? Where is it going to go? Is it secure? What are the energy requirements? Does it require special wiring? Is the space adequate?

There are very special considerations as far as the physical environment is concerned. Is your air conditioning adequate? Sometimes you think you have an air conditioning problem licked and it turns out that you don't. We had an instance in one of our computer installations where we went into the building and it had 24 hours a day, seven days a week, air conditioning to the computer room. Then the building went on an energy kick. Now all of a sudden their computer turns off our air conditioning at 12 noon on Saturday, and does not turn it back on until 8 o'clock Monday morning. When a situation like this occurs, you have to shut down your computer too. Without air conditioning, the computer cannot process.

Is your wiring sufficient inside to prevent an electrical fire? Do you have conduits? What kind of communications are you going to need, if any? If you are going to interface with the telephone company, where are you going to put the telephone equipment? Is your particular area already saturated, as we are in Houston, where we have so many people moving in that the telephone company has run out of regular telephone lines, and all of a sudden you need data lines and the cables aren't there? The telephone company tells us that it is going to take a year to put in a new cable. These types of problems you need to investigate.

Hardware

Now we finally come down to whether we want a mini or a micro, and now we come back to the buying. This is the first time that we have got up to the tip of the iceberg.

What kind of peripheral equipment are you going to have? Do you need terminals, printers? If you do, what kind of disk packs are you going to have on your machine? Are you going to have floppies or hard disks? You are going to have to worry about supplies. You will probably want to order checks and remittance forms and stock paper, to name a few of the items you are going to require.

Software

The most important feature of your new system, however, is the software, and that you might have a little tougher time finding out about. Basically, today any computer, from the smallest up to the largest, is going to work. The manufacturer has had the computer in test operations for years and years. The space program enhanced computer technology. The hardware will add one plus one and get two in an incredibly short period of time, and hardly ever mechanically goes wrong. Your biggest problem is going to be in the software area. So you ought to consider package software, if package software is available. If so, is it compatible with the computer hardware that you have finally decided on? You might have a good package written in COBOL, and it works fine on an IBM 3033, but it doesn't work on a Digital Equipment Corp. 11/34. You need to know if the software is capable. If you decide you are going to reinvent the wheel by bringing in a programmer off the street, you need to know if you have to reprogram the whole system.

From the hardware standpoint, you also have some software considerations to take into account. Languages and operating systems designed by manufacturers are software just like a report program. They are constantly in the process of finding bugs, correcting them, doing something different, doing something better, coming out with a revision. Who is going to implement these changes? Who is going to be the systems programmer? You need to find out what software, and there are several different phases of software, you are going to need.

Staffing

You will need to have a programming staff if you are going in-house. How many will you need? Are you going to go with just one? What happens when he gets sick? Where are you going to find programmers?—because you are going to need some programmers to maintain the system, keep it up, keep your machine alive, do what needs to be done. You will have operational staffing requirements. Somebody must sit down there to pump the paper through the machine so that reports get out on time. Somebody is going to have to back up the system so that you are never vulnerable to a system crash. You will need someone to decollate the paper, burst it, put it in the mail. You will need a routine operational staff. Who is going to check the quality control, make sure the reports are right; who is going to check to see that page 13 wasn't missing?

Finally, you will need backup support from your vendor. What happens if, in fact, all your staff are sick? You are going to have to ask your hardware vendor and software vendors if they have someone available on a consulting-type basis in case you have a problem.

Insurance

You will have to worry about insurance, catastrophe insurance and casualty insurance. There are two different types of insurance. You can protect yourself from a fire, theft or flood, and you can be compensated for the dollar loss—but can you really be compensated for information loss? What happens if your pension master file gets erased? Where are you going to go to retrieve it? Do you have a hard copy off-site? Do you have it on backup media some place, on a backup disk or a backup tape? If you really get down to it, the insurance company can compensate you for the loss of the hardware, but no one is ever going to be able to repay you for the loss of information if you haven't got information insurance.

The Obsolescence Factor

You also have to ask yourself if you want to lease or buy. You have the obsolescence factor to consider, if buying the machine. Historically, about every five years the computer you buy becomes obsolete. Something new has replaced it; something bigger, faster, and with more bells and whistles. Basically, however, if the machine is doing your job for you, it can be processing the same thing for 15 years and will not be obsolete. Therefore, you might want to consider the longer term investment. Your software can usually be leased or bought. Single CPU licenses are one way vendors like to package software to protect themselves. And, there are some additional considerations, like upgrades on the operational software which you will have to have on your main frame.

What I am trying to do is to outline the scope of the decision process, leading up to the tip of the iceberg... the computer itself. Mr. Jones will now lead you through what comprises a mini-computer.

Minicomputer Systems

If you will turn to the back, right before the Glossary, there are two diagrams, one labeled "Minicomputer Hardware Configurations," and the other one having to do with "Telecommunications." I separated these two because I feel as if they are two totally different industries.

Computer Components

As in the human body, the *central processing unit* is the center of activity of the modern computer. In broad terms, it is the CPU that converts software or stored instructions to electrical impulses which process data and control activities. The functions of the CPU can be put into three categories:

1. The arithmetic function, which most of your hand-held calculators can perform—things you expect a computer to do like add, subtract, multiply, divide
2. The logical functions, which include the computer's ability to check for less than, greater than, equal to, and, not, or, etc.
3. The control functions. They control the peripherals that are tied to the computer. This is done through a set of devices called interrupt commands.

The next major category is *memory*. This falls into two groups, core, which is non-volatile, and metallic oxide semiconductor, or MOS. MOS is faster and is cheaper. It seems logical that MOS would be the way to go, but the hidden factor here is its volatility. Basically, what this means is that if you lose power to your computer and you have core memory, the memory retains its state, so your systems people will be able to recover and continue processing whenever the lightning bolt hits. If you are processing with metallic oxide semiconductors, it has to be refreshed. In other words, if the power is lost for a few seconds you lose the state that the memory was in, so it involves a longer and more detailed recovery procedure. So when you are considering buying a computer, you need to look at, and your systems consultants need to advise you on, which type of memory you need to purchase.

The other major group is mass *storage*. This is the disk and the magnetic tape. The disk has an advantage: it is a random access device. You do not have to spin down the disk to obtain a piece of information. The head on the disk can go to the exact location where the data reside and pluck it off. I advise magnetic tape on any computer system because it is a universal transfer media. It is sequential, it is cheap and, if you have to transfer information from one computer to another computer, from an IBM to a Honeywell computer or any other vendor manufacturer, the magnetic tape is the medium that allows you to do so. It is not a very expensive peripheral, but I think a lot of the micro and minicomputers vendors try to sell today leave that important peripheral out. I think it is important. Also, many of the actuarial requirements and pension work that we provide to actuaries take the information from tape. So we don't have to produce a hard-copy report, which saves a lot of time and energy.

Input and output devices are the eyes and ears of your computer. The console I have separated because it is like a privileged communication device. It allows specific operating system changes. It usually allows a security bypass. Whoever is working at the console usually has access to your operating system, whereas your other terminal and peripheral devices may not allow that. There is a tremendous range of options when it comes to types of printers and drum printers, and a wide range of prices. Most of the major computer manufacturers do not build their own printers; they buy their printers from companies that specialize in the production of printers.

The other major device is the *multiplexer*. These are what your CRTs or teletypes will be tied to. They are really a microprocessor in themselves. They are a kind of device that interfaces the CRT device to the central processing unit. They fall into two major categories, the local multiplexers and those permitting communication over more than 2,000 feet. If you have to drive a line or have terminals located more than 2,000 feet from your computer site, then you are going to have to look into a telecommunication system.

Telecommunications

Diagram 2 shows some of the new technology and some of the options that are available in telecommunications. We will start at the top and come down. That is the most sophisticated one on the top.

The two boxes labeled STDM stand for *statistical time division multiplexers*. The distances involved there are 1,000 miles—I just picked 1,000 miles as being a good example. We have eight lines coming out of the multiplexer, or we have eight possible CRT connections, rather than having to run eight dedicated lines and absorb the communication cost for eight dedicated lines over a 1,000 mile distance. We have chosen to concentrate those lines onto a single line, and break them out on the other end. These devices are available today at a relatively low price. From a cost performance point of view, if you have to transmit over long distances, in my opinion this is about the only way to go. The manufacturers of the STDMs also put in error corrections, so you don't have to run on a high grade of line, as you did formerly. You get the same performance on a low grade line running 4,800 baud or 9,600 baud, or even at a higher speed.

The statistical time division multiplexer can be interfaced to another data set device, another modem device, or to a CRT. In our example here, I have seven CRTs and one modem, which means that in our example, if you wanted to put another CRT within a two mile radius, you could come out of the STDM, go into a modem, go across town and then drop your CRT at that location. The CRT can also be interfaced to a printer, which saves time because you don't have to have a line totally dedicated to output. It can share a line with an input/output device. The other eight lines at the bottom of the multiplexer fall into two different approaches, one being that of a dial up. You have a rotary-type dial system, it allows you to have seven or eight CRTs in the field communicating over five or six lines, the same way the telephone company does. The other option is your lease line; there are two examples of this at the bottom of the diagram. Here, you pay a fixed rate for a data line, and that line is dedicated 24 hours a day seven days a week.

There has been a long debate in the computer industry over where the computer is going to be located: whether you are going to have a central site location and your CRTs are going to be spread out all over the country, or whether you will have individual processors at each location where the computer is required. The communications industry today has kind of given the central site people an advantage. From a cost point of view, it is easier to keep all of your computer equipment at one isolated location and transmit over communication lines, and drop your CRTs wherever the job needs to be done. This has allowed us to fall back and regroup in the computer industry and rethink the solutions to some old problems.

Another possibility is in the deregulation of the communications industry, and this holds probably some of the best things to come. It started several years ago with the Carterfone decision, which allowed alien vendors to strap their equipment on Ma Bell's telephone lines. Now we have microwave and satellite transmission which is creating some competition for Ma Bell and, I believe, will bring the cost down to a very reasonable level.

In summary, I believe that where the computer is located or where the black box is going to be is really unimportant anymore. It can be just about anywhere you want to put it.

Mr. Bell will make the concluding comments.

Concluding Comments

Bennie has given you a brief summary leading to the tip of the iceberg, and what the tip is composed of. But what I would like to stress before I close is that whatever direction you take in data processing, it is a major, major, major decision. What you do will affect your plan for the next five to ten years—good or bad. If it is a poor decision based on a spur of the moment consideration, you will probably end up to regret it. If you don't have competent people, competent support, competent consultants and competent in-house people to run your machine, you will have undesirable results. But at the same time, if done right, it can vastly improve your operation.

Diagram 1

Minicomputer Hardware Configuration

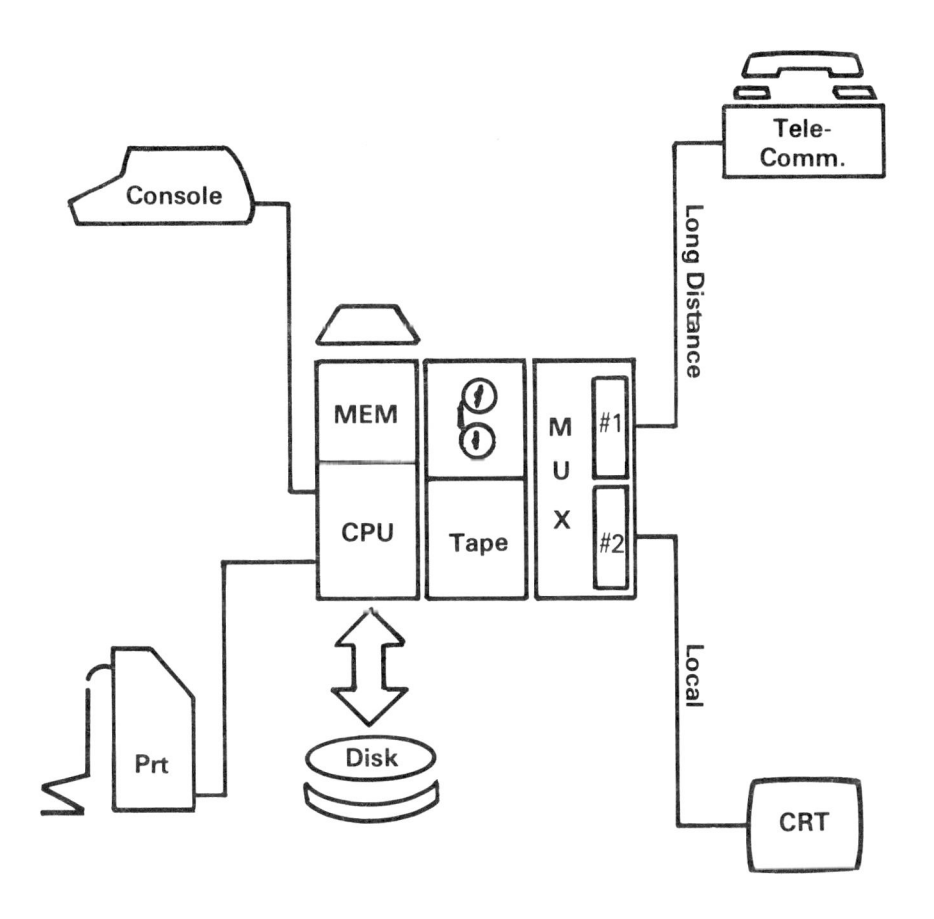

Diagram 2

Telecommunications

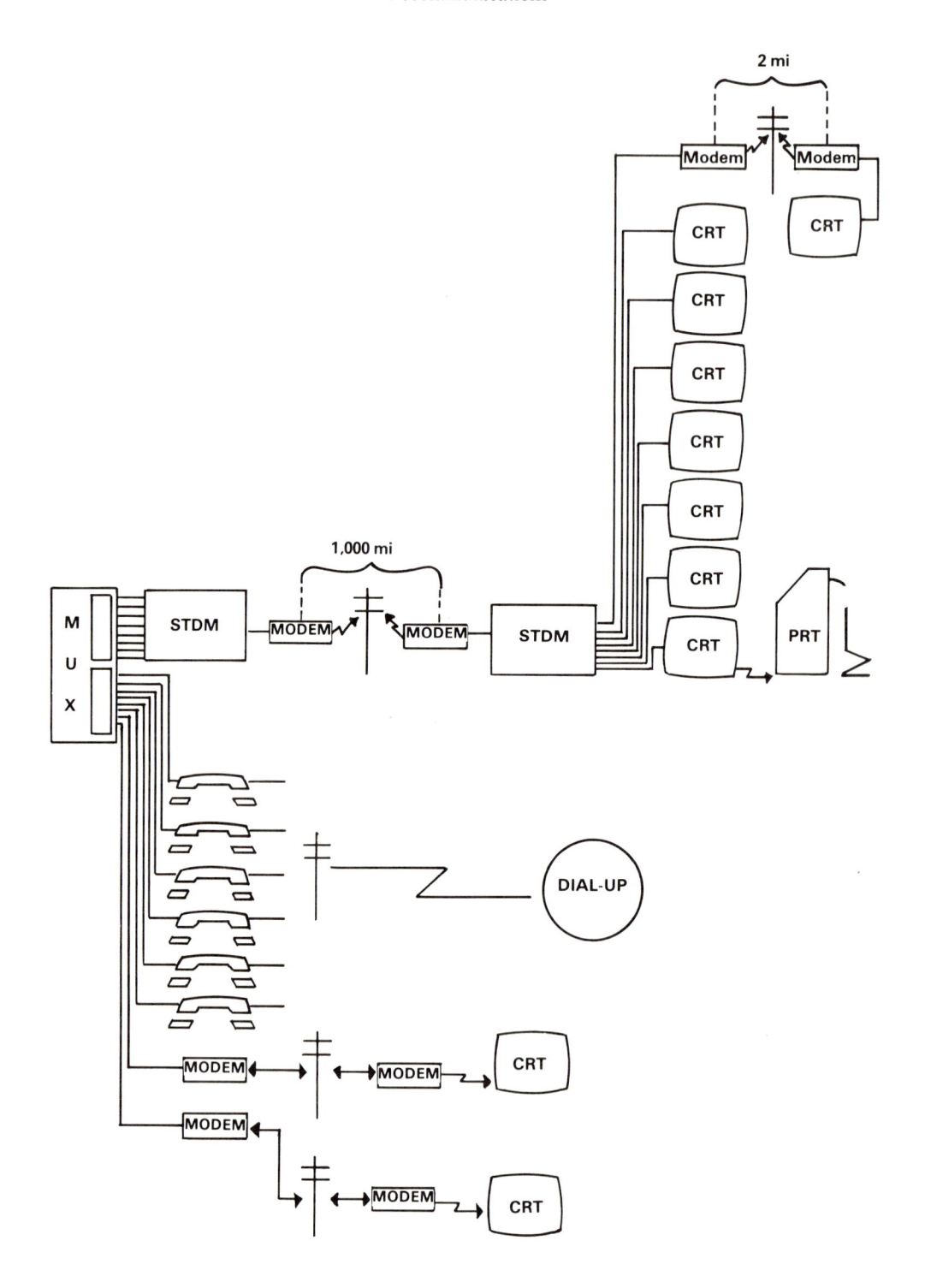

Glossary

Here are the terms a computer system buyer is most likely to encounter. Whether or not you can use the jargon well, though, require the dealer to speak *your* language. His ability to do so is one measure of his ability to understand your business.

applications software: the *software* programs written to perform particular business functions such as accounts payable, inventory control, and analysis of sales. Compare with *system software*.

backup storage: copies of data files, used as a safeguard against damage or loss. Usually *magnetic tape,* sometimes *floppy disk* or *hard disk*.

batch system: a *computer system* that handles input and output data in large chunks on a deferred or delayed-processing basis; for example, invoice data for an entire day are entered all at once before any of the invoices are printed. By contrast, an *interactive system* handles small amounts of input and output data in real time, and usually gives the user immediate results.

baud rate: a measure of the rate of data flow between any two devices, for example, between a *CPU* and its remote *terminal*. Baud rate specifies how many units of information can be transmitted along a telephone line in a second. The higher the baud rate, the faster you can transmit information. In a case where information is sent in single *bits,* 300 bits per second. (Pronounced "Bawd" or "Bod," depending on locale.)

bit: the smallest unit of information a computer deals with. A bit can have one of two values, generally represented as 0 and 1 or, in electrical terms, "on" and "off." Computers carry out all computations using binary (base 2) arithmetic, which involves rapidly manipulating strings of bits according to certain fixed rules.

bubble memory: a new form of computer *memory* that uses magnetized "bubbles" to store information. A major advantage is that information stored in a bubble memory is retained when electrical power is turned off. Bubble memories are just now coming on the market.

byte: a string of eight *bits*. Because of the nature of computer *storage* procedures, a byte is the amount of storage space needed to represent a character (i.e., a numeral, letter, symbol, or blank). Kilobyte and megabyte mean 1,000 bytes and 1 million bytes, respectively.

computer: a high-speed electronic machine that manipulates data by following sequential, programmed instructions. Strictly speaking, the term computer does not include *software* or *peripheral equipment,* but sometimes it is used more loosely to refer to an entire *computer system*.

computer language: the symbolic coding in which computer programs are written. Two of the most popular ones are COBOL and Basic. Most smaller machines use Basic.

computer system: a *computer* plus *software* plus one or more pieces of *peripheral equipment*

CPU (central processing unit): the part of a computer that performs calculations and processes data according to the instructions specified by the *software*. CPU is sometimes used interchangeably with *computer*. See also *microprocessor*.

CRT (cathode-ray tube): a video screen that displays prompting instructions, user responses, computer responses, and reports generated by the *computer*

data base management: a storage and retrieval system that allows easy access to stored information and efficient compilation of special reports. In data base management, a complete item of data (e.g., a part number and a description of the part) is stored in the data base only once and can be referred to by one or more short names or code numbers rather than having to be described in full each time it is needed (e.g., in each invoice file where the part appears).

debugging: the often time-consuming process of getting a computer program to execute instructions properly so it gives desired results without error

distributed processing: access to a *computer system* by many users at the same time in different locations. Each user has access to his own processor and file *storage,* and the individual processors may be linked to one another and to a common data base. (This is in which several users share a single *central processing unit*.)

dual density: a means of storing data on a disk at twice the density that formerly was standard

firmware: see *ROM*

floppy disk: a relatively inexpensive magnetic storage medium that looks like a flexible 45-RPM record permanently sealed in a paper jacket that has a small window. Standard sizes are 8 inches and 5¼ inches in diameter: the latter are called minifloppies.

hard disk: a disk similar to a *floppy disk* but larger and not flexible. Hard disks hold more data, allow for higher access speeds and are more expensive. There are two basic kinds: packs, which consist of several platters in a removable case, and cartridges, which usually contain one platter.

hardware: the computer itself or any item of *peripheral equipment*

interactive system: as compared with a *batch system*, an interactive system gives the user immediate results and allows an interchange of information between user and machine. For a manager, this is a particularly useful aid to decision making, because one can gain a desired piece of information (e.g., the cost of a projected 5% increase in inventory), enter a new command based on that information, and gain the next piece of information, all in a few seconds.

magnetic tape: a medium used primarily for *backup storage*, installing programs, and exchanging data files. Most common in business computer systems is the reel-to-reel format; other types include cartridge and cassette.

mainframe/maxi: these terms are used interchangeably to refer to "large" *computer systems*. There is no general agreement as to what the boundary is between a mainframe computer and a minicomputer.

memory: the part of the *central processing unit* that holds information being processed. Compare *storage*. See also *RAM*.

microcomputer/minicomputer: the distinction between these two is blurry. One could arbitrarily define microcomputer systems as those costing under $15,000 and minis as those costing $15,000 to $150,000. (Cost refers to complete systems, with all necessary *peripheral equipment* and basic *applications software*.)

microprocessor: the semiconductor "chip" that serves as the core of the *central processing unit* in many of today's computers. A microprocessor has virtually all the computing power of the early room-size computers, yet is only about a quarter inch square.

modem: a device that couples a computer or terminal to a telephone line. Used for long distance data transmission.

MOS (metal oxide semiconductor): the technology used to produce the microprocessor and memory portions of most computers. (Pronounced either "Moss" or "Em-Oh-Ess.")

peripheral equipment: input/output and data storage devices: printers, keyboards, *CRTs*, remote *terminals*, and tape and disk drives

RAM (random-access memory): the semiconductor chips within the computer that serve as a scratch pad. The *CPU* enters and retrieves information from RAM almost instantaneously, but unlike data in external storage or in the *bubble memories* just coming on the market, the contents of RAM are lost when electrical power to the computer is turned off. (Pronounced like the male sheep.)

ROM (read-only memory): if *RAM* is like a scratch pad, then ROM is like a printed book whose pages cannot be erased. *System software* is often stored in ROM. Situated in the twilight zone between hardware and tape-or disk-based software, ROM-based software is labeled, naturally enough, *firmware*. (ROM is pronounced either as a word or letter by letter.)

service bureau: a company that runs programs for a client for a fee. The customer need not have any computer equipment on his own premises, although a remote *terminal* and a *modem* are often used for convenience (and become necessary if *time-sharing* is involved).

software: the programs, or instructions, that tell the computer how to respond to specific user commands

storage: in contrast to *memory*, this generally refers to the external devices (cards, tapes, disks, cassettes) that store both data and software

system software: software programs that control the internal operations of the computer system, such as the translation of keyboard commands into a form that can be acted upon by the *central processing unit*. Compare *applications software*.

terminal: a point of input or output. Many terminals have a keyboard plus a printer and/or display electrically linked to a computer. Nonintelligent terminals simply transmit and receive. Intelligent terminals have some built-in computing power and can perform processing functions of certain kinds. In the middle are smart terminals, which permit some editing of data but no extensive processing of it.

time-sharing: simultaneous access by several users to one central processing unit. The CPU runs the programs for all the users at once, switching rapidly from one program to the other in such a way as to minimize the waiting time for each user. A time-sharing service is a company that provides time-sharing capabilities to customers for a fee. Each customer has a terminal; the computer itself is owned and operated by the time-sharing service.

turnkey system: an entire *computer system*, with *hardware* and *software*, assembled by a vendor and sold as a package. The term turnkey implies that the system will do everything it is supposed to as soon as it's turned over to the user. This should be thought of as an idea to be sought after, rather than an everyday reality.

CHAPTER 9

Investments

Peter Ladd Gilsey

Senior Portfolio Manager
L. F. Rothschild Asset Management
Washington, D.C.

Eugene B. Burroughs

Director
International Brotherhood of Teamsters,
Chauffeurs, Warehousemen and Helpers
of America
Washington, D.C.

Jon S. Brightman

Corporate Vice President
Meidinger, Inc.
Milwaukee, Wisconsin

Paul Sack

Real Estate Principal
The Rosenberg Real Estate Equity Fund
San Francisco, California

Donald A. Smart

Vice President
Deferred Compensation Associates, Inc.
Madison, Wisconsin

Roger C. Bransford

Corporate Vice President
Meidinger, Inc.
Louisville, Kentucky

Robert S. Waill

Vice President
Inverness Counsel, Inc.
New York, New York

Developing the Investment Policy Statement

BY PETER LADD GILSEY

I HOPE that as a result of what we will be discussing here we will all be even better prepared in the future to discharge our fiduciary role. This is one area of our work with pension funds where "A stitch in time—really does—save nine." You may think, after 30 years in this business, that I'm an investment expert. Well, just to put things in perspective, you should know that an investment expert is someone "you pay more money to help you manage your investments than you could possibly make out of them—even if you invested them right, instead of the way he tells you to!" In fact, there really are no experts in my business, only varying degrees of ignorance!

So, with those two humbling observations, I would like to say at the outset that under ERISA it is necessary for you and your board of trustees, along with your investment manager, lawyer and, if need be, your actuary or plan consultant, to establish a "funding policy." To do this properly takes time, and therefore I would urge each of you to be sure to take the time—a special meeting would be best—to see that this is done. There are no quick fixes or shortcuts to doing the job right, and once it's done and reduced to writing and agreed upon by all concerned, it should be reviewed at least annually to see if it is current and responsive to the needs of the fund and its beneficiaries.

Let's take a look at 16 factors that I have identified as being important insofar as developing an investment policy statement. You may have others which should be included, and some of mine may not be relevant to your situation, but at least the list provides a beginning or starting point for discussion and eventual agreement.

Sixteen Key Factors

Purpose of the Plan

We will begin with the HKM plan's purpose, which is to provide for, as I call it, "human depreciation," for those persons unable or unwilling to

Mr. Gilsey, a chartered investment counselor, is manager, Washington, D.C. office, and senior portfolio manager of L. F. Rothschild Asset Management. He previously was vice president and resident partner of Loomis Sayles & Company and was national sales manager for that firm. Holder of a B.S. degree in business administration from Georgetown University, Mr. Gilsey has lectured on investments at American and Georgetown Universities and taught courses in trust investments and security analysis for the Washington Chapter, American Institute of Banking. A former member of the International Foundation's Investment Management Committee, he has been a frequent speaker and moderator before many professional organizations, including the International Foundation of Employee Benefit Plans, where he has spoken at Annual Conferences, Advanced Trustees Institutes and regional seminars. He is a member of the Financial Analysts Federation and the Washington Society of Investment Analysts, of which he is a past president and currently serves as chairman of its placement committee.

work because of old age, infirmity, or other good and valid reasons. Every company likes to be able to provide adequate retirement benefits for those who have directed the greater part of their working lifetime to the company's business. Furthermore, attractively designed retirement programs can:

1. Influence the best people to remain with the company, particularly in some industries

where special technical or manual skills are required, which skills often are not fully developed until the employee reaches age 35, 45, or even 50. At present there is a shortage of many of these skills, and competition is vigorous.
2. Strengthen the company in a depression or recession, as the best and most senior people are likely to stay on if at all possible
3. Improve employee morale and loyalty by providing:
    a. Opportunity for advancement and reward for accomplishment;
    b. Financial security in later years for worker and family.

Age of the Plan

It is helpful to know how long a plan has been operating, and what its history has been of making contributions and paying benefits over the ups and downs of various business cycles. The longer a plan has existed and been successful in achieving its objectives, the greater reliance the investment manager may place on the likelihood of such a history continuing.

Type of Plan

It is helpful to know whether the plan is a defined benefit or defined contribution plan as, to a degree, the answer will or could affect investment policy. In most cases, Taft-Hartley funds are a hybrid, as the monthly retirement benefit is defined as a stipulated amount per month times the years of credited service earned, while the rate of monthly contributions has been collectively bargained for. The level of benefits is often determined by the plan's actuary based upon specific assumptions such as turnover, mortality, disability and interest earnings. The key assumption here, as far as the investment manager is concerned, is that involving interest, as it may be changed to reflect trustees' desires regarding a higher benefit payment and, if the investment manager hasn't earned it in the past and doesn't in the future, the plan will be in trouble at some point, and either benefits will have to be reduced or contributions increased—both unpalatable, and really an unacceptable alternative in the former case.

In the case of defined contribution plans (so much per hour), which are often preferred by many employers because they know their costs, there is no unfunded liability, since the benefit is only what the money will buy; and there is no government-required contingent liability for additional contributions beyond those shown in the plan. Ultimate payouts depend upon how successfully the monies are invested. Thus, there is a greater sensitivity among beneficiaries as to just how well the assets are being managed, and both trustees and the investment manager need to be aware of fiduciary responsibility insofar as preserving principal, reliable income flows, steady growth, and low portfolio volatility are concerned, as they often assume greater import than in defined benefit plans.

Industry Characteristics

Here, the investment manager needs to get a good feel for what the basic industry characteristics are which are likely to influence growth, employment trends, and stability and continuity of the contributing employers. Some industries, such as shoes, textiles and rubber manufacturers, could be labeled static or declining, while cement, building supplies and autos might represent cyclical growth and finally, computers, lasers and genetic engineering, rapid or high growth areas. Furthermore, it is helpful to know what the short and long range growth forecasts are for each industry. Relevant industry characteristics, then, can be listed as:
    a. Cyclical growth
    b. Static or declining situation
    c. Steady growth
    d. Rapid growth
    e. Short range forecast
    f. Long range forecast.

Obviously, when great industry cyclicality is present, or where a static or declining trend is identified early, one's investment posture should be more conservative, with greater emphasis on liquidity needs. In new technology or emerging growth industries where growth is rapid and a much younger employee age level is present, with most retirements occurring well down the road, a more expansive and aggressive investment policy may be followed.

Company Characteristics

Here again, once you have a good handle on the industry in which the company is situated, it is even more vital that you understand the specific company's characteristics as regards many of the same factors relating to growth, stability, financial status, geographic locations, past contribution record, and so on. The list of factors to be considered is not all-inclusive, but at least it is a good starting point.
    a. Cyclical growth
    b. Static or declining
    c. Steady growth
    d. Rapid growth

e. Short range forecast
f. Long range forecast
g. Geographic location
h. Employer financial status
—Strong
—Fairly strong
—Weak
i. Employer past contribution record
—Excellent
—Fair
—Poor.

Work Force Characteristics

It is generally helpful to develop an insight into whether the work force is growing, static, or declining; what the average age is; and what the workers' attitude might be toward taking early retirement. The answer to these questions will, to some degree, determine the fund's liquidity needs in the future, or even over the nearer term, and could have a bearing on how aggressively the portfolio is managed.

Work force characteristics:
a. Growing
—Moderate
—Rapid
b. Static or declining
c. Attitude toward early retirement
—May be encouraged by employer, as in auto and aerospace industries.
—Most plans provide for early retirement at age 61-62.
—In economic slump, many employees prefer to continue working until latest possible date.
d. Present work force average age (mid-50s for aerospace and milk industry employees)
e. Average worker's retirement age (best estimate)—
Before age 62
—Age 62 (when first eligible for tax free Social Security benefits)
—Age 65
—Later than age 65.

Actuarial Interest Assumption

Is the plan's actuarial interest assumption:
a. High?
b. Average?
c. Below average?
d. Likely to be raised?

This is a very vital area for the investment manager and the trustees to be concerned with, as the assumption refers to the actuary's best estimate of the various factors needed to estimate both the amount of expected benefits and the date at which these benefits will be payable. The investment manager needs to have an understanding with the trustees as to how he expects to obtain the actuarial assumption—though obviously there should be no reliance on the part of the investment manager that this is the end all and be all figure he must achieve, as his job is to maximize the total rate of return relative to the specific needs and objectives of each plan. It is useful to know whether the assumption is above or below the average for most plans, and it is also helpful to know if there is a likelihood that it may soon be raised. My own objective with my portfolios is to obtain the actuarial interest rate each year from current income flows alone.

Actuarial Soundness

Any investment manager who is working with the trustees to develop a sound investment policy needs to know whether he is managing an actuarially sound pension plan, which implies, at least in a general sense, that the market value of the plan's assets when divided by the present value of all accrued benefits is, in the actuary's opinion, sufficient to accomplish the plan's payout objectives. No manager would like to find himself in the position of having to liquidate portfolio securities during a depressed point in the economy, which implies a depressed stock and bond market and the strong possibility of large losses, if he can possibly avoid doing so.

Worst Case Reserve (WCR) Calculation

To anticipate the unthinkable, and in order for the investment manager and the trustees to feel relatively comfortable in the case of a very bad and prolonged decline in the economy insofar as the ability of their pension fund to meet its pension payments when due, it is helpful to prepare for a "worst case" contingency. This may be done by the process outlined in Exhibit 1, which immediately follows the text. The procedure which is used by various banks and money management firms throughout the country is to request the actuary to provide his best estimate of the *annual* pension payments expected to be paid beneficiaries for a period of five years ahead. He should also provide the annual expected contributions flows into the fund for the next five years, as well as a figure for the accumulated unfunded past service obligation and the time span over which it is to be funded. One should also know the actuarial rate and whether there are any contingency sums that should be provided for from the portfolio.

Once this information is obtained, the investment manager can then calculate, as Exhibit 1 portrays, a worst case reserve (WCR) ratio figure. This figure usually runs between 15-25% of the fund's total assets, and this sum (i.e., $743,600 in Exhibit 1) should be invested in U.S. Treasury or agency securities in the specific amounts that will be due and payable each year for five years. In this way if (a) no further contributions are made by employers for five years; (b) only one-half of the portfolio income is received; or (c) the economy is in a deep slump and therefore the bond and stock markets are completely demoralized, the pension fund could still meet its obligations to beneficiaries, without having to sell any of its assets in a very depressed market to do so. Such a calculation therefore can provide considerable peace of mind to both beneficiaries and contributing employers, as they know they can ride out a storm equivalent to the Depression of the '30s.

Vesting Provisions; Employee Reserve and Interest

An investment manager should also know the terms of any vesting provisions, so that he can anticipate the need for liquidity should there be a likelihood that substantial withdrawals will occur. It is also useful to know what reserve for employee contributions should be established, and what interest rate has been agreed upon.

Liquidity

The investment manager should give careful attention to the possible need for liquidity in some pension funds, arising from special industry factors such as possible layoffs, terminations and business mergers and/or failures. Also, funds with little or no cash flow have to adopt a more conservative investment posture to anticipate unpleasant surprises. Finally, and this applies mainly to profit-sharing, severance, annuity and welfare funds, adequate provision for large and unexpected payouts must always be anticipated, which obviously curtails the use of equities to a degree depending upon the specifics of each situation.

Compliance With ERISA

Every board of trustees and each professional associated with the pension fund must ensure that the requirements and tenets of ERISA are adhered to and followed. To do otherwise, unless sound legal advice to the contrary is obtained, is inviting trouble from any number of directions. Relevant in this regard are:
 a. Acknowledgement of duties as "investment manager" [Section 3(38) of ERISA] and "fiduciary" [ERISA §2(21)]
 b. Prudence/diversification requirements.

Trustees' Desires and Expectations

Any investment manager who is conscientiously trying to do a good job needs to know from the board of trustees what the minimum total rate of return objective is for the portfolio, per annum and over a complete market cycle. He also needs to know what his performance is going to be measured against, and I am of course assuming here that the fund's own objective is the paramount criterion he must satisfy. Trustees' expectations concerning investment performance may, for example, include the following:
 a. Actuarial assumption to be earned from interest and dividend flows alone. ___ Yes ___ No
 b. Minimum total rate of return accomplishment on the total portfolio to average ___ per annum over a complete market cycle.
 c. Minimum total rate of return accomplishment for equities over a 12-18 month period to equal the annual CPI inflation rate plus a premium of 50% (or something along these lines).
 d. Other.

The establishment of a time-weighted rate of return should be done in concert with the investment manager, as he must be able to feel that he can, in fact, accomplish what the trustees have in mind. Just to set an arbitrary figure of, say, 20% per year, without carefully reviewing with the investment manager the historical probabilities of his being able to achieve such a rate year in and year out, is an exercise in futility.

In previous comments, I have stated that I like to obtain the actuarial interest assumption from current income flows alone, and that I would like to obtain a time-weighted return on the total portfolio of 1.5 times the underlying imbedded inflation rate—currently about 10%—which would mean a 15% objective.

Investment Restrictions

These should be clearly identified and reduced to writing so that the investment manager knows in advance what areas he should avoid exposing the portfolio to. What is the attitude, for example, concerning:
 —Investment ratios?
 —Foreign securities?
 —Non-union firms?
 —Companies in the tobacco or liquor business?

—South African exposure?

A comment: Just the term "non-union" is not enough, as there are thousands of non-union firms which could be very attractive investments. What most trustees are concerned about is that the firm is not *anti*-union in a highly visible, aggressive sense. To date, the AFL-CIO has not published any blacklist of such "anti-union" firms, and just from a legal standpoint, it is not likely to do so. Each manager will therefore have to develop an understanding with his client fund of just what this term connotes and how he should respond to it.

Frequency of Meetings

Does your board of trustees meet quarterly, semiannually or annually? As a general rule, most boards like to meet quarterly and, of course, the majority of investment managers report to the board quarterly in writing if not in person. It should be made clear that it is vital and necessary to have *regular* meetings with the fund's investment manager at least semiannually, if not quarterly. This is so because a strong and viable communications link between the money manager and the board is absolutely essential if the manager is to do the job responsively that he is retained to do. He must be able to explain his investment philosophy, his investment selections, and his view of the economic outlook and investment markets and, of course, also adequately respond to whatever questions the trustees may have.

Overall Investment Objectives

The three investment objectives I have outlined here are those that happen to appeal to me—and, fortunately, to the clients I work for. They are not all-inclusive, and may not fit your particular circumstances at all. Each board, working with their investment manager and attorney, should develop their own statement along these lines. Whatever works for you and your manager, and that you both feel comfortable with as far as ERISA's language is concerned, is what you should use.

- The *principal objective* of our pension plan is to be able to so manage the assets of the plan that they will be unequivocally available, and therefore able to meet all legitimate beneficiary pension payments in the correct amounts and on the dates they are due and payable. We, therefore, deem it mandatory that *protection of principal* is the foremost consideration in the investment process, as without adequate principal we cannot honor our original commitment.
- The second vital and highly desirable, though not controlling, objective is to *maintain the "integrity" of the present and future beneficiaries' purchasing power*. This is important so that present and prospective retirees can expect to retire on incomes that will be adequate to preserve a reasonable approximation of their accustomed normal living standards when measured against the medium income attainment for pension plan retirees nationally adjusted for industry and geographical differences. (*See* Table 1—CPI.)
- A third desirable objective, though again not a controlling one, is to exceed the actuarial interest assumption by at least 50% in order to provide enough additional assets in the plan to enable benefit payments to be increased, while at the same time stabilizing, or even reducing if need be, pension costs, or some combination of the two.

We are in agreement with the observation that the real job of the investment manager is to enable the trustees, through development of an alert and responsive investment program, *to achieve the greatest possible benefits for the fund's beneficiaries at the most reasonable cost to its contributors*.

Investment Return Objectives

I have outlined in columnar form some logical considerations that you can use in developing useful criteria for each portfolio segment relating to

Investment Return Objectives

Rate of return (ROR) goals, assessed against other relevant factors.

	Our Fund Goal	Actuarial Assumption	CPI	Other National Portfolio Composites	DJIA	S&P 500	S.B.&H. Bonds	Lehman Bros. Kuhn Loeb Bonds
Total Fund	___	___	___	___	___	___	___	___
Fixed Sector	___	___	___	___	___	___	___	___
Equity Sector	___	___	___	___	___	___	___	___
Measurement Period		1 Yr.		2 Yrs.		3-5 Yrs.		Other

what you want your investment return accomplishment measured against. As for myself, I prefer to state a total return bogey for the entire portfolio on a time-weighted basis and this, as I've said, is 1.5 times the annual underlying or imbedded inflation rate.

Conclusion: Investment Guidelines for the HKM Pension Fund

Every pension fund should have its guidelines reduced to writing. The headings shown here are those that I have used with clients, and they have worked out well. You will obviously want your own, but these could form the basis of what you may be looking for. The balance of the tables, exhibits and charts should be useful to you as background "source" material to sharpen and refine your image and understanding of just what it is that you want in your investment policy statement. I hope, as Eleanor Roosevelt used to say, that I have "lit one candle rather than curse the darkness," and I wish you the best of luck as you search for the right answers in preparing your own fund's guidelines.

Investment Guidelines for the H.K.M. Pension Fund

Investment Ratios

1. Fund assets should be allocated on a 45:55 basis between fixed income and equity-oriented securities at market value. Equity assets at the end of any semiannual reporting period may exceed 55% of the total fund by 10% due to market appreciation for a period not to exceed 90 days after the end of a quarter, if the investment manager believes it is in the interests of the fund to permit such an increase.

Prudence

2. All investments should be limited to those that would be interpreted as "prudent" in accordance with Section 404(a)(3) of ERISA.
3. No investment in marketable bonds shall be made unless said bonds are rated A or better by Moody's and/or Standard & Poor's. No bond investment made shall exceed 5% of the total fund's assets under management, at market value.

Diversification

4. Equity investments in any one *industry* shall not exceed 15% of the total market value of the portfolio.
5. Equity investments in any one *company* shall not exceed 5% of the total market value of the portfolio, and 5% of the total outstanding shares of any one company. Individual stock positions which subsequently exceed the 5% limitation due to favorable market action need not be reduced or sold, if in the best judgment of the portfolio manager it would be disadvantageous to the portfolio to do so.
6. The portfolio should reflect an avoidance of "extreme" positions in either the fixed or the equity sectors of the pension fund.

Diversification—Small Company Investment

7. For purposes of further diversification to improve asset growth and to afford a greater degree of inflation protection, the investment manager may invest up to 5% of the total market value of the portfolio in the shares of smaller companies which have demonstrated well above average earnings growth over a minimum of five consecutive years, and which appear to have the requisite management, product and financial strengths to enable them to become large companies, and/or to be acquired by larger companies, within a relatively short span of years.

Real Estate

8. Real estate investment in debt or equity securities is permitted provided the investment manager has the requisite recourse, either "in-house" or through retention of outside experts, to knowledgeable and experienced personnel who can properly analyze and monitor such investments. Investments in REITs sponsored and managed by major life insurance companies and/or mortgage banking firms are permitted, and the fund may participate in FHA and/or VA insured loans originated and serviced by commercial banks, savings banks, insurance companies and/or savings and loan associations who are recognized by professionals in the financial field as being leaders of unquestionable standing and integrity in their respective industry groups.

Use of Options

9. Use of CBOE stock options may be employed where the investment manager justifies to the trustees and/or pension committee that such activity is clearly in the best interests of the fund. Such investment activities shall be limited to the writing of *covered* call options.

Restrictions

10. No investment in "foreign" securities shall be made without prior consultation with the trustees unless said securities are listed on a U.S. security exchange, except that Canadian provincial U.S. pay bonds may be purchased where the market is a reasonably liquid one. Investments in notoriously non-union firms are to be avoided.
11. No investments involving short sales, margin purchases, letter stock, private placements (unless approved by the trustees after a full explanation of such investment), commodities or situations otherwise generally recognized as highly speculative may be employed.

Exhibit 1

EXAMPLE OF WORST CASE RESERVE CALCULATION

1. *Projected Benefit Payments*   (3:00 9/7/78)

1978	$ 220,000
1979	248,000
1980	272,000
1981	296,000
1982	320,000
Total est. 5 year payments	$1,356,000

2. *Current Portfolio:* $4,250,000 market value

		% of Total
Fixed Income Securities	$2,550,000	60%
Stocks	1,700,000	40
	$4,250,000	100%

3. *Present Yields*

	Actual	Worst Case Assumption
Fixed Income	8%	4%
Stocks	4%	2%

4. *Projected Investment Income*—5 years to '82

Fixed Income Secs.	$2,550,000 at 4% for 5 years =	$510,000
Stocks	1,700,000 at 2% for 5 years =	170,000
Total estimated income flow for 5 years		$680,000

5. *WCR Calculation*

Projected pension payments	$1,356,000
Less estimated income flow	680,000
Desired reserve	676,000
Add. 10% safety factor	743,600

$$\text{WCR} = \frac{743,600}{4,250,000} = 17.5\%$$

6.

Projected Annual Payments		Average Income Flow		Provided by WCR
$220,000	−	$136,000	=	$ 84,000
248,000	−	136,000	=	112,000
272,000	−	136,000	=	136,000
296,000	−	136,000	=	160,000
320,000	−	136,000	=	184,000

Exhibit 2

HYPOTHETICAL ILLUSTRATIVE PORTFOLIOS
(principal amount $20,000,000)
(to reflect a range of investment policies and possibilities)

Assumed Investment Returns	Fund A 100% Stocks	Fund B 75% Stocks 25% Bonds	Fund C 50% Stocks 50% Bonds	Fund D 25% Stocks 75% Bonds	Fund E 100% Bonds	Fund F 100% Bonds[1]
1. A stock yield of 5.5% on S&P 400 as of April 1980	5.50	4.125	2.75	1.375	—	—
2. And bond yield of 10% on diversified high grade portfolio	—	2.500	5.00	7.500	10.0	11.0
3. Would produce a total yield of	5.50	6.625	7.75	8.875	10.0	11.0
4. Or, in dollars	$1,100,000	$1,325,000	$1,550,000	$1,775,000	$2,000,000	$2,200,000
5. Which when added to a stock appreciation potential of	15.00	11.250	7.50	3.750	—	—
6. Would produce a total return of	20.50	17.875	15.25	12.625	10.0	11.0
7. Subtracting the est. inflation rate of 9%	9.00	9.000	9.00	9.000	9.0	9.0
8. Would leave a "real" return of	11.5	8.875	6.25	3.625	1.0	2.0
In dollars it would look like this:						
9. Gross investment return	$4,100,000	$3,575,000	$3,050,000	$2,525,000	$2,000,000	$2,200,000
10. Subtracting the inflation rate of 9%	1,800,000	1,800,000	1,800,000	1,800,000	1,800,000	1,800,000
11. Would leave a "real" amount of	$2,300,000	$1,775,000	$1,250,000	$ 725,000	$ 200,000	$ 400,000
12. Which compares with the present return of 7.4%	1,488,000	1,488,000	1,488,000	1,488,000	1,488,000	1,488,000
13. Leaving an inflation-adjusted difference of	+$812,000	+$287,000	($238,000)	($763,000)	($1,288,000)	($1,088,000)
14. "X"ing out inflation, the gross $ inc. or (dec.) on an "income only" basis will be	($388,000)	($163,000)	$62,000	$287,000	$512,000	$712,000

1. Bond yield 11%.

Assumptions

1. Stocks yield 5.5%. Dividends increase at 5% per annum.
2. Stocks appreciate at 15% per year *on average*.
3. Bonds yield 10%—no capital appreciation assumed.
4. Inflation rate: 9%.

Table I-A

Consumer Price Index
(1967 = 100)

December of Year	CPI Unit Value	Annual Percentage Increase	5 Year Average Annual Increase
1949	70.8		
1950	74.9	5.79%	
1951	79.3	5.87	
1952	80.0	0.88	2.5%
1953	80.5	0.63	
1954	80.1	(0.05)	
1955	80.4	0.37	
1956	82.7	2.86	
1957	85.2	3.02	1.9
1958	86.7	1.76	
1959	88.0	1.50	
1960	89.3	1.48	
1961	89.9	.67	
1962	91.0	1.22	1.2
1963	92.5	1.65	
1964	93.6	1.19	
1965	95.4	1.92	
1966	98.6	3.35	
1967	101.6	3.04	3.8
1968	106.4	4.72	
1969	112.9	6.11	
1970	119.1	5.49	
1971	123.1	3.36	
1972	127.3	3.41	6.6
1973	138.5	8.80	
1974	155.4	12.20	
1975	166.3	7.01	
1976	174.3	4.81	
1977	186.1	6.77	8.5
1978	202.9	9.03	
1979	230.0	13.40	
1980 (first 8 months)	249.6	13.10 (annualized)	

Table I-B

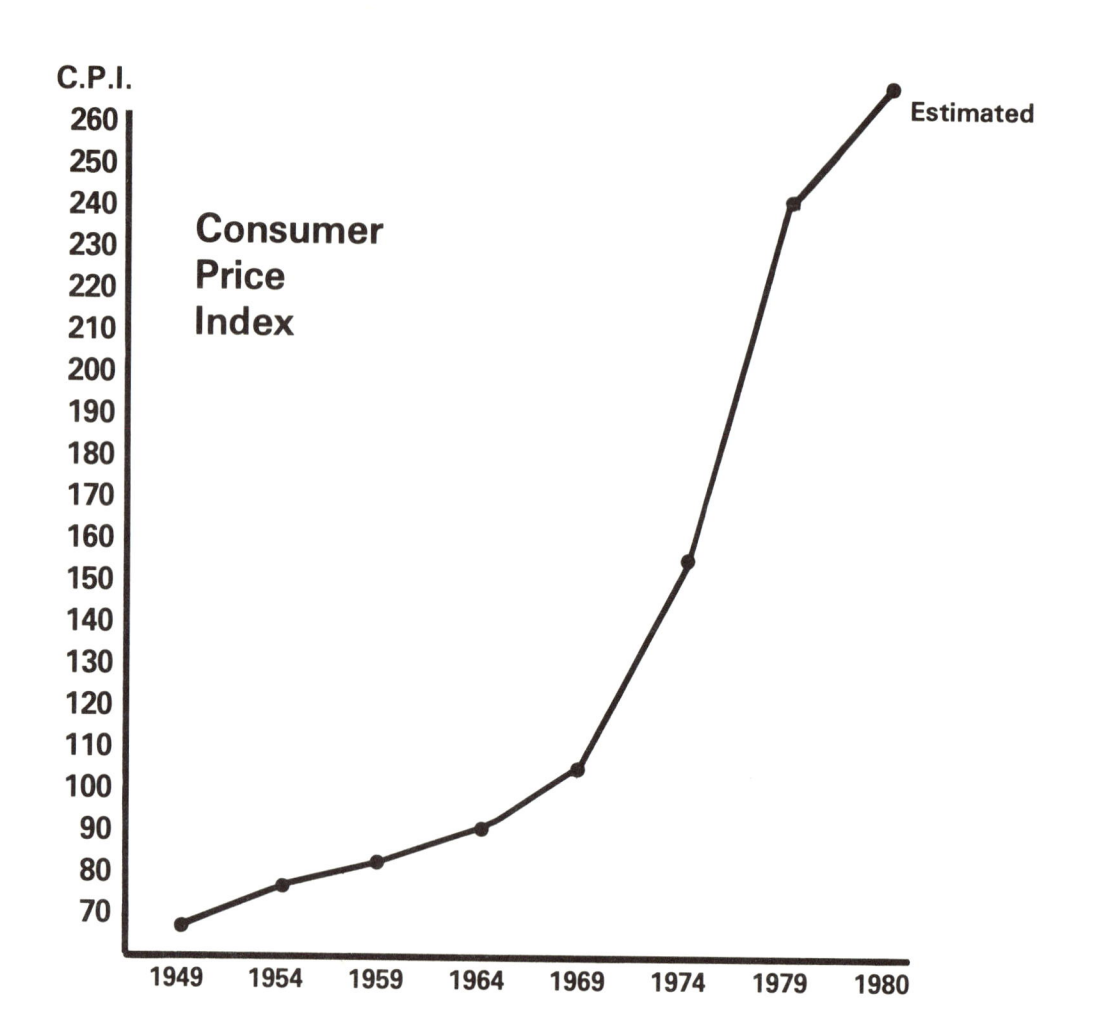

Consumer Price Index

Table II

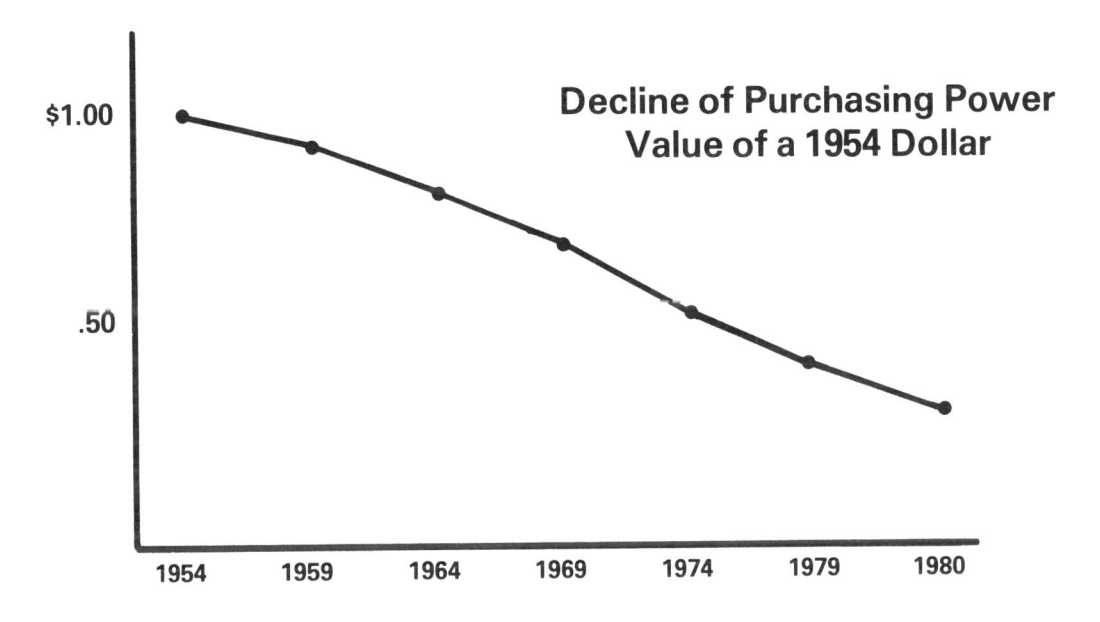

**Decline of Purchasing Power
Value of a 1954 Dollar**

Spectrum of Investments—1980

BY EUGENE B. BURROUGHS

Introduction

The purpose of this session, "Spectrum of Investments" is to offer you insight into what different classes of investments can do for a portfolio, particularly in light of the encouragement to diversify from the Department of Labor's regulations. We are going to use a case study approach. This session was first presented at the 1977 Annual Conference, which was in San Francisco. We looked at different classes of investments and their expected rates of return. We looked at this same portfolio again in 1978 in Atlanta and in 1979 in New York, and now we can compare what was *expected* in 1977 to what was *achieved* over the three years since then. This is no academic pie-in-the-sky exercise. It is a real live pension plan to which supervision is given—day by day. As we look down the highway of our investment objectives, it is always good to keep our eye on the rear view mirror. We need to learn from the past, as we face the future.

After we are finished, you will have an appreciation for the value of diversification, particularly in a volatile economic environment. During the past year, when the stock market and the bond market were both so volatile, we can really appreciate the fact that our employee benefit plans need to be more fully diversified. During inflation, certain classes of assets will go up in one period while others will go down. By having an appropriate mix in the portfolio, we should be able to achieve acceptable rates of return with limited portfolio variability from period to period, and thereby produce the pension promise over the longer term.

We are going to start on a basic level. In fact, we are going to start with the Department of Labor's regulations which came out in July 1979. Some people refer to their release as a "non-event" because, in fact, their definition of prudence for fiduciaries who are involved with employee benefit plans really is, in effect, just plain common sense. Fiduciaries who have been doing a good job for years have known the DOL's approach is essential to the decision making process. The "new" definition of prudence by the DOL is really the "old"

Mr. Burroughs is director of the investment department of the International Brotherhood of Teamsters, Chauffeurs, Warehousemen and Helpers of America. He is responsible for the research, development and recommendation of investment policy in the administration of the international union's operating monies and two related pension funds. Mr. Burroughs received his B.C.S. degree from Benjamin Franklin University. He is chairman of the Investment Policy Panel of the Pension Benefit Guaranty Corporation. A chartered financial analyst, Mr. Burroughs is a past president of the Washington Society of Investment Analysts and a member of the Financial Analysts Federation and the Institute of Chartered Financial Analysts. He has written articles for Pension World, *the* Journal of Portfolio Management, *the* Financial Planner, *and the* Employee Benefits Journal. *He currently serves on the Editorial Advisory Board of* Pension World. *Mr. Burroughs has spoken at several International Foundation educational meetings and serves on the Investment Management Committee.*

approach used by responsible fiduciaries prior to the "scare response" caused by ERISA when adopted in 1974.

We are then going to build upon that basic approach to the developing of a portfolio, using an actual portfolio. This is a portfolio that we supervise in Washington, D.C. You will see the way it was postured in 1977, why it was postured that way, what it did, both bad and good, what the economy's effect was on its results and, hopefully, out of this exercise we can come to an appreciation for the economy's effect on these different classes of assets.

We are going to end our session by putting our necks on the line regarding the various classes of investments as you might consider emphasizing or deemphasizing them in your particular plan depending upon the needs of your plan.

A Systematic Approach

One principle included in the Department of Labor regulations is the encouragement to develop a systematic, commonsense approach to solving your investment decision riddle. Whether it is a health and welfare fund or a large or small pension fund, a vacation plan, a dental plan, whatever it might be; you need to undertake a step by step process. This step by step process involves primarily the trustees and includes the investment manager, the actuary, the consultant, the accountant; whoever you use in your decision making process to attain your goal of producing rates of return that will help you meet the benefit payment promise.

It has been estimated that more than half of the future payments will come from the investment return. This results from the productive power of compounding interest, the power of the reinvestment of earnings. The average pensioner is 42 years old, and you have approximately 20 years to prepare for him. Consequently, your participants are looking to you to produce the investment return.

What Are the Facts and Circumstances?

The first place where we have to look is at the *plan* itself. There is no one who knows the needs of the plan better than you. You know the industry and the companies. You know the mentality and the attitude of the participants. You know the membership. You are the one that has the basic understanding, and you need to share this information with the investment manager.

In addition to knowledge of the plan, we need to have a knowledge of the *portfolio*. As you increase your knowledge of the portfolio, where it stands today and what you are trying to do with it, you and your fellow trustees will become more responsible clients. Unfortunately, many breakdowns in investment management relationships result from a lack of communication.

We are encouraged by the regulations to seek out *investment facts*. There are risks of ownership. Risk is a two-edged sword. There is the risk of reward and the risk of loss; consequently, we not only need to seek out the investment facts, but we need to *recognize the changing circumstances*. I don't think I need to remind anybody of the impact of the changing and evolving circumstances that occurred during the past year, starting October 6, 1979, with the Federal Reserve's Saturday night massacre. Do we have changing circumstances in this modern environment? Unfortunately, we have accelerating changing circumstances.

A portfolio needs to be its own best defense at any time. Therefore, as a trustee, you need to be comfortable with how your portfolio is positioned today to exploit the opportunities of tomorrow.

Concerns and Constraints

After we have considered the facts and the changing circumstances, we need to choose a *course of action*. You also have a *monitoring* responsibility. You have an *evaluation* responsibility and then, if it is in order, you *modify* whatever the policy has been. For what purpose? To ultimately produce the promises. What is the basic objective of our plan? To pay benefits. It isn't to beat the S&P 500. It isn't for a million other reasons, it is to *produce the promises.*

The DOL reminds us that it is the protection of principal through diversification which is very important. This is required by ERISA, but it really was the name of the game prior to ERISA—ERISA just called our attention to the importance of diversification. Those plans which have been more fully diversified over the last ten year period have had positive rates of return exceeding inflation. The other requirement that is called for is to provide for *adequate cash flow*. This is particularly important with a health and welfare plan that has a very short cycle in terms of using reserves for benefit payments. It is also very pertinent and relative if you have a mature pension fund. By that I mean a pension fund which has passed its accumulation phase and is in its termination phase. You are in the period where your benefit payments actually exceed the amount of contributions that are coming in. Therefore, the manager needs to know that you require cash from the investment program to pay benefits over the next year or next two or three years. It's very, very important, the DOL says, that you provide adequate cash flow.

What does your plan need? First of all, the *income level*. How much income does your particular plan need? Health and welfare plans and mature pension funds generally need a certain level of income. Does your plan need to *preserve principal value*? In 1974 and 1975, unfortunately, if you had a portfolio that was very heavily oriented toward common stock, in that two year period you could have been down 40% or 50% in principal value. Now, that was a short term aberration and the plan could have come back significantly since that period of time, and that event really made no long term impact on the fund. Conversely, a health and welfare plan which may have to pay out reserves over the next six months may have to put a lot of emphasis on the subject of preservation of principal value.

How much *volatility* can you really take? Remember that there is a price paid for stability. You can have stability. You can put all your money in certificates of deposit, but if the markets act efficiently, you will be rewarded for holding assets which have greater volatility and variability in value. If your planning horizon is long enough, then you can include investments that fluctuate in value and then earn a greater rate of return.

How much *liquidity*? This relates to your need to provide adequate cash flow. Common stock of IBM in a health and welfare plan may be inappropriate. It is highly marketable, but if something should have occurred yesterday in the fortunes of IBM and the stock drops 5% or 10% and you need cash to pay benefits, you will find the stock marketable but not "liquid." A price is paid for liquidity. Thus, it is important to only provide as much as is needed.

How much *management assistance* do you need? Generally, an investment management decision is only as strong as its weakest link. Therefore, it is incumbent upon all co-fiduciaries to have a full understanding of what is really involved in the process. Otherwise, in a market like we had last year, someone may say,"Look, I don't want to touch bonds with a ten foot pole. Get them out of the portfolio!" This, of course, could be completely inappropriate for the long term needs of the fund. Someone needs to decide how much management assistance is available and needed.

"Simplicity" in your program is also important. I think this is a cardinal rule, especially for funds with significant numbers of trustees. Now, that isn't to say that the results from simple strategies cannot be profound. They can be profound. We are sometimes led by the investment management community to overly sophisticated programs that we don't fully understand. This can cause problems. An *annual valuation* of your investments is extremely important. It was a good idea before ERISA. It is now required by ERISA. There has to be a periodic evaluation of your investments. Real estate is the toughest to frequently value. Appraisals can be very expensive. That is why many people go into real estate through the commingled funds that value their portfolio on a unit value basis.

Last, but certainly not least, is the concern for the *preservation of purchasing power* of the plan. How can we keep these plans competitive with inflation? The record shows that most of our funds haven't even kept up with the drop in the purchasing power of the dollar. One issue that will surface repeatedly over the next three or four years is the subject of post-retirement indexing of benefit payments. With inflation the way it is, we somehow have to figure out ways to keep participants at least equal to the standard of living they had when they retired. There are different ways to accomplish this, and one way is to tilt your pension fund toward those assets which have the potential and probability of increasing in value over time. Great emphasis should be put on the goal of preserving the purchasing power of the accumulated assets.

Selection of Investment Vehicles

What is available to you among the classes of investments? We have the *products of the insurance companies, fixed income securities* and *equity securities*. There are a lot more products for you now than just a few years ago. The toughest job you have is to separate the wheat from the chaff. Which ones are appropriate for your fund? This is where your use of consultants is very important.

You can go the fully insured route through the purchase of annuity contracts. This is laying off the mortality and investment rate risk on the insurance company. You can use deposit administration contracts or separate accounts. The separate account is where the insurance company acts just like an investment manager or a bank. You are hiring them just to manage investments for you. Insurance companies are financial department stores. They manage real estate. They supervise private placement funds and, of course, many of you participate in the guaranteed investment contracts (GICs). These are the ones where you can, for a fixed number of years, contract with them at a certain rate. The most significant feature is that they guarantee the reinvestment rate. That's a very valuable feature.

With fixed income investments we have money market instruments, bonds, mortgages, private placements, mutual funds and commingled accounts. Within equity investments, we have common stock, real estate ownership, index funds, mutual funds, commingled accounts, and stock options. Lots of alternatives for participating on the equity side of the business.

We are encouraged by the DOL regulations to seek out investment facts, the risk of ownership as well as the characteristics of different classes of investments. The different classes of investments respond differently to economic events. For instance, during the last couple of years, you've made lots of money by owning income-producing real estate. Why is that happening? Because real estate has a different personality than either stocks or bonds.

Risk. The first risk to consider is *interest rate risk,* commonly referred to as "market risk." When interest rates go up, the value of your fixed income securities drops in value. Thus, you have suffered interest rate risk. The market of stocks itself suffers from interest rate risk because there is a discounting mechanism operative. As interest rates go up, that attracts a lot of money to fixed income securities. Where is it coming from? It is withdrawn from stock ownership and produces a discounted rate of return from the stock market competitive to returns from buying bonds. If you have an active bond manager, and he is turning over your portfolio three or four times a year, chances are he is trying to anticipate the changes in interest rates. If interest rates are expected to rise, he wants to have you in CDs to protect the principal. If interest rates are expected to fall, he will extend the maturities, riding the interest rate curve to increasing principal value.

What about *purchasing power risk*? Go home and ask your accountant or actuary to convert the value of your fund today into 1967 dollars, and you will be shocked to find out the amount of loss in purchasing power. If you bought a bond in 1967, say for $1,000, by 1977 the value of that bond was $575.00; the value of that bond today is only $404.00. You experienced purchasing power risk. Next, we must consider the potential of *political or confiscation risk.* In the event there is a nationalization of certain industries, the investors in those industries will be compromised. Even if we are not yet at that point, we certainly should consider *social change risk* because we are feeling a great amount of regulatory influence from Washington. The real question is, in fact, should I be an investor or a lender? Most of you are from middle America. As an investor group you have preferred bonds. You have less than 30% of your money in common stock. You've made a decision. You've perceived that something fundamental is happening in this country. Risk is not being rewarded. Thus, you want to be a lender instead of an investor. You don't want to participate as the entrepreneur. Such a decision is in response to your evaluation of social change risk.

Finally, *financial or business risk* must be considered. Bonds are rated Aaa, Aa, etc., Aaa indicating superior investment quality, A, investment quality, Baa, still investment quality, but containing elements of speculation. These are measurements of financial risk. You might have a guideline with your investment manager requiring that all of your stocks meet certain investment criteria. The criteria would ensure a certain level of quality that all positions in the portfolio must meet.

Characteristics. In addition to the risks of ownership, we need to examine the characteristics of these investments. Their "personalities" are different. For instance, each class of assets differs in its *marketability.* Marketability is the degree to which you can easily sell, or buy, a particular security. Most pension funds can deemphasize marketability. For some reason, we have put a lot of value on marketability. Unfortunately, there is a price for marketability. If you have a strong positive cash flow in your fund, you can most likely deemphasize marketability and thus pick up increased yield as a result. With health and welfare plans, marketability is extremely important. You may have to sell those reserves because of an unforeseen level of claims.

Stability is a characteristic of investments. Common stock, as a class, is very unstable. Which classes have elements of stability? Money market instruments, of course, are very stable. Real estate can be relatively stable if it is attractive income-producing property, in a good location, with good tenants and negotiable leases. *Preservation of purchasing power:* Many feel that common stock over time will be competitive to inflation. Over the longer term, common stock has been very competitive to inflation. Bonds have not kept up with inflation, but the reinvestment of interest you receive in *higher* yielding bonds, over time, can produce a growing cash flow stream. *Growth in value:* Stocks have the potential for growth in value. The companies are reinvesting their earnings. They are taking advantage of strong research and development capabilities. They are compounding their resources over time, which results in growth in value. Real estate has shown us significant growth in value in the last few years. With the different classes, you can emphasize those classes that have high current income. Our plans are tax exempt. Market research has indicated that by emphasizing current income, you can achieve a higher total return over time.

The Portfolio's Performance

Now, let's look at our representative portfolio. Using a "case study" approach, let's look at the past and prepare for the future.

We have been reminded to diversify the portfolio, provide for cash flow, and compare expected and realized returns. Having "appropriately considered" all the facts and circumstances, we must *act*. That's fine, but I hope that people who eventually sit in judgment of what we do will understand the environment that we were acting in. We live in a time when the government certainly can't successfully predict or control the future. For them, the future is one week at a time. Secondly, we see that businessmen in this country are unwilling to invest in capital equipment because they are not convinced that they are going to get a decent rate of return. This is what the oil industry keeps telling us. The consumer is trying to balance between whether he should save because he is going to be laid off or spend his money because prices are going to go up. "What do they expect of the fiduciary of an employee benefit plan?" Our crystal ball isn't any better than theirs, therefore we can only hope that those who hold us accountable will keep in mind the circumstances and environment within which we made our decisions.

Initial Assumptions and Strategy

Let's move on and look at our portfolio (Exhibit 1). Now, this is not a hypothetical example. This is a pension fund with about 6,000 participants, now approximating $190 million. The time is May 1977. The yield at that time was 5½%. It was diversified among fixed income securities (43%) and equities (57%). The average Taft-Hartley fund would not have been tilted toward equity that much. But this fund has good, positive cash flow, was concerned with accelerating inflation, and therefore was trying to get into a position to take advantage of having some assets offering growth in value.

Asset Mix. What types of assets were used? Roughly half of the fixed income portion was in marketable bonds, rated A or better. About 24[c] of every dollar was invested in GICs—the guaranteed investment contracts of the insurance companies. Because of our concern about rising interest rates, 17% of the fund was invested in money market instruments.

Also, at that time, we were beginning to participate on a commingled basis in a "private placement fund." You can do this through banks, insurance companies, different mediums, but it is a way to participate in lower credit securities. The insurance company loans the money out, let's say, to Baa or Bbb companies that you may not feel comfortable with investing directly in your portfolio, but you can go through a keyhole of a commingled fund to achieve a higher yield. You have less liquidity,

Exhibit 1

THE PORTFOLIO
May 1977
Yield (at cost) 5.5%

Fixed Income	43%

Bonds	54%
GICs	24%
Money Market	17%
Private Placement Fund	5%

Equity	57%

Common Stock	
Actively Managed	44%
Index Fund	35%
Real Estate	21%

	100%

but you have the diversification offered by that insurance company, since you share with other investors in a portfolio of hundreds of loans to companies. You are "passively" invested, but reaching for higher yield than you can achieve with marketable bonds.

Now, what about the equity side? Our fund had had several money managers who had done relatively well but, unfortunately, several managers in the common stock area had done relatively poorly. Because of this experience, it was decided that a portion of the common stock should be passively invested in an index fund. An index fund is merely a way of replicating the return of a market, let's say, the S&P 500. By participating in all 500 issues, or 496 issues, or whatever it might be, you can achieve the market's return. No superior knowledge is involved. Active managers have to give evidence of possessing superior knowledge to provide you with value in excess of the market's return, so this fund's equity strategy embraces a combination of passive (index fund) and active management (two investment counsel firms). Now, part of the 57% in equity is allocated to equity real estate: warehouses, office parks, shopping centers and office buildings. Why? Because if inflation was going to get worse—and it did—then real estate could be a way of diversifying out of dollar-denominated assets into a commodity. We are going to see more of this. You are going to see pension funds participating as limited partners or in some other way in bricks and mortar, in commodities, oil, gas, timber, etc.

Exhibit 2

EXPECTED RETURN FROM PORTFOLIO
Projected at May 1977
(Assuming 5% rate of inflation)

	Expected Return
Fixed Income	8.0%
Bonds	8.4%
GICs	9.0%
Money Market	5.0%
Private Placement Fund	9.0%
Equity	12.6%
Common Stock	13.5%
Real Estate	9.9%
Combined Portfolio	10.7%

Expected Returns. What were the expectations at the time? (Exhibit 2.) After seeking professional counsel, we concluded that it was reasonable to assume over the next five or eight years an average inflation rate of 5%. Were we wrong? We were wrong! For decades, inflation had been 2%, 2½%, and then all of a sudden, it shot up to 6% and 7%. Now look where it is. The money market at that time was 5%. There was no reason to expect with inflation at 5% that money markets would pay any more than 5%. That's what the savings accounts paid. Private placement fund: Because of its reaching for lower credits, more illiquid investments, it was reasonable to expect 9%. Adding it all together and weighted accordingly, we expected a net of 8% from fixed income investments.

Now consider equity. Remember, we had a combination of common stock actively managed and also an index fund and real estate. Well, would you believe that at that time, many banks, many people doing this type of work, thought it was reasonable to expect an annualized rate of return of 13.5% from common stock. When I said that in the summer of 1977, I heard from the audience, "good luck." That was the attitude; very skeptical, as to whether you could get a 13.5% return. Today, what are they telling us? People who are doing the market research say you should be able to achieve 15% or 16% from common stock. That's how hard stocks have been hit. Now, real estate: 9.9% based upon the properties in the portfolios, what it looked at that time, never expecting inflation to be higher than 5% on a net basis.

These were reasonable assumptions at that time. Putting it together, based upon the mix in the portfolio and assuming a rate of inflation of 5%, we could expect a combined return from the portfolio of 10.7%.

The First Year

Now, what happened? (Exhibit 3.) We were assuming inflation of 5% and we said the combined portfolio should produce about 10.7%. We were looking then for a real return—the difference between the inflation rate and the combined portfolio return rate—of about 6%. Is it reasonable to expect a real rate of 6%?

Let's look at what occurred during the first year. Inflation started going up: from May 1977 to May 1978, it was 7.2%, higher inflation than expected. What happened to the various classes of assets? Look at fixed income. As inflation was going up, interest rates were following it. That's what happens. Consequently, our fixed income portion didn't do as well as we expected. The marketable bonds really got hit. In fact, during that period, there was perhaps, on a total return basis, zero return from the marketable bond portfolio. You got your 8% or 9% in clipping coupons, but principal dropped in value because interest rates were going up. The only way we were able to get the 5.4% is because, remember, part of the fund was passively invested in the GICs, and also in the private placements. GICs are not marked to market. Some people say they should be, but we know that we have a certain income stream out of the contract. Our fixed income return was hurt in an inflationary environment; not on target.

Now, from equity, we didn't do too badly. Remember, we said that we expected about 12.6%. Well, let's see how we realized it. Wow! Our active managers made some good strategic moves. They moved out of yield stocks into growth companies and, you know, if you look at the New York Stock Exchange as a total exchange over the last five years, if you could have purchased a share in the total exchange, you could have very high rates of return on a five year basis from 1974. A lot of smaller capitalized growth companies have done very well. So, inflation can be very disruptive. You can have winners and you can have losers, but in that particular environment our active managers did well. The index fund was a drag on our return, at least for that year. Real estate: We didn't reach the 9.9% goal. What happened? Well, we started accumulating the properties in

Exhibit 3

REALIZED RETURN VS. EXPECTED RETURN

	Expected Return at May 1977	Realized Return 5/77-5/78	Realized Return 5/78-5/79	Realized Return 5/79-5/80
Fixed Income	8.0%	5.4%	6.0%	4.0%
Equity	12.6%	12.0%	11.0%	20.0%
Common Stock				
Actively Managed	13.5%	16.8%	6.5%	12.7%
Index Fund	13.4%	6.4%	7.3%	18.5%
Real Estate	9.9%	8.4%	26.0%	33.2%
Combined Portfolio Return	10.7%	9.3%	9.2%	12.3%
Inflation Rate	5.0%	7.2%	10.9%	14.4%

the early 1970s. There was a real estate recession of 1974 and 1975. We were still suffering some leasing problems. The properties were not fully leased. Consequently, we did not reach the objective of 9.9%.

On a total basis, then, with inflation higher, although we had expected to get a rate of return of 10.7%, we got a combined rate of return when we put it all together of 9.3%—slightly above the inflation rate of 7.2%, but not nearly as much as we expected. The important thing in this review is not whether each class reached its objective on an annual basis, but that we may see the value of diversification. In that particular year, the active managers did very well for us. The index fund did not. Bonds were lagging because of inflation. Real estate lumbered along and gave us a good rate of return, although slightly under the objectives. A net return of 9.3%; I don't think we would apologize for that, but the point is, "What happened?" and "Why?"

The Second Year

Let's move to the next year (May 1978-May 1979). Remember, when we projected these expected rates of return we said that these rates were reasonable to expect over the next five or eight years. So, they should still be good. See what happened in May 1978-1979? From May 1978 to May 1979, point to point, the annualized inflation rate was 10.9%, *twice* as high as we expected.

What did it do to the assets? Look at real estate—up 26%! Not unusual during that period of time. Many of the commingled funds, PRISA, Coldwell Banker, a lot of these larger funds, had this type of return. How did they get it? Rolling over leases at higher per square foot rates, plus increased investor interest in real estate. They are willing to pay a higher price. Investors from Argentina, Italy, the U.K., Canada, are bidding up our real estate. And, they are willing to buy it today, believe it or not, at negative cash flows, counting on inflation to increase the value over time. They are seeking our stable political environment and seeking "hard" assets. Therefore, we realized 9% from net lease rentals for the period and added 17% from capital appreciation increases. Now, that shouldn't surprise you. Many of you live in neighborhoods in your own private residences where such increases took place. What has impacted real estate thusly? Inflation. Everybody is losing purchasing power in dollar-denominated assets; therefore, the purchase of real estate is a flight away from dollars into a commodity—in this case, bricks and mortar.

What happened in the other accounts? Well, during that period of time, the index fund returned 7.3%. It was very tough to make money during that 12 month period from common stock. Active managers didn't do as well as the index fund. So, at that point, you could say, "Well, maybe the index fund is good." We don't make these decisions year to year; we are looking for a ten, 12, 15 year period before we make any real changes. But, from equity, not necessarily with thanks to our common stock, but certainly from our real estate portion, we came up to 11%. Our targeted rate of return was 12.6%.

Bonds: Still problems. Why? Look what rising inflation is doing to fixed income contracts. Eighty-

Exhibit 4

REALIZED RETURN VS. EXPECTED RETURN

	Expected Return at May 1977	Realized Return (Annualized) 5/77-5/80
Fixed Income	8.0%	5.1%
Equity	12.6%	15.6%
Common Stock		
Actively Managed	13.5%	11.9%
Index Fund	13.4%	10.6%
Real Estate	9.9%	23.0%
Combined		
Portfolio Return	10.7%	10.5%
Inflation Rate	5.0%	10.7%

eight percent of your return from a long term bond investment is dependent upon the reinvestment rate. In the past, deflation has always followed inflation. What happens when we roll over these bonds over into maybe 5%, 6%, 7% paper? I'm not saying it is going to happen, but that's the risk that you run, and what can happen to bond portfolios. So, we didn't reach our 8% because the value of our portfolio was marked down as interest rates have gone up.

But, because of our diversified portfolio and thanks to real estate in particular, we achieved +9.2% for the year in the total portfolio.

The Third Year

Now, what about the most recent year, May 1979 to May 1980? Inflation at 14.4%! Thank goodness we had some bricks and mortar, a non-financial asset, real estate, up 33% (because of leverage). Conversely, fixed income contracts—couldn't even hold onto all of our coupons, up only 4%. Stock, index fund, up 18.5%, because of the amount of oil stocks and small capitalization companies in the S&P 500 index.

Now, let's put the three years together (Exhibit 4) and compare expectations to reality. We expected inflation to be 5%. It was 10.7%. You would expect real estate ownership to be profitable; it was, up 23%, far more than expected. Common stock kept pace with inflation; bonds, as expected, did not. Thanks to diversification and realizing the "unexpected," the real life portfolio worked out better than you could have written in a textbook; we *expected 10.7% per year,* we *achieved 10.5%.* That's the good news; the bad news is that that return is not good enough, because the purchasing power of the portfolio did not keep pace with inflation, which was 10.7% per year.

Have we learned something from the exercise? Yes, we had certain expectations. Now we have realities, and somehow or another, as we oversee these funds, we have to adjust from hope to reality. We have to learn from our experience. Now, unfortunately, we don't have the luxury of sticking with any 12 month period of time. We have to move ahead. In fact, just to remind you, we are encouraged to be mindful of changing circumstances—and wow, did we have changing circumstances over the past year—and we have to continue to choose a course of action. You are going to have some tough meetings ahead with your money managers, believe you me. They are facing them with concern about how you might respond. Obviously, the temptation is to make some serious changes in our portfolios. But we have to stir in an element of patience because, remember, we are dealing, those of us with pension funds, with 15-20 year time horizons. So, we don't want to do anything that is inappropriate which may reduce, may abort, what could be a successful long term strategy.

Looking Ahead: Current Strategy

So much for the past; where are we now? What are the advantages and disadvantages of the various classes in light of the changing circumstances?

Money Market Instruments

Money market instruments, particularly now, are providing a high current return. There are some people who say that because of the inflationary environment, there is a place in pension portfolios on a continuing basis for a certain amount of short term instruments. The most you are getting, though, is a current return that only matches the current level of inflation. Therefore, over a longer period of time, you are not realizing a real rate of return. High quality money market instruments, whether purchased individually or through commingled funds or mutual funds, generally provide a highly marketable and liquid asset source permitting health and welfare and other short term oriented funds an opportunity to raise cash with no loss of principal. Remember, though, that with short term money market instruments, you are not really making an "investment," you are just riding whatever the short term yield curve is, which can change significantly in a short period of time. Your return from money market instruments can drop 400, 500, or 600 basis points in just a few months. Thus, you may miss a long term investment opportunity and, for a pension fund, you may miss creating a high income stream if you keep too much of your money short. Another thing to keep in mind is that bankruptcies are up and, therefore, this is no time to be lowering your quality, particularly in the commercial paper area.

Make sure that you know about repurchase agreements, short term investment accounts, and corporate master notes. You should explore with your custodian bank how your fund can take advantage and receive income from what is known as "fail float." Fail float is cash available for investment resulting from a security which is to be delivered against payment; for some reason the broker is late in delivering the security, and the monies are idle past the original settlement date. Your fund should earn the income resulting from this fail to deliver.

With short term rates as high as they are, we dare not be sloppy in running our short term reserves. Lots of opportunities are available through money market instruments, but one needs to exercise caution since the unique administrative needs of the fund should be kept in mind.

Publicly Traded Bonds

Many of the funds represented at this conference have a larger commitment to publicly traded bonds than any other asset category. In the risk-adverse environment which existed from 1968 to the late 1970s, more money was made from clipping and reinvesting coupons from bonds than from stock, particularly the kind of stock we hold in our plans. Unfortunately, the last few years have been a disaster for those holding longer term bonds. However, we have to consider the high current income, as high as 13% and 14%, which is available. Also, remember that the power of compounding interest is working for you. For instance, on a long term bond, 88% of the ultimate return results from the level of the reinvestment rate from year to year. The good thing that you have going for you in your bond portfolios is (1) you are tax exempt; (2) chances are you have a positive cash flow and you will not be spending the income which you receive; and (3) all of that income can be reinvested at much higher rates. Therefore, the yield on your fixed income component is *increasing over time.* Time diversification is working in your favor. A painful disadvantage is the loss in purchasing power (for example, a $1,000 bond purchased today and held for 20 years and assuming the same 9% inflation rate that we had for the last five years, results in the value of that $1,000 being $171.93 at maturity). Another disadvantage to bonds is that any money that you allocate to bonds is obviously allocated away from common stock, and the large advantage of common stock in an inflation environment is that these premier corporations have the opportunity to reinvest their earnings at higher rates than you can achieve in the bond market. And, if they capitalize on their research and development, management skills, consumer acceptance, etc., your investment is being compounded by that company at higher rates than those which you can compound as a lender in the bond market.

The net bottom line is, if the risk posture of your board favors bonds, *this certainly is a time to be buying them, since we are back again at near the all-time high in interest rates.*

However, you should be aware that attitudes are changing toward bonds. Henry Kaufman (among other things) recently said that bonds should be bought for their potential for price appreciation and not for income protection, which is a real switch. He also calls attention to the advantage of the mortgage-backed securities in the bond area, and has said that financial futures are an integral part of any interest rate strategy. Therefore, if this is the case, then since the active managers of your bond portfolio will be using financial futures, it behooves you and I to try to at least understand what they are and how they may be used to hedge a portfolio.

Common Stock

In historical perspective, there is no question about it, all the statistics indicate that your premier companies are on sale at a discount. However, you can't always drive these portfolios looking into the rear view mirror. We have to look ahead. One has to be particularly concerned about the present traffic, so to speak, because there has been quite a difference in what have been the returns from the larger and smaller capitalization stocks. For instance, since the recession of 1974, the smaller, over-the-counter issues, the S&P 500 stocks, and the top 50 premier growth companies were all selling at about the same valuation level. During that six year period of time, the over-the-counter issues have increased in value fourfold, the S&P 500 almost 2½ times, and the premier companies slightly over two times. Thus, the premier companies are presently languishing in value compared to the over-the-counter issues.

The increasing levels of dividend payments and

the percentage change in dividends paid indicate that the companies are attempting to provide investors with a real rate of return. Obviously, the companies are in a good position to pass along their inflation costs to you and me the consumer. The S&P 500 index fund has done very well over the recent years, resulting from its exposure to the oil companies and to smaller capitalization companies. Thus, some funds which embraced the index funds some years ago have done relatively well compared to their active managers unless their active managers have also been in the right sectors of the market.

The disadvantages of common stock ownership are very obvious to all of you. As a group, you hold stock in low esteem because of your disappointment over the last 12 or 13 years. However, that just might be a technical sign indicating that stocks may be a good buy. Did you ever think of where all the money flowing into our funds is going to go? It's estimated that by 1995, the public and private funds will total $5 trillion. There is only $1.2 trillion currently in the stock market. What about all the Eurodollar money that is seeking haven in this country? There is only so much real estate to go around. Isn't it possible that the sheer weight of the dollars available could turn to be an advantage to the stock market of the future?

On a net basis, I have to give stock a *buy* rating.

Mortgages

Mortgages have similar characteristics to bonds in that they presently provide high current income, but they also have the additional advantage of periodically returning to you part of your principal for reinvestment at higher rates—if, indeed, rates will be going up in the future. This latter attribute is particularly evident if you buy the Government National Mortgage Association (GNMA, or Ginnie Mae) debentures.

Mortgages are becoming more advantageous to pension funds since more imagination is being used in packaging them. For instance, you now can get variable rate mortgages. You can get an inflation hedge by actually participating in the appreciation of the underlying properties securing the mortgages, and there are many different types of commingled funds through which you can participate in mortgages without having all the administrative details of checking them, warehousing them, etc. No question about it, the mortgage industry needs the pension fund dollar, as savings and loans and insurance companies (for different reasons) are strapped in providing funds for the mortgage market.

The disadvantages are similar to those of bonds as to the potential loss of purchasing power, and you do sacrifice growth in principal opportunities compared to equity investments. On average, mortgages, as bonds, present a *buy* opportunity for our employee benefit plans.

Equity Real Estate

In spite of equity real estate being the favored topic for discussion now among pension fund trustees, there is still only 1% of employee benefit money in this country invested in real estate.

One big advantage that we have now as pension funds is that, for the first time, real estate owners and developers are letting us inside their world since they need our money. With high interest rates, and mortgages almost impossible to get, they are sharing ownership opportunities and development opportunities on a joint venture basis, etc. The marriage of money and expertise is now available in real estate for the first time, and it is a good thing for both the real estate entrepreneurs and the pension fund managers. However, it's a very tough business and it has to be done right. You must be "location specific" and there must be intensive, expert management of the real estate portfolio.

Some would question whether real estate is fully priced, particularly when compared to common stock.

We, of course, as demonstrated earlier, have been very pleased with our real estate investment experience. However, real estate ownership is a complicated investment medium and one needs always to approach it with caution, weighing the advantages and disadvantages against the specific needs of your plan.

Conclusion

Within the context of the needs of the plan and keeping in mind the promises we are attempting to meet, we have examined the various asset categories and attempted to evaluate them in today's environment. Matching expectations and reality is an ever-changing challenge for each of us. Needless to say, none of us should get bored as we consider the challenges of supervising these employee benefit plan monies.

Insurance Company Investment Products

BY JON S. BRIGHTMAN

THE PURPOSE of this paper is to review the various investment vehicles available from insurance companies for pension plan trustees. To do so, I'm going to give a very brief refresher course in some basic information about insurance companies and pension plans and how they work together.

Characteristics of a Pension Plan

The Promise

First, what are the basic components of a pension plan? That may depend upon your point of view.

A participant looks at a pension plan as the source of retirement income. An administrator looks at a pension plan as a recordkeeping problem. A governmental agency looks at a pension plan as something to regulate. A consultant looks at a pension plan as an opportunity to solve problems and give advice. Trustees, of course, ought to have the broadest view of all, for they in fact are supposed to be keeping the thing under control.

A pension plan is all of these things, but primarily a pension plan is a *financial obligation*. The obligation is the promise to pay a benefit.

The final element of a pension plan is the fact that the benefit will be paid only upon the occurrence of some future event. That event may be death, it may be disability, it may be retirement, or some combination. It may be worthwhile for trustees to remember this when they are having a meeting, and ask, "Is this meeting about the financial obligation to pay a benefit at some time in the future?" If the meeting, or the sales pitch, or the speech, is not about these subjects, then perhaps the meeting, seminar or speech shouldn't be going on.

An Uncertain Business

Once a pension plan is established, it is important to understand that a pension plan is a very uncertain business. There are three major uncertainties to it: benefits, administration expenses and invest-

Mr. Brightman is corporate vice president and manager of the Milwaukee office of Meidinger, Inc. He previously was manager of the retirement and insurance department of the Air Line Pilots Association, representing 36 airlines, with fiduciary responsibility for pilot pension plans. Earlier, he held several positions with Travelers Insurance Co., including manager of pension services and portfolio manager in the investment department. Mr. Brightman received his A.B. degree from Bowdoin College and holds the professional designations of chartered property casualty underwriter (C.P.C.U.) and chartered financial analyst (C.F.A.). He is a member of the Institute of Chartered Financial Analysts, Washington Society of Investment Analysts, and Society of Chartered Property and Casualty Underwriters.

ment return. We could call them the three "true costs" of a pension plan.

The first, then, is the amount of benefits. How much money you'll have to pay out in benefits is a figure you won't know until long, long into the future. That figure depends not only upon what was negotiated at the bargaining table, but upon a lot of unknowns—how long the participants are going to live, the number of participants who enter the plan in the future and the various options available to the participants, such as early retirement or different ways of receiving benefits.

The second is the expense of administering the plan. This includes the fees paid to investment managers, trustees, administrators, attorneys, consultants, and so forth. Like the benefits, the expenses can only be totaled up after the fact—but these costs are not nearly as great as the cost of benefits, and are far more predictable.

The third uncertainty is the investment return. Unless the plan's trustees decide to put contributions into a shoebox and bury it under the apple tree, the money will be earning interest until it is needed to pay benefits. This income offsets the expenses of administration and the cost of benefits.

Characteristics of an Insurance Company

Now that we've talked about pension basics, let's talk about insurance companies. Since you as trustees may be dealing with insurance companies, it's worthwhile to take time to understand the basics of their business. Perhaps by knowing why *they* want to do business with *you,* you can figure out the conditions under which *you* want to do business with *them*.

When you go to buy a car, you have a pretty fair idea of how a car runs and how it's built. You also have a basic understanding of how the car dealers make their profits. You ought to have the same basic understanding of insurance companies before you go shopping for their products.

Insuring Risk: A Transfer of Uncertainty

An insurance company is in business to sell protection against risk. What is risk? The uncertainty of financial loss. You insure your house because you are not certain that it won't burn down, causing you to suffer a financial loss. In buying a homeowner's policy, you transfer the financial risk that your home might burn down from you to the insurance company. For a price.

You have only one house. The insurance company is going to issue policies not just on one house, but on thousands, and it's betting that *all* of those houses are not going to burn down. The insurance company has pooled a large number of risks, and the premiums on the houses that don't burn down will be enough to pay for the houses that do.

As the purchaser of an insurance policy, you transfer uncertainty from yourself to the insurance company. The cost of reducing your uncertainty is the premium. This is true whether you buy a fire insurance policy or an automobile policy or a pension plan product. When you give money to an insurance company to invest, you are buying an insurance product.

Structuring the Premium

How does the insurance company decide how much of a premium to charge? This is based on four factors.

First, the *probability of loss*. Just how likely is it that the house is going to burn down? With a large pool of similar risks, exposed to the same hazards, an actuary can determine with a great deal of accuracy what the probability of loss for a certain event is.

If you are 65 years old, nobody, including an insurance company, would venture to tell you how much longer you have upon this earth. Not only is your health an uncertainty, but so is the question of whether you'll get hit by a bus the next time you cross the street. But if you are one of a million people who are 65 years old, the insurance company can tell you fairly accurately that the average for those million is another 13.6 years of life. This information allows the insurance company to predict, fairly accurately, the cost of paying benefits on those million people's lives. That's the first and the major component of the insurance company's premium—expected loss.

The second component is *reserves*. If insurance companies didn't have a certain amount of money hedged against unforeseen circumstances, they would go broke as soon as the law of averages went the slightest bit against them. If the company had figured, for instance, on 562 houses burning down each year, and only had that much money available to pay claims, then it would be in trouble when the 563rd house went up in flames. So a certain amount has to be set aside out of the premium dollar for reserves.

The third component is *expenses*—paying the clerks who process the claims, the agents who sell the policies, the gas and electric bill.

The final component is *profit*. Insurance companies do not operate as charitable institutions; they are in business to make money. If they're stock companies, they make money for their shareholders. If they're mutual companies, they make money for surplus.

Insurance Company Objectives

Whenever you are contemplating doing business with somebody, you ought to wonder what the person is interested in and why that guy is sitting at your meeting. Insurance companies are not much different from other business organizations in the free enterprise system.

Their first objective is to increase sales.

Second, and in some cases very important, is to

enlarge their asset base. Insurance companies really love assets. They are often ranked by trade journals by the size of their assets; presumably the larger the base, the better they are doing. When Prudential Insurance Company's assets passed Metropolitan's, there was a great hoopla in the industry.

Finally, their objective is to make a profit. An insurance company will not offer a product unless there's a reasonable expectation of making profit on it. This is not something you should hold against them; just be aware of it.

I have a great deal of respect for insurance companies. I used to work for one, and I can assure you they spend a great deal of time in designing policies, contracts and premiums which reduce the probability of the company's losing money. They want very much to be able to make a profit—on every insurance product they sell. There are no loss leaders in the insurance business, as there are in the grocery business.

This is important for a trustee to remember when talking to an investment broker about investment opportunities.

The Regulatory Environment

Let me make one last important point about insurance companies. They do not operate in a vacuum. Since they handle huge amounts of money and are dealing with individuals as a sort of public utility, it is natural that they are regulated by the government.

Most financial institutions are regulated by the federal government, but insurance companies are specifically exempted from federal regulation under the McCarran Act of 1944. Instead, insurance companies are regulated by state governments—the state in which they are headquartered, and often the states in which they operate as well. Because the ground rules are different, the products available from other institutions like banks or investment brokers are different from those of insurance companies.

Although each state has its own insurance commissioner who regulates activities within that state, there is a great deal of similarity among the various states in terms of general approach. The New York State Insurance Department is generally regarded as the strongest state regulatory body, and other states tend to follow suit, eventually. What all insurance commissioners have in common is a mandate to protect the public—in this case, those members of the public who purchase insurance. The major concern of an insurance purchaser is that the company he buys insurance from stays in business, so commissioners insist that insurance companies use very conservative assumptions and operate in an extremely prudent manner in order to remain solvent.

Annuities

The Basic Product

Now that we've briefly gone through the basic idea of a pension plan and the basic idea of an insurance company, it's time to bring the two together. How does an insurance company serve the pension industry?

Insurance commissioners tell insurance companies that there's one and only one way they can do business with pension plans, and that's by offering annuities. An annuity is a contract that provides a regular income for a certain period of time—such as for the rest of one's life. The annuity is the basic insurance company pension product. In fact, it's a *required* part of any insurance company pension product. Somehow, somewhere, in every insurance contract you buy, or in every separate account investment vehicle that you enter into as a pension plan trustee, or in every GIC you have, you will find a reference to an annuity. The reason is this: If they did not refer to an annuity, or give you the option to buy an annuity, or in fact provide you with an annuity, the insurance commissioner would not allow them to take your money.

This being the case, we ought to know a little more about annuities.

An annuity is like other insurance products: it allows you to transfer risk to the insurance company, by paying a premium. Remember what we said a few minutes ago about the three basic risks or costs associated with a pension plan—benefits, administration expenses and investment return. If you as a pension plan trustee have absolutely no sense of adventure and abhor risk taking, you can go down to your friendly neighborhood insurance company and buy an annuity for each participant in your plan.

You have just wiped out all your risk. No matter how long your participants live, no matter how much clerks and attorneys cost, no matter what happens to the stock market over the next 35 years, you have fulfilled your financial obligation. And, because insurance commissioners require companies to use conservative assumptions, you can be pretty sure that the insurance carrier is making promises that can be kept.

Variations on a Theme

Let's have a history review, and briefly go over the different steps in the development of modern insurance company products for pension plans. We'll also talk about cost, and for purposes of illustration, let's assume that we're always talking about the same situation: a 45 year old employee who is going to retire at age 65, to whom we have promised a benefit of $100 a month.

Life Insurance. The basic product which life insurance companies used to sell to pension plans (and would still like to sell to pension plans) is life insurance. As a trustee, you can purchase a policy for each participant in your pension plan. Not only does this pay a benefit should the employee die before retirement, but it builds up a significant cash value over the years. When the employee reaches retirement, the insurance policy is canceled, and the cash value is used to buy an annuity for the employee, which will provide the monthly benefit for life. For our hypothetical employee, we would buy a $10,000 policy, which would then be converted into an annuity upon retirement. Our annual premium would be $400.

Deferred Annuities. Many plan sponsors, however, weren't satisfied with this product. Either they didn't want to buy life insurance at all, or they'd just as soon work out that coverage separately from their pension obligations. All they wanted was the annuity—so insurance companies obliged, removed the life insurance and went straight to the annuity. This cut the cost, of course, because the insurance company no longer bears the potential danger of having to pay out $10,000 if the employee dies before retirement. For our hypothetical employee, the premium would go down from $400 to $360.

Each year, then, you as the plan trustee would purchase what's called a deferred annuity for each participant in the plan. When the employee reached retirement, all those small annuities would add up to the promised monthly benefit.

Deposit Administration Contracts. The next step in the evolutionary process came when the plan sponsors decided they didn't need to transfer to the insurance company the risk of investment return and expenses during the active working period of the employee. Instead of purchasing deferred annuities throughout the working years, the trustees would invest the money until the employee was about to retire, and only then would they go to the insurance company to buy the annuity.

There was an added degree of risk in this procedure: the pension plan might lose money in the market or suffer some other financial catastrophe in the 20 years before our hypothetical employee retired and, if so, there might not be enough money left to buy his annuity. But if the trustees were willing to accept that risk, they could cut their costs even more by postponing the transfer of risk to the insurance company.

This kind of situation is called a deposit administration contract. As the plan sponsor makes contributions through the years, the money is actually put "on deposit" with an insurance company, just about the way you would put it on deposit at a bank. For the time being, it is invested and the pension plan receives whatever investment return the market yields, whether it's good or bad. When each employee reaches retirement age, the trustees simply tell the insurance company to take enough money out of the general fund to purchase an annuity.

For our hypothetical employee, there now is no annual premium. Instead, we take $12,000 out of the pot when he reaches age 65 to buy his lifetime annuity

IPG Contracts. Onto the next step in the evolution of insurance company contracts. Plan sponsors felt they could handle the risks not only during the pre-retirement years, but after retirement as well. So insurance companies developed a product called the immediate participation guarantee (IPG) contract. This consisted of a big pool of invested assets, just as in the deposit administration contract. The pension plan took the risk of whatever return its assets brought in the market. When an employee reached retirement age, though, instead of buying a lifetime annuity for him, the trustees would only take enough money out of the pool to buy a one year annuity. Next year, they'd again have to purchase one year annuities for all living retirees.

Basically, the insurance company is simply providing investment services, just like those you could get from a bank or an investment manager. There is one small vestige of "insurance" left to the immediate participation guarantee contract, and that is the fact that the insurance company is required to maintain certain reserves on your behalf—enough to purchase all the annuities required by your participants, in case you decide to stop doing business with the insurance company.

From this point, it's only a little way to the last step. Plan sponsors said they were willing to assume every risk associated with their pension plans. All they wanted was a good place to invest their money before it was needed for benefits. So insurance companies developed what are called "investment only contracts." However, such contracts do provide for "optional annuities." The big question, of course, is at whose option—the insurance company or the plan sponsor?

'Investment Only' Contracts

First, Read the Contract

Anytime you become involved with an insurance company, your first task is to look at the *basic pension contract* you must purchase to get into the game.

When you deal with a bank or investment manager, it is not necessary to analyze your contractual relationship, because they are not required to go through the machinations of pretending they're selling you annuities, when in fact they're only going to invest your money. But it's a different story with insurance companies. It is not unusual that an organization has used an insurance company as an investment vehicle and, to its utter surprise and consternation, has discovered a few years later that the annuity contract they signed is a real restriction upon their freedom to use their money or get their money back. They may have difficulty getting money back from the insurance company, or moving it to a different investment manager, or even in switching money from one separate account to another at the same company.

For this reason, contract analysis is becoming a big growth area in the pension consulting business. Remember, an investment only contract is still an insurance contract; as such, in one form or another, it must provide for the purchase of annuities.

I have spent this much time going through the history and evolution of the investment only contract because I think that's necessary to understand the product as it's being offered today.

The reason these products developed was the pressure of the competitive marketplace—and that pressure still exists. Many large pension funds reached the point where they no longer needed to transfer risk—in other words, they didn't need insurance companies at all. What they *did* need were certain specialized services to help administer their plan's operations.

And there are lots of businesses out there to help. Banks for instance, can keep and account for your money, and make benefit payments as directed. Third party administrators, actuarial consulting firms, investment advisors, law firms, all are happy to sell their services to pension plans—and they are unencumbered by a lot of the restrictions placed upon insurance companies. They don't have to use conservative assumptions; they don't require their customers to purchase annuities; and in general they have more freedom to sell what the customer needs. So insurance companies, unwilling to be shut out of the game, unbundled their services. They started offering a la carte menus of actuarial services, legal services, benefit payment services and investment services.

Separate Accounts

In the early 1960s, insurance regulatory agencies, following the lead of the New York State Insurance Commissioner, allowed insurance companies to segregate certain assets from their overall portfolios into small accounts. Instead of simply taking your share of the general account, which was a diversified investment portfolio, you could elect to put your assets into one of the separate accounts.

I'm sure you're all familiar with the mutual fund families that have become so popular in recent years. If you have money in any of their funds, you can switch it into another by a telephone call, getting into blue chip stocks, or speculative stocks, or bonds, or cash equivalents, or gold as the spirit moves you.

This is exactly the same concept as the separate accounts offered by insurance companies. When separate accounts first started, insurance companies would offer one or perhaps two common stock commingled funds. Now they offer many separate accounts:

- Common stock funds
- Bond funds—either publicly traded or private placement
- Real estate accounts
- Mortgage accounts,

and many other accounts similar to the array of investment vehicles available from banks or other financial institutions.

In addition to allowing participation in any of the separate accounts, insurance companies may permit a large fund—$5 million or so—to have its own separate account with an investment program tailored to that fund's particular objectives. There's a hitch, however, stemming once again from the particular restrictions placed upon insurance companies. Pension funds are not allowed to participate directly in the separate accounts. Instead, you must first "purchase" a pension contract which involves annuities. Then you can flow your money through the annuity contract into the investment funds—but watch out for the insurance contract.

General Account Investment Vehicles

A recent evolution in insurance company products has been the aggressive marketing of their general accounts. The general account, basically, is a diversified portfolio of stocks, bonds and real estate, usually measured in the billions of dollars.

A recent breakdown of the general account of one very large insurance company looked like this:

	Billions	%
Mortgages	$ 5.9	52%
Bonds	5.2	45%
Real Estate	.2	2%
Stock	.1	1%
Total	$11.4	100%

The yields that insurance companies get on their investments are not much different from those available to any other financial institution. Insurance companies hire good people for their investment departments, just as banks and investment counselors do, and they try to make good decisions ... but sometimes they make mistakes, just like banks and investment counselors.

In comparing the total portfolios of various insurance companies, the difference in yield of the general accounts is relatively small—usually measured in tenths of percents rather than in full percentage points. In fact, since insurance companies generally work the same turf, many substantial financial deals, such as loans to major corporations or large real estate projects, have more than one insurance company participating. In such a case, they all would be earning the same return.

For that matter, banks and other financial institutions often get in on these deals, too. So what's the difference whether you put your money with a bank or insurance company, if it's going to end up in the same kind of investment?

An Important Difference

Book Value vs. Market Value. Actually there *is* a difference, and I'd better make this point very clearly because it's probably the most important point of my presentation. Because of the peculiar regulations affecting insurance companies, they are required to value their general accounts investments at book value—that is, to assume that bonds and real estate investments will be held to maturity even though they may be traded. In contrast, banks are required to value their investments at market value.

Why do insurance companies value their assets at book value? Remember that insurance commissioners, whenever they have a choice, require insurance companies to take a conservative approach. That is because insurance companies are taking in money now and promising to pay it back in the future, and to protect the public there must be a strong guarantee that the money is going to be there when the time comes to pay it back, to settle the claim. So, insurance commissioners insist that insurance companies keep large reserves on hand to back up their promises, and the reserve requirements are set according to certain formulas. These formulas assume that the assets will be held until their maturity—so they are priced at their face value. An outside influence, such as rising and falling interest rates, is ignored when pricing these assets.

What Does It All Mean? So what difference does it make to you the investor if you use market value or book value to value your assets?

First, short term results appear to be more consistent and less volatile if you use book value. Even though the value of your bond is fluctuating according to the market, it is still reported as $1,000. Book value asset values are held constant even though the true market value of the bond is always more—or less—than book value.

Second, the actual value of your investment will never be exactly what the book value accounting report says it is. The value of an investment is whatever you can get for it. As long as you don't have to sell, or leave the insurance company, you can afford the luxury of telling yourself its book value is equal to the market value. But as soon as you must have that investment, you're at the mercy of the insurance company, or the economic environment.

Third, in the case of an investment only contract, the true value of your investment can only be calculated when it comes time for the insurance company to settle up with you, either at the end of the contract term or if you break the contract early. You'll get back the market value of your investment pool, which is the book value, minus the insurance company's profit, and minus (or plus) market value adjustment.

Fourth, your total return is unaffected by interim value. In order to calculate the rate of return you are receiving, you must take into consideration the amount and the timing of your payments into the contract. Whether or not the true market value of your assets was correctly reported to you in the interim period has no effect whatsoever on the total return you get from your investment.

Fifth, you should always remember that insurance companies have to make a profit, just like your bank or investment management firm. Their expenses and profit will reduce the returns you can expect from your investment. Book value reporting does not affect expense.

Last, I should point out that the eventual costs of a pension plan will be the same no matter whether you use book value or market value reporting.

Making It Work For You

I'd like to make a few comments about some particular ways that guaranteed contracts can be of great use to pension plan trustees. There are certain situations in which you do want to transfer the risk of benefits, investments or expenses away from your pension fund.

For instance: Your retirees may have become an inordinate burden upon your fund. If your retired population is significantly greater than your active population, you simply may not be able to take the risk that a bunch of them will outlive the odds. Even though the actuaries say you'll probably be able to cover their benefits, you just don't have enough money to gamble that they won't all live to be 100. Perhaps in this case it would be appropriate to "sell off" your retired life reserves—that is, buy annuities for those employees from an insurance company. Let the insurance company take the risk of them living a long time—which it will be happy to do, for a price. Perhaps, if your present actuary is using more conservative assumptions than the insurance company uses, you may even be able to sell off those lives for less than you're paying to carry them. In that case, you might even be able to achieve an actuarial gain in your pension plan.

Another example: If a plan is terminated, it may be advantageous for you to turn over the whole shebang to an insurance company. They'll take over the plan's assets and liabilities—for a price—and the trustees won't have to worry about whether the participants will outlive the odds.

Third example: In the new climate of multiemployer legislation, unfunded vested liabilities are a commodity no pension plan wants to have much of. Both unions and employers may well be hesitant to increase benefits, because they realize it will increase unfunded liabilities. (Unions don't want this, because it might put too much of a burden upon future active employees. Employers don't want it either, because they may be held liable for further contributions to cover such shortfalls.) But plan trustees may be able to use some of the newer concepts available in insurance company investment products, whether bond immunization or guaranteed contracts, to reduce unfunded liabilities or even sell them off entirely. My firm has done some work in this area, and there are some rather creative techniques that trustees can look at—although they are certainly not appropriate in every instance.

And now my closing word. Whether you are dealing with an insurance company, a bank, an investment counselor, a consultant or any other business associate, remember this: there ain't no free lunch. You get what you pay for—so be sure you *know* what you're paying for.

Real Estate as a Pension Fund Investment

BY PAUL SACK

IN 1975, when we first established the Rosenberg Real Estate Equity Funds (RREEF), only 35% of all pension funds were even thinking about diversifying into real estate, and those funds were considering investing 2-5% of total assets. As of 1980, over half the pension funds—including most of the larger and more sophisticated ones—have made the decision to invest in equity real estate, and they are talking about 10-20% of their total portfolios.

What are the reasons for this dramatic change? To answer this question, I think we must examine the motivations of real estate investors.

Real Estate as a Hard Asset

Stability

One important motivation is, no doubt, the desire to increase the stability and reduce the volatility of returns—both current cash income and principal value. Because leases on real property typically are written for five years or more, current cash returns of real estate change more slowly than the profits of businesses where sales respond directly to consumer demand, finance, and so forth. There is no single market common to all real estate transactions, comparable to the stock and bond markets reported on daily in the financial pages. Instead, real estate practitioners such as buyers, sellers, brokers and developers, must constantly ask each other what is happening to yields.* Typically, it takes three to four months before a move of 25-50 basis points is generally recognized. In such an atmosphere, it seems fair to say that principal values are more stable than for stocks or bonds. In the 22 years that I have been in the real estate business, "cap" rates on the type of properties which institutions are now buying have moved between 8%

*In real estate, "yield" is called the "capitalization rate" or, for short, "cap rate." The latter terms will be used for the balance of this article. For those unfamiliar with real estate: current income divided by price equals the capitalization rate.

Mr. Sack is one of the real estate principals of the Rosenberg Real Estate Equity Funds (RREEF). As such, he is responsible for real estate acquisitions, including property selection, financial analysis, market study, negotiation and subsequent supervision of management. For 16 years prior to joining the Rosenberg Funds, Mr. Sack's principal business activity was acting as a principal, not a broker, in the acquisition, development and management of properties. Mr. Sack received a Ph.D. in political economy from the University of California-Berkeley, an M.A. from the Harvard Business School and an M.B.A. in economics from Harvard, where he graduated magna cum laude.

and 10%. Comparable stability in the stock market would require that price/earnings ratios vary only from ten to 12 over a 22 year period.

Inflation Protection

Inflation protection, however, is clearly the most important motivation for diversifying into real estate. The increasing interest in real estate by pension funds in the past few years partially reflects their greater comfort with the medium but to a greater extent reflects the increasing expectations for inflation on the part of all of us. In 1975, prolonged double-digit inflation seemed unthinkable, and 6% seemed a reasonable expectation. Now, double digits seem probable to many of us, and 8% seems a satisfactory goal for "stability."

Real estate is an inflation hedge because it is a hard asset. Inflation, after all, is an increase in the price of "things." Real estate is really a bundle of "things"—cement, steel, plywood, asphalt paving, roofing and so forth, plus land and the labor it takes to put these "things" together into a building. Traditionally, the price of the things that go into a building and the price of construction labor have gone up more rapidly than the Consumer Price Index. There is a tremendous energy component in many construction materials such as cement, plywood, steel and, of course, the petroleum-derived roofing and paving materials. Thus, it seems highly likely that the price of construction will continue to rise more rapidly than any of the general price indices.

When a new building is constructed five years from now, its rents will have to be sufficiently high to pay for construction costs at that time—at whatever level inflation has driven them to. Well-located, well-designed older buildings which are able to compete with new buildings five years hence will be able to raise their rents almost to the rent levels in new buildings. This is where the inflation protection or "incremental value" lies in real estate investment: for as rents go up, both current income and principal values go up.

Intrinsic Value. Underlying it all is "intrinsic value," the costs of the materials and labor inherent in the property. For existing properties, we call this the "replacement cost." In purchasing properties for their potential as inflation hedges, it is important that one never pay more than the intrinsic value or replacement cost—for if one paid more today than it would cost to replace the property, one would be giving up part of the incremental value one expected to achieve as the cost of the components of the building increased over future time with inflation.

Setting replacement cost as a ceiling on price and tying incremental value to the prices of the component parts of a building sets the valuation of real estate sharply apart from that of stocks or bonds. The latter are valued essentially in financial markets. For instance, supply and demand for bonds can be brought into balance by the issuance of more debt instruments or variations in the interest rate or yield. The financial markets themselves comprise the entire process. Real estate, on the other hand, operates in two separate markets—the financial markets and the markets for physical space. One cannot create additional warehouses or office buildings unless demand for warehouse or office space exceeds its supply. Thus, in the financial markets for real estate, there is an *external constraint* on the supply side. Moreover, in these real estate markets, rents in new buildings are tied very closely to the costs of construction. If the return on new construction exceeds the minimum demanded by developers or owners as a return on capital, more properties will be created. There is no reason for anyone to pay more than replacement cost, because it would be cheaper to develop a new building.

Potential for Appreciation. While intrinsic value sets an upper limit on cost, not every piece of real estate offers the potential for incremental value or inflation protection. Three broad criteria are relevant:

1. The importance of quality in location and design cannot be overemphasized. It is only the well-designed, well-located properties which can be counted on to compete with new buildings constructed five years hence and to increase rents to the levels of those new buildings.
2. It is important also that the building appeal to a large number of tenants and not be constructed to the unique requirements of a single tenant. Otherwise, when the initial lease expires, the owner may find that the market for his building is so limited—if, indeed, it exists at all—that no one else will pay even as much as the first tenant did five years earlier. Examples of single purpose buildings are: sophisticated research laboratories, refrigerated warehouses, chain restaurants.
3. Unless the existing leases in the buildings are for relatively short periods of time, it will not be possible for the owner to raise rents and capture for himself the incremental value that lies in the property. Long leases leave this incremental value in the hands of tenants and inaccessible to owners.

What Rate of Return Can You Expect?

At RREEF, we strive for a time-discounted rate of return four percentage points higher than any assumed rate of inflation. That is to say, if we assume inflation at the rate of 8%, we would expect a discounted rate of return of 12% over a holding period of ten years. If we assume inflation of 15%, we would expect a discounted rate of return of 19% over the same holding period. This is what economists call a 4% "real return." For pension funds interested in inflation protection, the possibility of a return in excess of the rate of inflation should be most attractive. Some implications of these goals:

1. You should be more interested in the return over a ten year period of inflation than in the initial return the first year. For example, assume you are purchasing a building whose tenants have ten year leases that were written at a rent of $5 per square foot eight years ago but which will be expiring in two years, when rents are expected to be $13 per square foot. Clearly, very little significance should be attached to the return the first year. After all, it will more than double after only two years.
2. Since a dollar today is worth more than a dollar five years from now, the return should be measured on a time discounted basis.**
3. Real estate is a long term investment—and by long term, I mean at least eight to ten years. After all, if you purchase a property because the leases are below present market rates and will be expiring in five or six years, nothing will happen to the current income until that time. Full increase in value will not be achieved until the new leases have been written.

How Do Business Cycles Affect Real Estate?

For owners of *existing, occupied properties*—which is what we recommend for investment by pension funds—the periodic recessions to which the American economy recently has been subject have only a minor effect. Since leases are typically for five years, no more than 20% of the leases expire, on the average, in any given year. Furthermore, at least 60% of tenants generally renew their lease. Therefore, if the recession were so severe that it became impossible to secure any new tenants whatsoever for the space that became vacant, an increase in vacancy of only 8% (40% of 20%) would be experienced. For an unleveraged owner, the result would be a decline of approximately 100 basis points in the current cash return during a one year recession.

**Here is a brief explanation of "discounted" value for those who are not familiar with the concept: Since $50 today will be worth $100 in six years if invested at a compound rate of 12%, we say, "The present value of $100 six years from now discounted at 12% is $50." Thus, a discounted rate of return of 12% over a ten year holding period means that the purchase price could be invested at 12%, and all the projected annual income in the form of rents and increases in rents could be taken out of the account and, at the end of ten years, there would be an amount remaining equal to the estimated sales price of the property at the end of the ten year holding period.

It is appropriate to mention leverage (i.e., mortgage debt) when considering the effects of the business cycle on returns from real estate. Leverage increases the effects of the vacancies that might be caused by the recession.

For example, let's consider a property whose purchase was financed with a loan for 60% of the purchase price at 10% interest. Such a property would break even at approximately 70% occupancy. Thus, as vacancies went from a normal 3% or 5% to 70%, the current cash income would fall from 7% to zero. The same property, if purchased on an unleveraged basis, would break even at around 30% occupancy; and the return would drop from 9% to a little over 6% if occupancy dropped to 70%. If one of the goals of a pension fund in diversifying into real estate has been to increase the stability of current income and principal value, leverage should not play a significant role in a real estate program. It also should be clear that an unleveraged portfolio is relatively unaffected by the type of mild recession that the United States has experienced periodically.

The effect of such recessions on *development deals,* however, is very different. Real estate developments are generally of long gestation. It takes two to four years to bring an office building or shopping center from the point of inception to the time at which construction and leasing have been completed and cash flow to the owners commences. This time period can be stretched out enormously by a recession. During these times of economic slowdown, two things happen. The demand for new office, retail or warehouse space falls away to virtually nothing, and the financial carrying costs increase. Thus, if the developers contemplated carrying the project at 14% interest for two years, the returns can be affected disastrously if it takes four years to find tenants because of the recession and the building has had to be carried at two points over a prime rate of around 20%. Thus, recessions can have a dramatic—or even disastrous—effect on development deals. We at RREEF do not feel that the risks of development deals are really suitable for the conservative money that pension funds represent.

Similarly, recessions can stretch out the time period for maturing of the prospects for *raw land.* With the type of stop-and-go economy that has resulted from our attempts to control inflation through bringing periodic recessions, ownership of raw land has become increasingly speculative.

Curiously, recent recessions have not seriously affected the price of *well-located, well-designed, occupied properties.* The purchasers of these properties are looking at returns over a long term holding period, and are therefore little concerned over such short term fluctuations. In 1980, for instance, in spite of the combination of very high interest rates, tight money and recession, capitalization rates on high quality, occupied properties moved up no more than 25-50 basis points at the very most.

What Types of Properties Are Suitable?

Existing, substantially occupied office buildings, industrial buildings and shopping centers are generally regarded as the most desirable types of properties—although there is no consistent agreement concerning rankings among these Big Three. Even in purchasing these types, however, it is important to set a high standard for location and design. Only the well-located, well-designed properties will be able to compete with new properties built five years hence and to secure top rents.

Quality Characteristics

Quality characteristics can be described as follows:

1. *Industrial buildings.* Look for locations near four-way freeway access, airports, and/or located in well-designed industrial parks. For larger buildings, rail service and ceiling heights in excess of 20 feet are important in most markets. Truck turnaround space and easy in-and-out are important. Beware of too much highly developed office space. Less than 15% is normal, and most tenants will not pay for more. Rectangular warehouses with a depth no more than 250 feet are easy to break up for multiple tenant occupancy, so are much more desirable than, say, a square warehouse.
2. *Office buildings.* Bay depths (the distance from hall to window) must be proper for the market. Too long a bay depth, such as 50 feet, leaves tenants in a small-user market with long thin spaces which are difficult to lay out. Parking ratios, elevator ratios, the size of air conditioning zones are all important. Location should be convenient to the preferred modes of transportation and to the type of amenities office workers demand during noon hours. Ceiling heights and lobby decor are also important.
3. *Shopping centers.* Demographic characteristics of the trading area, location of present and future competition and access to highways or major arteries are basic. Bay depths, tenant mix and parking layout all also strongly influence success.

The purpose of this brief catalog of quality characteristics is not to make the reader an expert, but to give an appreciation of the types of expertise necessary to make real estate investments. A pension fund manager entering a commingled fund should study the decision making process of the fund and, if possible, meet the people who actually will visit the properties and make the decisions. Quality characteristics which may be readily evident to an experienced, entrepreneurial operative may be unknown to a recent hire direct from one of the prestigious business schools.

Some Other 'Opportunities'— Cautions, Considerations

As pension funds strive to acquire more property in a seller's market, there will be an increasing tendency to go into "development deals" or partnerships with developers. These are fraught with risk, especially in these times when the Fed fights inflation by periodically bringing on recessions through tight money and high interest rates. As a result of such stop-and-go economics, development projects which were planned to be brought on stream in two to three years may take twice as long. There simply is no demand for new *warehouse space* when real GNP and inventories are down. At such times, there is also little or no demand for new *office or retail space.* Not only will developers have to carry empty properties for longer periods of time, but the interest rate they will be paying may be 22% instead of 14%.

Remember: there may be bad development deals, but there are no bad *pro formas.*

Periodic recessions similarly make investment in *raw land* hazardous by stretching out the amount of time it may take before the land is ready for development. To investors in raw land, time is all important. If the value of the land doubles in six years, the owners will have had a 12% return; but if it takes 12 years, they will have had only a 6% return. If the land is rezoned as a park, no one knows what it may be worth.

Most institutional investors agree that *apartments* should be avoided because of the threat of rent control.

Ownership of *hotels and motels* by pension funds is an open question. They seem attractive for inflation protection, as the rent can be renegotiated every night. On the other hand, operating a hotel or motel is more like running a business than a capital-intensive investment. There are all the problems of labor costs and productivity in addition to fashion features of the convention business, decor and general marketing. For real estate investments, we at RREEF prefer something capital-intensive, like the warehouse complex which we recently purchased in the Seattle area for $10 million which has not a single employee.

To be strictly avoided are *single-purpose properties* for which there may be no ready market when the first tenant, to whose requirements the improvements were constructed, terminates his lease. Examples would be a laboratory built for exotic research requirements, a refrigerated warehouse or a fast food restaurant. While no one can guess what McDonald's requirements will be ten years from now, it seems certain that they will be for a very different building than McDonald's is renting today.

Agricultural land has certainly produced large profits for owners in recent years, but requires specialized knowledge of the agricultural business. For those with access to that specialized knowledge, putting a portion of a portfolio into agricultural land makes good sense.

Is Real Estate Overpriced?

Real estate prices have responded to investors' increasing concern over rates of inflation. Just as those investors have demanded a higher interest rate on fixed income securities to compensate for inflation, the same investors have been willing to accept lower returns in the initial years on real estate which offers the potential for protection against inflation.

The investor's best protection against overpricing in real estate is to pay strict attention to intrinsic value. Real estate is a hard asset being purchased on the basis of the anticipation that inflation will drive up the cost of all the "things" that went into construction of the building. Thus, if one does not pay more than those "things" are worth today, there should be little concern about overpricing—provided, of course, that anticipations concerning inflation do not change.

Current real estate prices are based on the expectation of inflation of at least 7-8%, and possibly pushing periodically into double digits. If the expected rate of inflation should decline to below 6%, there would be a one-time loss of value for real estate, as the inflation premium built into current prices was lost. Curiously, however, if expectations concerning inflation fell to the 0-3% range, real estate would again be priced as a fixed income asset at capitalization rates roughly two to three percentage points above the long term mortgage rate. Assuming that under such conditions of price stability the long term mortgage rate would return to 6%, capitalization rates on real estate would be 8-9%—or exactly where they are today. This potential role for real estate as a fixed income asset if there is a return to conditions of price stability imparts downside protection.

Conclusion

Pension funds weighing the role of real estate in their plans should consider carefully how they are protecting income and principal against their expected rates of inflation. For rates of inflation of 7-8% or more, real estate appears to be a better protection than either stocks or bonds. While bonds appear to be a good hedge against a return to lower rates of inflation, real estate should play a major role in the portfolio of any managers who believe they should be protecting against long term continuance of inflation rates of 7-8% or more.

Investment Targeting: Is There a RAM in Your Future?

BY DONALD A. SMART

"IT IS NOT CONSISTENT with the prudence standard for the fiduciary to make his or her investment decisions based on other objectives, such as to promote job security."

This statement by Ian Lanoff in his speech before the International Foundation's Legislative Update in Washington, D.C. in June 1980 clearly draws the battle line between the proponents and adversaries of socially beneficial investing. Many proponents today are suggesting that the investment of pension fund dollars is literally costing thousands if not millions of workers their jobs. This is happening because a company's pension fund is being invested in the securities of its competitors; union pension funds are being invested in anti-union companies; Northern pension funds are being invested in Sunbelt industries, producing runaway shops and closing factories where workers simply cannot be reemployed or easily relocated. Carried to its logical conclusion, those workers for whom the pension dollars are being contributed will lose their jobs and not be able to receive the pensions to which they otherwise would be entitled. Thus, the proponents of socially beneficial investing believe that the failure to consider an investment's impact on the workers' daily economic lives is imprudent because it undermines the basic philosophy of a retirement plan.

The Legal Perspective

Michael Leibig, an attorney with the Washington, D.C. firm of Zwerdling, Maurer & Weinberg, was recently retained by two public interest foundations to analyze the whole question of socially beneficial investing from the legal perspective. Drawing heavily on previous analyses by James Hutchinson, Ian Lanoff's predecessor at the Department of Labor, and Roy Schotland, a professor of law at Georgetown University and a well-known adversary of socially beneficial investing, Mr.

Donald A. Smart is vice president and manager of the Madison, Wisconsin, office of Deferred Compensation Administrators, Inc. (DCA), a Minneapolis-based consulting firm. Prior to joining DCA, he directed an extensive two year study of the Wisconsin State Investment Board. The study examined alternative investment policies for the state's public employee pension funds and looked into ways the funds could be invested locally without increasing the risk or reducing the return on those investments. Mr. Smart is a graduate of Lawrence University, and received his M.B.A. from the University of Idaho. He has testified before the President's Commission on Pension Policy and has written numerous articles on the subject of socially beneficial investing.

Leibig nevertheless concluded that "the paramount duty of the prudent pension trustee is a full commitment to the best interest of the beneficial owners of pension assets. Full and honest consideration of the impact of investment decisions on the interest of pension participants and beneficiaries, unencumbered by self-interest or self-dealing, is required. The duty is not limited to a sole or simplistic consideration of 'maximum financial return with minimum risk'—a rubric which should never be available to camouflage detriment to the real interest of pension participants and beneficiaries." Mr. Leibig concludes that there is a legally enforceable duty of social prudence in the investment of pension funds.

The problem, however, isn't that job maintenance and retirement income security are necessarily divergent goals, but rather when is one of the goals being reached at the expense of the other? In other words, when are you using the siding on your house as fuel to keep your family from freezing? Proponents, of course, claim that if pension fund dollars are being invested in a way that is costing a participant his job, then effectively someone is already stripping the siding off his house to fuel the fire.

But, based on recent articles and speeches by both sides of this issue, we may be coming down to a game of inches. Both James Hutchinson and Ian Lanoff have provided considerable leeway in their interpretations of the legal requirements that would allow for a great deal of social consideration in investing.

The 'All Things Equal' Myth

Almost everyone agrees that the basic purpose of a pension fund should not be undermined in the pursuit of social goals. But what constitutes an undermining of the primary purpose? Most adversaries would agree that it is permissible to consider social factors as long as the financial criteria of a considered investment are met first. This has also been referred to as the "all things equal" tenet: if there are two investments of equal merit, financially, then either may be chosen on its social merit. The fallacy of this statement is that hardly ever will an investment manager be presented coincidentally with two investments of equal financial merit. There will always be a measure of subjectivity introduced and, in considering an investment in the framework of the total portfolio approach, it is well conceivable that two investments of unequal financial merit are nevertheless acceptable investments for the portfolio. Trying to couch a social investment in the false imagery of "all things being equal" will rarely lead to an investment being made with at least some measure of consideration for its social impact.

The issuance of regulations by the Department of Labor in 1979 served to dispel much of the concern managers had about being judged imprudent on the basis of perhaps one or two investments in small or risky ventures. By providing a safe harbor approach and judging an individual investment with regard to the role that investment plays in the pension plan's overall portfolio, considerable leeway is given to managers who are instructed to include certain social guidelines. It is reasonable to suppose that certain investments, having a higher risk than others previously considered for the portfolio, can now be included. Additionally, it should be noted that nowhere in ERISA will a mandate be found that requires a fiduciary to maximize the return. As Michael Leibig has pointed out, there has never been a case where legal sanctions were imposed when an investment manager has given non-self-serving weight to the social or non-economic impact of an investment, even when investments promising a higher return were available.

Finally, Mr. Lanoff himself has stated, "While fiduciary considerations such as investment performance may not properly be sacrificed in order to advance the social welfare of a group or region, an investment is not impermissible under ERISA solely because it has social utility."

'Exclusive Benefit' vs. Exclusionary Investing

Where the advocates of socially beneficial investing start to get into trouble is when, in the euphoria of social purpose, they lose sight of the fact that the funds have been set aside to benefit a specific group of individuals. Thus, in looking for social benefit, proponents have been too quick to suggest how the funds can speak to a host of social problems which may or may not bear any close relationship to the participants' and beneficiaries' lives.

Exclusionary policies of investment are a case in point. While a good deal of the hullabaloo that has surrounded socially beneficial investing has focused on such items as J. P. Stevens, South Africa disinvestment, sanctions against alcohol and tobacco stocks and the like, this is also the area where it is often the most difficult to show any strong economic benefit to the participants and the beneficiaries. And, this is the area which is getting the greatest resistance from adversaries of socially beneficial investing. Ian Lanoff recently stated, "Anyone interested in social investing by funds would be well advised to forsake a policy of exclusion.... [The policy of exclusion] should not be expected to succeed when subjected to legal analysis of the fundamental ERISA fiduciary standards." Instead, Mr. Lanoff suggests, "The more promising approach is to broaden the number and types of investment vehicles money managers will examine for investment purposes." There seems to be much less dispute between proponents and adversaries when a suggested social investment provides economic benefit, even sometimes indirect economic benefit, for the participants and beneficiaries.

Targeting Pension Fund Investments

Current Programs

In the last several years, unions and public pension funds have taken the lead in developing and investing in certain otherwise prudent investments that have social utility. Unions for years have targeted portions of their members' pension funds for investment in projects that provide jobs and other benefits. The Wisconsin State Carpenters, a Taft-Hartley fund, invest up to 10% of the fund in mortgages of projects that their members are involved in building. Recently, a group of southern California unions pooled almost $2 billion in pension fund assets with the objective of investing over half that sum at the rate of almost $100 million per month in southern California real estate. Regardless of whether or not the investment provides jobs for them, union members feel that real estate in their area is a good investment.

Another recent union investment which received quite a bit of publicity was in Florida, where the International Union of Operating Engineers, Local 675, invested $2 million in land that was to be developed by the union's apprentices and then used by its members. Besides being an attractive investment, the project enhanced the value of the land, allowed apprentice members to improve their skills and gave members a place for recreation. In addition to a recreational center, the project includes a park, administrative office building and industrial park.

Public pension funds have a history of targeting investments to projects that benefit their geographic area. In Alabama, in 1973, the investment board adopted a policy to encourage public pension funds to invest in the state. By the end of 1979, 47% of the $1.6 billion under management was invested in Alabama. These investments include not only companies headquartered or with substantial operations in the state, but also GNMAs packaged exclusively with Alabama mortgages and short term funds placed with in-state banks. In Hawaii, almost one-third of the state's public pension fund money is invested in home mortgage loans to its members. Although the loans are offered at ½% below prevailing rates, the investment board nevertheless believes this type of investment has benefited the fund, its members and the Hawaiian economy.

The Kansas public pension fund actively supports economic development in the state. Up to 20% of the $600 million fund is invested in stocks and bonds of companies that "provide a positive economic impact to the state." The pension fund also has purchased up to $16 million in Kansas Development Credit Corporation (KDCC) packaged loans. The KDCC has been a successful intermediary for SBA loans to needy areas of the Kansas economy. Late in 1979, the pension fund began making short term funds available to banks and savings and loans in the state in an effort to ease a growing liquidity problem.

In Massachusetts, the public pension funds recently purchased $10 million of packaged SBA loans made up exclusively of Massachusetts businesses.

Perhaps one-third to one-half of all the states have targeted a portion of their public pension funds in investments to be classified as socially beneficial. Of course, the key to all of these investments is that they be made in the members' best interest and not for some ulterior or self-serving purpose. While public funds are not held to the ERISA standard, the ERISA standard nevertheless provides a benchmark that all pension funds are wise to consider. Nowhere in ERISA is there language which prohibits an investment being made for socially beneficial purposes. Nevertheless, self-dealing is specifically prohibited. Thus, it should be underscored that if a consideration for the social elements of an investment is to succeed, even the aura of self-dealing must be carefully and completely excised from the investment process.

Conflicting Concerns?

The current success rate of socially beneficial investments notwithstanding, the vast majority of money managers remain shoulder to shoulder in their aversion to the whole idea. They believe that no investment should attempt to do more than further the primary purpose of the pension fund: to provide at least a measure of income security in retirement. Despite evidence to the contrary, pension fund managers feel that this primary goal may somehow be abrogated if other social and economic goals must also be considered. Yet, with a fair measure of justification, the proponents of socially beneficial investing cast a cynical eye on computer models and the mathematical processes (most notably modern portfolio theory, a.k.a. beta) which money managers have so carefully groomed and point to as the paragon of prudent investment technique—only to have certain other investment experts question their validity. And all this against the backdrop of a decade of modest if not abominable returns.

A lingering question remains: What if there were an investment that addressed the concerns of both the proponents and the adversaries? What if there were an investment that not only coincided with the primary goal of pension funds but, at the same time, served an ulterior social and economic goal of the fund members? Perhaps such an investment will be found as gerontologists and pension experts link arms to solve the current plight of the elderly.

Structural Problems in Our Pension System

Despite the remarkable growth in the pension systems of America, over 3 million persons age 65 or older in 1977 were living in poverty, as defined by the official Poverty Index. This represents 14% of our retired population. Over 80% of these people were receiving Social Security, but it was insufficient to keep them from being poor.

When Social Security was established, it was intended to provide a minimum floor for retirement income. It was expected to supplement the other two usual sources of retirement income: private pensions and personal savings. Together, these three sources of income, often referred to as the three-legged stool, were to provide adequate retirement income.

Yet they fall far short of this goal. Welfare and other forms of "in kind" assistance programs currently are a major source of income support for the aged. The growth of these support programs in recent years is due in large part to the failure of our retirement income programs to provide adequate benefits for a significant block of our elderly population. Thus, millions of Americans age 65 and older are learning the hard way that their pensions will not buy them the dignified economic existence which they once were promised.

As a greater percentage of our population moves into their twilight years, this situation can only become worse. And layered on this is a fiscally strained, pay-as-you-go Social Security system. Many multiemployer plans and public systems upon which millions of people are counting for retirement benefits are in similar financial straits. The upshot has been a series of proposed and instituted remedies that, while offering a measure of protection to the immediately affected elderly populace, create even more severe strains that simply postpone the problems to a later time— when they will have increased to a far greater magnitude. COLAs (cost-of-living adjustments), one time adjustments to pensions, jacking up the contribution levels to Social Security, and the President's Pension Commission's suggestion of a mandatory private pension system are all extremely costly. Other remedies such as relaxing the mandatory retirement age and encouraging the elderly to get other or part-time work (hence, a fourth leg to the retirement income stool), represent options not always feasible or available to many, and offer only a partial solution at best.

We, as retirement plan professionals, are entrusted with solving these problems. Yet the answers are far from obvious and, while the typical government remedy of throwing more money at it would certainly do the trick, enough money is simply not available. Still, there are those optimists among us who would say that a little creativity and one or two adjustments here and there could provide the answers. The present pension system is like a huge ocean-going vessel. While that vessel may respond slowly, seemingly insignificant movement at the helm will produce definite changes in course. And just such a course change may be that form of social investing which complements a pension fund's primary purpose.

Home Equity Conversion Programs

Now in the development stage are a host of investment mechanisms that fall under the general category of home equity conversion programs. If the pilot studies of these programs succeed, the end result will be an investment mechanism suitable for pension funds that allows pension dollars to be targeted in such a way as to provide a comprehensive package of direct benefits to participants and beneficiaries.

Most older people own a home and want to remain living in it. While inflation is boosting their home's value, it is also eroding their already low or moderate income. They are becoming increasingly "house rich" and "cash poor." Unless they sell their homes and move, many older people will not be able to cash in on their most important long term investment. They spend a lifetime acquiring this nest egg of home equity, but they can't use it when they need it most unless they give up their home.

In recognition of this problem, the Wisconsin legislature in 1978 authorized a project to study ways of converting equity into income without relinquishing residency. This project has become the catalyst and hub for other projects that are blossoming throughout the nation. Currently five cities—Buffalo, San Francisco, Milwaukee, Madison and Monona, Wisconsin—have pilot projects underway. These pilots began independently from one another and, although their goals are similar, they have different funding sources. Seattle, Washington, Lancaster, Pennsylvania, and Orange, New Jersey, are also considering pilot projects of their own.

To help coordinate these pilot efforts, the U.S. Department of Aging has awarded the State of Wisconsin a $250,000 two year grant. The state agency responsible for the grant will act as a centralized clearinghouse for consultant input and individual experiences from throughout the country. The ultimate goal will be to develop a sound equity conversion program for older homeowners.

Suitability for Pension Fund Investment

Pension funds are considered a likely financing source for a venture of this nature for two reasons. First, a pension fund's cash inflow (contributions to the fund over a period of many years leading to a lump sum distribution or annuitized payout) appears to complement the cash outflows of a home equity conversion program (monthly payments over a period of time leading to a lump sum payback). Second, the primary purpose of the pension plan—to provide income security in retirement—could be enhanced significantly if, in addition to providing direct income payments, the pension fund also invested in home equity conversion plans that allowed retirees to use the principal in their home—an otherwise frozen asset.

This approach to pension fund investing is not necessarily free of problems. It is a new concept and there has been little if any experience with specific mechanisms. A new, specialized intermediary would likely be needed to package and manage the home equity conversion investments being sold to the pension fund. Because of this, there are bound to be development costs which may inhibit returns, and there's also a potential for added risk due to the lack of experience with this form of investment. But home equity conversion is an idea that has come of age. It is a natural for the pension fund concerned with targeting investments for the beneficiaries or to a particular geographic region.

Key Criteria

There are numerous variations of the home equity conversion arrangements, from monthly income plans to the postponement of real estate taxes. But surveys of older homeowners and financial analyses of theoretical models indicate several important criteria for a sound equity conversion plan: affordable cost; insurance against foreclosure; low potential for consumer abuse; administrative simplicity; financial flexibility and future adaptability; easy to understand; no outside interference with personal management of the home; options for equity preservation; substantial income benefits that rise over time; strong market appeal; neutral effect with respect to taxes and public benefits; and on-going consumer choice.

As one might expect, almost all of the plans currently in existence or being studied fall far short of these requirements. Some fail to meet key criteria such as cost and market appeal. Others require substantial development time and cost. For example, one of the most interesting programs is the reverse annuity mortgage, or RAM. Under a RAM, the homeowner would receive monthly payments in exchange for equity in his house. But by themselves, RAMs carry no foreclosure protection. Another type of home equity conversion is a private sale/leaseback where the homeowner actually sells his house and then leases it back from the new owner. But private sale/leasebacks are complicated, and they require the sale of the home. Currently, the State of Wisconsin is most interested in the home equity conversion program that postpones real estate taxes. The idea has received wide favorable response, has the backing of the Governor, and seems to meet many of the above criteria that are necessary for its success.

The RAM

The reserve annuity mortgage (RAM) may offer the best potential for pension funds. As mentioned above, the homeowner using a RAM is borrowing against the equity of his or her home to supplement monthly income. The size of the payments to the homeowner would depend on five factors: the administrative cost of the loan; the value of the security property; the life expectancy of the borrower/homeowner; the prevailing interest rate; and the mortality risk (the chance that an individual borrower will live precisely as long as his or her actuarial life expectancy; i.e., will the homeowner be paid too much or too little for the equity in his or her home?).

The addition of low cost insurance would eliminate the threat of foreclosure. Also, a contractual obligation could be built into the arrangement that would give the lender a percentage of any increase in market value. This added feature would make the RAM a hybrid between an outright sale and a loan, and would increase the amount of the payment to the homeowner.

Regardless of what the final instrument is that allows the elderly homeowner to unlock the equity in his home—whether it be postponement of real estate taxes, a sale/leaseback, or a RAM—one of the key ingredients will be the development of an intermediary that handles the administrative and financial details and is able to put each individual homeowner's stake in a package that represents a workable investment for a large institutional investor. The beauty of home equity conversion, however, is that it is an idea which deals in part with the enormous problems of an aging American population and the growing pressures on Social Security and pensions. These are problems that relate directly to the pension fund's primary goal. Thus, from an economic and philosophical standpoint, home equity conversion is one of the most appropriate pension fund investments a manager can make.

Conclusion

There will come a time, I predict, when we will have advanced the art of pension fund investing to the point where it will be imprudent *not* to consider a wide range of social criteria. And these criteria will rank on a par with traditional financial criteria. There will be no question that for an investment in a pension fund to be prudent, important social objectives will have to be realized. We may be years away from this; but if it happens at all, it will likely be prior to the year 2000, when pension fund dollars will top the $3 trillion mark. The role pension funds collectively will then be playing in our financial communities and daily lives may transcend all else, save perhaps the federal government.

Perhaps then the importance of considering an investment's impact on the current lives of the plan participants and beneficiaries will be clearly understood. Perhaps then, financial and social criteria will be considered on a par. For now, however, home equity conversion programs offer an innovative compromise to the social investment dilemma.

Selecting an Investment Manager

BY ROGER C. BRANSFORD

HOW DOES ONE select an investment manager?

To answer this question, I'd like to develop an analogy which I think will be very helpful. That is, selecting an investment manager can be regarded almost exactly as you would an individual personnel decision—how to hire a new employee. You, of course, are the employer; the investment manager is the employee.

If you keep this analogy in mind at every step of the process, it will help you put the proper perspective on the decisions you must make in "hiring help" for your plan's investment activities. Perhaps the major mistake trustees make in choosing investment managers is to lose control of the process. They assign assets to managers without properly determining how the job ought to be done, and they select managers almost by accident. This happens because this process is kind of esoteric and complicated, and it's easy to forget just how simple the essential relationship is—you're the boss, and the manager is your employee. Remembering this analogy can give you the right outlook on what you need to do when it's time to do something about your investment manager.

The first question you have to ask is, "Do I really need a new employee?"

There are several factors that might make you answer "yes." The first is the magnitude of the work load—have you grown so much, either in terms of assets or in terms of plan complexity, that you need additional help? An interesting question came up recently. A trustee said, "If I have $100 million, is it time to split my fund?" When I was involved in some similar sessions five or six or seven years ago, people used to ask the same question, except then they would say $10 million or $25 million! Such is the impact of inflation.

I don't believe there is any magic number, $100 million or $10 million, that can tell you when it's time to choose another manager. But there may well come a time when the sheer size of the assets leads to an overload of work for one manager. More likely, you are concerned about diversifica-

Mr. Bransford is corporate vice president and director of marketing services for Meidinger, Inc., in Louisville, Kentucky. Among his responsibilities are the investment-related consulting activities with multiemployer, public and corporate employee benefit clients. Prior to joining Meidinger in 1978, Mr. Bransford spent seven years with A. G. Becker. After receiving a B.A. degree from Cornell and an M.B.A. from Columbia, he worked with Citibank. Mr. Bransford has spoken at previous Foundation educational programs.

tion rather than just the sheer size of the assets, because when you reach a certain level of size you can reap the benefits of diversification without sacrificing market leverage.

There is a second reason you might want to consider "hiring a new employee"—if the job is not being done well by your current employee. If your manager is not delivering the kind of investment performance record you want, for whatever reason, you clearly might consider selecting a new manager.

Once you come to that kind of conclusion, you have to make another basic personnel decision: should I hire somebody new, or should I promote from within the company? In other words, should I give more responsibility to an existing employee? All too often, trustees who already have more than one investment manager immediately dismiss the notion that they should give incremental dollars or incremental work to one of their existing managers. They just go looking for yet another manager. This is not necessarily the best decision to make, particularly if you have been pleased with the performance of one of your "existing employees."

The Manager Selection Process

Write a Job Description

Let's assume that you have decided to hire a new employee. The first step is to write a job description. Yes, just like they do in classified ads. If you can't put it down in black and white, you probably haven't done your homework well. Exactly what do you expect this employee to do for you? Will the new manager handle all or part of your asset base? What is that investment manager supposed to do, other than buy low and sell high, get maximum return with low risk, and all the other wonderful things we would like to have happen?

Now, just as you would be foolish to hire a new person to come work in your organization without telling him what he is supposed to be doing, it's important that you tell this "job description" to your investment manager. All too often in the ten years I have been in this business, I have seen that people don't communicate terribly well. The investment manager thinks he is supposed to be doing one thing; the trustees think he's supposed to be doing something else.

Goals and Objectives. Of course, before you can write a job description it really requires a good understanding on your part of your investment goals and objectives. If you haven't done front end work on goals and objectives, if you don't have a specific statement of what you're trying to accomplish with your assets, you have a problem. Goals and objectives do not have to be elaborate documents three inches thick; as a matter of fact, the more stuff you get in there, the bigger it is, the less intelligible and the less useful the statement is. I saw one the other day—probably one of the better statements of goals and objectives I've ever seen—and it was one page long.

You have to be very careful in distinguishing between goals and objectives and investment policies. You may have a policy that prohibits certain kinds of investments—that is a policy, not a goal or objective.

It is not my purpose here to talk about goals and objectives, but unless you really understand the goals and objectives of your plan, you are very likely going to have problems in your relationship with your investment manager. If you don't know exactly what basis you're measuring the organization against, how can you tell whether they're doing a good job? We can apply the personnel analogy to goals and objectives. A good statement of goals and objectives is one which gives a *maximum of quantifiable standards* and a minimum of subjective judgment. It's difficult and unfair for a boss to sit down with an individual employee and deliver an unfavorable salary review if it all comes down to how the boss feels about the employee. But if you had the foresight to write a set of criteria for the salary review—in the next year, you will bring in $239,000 worth of new business, or some such—it's very easy to reach a judgment on that employee's performance, and justify it. Similarly, it's easier for the employees, because they know how they are doing in between salary reviews. Exactly the same considerations apply to investment managers—and the goals and objectives of your plan function just like the salary review criteria for an individual employee.

Here's another reason why you need a written job description and a written statement of your goals and objectives: because otherwise you may fall prey to a "door-to-door salesman." You may be talking to a candidate and you find yourself listening to all the nice words and superficial things that come out in the spiel—things that actually have no relevance at all to your plan and its particulars. Often trustees looking for an investment manager simply parade in five or six different people, just like a beauty contest. Each one does his little talent sketch—whichever one has the most persuasive sales pitch gets your attention. But then, when they've all come and gone, and you try to decide which one was the best, you have no basis for comparison.

Priorities and Specific Needs. You need to get your own priorities straight before you interview. You have to decide which qualifications are required. Here are some things that people are often interested in. I don't mean these as specific suggestions, but to give an idea of the sort of things that might be important to you.

- Breadth of coverage—does the organization invest in real estate? Does it do stocks? Does it do bonds? What about its research capabilities, if that is an important issue to you?
- Size of the organization—does size make a difference? Perhaps it does when you're talking about bond transactions, because a larger organization can get together enough capital to get better interest rates. Probably size doesn't matter for other kinds of investments. You are going to have some preferences, very likely, as to the size of organi-

zation you want to deal with, but that's more a question of what you feel comfortable with, not that it will have an effect on investment results.
- Geography—does it make a difference where your investment manager(s) is located? It may or may not, but you need to establish some sort of criteria.

If you don't have criteria in mind, if you haven't established in advance what it is that you really want to do, you end up talking about irrelevant things that really don't make any difference.

Narrowing the Field

Now that you've gotten your job description written down, it's time to try to create a universe of candidates for the job. Obviously, you can't interview every investment manager in the United States—there are about 4,000 of them floating around—you have to pare down that universe to manageable size or you'll never be able to live through the selection process.

How can you pare down the universe to a small number of possibles? First, look in your files. You may have people who contacted you in the past; you may have clipped articles out of magazines; you may have seen information from investment performance reports from various organizations on a particular organization; you may have seen something in the newspaper, or whatever.

Another method of getting names is through the grapevine—people in your industry or others whose judgment you respect may well be able to give you suggestions. There may be certain investment managers who have good reputations in your circle of associates. You may get some good names off the grapevine, and you may get some lousy ones; but you need to ask around.

Of course, there is another alternative—you can simply say this whole thing is much too complicated for me, so I'm going to go out and get a consulting firm to help me. For some organizations this is a waste of time and money. All too often, people try to solve their problems before they have figured out what their needs are. In a lot of situations you can do the work yourself, or at least some of the work. There may be situations where you might need help. Very frequently a consultant can do the most good for you in getting the process in order—getting involved at the very beginning instead of at the tail end, the way many do. That means the consultant helps set the goals and objectives, or helps create the universe of investment managers for you to interview.

Most people get involved with consultants at the end of the road. But if you haven't done the front end work, the poor consultant is not going to have as much success as you would like, and you're probably not going to get your money's worth out of the deal.

The Interview: An Information Exchange

Now let's move on and talk about the job interview itself. The most important thing about the interview is that you need to set an agenda for the discussion.

Think back to some experiences that you may have had in the past. You call up the investment manager and say, I want you to come in on December 2 and tell us about your organization. With no guidelines on what you want them to say, you'll get a real variety of presentations. Some people will make their pitch in 15 minutes; some will take three hours. And, when they're done, you find it difficult to digest what they've told you. What you need is a specific list of things you want to talk about. Things that are relevant to you may not be the most important things to the investment manager, but so what? You're the boss in this relationship—talk about what's most important to you.

Again, I'm a great believer in a written list. It doesn't have to be an elaborate list, but tell the investment manager *before the interview* the kinds of things you want to know. Most investment managers want to know the kinds of things that are on your mind—they don't want to waste their own time talking for an hour and a half on something that isn't going to nail down the job for them.

At the same time you give the candidates the agenda, you should also provide them with the information about your plan that they will need to make an intelligent presentation—basically, the same kinds of information you should be giving to your existing manager all along. An investment manager can't make intelligent decisions if you're going to be mysterious about yourself and conceal relevant information about your plan. In my own consulting work, I like to send virtually everything about an organization to a prospective investment manager: the summary plan description, financial documentation about the sponsoring organization if it is appropriate, some of the history of the plan, current asset configuration, statements of goals and objectives, whatever.

This means that the candidate will be fully prepared and understanding of the situation that they are going to be dealing with. I would rather give them too much information than too little. It's often interesting, when the interview is over, to notice whether the candidate has spoken specifically about your situation instead of in broad generalizations: i.e., here's what we would do with the typical $25 million fund. See whether they relate their recommendations to your fund's goals and objectives, or to your present portfolio, or otherwise give evidence of having looked at the materials you sent them. You save yourself a lot of time and learn a lot about a prospective investment manager.

Assessing the Candidate

Now, with the "job interviews" over, what factors are going to influence your decision? Basically, you want to examine the thought processes and the communication skills of the manager

Overall Strengths

Let's talk first about the "resume." The first thing you would probably look for is the candidate's specialization and expertise. Just what is this organization good at doing—do they have a particular approach in fixed income, real estate, stocks, international investing, options, whatever? Do they specialize in multiemployer plans or in corporate plans, are they dealing mostly with large plans or small plans?

Second, I would look at the overall profitability, stability and earnings pattern of the organization. If an organization is having problems and people are coming and going very rapidly, what kind of a situation are you faced with? Paramount in their minds is their own pocketbook—they just aren't going to be worrying full time about your assets. There are ways of asking questions about the financial stability and profitability of an organization, and I shouldn't think that you would be too reluctant to do that.

Size and Growth Patterns

Another factor is size. What difference does size make? A lot of it is in the eyes of the beholder, but there are certain things that I think are critical to look at. One is the rate of growth that the organization has experienced. Have they been able to adjust and adapt to their growth over the last several years? If an organization started out with $150 million three years ago and is now managing $1½ billion, what does that suggest in terms of potential organization problems? Maybe nothing—but it's clearly worth looking at anyone who grows that rapidly or changes investment philosophy that rapidly. There might be something to look at behind the scenes. Is this the same organization that really brought you the initial performance?

How about an organization that developed its reputation with rather aggressive tactics and has now retreated; they say, why should we take the chance anymore, market timing was nice back then, or investing in small capitalization stocks was nice back then, but now we have become a risk-averse organization. This may be a prudent business decision on the part of the investment manager, but it sure changes the basic type of organization you think you're dealing with. Anytime you see a manager with numbers that are shooting off the top of the charts, you need to take a very serious look at what's behind it. Is this fundamentally the same organization that produced the performance?

There is another issue relating to size and growth: the question of whether a firm has perhaps grown too big. I don't know what too big is—that's all based on where you start from. For a firm that started at $50 million a couple of years ago, $300 million may be big; $2 billion may be big for another firm. If it's become too big, what kind of control can individuals have over investment policy? If you have a very automated shop, why in fact would certain types of individuals want to work in there at all? How are you going to still attract the same kind of good people who made you what you are today? In a total top-down operation, where they're making all the decisions at the top, a portfolio manager is merely an implementer. He's deciding whether to put 5.2% vs. 5.3% of IBM in your portfolio.

With other people, location really makes a difference. Trust powers are another issue—do you want an organization that can be self-contained from a trust power point of view, or does it make any difference? Do you have a master trustee already? Those are some items that you can look at from the candidate's resume.

References

Now let's move along with the personnel analogy and talk about checking references. I think a lot of times we make up our minds we want to do something and we don't really go through the kinds of procedures that we should go through—like checking references.

Just how do you go about checking the references of an investment manager? You don't want to just ask the candidate for a list, because you're going to get back a list of all their satisfied clients. Instead, ask for a reference list to *your* specifications: a plan like yours, someone from your industry, someone with an asset size or configuration like yours. I would also look for some people that have recently hired and some that have recently fired this organization. Find out the reasons behind these decisions (bearing in mind that none of us have a lock on wisdom in this business).

Now that you have the references, call them up and talk to them. Ask them for their bottom line impression—has the organization delivered what they said they were going to deliver?

Decision Making—
What Does It Tell You?

Another area that is important is looking at what I call work samples—reviewing and comparing actual portfolios. I like to hear the words, but also like to see the work that the organization has done. One of the things I like to do is to go back and get statements of investment procedures and policy that an investment manager has produced over the last two or three years. It doesn't have to be every one. If they produce monthly letters, take random letters or take ones at turning points in the market. Request a sample from the manager; they will give it to you if they produce them, even if it's an internal document. Check it for consistency. What kind of thought process did the organization demonstrate—was it logical, was it intelligible, did they implement and manage the portfolios according to what they said they were going to do?

Now look for evidence that the manager can strike the delicate balance between flexibility and discipline. We need a framework for making decisions—but we also need to cope with change. You need to look for examples of adaptability.

Another thing that I would suggest to do is to try to track a recent investment decision of the manager. Pick one out—maybe the organization just bought Weyerhauser or just bought Georgia Pacific—ask them why. Would you walk us through that process from beginning to end? Where did that idea come from? Who did the work on it? Who made the ultimate decision? Why did you buy 3,000 shares as opposed to 5,000 shares? All you're trying to do is to understand the thought process, not why Georgia Pacific or Weyerhauser are good or bad stocks.

I think you can find some very revealing things from looking at some actual listings of assets at various points in time, looking at transaction statements to understand how they moved from one particular asset position to another. Try to focus on a few of the changes to determine why they did those—not questioning the decision to buy or sell IBM or anything else, but why *they* made the decision, whether that is consistent with *your* investment philosophy.

Let's talk about investment philosophy for a minute, in terms of the thought process. What's an investment philosophy? I don't really know what it is, but I can show you something that it isn't; you hear it all the time: "Buy low, sell high." (Fortunately you don't hear that too much anymore; people can't say it and keep a straight face.) But you find other "philosophies" like it: "We buy value." What the hell is value? "We're looking for secular change in the economy"—and so on.

Performance Measurement

There is another area that we all get involved in, and that is the question of performance and how it fits into the selection process. You've got to be very, very careful of the performance numbers that investment managers provide, because there aren't any plans that are exactly like yours. It's really a question of how that manager's going to perform with your type of plan and the constraints or restrictions on your plan. Performance should be related to objectives of the plan.

One of the things I think is interesting to do is to ask the investment manager how he likes to be measured, how he likes to be evaluated. If the response is "against other managers," how relevant is that to your particular plan? I think you need to ask that question. I'm not sure if there is a right response to it, but it should give you some interesting things to listen to.

Ability to Communicate

Another very important thing you need to assess in your job candidate is communication skills. You may have a problem with the thought process, but it also may be the inability of the organization to communicate effectively.

Let's talk about communication skills. It is not sufficient for an investment manager to simply send a statement every month or every quarter. Does the organization communicate effectively, or does it produce a lot of mumbo jumbo? Here's something I received on October 29th from an investment manager in the East, and I'm going to just give you the last paragraph (we took it off the original stationery to protect the guilty or innocent): "Lofty interest rates and weaker business conditions ahead will probably pose roadblocks to any further major advance by stocks, notwithstanding the reasonable valuation levels that exist today in the equity market—heightened speculative activity is also worrisome. We believe some cash reserves continue to be justified. We also remain convinced that the secular case for equity ownership is very strong and must outweigh the problems that we have outlined." Mumbo jumbo. What the guy is basically saying is, "I want to invest in stocks and I know there are a lot of things that suggest I shouldn't." Actually, if you read the whole thing, the manager happens to be 75% invested in stocks and is trying to alert his client to the fact that there may be some up and down movement of a pretty dramatic nature. That's an important message—but did it come through to the reader?

If you get letters like this, will they really tell you the kinds of things you want to know? That's really for you to determine.

The Bottom Line

Now that you've gone through this extensive and thoughtful process, the bottom line really comes down to a question of personal chemistry. The individuals that you work with do make a difference. You have to be able to relate to them, and you have to be able to understand them. The firm that you will be dealing with has its own character, which you may like or dislike. That may not be the most rational way we can approach the procedure, but personal chemistry can make your relationship sink or swim. Don't ignore it.

The Investment Manager—Differences in Philosophy and Style

BY ROBERT S. WAILL

Introduction

Selecting an investment manager is an extremely difficult task. How can you tell which one to pick? And how can you avoid disappointment with your existing manager?

It is worth making the effort to have a good relationship, because changing managers is very costly —especially to the portfolio. Usually the new manager sells out the old manager's securities and substitutes his own. Now, no one would want to deny the brokers their well-deserved double commission, but some pretty unpleasant losses are often realized in this process. More important, all of us are familiar with cases where performance got worse under the new manager, while the organization which was fired promptly turned in the best performance of its life for its next client.

The test of the relationship doesn't occur when performance is good, security markets are functioning well, and the manager seems to be acting sensibly. The real test takes place during moments when performance is poor, markets are in extreme circumstances, and the manager appears to be stubborn and irrational. Then, sometimes, the trustees can't stand it any longer—and they change managers.

While, over the long run, good statistical performance is essential, a feeling of remoteness can develop over the *short* run—a sense of not being on the same wavelength—a feeling on the part of the trustees that the manager's approach and philosophy are incomprehensible and just plain wrong. This loss of confidence can lead to sizable and unnecessary losses and mistakes, including buying at the top and selling out at the bottom.

Two Views of Investments—And the World

Trend vs. Fluctuation

Most everyone agrees that differences in investment styles are usually based on differences in

Mr. Waill is vice president, economist, director of research and chairman of the Investment Committee of Inverness Counsel, Inc. His firm is an international investment counseling organization with headquarters in New York and offices in Denver, Houston, Palm Beach and Geneva. Mr. Waill is a graduate of Cornell University and received his M.B.A. from Columbia University. He is a chartered financial analyst, a member of the New York Society of Security Analysts, and a past president of the Money Marketeers of New York University. Mr. Waill is a member of the faculty at the New School for Social Research and previously taught investments at the Bernard M. Baruch School of Business of the City University of New York. Currently a contributing editor and columnist for Trusts & Estates *magazine, he has also written articles for the Foundation's* Employee Benefits Journal, Pension World, The Financial Analysts Journal, The New York Times *and other publications. Mr. Waill has appeared on previous Foundation educational programs.*

philosophy. But I think that differences in philosophy are based—at least partially—on something more fundamental about each individual. In my opinion, almost all people can be divided into two groups: those who believe that life is made up primarily of trends, and those who are convinced that the essential characteristic of the world is fluctuation.

Trend people say that companies and cities which are rising will tend to keep on rising, while currencies and civilizations which are skidding will keep on skidding until they go away altogether. A winning baseball team is apt to continue winning, while declining stocks are likely to keep on declining and should be avoided unless and until they turn up with conviction.

Fluctuation people disagree. They say that life has ups and downs, winter follows summer, and good days are followed by bad days. Companies and industries have good years and bad years, and even nations can rebound after disaster. (Who would have imagined, at the end of World War II, that Japanese cars would someday capture 20% of the United States market?) And, finally, a depressed stock can rally strongly.

The controversy over trends and fluctuations defines a great many questions—including some which are truly profound. The most important issue in astronomy today, for example, is whether the universe will keep on expanding forever or whether it will simply go through a repetitive cycle of expansion and contraction.

There is no right or wrong to most of these observations. Many are subjective "eye of the beholder" evaluations. What is important is that the psychological tendency of an individual to interpret events as either trends or fluctuations is usually very clear and very strong.

Alternative Theories of Investing

These two different perceptions of how the world is underlie the major theories of investing. They also often explain individual reactions to these theories.

The *growth stock approach* is based on the idea that trends tend to persist. Find a rising trend of earnings and stock prices which looks like it will continue—hitch your wagon to the right star—and stay with it. The *technical approach* is quite similar to the growth stock approach, except that its time horizon is days rather than months or years. A stock that has gone up lately is technically strong and should be bought, because trends tend to continue. A stock that has gone down lately is technically weak and should be avoided or sold.

The *fundamental* or *valuation approach* assumes that a company and its stock can be appraised—like a building—and that the appraisal will change only slowly. Further, the price of the stock will tend to fluctuate around the valuation. Under this approach, the lower a stock goes, the more attractive it becomes.

These two approaches to investment are completely contradictory. Nevertheless, there have been many attempts to reconcile them. "Look for a stock selling at 40 which is really worth 60—but don't buy until it starts to move up and reaches 45." Most such attempts have failed, partly because they forego some of the large discrepancy between price and value on which the success of the valuation approach depends. More important, the attempt tampers with a person's basic human nature.

The side that one is on—trend or fluctuation—is hardly casual or accidental. And, it is probably not based on intellectual reasoning or experience. More likely, the tendency is innate, deeply embedded in one's personality. Conceivably it has some genetic basis. In any case, the two tendencies are almost impossible to change—and very difficult to overcome.

Roadblocks to Understanding

When the trustees are in one camp and the manager is in another, the stage is set for trouble. For example, the "fluctuation" manager, who believes in value, buys a stock at 40 and adds to the position when it falls to 35. The trustees, who believe in trends, begin to feel a bit uneasy. When the price falls to 30, the manager is still enthusiastic and finds it a better value than before. The trend thinkers, however, view additional purchases as throwing good money after bad. They feel in their bones that any stock that goes from 40 to 30 could be on the way to zero.

When the manager persists in this approach and prices weaken further, the manager is fired. A new manager is hired who knows better than to average down. He looks at the portfolio of losers and sells them. But by now they are really deflated, and they promptly double—for the benefit of the old manager's new clients.

Another example might involve the "trend" manager who buys a stock at 40 and sells it at 35 because it is "acting poorly." The trustees, who are fluctuation types, find this outrageous and incomprehensible. "If you liked it at 40, why isn't it more attractive at 35?"

The problem is made worse because communication between the two kinds of people is very difficult. Since the two approaches derive from different personalities—and maybe from different biological backgrounds—people in one group will very often find the other approach hard to accept and actually unpleasant. Whatever understanding does exist will generally be intellectual, superficial and fragile.

Seeking Competence and Compatibility

Under the circumstances, what should trustees do? First, without doubt, seek investment competence. Then, look for some compatibility of mind. This may not always be possible. The trustees may already have a manager. And, the trustees themselves may be diverse. What then?

Try to understand the manager you have or are getting. The investment approach must seem sensible and reasonable to you. The success of the relationship—which inevitably will be tested—will depend on your willingness to support the manager's approach at some critical time in the future.

Those manager organizations which are clearly in one camp or the other are usually dominated by a single person. Other organizations, however, won't allow this to happen, and their policies reflect the contribution of different individuals.

Trustees also should educate themselves about the nature of the securities markets, including the volatility of security prices and the psychological forces which are part of such price movements. An understanding of both the action of the markets and the philosophy of the manager will make it possible for trustees to prepare each other for the emotional challenges to come.

It may be helpful in screening new managers to include in the questionnaire some items dealing with trend and fluctuation: e.g., "Other things equal, how do you view a stock which has gone from 40 to 35?" Also, it is far better to stay with one approach—whatever it is—than to flit back and forth between various approaches. That will definitely lead to bad results.

While professional management organizations can often contend with the trend/fluctuation problem, the trustees frequently cannot, and they may be the more vulnerable and susceptible. Accordingly, an initial, private questionnaire should really be filled out by the trustee! (It need not be shown to any other person.) Find out. Are you a trendie or a fluctuation type? Find out what you are before interviewing new managers—or firing the old one. A sample question might involve an honest coin which had just been flipped heads seven times in a row. "Would the next flip be more likely to be heads or tails?" (Only a coldblooded professional would say it was still a 50-50 chance.) "And how do you feel about averaging down?"

So, find out about the financial markets and your manager, and the other managers to pick from. But, most important, first find out what *you* are.

Index

Author Index

Bader, Lawrence N.: 445-453
Bell, Spencer V.: 515-527
Beres, Robert J.: 486-489
Berman, Richard A.: 304-307
Bohrer, Robert A.: 344-358
Bransford, Roger C.: 572-577
Brightman, Jon S.: 554-560
Brown, Leo: 102-125
Burroughs, Eugene B.: 544-553
Butler, Walter J.: 383-391
Cole, Gerald E., Jr.: 40-42
Cooper, Robert D., Ph.D.: 459-477
Davidson, Phil E.: 99-101
Dawson, James M.: 181-184
DeCori, Robert A.: 481-485
Donaldson, Richard P.: 61-72
Duffey, Robert J.: 185-189
Earhart, William C.: 219-220
Ehrlich, Harold B., Ph.D.: 9-15
Eichenholz, Joseph: 48-51; 392-400
Finkel, Madelon Lubin, Ph.D.: 314-319
Frank, George A.: 240-242
Gaines, Sidney: 221-224
Georgine, Robert A.: 16-20
Gertner, Marc: 367-382; 401-424
Gilsey, Peter Ladd: 531-543
Giuntoli, David A.: 149-164
Haber, Jonathan F.: 429-444
Handel, Bernard: 327-332
Haneberg, Ronald L.: 136-143
Hillmer, Siegfried O.: 190-193
Howitt, Stanley: 225-230
Johnson, Richard C.: 93-98
Jones, Bennie: 515-527
Jost, Lee F.: 335-343

Korbee, Harold G.: 214-218
Lewis, Sheldon P.: 425-428
Lind, Matthew M., Ph.D.: 129-135
Lipton, Mark H.: 194-199
McCarthy, Eugene G., M.D.: 308-313; 314-319
McCarthy, Hugh J., Jr.: 73-76
Matook, Douglas F.: 251-303
Mele, G. A.: 494-514
Miller, Dan: 314-319
Mundt, Daniel H.: 209-213
Nagle, Robert E.: 27-35
Perreca, John S.: 165-174
Pritzker, Malcolm L.: 23-26
Putman, Patricia K.: 52-57
Rinfret, Pierre A., Ph.D.: 3-8
Rowcliffe, Donald H., Jr.: 490-493
Ruchlin, Hirsch S., Ph.D.: 308-313
Sack, Paul: 561-565
Saltzman, Warren H.: 93-98
Schanes, Steven E., Ph.D.: 43-47; 233-235
Semenza, Robert A.: 454-458
Shapiro, Kenneth P.: 144-148
Sherman, Carlton R.: 320-326
Sickles, Carlton R.: 36-39
Silverman, David W.: 77-85
Smart, Donald A.: 566-571
Stanton, Thomas E., Jr.: 86-92
Susskind, Howard S.: 359-366
Tannenbaum, Kenneth A., D.D.S.: 243-250
van Steenwyk, John: 52-57
Wackett, Ronald D.: 203-208
Waill, Robert S.: 578-580
Ward, Ben D., Sr.: 236-239
Ware, John K.: 175-180
Watanube, Orlando K.: 52-57

Topical Index

A

Accounting and auditing, 425-428, 429-444, 445-453, 454-458
  APB #8, 456, 457
  audit trails, need for, 489
  average expenses of multiemployer pension funds, 465-466, 469, 472
  FAS #35, 445, 455-456
  FAS #36, 445, 446, 456-457
  FASB, 454, 457
  reporting of unfunded liability, 445-453, 454-458
Actuary and actuarial process
  actuarial assumptions, effect on investment policy, 168-169, 533, 534
  actuarial assumptions, effect on pension costs, 166-168
  actuarial assumptions, effect on unfunded liability, 446-449
  average expenses of multiemployer pension funds, 466, 473
Adams v. Hercules, 348
Age Discrimination in Employment Act (ADEA), 141
Alcoholism and counseling benefit programs, 240-242
Allen v. Atlantic Richfield Retirement Plan, 67, 347
Amato v. Bernard, 69
Amax Coal Company v. National Labor Relations Board, 61-62
American Communications Association, Local 10, IBT v. Retirement Plan for Employees of R.C.A. Corporation, 71
Annuities, structures and types, 556-557
Arbitration
  as alternative to litigation, 364
  in withdrawal liability cases, 39
  mandatory, 69
Administrative services only (ASO) contracts, 393-394, 395, 397, 400
Auditing of hospital bills, 261-263, 289-303
  cost savings, 263
  procedures, 262-263
  purpose, 261-262, 289
  sample forms, 290-303
Auditing standards *see* Accounting and auditing
Audits, payroll *see* Collection of contributions

B

Bonds, 550-551, 552
Buczynski, et al. v. General Motors Corporation, 192, 198
Bunnell v. New England Teamsters and Trucking Industry Pension Fund, 62-63

C

Cafeteria approach to employee benefits, 204-207
Calhoun v. Falstaff Brewing Company, 69
Castillo v. Camacho, et al., 347
Challenger v. Local Union No. 1 of the International Bridge, Structural and Ornamental Iron Workers, A.F.L.-C.I.O., et al., 69
Claims and utilization, effect of recession, 337-339, 343
Coffy v. Republic Steel Corp., 216-218
Collection of contributions, 359-366
  averages, multiemployer pension funds, 461
  bonds, 360, 363
  collective bargaining agreement provisions, 359-361
  court cases, 63-64
  effect of recession, 335-336
  employer reports, 360, 488, 492-493
  health and welfare eligibility (delinquent employer), 365-366
  legal obligations of corporate employer, 77-85
  litigation vs. arbitration, 364-365
  MPPAA provisions re return of mistaken contributions, 98
  PTE 76-1, 336, 361, 365
  payroll audits, 83-84, 359-360, 362-363
  pension eligibility (delinquent employer), 365
Communication to participants
  communications checklist, 357-358
  computer's role, 484-485
  individual benefit statements, 351-353, 354-355
  plan booklets, 348-349
  self-insured plans, 385
  statements made by individuals, 349-350
  statutory requirements, 344-347, 354-358
  trustees' liability, 66-67, 199, 350-351
Computers and data processing, 482-485, 486-489, 490-493, 494-514, 515-527
  glossary, 507-514, 525-527

minicomputers, 515, 520-521; *diagram,* 523
personnel needs, 496-497, 498-502, 519-520
plan applications, 482-485, 487-489, 492-493, 495-496, 504-505
security aspects, 491, 505
systems selection and design, 486-487, 491-492, 497-498, 502, 503-505, 515-520
telecommunications, 521-522; *diagram,* 524
Consumer Credit Protection Act, 89-90
Contributions, non-cash
deductibility of, 107-108
Coordination of benefits (COB), 251-260, 264-273, 274-281
administrative processing, 254-259
definitions, 252
order of benefits determination, 252-254, 259-260
sample forms, 264-273
sample plan provisions, 274-281
Cornell-New York Hospital second surgical opinion program, 308-313
cost/benefit analysis, 310-313
program design, 309-310
Cost-of-living adjustments (COLAs)
of pension benefits, 153, 154-155, 165, 170-171
of Social Security benefits, 144, 152, 164, 173, 177
Court cases *see* specific cases

D

Defined contribution plans, 153-154, 176-181, 451, 532
conversion from defined benefit plan, 178-179
Delinquency *see* Collection of contributions
Demographic changes, effects on plans, 10, 154, 170
Dental benefit programs, 243-250
cost control and plan design, 244-246
cost control and provider options, 248-250
Disability benefit programs, 190-193, 194-199
conflicting definitions of disability, 68, 191-192, 193-194, 197-198
short term, 194, 195
types, extent of coverage, 194-195
workers' compensation issues, 190-192
Drug benefit programs, 236-239
cost containment aspects, 237-239

E

Economy, international, role of U.S., 3-6, 13, 15
Economy, U.S.
government policies' impact, 6-7, 9-11, 13-15, 173, 174-175
growth in labor force, 132
key industries' outlook, 11-12, 132-134
need for investment capital, 173-174
recession's impact on plan administration, 335-343
Electronic data processing (EDP) *see* Computers and data processing
Employee Assistance Program (EAP), 241-242
Employee benefits as compensation component
flexible benefit concept, 204-207
prevalence and cost, 206, 209, 210
tax treatment, 205, 206, 209, 211-213, 215, 221-223
Employer liability *see* Withdrawal liability

F

Feher v. Local 381 Pension Fund, 68
Financial statements *see* Accounting and auditing
Funding alternatives and media, 168, 392-400
see also Self-funding

G

Gilliam v. Edwards, 70
Guaranteed investment contracts *see* Insurance company investment products

H

Hawaii Prepaid Health Care Act, 52-57
coverage and impact, 53-54, 56-57
legal and legislative background, 54-55
Health care benefits, state-mandated, 53, 393
Health care costs
growth and major areas, 233-234, 251, 327-328, 329
hospital care as component, 261, 305, 307, 328, 331-332
surgery as component, 308-309
Health care costs, containment techniques
administrative: auditing of hospital bills, 261-263, 289-303; COB, 251-260, 264-273, 274-281; subrogation, 260-261, 282-288
benefits design: alcoholism programs, 241-242; dental programs, 244-246, 248-250; drug programs, 237-239; preventive care, 207-208, 233-235, 307; second opinion programs, 310-313, 315-319
HMOs, 323-324
NHI, 44, 45-46, 47, 49
national health planning efforts, 327, 328-332
New York State hospital cost containment program, 304-307

Health maintenance organizations (HMOs), 45, 234, 320-326
dental, 247
evaluation of, 323-324
HMO Act, 321-322, 323, 324; *excerpt,* 325-326
independent practice association (IPA), 320-321
Health systems agencies (HSAs), 329-332
goals and functions, 331-332
structure and organization, 329-331
Hodgins v. Central States Southeast & Southwest Areas Pension Plan, 347
Home equity conversion programs, 569-571

I

Indexing of retirement benefits *see* Cost-of-living adjustments (COLAs)
Inflation
CPI vs. purchasing power, *tables,* 541-543
effect on pension adequacy, 149, 152-155, 169-170, 177
effect on real estate investment, 561-564, 565
overstated by CPI, 170-171
related to government policies, 6, 10-11, 13-14, 173-174
Insurance, alternatives to traditional premium arrangements, 392-400
ASO contracts, 393, 394, 395, 397, 400
alternative premium structures and savings, 395-400
goals, 392-395
premium tax aspect, 393-394, 395
see also Self-funding
Insurance, purchase by funds, 401-424, 557
DOL investigations, 70-71, 73
fiduciary standards, 403-404, 405, 406, 407-408, 410
PTE 77-9, 403, 406, 408
sample forms, 411-418
Senate Subcommittee Report: recommendations, 401-410; *summary,* 419-424
Insurance company investment products, 546, 555-560
annuities, structure and types, 556-557
IPG contracts, 557
valuation of assets, 559
Investment targeting, 19-20, 566-571
exclusionary policies, 534-535, 567
prudence, 19, 566-567, 571
Investments, plan asset management
asset mix strategy, 546-549
assets and investment practices of multiemployer pension funds, 461
average costs of multiemployer pension funds, 463-464, 467, 470, 476
investment manager selection, 572-577, 578-580
investment policy statement development, 531-540, 545-547: defining plan needs and constraints, 168-169, 177, 449-450, 531-536, 545-547; investment objectives, 535-536; *sample guidelines,* 537-538
objectives of SUB funds, 215
portfolio performance, 1977-1980, 544-551
prudence, 71; *see also* Investment targeting
Investments, vehicles
bonds, 550-551, 552
debt instruments, 8
GICs, 558-559, 560
gold and silver, 7
home equity conversion programs, 569-571
insurance company products, 555-560
international investing, 8
money market instruments, 551-552
mortgages, 553, 570-571
real estate (equity), 7, 553, 561-565
reverse annuity mortgages (RAMs), 570-571
stocks, 7-8, 545-546, 552-553, 578-580

K

King v. Wagner Electric Corporation Contributory Retirement Plan, 66-67

L

Labor relations
common interests of labor and business, 16-20
Legal services benefit plans, 221-224, 225-230
administration, 228, 229-230
costs, 224, 225, 228
plan design options, 223-224
restrictions on services provided, 223, 226-228
tax qualification requirements, 221-223, 225-226
Legislative process, potential plan involvement, 23-26
Ludden v. Commr., 108

M

Martin v. Hamil, 64-65
Mergers of plans, 182-184, 450-451
Minimum universal pension system (MUPS), 134, 142-143
Money-follows-the-man *see* Reciprocity
Money purchase plans, 175, 176-177, 180
Multiemployer multiunion plans, 74-75
Multiemployer Pension Plan Amendments Act of 1980 (MPPAA), 28-35, 130

collections provisions, 29-30, 64, 65, 98
communications requirements, 346-347
funding requirements, 29, 33, 40
guarantees and premium levels, 29
key provisions, *table,* 31-35
legislative history, 18, 23-26, 40
mergers, 450-451
withdrawal liability, 36-39, 40-42, 446, 447, 450-451, 456-457

Multiemployer pension plans *see* Pension plans, multiemployer

N

National health insurance (NHI), 43-47, 48-51
cost containment aspects, 44, 45-46, 47, 49
gaps in existing health care coverage, 48-49
Hawaii Prepaid Health Care Act as model, 53, 57
history and development, 43-47
legislative status, 48-51
Medicare as model, 44

National Health Planning and Resource Development Acts, 328-329

O

Oakton Distributors, Inc., v. Commr., 108-109
Operating Engineers v. Lionberger, 65
Owner-operator participation, 82-83, 93-98, 99-101

P

Participation of owner-operator, 82-83, 93-98, 99-101

Pension plans, 149-164, 165-174
as capital source, 19
characteristics and objectives, 531-532, 554-555
costs as percentage of payroll, 166
government involvement, 136-143
history and development, 149-150
retirement income goals, 150-154, 163; *charts,* 156-162
unfunded liabilities, 445, 446-453
see also Pension plans, defined contribution; Pension plans, multiemployer

Pension plans, defined contribution, 153-154, 175-180, 532

Pension plans, multiemployer
administrative costs (International Foundation study), 459-477; *sample calculations,* 468-477
effects of recession, 340-341
industry distribution, 130, 131-132, 460

pre-ERISA, 16-17
size, 459-460
trends and outlook, 129-135

Pension rights of ex-spouse, 65, 87-92

Plan administration, effect of recession, 335-343

Plan termination *see* Withdrawal liability

Podiatry
need for plan benefits, 314-315
second opinion program, 315-319

Ponce v. Construction Laborers Pension Trust for Southern California, 67-68

Preemption of state laws, ERISA
domestic relations laws, 86-92: intent and background, 86-87; pensions as community property, 86-92
Hawaii Prepaid Health Care Act, 54-55, 87
workers' compensation offset issue, 199

President's Commission on Pension Policy
report and proposals, 134-135, 142-143
Social Security recommendations, 148

Preventive care/wellness intervention programs
as cost containment measure, 207-208, 234, 235
dental, 243, 244
Stay Well Plan, 207-208

R

Real estate as plan investment, 550, 553, 561-565
types of properties, 564-565
yield and return, 550, 561, 562-563

Reciprocity, 181-182, 185-189
combination approach, 185-187
health and welfare, 182
money-follows-the-man, 181-182, 185
pro rata, 181-182, 186-187; *sample agreement,* 189-190
recordkeeping, use of EDP, 488-489

Recordkeeping requirements, 351-353, 356, 481-482, 487-489, 495-496, 503, 504-505, 516
see also Computers and data management

Reserves, health and welfare, 367-382
developing a reserve model and policy, 367-368, 370-377
ERISA guidelines, 369-370
effect of recession, 339-340
IRS (TAM) guidelines, 368-369
sample trust agreement provisions, 378-380
self-insured plans', 389-390

Retiree benefits, health and welfare, 67, 219-220

Retirement ages and policies, 141, 168-169, 172
see also Social Security

Retirement income goals, 149, 150-151, 163
see also Pension plans

Reverse annuity mortgages (RAMs), 570-571

S

Second opinion programs
  cost/benefit analysis, 310-313, 318-319
  elective surgery, 308-313
  podiatry, 314-319
Self-funding
  ASO contracts, 393-394, 395, 397, 400
  COB, 389
  combined with insured benefits, 390-391
  communications, 385
  conversion option, 385-386
  cost comparisons, 384-385, 386, 388, 389-390
  dental plans, 247
  financial statements, 427
  reserves levels, 339-340, 342, 389-390
  SEIU welfare plans, 383-391
Self-pay options, effect of recession, 336-337
Social investing *see* Investment targeting
Social Security, 143, 144-148, 149, 150-152, 164, 171-174
  coverage issues, 139, 146-147, 148
  disability definition, 192, 196-197, 198
  PCPP recommendations, 148
  problems and suggested solutions, 137, 139, 145-146, 147-148, 172-173
  retirement income replacement levels, 137-138, 144-145, 149, 150-152, 154-155, 162, 164, 569; *charts,* 156-161
  sex discrimination issues, 147
  tax levels, 173, 175
State health benefits mandates, 53, 393
State laws, preemption *see* Preemption of state laws, ERISA
Stay Well Plan, 207-208
Stocks and stock market
  performance over time, 545-546, 552-553
  "trend" vs "fluctuation" theory, 578-580
Stone v. Stone and S.I.U.-P.M.A. Pension Plan, 65, 72, 88
Subrogation, 260-261, 282-288, 337
  sample forms, 284-288
  sample plan provisions, 282-283
Supplemental unemployment benefit (SUB) plans, 213-218

T

Talarico v. United Furniture Workers Pension Fund A, 71-72

Target benefit plans, 180
Tax laws, effect on benefits design
  benefits viewed as compensation, 205, 206, 209, 211-213, 215, 221-223
  effect on pension planning, 139-140
Taxpayer Compliance Measurement Program
  audits of benefit plans, 102-109
  Form 5500 *sample,* 120-125
  Form 6080, 110-111; *sample,* 112-119
Thomson v. I.A.M. National Pension Fund, 66
Tionesta Sand and Gravel, Inc., v. Commr., 109
Toland v. McCarthy, 68
Trombly v. Marshall, 348-349
Turner v. Teamster Local 302, 67

U

Unfunded liabilities, 445, 446-453, 454-458
  actuarial assumptions' effect, 446-448, 449
  reporting and disclosure requirements, 445-446, 454-458
  sources and types, 445, 452-453
Union Trustees and Employer Trustees of the Operating Engineers Pension Trust, 71
United States v. Andreen, 63
United States v. Ford, et al., 63

V

Vacation plans, 339, 365

W

Washington Area Carpenters Welfare Fund v. Overhead Door Company of Metropolitan Washington, 63-64
Western Washington Cement Masons Welfare Trust v. Hillis Homes, 63-64
Withdrawal liability
  in multiemployer multiunion plans, 74-75
  under ERISA Title IV, 27-28, 31
  under MPPAA, 31, 36-39, 40-42: liability allocation methods, 37-39, 41-42; withdrawal defined, 36-37, 41
Workers compensation
  disability standard, 190-191
  pension offset issue, 75, 191-192